Jewish Studies at the Crossroads of Anthropology and History

JEWISH CULTURE AND CONTEXTS

Published in association with the Herbert D. Katz Center
for Advanced Judaic Studies of the University of Pennsylvania

David B. Ruderman, Series Editor

Advisory Board
Richard I. Cohen
Moshe Idel
Alan Mintz
Deborah Dash Moore
Ada Rapoport-Albert
Michael D. Swartz

A complete list of books in the series is available from the publisher.

Jewish Studies at the Crossroads of Anthropology and History

Authority, Diaspora, Tradition

EDITED BY

Ra'anan S. Boustan,

Oren Kosansky,

and Marina Rustow

PENN

UNIVERSITY OF PENNSYLVANIA PRESS

PHILADELPHIA

Publication of this volume was assisted by a grant from the publication
fund of the Herbert D. Katz Center for Advanced Judaic Studies,
University of Pennsylvania.

Published by
University of Pennsylvania Press
Philadelphia, Pennsylvania 19104-4112
www.upenn.edu/pennpress

Printed in the United States of America on acid-free paper
10 9 8 7 6 5 4 3 2 1

Library of Congress Cataloging-in-Publication Data
Jewish studies at the crossroads of anthropology and history :
authority, diaspora, tradition / edited by Ra'anan S. Boustan, Oren
Kosansky, and Marina Rustow. — 1st ed.
      p. cm. — (Jewish culture and contexts)
   A collection of essays written by scholars invited to the Herbert
D. Katz Center for Advanced Judaic Studies at the University of
Pennsylvania in 2003–2004.
   Includes bibliographical references and index.
   ISBN 978-0-8122-4303-1 (hardcover : alk. paper)
   1. Judaism—Study and teaching. 2. Jews—Study and teaching.
3. Authority—Religious aspects—Judaism. 4. Jewish diaspora. 5.
Tradition (Judaism) I. Boustan, Ra'anan S., 1971– II. Kosansky,
Oren. III. Rustow, Marina. IV. Herbert D. Katz Center for
Advanced Judaic Studies. V. Series: Jewish culture and contexts.
BM42.J485 2011
296.071—dc22

                                          2010034237

Contents

PART II. DIASPORA

PART III. TRADITION

Preface

This volume of important essays emerged from the yearlong deliberations of a talented group of scholars invited in 2003–4 to what is now the Herbert D. Katz Center for Advanced Judaic Studies. Their charge was to explore the theme "Prescriptive Traditions and Lived Experience in the Jewish Religion: Historical and Anthropological Perspectives." As always, the year was devoted to interdisciplinary scholarship of the highest order, to the rigorous discussion of differing academic perspectives, and to a breaking down of the barriers set up by specialized training and circumscribed fields of study. In this instance, historians with specialties ranging from antiquity to the present were partnered with anthropologists, folklorists, and sociologists for an invigorating conversation about how their methods of scholarly inquiry could intermesh. How might a focus on texts complement or clash with a focus based on lived experience? And how might this fascinating dialectic play out in the traditionally text-oriented fields of Jewish studies?

The exciting results of much of this conversation are now before the reader. It would not be an exaggeration to consider the volume at hand as field-defining, even as expanding and moving Jewish studies into a new era and into a new self-perception of what constitutes Jewish learning. It would also not be an exaggeration to say that just as the conversations upon which it was based were not easy to stage, this volume was not easy to produce. It is one thing to encourage a dialogue between historians and anthropologists; it is quite another to reach a consensus and a common language about the subject of these inquiries. The credit for this achievement rests in the prodigious efforts of the volume's three editors: Ra'anan Boustan, a scholar of rabbinic literature and ancient Jewish history; Marina Rustow, a historian of medieval Jewish culture and society; and Oren Kosansky, an anthropologist who works on Jewish communities in Muslim North Africa. Besides their efforts to shape a coherent volume, their introduction stands as a bold and thoughtful statement about their respective disciplines and places within the study of Jewish culture and society. I wish to thank these three individuals for their achievement; I also wish to thank the other contributors to this volume as well as the fellows who are not represented in the book but who contributed significantly to the intellectual community from which it has emerged.

DAVID B. RUDERMAN
Joseph Meyerhoff Professor of Modern Jewish History
Ella Darivoff Director, Herbert D. Katz Center
    for Advanced Judaic Studies

Anthropology, History, and the Remaking of Jewish Studies

Ra'anan S. Boustan, Oren Kosansky, and Marina Rustow

This volume is organized around three terms—authority, diaspora, and tradition—that have exerted a tenacious hold on the field of Jewish studies. The centrality of these terms reflects their analytical utility for the study of the Jewish past and present: Jews from antiquity onward have made use of competing sources of legitimacy, followed patterns of geographic dispersion, and lodged claims to historical continuity; print capitalism, the existence of a Jewish state, and post-Enlightenment secularism have not rendered these terms outmoded in the least. The rough correspondence between these concepts and "native" Jewish ideas such as *masoret* (authoritative tradition) and *galut* (exile) further helps to explain their enduring status in the field. Indeed, the terms authority, diaspora, and tradition refer not only to conceptual tools derived from modern social philosophy and postcolonial theory, but also to domains of discourse within Judaism itself.

The seductive congruence between analytical and indigenous categories signals the fundamental problem that the present volume addresses. One major challenge of Jewish studies in the twenty-first century is to rethink these governing categories of inquiry and their relationship to the historical phenomena they are meant to capture. This challenge, as the field is already taking it up, begins with the recognition that analytical categories provide neither natural nor neutral frameworks of inquiry and that they can distort Jewish historical experience as much as illuminate it. It is clear enough, for instance, that the reduction of Judaism to a matter of private conscience and personal faith, following the Protestant model, risks obscuring the institutional forms and embodied practices that have created Jewish tradition from the ground up. Analytical categories derived from normative Jewish discourse are equally limiting: for instance, paradigms of diaspora that unequivocally valorize a sacred center can hinder an appreciation of the ways Jews have sanctified certain places in diaspora; approaches that see Jewish law as the reflection of actual behavior, or even as a set of authoritative ideals, often fail to account for the fact that authority is not an imminent property of canonical texts but rather an emergent effect of the social institutions and practices in which they are embedded.[1]

The field's most important response to an excessive reliance on normative categories has been to take a more inclusive stance toward the study of Jews. Over the past forty years, Jewish studies has been characterized by a phenomenological approach that embraces all varieties of Judaism rather than privileging certain dominant ones. At its best, this particularizing approach hesitates to favor any single Jewish variant (e.g., *rabbinic* authority, *Zionist* conceptions of diaspora, *Ashkenazi* tradition), and thereby avoids the analytical pitfalls of anachronism, teleology, and ethnocentrism. Such pluralistic strategies have been especially evident in comparative projects organized around Jewish "traditions," "diasporas," "cultures," "societies," and "identities," now typically rendered in the plural.[2]

The multicultural turn in Jewish studies is the culmination of developments that reach back to the mid-twentieth century. The "new Jewish studies," as one commentator has dubbed this pluralist trend, is characterized by increasing emphasis on several forms of heterogeneity. First, pluralists have turned to a much wider assortment of texts, including previously overlooked genres and authors (qabbalistic and Hasidic writings, women's prayer manuals), newly uncovered sources (the Dead Sea Scrolls, documents from the Cairo Geniza), and recently exploited archives in Europe and its former colonies. Second, scholars are now looking beyond the text to other modes of expression, including ritual practices, spatial arrangements, artistic production, and oral performances. Third, numerous studies now pay attention to previously neglected social groups: the study of women, children, magical practitioners, tradesmen, peasants, and laborers indicates the extent to which social heterogeneity has moved to the center of Jewish studies. Finally, the field now attends more systematically to temporal and geographic heterogeneities, focusing increased attention on periods and regions previously relegated to its periphery.[3]

While recognition of these types of heterogeneity productively challenges essentialist conceptions of Judaism, the regnant pluralistic framework has its own potential limitations. Nominalist views that judge a phenomenon as Jewish according to whether some Jews recognize it as such re-essentialize the boundaries of Jewish tradition by adopting a monothetic approach, in which inclusion in the category rests on a single criterion—in this case, what Jews recognize as Jewish. Polythetic approaches to "Judaisms" and "Jewish traditions" avoid this problem by refusing to rely on any single criterion. But they just as often fail to attend adequately to the historical processes that have led to the domination of certain traditions over others, suggesting instead that each bears equal importance. The chapters in this volume put power at the center of analysis by demonstrating how the heterogeneous elements of Jewish civilization can be studied as the products of asymmetrical social relations, global political forces, and instituted textual practices. Embracing certain aspects of pluralism but also moving beyond it, the authors gathered here foreground the practices that authorize texts, artifacts, beliefs, customs, places, and populations as Jewish in the first place, and then transmit them as such throughout their historical duration.[4]

Our claim is that the best response to the dangers of essentialism is neither to give up on the potential of analytical categories such as authority, diaspora, and tradition nor to treat them merely as catchments for the empirical study of Jewish diversity. What is required, rather, is to rethink these categories in a manner that not only makes room for Jewish heterogeneity, but that also accounts for hegemony in determining the scope and substance of what has historically been incorporated into the Jewish tradition.

Beyond Disciplinary Pluralism

The increasing number of academic disciplines included within Jewish studies is one hallmark of the multicultural turn. History, religious studies, and the philological fields (most often included in departments of Near Eastern and Middle Eastern studies) still operate at the core of Jewish studies and continue to play a role in maintaining the textual emphasis that, in the past, circumscribed the field more completely. Now, however, anthropology, comparative literature, the history of art, and other disciplines are bringing non-textual and non-Western phenomena under fuller consideration. Yet accumulating a larger repertoire of methodologies to capture more levels of Jewish experience, or turning to new academic disciplines to expand our coverage of the globe, does not necessarily help us to rethink the analytical categories and frameworks with which the field continues to work.

The current trend to include anthropology, in particular, within Jewish studies' inventory indicates the advantages as well as the potential pitfalls of disciplinary expansion. There are good reasons to applaud the recent anthropological turn: ethnographic methods shed light on social categories and processes that textual sources never fully capture, and often obscure; anthropology's still-reigning orientation toward the non-Western world facilitates the collection of detailed knowledge about previously understudied populations; and anthropology's focus on the present expands the scope of research on living Jewish communities. Anthropology has, for these reasons, taken its place as one of the privileged social sciences within a field increasingly oriented toward representing Jewish diversity on a global scale.[5]

Although a big-tent approach that includes anthropology is commendable, it also reproduces the major fault lines that continue to underlie pluralistic approaches to Jewish diversity. Within Jewish studies, anthropology functions largely to help fill the lacunae left by disciplines that typically focus on masculine, textual, and Western Jewish traditions. One less salutary effect of this disciplinary division of labor is that, beyond simply increasing our appreciation of Jewish heterogeneity, it also naturalizes the geographic and cultural boundaries according to which Jewish diversity is mapped. Indeed, because anthropology has tended to cover the more quotidian aspects of Jewish experience and its geographically "exotic" forms, there remains the danger of reinstating the old distinctions along disciplinary lines. An alternative approach requires not only new methods and topics but also new concepts that situate Jewish phenomena on both sides of the borders between texts and practices, the elite and the popular, Jews and non-Jews, the past and the present, and the East and the West.[6]

Recent developments at the crossroads of history and anthropology have helped move Jewish studies in this direction. The old distinctions between the two disciplines—one diachronic, the other synchronic; one textual, the other ethnographic; one focused on the elite, the other on the popular; one oriented toward the West, the other toward the rest—no longer hold. The revision of these vulgar contrasts and the emergence of a research agenda situated at the boundaries between them suggest alternatives to a naïve pluralism. In what follows, we delineate three such alternatives and indicate how they are already taking hold in Jewish studies. The first, following on the textual turn in anthropology and the hermeneutic turn in history, focuses on what we call textual hegemony as a way to rethink Jewish authority. The second uses the lens of postcolonial theory to refocus the study of Jewish diaspora. The third suggests that discursive tradition, as the concept is being developed especially in anthropology and religious studies, offers a productive frame for rethinking Jewish tradition.

Textual Hegemonies

The "historical turn" in twentieth-century anthropology reflected a recognition that history and anthropology, despite their methodological differences, shared the common hermeneutical problem of interpreting unfamiliar cultural "texts." Texts had previously been a point of differentiation between the two disciplines, with anthropology focused on preliterate societies and history attending to civilizations documented in written records. By the 1970s, the text, taken metaphorically to include the social actions that ethnographers observed as well as the archival evidence that historians gathered, emerged as an idiom of common purpose. Written texts themselves have also become a concrete point of intersection between the two disciplines: anthropologists attend to the textual artifacts and practices that circulate even in "ethnographic" societies, while historians look to anthropology for conceptual tools, modes of analysis, and cross-cultural comparisons to assist in the interpretation of textual sources.[7]

This interpretive and methodological rapprochement has been palpable in Jewish studies. Historians of Judaism now regularly draw on anthropological concepts and cases in the study of texts, and not only when dealing with characteristically ethnographic topics such as magic, pilgrimage, sacrifice, and rites of passage. Anthropologists, for their part, approach Jewish texts as sources of cultural history, objects of ritual and pedagogical practice, and artifacts of symbolic value. The chapters in this volume demonstrate some of the ways in which research in Jewish studies is capitalizing on the overlapping interests in textual materials and material texts that have defined the crossroads of anthropology and history.[8]

Recently, scholars working at this crossroads have moved beyond the treatment of texts as repositories of meaning, prescriptive blueprints for social life, or objects of ritual significance. This shift has been motivated by a recognition that texts are embedded within regimes of power, as are the practices with which they are associated and the institutions that mediate their production, dissemination, and use. The turn toward the study of textual hegemony entails a focus on how concrete textual forms (legal documents, census reports, textbooks, prayer manuals, ethnographic accounts, amulets) and institutions (synagogues, mass media, courts of law, schools, archives) operate in the variable contexts of state structures, colonial empires, and global economies.[9]

Textual hegemony, as we use the idea, does not refer primarily to the power of texts to fix singular versions of otherwise heterogeneous oral narratives, or to displace previously non-textual modes of expression. While these processes have occurred in the history of Judaism, a restricted focus on the hegemony of texts fails to account for the more dynamic relationship between textual codification and non-textual forms of expression. The ascendancy of textual authority—whether represented by the early modern canonization of the printed Talmud and the *Shulḥan ʿarukh* or late-modern orthodoxy's reliance on offset printing—has never entailed a monopoly of texts within Jewish life. Indeed, medieval and early modern efforts to fix the form of the Jewish liturgy led to a proliferation of diverse and competing prayer manuals rather than their reduction to a single form. Moreover, Jewish prayer books continued to mediate liturgical experiences that entailed oral recitation, bodily comportment, and a range of visual practices.[10]

Jewish textual hegemony is characterized, then, not necessarily by the supremacy of texts but by the variety of positions they occupy within an array of oral, corporeal, and visual forms of expression.[11] Because those positions have been subject to radical transformation, we use the concept of textual hegemonies to refer to the ways in which texts and textuality have crystallized into relatively enduring structures of authority. Consistent with the pluralistic approach, this analytical strategy insists that the significance of Jewish texts must be understood in their contingent historical contexts. But unlike many pluralistic approaches, the study of textual hegemonies stresses the hierarchical arrangements among various expressive media and among competing textual regimes.

To take an early example, the formation of a scribal hegemony in the temple polities of antiquity entailed the ascendancy of a restricted class of textual specialists who commanded both religious authority and political power. The monopolization of public performances of writing, reading, recitation, and textual interpretation was crucial to the consolidation of priestly and dynastic power. In the Hellenistic and Roman periods, a competing set of sociopolitical institutions and pedagogical disciplines formed an alternative mode of Jewish textual hegemony. Dominated by the elite citizenry of the emergent polis, this rhetorical hegemony centered on the mastery of grammar, persuasion, and memorization as filtered through oral practices that competed more vigorously with textual ones. Rhetorical hegemony, however, did not replace scribal hegemony: the two overlapped in a productive tension out of which novel forms of textual power emerged.[12]

Jewish textual hegemonies are never fully autonomous, but always embedded within more extensive forms of textual domination that reach beyond Jewish society. The Temple in Jerusalem, dominated by a priestly class at the center of a sacred polity, was situated within patterns of priestly oligarchy that operated throughout the ancient Mediterranean. The emergent rabbinic movement, within which the rhetorical arts were transmitted through master-disciple relationships, was part and parcel of Greek *paideia*. A similar embeddedness can be seen with respect to the forms of the liturgical-legal hegemony that emerged in the medieval period, when the biblical text, the prayer service, and the Jewish legal corpus were canonized into written form. The attempt to fix Judaism according to textual standards controlled by rabbinic literati reflected the more widespread distribution of new technologies (for example, paper and the codex) that had measurable effects on Christianity and Islam as well. Likewise, the development or adoption of new textual genres such as responsa, institutions such as law courts, and authorities such as judges and court clerks went hand in hand with emerging forms of law, administration, and governmentality that remade both Christian and Islamic societies.[13]

The concept of textual hegemony shifts the focus from Jews' acculturation to "outside" forces to their engagement with communicative regimes across religious boundaries. Beyond taking into account the "broader" forms of textual discipline and domination that function at any given historical moment, the study of Jewish textual hegemonies examines how Jewish institutions and practices constitute those "broader" processes themselves. Thus, when a modern Jewish textual regime emerged with the return to Scripture, the standardization and diversification of prayer books, and the textual objectification of Judaism, a new denominational hegemony recast the Jewish text alternatively as a vehicle of confessional faith, a source of universal ethics, and an incontrovertible locus of tradition and authority. This happened precisely as print capitalism and the nation-state reconfigured the confessional landscape of Christian Europe. It would be wrong, however, to conclude that the modern textualization of Jewish authority was simply derivative of the Christian enlightenment or dependent on new technologies of mass communication.

Rather, Jews were an integral part of European religious transformation, just as the Jewish press was formative in the expansion of public literacy in Eastern European and Ottoman society.[14]

This reappraisal also refines pluralistic approaches that continue to rely on facile—and teleological—distinctions between modernity (conceived of as secular, democratic, and global) and tradition (conceived of as religious, stratified, and provincial). As recent research in anthropology and history makes clear, the "secular" emerged through new relationships between religion, polity, and power rather than through their slow disaggregation. The modernness of Jewish denominational hegemony, in this light, is characterized not by the receding reach of religion into politics, but rather by a reconfiguration of the relationship between the two. The maskilim of early modern Europe were no less implicated in states and empires than were the priests of antiquity. Along the same lines, the effects of modern mechanical reproduction and mass dissemination cannot be reduced to the secular fragmentation and democratization of Judaism. Jewish textual traditions had never been monolithic, and they continued to be structured by hierarchies of authorship, production, and distribution. The contemporary technologies and economies of Judaism are modern, rather, primarily insofar as they have exposed increasingly literate Jewish publics to textual discipline through institutions such as publishing houses, schools, universities, and seminaries.[15]

Similarly, the modernity of Jewish denominational movements is not reducible to their global scale. Jewish mobility is not, of course, unique to recent centuries: trans-regional trade networks, pilgrimage routes, charitable missions, travel in pursuit of learning, and forced relocations have facilitated the dissemination of Jewish textual hegemonies across global empires since antiquity. Movements such as the Alliance Israélite Universelle, with a network of Jewish schools that once extended across several continents, and Ḥabad Hasidism, with its worldwide outreach, are modern because they have relied on modes of communication (print media; the Internet) and transportation (steamships; air travel) that reworked, rather than created, Jewish diasporic globalism. As significantly, these movements are modern because they were made possible by European and American empires: the Paris-based Alliance was an extension of the French imperial project; the missionary reach of the Brooklyn-based Ḥabad movement reflects the expansion of American political and economic power. Accordingly, new directions in Jewish studies focus on how colonialism and empire reconstituted the diaspora as a terrain of Jewish diversity and an object of knowledge.[16]

Trans-regional historical processes are, therefore, inseparable from the formation of Jewish textual hegemonies. For this reason, a fully adequate approach to Jewish authority demands consideration of the circulation of people, objects, and practices across global terrains.

Beyond Diaspora Essentialism

A second salient point of intersection between anthropology and history is diaspora studies. The study of diaspora is no longer associated primarily with the Jewish case, but also with colonial and postcolonial migrations and with global circuits of labor. This broader conception of diaspora has productively destabilized the boundaries that were once thought to define relatively isolated societies and national territories. Insofar as the Jewish diaspora preceded recent patterns of mobility and fragmentation, the study of Jews has provided a historical counterpoint to postmodern inclinations to view diaspora as a resolutely contemporary condition.[17]

Surprisingly, the concept of diaspora has played a largely conservative role within Jewish studies. While Zionist-oriented scholarship has cast the diaspora as the defining counterpoint to a more genuine national-territorial Jewish identity, a countervailing tendency has been to claim extraterritoriality itself as the principle locus of Jewish historical identity. Even some scholars who otherwise insist on flexible and non-hermetic forms of identity have asserted that the diaspora is the sine qua non of Jewish authenticity. The substitution of the diaspora for a territorial homeland as the uniquely genuine space of Jewish identity reverts to the very forms of essentialism that the concept has so usefully disrupted when deployed in other cases. Recent academic disputes over whether the Israeli nation-state represents the zenith of Jewish vitality and the fruition of Jewish national destiny or Jewish agency and creativity have thrived primarily in the diaspora demonstrate the point. Both sides of this hoary debate share the reflex to search for a single mode of authentic Jewish identity that excludes others. Discounting territoriality, in any of its ancient or modern forms, as a central Jewish motif bears as much potential for essentialism as does rooting Jewish identity exclusively in a territorial homeland.[18]

Other scholars have avoided the question of authenticity, preferring to demonstrate the intricate dialectics of Jewish homelands and diasporas.[19] Research in this vein shows, for example, how Jews have identified with diasporic homes by creatively revising and reapplying Jewish idioms of sacred homeland. The existence of "little Jerusalems" across the globe provides only a glimpse of the social and semiotic mechanisms through which Jews have made diasporic places into Jewish homelands. Conversely, even Jews motivated partly by liturgical fervor to return "to Jerusalem" have experienced modern Israel as a place of exile. The celebration of the Moroccan festival of *mimuna* in Israel, for instance, is partly an expression of postcolonial nostalgia for a lost North African homeland. At their best, studies of such phenomena destabilize the homeland-diaspora paradigm by demonstrating that it has never provided a single, simple, or uncontested map of Jewish space.[20]

Yet even the most nuanced approaches to diaspora and homeland, in which they are taken as mutually constituting categories and geographically fluid spaces, do not necessarily call into question the dualistic terms of the model itself. This oversight partly reflects the analytical internalization of native Jewish and Zionist categories. But it also points toward the fact that Jewish studies emerged as a Western academic discourse in an age of European colonialism and nation building. A deep-seated dualism also reflects discourses of empire that bifurcate global space in other binary terms, such as Occident and Orient, metropole and colony, and First World and Third World. Indeed, Jewish studies emerged as part of a long history in which Jews were both objects and propagators of orientalist discourses and colonial projects. Only recently has the field started coming to grips with what Ivan Kalmar and Derek Penslar have identified as a significant relationship between orientalism and the Jews.[21]

Within Europe, Jews were for centuries cast as others whose semitic bodies, Levantine roots, and Eastern mentalities placed them outside the religious, racial, geographic, and civilizational sphere of the West. European Jews were subjected to forms of ethnographic representation, administrative regulation, residential segregation, and bodily violence that were concurrently and subsequently applied to colonized societies.[22] But Jews were not only the passive objects of representational and regulatory practices. Although over the course of the Enlightenment, some Jews (and Christians) attempted to recuperate the oriental Jewish past as the origin of Western rationality and spirituality, the rhetoric of European Jewish emancipation relied heavily on teleological narratives in which that past gave way to a modern European or Zionist future. Indeed, European Jews applied their own orientalist discourses to non-European Jews, representing them with the same oppositions—between civilized and savage, rational and superstitious, literate and oral—that justified the Western imperial project and that framed the implementation of colonial rule. In the Jewish case, orientalism also reflected a unique investment in the teleological narratives of Jewish emancipation, which cast Arab, Turkish, Persian, and Russian Jews as exemplars of the feudal, superstitious, and parochial past that Western Jews had already escaped. As colonizers, Jews established their own imperial ventures couched in term of education, philanthropy, and advocacy for their Eastern European, North African and Middle Eastern coreligionists. Organizations such as the Alliance, and later the American Joint Distribution Committee, reproduced imperial hierarchies of cultural difference and mapped the Jewish diaspora accordingly.[23]

One enduring effect of Jewish orientalism has been the resignification of the terms "Sefaradi" and "Ashkenazi" to encompass the entire Jewish diaspora and to divide it along a single axis of difference. The globalization of these terms partly reflected the late medieval and early modern migrations and expulsions that led Sefaradi and Ashkenazi liturgies, customs, and legal precepts to dominate those of local Jewish communities. The meaning of the term "Sefaradi" ultimately expanded to include not only Jews who traced their ancestry directly to the Iberian Peninsula but also all those located within Europe's Islamic colonies; this semantic generalization entailed the leveling of locally salient distinctions between Sefaradi immigrants and native Jewish communities (such as *megorashim* and *toshavim* in Morocco and Sefaradim and Romaniote in Ottoman realms). In the lexicon of Jewish ethnicity in Israel, the term "Mizrahi" ("oriental") has largely replaced Sefaradi, with the new term retaining, and even augmenting, the capacity to encompass and homogenize Jews from Europe's former colonies.[24]

The academic representation of the Jewish diaspora has perpetuated these modern topographies of European hegemony. Jewish studies continues to be organized into subdivisions, research centers, conference panels, and edited volumes that follow from the colonial heritage. "Sefaradi studies" and "Mizrahi studies" are marked categories in Jewish scholarship in a way that, with rare exceptions, "Ashkenazi studies" is not. Likewise, the study of Jews in the modern Islamic world remains predominantly an anthropological and folkloric enterprise, whereas Jews of the Christian West have been taken up primarily as objects of historical and sociological inquiry.[25]

The growing number of ethnographic studies that deal with Jewish communities in postwar Europe as well as of historical monographs about Jews in former colonies represents a welcome change from disciplinary conventions that follow closely from the colonial bifurcation of the Jewish diaspora.[26]

Likewise, other conventional dichotomies are now being questioned. Rather than retrojecting binaries such as Christians and Jews, priests and rabbis, and Qaraites and Rabbanites onto periods before they existed, scholars are now attending to the gradual and uneven processes through which these categories emerged.[27]

Along these lines, recent research in Jewish studies works explicitly across imperial and national boundaries. In the wake of 1391 and 1492, Sefaradi identity functioned as a mode of Jewish cosmopolitanism that reached from Europe across the Mediterranean and into the Levant. In the nineteenth and twentieth centuries, Jews continued to play an important role as diplomatic, economic, and cultural intermediaries between Europe and its colonial possessions. As North Africans and Middle Easterners, Jews were selectively cultivated as colonial intermediaries through the efforts of institutions such as the Alliance and through diplomatic regimes such as the protégé system by which European powers granted some Jews limited legal protection. Recent research has demonstrated how Jewish trade networks, commodity exchanges, diplomacy, philanthropy, and ritual practices linked empires (e.g., European and Ottoman) and moved between metropoles and colonies.[28]

The study of global networks within the Jewish diaspora also prompts a reconsideration of the nationalist scaffolding that still girds much work within Jewish studies. For the most part, pluralistic approaches have moved well beyond the competing nationalisms, both European and Zionist, previously embedded in the practice of Jewish history. Devoid of such commitments, the study of Jewish diasporic diversity along national lines succeeds best in documenting the wide variety of traditions and identities that took shape in local and national contexts. A growing set of historical and ethnographic monographs dedicated to premodern and non-European Jewries moves even further by questioning the applicability of nation-state idioms to Jewish society.[29]

Even so, the uneven mapping of the Jewish diaspora continues to reflect postcolonial and nationalist legacies. In comparison with the vast library of meticulous historical monographs on Jews of Western Europe and North America, there are fewer full-length studies about colonial and postcolonial Jewish communities. The nation-states that emerged from former colonies tend to be lumped together into regions that recapitulate orientalist topography. The recent spate of edited volumes on Jews from non-Western regions of the world is an important development, but such collections bear the potential to reinscribe a colonial divide on the far side of which lie the cumulative populations of the East.[30]

Explicitly comparative studies also tend to portray a world divided along the lines of the nation-state. To take one prominent example, it has been proposed that the diaspora offers "laboratory-like" conditions for the study of Jewish adaptation to diverse national environments. But national contexts are not naturally bounded ecosystems; they come into being and change through long histories of interaction that contaminate the purity of the samples (the local Jewish communities) upon which the model depends for its coherence. This model also focuses on how Jews (as dependent variables) adapt to their environments, while paying less attention to the converse process. Medieval European religious disputations, for example, did not merely force Jews to respond to their Christian environment; such events were part of the processes though which medieval Christianity came into being and defined itself. The same can be said for German National Socialism, Moroccan monarchism, or the American civil rights movement.[31]

Comparative projects of this sort also represent the stubborn persistence of "host society" models, in which the diaspora appears to be made up of bounded national or imperial contexts into which Jews intruded or, at the very least, in which they remained a discrete minority. The analytic approach to Jews as "guests" is, of course, not the same as characterizing them as "parasites," but both implications of the "host" society metaphor follow the same exclusionary logic according to which Jewish difference is objectified and taken as the axiomatic starting point for analysis. Conversely, the host-society model implies a homogenous national context against which Jewish difference is thrown into unique relief. Insofar as ancient and modern empires were linguistically, ethnically, and religiously diverse, applying the concept of a host society to premodern contexts seems to retroject a nationalist logic onto contexts from which that logic was largely absent.[32]

In its blunter forms, the host-society model has framed studies of Jewish "assimilation" and "acculturation" into societies presumed to preexist the Jews. Critiques in the pluralist mode have pointed to this model's failure to recognize that Jews also contributed to the creation of those societies. Among the insights to emerge from this more nuanced and dialectical approach is the recognition that Jews have crafted their own distinctive identities by borrowing and subverting motifs from the cultures in which they live—a process that Ivan Marcus has termed "inward acculturation."[33] But the underlying structure of the host society–minority model persists even in some pluralistic approaches that dispense with those terms. One is left confused, for example, by contradictory exhortations to avoid seeing Jews as outsiders who "borrowed from" surrounding cultures, and at the same time to appreciate how Jewish minorities "adopted non-Jewish beliefs or practices but infused them with traditional Jewish symbols."[34] The idea that Jewish communities should be viewed as one organ in a larger organism corresponds with old sociological models that presupposed a boundary of discrete identity (the organ) within an encompassing context (the organism). Likewise, "acculturation," "assimilation," and "adaptation" have surprisingly remained part of the analytical tool kit of Jewish studies even as those terms have been increasingly challenged in history and anthropology.[35]

An acute contradiction, then, characterizes the pluralistic turn in Jewish studies. On the one hand, new approaches offer a better appreciation of how Jewish beliefs, practices, and identities come into being at the social and cultural border between Jews and others. On the other hand, such studies continue to rely on concepts, models, and metaphors that presume that the boundary has already been fixed. Moving beyond these approaches requires a full-fledged revision of how we understand the scope and substance of diaspora. It also requires accounting in a more complex fashion for Jewish tradition and the formation of Jews within it.

Judaism as a Discursive Tradition

Tradition, as the concept has been revised at the junction of anthropology and history, is no longer a catch-all category for everything premodern. The study of tradition is now characterized, rather, by a more complex understanding of the relationship between a putatively static past and a dynamic present. The distinguishing elements of colonized cultures (social structures, religious rituals, legal systems, languages) no longer appear as timeless holdovers, but instead as traditions "invented" by ethnographic practices of representation and harnessed to administrative strategies of control. Modernity, in turn, is no longer studied as the successor to tradition, but rather as its golden age, within which both long-standing cultural practices and new ones are institutionally objectified by reference to the legitimating past.[36]

Within Jewish studies, cataloging the varieties of Jewish historical expression across time and place goes a long way toward dispelling the view that tradition is a homogenous counterpoint to modernity. Examining Zionism as a manifestation of Jewish modernity, for example, suggests some of the ways in which novel political forms rely heavily on traditionalizing claims to communal and territorial continuity. Other modern Jewish projects that claim to be deeply conservative, such as denominational orthodoxy, have utilized modern means (bureaucratic, mechanical, capitalist) to objectify "tradition" and make it into a new kind of authorizing discourse. The geography of tradition and modernity is likewise being remapped. Jewish law in the "traditional" Middle East, for example, has been shown to be at least as flexible as its "modern" reformist and orthodox counterparts in the West.[37]

An emphasis on the multiplicity and dynamism of Jewish traditions does not, however, necessarily lead to an effective critique of the analytical models that continue to essentialize tradition within Jewish studies. Pluralistic scholarship has yet to offer a fully developed alternative to the essentialization of either Jewish textual unity ("the Jewish tradition") or Jewish heterogeneity ("Jewish traditions"). We suggest that the idea of discursive tradition, as elaborated by Talal Asad, can productively reorient our approach to the various types of Jewish heterogeneity (textual, expressive, social, and temporal/geographic) that pluralistic approaches to Jewish traditions have highlighted but not adequately reconceptualized.[38]

Judaism is a discursive tradition only partly because it makes reference to a set of foundational texts. Those practicing in the name of Judaism have generally agreed on the authority of texts, but just as significantly, Jews have contested which texts are canonical, which interpreters authoritative, and which hermeneutical methods legitimate. The notion of discursive tradition, then, takes us beyond a limited corpus of foundational texts and instead focuses our attention on the processes through which *every* Jewish text potentially participates in the creation of a canon and the modes of authority associated with it.[39]

The study of Jewish textual heterogeneity cannot, therefore, be simply a matter of collecting texts while presuming or leaving unquestioned the processes that made them canonical or failed to do so. This is one insight that follows from the phenomenological turn in Jewish studies, in which Gershom Scholem and Jacob Neusner stand as towering figures. As a result of their work, the field attends more carefully to what is at stake in the dynamic processes of textual canonization. Subsequent scholarship has extended their phenomenological approach from the centers of Jewish canonical authority deeper into the peripheries. Studies in this vein demonstrate that even the most "marginal" of hagiographic, magical, mystical, millennial, or paraliturgical texts do not simply draw on more authoritative textual traditions; marginal texts themselves are constitutive elements of those traditions.[40]

Ethnographic research can be especially useful in forging an appreciation of how even the most marginal of Jewish texts are read, understood, and employed as full constituents of "Torah," that is, of authoritative textual tradition—only sometimes against the grain of competing elite propositions. A Moroccan Jew, for example, can see a twentieth-century Judeo-Arabic hagiographic text as an exemplar of Torah by virtue of her familiarity with the graphic forms—typefaces, page arrangements, decorative motifs—it shares with the prayer books, volumes of Talmud, Hebrew texts framed for home decoration, Torah scrolls, and mezuzot that she knows from the bibliographically dense Jewish landscape she inhabits. Such a phenomenological rethinking of Jewish textual canonicity moves well beyond the now largely suspect model of "great" and "little" traditions, which presumed a wide gap between the universal, textual, and elite aspects of "world religions" and their local, ritual, and popular manifestations. The well-recognized problems with this model pertain no less to Judaism: "local" Jewish beliefs and practices have their cosmopolitan dimensions; texts circulate among illiterate Jews; religious elites engage in ritual practices from which they draw much of their authority.[41]

It would therefore be a mistake to limit the phenomenological investigation of Jewish canonicity to the ethnographic study of how texts are received by the Jewish "masses." Rather, ethnographic and textual approaches must converge in a phenomenological approach to the expansion and experience of the canon itself. The marginal books, vernacular hymns, and local liturgies encountered by Jews less well versed in texts are likely to have been written by rabbis schooled in the canonical arts of Jewish learning and literacy. Local Jewish authors compose texts using rhetorical and generic strategies that determine Jewish canonicity more universally. Such authorizing strategies include the use of Hebrew, Hebrew characters, rabbinic attributions, biblical quotations, commentary in the midrashic style, ancient and medieval liturgical forms, and so forth.[42] Those who deny the canonicity of "heterodox" texts must ignore, willfully or not, the densely packed literary mechanisms that function to authenticate the work in question.

Neither the masses nor the elites, then, monopolize textual canonicity. The rabbi who writes a hagiography, those who read it to themselves or to their children, and those who hear it all partake in the text's incorporation into the Judaic canon. Moreover, rather than dividing Jewish societies into elite and popular classes, it helps to recall that most Jews are situated somewhere in the middle as semiliterate, modestly schooled, and institutionally intermediate social actors. Circumcisers, ritual butchers, cantors, schoolteachers, scribes, mortuary guardians, minimally trained bar mitzvah boys, pious lay-people, and anyone who can recognize and appreciate the formal qualities of a Jewish text without necessarily being able to read it him- or herself all confirm the authority of situated canonical Jewish texts without necessarily being able to compose or even read them.[43]

Understanding Jewish textual heterogeneity is not simply a matter of pushing back the boundaries of the Jewish canon; it requires rethinking the idea of the canon itself. Jewish texts do not naturally sort into an authoritative hierarchy based on relative proximity to a canonical core, whether defined by the Hebrew Bible, the Talmud, or other formative Jewish texts. Putatively foundational and marginal texts alike become and remain canonical as the result of concrete social, semiotic, and rhetorical mechanisms with which Jews authenticate, promote, and contest the inclusion of certain texts as "Torah." That even those Jewish texts whose normative status has been most widely accepted harness such mechanisms more or less effectively is clear from the myriad works rejected as noncanonical, from modern reform movements back through the long processes of rabbinic redaction and biblical canonization.[44]

To ignore these points is to substitute the leveling aesthetics of multiplicity, pluralism, and conversation for the historical realities of imposition, debate, and dissension. Approaching Judaism as a discursive tradition, by contrast, entails recognizing that the assertion of power is integral to the formation of any recognizable canon. The discursive quality of Jewish tradition alludes to what Brinkley Messick has called the authority *in* texts, by which he means the way their authority emerges formally, rhetorically, and graphically in relationship to other texts, both within the tradition and outside it. Messick also calls our attention to the authority *of* texts as they function in relationship to non-textual modes of practice. What makes a tradition discursive, then, is not only that it is textually mediated, but that textual mediation itself takes place within a broader range of expressive forms that have their own authoritative weight.[45]

While the pluralistic turn has brought Jewish studies to this important recognition, most scholarship continues to presume that texts provide the anchor for other modes of Jewish expression. Even the pluralists within Jewish studies continue to proclaim the text as the authoritative and centripetal force that binds together diverse Jewish traditions. Of course, historians must rely on texts when other evidence is absent. Yet, the textual emphasis that still dominates Jewish studies has its own modern genealogy. Although textual authority has obviously operated within Judaism since antiquity, modern communicative regimes recentered the text as the unequivocal source of "normative," "traditional," and "authentic" Judaism; the scripturalist values of religious reformism converged with print capitalism to reify the text as both the unparalleled receptacle of divine revelation and a fetishized commodity with its own generative power. This is not to say that texts were insignificant to Judaism before the modern period. It is simply to point out that modern modes of producing, distributing, and reading texts have determined how scholars of Judaism conceive of Jewish textuality. The scholarly focus on the text also reflects modern Judaic aversions to the material, embodied, and visual manifestations of Jewish tradition.[46]

In recent decades, historians and ethnographers of Judaism have begun to work against the textualist grain by studying Jewish artifacts (art, crafts, architecture, gravesites, amulets, clothing, tools, machines, broadsheets, codices) and practices (pilgrimage, magic, pietism, gastronomy, life-cycle events) as integral constituents of Jewish tradition. Yet, even as Jewish studies attends more closely to non-textual forms of expression, textual analysis remains the default mode of research in the field.[47] Moreover, the balanced attention that some scholars now give to the interactions between texts and practices has not extended equally to the study of Jewish traditions across the globe. In some cases, in fact, the challenge facing Jewish studies is to focus more intently on texts. The long Christian history of representing Jews as carnal rather than spiritual, material rather than philosophical, orthoprax rather than orthodox, is still evident in scholarship on Middle Eastern Jews that overemphasizes the practical and material sides of Judaism and neglects the textual. The folklorization of North African and Levantine Jews reflects the once dominant scholarly inclination to view these groups as "traditional"—illiterate, oral, practical, superstitious—and therefore as more appropriately studied with ethnographic methods than textual ones. Judeo-Arabic, Judeo-Spanish, and Judeo-Persian literatures were seen to occupy non-serious popular genres; scholars mostly overlooked the prolific textual production and venerable literary traditions that extended well beyond what was preserved in the Cairo Geniza or produced during the Andalusian golden age.[48] Only recently have scholars begun to redress these oversights by looking more closely at the pervasive textuality of non-European Jewish communities: historical studies now focus more regularly on Middle Eastern rabbinic and literary traditions, and ethnographic studies deal with the production of textual artifacts, the centrality of textual institutions, the circulation of textual materials, and the practice of textual rituals in North African and other societies.[49]

The pluralistic turn in Jewish studies also represents the recognition that the placement of texts in evaluative and experiential Jewish hierarchies is always subject to negotiation. Texts are rarely absent from fields of Jewish experience and authority, even when books are relatively unavailable and illiteracy prevalent; but neither does textuality always dominate within hierarchies of expressive authority that include other practices as well.[50] Beyond this insight, however, the relationship between text and practice remains ill conceptualized. Judaism is composed not only of texts and practices, with the latter either flouting or enacting normative written prescriptions; it is also composed of textual practices through which the tradition performatively emerges. A discursive approach highlights the capacity that such textual practices harbor to endure as citable marks of Jewish tradition, a tradition that is thereby inscribed in the writings, images, sounds, and habits that, transmitted across generations, contribute to the formation of Jews as Jews.[51]

Attention to the transmissibility of Judaism across a range of media also provides an alternative to pluralistic approaches: a discursive approach to Jewish tradition shifts focus from seemingly static social divisions across lines of gender, class, education, and prestige to the social production of internally differentiated Jewish subjects. Such an inquiry begins with the instituted practices through which Jews are disciplined into Jewishness across the entire range of expressive media and contexts. This approach requires the study of Jewish education and pedagogy, but also of the pietistic, artistic, professional, medical, judicial, and other institutions through which Judaism is daily transmitted. Every iteration of Jewish expression is necessarily an act of transmission for those who experience and witness it, just as every strategy of Jewish transmission is also a form of Jewish expression. Like all traditions, Judaism is, in this sense, a performative one. The fact that its transmission is always imperfect—characterized by both rupture and continuity—need not be viewed as a threat. It is an inherent feature of all living traditions, which must remain mutable in order to survive.[52]

Even practices performed and identities cultivated against the grain of the dominant forms of Judaism in any given context are part of the discursive tradition. This seems clearest at those formative moments when the difference between the Jewish and the non-Jewish was unclear and debated. But the principle holds no less with respect to crypto-Jews in Spain and the Sefaradi diaspora, Ethiopian Hebrews, or modern Jewish messianists ("Jews for Jesus"). Our point is not the nominalist one that all those who call themselves Jewish are part of the tradition, though this is a conclusion to which the present analysis may lead. Our point is rather that the supposed boundaries of Jewish tradition are the emergent effects of social interactions, theological apologetics, heresiologies, legal pronouncements, and other statements and iterations of power. The boundaries are not intrinsic or transcendent features of Jewish tradition itself.[53]

Likewise, the boundaries that distinguish Jews from others are determined neither entirely by Jews, as theorists of Jewish agency would have it, nor by others, as ideologues of Jewish victimization in the diaspora once held. Rather, Jewish identity is established dialogically by Jews and non-Jews who possess, wield, and resist the power to set those boundaries. In some cases, boundary setting occurs collusively, as when the Jews of modern France denied their racial distinctiveness (as *juifs*) while emphasizing their spiritual inclusion in what elsewhere came to be called the Judeo-Christian ethic; non-Jewish republican apologists accepted and elaborated similar discourses of French national identity within which secularized Jews appeared as exemplary citizens whose confessional religious identity (as *israélites*) properly receded into the private sphere of civil society. In other cases, Jews have had identities inescapably foisted upon them, as when those very same claims to citizenship came under fire from countervailing discourses of French national purity and racialized semitic difference.[54]

The boundaries between competing Jewish identities and variant Jewish traditions come into being though a similarly dialogic process. European Jews represented themselves as "brethren" to Jews in the colonies, often by reference to common ancestral identity. At the same time, European Jews also emphasized both the superiority of their own civilization, in which they positioned themselves as beneficiaries of emancipation, and the backwardness of their Arabic-speaking coreligionists. Colonized Jews did not remain silent, as when local rabbinic authorities called into question the Jewish authenticity of religious educators in the Alliance schools. At the same time, colonized Jews resisted their treatment as undifferentiated natives (*indigènes*), often by denying the Arab identity imposed upon them.[55]

This fraught play of identities indicates that Judaism and Jewishness are not transmitted homogenously through disciplinary institutions with a monopoly on determining what remains inside and outside the boundaries of tradition. Rather, the tradition is transmitted heterogeneously through competing institutions. The Alliance schools, for instance, never fully displaced other institutions of Jewish socialization in shaping the subjectivities of their colonized Jewish students: students cut class to make pilgrimages to saints' shrines; Jewish parents who sent their children to study science continued to patronize magicians and amulet writers; just when the Alliance had successfully inculcated Francophonie and French came to prevail over Arabic in quotidian Jewish conversation, the popular Judeo-Arabic press experienced unparalleled growth. Moroccan Jewish subjectivity, like all forms of subjectivity, is not merely divided along lines of class, gender, educational achievement, and so forth; it is divided within every individual.[56]

This view of discursive subjectivity also puts us in a position to rethink the local and global extents of Jewish tradition. Calling Judaism a "total way of life" is misleading if, by that claim, one means that Jews in the "traditional" past led lives determined entirely by precepts of Jewish law and custom: the Jew who served time in an Ottoman jail, paid port taxes in Aden, apprenticed as a metalworker in Tunisia, composed a sonata in Germany, or went to a baseball game in Brooklyn indicates otherwise. Judaism has never had the exclusive capacity to form the identities and subjectivities of individual Jews. Judaism is a total system only in the sense that every act committed in its name indexes a set of institutional practices that does not necessarily respect the boundaries that ideally define the autonomous realms of modern civil society (religious, legal, educational, economic, domestic, and political).[57]

Nor should the totality of Judaism be confused with the assertions of particular orthodoxies, whose power to shape what is normative is always limited. The secular American Jew who gives money to the Ḥabad movement represents both the power and weakness of normative Jewish projects. This does not mean, as some have asserted, that Jewish normativity is characteristically sectarian in the absence of a centralized Jewish clergy. Jews have established numerous structures of centralized authority—from the Jerusalem Temple and the gaonic yeshivot to the Consistoire and the Israeli state—and those structures possessed or negotiated access to coercive power.[58] Likewise, Jewish normativity is not distinctive by virtue of reference to the past or rejection of it; as in other traditions, the Jewish past is a normative benchmark to be variously utilized or deliberately ignored. Jewish orthodoxies are normative, then, not because they successfully discipline every Jew, fully monopolize Jewish authority, or maintain continuity with the past. Orthodoxies are normative because they assert, more or less successfully, disciplinary, authoritative, and rhetorical power. In this regard, the pluralist inclination to move "beyond" Jewish normativity by dismissing it as a "second order" construct that produces an illusory essentialism fails to account for the ways in which orthodoxy is, in fact, a mode of power. Normative Judaism is a very real effect of the discursive construction of the Jewish tradition and the disciplinary processes that form Jewish reasoning minds and practicing bodies.[59]

Finally, if Judaism is in any sense a global tradition, this is not because it brings together a worldwide community within a stable discourse of common identity. Indeed, Jews have often experienced difficulty in establishing common ground, whether they have found themselves circumscribed within relatively local contexts or troubled by the conflict between diasporic identities and Zionist ones.[60] Rather, Judaism and Jewishness are global because they circulate in cosmopolitan networks of mobility and communication, within which relatively autonomous religious traditions and identities reflect and refract each other. As we have been arguing, Jewish tradition is always contaminated by others and contaminates them in return. In this sense, Judaism is discursive because it is heteroglossic and hybrid—constituted, and not merely modified, at the boundary between "interfering" religious systems, whether the local and imperial religions of the ancient Near East and Mediterranean or Christianity and Islam.

Jewish studies, especially in its pluralist incarnations, has moved well beyond the evaluative discourses of orthodoxy and nationalism, which, for different reasons, cast Judaism as an essentially autonomous tradition. Notions such as hybridity have become key frames of analysis that have reoriented Jewish studies to the borders between Judaism and other discursive traditions. Indeed, even potentially outmoded analytical categories such as acculturation and syncretism have recently been revised so that they no longer follow derivatively from native concepts, such as heresy and apostasy (*minut, kefira*), that make hybridity appear to be the exception rather than the rule. Attempts to recuperate these analytical categories, once associated with naïve essentialism, represent one important step in the remaking of Jewish studies at the crossroads of anthropology and history. The recuperation of other such categories—including authority, diaspora, and tradition—represents a next step forward.[61]

Authority, Diaspora, and Tradition

We have argued that the three rubrics into which we have divided this book—authority, diaspora, and tradition—remain indispensable to the field of Jewish studies, despite their overburdened genealogies within various Jewish discourses as well as in the field itself. When properly reconceptualized, all three bear the potential to remake Jewish studies in fundamental ways. We are also convinced that these three critical terms are viable as analytical categories only when understood and deployed in concert. With that in mind, we offer the reader a guide to the book's contents.

The book's first section includes studies that move beyond abstract or prescriptive statements about where authority resides "in Judaism" and attend, instead, to how various institutional modes (political, religious, cultural) and media (texts, practices, artifacts) have, in practice, served to establish and contest authority in specific Jewish contexts. The chapters in this section thus emphasize the constructed nature of authority and, more interestingly, the conditions for its transformation and even corrosion.

Riv-Ellen Prell's fine-grained account of an intense social drama that unfolded at Camp Ramah during the summer of 1965 presents a case in which conflicting claims to authority drew upon competing Jewish discourses. Prell analyzes how campers and staff reacted to a group of Black Jews who spent a Sabbath on the Ramah campus. She argues that the partial accommodations that the various participants reached regarding the eligibility of Black Jews to be called to the Torah heralded the emergence of a novel form of Jewish subjectivity that was grounded in American discourses of racial justice. As Prell demonstrates, the controversy brought to a head unresolved tensions between Conservative Jewish views of halakhah and what some in the camp community viewed as the equally authoritative Jewish imperatives embodied by the civil rights movement.

J. H. Chajes's chapter on the discourses and uses of magic within rabbinic culture analyzes the capacity of individual rabbis to navigate competing modes of authority. Chajes attends to rabbinic elites' tactical participation in activities that they themselves deemed to be illicit and potentially dangerous. From antiquity to modernity, these elites exhibited a finely tuned sense of how best to negotiate this fraught but also potentially empowering domain. Chajes shows that rabbis adopted a wide range of postures, at times distancing themselves from potentially suspect practices while also claiming magical expertise in order to bolster their own authority in the context of widely held ideologies of supernatural efficacy.

As Yoram Bilu demonstrates, audiences, no less than authors, participate in the construction and deterioration of authority. In his analysis of the rise and fall of a saint's shrine in contemporary Israel, Bilu charts the space between the personal dreamworld of a single individual and the shared cultural framework of a wider community. Bilu examines how the ongoing process of dream narration initiated by the shrine's impresario authenticated devotional practice at the shrine by using a recognizable vocabulary shared by others. The site thus owed its short-lived success to the formation of an identifiable, if relatively transitory, community that came together through the "public" circulation in speech and writing of "private" dream experiences.

Like Bilu's chapter, Shalom Sabar's study of Jewish marriage contracts (*ketubbot*) accords special prominence to the performative dimension of authority. Sabar focuses his analysis on the interplay between widespread rabbinic norms and divergent iconographic conventions. Sabar asks how the written formulas prescribed by rabbinic law, the ornamental motifs of local artistic traditions, and the materiality of the object itself have worked in concert to produce legally binding agreements as well as affectively charged artifacts. He finds that the authority of marriage documents emerges from their performative force in the ritual settings that transform inert objects into both legitimate contracts and protective amulets.

The second section of this volume ranges over the *longue durée* of the Jewish diaspora, from Mediterranean antiquity to the period of modern Jewish nationalism. The authors in this section demonstrate how Jews have regularly contested both the primacy of a single sacred center in the Holy Land and the meaning of dispersion, often undermining the very dichotomy between diaspora and sacred center.

Ra'anan S. Boustan's essay on the fate of the Temple vessels in rabbinic sources from the centuries after the Roman destruction of Jerusalem invites us to reconsider the tension between views of diaspora as either the unequivocal site of Jewish degradation or the unparalleled context of creative authenticity. He argues that new modes of religious authority grounded in rabbinic practices of Torah study did not entirely displace the authority of visual experience, especially with respect to the material artifacts associated with the Temple in Jerusalem and its priestly rituals. Rather, the materiality of authority as it had been elaborated in the cultic center remained a frame of reference even within a self-consciously text-centered rabbinic Judaism.

Lucia Raspe's study of medieval mortuary practices focuses on how the "graves of the righteous" contributed to the formation of Jewish identity in the diaspora. Extending research on Jewish pilgrimages and shrines that has focused primarily on North African and Hasidic contexts, Raspe traces the development of similar traditions in the heart of Ashkenaz. She shows that enshrinement in the medieval German context corresponded with corollary Christian traditions, but also took shape in the crucible of relatively autonomous Judaic ideologies, liturgical customs, and rabbinic debates. Raspe argues that the graves of the righteous served to establish diasporic places as sacred Jewish homes, even as those homes came to be imagined in ways that reinforced the paradigm of an orienting Jewish center in the Holy Land.

Andrea Schatz's analysis of Samuel Romanelli's *Masa' ba'rav* reminds us that Jewish diasporic identity is not always negotiated with reference to territorial homelands and diasporas. Her essay explores how an eighteenth-century Italian maskil, in his depiction of the Jewish communities of Morocco, used a set of rhetorical tactics that recapitulated orientalist representations of the East as a distant place of radical otherness. Yet Schatz also insists that Romanelli inflected Christian orientalism by invoking points of identity that linked him to his North African interlocutors. Schatz provocatively concludes that Romanelli's text constructs the diaspora as a new kind of Jewish home, one that is located in the rational and mobile epistemology of the Enlightenment rather than in any territorial location.

Tamar Katriel's essay on "rescue narratives" in modern Israeli culture examines the legacies of orientalism in the context of modern Jewish nationalism. Katriel analyzes mass-mediated Israeli discourses that have represented communities from Africa and Asia as passive populations in need of heroic intervention by the Jewish state. In these narratives, the diaspora emerges as both the common ground of idealized Jewish unity, to be fully realized through "the ingathering of exiles," and a zone of Jewish difference and hierarchy, inhabited by those supposedly incapable of redeeming themselves. At the same time, Katriel demonstrates that the "rescued" communities have voiced counter-narratives that recuperate diasporic locations outside Israel as spaces of nostalgic longing, heroic sacrifice, and historical agency.

The final section of this volume is composed of chapters that destabilize the notion that "traditions" emerge neutrally from a preexisting and fixed repository of past beliefs and practices. Each chapter examines key moments in which the idea of "the Jewish tradition" appears to take an active and self-conscious role in its own construction. The section also demonstrates that Judaism provides a context particularly well suited to studying the uses of tradition in legitimizing claims to continuity.

Albert I. Baumgarten and Marina Rustow's essay on Jewish discourses of tradition from antiquity to modernity argues that claims to continuity emerge precisely during periods of rapid change. Their analysis invites us to reconsider the distinction between genuine and spurious traditions and to question the standard periodization that holds "the invention of tradition" to be a uniquely modern phenomenon. Their survey of key moments in the genealogy of "tradition" as an object of Jewish discourse demonstrates that the insistence with which Jewish authorities assert fidelity to the past tends to be diagnostic of historical moments in which structures of authority are undergoing significant challenges and transformations.

Sylvie Anne Goldberg's essay on the controversy over the calculation of the calendar in medieval Judaism similarly takes up the dialectic between discourses of continuity and contexts of change. At the heart of the essay is what Goldberg calls the "troublesome" situation in which Se'adyah Ga'on (882–942) instituted radical changes and reforms while justifying them as the seamless continuation of past practices. Goldberg demonstrates that Se'adyah brought together two competing Judaic discourses of tradition: the biblical notion that it is handed down unchanged as a sacred legacy and the rabbinic idea that it is something constructed over time.

In his essay on the liturgical practices of medieval European Jews, Ephraim Kanarfogel focuses on the realm of prayer to investigate the relationship between the oral and the written in the performance and transmission of Jewish liturgy in Ashkenaz and Sefarad. The question of orality and literacy was particularly fraught in late antique and medieval halakhah, which regulated what could be transmitted in oral and written form. Kanarfogel demonstrates that far from being immutable, this legal corpus exhibited flexibility depending on the availability of written prayer books. He also argues that close readings of textual sources produced by the elite can provide precious evidence of popular practices and competences.

Tamar El-Or's contribution focuses on the transmission of tradition among Sefaradi ultraorthodox and *ḥaredi* women in contemporary Israel. El-Or studies women "returning" to traditional Jewish practice who have developed a new method of fulfilling the halakhic obligation to bake Sabbath bread and to sacrifice part of the dough symbolically. In these women's hands, a ritual that had previously been relegated to the private space of the kitchen has been transformed into a public act that attests to their embrace of "tradition." El-Or's analysis situates this transformation in the context of global and postmodern religious discourses in which public "spiritual experience" has emerged as a form of women's resistance to the patriarchal relegation of women to the domestic sphere.

Concluding a set of chapters that touch on moments in which Jewish practices comment on their own relationship to previous traditions, Michael D. Swartz offers a study of what he terms "ancient ritual theory" in early Judaism. Comparing late antique prescriptive and liturgical sources regarding the defunct sacrificial rite for the Day of Atonement (the 'Avodah), Swartz argues that rituals often include systematic metadiscourses about themselves. Building upon theories that highlight the opacity of ritual and its inherent resistance to exegesis, Swartz suggests that at moments when new forms of authority emerge, rituals can become public acts of interpretation in which the recitation of a bygone practice is transformed into a performative constituent of tradition itself.

Finally, Harvey E. Goldberg's epilogue to the volume reflects on the transformation of Jewish studies over the past generation by tracing key moments in the emergence of the anthropology of Jews and Judaism. One of the field's founding and most influential scholars, Goldberg offers a compelling account of these developments that is at once personal and synthetic, autobiographical and analytic. He situates the preceding chapters within the scholarly currents of anthropology and Jewish studies, and offers them as evidence of the productive "cross-fertilization" between the fields. Goldberg concludes with the suggestion that the remaking of Jewish studies depends on the willingness of scholars to move collaboratively beyond the conventional methodological and substantive boundaries that previously separated anthropology and history.

As we have suggested, and as the integrative approach taken in the epilogue makes clear, the rubrics of authority, diaspora, and tradition cannot be considered effectively in isolation from one another. The tripartite division of this volume, therefore, should not be regarded as constraining the themes that the individual chapters address. Thus, for example, Prell's account of the contested Torah service at Camp Ramah, though it appears in the section on authority, is as much about a sphere of traditional practice as about the dynamics of halakhic and ethical authority. Schatz's analysis of Romanelli's travel writings, which appears in the section on diaspora, attends to the emergent authority of Enlightenment epistemology as much as it sheds light on the diasporic encounter between Jews from different worlds. Swartz's argument about ancient ritual theory is both about the creation of new exegetical and liturgical traditions and about how such traditions reflect the efforts of Jewish authors and functionaries to bolster their own authority. Although Bilu's chapter is situated in the section that deals with authority, his case study of a Moroccan shrine in Israel also reflects the reconfiguration of the Jewish diaspora after 1948. Similarly, Katriel's discussion of "the rhetoric of rescue" in the Israeli mass media focuses not only on the problem of diaspora but on the contested forms of narrative authority asserted by the Israeli state apparatus and subaltern ethnic communities.

The volume as whole, then, suggests that authority, diaspora, and tradition are not independent facets of Jewish historical experience but interconnected frames of reference. Keeping the connections among them in mind prevents a return to essentialism and, more importantly, to those modes of analysis that celebrate diversity from the pluralistic standpoint of liberal modernity. Having authority on one's mind when thinking about tradition serves to hedge against normative approaches to tradition and to clarify the contested nature of institutionalized Jewish discourses. Considering diaspora in its historical specificity and its global expanse disrupts approaches that rely on implicit hierarchies of place and obscure the relationships between them. Tradition, likewise, can no longer be understood comparatively, as the heritage of relatively isolated communities, or relativistically, as a mosaic of colorful varieties; Jewish tradition comes into being through trans-regional processes and within social fields of authority and debate. We hope that the reader will appreciate the following chapters as an ensemble that suggests future directions for Jewish studies.

PART I. AUTHORITY

Chapter 1

"How Do You Know That I Am a Jew?": Authority, Cultural Identity, and the Shaping of Postwar American Judaism

RIV-ELLEN PRELL

In 1955, Bernard Malamud, a writer much taken with metaphorical relationships between Jews and African Americans in the United States, wrote "Angel Levine," a story that might be read as a comment upon authenticity and authority in Jewish life.[1] In Malamud's fiction, a modern-day Job, a tailor and pious Jew whom he calls simply—and not without irony—Manischewitz, suffers a tragic reversal of fortune.[2] He loses his business because of a fire and is left in penury despite insurance. His son has been killed in the war, and his daughter has married "a lout" and disappeared. He is wracked by debilitating physical pain, and his beloved wife, Fanny, is near death. Finally, in desperation, he prays to God for help.

Later that evening, he feels the presence of another person in his tiny apartment. In the next room, he discovers "a Negro reading a newspaper" seated at his table. Manischewitz, after some time, finally asks him, "Who are you?" and is "amused" by the man's reply: "I bear the name Alexander Levine." This obviously Jewish name strikes the tailor as incongruous for an African American. Malamud writes of Manischewitz, "Carrying the jest farther, [he] asked, 'You are maybe Jewish?'" Levine replies, "All my life I was, willingly."

Manischewitz feels by turns mocked and dubious when Levine offers him his "humble assistance" because he declares that he is an angel of God, albeit one who has recently been "disincarnated." Thus he begins his attempt to authenticate Levine both as an angel and as a Jew. He inquires about his wings, asks him to recite the blessing over bread, and finally inquires why God has sent a black angel. Levine explains obliquely that he had lost his wings, provides the blessing over bread in a rich Hebrew voice, and notes simply—in response to why a "Negro angel"—that he was next in line to appear. Unsatisfied, Manischewitz proclaims, "Is this what a Jewish angel looks like? This I am not convinced." Confronted with the denial of his authority and authenticity, the angel takes his leave for Harlem.

Ultimately, however, Manischewitz does seek out the angel Levine's help. Malamud takes this Job to the brink of belief and pulls him back finally to have him affirm to a disheveled, drunken Levine in the arms of a very human woman, "You are Jewish. This I am sure." Then, prompted by Levine, he adds, "I think you are an angel from God." Weeping, Levine declares, "How you have humiliated me," and then changes his clothes, walks with Manischewitz to his flat, and from there ascends. At home, the tailor discovers his wife restored and tidying their apartment, and he, too, regains his health and ability to work. Manischewitz's prayers have been answered, and he proclaims the final words of the story: "A wonderful thing Fanny. . . . Believe me, there are Jews everywhere!"[3]

Although "Angel Levine" has rightly been read as a theological work concerned with embodiment, as well as a meditation on relationships between Jews and African Americans, it offers an equally incisive reflection on the nature of authenticity and authority for Jews immediately after World War II. In Manischewitz's meeting with an angel who is "other," that is, a "Negro angel," he must ask himself what makes a person, or an angel, for that matter, a Jew. Is genealogy, religious competence, or race the most relevant, or even necessary, criterion to authenticate Jewishness? Could a man in Harlem in 1955 be a Jewish angel? Could black Jews, whom Manischewitz encounters in Harlem, be Jews like himself? Malamud's fictional tailor is persuaded that Jews are everywhere, and Malamud's readers are similarly asked to consider what Jewishness is, and how one can know who and what is Jewish.

Malamud was prescient precisely because his story did not focus on institutional life; he did not confront his crisis in the spaces of synagogues or organizations. Rather, Manischewitz must confront the problem of authority through his own choices and actions. He must, in a time of crisis, decide not *what* to believe, but *whom* to believe. He must face the problem of how to bring order out of what he experiences as the contradictions of race, ethnicity, and Judaism in the midst of personal crisis. Further, Malamud writes of

Manischewitz's quandary, "Was a man ever so tried? Should he say he believed a half-drunken Negro to be an angel? The silence slowly petrified. Manischewitz was recalling scenes of his youth as a wheel in his mind whirred: believe, do not, yes, no, yes, no. The pointer pointed to yes, to between yes and no, to no, no it was yes. He sighed. It moved but one still had to make a choice."[4]

Thus, Malamud offers a story of how one man makes sense of cultural and religious contradictions in order to restore order to his life. Through the story's juxtaposition of whiteness, blackness, Jews, and Judaism, it frames a discussion of authority with the problem of identity. It reveals that competing ideas of authority are at play in the ways in which individuals and communities understand themselves to be Jews, to engage in Jewish life, and to make Jewish decisions and choices.

But if Judaism and Jews are not, to use Malamud's formulation, what they first appear to be—something given, immutable, and transparently identifiable—then scholars of culture must find the right settings to ask how religion in general and Judaism in particular "work." How does Judaism, as a total system of claims on the individual, constitute specific practices and discourses as Jewish? This process revolves around the problem of authority or of multiple—and, at times, competing—sources of authority. Thus, over and beyond the historical issue of placing Judaism within a particular time and place, the central question must be how Judaism is made authoritative through specific sets of relationships and processes. How does the negotiation of multiple authorities, both communal and individual, translate to the formation of culture and identity? What are the sources of self and communal identity that put Jews into relationships of power that are continually being constituted and challenged?[5]

Malamud's short story "Angel Levine" serves as a literary metaphor for the case study that is the focus of this chapter, a crisis concerning the authenticity of the Jewishness of a group of young Black Jews who visited a Conservative Jewish summer camp in the mid-1960s. In the summer of 1965, teenage campers and their counselors and teachers at Camp Ramah experienced a version of Manischewitz's problem when the camp was asked to host a Sabbath visit with Black Jewish teenagers who belonged to an organization called Hatzaad Harishon (The First Step), which was devoted to linking Black Jews and Jews of European descent, groups that had rarely recognized each other's legitimacy or claims to Jewishness.[6] It is no surprise that the authenticity of the Jewishness of the camp's guests became a source of crisis, making visible the often implicit conflict among competing ideas about what constituted the central values and symbols of postwar American Judaism.

In these events, Jewish authorizing processes were made manifest. The classical rabbinic system of authoritative legal-religious discourse (halakhah) was evoked in relationship and contrast to American concepts of democracy, racial liberalism, and personal meaning in the context of a nationwide mobilization around race relations and civil rights. The events reveal how these various systems of authority were integrated, fractured, and reshaped—in short, how they became an authorizing process for Jewish life. More than showing systems of authority in conflict, the case study reveals the dynamic process by which identity and authority interacted. In the 1960s, Jews faced a growing number of possible definitions of what it meant to be a Jew and how to act like an American Jew. A close study of this dynamic suggests how they formulated choices and asserted authority. It also reveals the existence of a surfeit of authorities, all claimed and legitimated by those within the Conservative movement.

In this essay, I offer a reading of the context of Jewish life in the postwar period that locates Jewish summer camping as a critical site for understanding Jewish socialization as it was conceived by rabbis and educators. These contexts provide an ideal venue for the study of competing ideas and visions of Jewish life and how those are central to the problem of authority. I will then look at the unique role that civil rights programming played at Camp Ramah in the 1960s, how leaders of these camps translated ideas about Judaism to contemporary events, and how their translations created an American Jewish identity authorized by a particular reading of halakhah. In short, these events, like so many forms of socialization, reveal authority as a process. In so doing, they allow us to analyze the construction of identities.

The historian Ivan Marcus provides a helpful starting place for a discussion of authority as a dynamic process. His study of rituals of childhood in medieval Ashkenaz moves well beyond traditional definitions of Jewish authority. He argues that the important question to ask is how Jews of a particular period made sense of the world in which they lived. He counsels that one cannot focus on "the culture of the Jews," since in that period, "culture" privileged a world of written texts authored by rabbis, all of whom were men. The perspective is distorting because it narrows in advance what counts as authority and experience. Rather, he counsels would-be interpreters to examine the "Jews as culture," that is, what Jews did in making Jewish lives, how their metaphors and media made sense of the world.[7] His focus on practice and action makes the study of authority dynamic rather than static, and behavioral rather than solely textual.

While Marcus points clearly to the interpretation of culture in studying the making of meaning, other scholars of religion focus on linkages among religion, authority, and power. For example, the anthropologist Talal Asad, long a critic of studying religion as a matter of disembodied attitudes and beliefs, argues that instead, one must train analysis on the "authorizing processes" that define religion in society.[8] Asad asks how the symbols and discourses that those who teach, embrace, and challenge religious traditions use become real and compelling. How do they deploy and question those discourses in power relations and in politics? He asks us to focus on religion as a dynamic system embedded in society, not a sphere separated from power.

These approaches share an interest in how people exercise authority rather than in how authority functions institutionally. Marcus and Asad both focus closely on the symbolic and discursive media through which such relationships are expressed. Marcus does, however, emphasize issues of cultural adaptation, how Jews reorient the rituals and ideas of a larger (Christian) culture, and how those rituals and ideas in turn reorient Jewish daily life. Asad argues for the centrality of political processes. In their work, I find a nexus point between cultural adaptation and political processes that is helpful in understanding why authority became the focus of both powerful symbolic discourses and conflict as Conservative Jews, in particular, established a postwar American Judaism.

The Social Drama's Sources and Gaps

The events I analyze in this chapter occurred more than forty years ago. I have drawn on many types of sources not only to re-create those events, but also to view them retrospectively through the eyes of some of the participants, who felt their impact for many decades. Materials drawn from the Camp Ramah archive and the papers of Reform summer camps allowed me to survey civil rights programming in the camps in the early 1960s. Interviews with six of the Ramah participants—campers, the camp director, the scholar in residence, and a counselor—provided me with the "data" for reconstructing the events. It is important to stress from the outset that there is no consensus among the various participants about exactly what happened. They offered overlapping versions of the events and memories imbued with strong and varying emotions. What transpired is best understood as an open-ended "text," that is, a set of narratives about what occurred that reveal attitudes and understanding as well as fading memories. Its ambiguities and differing scenarios play quite directly into the task of understanding how authorizing processes become visible through the partisans' conflict over what is Jewish, what is halakhic, and what is racist.

What is lacking in this account is the point of view of the Black Jews who experienced these events—and who served as one of the catalysts for the process analyzed here. I have located archival sources about the group to which they belonged and have learned about how issues of authority and authenticity ultimately undermined it.[9] But there were no specific sources about who among them attended that particular Sabbath at camp. In any case, this is a story from the perspective of those Jews who were participants in the American Seminar at Camp Ramah that summer.

New Spaces for American Judaism in the Postwar Period

Postwar Jewish life was characterized by a series of changes in the ways American Jews organized their lives. Following World War II, Jews in America moved south and west. Virtually everywhere they settled, they moved to the suburbs for the first time in significant numbers. The dense urban enclaves where Jews had lived for decades in neighborhoods that were overwhelmingly Jewish did not disappear. But they were supplanted by residential patterns in which Jews were not in the majority, and the synagogue, once just one among a number of institutions of Jewish urban life, rapidly became the dominant one.[10]

The aspirations of young parents for their children drove many of their key decisions following the war, and Jewishness was surely among the most complex. The decision to join a synagogue was in large part motivated by the desire—or pressure, depending on one's point of view—to educate children of the postwar baby boom about Judaism. Often, but not always, the settings where Jewish children were sent—Hebrew schools, summer camps, youth groups, and day schools—were battlegrounds for their hearts and minds, often tugs-of-war between educators and rabbis firmly holding one side of the rope, with parents at the other end.

Some suburban parents in the 1950s and early 1960s demanded religious curricula that did not require families to practice or believe what their children were learning. Occasionally, they even insisted that educators exclude the very concept of God from their children's Jewish educations. Some parents were, of course, quite enthusiastic about Judaism, increasing their participation in synagogue and Jewish practice in concert with their children's involvement. But most families fell into the middle, and the parents who felt strongly about their Judaism were more likely the exception than the rule.[11]

After the war, a variety of Jewish cultural spaces—both new and old—flourished in unprecedented ways. Many of these became cultural battle-grounds of Jewish life. Educators and rabbis who were passionate advocates for a new Judaism created summer camps that were among the most central of these new spaces. They arose out of newly invigorated Jewish denominations that were enjoying a boom in synagogue membership and institution-building. They offered Jewish children and teenagers a different vision of Jewish life from the one that they encountered in their homes and even synagogues. Although summer camping was embedded in the institutional framework of Jewish denominations, it often provided a counterpoint to them. Camps advocated ideas, activities, and ways of being Jewish that were not identical to those put forward in the synagogue and certainly not to the Jewish practices of most families. Indeed, much of the camp leadership was critical of synagogues and families for a lack of "authentic" Jewish practice. As a result, summer camps were often viewed—and viewed themselves—as competitors for the loyalties of young Jews.[12]

Postwar denominational summer camps built on a more-than-fifty-year history of camping as a response to a variety of issues that confronted American Jews over these decades, including poverty, nationalism, and Americanization. Jewish summer camps began in the late nineteenth century in the United States to provide opportunities for poor children to enjoy a better diet and climate. The first Jewish educational camps were established after World War I. Camp Cejwin began in New York in 1919 and Camp Modin in Maine in 1922. Camp Achva, the first Hebrew-language camp, was founded in 1927, and Camp Boberik, a Yiddish-speaking camp, in 1928. The Labor Zionist youth movement in North America began Kvutz Habonim camps in 1932, called Kvutz, with campsites throughout the United States and Canada. Camp Massad, founded in 1941, offered a "second generation" of camping devoted to Hebrew-language instruction. Several other small educational camps were also established in the 1930s.[13]

At the end of World War II, a new type of educational camping developed that was closely linked to the larger structural changes in American Jewish life. Denominational camps emerged in this period. The Reform, Orthodox, and Conservative movements sought to bring children into year-round education and Jewish experience through their summer camps. Their aim was to link the Jewish activities of the school year in religious school, Hebrew school, religious day schools, and youth groups to intensive summer experiences, and thus to shape, or more likely reshape, children's Jewish environments.

Conservative Judaism's Camp Ramah was begun in 1947, and Reform Judaism developed its first summer camp (referred to as an "institute") in 1951. Each was located in Wisconsin, but other campuses appeared throughout the Northeast, the West, Canada, and the South. While the Orthodox movement did not sponsor a specific camp, Camp Moshava, affiliated with the Orthodox-Zionist movement B'nai Akiba, drew Orthodox campers who were often part of the Orthodox Union youth movement.[14]

There were obvious differences among these camps with regard to levels of observance, their commitment to Hebrew education, the extent to which they included Yiddish culture, and their relationship to Israel. Yet, for all their variations, they shared some striking similarities. The remoteness of Jewish summer camps from cities and their isolation allowed them to create a new world and landscape. They provided an alternative environment to home, school, and synagogue for the transmission of Judaism. The authority figures, teachers, counselors, and rabbis at the camps interacted more personally with campers through communal living, sports teaching, and conversations than they could in the school or synagogue setting. These leaders became crucial role models for a new way of practicing Judaism.[15] They emphasized a Judaism that was often more rigorous than campers found at home, across the denominations, but also one that was, by campers' accounts, more joyful and pleasurable. The Jewish calendar structured each day and each week of the camp session. The Sabbath, however it was observed, was a focal point. Judaism and Jewishness were the norm of the camp experience. The camps' activities emphasized Jewish culture—music, dance, Bible, and history—as well as American culture—music, dance, and citizenship.

Most Jewish educational camps, then, aimed at more than merely offering a summer of fun and entertainment. They intended to provide a form of socialization, a process that I will discuss at length below. Ideas motivated these educational camps: What is the language of the Jewish people? What are Jewish arts? How should a Jew live? These ideas were most effectively communicated by creating the camp as a world set apart, a space that was liminal both physically and culturally, in which children were separated from home, school, and synagogue, and experienced new relationships, experiences, and authorities.[16] Summer camp was classically "anti-structural," outside the ordinary routines of life. The camps' goal was to have children return yearly, to move from being campers to becoming counselors and even to assume the role of director. Most of these camps were available for children from ages ten to sixteen or seventeen. A significant number of children and teenagers who attended camp throughout their young lives came to see themselves and their Judaism through the prism of their camp experience, and that was precisely what educators had in mind. Moshe Davis, a founder of Camp Ramah and a counselor at Camp Massad, summarized the philosophy of many camps: "The whole day was now under our supervision. Until then you would come to a [prayer] service and you would come to [afternoon] school, but you didn't live as a Jew in a civilization."[17] Re-creating what Davis and others thought of as Jewish civilization required a world set apart as well as yearly participation.

The remaking of Jewish authority became an unfolding saga in denominational camps that brought together concerns for children's identification as Jews, their moral and educational development, and their practice of Judaism, however that might be defined. These camps, in contrast to Zionist camps, for example, were committed to making children American Jews as well. They therefore contended with how to define Jews as Americans and how to negotiate competing claims on children's lives. It was these negotiations that contested the older modes of authority, both religious and cultural, and revealed how postwar American Judaism was being reshaped.

The majority of Jewish children who attended summer camps did not enroll in educational or Zionist ones. Most attended private camps that catered exclusively to Jews and emphasized recreation. Mordecai Kaplan once expressed his frustration with this form of camping when he famously asked why Jews sent their children to camps to learn how to be American Indians rather than Jews. The norm of recreational camping was to appropriate Native American customs, terms, ideas, and outdoor skills in an evocation of a "return to nature."[18] Well into the 1960s, the key premise of Jewish camps was that Jews were most comfortable around other Jews.

Educational camps, whether they were denominational, Yiddish, Zionist, or Hebraist, were engaged in the transmission of Jewish culture and not simply in building Jewish relationships. Because they sought to create Jews, they drew on symbols, language, rituals, and practices that shaped Jewish experience as authentic. It is within the context of transmitting Judaism and creating postwar American Jews that I situate my discussion of the crucial role that ideas about justice and Jews' responsibility to address racial oppression played in remaking the dynamics of authority within Jewish culture.

Civil Rights, Jewish Racial Liberalism, and Summer Camp

In the first half of the 1960s, civil rights became a critical form of discourse within liberal denominational Jewish summer camps. This discourse served as a medium for reflecting on and shaping Jewishness for Americans, just as the Holocaust and Israel would do in the following decades. The civil rights movement briefly played this role because it helped to define what it meant to be a Jew in America, powerfully articulating a view of Jews as people who could draw on their own cultural traditions to serve larger American democratic and liberal ends. Depending on the denomination, Jewish values, Jewish law, and the Hebrew Bible, in addition to other classical texts, provided the grounding to guide contemporary Jewish lives effectively. From this perspective, Judaism was completely compatible with a liberal democracy. In turn, Jews were fully capable of participating in that liberal democracy and were obliged to see themselves as working for social justice. If we follow Marcus's reasoning, "the culture of the Jews" in the world of denominational summer camps made liberal values into fundamentally Jewish ones, and a progressive and inclusive outlook compatible with the specific practices of Jewish life.

Liberal political values did not define Judaism exclusively in these summer camps. Jewish prayer, the study of Jewish texts, and the importance of the rabbi or scholar were all critical to the life of the camp. What made denominational summer camps a site of this version of the liberal culture of the Jews was its ability to integrate Jewish practices with civil rights concerns. Political issues that swirled around adolescents at home and at school became Jewish issues in the context of camp. The same environment that promoted more rigorous ways of observing Shabbat, learning Jewish history, and posing ethical dilemmas became the context for learning about the civil rights movement. Hence, these issues became Jewish issues, issues that were sanctioned by the same authorities as the other activities at camp. How were Jewish authority and authenticity harnessed to produce this particular Jewish cultural formation?

Between 1961 and 1965, Conservative and Reform camps offered regular programs that addressed the struggle for justice within the civil rights movement. In 1961, campers at the Reform camp Olin-Sang-Ruby Union Institute, for example, created a play in which they role-played the oppressed (Bliks) and the oppressor (WASPs). The camp newspaper featured discussions about this activity, and in subsequent services, students delivered sermons about it.[19] In 1962, Camp Ramah in California engaged in a related but more elaborate experiment in the experience of oppression by turning a group of blond campers out of camp for the better part of the day to demonstrate the lessons of arbitrary discrimination.[20]

Retrospective interviews with the counselors and camp directors involved in these wide-ranging events evoked a remarkably similar set of reflections. Their goals were, first, to teach campers the meaning of justice by learning to empathize with victims of oppression and, second, to use Jewish "values," texts, and history to teach campers that Judaism was relevant to contemporary issues. Camp leaders believed that Jews should respond to injustice "as Jews," and camp programming was critical to teaching that process. Looking back on the dramatic, if not traumatic, role-play that exiled a group of children from camp to provide a lesson in racism, Walter Ackerman, the camp's director, who created the experiment and trained his staff for it for one week, explained to me why the event was so important:

> It took the kids four hours to figure out who was left in and who was forced out. They understood that the decision was based on arbitrariness. The impact was tremendous. The kids cried, yelled, and begged to be let back into camp. We finally did after the regular dinner. They gathered at the place in the camp where I spoke before *tefillot* [prayers] on Friday night. The occasion required it [a place that important]. I wanted them to understand civil rights, to know what they are talking about. This was an American issue that I turned into a Jewish issue. We have an obligation because of who we are in this struggle. We have an obligation to social justice. It was as simple as that. I feel highly identified with blacks—as a Jew.[21]

For Ackerman and others, that sense of identification led not only to engagement with civil rights issues, but to action and an attempt at change.

Similarly, Rabbi Shalom Podwol, who served as counselor at the Camp Ramah Poconos campus while he was a rabbinical student in 1963, created an elaborate performance with ninth- and tenth-graders of the integration of a school in Alabama. He included other moments in the civil rights movement, including the assassination of Medgar Evers, which had occurred at the beginning of camp that summer. He recalled that his campers felt that they were "doing something that they realized was going to have very lasting historical significance." Podwol described to me how he recalled thinking about the conjunction of civil rights and Judaism: "We would mention Hebrew prophets and that this is the right thing to do. We, the Jewish people, have to identify strongly with what the Negroes are going through. No one challenged that [at camp]. I thought that the connection between civil rights and Judaism was very clear. I wanted to show that this was something very much related to the teachings of Judaism."[22]

Podwol and other counselors spent the summer discussing the issues, teaching their campers about the events and figures, and even translating some of the civil rights speeches into Hebrew. The translations were especially important not only because the camp was committed to teaching Hebrew language, but because they further emphasized the vital connections between Judaism and civil rights.

One group of Ramah campers in the early 1960s staged an original opera in Hebrew on the themes of oppression and racism, written by the camp's music director, Rabbi Efry Spectre. The opera featured as a character the Mississippi sheriff Bull Connor's terrifying dog. Campers who participated in Hebrew musicals received study sheets with Hebrew and English vocabulary and memorized all their words and music. Campers that year learned Hebrew terms for "the Negro Race," "the brotherhood of man, and "the real estate value of the neighborhood," among many other phrases that taught about social injustice and racial indignity. Other Ramah camps staged several classic pieces of American musical theater about race: *Showboat* in 1955, *Finian's Rainbow* in 1959, and *Porgy and Bess* in 1962. All were performed in Hebrew.[23]

Chaim Potok, the late noted American Jewish writer, served as a head counselor at Ramah in the 1960s and looked back on the production of *Porgy and Bess* as the event that he was "proudest of at camp" because he said that the "campers could get under the skin of black men and women."[24] Potok's "pride" resulted from his ability to teach campers a deep empathy that would enable them, in his words, "to transcend their own world and to inhabit the experiences of others." His language captures the sensibility of the period: to begin to address injustice, one had first to experience the world of racial oppression. His formulation, that one could "get under the skin" of others through performing a musical, seems naïve at best.

Encouraging campers to identify with oppressed African Americans in a struggle that, at that point, was focused in the South, was both an emotional and cognitive strategy that had a profound impact on the postwar liberal denominational culture of the Jews. The Jewish world built within the camp sought to make Judaism "natural." The juxtaposition of Judaism and civil rights aimed to achieve on the political plane what virtually every other aspect of camp sought to do on the Jewish one: to instill campers with an intuitive and experiential sense of something that, until that point, may have been unfamiliar. Nathan Glazer wrote in *Commentary* magazine in 1956 that the purpose of teaching children to say "pass the butter" in Hebrew at Camp Ramah was "to provide an example of a Jewish life so that it will not be necessary to argue and put out apologetic literature—it will only be necessary to say: 'Be a good Jew' and give an example."[25]

Within a few years, at Ramah and other camps, children learned to identify racial justice as intuitively Jewish, one of the parade of examples of how to "be a good Jew." The empathic and the intuitive became authorizing processes in the socialization of American Jewish youth—a new form of authority within American Jewish life.

Liberal Judaism and Race in America

The denominational camps' engagement with the civil rights movement did not occur in a vacuum but simply constituted one more aspect of American Jews' complex relationships with African Americans and the ongoing struggles for racial justice.[26] Eric Goldstein's recent historical work on Jews and race demonstrates that Jews' own sense of racial identity was anything but stable or unitary throughout the nineteenth and early twentieth centuries. Jews from different parts of Europe did not always share the same ideas about race. In some periods, Jews thought of themselves as constituting a unique race in order to emphasize their difference from non-Jews. In other periods, they rejected racial designators for fear that, like African Americans, they would be unable to integrate into the broader American society. Early in the twentieth century, those Jews who were most committed to issues of racial equality for African Americans, men and women who were part of the progressive politics of the time, were usually the most remote from the Jewish community.[27] Eastern European immigrants often took up issues of racial equality through socialism, communism, and the union movements, but they were not a majority by any means.

Only beginning in the 1940s did a substantial majority of American Jews begin to express profound empathy for African Americans. Goldstein, among other scholars, describes the emergence among Jews of a "racial liberalism" that claimed that racial prejudice was un-American and antidemocratic. He argued that racial liberalism emerged once Jews' own racial identification was firmly secured as white.[28]

Denominational camps, then, may be seen as an important site for the transmission of racial liberalism as part of a postwar "culture of the Jews." Indeed, it was one component of what the historian Arthur Goren has identified as the "functional consensus" that developed in the decade following the end of World War II. That consensus was built on two key public commitments: ensuring Israel's security and striving for a liberal America.[29] Denominational Jewish summer camping clearly embraced that consensus. However, it grounded it in a different type of authority from the common one among American Jews. Goldstein astutely points out that racial liberalism did not provide a strong "Jewish particularism."[30] Jews' historical experience, their commitment to the New Deal consensus, and their newfound access to American society all shaped Jewish life after the war. Denominational camps attempted to root those experiences within Jewish practice as well.

At the same time, the denominational camps (as well as the Zionist ones) were leaders in establishing the centrality of racial liberalism. The historian Cheryl Lynn Greenberg argues that throughout the 1940s, Jewish organizations remained conflicted about the degree to which they could support African American civil rights as well as about how to express that support. Even as they cooperated increasingly with African American organizations, the alliances were slow in coming.[31]

The potential conflicts in the culture that denominational camps both created and transmitted came into dramatic relief on a Sabbath in 1965 at a campus of Camp Ramah. The unfolding events constituted what the anthropologist Victor Turner termed a "social drama," a process begun by a breach of norms that leads to mounting conflict and finally to a resolution that usually creates another conflict.[32] These social dramas often lay bare key conflicts— indeed, the most fundamental contradictions of a community, nation, or group. Asad's argument for the importance of struggle in establishing authority supports Turner's assumption that social life is most effectively revealed through conflict. In this social drama, the authorizing processes of Judaism, racial liberalism, and the postwar Jewish consensus came into juxtaposition and, indeed, conflict.

Black Jews? Camp Ramah and the Crisis of Authority

In the summer of 1965 over a Shabbat at Camp Ramah in Nyack, New York, the organic links between justice, Judaism, and Jewish identity were to be challenged. That summer, Ramah experimented with a program for sixteen-year-olds called the American Seminar. Rabbi Joseph Lukinsky, an instructor at the Jewish Theological Seminary, introduced a new vision of Jewish camping that included three related goals: traditional study, creating community, and social action. Campers were expected to learn to live together for eight weeks and work out their differences. From the directors' point of view, these lessons in moral responsibility—learning to balance freedom and obligation—were central to the camp experience.[33]

Campers in the American Seminar were required to engage in "social action" by participating in a project in nearby cities for three hours a day. Many took part in voter registration with the NAACP. Some painted houses for impoverished African American residents, while others worked at Rockland State Hospital with severely mentally ill children and adults. Those who were frightened by these alternatives—and there were some—could also work in the Ramah day camp. Lukinsky received support in this experiment from a group of counselors with whom he had worked for many years in Ramah camping and who shared his vision. Many of them had grown up in the Boston synagogue where the young Lukinsky served as a rabbi who worked with youth. One of the counselors, Robert Cover, had participated in the Student Nonviolent Coordinating Committee's voter registration in Georgia in 1962.[34]

In the mornings, campers studied for three hours, part of which was devoted to learning Talmud with a distinguished member of the Jewish Theological Seminary's Talmud faculty, Israel Francus. Francus also served as the camp's professor in residence and its religious authority, the Seminary's representative who assured the halakhic legitimacy of what took place at the camp. Given their teacher's virtuosity and their ignorance, one former camper likened the process of studying with him to learning to play "Heart and Soul" on the piano with Mozart.[35]

Lukinsky and Francus represented cleavages within the Jewish Theological Seminary of the 1950s, 1960s, and 1970s. Lukinsky was American-born and had received a secular education prior to entering rabbinical school. He was passionate about baseball, sports, and Judaism. He received a Ph.D. in education from Harvard long after his rabbinical ordination and saw himself as an educator. By contrast, Francus was born in Poland and came to the United States after the war. He was educated entirely at the Seminary and Columbia University and held one of the first joint undergraduate degrees between the two institutions. The Talmud faculty was the Seminary's most prestigious because it represented the highest form of classical learning. During the 1960s, most of its members hailed from Europe and had been educated there in the rigorous academies of Jewish higher learning. Europe and America, traditional learning and a postwar adaptation of Judaism to the United States met in camp that summer. In the context of the American Seminar, it was clear to all that Francus had been assigned as the legal authority of the camp to keep a firm hold on an experimental summer.

Many former campers and counselors recalled the 1965 American Seminar as a summer that changed their lives, moving them to professional commitments, to the rabbinate, or to work with troubled children. But what many remember most vividly was the Shabbat fairly late in the season when a group of teenage African American Jews (then called Black Jews) from Hatzaad Harishon came to Camp Ramah Nyack following a request from one of their leaders to visit the camp.[36]

Hatzaad Harishon had been founded one year earlier in New York City. Its first executive director and one of its founders, Yaakov Gladstone, a Hebrew teacher, wanted to bridge the gap between black Jews and white Jews in the United States.[37] The group was committed to *kelal Yisra'el*, the unity of the Jewish people throughout the world. It was also committed to Israel as the spiritual and national center of the Jewish people.[38] The group sponsored a youth and young adult organization for ages sixteen to twenty. Several members of the youth group formed a dance troupe that performed Israeli folk dances and attracted media attention.[39] Gladstone and the organization were especially committed to ensuring that Black Jewish children and teens received a traditional Jewish education, and Gladstone raised funds for that purpose. The request for an invitation to Camp Ramah clearly came in the spirit of integrating Black Jewish youth into the "mainstream" of Jewish youth culture.

One Ramah camper from that era remembered how she felt when the group was informed about the visit. "Most of us came from liberal homes. We knew about Falasha—Ethiopian Jews—but black Jews in America was something very new. The majority sense was that we were proud to do this. They were our own."[40] The rabbis who ran the American Seminar anticipated that the visit would be important but complex, and they held many discussions about it in the preceding weeks. Would there be resistance, awkwardness, or difficulties? How could they best prepare campers who had little experience with African American teens and who might harbor prejudices and racist attitudes?

They also broached the problem of Jewish law. Were the Black Jews actually Jewish according to Jewish law? Some Black Jewish groups' practices were by no means identical to those of either European or Mizraḥi ("Oriental")

Jews and their descendants. Their claims to Judaism differed, too: many Black Jewish groups viewed other Jews as usurpers of an authentic Judaism linked to biblical texts. Harlem was an important site of Black Jewish life, but by no means the only one. Beginning in 1915, Black Jewish churches could be found throughout the East. Harlem, however, was the site of a significant transformation in the practices of Black Jews. It was in that New York neighborhood that they encountered European Jews and their descendants. Through contact with European Jews, Black Jews began to change some of their practices, and a sect who called themselves Ethiopian Hebrews evolved. There was rarely mutual recognition between Jews of European descent and Ethiopian Hebrews.[41]

The organization Hatzaad Harishon had a constitution that accepted a "normative" definition of Judaism, that a Jew "was defined by being born of a Jewish mother or reaffirming Judaism before a *beit din* [through conversion before a religious court]."[42] However, how the group defined Judaism and what its relationship was to other black Jewish groups was unclear to those running Camp Ramah. If Black Jews were not "really" Jews according to Jewish law, the visit would present certain obvious problems. Could they pray together? Could the visitors be invited to take honors associated with the Sabbath, such as chanting the blessings at the Torah reading (aliyot)? Their discussions centered on the purpose of the camp, namely, how to integrate traditional Judaism with an American life built on democratic principles, personal responsibility, and what the group's leadership deeply believed was a Jewish critique of American injustice.

The staff agreed to pray, or *daven*, together with their guests, a decision that put them on a potentially confrontational path with the camp's "traditional" sources of authority. Like Manischewitz of Malamud's tale, the staff had to decide not *what* to believe, but *whom* to believe. They did not find it sufficient to accept the self-proclaimed Jewishness of their guests. They had to authenticate their Jewishness because they were not simply socializing or hosting a meal; rather, they were moving into the territory of Jewish practice, engaging an entire system of understanding concerning what and who were acceptable. The multifaceted purposes of the camp were brought into conflict because the event brought the very tensions of living an American Jewish life into play. They, too, had to discern "if Jews were everywhere."

In anticipation of the visit, the camp leaders consulted Professor Francus about whether they could offer aliyot to their visitors. Francus, in turn, consulted the halakhic authority of the entire Ramah movement, Rabbi Moshe Zucker, also a Seminary faculty member.[43] Zucker's decision was calculated to be both sensitive to the visitors and legally rigorous. He ruled that any male in the group past the age of legal majority (bar mitzvah) who was enrolled in a yeshiva or Jewish day school could receive an aliyah. (This was before the Conservative movement equalized women's rights and obligations in Jewish practice.) Zucker reasoned that the educational institution would vouch for the "authenticity" of the young man's Judaism. This ruling was agreed upon by the camp director, Lukinsky, and Francus, the scholar in residence and Talmud instructor.

Breach and Crisis

The guests and the campers arrived on Friday afternoon. They shared a Shabbat evening meal, talked amiably in their bunks, and the staff was satisfied that the initial encounter had gone well. The following morning, however, when the campers and guests assembled for the Sabbath morning prayer service, Lukinsky faced a dilemma. He described how he felt that morning when he entered the house of prayer. He knew that he was obligated to go up to the young visitors and inquire whether they were enrolled in Jewish educational institutions. He discovered, he said, that he simply could not bring himself to do this. In any other Jewish setting, he reflected, if a person were to present himself as a Jew, the inquiry would stop there. There was only one reason he found himself asking young men on a Shabbat morning if they attended a yeshiva, and it was because they were black. Therefore, he simply assigned aliyot to the visitors, as one would do for any synagogue guest who was a Jew. He ignored the carefully worked-out compromise between tradition and courtesy to guests whose halakhic status as Jews was unclear to the hosts.

Most of the former campers and staff who spoke to me recalled that the Shabbat morning service was uneventful. Campers remembered that they all went to lunch together. During the meal, however, a murmur spread among the campers. They told one another that, following the service, their Talmud instructor, in his role as halakhic authority of the camp, had asked several male Ramah campers to stay after the service so that they might repeat the entire Torah service. Francus explained that the aliyot performed by the Black Jews had rendered the service illegitimate; it had to be redone.

This version was only one of the four variations I recorded from various participants. The most dramatic variant described a rupture in the service when the Talmud instructor declared that the Torah service was not *yotse'*, legitimate, and marched out with some campers. Others recalled the order of events differently. But all agreed that the Torah service was restaged as a result of the aliyot performed by the guests from Hatzaad Harishon. Most of the young men who had been asked to stay behind were outraged, according to one whom I interviewed. The campers were embarrassed for their guests, though they did not challenge their Talmud teacher by refusing to participate in the second service. One former camper remembered his own feelings that day: "I felt embarrassed. Why did we invite them if they weren't Jews? Why did we do this? I don't remember if I went out with Francus. I think that I did go out. It was right; I should do it, even though it upset me. There was pain and anger in the air. I was very conflicted about him thereafter."[44]

The campers were sufficiently outraged that they turned to their two rabbis, Lukinsky and Francus, and demanded a meeting. That demand was consistent with their experience of the American Seminar. All summer, the camp leadership had emphasized the importance of personal responsibility. Meetings were the medium for settling disputes and airing conflicts. Lukinsky's educational philosophy emphasized discussion and reflection. Meetings allowed campers to create the link between tradition and daily life in order to become moral thinkers.

Redress and Resolution

One of the campers, Ann Mintz, recalled the scene that afternoon vividly. Almost all of the campers and many of their visitors were seated in a grassy area of the camp outside the chapel in the late-afternoon sun. Lukinsky and Francus were respectful, even "deferential" to each other, but each staked out a different position. Mintz described what happened that day as "an honest-to-God difference, the only *maḥloqet* [formal rabbinic legal dispute] I have witnessed in my life."[45] The *maḥloqet* enjoys an almost sacred status within the talmudic tradition, which holds that only through debate and dispute in the name of heaven could one arrive at the correct legal position.

She recalled their Talmud instructor, Francus, explaining repeatedly that he did not doubt the Jewishness of their guests but rather that he simply did not know whether they were Jewish. In an interview that I conducted with Professor Francus in 2004, he described those difficult events. He explained that, walking around camp that Shabbat, he had heard their guests talking about their churches. "Fine," he said. "They can say that they are Jews, but does that make them Jews?" More importantly, he saw the decision taken by the camp director to be the betrayal of a promise. "We all agreed that this is what we would do, and he didn't do it."

That afternoon, however, Lukinsky explained his reasoning to the campers. "If there were a group of poor Jews from the Bronx who were white, would we have questioned them? No. It was only because of their skin color that I was expected to ask that question."[46] How could he reject the principles of justice and the commitments to civil rights on which they had worked all summer precisely when it counted most, with black guests who were Jews?

Ann Mintz, reflecting on what had happened thirty-five years earlier, told me: "I know now that our teacher [Francus] followed his teacher, Zucker (the authority for the entire camp system), and that is what the halakhic system required. But we heard the rabbi [Francus] say, 'I was just following orders.' We had all seen [the film] *Judgment at Nuremberg* that year, and here he was saying that he should have followed orders. He heard it, too, and tried to explain ten to fifteen more times that this was a halakhic requirement."[47]

This association with Nazi-like authority was surely not uncomplicated. Each day when Rabbi Francus taught Talmud in shirtsleeves in the summer heat of the Poconos, the Ramah campers could see the blue number that had been tattooed on his arm at Auschwitz. His entire family had been killed in the Holocaust. Nevertheless, their great and revered Talmud professor had, in some sense, betrayed them by demanding an accounting from Black Jews.

Mintz recalled Ernestine, a nineteen-year-old visitor who spoke up at the meeting and, in Caribbean-accented Hebrew, asked, "Am I not flesh and blood . . . *basar ve-dam*?" evoking Shylock's discovery of his daughter Jessica's apostasy in *The Merchant of Venice*. Mintz wondered how anyone could doubt Ernestine's Jewishness. Danny Margolis, a staff member that summer, remembered "kids saying, 'How can he prove he's Jewish, that I'm Jewish?' Why aren't these kids as Jewish as anyone else?"[48] Teenage campers pushed the issue to its extreme by questioning the basis of Jewish identity. How, they asked, does anyone know who is really Jewish?

Mintz recalled that "none of us had experienced a conflict in rabbinic authority before. The head of a Ramah Camp, Joe Lukinsky, stood up to Moshe Zucker, the legal authority for the entire system. He stood up to the weight of halakhah in favor of social justice. It was as though we had our own conflict between the prophetic and the legal." Mintz sighed and concluded: "I can pinpoint that day coming to a decision to take the road less traveled. I followed Joe to pursue social justice over halakhah. It was a subversive summer, thank God."[49]

The visitors left, and there was no formal resolution of any kind. Many decades later, both Francus and Lukinsky reported that Lukinsky had apologized to Francus for breaching the agreement that they had struck. But some of those involved believe that the conflict continued to play itself out in the lives of the teenagers, in conflicts among faculty at the Jewish Theological Seminary, and in ideas about what the goals of Camp Ramah and Conservative Judaism should be.

Authority and Authorizing Processes

The social drama laid bare powerful tensions and conflicts in the formative elements of Jewish life at Camp Ramah—Jewish practice, Jewish identity, and moral development. More specifically, it revealed some of the complexities of the project of racial liberalism as it strove to unify Jewish experience. These tensions were by no means circumscribed by the camp experience; they were deeply embedded in postwar American Jewish life. The crisis first demonstrated competing visions of Jewish authority and their implications for Jewish life in America. That contestation partly explains why there are so many competing versions of what happened on that Shabbat, over and beyond the passage of time and the unreliability of memory. Competing ideas about American Judaism could be directly mapped onto how the events were recalled. Each of the positions staked out in the crisis stage of the social drama revealed a vision of how to reproduce Judaism for Americans. But they differed profoundly regarding the role of halakhic authority and the meaning of Jewish "tradition."

All the rabbis in this social drama identified with the project of Conservative Judaism, which is committed to a Jewish law that changes as it unfolds over successive stages of history and is thus able to respond to contemporary life. Indeed, each of them believed that authenticating the Jewishness of the Hatzaad Harishon visitors should be done with sensitivity. Neither Lukinsky nor Francus rejected the authority of halakhah. Nevertheless, the American Seminar revealed their radically different ideas about Judaism and the nature of Jewish authority.

Israel Francus described himself to me as uncomfortable with the principles of the American Seminar. He rejected the way Judaism was, to his mind, made less important than the ideas and political activism of the African American leaders about whom campers learned that summer. He felt that parents had been "cheated" because their children were not experiencing Judaism at camp, but something quite different. He complained that camp counselors affirmed radicalism. Camp leaders' focus on the civil rights movement troubled him, he said, because he did not need any other group to teach him about justice. "I learned about justice from my grandmother," he told me. "Every Friday, I went with her as she delivered food and money to those in need. I did not need someone to tell me what was justice. Jews don't need a camp with ideas from others to learn that." "Why," he asked, "did they run to paint the houses of Negroes in town when there was a Jewish old-age home a short distance away? Why didn't their needs matter?"[50]

Professor Francus thus rejected the principle that empathy for other groups was the proper way to socialize young American Jews to Judaism; Jewish values taught youngsters to care for the elderly and to address the needs of other Jews. His evocation of his grandmother, who taught by the example of helping others in the community, was the most eloquent for him, and he believed that it was wrong that this model was not being transmitted at a Jewish camp. From his perspective, Judaism provided a whole, organic system that did not require translation or bridges to other systems. Judaism was fundamentally about treating others justly, and it did not need to draw on the civil rights movement, for example, to teach what was inherent to halakhah.

Joseph Lukinsky offered an alternative symbolic discourse built on theories of education. He articulated his vision for the American Seminar in a dissertation about the next year's camp session. He explained that he considered the weakness of the 1965 session to be his failure to make explicit the links between communal service outside the camp and studying classical Jewish texts. Ultimately, he worked to develop a view of tradition that recorded "how past generations [had] oriented themselves to the world." Campers, he believed, "could develop a critical approach to tradition and free inquiry into it." Their Jewishness would be better secured by understanding that "growth and change take place in the context of a tradition which is responsive to the real problems of the community and the individual."[51] Therefore, the American Seminar's focus, from his perspective, was on integrating traditional texts and ideas with the compelling issues of contemporary society. As he understood and presented his own actions, he did not aim to challenge halakhah. Rather, he believed that authority was most powerful when it was freely chosen and when its relevance could be established.

Indeed, only a few years later, Lukinsky would find himself again confronting European-born Seminary faculty with different visions of Judaism and Jewish authority. In 1968, at the height of the student movement, police brutally broke up protests at Columbia University. Many of the students were enrolled at both Columbia and the Jewish Theological Seminary, which were separated by a few blocks. Student activists at JTS, many injured on campus the day before, asked the chancellor, Louis Finkelstein, to issue a statement condemning the violence. He refused to do so, saying that he needed more information first. Lukinsky rose to say that halakhah demanded that he make such a statement, but was quickly dismissed by the chancellor and others (though he did receive support from some of his colleagues).[52]

Some campers from the American Seminar whom I interviewed articulated retrospectively the vision that guided their program. Rabbi Joshua Elkin told me that the American Seminar had a tremendous impact on his life and that his counselors and teachers provided role models for living a Jewish life.

> I don't put myself on the extreme radical, liberal end. I do feel that how I have viewed civil rights, how I viewed the Vietnam War, how I came to view Columbia's relationship to its Morningside Heights neighbors were shaped by that summer. I think that being in the camp and being exposed to these things inducted me into a social activist agenda that never was fully realized, but it has contributed to a value system I have, which tends to be sympathetic to the black community, and which tends to resonate with [views about] the evils of the corporate industrial complex. Bob Cover was a bigger-than-life figure. He was the first example in my life of a real social activist liberal who was putting his energy where his mouth was. He was not the most knowledgeable Jew there, but he was there, participated in *tefillah* [prayer] and everything else. He made me see that it was OK to be involved in social activism and to be Jewish.[53]

Stephen Donshik also recalled how important American Seminar staff members were to his developing ideas about how to be a Jew. "When I think back to Danny Margolis and other *madrikhim* (counselors), their attitude was 'this [social activism] is part of life and you're not Jewish unless you do it.'"[54]

Some former campers recalled tensions between what they termed "the prophetic and the legal"—the contradictory demands of justice and Jewish law. Others described bridging and integrating activism and Jewish traditions. The mix itself clearly formed the culture of the Jews in 1960s camp life. Virtually all of them affirmed the centrality and importance of classical Jewish texts, and with them the system of halakhic authority as personified in the figure of the legal scholar.

Within this context, the specific culture in which this drama unfolded involved a surfeit of authorities rather than a challenge to one principle of authority or another. The authority of reason, of empathy, of experience, and an internalized sense of what was right were all seen not only as intrinsically Jewish but as authoritative in guiding a Jewish life. In the context of the camp, those modes of authority were particularly compelling in personal relationships. The camp director and counselors personified Jewish authority and modeled a Jewish life.

Shaped as it was by discourses of empathy and justice, the confrontation may have been inevitable, but it was hardly a deathblow to the system of hierarchical, halakhic authority. Indeed, the whole experiment in denominational camping and that difficult summer day in 1965 reveal an emergent authority—how it operated and what it achieved. This work grounded the educational mission of camps dedicated to making young Jews American Jews.

The visit of Black Jews precipitated a crisis for this vision because it revealed that traditional Jewish authority had its limits; it could not accommodate every version of liberalism. That fundamental conflict challenged the key lessons of the summer for campers. They were forced to question the Judaism of the visitors whose presence affirmed that Judaism transcended race and other differences. They were torn between the very principles that they believed to be unified: justice and Jewish law. Above all, the Shabbat crisis revealed that the camp staff contested the core principles of the American Seminar. The experiential as a medium to bridge past and present as well as Judaism and American liberalism failed. What felt intuitively correct was ruled as outside the bounds of Jewish authority. And who was "really" a Jew emerged as a disturbing question, as did the potential incompatibility between Judaism and liberalism.

Authorizing Processes and Identity

Authority is worked out in real relationships. For American Jews, many of those relationships reside in institutions, law committees and governing bodies of institutions, rabbinic courts, and other adjudicating systems that regulate Jewish behavior and decisions. Halakhah does not guide all of these bodies and organizations, although all of them claim that authority resides beyond individual choices. At the same time, the majority of America's Jews are more or less indifferent to these processes. How can an analysis of the culture of postwar Jews understand how authority works beyond acknowledging its complexity and absence of universal acceptance?

Authority, as I argued at the outset, is discursive. It is a system of symbols and images, a language for defining experience, for preparing Jews to claim what is and is not Jewish. It is critical to understand how this system operates, both within traditional authority structures and beyond or outside of it. The emergence of denominational summer camping, which so heavily focused on transmitting Jewishness and socializing young Jews, is a useful venue for that analysis. The summer camp created Jews by having them behave like Jews. Prayer services, study, observance of the Sabbath, Jewish dance and music, and an environment made up of Jews—all shaped behavior and relied on a growing repertoire of cultural competence and knowledge.

But the authorizing processes of camp, what made Judaism for many *convincing*, involved particular ways of perceiving. In this sense, the culture of American Jews that the camps disseminated aimed to create a shared identity and to fashion a particular outlook—indeed, a comprehensive worldview. In the end, civil rights movement programming allowed a variety of camp leaders to shape and frame what it meant to be an American Jew. It drew on a variety of ideas and modes of educating to assert the link not only between Judaism and liberalism but between Jews and those battling oppression. It built Jewish practice and Jewish identity on a discourse about one's responsibility to change the world while claiming that changing the world was intrinsically Jewish. Put another way, within this discursive universe, the particular and the universal were essentially the same.

As American politics changed and social movements realigned, many Jewish discourses shifted as well. Israel and the Holocaust became ways of asserting a unique experience of oppression and a nationalist vision. Appeals to authority were built less on bridging worlds than on re-creating "authentic" Jewish spaces engaged with a highly particular history. The liberal synthesis was clearly under attack, as Jewish youth, like their peers nationwide, challenged all forms of authority, questioned any rules at camp, and demanded more far-reaching changes.

The social drama of the American Seminar provided me the occasion to reflect on the meaning of Jewish authority for Conservative Judaism in the early 1960s. It reveals that the classic binaries that scholarship has used to understand American Jews of this period are not entirely convincing. American Judaism of this period is still largely viewed as a "folk" Judaism in contrast to an authentic "elite" formulation, or a Judaism that abandoned halakhic authority for a generalized American religion, or reshaped ethnic attachment into synagogue-based Conservative Judaism.[55] These interpretations share the view that Judaism failed to exercise authority over its followers beyond a generalized sense of tradition and memory.

The summer camp, envisioned as a utopian space in which to create a new postwar Judaism, took the issue of Jewish authority very seriously. These summer camps were not so different from the yeshiva or the Islamic madrasa, where learned teachers aim to socialize children and youth in ways that challenge or simply differ from religious practice in the home. Camp Jewish observance was almost always more intensive than home observance, and different from that in the synagogue. The summer camp deepened Jewish practice and knowledge. But it did more than that because its leaders created a complex discursive universe that made Jewish authority central to transmitting Judaism. They created authorizing processes that depended on an intuitive understanding that what was Jewish was just, moral, ethical, and right. The American Seminar was predicated on an absolute conviction that Judaism was entirely relevant to the problems of social injustice and that it provided a sturdy and effective bridge between daily Jewish practice, textual study, and the ability to make the world more just.

The culture of the Jews envisioned by those camp leaders was frankly liberal and pluralist, grounded in the commitment to make Jews unique, to avoid assimilation, and to respond to the politics of the time. In creating their position, the rabbis and teachers of the movement were influenced by the Holocaust, Zionism, and antisemitism—not to mention such educators as John Dewey—and there was nothing inevitable about that synthesis. In other generations, efforts to link democracy and Judaism in America had not shaped the vision of Jewish authority that these men and women embodied. Their embrace of the discourses of political, cultural, and racial liberalism embedded postwar Judaism in a new set of imperatives that relied on the importance of the individual in a framework of responsibility and obligation.[56]

The surfeit of authorities that collided during the visit by young Black Jews reveals the inevitable: there were competing discursive universes, and liberal Judaism and some interpretations of halakhah would inevitably collide. How the collisions were negotiated allows us to see more clearly the power of Jewish authority and authorities at work—and *not* the absence of authority for American Jews, as the story is more traditionally told.

Ultimately, what was the impact of this process? In contrast to socializing systems that attempt to contain and control dissent, Camp Ramah welcomed it. Does this partly explain the ferocity of youthful rebellion, the refusal to accept any authority in the years that would follow? Does a surfeit of authorities ultimately share the consequences of highly repressive authority, both so often leading to revolt and reaction? In the case of the American Seminar, as well as many other ideological and denominational camp experiences, it is clear that the impact of creating a highly experiential Judaism that focused on the issues of the day was powerful for the men and women who looked back on those years as essential in shaping who they became.

This analysis invites scholars of American Judaism to keep their eyes on the ways in which the culture of the Jews is shaped by religious discourses—even liberal ones—that may represent forms of authority long thought lost to postwar America.

Chapter 2

Rabbis and Their (In)Famous Magic: Classical Foundations, Medieval and Early Modern Reverberations

J. H. Chajes

"The Laws of Sorcery Are Like the Laws of Sabbath"

Is magic something distinct from religion? If so, is the difference to be found in social organization (individual or group engagement with the divine realm) or in intentionality (coercive versus petitionary)? Might certain beliefs or practices be inherently magical, or is the magical valence of a belief or practice found exclusively in the eyes of the beholder? If the term is subjective, is it invariably pejorative—that is, what we do is good (religion), and what they do is bad (magic)? These are central questions in anthropological, sociological, and historical studies of the most variegated human cultures; they are also some of the very questions that Jewish sources have asked themselves.[1]

Indeed, self-conscious agonizing over the legitimacy, role, status—and even definition—of magic in Judaism has the distinction of characterizing internal and academic discourses alike. I would submit that the self-conscious and remarkably nuanced discussions of magic in classical Judaism paved the way for later Judaisms to develop postures more ramified than the rigid options set forth as possibilities by modern scholarship. If magic and idolatry (the Hebrew term *'avodah zarah* literally means "foreign worship") are largely conflated in biblical sources (Deuteronomy 18 foremost among them),[2] early rabbinic literature articulates a distinct realm of magic that is not merely the inverted reflection of the licit cult.[3] This realm is denominated generically as *kishshuf*, although other terms are introduced as well.[4] The rabbis offer an etymology of the term *kishshuf* that stresses its theological, or better, its theurgic threat: "Why are they called *keshafim* [sorcery or sorcerers]? Because they confound [*makhishim*] the supernal household [*familia*]" (bSan 67b).[5] This distinction is based on the intention of the one engaging the divine realm; *keshafim* implies the attempt to force and control rather than to supplicate these higher powers. Often regarded as arising in the context of the early Protestant critique of Catholicism, this was the regnant working definition of magic among anthropologists in the nineteenth and early twentieth centuries.[6] And here it is, alas, in the Babylonian Talmud.

Given this approach, it would certainly be reasonable to assume that the rabbis did not countenance any magical activity, or to be more precise, any activity that they would have defined as falling under the rubric of *kishshuf*.[7] Yet in rabbinic thought, things are not so straightforward. A scant few lines later, the rabbis take us by surprise: "Abbaye said: The laws of *keshafim* are like those of the Sabbath. Certain actions are punished by stoning; some are exempt from punishment, yet forbidden; others are permitted ab initio. One who carries out an act is stoned; if he creates an illusion, he is exempt, yet it is forbidden; and there are those that are permitted ab initio, such as was performed by R. Ḥanina and R. Oshaia, who spent every Sabbath eve studying the Laws of Creation, by means of which they created a third-grown calf and ate it."[8]

To my mind, this text exemplifies the complexity of the rabbinic approach to magic in Judaism's classical period. If Deuteronomy 18 clearly presents magic as the religion of the other, and rabbinic discussions explain *kishshuf* as a rebellion against the divine will, we would expect that, euphemisms aside, the learned tradition would strictly condemn anything defined as *kishshuf*. And yet it does not. Instead, we find forbidden and punishable *kishshuf*, forbidden but unpunishable *kishshuf*, and permitted *kishshuf*—all three using the same ostensibly pejorative term, now suddenly purged of what seemed its indelibly negative connotations. Indeed, to sharpen things just a bit: this term of "disapprobation" is applied as a compliment to a pursuit regarded as worthy of the highest approbation.

Medieval rabbinic authorities anticipate our surprise. "Permitted *kishshuf*" seemed to many an oxymoronic formulation that could not possibly mean what it said. R. Shlomo Yitsḥaqi (Rashi) (France, 1040–1105) thus comments here that the permitted magic in question is not *kishshuf* (he uses the term *makhshefut*) but rather "an act of the Blessed Holy One by means of a Name of Holiness that is his alone." To make that point even clearer, he interpolates *u-mimeila'* ("of itself," that is, without having been forced by the operators) into the last line of the text, rendering it: "by means of which a third-grown calf was created (of itself) and they ate it." The later R. Shmuel Eidels (Maharsha) (Poland, ca. 1555–1632) agrees, and he attempts to explain the strange terminology as deriving from the similarity between these permitted acts and forbidden *kishshuf*—itself a provocative observation (*Ḥiddushei aggadot*, bSan 7). The classical rabbinic text was too audacious for medieval rabbis to allow readers to take it at face value. As pedagogues, Rashi's and Maharsha's forced readings may indicate their unease with leaving talmudic students with the sense that *kishshuf* could be licit and even laudable—at least at the semantic level.[9] It certainly indicates something of a medieval retreat from the complexity of the classical rabbinic discussion.[10]

There is clearly more to say about this exceptional talmudic discussion, but for my present purposes, I should like to emphasize the internal tensions of this canonical appraisal of the place of magic in Judaism. In it, magic and its practitioners are placed at opposing extremes of the axiological spectrum, establishing a legacy that is the patrimony of saint and sinner alike. The association between absolute piety (sinlessness) and magical prowess in this talmudic discussion would certainly have contributed to the acceptance of such prowess as a constitutive property of piety in later Jewish cultures. Although it could not be said that all magicians were pietists, it could very well be said that all pietists were (or had the power of) magicians.

Magic and the Judgment of Jewish Historiography

In the academic context, magic has been subject to value-laden treatment from the start. The central trajectory of twentieth-century historiography from ridicule or apologetics to revisionist acceptance is too well known to require reiteration; the triumph, at least for now, of the "post-rationalists" seems assured.[11] Most scholars acknowledge today—without judgment—that magic has been at the heart of Jewish life from time immemorial.[12] Once scorned and dismissed, magic is now increasingly studied, its centrality in most historical Judaisms rightly emphasized.[13] Biases for and against notwithstanding, we remain in the infancy of scholarship on magic in Jewish society, whether with regard to textual sources or their *Sitze im Leben*.[14] The study of Jewish magic has been chiefly concerned with the analysis of the content of prescriptive literature and relatively less with the social context of its performance. Like any body of prescriptive literature, the magical *grimoire* cannot tell us much about enactment, about what practicing magic was actually like. We get far closer to understanding what practicing magic meant—at least to rabbinic elites— by exploring the personal documentation (sometimes called "egodocuments") left by a number of sixteenth- to eighteenth-century figures who were themselves involved directly in magical activity or who reflected on others in their surroundings who were.

These sources open up the possibility of exploring the place of magic in the constitution of rabbinic authority, and we will make extensive (though not exclusive) use of them in what follows.[15] Among the questions to be considered: What was the status of a rabbinic magus? How did one become a rabbinic magus? Did the syncretistic dimension of magical activity reinforce or undermine the authority of the rabbinic magus? How did the perceived danger of magical practices contribute to a heroic, if teasingly transgressive, image of the rabbinic magus?

What follows, then, is an exploration of the simultaneous valorization and disapprobation that mark the nexus of magical prowess and rabbinic authority. Although my analysis will emphasize medieval and early modern Jewish cultures, it will be augmented, as it already has been, by comparisons with sources classical to modern, thereby exposing tensions and equivocations that belong to the *longue durée* of Jewish history.[16] I am not arguing that magic is a transhistorical phenomenon but rather that learned Jewish cultures worked with a repertoire of traditions that tended to favor the development of what might be called a "charged ambivalence" with regard to this cultural domain.[17] The Jewish magus might benefit from the prestige and mystique of those talmudic exemplars of the nexus of piety and power, but magical prowess also situated him beyond normative religion and its conventional concerns.[18] Internal traditions were, of course, in constant dialogue with the myriad environments in which Jews lived. Cultural exchanges produced articulations of the Jewish magus inflected by each historical context, from ancient Babylon to medieval North Africa and the Rhineland and from Renaissance Italy to the eighteenth-century Carpathians.

The Rabbi Makes It Kosher

Rabbis deployed complex strategies to negotiate their relationship to magic. Tensions within the categories "magic" and "magician" to which we have already pointed allowed rabbis to decry certain practices without necessarily refraining altogether from partaking in their performance. As we will see, this could take place through a casuistic renaming, creating a licit twin of the taboo, as well as through the deployment of a number of more complex analytical and behavioral strategies. Ultimately, it seems that in the realm of magic, the most significant consideration was *who* was doing something, followed by *why* he was doing it. The legitimacy of what one was doing—indeed, the very question of *what* one was doing—would largely be determined within this specific social context.

We have seen that in the formative strata of Jewish tradition, magical prowess was construed as straddling the extremes of piety and impiety. Indeed, the magic of saints and sinners was formally all but indistinguishable. In his classic and still-unsurpassed *Jewish Magic and Superstition* (1939), Joshua Trachtenberg noted that Jewish tradition was largely uninterested in the distinction between white and black magic that so preoccupied other cultures.[19] Trachtenberg suggested that rabbis accepted the overarching halakhic principle that harming another was forbidden; thus no special prohibition against *maleficia*, or "black magic," was necessary. In effect, then, if Trachtenberg was correct, the resulting inference must be that, if a rabbinic authority is engaged in a magical practice, it is ipso facto white/licit magic. Yet matters are not quite so black and white. Before us lies a combustible constellation of factors. Magical prowess is linked at once to saints and sinners, yet magic itself is bound to worlds of divinity and secret knowledge outside the domain—threateningly so, dangerously so—of the normative sacral tradition.[20] Magical prowess is the human expression of divine power and, in the case of rabbinic exponents, the witness to their sublime piety. Piety, power, and danger converged in the rabbinic magus, though their contribution to the constitution of rabbinic authority demanded ongoing cultural negotiation.

The Rabbinic Elite and the Dignities and Indignities of Magic

Magical prowess could be conceptualized as the highest possible human achievement, claiming pride of place in the ideal Jewish curriculum.[21] As represented in classical sources, such gnosis all but erased any distinction between Creator and created. What constituted this gnosis? The dominant conceptualization held that the rabbinic magus wielded sublime and secret names of God. The centrality of divine names in Jewish magic was grounded in the ancient idea that Hebrew was the very language of creation, a language expressing its referents' essences rather than mere social convention.²² To wield a name was to assume the power of that which it denominated; Moses' sword—being the divine name by which he was understood to have smitten the Egyptian—exemplifies this notion and is itself the name of an ancient Jewish magical text (*Ḥarba de-Moshe*).²³

Being a master of divine names, however, did not guarantee respect. The very designation *ba'al shem* (master of the name; the Jewish magus) served as a polemical term of marginalization and as an appellation of authority, at once repellent and attractive. Thus, in a query to Hayya b. Sherira, ga'on of Pumbedita in Baghdad (1004–38), the Jews of Qayrawān referred with cautious admiration to wonder-workers as *ba'alei shem* (pl.); these men were reputed to traverse long distances in the blink of an eye, a technique they referred to as "path-jumping."²⁴ Such feats, even recounted secondhand, bred awe and anxiety among these Jews, as their tense correspondence with the ga'on attests. The ga'on's response evinces a skeptical, even scornful posture that displays his affinity to the "rationalist" philosophical trends popular among his learned Baghdadi contemporaries. He has only disdain for what he regards as charlatanism and cheap trickery. (Yet, tellingly, fear and trembling are not absent from his remarks on the Jewish *grimoire* known to him, including *Ḥarba de-Moshe*.) Moshe Idel has shown how disparaging even logomaniac Jewish mystics could be toward those who applied divine names to prosaic ends.²⁵

Indeed, the practical application of magical knowledge seems often to have been associated with indignity, recalling the medieval dependence upon and disparagement of the barber-surgeon.²⁶ This sentiment is made explicit in the extensive ethical will written by R. Pinḥas Katzenellenbogen (1691–1765/67), *Yesh manḥilin*.²⁷ Katzenellenbogen describes a situation that he felt called for the application of a magical technique known to him that could heal a child stricken by witchcraft. The technique had been explained to him by a *ba'al shem* whom he had hosted in the spring of 1720, R. Joseph of Jerusalem, a year before a number of children in his community died—"clearly [killed] by women witches." Katzenellenbogen, however, felt disinclined to carry out the technique. "It was beneath my dignity to do this myself, by my own hand."²⁸ The technique, it must be said, was cruel, calling for the bloody grinding of a child's gums on the stone wall surrounding a well. This disturbed Katzenellenbogen, who was "soft-hearted" by his own account. Had the cure involved the recitation of divine names alone, the rabbi would likely have been more amenable. Indeed, magical techniques that involved object manipulation were always more suspect and problematic than mere speech acts in rabbinic discussions, evidently in keeping with the talmudic position that "one who performs an action [*'oseh ma'aseh*] is culpable."[29]

R. Hayyim Vital, whose egodocument *Sefer ha-hezyonot* attests to his insatiable attraction to all things magical, could still lament having wasted time engaging in the study of alchemy as a youth, as if it were a vice to be overcome.[30] Despite such disavowals, Vital left an extensive manuscript dating from his late period in Damascus that leaves no room for doubt that he was deeply engaged in *qabbalah ma'asit* ("practical qabbalah") throughout his adult life.[31] Vital's teacher, R. Isaac Luria, had shied away from carrying out certain patently magical procedures, even when they emerged from his own inspired innovations. He would thus send his young apprentice Vital to exorcize the possessed rather than do so himself.[32] And what of the fact that the use of holy names was an indispensable component of Lurianic qabbalah?[33] Here a semantic sleight of hand was sufficient to deal with the problem: in the words of R. J. Z. Werblowsky, Vital posited an "unprecedented and original distinction between 'magic formulae' [*hashba'ot*] and 'mystical formulae' [*yihudim*]."[34] The rose, by any other name, would not smell as sweet.

The *ba'al shem* who lacked elite rabbinic credentials might be ridiculed as little more than a profiteer exploiting the powerful image of the qabbalah, more snake-oil salesman than scholar. Solomon Maimon (1754–1800) prefaced his autobiographical account of a visit to the Hasidic court of the R. Dov Ber (1710–72), the "Maggid of Mezerich," with a brief history of the *ba'alei shem* whom he regarded as the precursors of the leaders of the new movement.[35] Hardly objective, though always interesting, Maimon explained to his German readers that *ba'alei shem* actually effected their cures through natural means, but in the interest of increasing their prestige, attributed their success to magical prowess. "With their cures the process was quite natural. They employed the common means of medicine, but after the usual method of the conjurer they sought to turn the attention of the spectator from these, and direct it to their Cabbalistic hocus-pocus."[36]

R. Jacob Emden (1697–1776) vehemently condemned R. Samuel Falk (1708–82), the "*Ba'al Shem* of London," in a letter published in his *Sefer ha-hitavkut*, and ridiculed the *ba'al shem* Moshe David in his autobiographical *Megillat sefer*.[37] Yet Emden was himself willing to work occasionally as a qabbalistic healer, fashioning a name-engraved gold ring for a sick girl he sought to cure.[38] Katzenellenbogen also copied instructions on how to fashion a magical ring to treat epilepsy into his ethical will from the ethical will of his grandfather. This grandfather, it should be stressed, had strenuously urged his descendants to have nothing to do with magic and divine names, but the benefit of magical rings (there was another to ward off nocturnal emissions) was too great. They were, apparently, the exceptions that proved his rule.

The most famous of the *ba'alei shem*, R. Israel Ba'al Shem (1700–1760), seems to have been initially rebuffed by rabbinic figures in Miedzyboz who were disinclined to accept a *ba'al shem* as a colleague.[39] Although social standing was also likely an issue in the elite rabbinic disdain for *ba'alei shem*, their social and intellectual backgrounds were varied, and the ambivalence toward them should not be viewed as merely an expression of class antagonism.[40] The perceived nature of the magical activity seems to have been of paramount concern. The typical *ba'al shem* pursued his art with an eclectic grab bag of approaches.[41] He might deploy any combination of incantations, adjurations, amulets, potions (mineral, vegetal, or animal), mystic contemplations, and shamanic ascents. Magical know-how could be gathered from written sources—books and, especially, manuscripts—and from elder practitioners of all kinds. Such learning, not unlike advanced Jewish education in the Ashkenazi Middle Ages, required the student to travel from teacher to teacher, from *ba'al shem* to *ba'al shem*, as did the young R. Moses Zacuto. Zacuto's desire to learn magic led him to Poland and its Jewish wizards.[42] *Ba'alei shem* were often itinerant themselves, increasing all the more the possibilities for information sharing, as R. Katzenellenbogen discovered while hosting one such figure.

Ultimately, the resulting practitioner was a hybrid creature who resisted easy classification.[43] On the one hand, such a Jewish magus could have a learned background and could have mastered sublime traditions; on the other hand, he could be practicing magical lore received from his mother. This latter possibility is already attested to in the Babylonian Talmud (bShab 66b), in which the reader may find magical healing techniques recommended by Abbaye in his mother's name. We have already noted R. Katzenellenbogen's belief that powerful and magically adept women were murdering the children in his community, and Jewish sources had long accepted a natural female proclivity for witchcraft.[44] Class and gender associations may thus have contributed to the sense of indignity that adhered to magic and to the equivocal status of its practitioners in Jewish society.

Few documents shed light on the gendered aspects of Jewish engagement in magic to the extent that we find in Vital's *Sefer ha-ḥezyonot*. Vital describes in detail his consultations with women who were gifted clairvoyants, mediums, wise women, dream interpreters, and practitioners of divination techniques.[45] To complicate the picture, however, I would borrow a phrase from the *Brantshpigl* and point out that there were a number of men mentioned by Vital who were like these women, with very similar areas of expertise.[46] Vital respected and consulted men as well as women who were accomplished practitioners of divinatory techniques (just as he consulted Jews and Gentiles with equal nonchalance when a magical service was required).[47] Thus we have male palm readers and lot casters; female lecanomancers (oil diviners); male and female clairvoyants and demon adjurers. One clear difference, it should be noted, is the lack of women among the practitioners of manuscript-based learned magic.[48] This is not to say that women could not have possessed sophisticated bodies of orally transmitted magical traditions, as indeed Abbaye thought his mother did.

Given the equivocal status of the magical practitioner, possible aspersions might also be attenuated through a division of labor. Collaboration seems to have been a preferred method of surmounting the countervailing pressures on rabbinic authorities to remain disengaged from praxis and its indignities without shirking expectations that their esoteric know-how would benefit their communities. Thus Katzenellenbogen sought another rabbi to carry out the technique he knew perfectly well but was loath to perform himself. Luria, as noted, regularly dispatched Vital with explicit instructions, excusing himself from performing a task long associated with magical traditions.[49] And Vital himself left an extensive record of his collaborations with R. Joshua Albom.[50]

Albom was Vital's partner in treating a case of spirit possession in Damascus in the late summer of 1609. As a part of their treatment of the young female victim, Vital directed Albom to fashion an amulet to prevent her repossession by the exorcised spirit. Vital did not merely instruct Albom, however; he also took interest in the magical knowledge possessed by his less rabbinically accomplished associate. Vital, in fact, preserved material from Albom's *grimoire* in his own comprehensive magical manuscript.[51] In Vital's account of the possession episode, the spirit is noted to have complained that Albom did not help him "by means of the techniques in the book in his possession," yet praised him for his mastery of adjurations.[52] This mastery the spirit credited to the excellence of Albom's teacher, R. David Mughrabi, a mysterious figure described by seventeenth-century historian R. Joseph Sambari as "of crippled hands and lame, a skilled scribe who wrote tefillin, mezuzot, and Torah scrolls with his mouth."[53] If his collaboration with Vital linked Albom to a member of the rabbinic elite, Albom was not opposed to collaborating with figures whose authority was more contested. The young woman whom he and Vital had exorcised subsequently "mastered the spirits" and became something of an oracle in her community.[54] Vital recorded in his journal the rather surprising scene of Albom working together with this young woman to draw down angels to appear in a mirror for her consultation.[55]

Finally, although not so much out of a sense of the indignities involved with magical operations as in these previous examples, the egodocuments left by the Ba'al Shem of London and his assistant make clear the extent to which Falk depended on his associates (who were of a lower social and intellectual profile) to enact magical ceremonies.[56] His assistant, Zvi Hersh, recorded in his notebook many of the duties assigned to him by his master. These demanded varying degrees of competence and religious expertise. Recitation of Psalms was the most frequent duty of the associates, but assignments might also include magical writing, seal making, and other technical tasks.[57] Though Falk took frequent visits to a nearby forest to carry out solo night vigils, the details preserved in the notebook of his associate indicate just how extensively magical practice was pursued collaboratively and hierarchically.

As we consider issues of authority and magic, the significance of the location or space in which magical practices are undertaken must not be overlooked. Early reports of spirit possession from the sixteenth century place most exorcisms in the homes of the possessed; later accounts show them to have moved into synagogues. The magical performance of an exorcism was, whether in private home or synagogue, almost always a public event; a quorum was actually required before a *ḥerem* (ban) upon a recalcitrant spirit could be invoked.[58] Communal presence—even participation—was therefore integral to these displays of divine power. This made for a kind of sacred theater likely, and perhaps even consciously designed, to reinforce rabbinic authority.[59] The exorcism of the Dimona resident Yehudit Sigauker—widely distributed in Israel on audio- and videocassettes—featured a spirit who attested to the supernal popularity of the Shas party, and is a particularly crass contemporary example of such a phenomenon.[60]

Other kinds of magical activity, however, are described in personal documents as taking place in dedicated locations akin to laboratories. This makes a good deal of sense when the magical activity included alchemical experimentation, as described, for example, in the autobiographical *Ḥayyei Yehudah* of the seventeenth-century Venetian R. Leon Modena. Modena describes his son Mordecai's apprenticeship at the hands of the priest Joseph Grillo; as soon as he was sufficiently adept, Mordecai "arranged a place in the Ghetto Vecchio and with his own hands made all the preparations needed for the craft."[61] Here again, the notebooks left by Samuel Falk and his assistant are particularly illuminating and informative. Falk and Zvi Hersh refer throughout their writings to their dedicated space for magical work with a variety of terms: *gevul* (boundary); *ohel* (tent); and *maḥaneh* (camp). This dedicated space was treated with extreme care, especially when lengthy ceremonies were under way. During such times, the associates were called upon to remain in the space throughout the night, awake and reciting the Psalms, lest demonic forces invade and fill its void.[62]

Falk and these associates did not live in or adjacent to such dedicated spaces. For a time, Falk used rented space on London Bridge for his magical work. The London Bridge space ensured ready access to water, indispensable to the work itself as well as to the handling of work-related emergencies, typically explosive conflagrations. The positioning of a magical laboratory in such a central public location also made it easily accessible to clients, not an insignificant consideration for a *ba'al shem* whose livelihood depended on providing services to a wealthy clientele. The notebooks of Falk and his assistant indeed shed considerable light on the economics of magical activity, providing a window into the financial dimension of running a "magic business." Efforts to obtain costly but essential materials, such as the gold used for specially engraved tablets and the cash needed to rent the space, are documented in detail. More often than not, cash was obtained by pawning household objects—such as Mrs. Falk's candelabrum. (The *rebbetsin* was not pleased.)

Falk's location in the heart of London raises the compelling question of how the trans-confessional applications of magical practice intersected with perceptions of religious authority. In which contexts might the identity "magician" have served Jewish authority figures as a source of their authority? Was there a difference between operating in a Jewish and non-Jewish setting in this regard?

The syncretistic elements of magic have been widely acknowledged by scholars, largely on the basis of foreign linguistic elements—and even deities—in prescriptive magical literature. Personal documentation reveals other aspects of the pragmatic dimensions of magical work that routinely led to cooperation between practitioners of different religious communities. Vital writes, for example, of his journey to Ṣalāḥiyya, just north of Damascus, to consult a sorcerer (he uses the term *mekhashshef*) by the name of Sheikh ibn Ayyūb, whose expertise was the healing of those whose illnesses were brought on by demons. Vital writes of his general curiosity with regard to this man—"I wanted to examine his wisdom"—as well as of his intention to take advantage of the sheikh's expertise to relieve a debilitating eye condition. Ibn Ayyūb ultimately deploys a technique similar to one Vital described elsewhere as having been used by Albom, adjuring seven demon kings to assist him. In this case, however, Vital writes that the sheikh was unable to help, since the demon kings demurred: they could not be in the same room with him because of his holiness. Without them, the sheikh was powerless to help. Other visits to non-Jewish sorcerers by Vital and others, recorded in Vital's journal, were, however, more successful. In a similar vein, Vital's son Samuel wrote that his first recommendation for the treatment of a possessed girl in Egypt in 1666 was for the family to call in a Gentile sorcerer.

Rabbis were thus well aware of the magical prowess of their Gentile peers, although they could not accept the magical lore in the hands of the latter as on par with their own traditions. Even when similarities were overwhelming, as was the case in areas such as astrology or alchemy, rabbis could argue for the superiority of Jewish traditions on the basis of modest Hebraic overlays. Jewish astrology, then, was incomparably superior to that practiced by Gentiles because Jews knew the twelve permutations of the tetragrammaton and their zodiacal associations, a gnosis posited as something of a quantum upgrade of the universally held lore. Such claims also evince the unease in the early modern period over the influence of Arabic magic upon Jewish traditions.[63]

Danger and Heroism

The permeable cultural boundaries on display in so much magical lore and praxis constitute but one aspect of their liminality. Magical performance took the practitioner beyond the domesticated space of normative religious life to a realm sacred but untamed, perceived as dangerous in a variety of ways. This perception of danger may have amplified the sense that magical acts were efficacious and their performers nothing less than heroic. There was, of course, the obvious danger of transgression. The material aspects of magical activity were often taken as the most problematic. The nonkosher ingredients of many a potion were problematic so long as the cure was not deemed vitally necessary and its effectiveness assured; acts such as the burning of incense or the use of astrological talismans or amulets could easily be interpreted as idolatrous.[64] Magical acts invariably involved the use of divine and demonic names, and, as we shall see, the transmission of a divine name was no light matter. The use of a demonic name, certainly the beginning of what would be called demonic magic, was often accepted as unavoidable when opposing malevolent spirits. If we may adapt the old adage, it takes a demon to catch a demon. Use of such names was generally not considered a transgression so long as the ends were justified.[65] Nevertheless, medieval traditions warned against such involvement even if the actions were not technically forbidden. The most famous and oft-repeated warning against even licit magical activity was that written by R. Judah of the medieval German pietists (d. 1217):

> One who engages ['oseq] in adjurations of angels or of demons or magical incantations [be-leḥishat keshafim]—his end will not be well, and evils will befall him or his children all his days. Therefore one ought to distance himself from doing all of these, and also resist [engaging in] dream questions[66] [e.g.,] in order to know what wife to take or in what matter he will or will not always succeed. And do not [use] bouquets[67] that are called in the language of Ashkenaz wegerich, for adjuring the wegerich is forbidden, as it is written, "be simple with the Lord your God" (Dt 18:13), and [one should not adjure] with anything. For ultimately his situation will be irreparable—how many did [adjurations] and how many asked [dream questions] and were diminished or apostatized or fell seriously ill, they or their children? And one should not ask others to do so for him. Nothing is thus better for a person than to pray to the Blessed Holy One for all his needs. He is merciful and compassionate and repents of the evil [that he has decreed]. And how many prophets have been killed rather than adjure with a Holy Name? Rather they stood in prayer and said, "If our prayer is not heard, we will know that we were not worthy of being saved," and they acted exclusively by means of prayer.[68]

R. Katzenellenbogen thought it important to adduce these warnings from Sefer Ḥasidim in his ethical will, along with the evidence of his own experience: "And I, the small, know and am witness to this matter, for I, too, have known in our day ba'alei shem who worked with [names] in these times, and I know that hardly a one has emerged unscathed [rubam ke-khulam mamash lo yatsu neqi'im]. Some were injured themselves; some died prematurely; others, childless."[69] He goes on to note specific examples, including elite scholars who were also ba'alei shem who lost their children or their sanity. And as if to demonstrate the irrepressible attraction of magic even in light of such dangers, Katzenellenbogen then goes on to copy a number of magical techniques in the pages that follow—including the magical rings. How was such a thing possible? Even the rabbi realizes that his readers may be mystified. The answer: there is always room for an important exception, and "even he [his grandfather, who expressly forbade such things,] was unwilling to forgo this [the magical technique] in deference to [his own] ethical will, and he had his reason and justification."[70]

If various forms of magical activity "bothered" the spirits and exposed one or one's children to grave danger, the mortal threat involved in direct confrontation with the demonic in an exorcism was immediate.[71] One who would command a spirit to dislodge from the body of the possessed has made an enemy; once dislodged, the spirit could be expected to exact revenge. Such concerns are articulated explicitly in many exorcism liturgies. In these formulas, adjurations designed to expel the spirit are punctuated by negotiations, conditional promises, and demands that the exorcist be guaranteed his safety following the expulsion. The ancient *Havdalah de-Rabbi Akiva*, designed "to nullify witchcraft, [to rescue] one harmed by an evil spirit, as well as [to help] one bound from his wife [i.e., unable to perform sexually], and to open the heart [i.e., improve the memory]," thus includes a special defensive adjuration to ward off harm to the person who performs the rite as well as to the others present.[72] An elaborate technique preserved in R. Abraham Alnakar's personal copy of the seventeenth-century Hebrew magical name *grimoire*, *Shorshei ha-shemot*, also includes repeated refrains to this effect.[73] Early in the ritual, the exorcist is to ask God to "give me power to carry out this action successfully" and to spread over him a kind of sefirotic force field (*ḥashmal ha-binah*; cf. Zohar II 78a–b) to protect him "lest the foreign spirit in the body of X injure me now or after his departure, nor that he command any of the injurious spirits among his comrades to injure me now or at any subsequent time."[74]

Although it is true that rabbinic exorcists might acknowledge and even seek out the expertise of non-Jewish practitioners of magical healing, the ability to conduct a successful exorcism—to wage a winning battle against the malicious spirits—could only redound to the glory of the rabbinic exorcist and the tradition he represented.[75] The performance of an exorcism by a rabbi demonstrated personal courage as well as the power of the authority vested in him by tradition: he could administer oaths and bans; he had mastered the qabbalistic arcana out of which the rite was constructed; he could convene quorums and command that shofar blasts be blown to terrify his demonic opponent. The rabbi's piety was generally construed as essential to his success in deploying these spiritual weapons; the abilities of non-Jewish magical healers were, on the other hand, ascribed to their proficiency in the arts of "black magic" and personal impurity.[76]

The sustained talmudic discussion of magic had clearly already made such a distinction. Indeed, the magical prowess of the talmudic rabbis is adduced as a proof—or, more precisely, as a consequence—of their righteousness earlier in the same extended talmudic discussion (bSan 65b). In this earlier passage, these rabbis, as well as others, are cited as examples of men whose righteousness (here constituted as "freedom from sin") has left them with the magical creative power—well-nigh indistinguishable from God's—that, were it not for sin, would be humanity's birthright. Magical power is also available—and much more easily, at that—to those willing to manipulate the energies of evil; only the rare sinless man wields anything like the magical power readily accessible to an evil magus. Consideration of this disparity was enough to make R. Akiba cry, we are told. Given this presumption, the magical prowess of a pietist rabbi was all the more heroic and impressive, divine acknowledgment of the rabbi's supreme piety.

Magic and Everyday Judaism

Did magic in some sense "compete" with the quotidian religious obligations of Judaism?[77] The classical account with which we began indicated compatibility: R. Ḥanina and R. Oshaia's magical arts and calves project (bSan 67b) was clearly not a quotidian religious obligation.[78] Audacious as it was, however, it hardly conflicted with normative religion (whatever *that* was). The narrative, in fact, showed magical activity as arising from textual study, a preeminent rabbinic value, and producing a material benefit that supported another: Sabbath dinner.[79]

Early modern egodocuments reveal in distinct ways the place and prominence of magical activity in the lives of very different sorts of rabbinic figures. The journals of Zvi Hersh and Falk show them as engaged, day in and day out, in Jewish magic. Their practice is quite technical and requires special expertise. Modena's autobiographical work, on the other hand, reveals the everyday engagement with magical practice in the life of a nonspecialist. Alchemical pursuits, astrological queries, palmistry, and dream questions punctuate Modena's account.[80] Egodocuments clearly reveal the dream question in particular as a magical technique borne of acute emotional distress. Modena's dream questions figure in the context of his uncertainties and anxieties around life-cycle events. Another example is to be found in Azikri's heartbreaking personal notes following the death of his two sons. His yearning for a son pained him through old age, prompting countless dream questions relating to his frustrated desire for an heir.[81] R. Asher Halevi (1598–1635), a learned Alsatian Jew who left a stunningly unusual egodocument that has not been sufficiently appreciated, does not discuss magical arts. Yet near the end of his lachrymose account, we discover that R. Asher deployed a magical modality when he lost hope for his son's recovery from an illness in the summer of 1634. In his account, R. Asher relates that two weeks of medical treatments did not alleviate his son's condition. Taking matters into his own hands, he tells us with no special emphasis or justification, "I prepared an amulet—written on his limb—and he recovered over five days."[82]

I have already pointed to Vital's comprehensive magical and alchemical manuscript, the very existence of which testifies to the significance of magic in his life. *Sefer ha-ḥezyonot* allows us to understand his attitudes toward the lore gathered there, as well as to the magical prowess to be found outside of learned rabbinic circles. The regularity of Vital's visits to female diviners and his nonchalant attitude toward these consultations are implicit in his repeated insertion of the phrase "as is customary" whenever he describes a visit to one of these magical service providers.

But what happens when magical activity competes with normative religious obligation? In *Sefer ha-ḥezyonot*, Vital describes a disagreement with a spirit that he was in the process of exorcising over his obligation to participate in communal prayer. In the midst of his negotiation with the spirit about who would participate in the exorcism, Vital abruptly declares, "I will go and recite the *shaḥarit* prayers." The spirit responds, "This is more important than prayer." "I do not miss the prayers under any circumstances," Vital counters. "As for what will be thereafter, may God have mercy."[83] This dialogue, which Vital recorded in his journal as though it were a script for a screenplay, gives a good indication of the commitment to routine religious obligations amid a dramatic exorcism.

A similar impression is given by Zvi Hersh's notebook, where we read of the fulfillment of quotidian obligations along with the performance of complex and innovative magical ceremonies.[84] At one point, Zvi Hersh records that Falk "said to us that we have permission to perform the morning prayer and to recite Psalms or *Sha'arei Tsiyyon*[85] or other supplications [*baqqashot*], but that every ten minutes we had to say the [particular] chapter [of Psalms] with the 'intentions' [*kavvanot*] that he transmitted to us, and [he ordered us], God forbid, not to sleep."[86]

Magical performances might be undertaken day or night, depending upon the type of work being done. It is no doubt because so much of this activity entailed "work" in the halakhic sense—writing often playing a central role—that magical rites were generally not carried out on the Sabbath. While they could not be written, amulets might nevertheless be worn on the Sabbath without violating prohibitions against carrying objects so long as they were approved (in other words, proved efficacious) and were made by an expert; this had been established already in the Mishnah (bShab 60a; "One may not go out [on the Sabbath] . . . with an amulet written by one not yet recognized as an expert"). This passage is a classic locus for the nexus between rabbinic authority and magical prowess. Magical techniques might also piggyback on normative practices; rather than competing with such obligations, they would exploit their potential efficacy. The *Havdalah de-Rabbi Akiva* noted above is a singularly bold example of such a practice, weaving anti-demonic magical formulas through the conventional Saturday night liturgy to take advantage of the auspicious (albeit liminally dangerous) hour.

In the Ba'al Shem Tov's famous "Epistle," an egodocument that is the most significant extant text composed by the master, the Besht recounts his own soul ascents, describing them as having been accomplished "by adjuration" on two separate Jewish New Year (Rosh Hashanah) holidays.[87] *Shivhei ha-Besht* preserves an account of a similar ascent of the Besht's in the final hours of the Day of Atonement (Yom Kippur).[88] The auspiciousness of Yom Kippur for magical activity is also evinced in the numerous vision-inducing and memory-enhancing techniques to be enacted on Yom Kippur night preserved in magical manuscripts.[89] The latter goal should suffice to remind us of the potential of Jewish magical practices to reinforce the ethos and practice of the normative commitments of Jews and of rabbinic authorities in particular. Most prominently, the concern over forgetting one's learning was evinced in the writings of Judaism's scholarly elite for over a millennium. Along with pedagogical strategies and dietary tips, rabbis frequently adopted magical techniques to help them retain the vast stores of information that had to be at their ready disposal before the era of the CD-ROM.[90] No less a figure than R. Joseph Karo (1488–1575), author of Judaism's most universally accepted presentation of Jewish law, recorded a dream question that he put to his angelic spirit-mentor, the *maggid*. In it, Karo requests a technique that would transform him into a "cemented cistern that loses not a drop."[91]

The Irresistible Image of the Rabbinic Magus

One of the most perplexing expressions of the liminal status of the magus-rabbi in Jewish culture is the attraction-repulsion evident in contradictory traditions associated with such figures. Simply put, rabbis who condemned magic seem often to have engaged in practices indistinguishable from those they condemned. And if we find no indication that a saintly rabbi engaged in magical activity in his lifetime, chances are good that hagiographical traditions have immortalized him as a powerful magus all the same. The sharp tension between the valorization and disapprobation of the magus apparent in such contradictions has given rise to explanations both apologetic and harmonizing. Rather than merely reviewing and reinstating such contradictions and rationales, their nature and function must be analyzed.

We recall R. Judah the Pious's warning, cited above, lest one engage in any form of magical activity—even one considered legally permissible. This strong statement would certainly lead one to conclude that few could have opposed magical praxis more vehemently than its author. Such a conclusion was indeed reached by the many authorities who cited it over the centuries; later sources thus preserve traditions featuring a R. Judah who preferred certain death to salvation by magical means. The sixteenth-century *Yakhin u-Vo'az* includes a responsum that recounts a story about students of R. Judah who saved themselves from bandits by using a magical name (§135). According to the story, R. Judah warned them that they would lose their share in the world to come if they did not retrace their steps and pass through the place of danger without using the name. Upon this second pass, they resisted using the name, but were killed by the bandits.[92]

An even more manic tradition is recorded by R. Menaḥem Azariah of Fano in his *Qanfei yonah* (Wings of a dove). According to this tale, students of R. Judah (some say R. Jonah the Pious) wanted to try out the holy names and went to a wilderness teaming with bears, lions, and other wild beasts. Using the names, they were unharmed. In the morning, their teacher told them that in order to avoid next-worldly punishment, it was upon them to return to that very spot and desist from using the names: "The wild beasts ate their entire bodies other than their hands and faces. The rabbi sent [other students] in the morning to see what had become of them, and found them [their hands and faces]. They were brought to the study hall where the rabbi expounded over them that their death was their atonement. He explained that since they had used [the names], they were eaten, but that the face and the hands—they

had read the names with their eyes and held the books [with their hands]—
merited to be saved."[93]

The passive engagement with magical names indicated by merely holding
a book or reading its words is thus granted salvific power (at least to discrete
organs). The uneaten face and hands are nothing less than relics to this effect,
objects worthy of a place in the pietists' study hall. That the magical names
were deployed, however, was a heinous sin that could be atoned for by nothing short of the students being eaten alive. Indeed, *Sefer Ḥasidim*'s warnings
against magic indicate little interest in distinguishing varieties of magic; they
conflate sorcery, demon magic, and the use of divine names. Thus "work of
sorcery [*ma'aseh keshafim*], work of demons [*ma'aseh shedim*], or work of the
tetragrammaton [*ma'aseh ha-shem ha-meforash*]" are all considered to be acts
that "bother the angels" and endanger the operant.[94]

The disapprobation of magic and its performance evinced in this trend
nevertheless existed along with other antithetical perceptions of R. Judah, his
father (R. Samuel), and his successor R. Eleazar. The last was responsible for
a vast work devoted to the tetragrammaton, *Sefer ha-shem* (The book of the
name). Early in the work, R. Eleazar describes the ceremony in which a worthy
disciple receives initiation into the knowledge of the name from his master:

> The [name] is transmitted only to the meek, who do not get angry,
> and to the God-fearing, who perform the commandments of their
> Creator. It is transmitted only over water, as it is written, "the voice
> of the Lord is over the waters" (Ps 29:3). Before the master teaches
> his disciples, they should bathe in water and immerse themselves
> in [the ritual bath that measures] four *se'ah*. They should don white
> clothes and fast on the day he will teach them [the names], and they
> should stand in the water up to their ankles. Then the master opens
> his mouth in fear and says, "Blessed are you, O Lord, our God, king
> of the universe, Lord, God of Israel, you are one and your name is
> one, and you have commanded us to conceal your great name, for
> your name is awesome. Blessed are you, Lord, who reveals his secret
> to those who fear him, the one who knows all secrets."[95]

The solemn dignity of this ritual—the liturgical expression of the belief
that the transmission inducted the student into an apprehension of the most
august divine mysteries—marks the attainment of magical knowledge as a
glorious pursuit appropriate to the very highest echelons of Jewish society.

And such rites promised more than speculative or visionary achievements; a parallel ritual from *Sefer ha-malbush* provides a more fanciful garment for the initiate, who is promised irresistible strength upon donning it.[96] R. Eleazar's account of the transmission tellingly forgoes this assurance.

If we examine the traditions of the medieval German pietists, R. Judah, R. Samuel, and R. Eleazar figure as arch-magi in an abundance of tales.[97] R. Samuel is imagined "creating a Golem, riding a lion, triumphing over Christian priests in a contest of sorcery and rescuing a doomed Jewish community from an evil decree."[98] Judah himself is described as writing an amulet with the power to revive the dead: "Then the pious man wrote a charm with holy names on it and placed it in the hands of the dead man. The dead man rose up, turned around and saw the murderer hiding behind another man. . . . The man who had been killed had many rich friends who offered a great deal of money to R. Judah and begged him to let the man live. But R. Judah had no such intention, for he said he was not allowed to do it. He took the charm away from the man who had been killed and he fell down again and lay dead like any other corpse."[99]

R. Judah is also imagined pronouncing "certain mystical names of God" to allow a Jew who had been falsely accused of stealing to see the true thieves.[100] R. Judah's instruction to his foremost disciple also is imagined as having been a magical initiation: "'I will teach you something.' Then R. Judah took the staff that he had in his hand and wrote some mystical names in the sand. Then he said: 'My dear R. Eleazar, read what I have written here.' As soon as he read it, he knew as much as the pious man himself. Then the pious man erased the writing and covered it with sand. Immediately, R. Eleazar forgot everything that he had learned before."

Eleazar finally licks up the names and remembers everything. "The pious man blessed him with the priestly benediction and pronounced so many mystic names that R. Eleazar soon saw Mainz, and in a short while found himself at home."[101] Finally, R. Judah is pictured defeating the bishop of Salzburg, who had come to Regensburg to kill him. Encouraging the bishop to look out of a window, "R. Judah, by means of mystic names, made the window grow longer and narrower so that he could not get his head out again and was nearly strangled."[102]

The late thirteenth-century qabbalist R. Isaac of Acre regarded R. Judah as an expert in magic, black no less than white, who "knew how to do good and evil; he knew how to use the name of purity as well as the name of the opposite of purity."[103] Note that R. Isaac used euphemistic language to denote the black-magical realm that R. Judah also was thought to have mastered. This itself is an indication of the fraught nature of this realm of expertise. Judah's uses of adjurations, names, and amulets are all in addition to the clairvoyance that enables him to know when someone will be vulnerable to conversion to Christianity or simply when someone is coming to see him. Thus, Tamar Alexander's conclusion that "the hagiographic character of R. Judah" is "not all that far from his historical personality" is curious.[104] The principled anti-magical stance of R. Judah in *Sefer Ḥasidim* may reflect his historical personality, but it seems certain that the R. Judah of hagiography acts in a manner that the R. Judah of *Sefer Ḥasidim* would have had to condemn.

Much the same could be said of the historical Maimonides (1135–1204) and his hagiographical image. If R. Judah's German pietism was replete with magical elements that made the transformation of a magically-capable-but-principally-opposed figure into an arch-magus possible, Maimonides represents the most prominent exponent of the uncommon view that magic, including those forms prohibited by the Torah, did not even exist.[105] In addition to the stories in which he figures as a magus capable of walking through walls or metamorphosing into a lion, he was depicted as having recanted his rationalism in favor of a profound appreciation of magical names and their efficacy. In a pseudepigraphic epistle that seems to have been composed in late fourteenth-century Spain, Maimonides explains to his student (in a tone mimicking the authentic letter that introduces the *Guide to the Perplexed*) that through divine names, the prophets "apprehended the future, and acted in strange actions outside of customary nature. . . . And I know all the weighty doubts that I had in the past, but the doors of perplexity were opened before me and the keys to wisdom were given, along with the explication of all that had been hidden from me. And I hereby adjure you not to reveal these fine secrets and awesome insights to anyone other than one who is of fine mind and clean in his deeds, low in his own eyes, and who walks in the ways of learning and knowledge."[106] With that, pseudo-Maimonides begins his discussion of divine names and their powers.

Is it sufficient to argue that the fashioning of magi out of anti-magical rabbis is indicative of the lack of historical sensibility among the makers of such traditions? Or of the community's need to feel protected by the magical prowess of quasi-divine rabbis in the face of never-ending jeopardy? A folk-religious tendency rather than an expression of the high church? These and other arguments may have more than a little truth to them without exhausting the full cultural significance of this phenomenon. The attraction to and repulsion from the magical realm shot through each source in this discussion are indeed epitomized in the very production of such traditions. Whoever wrote the pseudo-Maimonides epistle on the true worth of magical pursuits was hardly unaware of the real Maimonides. The letter mimics the opening epistle of the *Guide to the Perplexed*, and indeed presents itself as something like its sequel. It is nothing if not a sign of unease with the prospect of leaving a cultural hero's posthumous image devoid of the mighty charge of magical prowess.[107] This charge is as strong as it is precisely because of its origins in the manic oscillations between the poles of attraction and repulsion, of valorization and disapprobation, that stake out the realm of the magical in so many historical Judaisms.

Chapter 3

Dreamers in Paradise: The Rise and Fall of a New Holy Site in Beit She'an, Israel

YORAM BILU

In recent years, Israel has witnessed a proliferation of holy sites and cultic practices related to saint worship. Old-time saints' sanctuaries are enjoying renewed popularity, new ones are being added to the native "sacred geography," and the list of contemporary charismatic rabbis acknowledged as zaddikim is growing.[1] While this revival is too widespread to be the monopoly of one particular group, Jews from Morocco have emerged as a major force behind it, impregnating the cult of saints in contemporary Israel with a distinctive Maghribi flavor.[2] The case I am presenting here may be viewed as part of the contribution of Moroccan Jews to Israel's holy map. This chapter traces the life cycle of a new shrine, modest in scope but pretentious in its vision, that was precipitated and later sustained by a torrent of visitational dreams. I analyze the decisive role played by these dreams in validating the new shrine and in empowering the community around it. But I also draw attention to the limitation of the dreams as sources of authority and legitimacy—in the absence of other, more tangible, sources of support, such as endorsement by rabbinical and municipal authorities.

According to a talmudic legend, the entrance to the Garden of Eden in its terrestrial form is located in the town of Beit She'an in the central Jordan Valley.[3] In 1979, a man of Moroccan background in his late thirties named Ya'ish, the leader of a cleaning crew in the local municipality, announced that he had discovered the Gate of Paradise in the backyard of his house. Elijah the Prophet, the protagonist of the visitational dreams that triggered Ya'ish's discovery, was declared the patron saint of the site. The *hillulah* (annual celebration) for Elijah was conducted in Ya'ish's backyard at the beginning of the Jewish month of Elul, near the small synagogue that had been erected over the presumed Gate of Paradise. Throughout the first half of the 1980s, when I was doing fieldwork in Beit She'an, the Gate of Paradise functioned as a modest but regularly frequented shrine. It enjoyed a constant flow of female supplicants, primarily from the local neighborhood. The site became a healing shrine for many of the visitors to the neighboring Kupat Holim health-care clinic, supplementing rather than supplanting its medical interventions. But all this activity came to an end in the early 2000s, when Ya'ish sold his house and moved to Yavneh, a town twenty miles south of Tel Aviv, and the site ceased to exist.

In what follows, I will situate the case of the Gate of Paradise in the broader context of saint worship in Morocco and explore its vicissitudes through the analytic prisms of authority and legitimacy. Specifically, I am interested in the different effects of several potential sources of legitimacy on the "life course" of the shrine, from its onset to its demise. First, I will analyze the processes by which Ya'ish was initially successful in exerting his authority and attracting believers to his project, despite his humble standing, his non-charismatic personality, and his scant resources. The peculiar nature of the Gate of Paradise as one man's apparently idiosyncratic initiative, lacking institutional support and based primarily on his dreams, makes the questions of authority and legitimacy all the more compelling. Without the backing of municipal and rabbinical authorities, Ya'ish's initiation dreams, which guided him to the holy site and transformed his life, served as an alternative means of lending the project legitimacy. Self-generated and relatively independent of scriptural sources of authority, his dreams functioned as "charismatic significants"[4] and provoked a flood of visitational dreams among members of the local community, endowing the dreamers with rich and engaging subjective experiences associated with saint and site.[5] To this end, I will discuss Ya'ish's initiatory dream sequence as the apex of his life story, and then analyze two other dreams reported by local inhabitants involved with the shrine from a corpus of 150 dream reports that I collected in Beit She'an from 1981 to 1983.

Second, I will argue that visitational dreams enhanced the legitimacy of the Gate of Paradise because they functioned as "swing concepts,"[6] bridging mental, intrapsychic processes and collective, interpersonal and intersubjective ones. Unlike the modern psychological view of dreaming as emblematic of private, subjective, and largely ineffable experiences, these visitational dreams stemmed from an established tradition of dreaming and relied on a widely shared vocabulary of cultural symbols, given that visitational dreams played a central role in the Jewish and Muslim cults of the saints in Morocco.[7] The authority of visitational dreams and their power to bind people to the shrine were predicated on this shared vocabulary, in which saint and site were major cultural idioms. The dreamers employed the idioms of Elijah and paradise in order to articulate and cope with a wide variety of personal experiences, but while their dreams served a "therapeutic" function that enhanced the attraction of the shrine, they also served an "authorizing" function, supplying corroborative evidence for the validity of the revelation underlying it. This authorization process was predicated on the Janus-faced nature of the idioms of saint and site as personal symbols, mediating subjective experience and collective representation, biography and community.[8]

Third, I will make the methodological argument that, in order to understand the processes through which these dreamers projected their individual visionary experiences on the public arena and corroborated them by means of it, one must study the dream-based discourse that evolved in Beit She'an from two perspectives. We must focus our analytic lenses on the performative and rhetorical aspects of the dream as narrated orally and textually, and on the domain of dream psychology and the experiential aspects of the dream as remembered.[9]

Even if we accept that visitational dreams functioned in Beit She'an as self-generated sources of authority, one must still evaluate their efficacy relative to other, more official and hierarchical, forms of authority, the paucity of which alerted me in the first place to the role of dreams as substitute modes of legitimacy. My final argument is that the eventual demise and disappearance of the shrine may be taken to indicate the limits of dreams as loci of empowerment on the micro-level. Dreams were easily available and widely distributed among the rank and file; the religious authorities viewed them as too facile, fanciful, and "contagious" to constitute a valid means of authenticity and legitimacy. But this after-the-fact assertion could hardly be predicted during the heyday of the shrine in the early 1980s, when many local inhabitants, inspired and guided by their dreams, flocked to the Gate of Paradise. To shed light on the two-decade life span of the shrine and the dynamics of its eventual demise, I take a diachronic approach, against the once-prominent anthropological genre of "writing in the ethnographic present."

In the contested territory of saint worship, the life cycle of many sacred sites is very short.[10] "Failures" appear to outnumber successes, since the limelight of research is usually cast on functioning shrines. But the postmortem examination of the vanished shrine shows that it continued to have interesting reverberations in Beit She'an—a type of "afterlife." This afterlife, too, was intimately associated with the legitimizing power of visitational dreams.

Maghribi Roots

In form, style, and prevalence, the folk veneration of saints among Moroccan Jews in the twentieth century bore the hallmarks of indigenous saint worship, a cardinal feature of Moroccan Islam.[11] At the same time, Jewish saint worship drew on the deep-seated conception of the zaddik in classical Jewish sources and its mystical amplifications in qabbalistic literature.[12] Most of the Jewish Moroccan saints were charismatic rabbis, distinguished by their erudition and piety and believed to possess a special spiritual force that did not fade away after their death. This force, akin to the Moroccan Muslim concept of *baraka*,[13] could be utilized to benefit the saints' adherents.

But in contrast with their Muslim counterparts, most of the Jewish Moroccan zaddikim became identified as such only after their death. Their miraculous feats thus usually became associated with their tombs. In addition, the strong sense of inherited blessedness contained in the Jewish notion of *zekhut avot* (the merit of the ancestors) allowed for the emergence of some dynasties of zaddikim, the best known of which were Abū Ḥaṣera, Pinto, and Ben Barukh.[14]

Virtually every Moroccan Jewish community, including the tiniest and most peripheral, had one or more patron saints.[15] While the popularity of most of these saints was quite circumscribed, some of them acquired reputations and followings that transcended local boundaries. Some were well-known historical figures, while others seemed to be legendary characters, recognized as blessed with holiness only after a posthumous apparition—most typically, in dreams.

Generally speaking, the presence of the saints was a given among Moroccan Jews and a central idiom for articulating a wide range of experiences. The main event in the veneration of each saint was the collective pilgrimage to his tomb on the anniversary of his death and the *hillulah* there. In the case of the more renowned saints, a massive flow of pilgrims from various regions would gather around the tombs for several days, during which they feasted on slaughtered cattle, drank *mahia* (also known as arrack, an anise-flavored liqueur), danced, chanted, prayed, and lit candles. They conducted all these activities in honor of the zaddik, combining mundane concerns with marked spirituality and high ecstasy.

In addition to collective pilgrimages, Moroccan Jews visited saints' sanctuaries on an individual basis in times of distress. As intermediaries between God Almighty and the believers, saints were considered capable of solving problems encompassing the full range of human concerns. The presence of the saint was also strong in daily routine, when people would cry out his name or dream about him when they faced a problem. At home, people lit candles and organized festive meals (*se'udot*) in his honor and gave male newborns his name. In many cases, the relationship with the saint amounted to a symbiotic association spanning the entire life of the devotee.

The Jewish cult of saints in Morocco was not a frozen set of cultural vestiges but a dynamic system that accommodated itself to shifting circumstances in which new saints and shrines successively emerged, sank, and resurfaced. It was also a very local phenomenon: a country beset by a volatile history of feuds and warfare between various tribes and factions never possessed the preconditions for developing major pilgrimage centers that attracted visitors from remote areas. As a powerless minority, Jews in particular were bound to the places in which they lived under the aegis of local Muslim patrons.

The 1940s and 1950s, decades of rapid modernization, were the golden period of saint worship among Moroccan Jews. The rapid social changes that the French Protectorate (1912–56) brought about—including massive migration, urbanization, and secularization—shattered the traditional Jewish communities.[16] The resultant disorientation increased the salience and appeal of the traditional dispensers of solace and protection. Following a period of French-enforced pacification, communication and travel between the Jewish communities became more affordable. The improved economic and political conditions facilitated organizational efforts that drew large numbers of visitors to the tombs of the saints.[17]

The massive waves of immigration from Morocco to Israel during the 1950s and 1960s further ruptured the social fabric of Moroccan Jewry, including their hagiolatrous traditions. The predicament of "homecoming," including cultural shock and enormous economic difficulties, became all the more painful with the disengagement from the saints whose tombs the immigrants had left behind. Indeed, in the first years after immigration, Moroccan Jewish *hillulot* were diminished and decentralized, celebrated modestly at home or in local synagogues.[18] Once the newcomers became more rooted in the local context and more confident in their Israeli identities, they forcefully and ingeniously revived practices of saint worship as an emblem of ethnic pride. Substitutes now compensated for the deserted shrines and the immigrants employed them in flexible ways. All this contributed to a renaissance of Moroccan Jewish hagiolatry in the new country.[19]

Most accessible among these new alternatives were tombs of local zaddikim, mainly from the talmudic era of Roman and Byzantine rule. These shrines had been cherished as pilgrimage loci as early as the Middle Ages, but their Maghribization is a much more recent phenomenon. Most notably, the popular *hillulah* of Rabbi Shim'on bar Yoḥai in Meron near Safed now brings together as many as 350,000 celebrants annually. Regional celebrations, such as those honoring Ḥoni ha-Me'agel near Ḥatsor ha-Gelilit and Rabban Gamliel in Yavneh, have also grown in recent years, and there are new pilgrimage centers around the tombs of modern rabbis who were granted saintly status during their lifetime or posthumously. The most celebrated of these was Rabbi Israel Abu Ḥaṣera (nicknamed Baba Sali, d. 1984), a pious sage and a descendant of the most respected family in southern Morocco. Baba Sali's sanctuary in the southern town of Netivot has become a national pilgrimage center, second only to Rabbi Shim'on's shrine in popularity.[20]

In recent years, the reburial in Israel of pious rabbis from Morocco has been growing despite the opposition of the Moroccan government to this practice. The most popular site in this group is the quadripartite shrine in the town of Kiryat Gat housing four sainted figures of the Pinto family. No less prevalent is the symbolic translocation of saints from Morocco to Israel. These projects were inspired by visitational dreams in which the saint announced his move to Israel following his adherents and urged the dreamer to provide him with a proper abode. The most popular shrine in the category of "migrant saints" is the House of Rabbi David u-Moshe in Safed.[21] Dreams were also the trigger for the erection of shrines associated with native Israeli traditions rather than imported ones. The case discussed here belongs to this category.

The Road to Paradise: Ya'ish's Life Story

In accounting for the welcoming reverberations that Ya'ish's revelation stirred in the local community, we should note again that the vision that inspired him drew on all these traditions. He and other "saint impresarios"[22] employed personal symbols with Janus-faced typification, at once mental and collective, private and public, internal and external. The associations that Ya'ish made between the Garden of Eden and Beit She'an and, to a lesser extent, between the Garden of Eden and Elijah, had textual precedents; since many local inhabitants knew the talmudic tradition connecting their town to paradise, Ya'ish could rely on the authority of a canonical text in seeking to propagate his revelation.[23] Still, Ya'ish alone appropriated this tradition by claiming that the gate of paradise was located in his own backyard. We must account for Ya'ish's singular undertaking by asking what individual experiences had fashioned his internal schema of paradise into a cognitively salient, life-transforming, motivating, and authorizing system.[24] Hence, before discussing how the community came to accept his vision, I will portray his personal journey to the Garden of Eden, dwelling on the events and experiences that endowed his personal notion of paradise with rich subjective meanings, culminating in the authorizing voice of the revelation.

Ya'ish was born in Oulad Mansour, a village in southern Morocco on the Marrakech-Demnat road, most of whose Jewish inhabitants made their living in agriculture and animal husbandry, including Ya'ish's father.[25] The patron saints of the village, whose collective burial site adorned the local cemetery, were called *il-kuhaniya* (the priests), unknown zaddikim of priestly descent believed to have come to Morocco from the Land of Israel in ancient times.[26] Ya'ish's mother boasted her own line of pious ancestors and told her children many stories of their miraculous feats. Ya'ish's great-grandfather, a renowned healer and mystic, was believed to have had absolute control over the *jnun* (demons).[27] His grandfather Rabbi Issakhar Amar was considered so pious and devout that he could stop a flowing river with prayer. In contrast, Ya'ish's father came from a plebeian background and was a plain, hardworking man who always struggled to sustain his family. Ya'ish acknowledged his father's kindheartedness and assiduousness with great affection but was careful to note that in terms of learning and spirituality, his father was a far cry from his maternal forefathers. The awareness of this gap might have left Ya'ish in an ambiguous state of "distant proximity" vis-à-vis the family blessing. Is it farfetched to see in his grandiose initiative an enduring wish to affirm his share in his forefathers' *zekhut* (merit)? While I could not examine this psychodynamically informed conjecture directly, even a debatable *zekhut*—or perhaps especially a debatable one—could provide Ya'ish with a sense of conviction and an authorizing voice conducive to his future project.

Ya'ish viewed his childhood with nostalgic affection, portraying life in Oulad Mansour as idyllic. In his recollections, the community enjoyed abundant, unspoiled natural resources. Relationships among people were harmonious, and there was a special spiritual ambiance. "Everything was plentiful there. We had beans, pears, grains; we used to fill up sacks with all sorts of fruits and dry them. From the river we brought large quantities of fish. . . . People were strong and healthy, and happy, too. The water was pure, the air fresh and clear. Nothing got spoiled there. All the inhabitants of Oulad Mansour, Jews and Arabs, were like brothers. . . . We studied Torah in the synagogue from sunrise to sunset. We were strong there. We knew our way."

Ya'ish was twelve years old when his family immigrated to Israel. Their aliyah shattered his secure childhood world. The harsh living conditions in the *ma'abarah* (transit camp) that housed many new immigrants temporarily, the shaky economic situation, and the negligent atmosphere in the local school led Ya'ish to abandon the path of learning permanently after just one year in the new country. To this day, he laments his truancy and seeks to undo it by maintaining a life of piety and learning. In the synagogue erected on the site, he established a Talmud Torah (religious school) for wayward youth. He was well aware that in building and running the school, he was healing his own wounds. Moreover, given his nostalgic and idealized depiction of his native community, his claim to have discovered the entrance to the Garden of Eden seems like a fantasy to re-create the lost paradise of his childhood in the backyard of his house in Beit She'an. By employing the shared tradition or public myth of the Garden of Eden, Ya'ish acted out a private childhood myth and, in the process, became a cultural broker, providing his fellow believers with a place to engage in saint worship. More specifically, his remote memories of scholarly success and relentless spiritual pursuit, idealized as they were, could serve to boost his self-conviction and authority, despite his later failings.

After dropping out of school, Ya'ish began to work as an agricultural laborer in the fields of neighboring kibbutzim. He later made a living excavating archaeological sites in Beit She'an and soon established himself as a skilled, dependable worker. From Beit She'an, he moved to Masada, where he took part in the reconstruction of the archaeological site, but he missed his family badly and soon returned home. After a short time as a textile worker at a local plant, where he met Ḥannah, his wife, he joined the workforce of the local municipality, where he remained until his retirement, moving among various manual jobs. On the eve of the revelation, Ya'ish was already married with four children (three girls and one boy). While the archaeological chapter in

Ya'ish's life was not lengthy, it might have informed his initiative to expose a sublime past.

One of the triggers of Ya'ish's initiation dreams was acute psychological distress. Introverted and ill at ease in dense social situations, Ya'ish suffered from severe anxiety attacks during synagogue prayers. His initiation dreams assuaged the problem. In the wake of the revelation, now exempt from attending the neighborhood synagogue, he began to pray dutifully in the relaxed atmosphere of the tiny synagogue he had founded at home. Now relieved of his problem, he became religiously devout. His otherworldly tenants at the Gate of Paradise, Elijah the Prophet and other zaddikim, would not let him skip a prayer or omit a precept of Jewish law.

To have an impact on the community at large, Ya'ish's revelation had to be made known and written down. With the help of learned neighbors, Ya'ish wrote down, edited, and promulgated his initiation dreams in a text titled "Announcement to the Public," which was circulated in Beit She'an and the surrounding area. The text is presented here verbatim, followed by a short exegesis.

> I, Oḥanah Ya'ish, who live in Beit She'an, Neighborhood D, 210/2, have been privileged by the Lord to see wonders. In my first dream, a zaddik revealed himself to me and told me to dig in the yard behind my house. I started digging, and suddenly a gate was disclosed to me. I entered through the gate, and marvelous things were revealed to my eyes. I saw a pool with freshwater and many plants around it. I kept going and saw a splendid, bountiful garden, and rabbis walking around the garden, enjoying the brightness of the place. One of the rabbis turned to me and told me that I must take good care of the place because it is holy. He also told me to inform anyone who would like to come to the place that first he must cleanse himself.
>
> I didn't pay attention to the dream, even though it came back every day that week. But then, in the second week, I was bothered again [by another dream]. I dreamed that I was standing between two cypress trees in the yard of my house and I heard a voice calling to me in these words: Listen, listen, listen. Three times, the voice was heard. I stood there trembling from head to toe, and the voice continued, telling me that the place where I stood was holy and that I must maintain its holiness.

And again in the third week, on Sabbath eve, I went to the synagogue to pray. After the prayer I came back home, did the kiddush, and sat down to eat. After dinner, I went out to the yard, and suddenly a gate was revealed to me in the same place, and I saw light burning in the entrance. And again, I heard the same voice calling me in the same words: Listen, listen, listen. And this time, it was a reality, not a dream. And I was told that this was the gate of paradise. And I was asked to build an iron gate and to clean the place, and to put it in order. I was also asked to announce in all the synagogues and to inform the public at large that those who would like to frequent the place must first cut their fingernails and purify themselves and repent.

Then my wife had a dream in which I came to her and told her that we have to prepare a *se'udah* [festive meal] and call it after Elijah the Prophet.

The events depicted in the "Announcement" spanned three weeks during the month of Elul, the month of penitence that leads to the High Holidays, during which Ya'ish gradually and reluctantly came to the recognition that the gate of paradise was located in his backyard. His initial disregard of the recurring nightly messages and his ignorance of the identity of saint and site convey his innocence. This innocence recurs in Jewish Moroccan visitational dreams as a rhetorical device—a credibility-enhancing stance.[28] Aside from the visual images of the unearthed site, which resonate with Jewish folk depictions of the Garden of Eden—a bountiful, oasis-like location inhabited by sages—the site's identity is implied in expressions such as "a wonderful garden" and "I must take good care of the place" (cf. Gn 2:16).[29]

The voice of the announcement is double-edged. On the one hand, in accord with the theme of innocence, Ya'ish presents himself as a receptacle for external messages from authoritative beings. On the other hand, the narrative is fraught with active imagery—"I started digging," "I entered," "I kept on going"—that bespeaks the personal nature of the revelation and anticipates the industrious phase of site building. Following the first dream, Ya'ish found himself exposed to vocal messages that repeatedly emphasized the holiness of the site. The messages seem to have been informed by prototypical biblical revelations, from Jacob's dream in Bethel to Moses' encounter with God in the burning bush and Samuel's initiation at Shiloh. The latter episodes may be encoded in the phonetic similarity between *tishma', tishma', tishma'* ("listen, listen, listen") and the Hebrew names of Moses and Samuel uttered by God—*Mosheh, Mosheh* (Ex 3:4) and *Shemu'el, Shemu'el, Shemu'el* (1 Sam 2:10). Moreover, the dream message that Ya'ish received—"telling me that the place where I stand is holy"—is almost identical with the biblical injunction to Moses—"the place where you stand is holy ground" (Ex 3:5).

The revelatory sequence reached its apex at the end of the third week, when the identity of the place came to Ya'ish in a direct revelation. The fact that this peak experience took place in waking reality probably endowed it with extra validity and added to its authority. The timing of the revelation, Sabbath eve at the end of the month of Elul, and the activities preceding it, evening prayer in the synagogue, the ritual of kiddush, and the Sabbath meal, all converged to produce the apposite framework for the revelation—an intersection of sacred time, sacred space, and ritual.

Rhetorically, this confluence of sacred elements may have served to increase the authority of the announcement in the eyes of its readers. But first and foremost, it had a special bearing on Ya'ish's own willingness to accept his revelatory experiences as authoritative and dependable. To understand Ya'ish's move from skepticism ("I didn't pay attention to the dream") to receptiveness, we have to juxtapose the majestic nocturnal drama of the revelation to another, real-life drama that tormented Ya'ish during this period. Under persistent family pressure and especially that of his wife, Ya'ish reluctantly consented to leave Beit She'an for Yavneh, where Hannah's siblings lived. On the Friday morning when the climax of the revelation arrived, Ya'ish had finished preparing for their departure. They planned to leave Beit She'an permanently on the coming Sunday. But the sudden apparition of Elijah and the discovery of the Gate of Paradise forestalled the decision and bound the family to their home-turned-shrine. The powerful convergence of the two plots, with its obvious psychological gain for Ya'ish, made him more ready to accept the revelation as a reliable source of authority and guidance.[30]

The vocal messages that Ya'ish receives at the end of the revelation include specific injunctions that he hastens dutifully to fulfill. The laconic and apparently marginal *se'udah* dream, which seals the revelatory sequence, bears special significance to the announcement's acceptability: it provides the site with its patron saint, Elijah the Prophet, thus situating it within the cultural bounds of the folk veneration of saints. Elijah's apparition is highly compatible with his established position in Jewish folk traditions as divine messenger and conveyer of esoteric knowledge, and with his central role in Jewish Maghrebi saint worship in particular.[31] Against the common idiom of *gillui Eliyyahu* (the revelation of Elijah), the identity of the site's patron may have added credibility to Ya'ish's initiation dreams and augmented the authority that his announcement conveyed. Similarly, in the final dream of the "Announcement," the dreamer is Ḥannah, Ya'ish's wife, but Ya'ish himself is the dream's protagonist who discloses to her the identity of the new site's saint.

From Oneirobiography to Oneirocommunity

The enthusiastic response to Ya'ish's announcement provides powerful testimony to the impact that the dream exerted on his community at the collective level. What had started as a representation of experience, *of* the world, became a cultural thing *in* the world.[32] But the role of dreams in this context went beyond nocturnal revelation. First, in critical moments before and after the building of the shrine, Ya'ish received further dream-based messages from sainted figures. Second, the community registered its approbation in an outpouring of dream apparitions related to both the site and the saint. Two analytic avenues can be discerned in this dream-saturated soil. One is intrapsychic, reflecting the fantasy life of the site builder; the other is interpersonal and intersubjective, reflecting the various imprints and reverberations of Ya'ish's announcement on his audience.[33] I have coined the terms "oneirobiography" and "oneirocommunity" to refer to this twofold process, in which a dream-based vision, after infusing an individual's life with surplus meaning, is projected onto a community to produce an elaborate dream dialogue among its members.[34] It should be noted, though, that the bifurcation of the intrapsychic and interpersonal aspects of dreams is merely schematic, since each of the dreams embedded in the communicative network of the community also conveyed personal concerns reflecting the psychological characterization of the particular dreamer. At the same time, Ya'ish's fantasy life was grounded in collectively shared cultural idioms.

The following two dreams illustrate how individual dreamers employed the cultural idioms of saint and site to articulate personal wishes and concerns. The first dreamer, Me'ir, belonged to the inner circle of activists who emerged around the Gate of Paradise. His dream was a direct response to Ya'ish's initiation dream.

> I am walking near the junction of Kittan [a local textile factory] on the old road to Beit She'an. There was some sort of a hut, and I saw

someone there, looking like a religious kibbutz member, with *kova'
tembel* [a hat popular among blue-collar workers in Israel's formative years] on his head. He was sitting there, and I saw myself as if I
was going to work [in Kittan]. He says to me: "Shalom, Me'ir, how
are you?" and I reply: "Shalom, what are you doing here?" And he
points at this house [Ya'ish's], toward the wadi, indicating that they
are working there with compressors, digging some sort of stream. I
ask him why, and he says to me: "Look, the stream as it exists today,
the rain always blocks it. The passage they dig, it's in the direction
of this [Ya'ish's] house." And I ask him: "What happened?" And he
says: "Look, here it always overflows; that is, it disrupts the traffic.
So we would like to dig a stream here." And he shows me how they
are working.

Suddenly I meet another person, and he also asks me how I
am. And the place is full of trees; really, trees all over, and people
are coming out of the place, old-timers, like Yemenite Jews. And a
young man was standing there, as I told you before, a kibbutz member with *kova' tembel*. And I ask him: "Who are these people?" And
he replies: "This is an old moshav, and in the morning everyone is
going to work." And I see them, one with a basket, another with
a bicycle, and so on. I asked him: "Can I see this?" And he says:
"Sure." I entered that place and, instead of seeing some sort of a
moshav, I saw something like his [Ya'ish's] house. And I see something like a hospital, a Kupat Holim clinic, girls with white gowns.
And I see a man sitting there, with three bottles of wine near him,
and inside the bottles there are myrtles. I ask him: "Tell me, are
these myrtles? I would like to ask you a question." And this is what
I asked him: "Why isn't every plant successful?" He replied: "Look,
this is a secret I can't reveal." And I see the people, like sick people,
sitting there, as in a Kupat Holim clinic. And he tells them to take
some arrack from the bottles, as if they threw away [the pills] . . . as
if they took some pills or something, and now they don't take these
pills any more. And he gives them some arrack to drink; this is their
medicine. And I ask them: "Well, how do you feel?" And they say:
"All the pain that we had—with the stuff he has given us, it's OK,
it's gone." And I go on and I see a third man, and I ask him: "What
are you planting here?" And he says, "Look mister, here, near the
entrance to Beit She'an, we already planted something one year

ago, but the inhabitants spoiled what we had planted." Then I say: "You should blame no one. You informed us neither by letters nor through the Ministry of Religion or the local municipality." Then he says: "You'll receive a letter, and then you'll know." That's what he said to me.

The dream elucidates the motivational basis of Me'ir's immediate attraction to the site. Unlike Ya'ish's initiation dreams, which took place in a contextual vacuum, Me'ir's report is replete with places and characters from the local scene: Kittan Junction (named after the biggest industrial plant in town, where Me'ir was working), a religious kibbutz member and a moshav of veteran Yemenite Jews (compatible with the fact that the valley of Beit She'an is dotted with religious kibbutzim and moshavim), the Kupat Holim clinic, and Ya'ish's home. The diversion of the stream in the direction of Ya'ish's place alludes to the identity of the site, since "a river issues from Eden to water the garden" (Gn 2:10). The flow of water will ensure the growth of the plant, which stands for the shrine. The road construction, which will enable fluent, undisturbed traffic to the site, may represent the dreamer's wish to see the popularity of the shrine growing, and perhaps also to unearth the gate (of paradise)—the "passage" in the dream. (Indeed, Me'ir sought to promote a large-scale archaeological dig at the site.) The sequence of characters and places in the dream may indicate that for Me'ir, the road to the Garden of Eden, which ends in Beit-She'an, a development town mainly populated by North African Jews, starts in a religious kibbutz and goes through a Yemenite moshav. This is a clue to Meir's integrative vision of the site, which resurfaced in other dreams that he had. The transition in the dream from the domestic shrine to the Kupat Holim clinic is based on a functional similarity, healing, enhanced by the fact that Ya'ish's house is adjacent to the neighborhood clinic. This transition, which occurs in many other dreams, not only highlights the therapeutic functions of the site but also emphasizes the superiority of traditional agency over the modern clinic. The arrack and the myrtles, traditional symbols of well-being, supplant modern medication as the therapy of choice.

The generally optimistic mood of the dream is marred by uncertainty, epitomized by the question, "Why isn't every plant successful?" The answer is given only at the end of the dream. The plant, standing for the site, had been put in the ground near the entrance to the town a year earlier (indeed, Ya'ish's house was near the western entrance to Beit She'an), but "the inhabitants spoiled what we had planted" (by disregarding it?). Me'ir's yearning in the dream for a reassuring sign regarding the success of the plant is congruent with his relentless attempts to legitimize the revelation by soliciting approval from celebrated rabbinical figures outside Beit She'an. The fact that, in the dream, the Ministry of Religion and the local municipality were not notified about the site might indicate Me'ir's concern over their reluctance to acknowledge the holiness of the place. The promised letter at the end of the dream probably alludes to Ya'ish's "Announcement to the Public." Against the backdrop of the dream as a whole, the three figures that guide Me'ir to the site probably represent the shrine's patron saint, Elijah the Prophet, known in Jewish folk traditions for his unpredictable appearances under a wide range of guises.

To conclude, Me'ir's vision situates Ya'ish's revelation at the epicenter of the community, endowing it with meanings derived from the local scene in Beit She'an. The dream lucidly conveys the immense importance that Me'ir ascribed to the site as a place for integration and healing as well as his ambition to play a central role in its development.

The second dreamer, Raḥel, was the most prolific dreamer in the community. Her profound involvement with the Gate of Paradise manifested itself in many dreams that portrayed the site as warm, hospitable, and nurturing—a panacea for life's problems. While the exchange of food between the zaddik and the dreamer is a common theme in visitational dreams, the compelling way in which it resurfaced in Raḥel's dreams indicated the strong personal motivation with which it was charged in her case. One possible source for this motivation was an early loss she had suffered, as manifest in the following dream.

> I dreamed that I was going to Ya'ish's house and standing before the gate there. I knock on the door and a tiny old man with a hat comes out. I ask him: "Where is Ya'ish?" He says: "Ya'ish isn't here. I am replacing him. I take care of the house. What do you want?" I say: "I came because I don't feel well, I have problems with my pregnancy. Give me some arrack from the place." Then he asks me: "Have you taken a ritual bath?" And I know that I am supposed to take the bath [for purification after the menstrual period] the next day. I say: "No, I'll go tomorrow." He says: "No! I don't agree, no one will enter this place without taking a ritual bath." I say to him: "But Ya'ish, whenever I ask him, says that I don't have to take the bath if I am clean." He says, waving his hand: "No, you are not

allowed to enter! And Ya'ish should know that from this day on, no woman can enter this place without first taking a ritual bath." I said, "OK." He didn't let me in. He stood with me at the entrance. Then he says: "Wait here, I'll bring you something." He gave me a glass of arrack and an orange, and I went home.

And my mother—I lost her when I was fourteen. And then I see her waiting for me at home. She says: "Where have you been? How come you've disappeared? I have been waiting for you for so long." I told her: "Mother, we have a place, what shall I say, in this house every wish is granted." She said: "Come on, take me there, to that place." I took her there. And I saw her standing, holding a baby and feeding him with milk.

The dream is divided into two separate, though thematically related, parts. Raḥel is coming to the place as a supplicant, with an actual problem related to her pregnancy. She meets the gatekeeper of the site—standing for the zaddik—and asks him for a remedy, some arrack from the place. The zaddik's refusal to let her in might have been related to the religious concerns that engrossed Raḥel when she had this dream. Fighting with herself and her husband to adopt a more religious lifestyle, she found in the "Gate of Paradise" a major source of support in her struggle. The dream articulates her concerns about her religious stance through the idiom of limited access to the shrine, employing images of smooth and easy versus difficult and limited access to convey feelings of self-efficacy and self-aggrandizement, on the one hand, and self-depreciation and doubts, on the other. Here Raḥel fails to gain entry into the shrine; but her sense of failure is softened first by redirecting the responsibility to Ya'ish for not enforcing female purity laws in his abode more strictly, and then by the arrack and orange she receives from the zaddik. Receiving this oral sustenance indicates that, despite the saint's reproach, she is entitled to enjoy his blessing. Moreover, the gift from the zaddik assures her that her difficult pregnancy, the reason for her visit to the site, will end well.

In the second part of the dream, Raḥel meets with her late mother. Raḥel deemed her mother's sudden death when she was fourteen the most painful loss in her life. The mother's complaint—"Where have you been?"—is a sheer projection of the dreamer's own sense of privation following her mother's death. The dynamic association between the reunion with her mother and access to the site appears in their joint visit to the place. The final scene openly reflects Raḥel's strong wishes to be taken care of and nourished. It is hard to say whether the baby in the dream is Raḥel herself, enjoying her mother's milk as compensation for her painful disappearance, or her own baby, soon to be born, an indirect assurance that her pregnancy problems will be resolved. For her, the site is a mother surrogate, endowing her with nourishment and protection. In her own words, "in this house every wish is granted." The two sections of the dream also correspond symmetrically. In both of them, the dreamer meets with a parental figure who provides and nurtures, and the resources that figure provides are meant to protect a newborn, before or after birth. The dream indicates the multi-determined way in which Raḥel uses the Gate of Paradise. While dealing with a current medical problem, she is also coping with a past trauma.

The dreams presented here do not offer a complete representation of the oneirocommunity that emerged in response to Yaʻish's initiation dreams. They do, however, illustrate the highly personalized ways in which the saint and his site were incorporated into the life worlds of different dreamers. While the basis of Yaʻish's authority was not charismatic leadership, his dreams served as "charismatic significants," igniting the imagination of many in the community and drawing them to the domestic shrine he erected. The rich dream-based discourse that engulfed the community germinated in the common cultural heritage of saint worship and visitational dreams. As veteran members of the cult of saints in Morocco, many residents of Beit She'an could accommodate Yaʻish's extraordinary initiative to previous, well-established, legitimizing patterns of saint worship at holy sites and therefore accept it despite its relative paucity of formal sources of legitimacy.

Dreaming Is Not Enough: The Expulsion from Paradise

Today, nothing in the house that once hosted the Gate of Paradise indicates its past glory. The shrine and its builder have both vanished from the scene. A fire that consumed the synagogue in 1997 dealt the coup de grace to the shrine, which had been already struggling throughout the 1990s. Suspecting arson, Yaʻish grew embittered and morose and refused to restore the shrine. Three years later, he moved his family to Yavneh, thus completing the move that had been forestalled twenty-two years earlier. This time, Elijah the Prophet did not intervene to stop him.

What were the reasons for the shrine's demise? In the densely populated holy geography of Israel, the life span of most new, individually based projects in the peripheries is not long. While saint worship is thriving in contemporary Israel, it is also a fluctuating and contested phenomenon. Even in its heyday, the Gate of Paradise enjoyed a bounded popularity critically dependent on the support of the local community, and it remained a minor shrine. I suspect that the grandiose nature of Ya'ish's initiative placed an extra liability on the Gate of Paradise in comparison with other shrines. Even though the revelation was grounded in a well-known tradition, one layperson's project of exposing a mythic *axis mundi* in his modest house was too pretentious for many who were outside Beit She'an to accept. The blatant character of the discovery also made the local rabbinical authorities reluctant to grant recognition to the Gate of Paradise. Ya'ish, Me'ir, and other activists relentlessly fought to change their minds, but to no avail. As a last resort, they sent a group of female dreamers to the chief rabbi of Beit-She'an, including Ḥannah (Ya'ish's wife) and Raḥel (the prolific dreamer), to inform him about their exciting nocturnal experiences. But the chief rabbi refused to endorse the shrine without extra-oneiric corroboration.

Following this futile encounter, Ḥannah had a dream that vividly articulated her concern over the unresolved issue of rabbinic approval.

> In the evening, while I was sleeping, I dreamed that a rabbi I didn't know came in through the gate [of the garden], but he didn't enter the house. We didn't care about him . . . he didn't care about us. And I said to myself in the dream: "I will follow this rabbi, to find out why he came here." And he went to the exact place where the synagogue was. At that time, we hadn't yet built the synagogue. And I see there a tomb of a zaddik, and he sees it, too. And the tomb was deserted, without candles, without anything. It reminded me of King David's tomb. Then this rabbi cried out three times, in a loud voice: "*Kohen ha-gadol, kohen ha-gadol, kohen ha-gadol* [high priest, high priest, high priest]!" Three times . . . [pause]. "So I am waiting for an answer" [he said]. He didn't ask us for anything, and he went out the same way, through the gate.

The rabbi's visit to the site might be viewed as a gesture of recognition and legitimacy, but insofar as Ya'ish's family is concerned, it conveys a message of total indifference ("he didn't enter the house". . . "he didn't care about us". . . "he didn't ask us for anything"). In Ḥannah's dream, the shrine is transformed into a tomb of a zaddik, perhaps even the tomb of King David—

whose presence in paradise reverberated in other dreams—but it appears desolate, devoid of holy paraphernalia and thus of public recognition. The unanswered triple proclamation of the rabbi stands in contrast to the unsolicited triple message to Ya'ish in the same place ("Listen, listen, listen"). The revelation bestowed on Ya'ish is kept from the rabbi. Could this gap be viewed as a reprisal for the rabbi's arrogant and insulting behavior—a nocturnal wish fulfillment? Ḥannah's slip of the tongue in recounting the dream— "and we didn't care about him" immediately rectified to "he didn't care about us"—perhaps betrays some of her animosity toward the inattentive rabbi. But even if this interpretation is valid, the rabbi's rude conduct, together with the fact that he left without answering, indicates that he did not grant the Gate of Paradise recognition. The thrice-repeated address, "*kohen ha-gadol*," refers to the ancient Temple of Jerusalem (see below), but it can also be taken as a clue to the identity of the visiting rabbi. The chief rabbi of Beit She'an, Rabbi Eliyyahu Kohen, frustrated and enraged Ya'ish and his supporters by persistently refusing to give his blessing to the new shrine. Ḥannah herself was among the female dreamers sent to the rabbi in a vain attempt to change his mind; but, unmoved by their accounts, the rabbi told the women halfjokingly that he would not embrace the shrine as legitimate unless "the one who frequented Ya'ish's dreams visits me, too." Thus, the dream's plot puts to the test the condition that the rabbi placed on the shrine by portraying his abortive attempt to establish a liaison with its saintly patron. Ironically, the rabbi, a namesake of the site's patron, is deprived of Elijah's appearance, *gillui Eliyyahu*.

The association with the Jerusalem Temple in Ḥannah's account does not seem incidental. In her dream, she transforms the shrine into the tomb of King David, the king who first sought to build the Temple (1 Chr 14:1–15); in another dream, she dubbed the site *qodesh ha-qodashim* (the Holy of Holies, the inner sanctum of the Temple). Notwithstanding her emphasis on this holiness, in her dreams Ḥannah also gave ample voice to her misgivings regarding the shrine's prospects, conveyed here by the fact that the only visitor to the desolate site ignores its owners and cannot get an answer to his query. In all probability, the qualms and doubts that pervaded Ḥannah's dreams reflected her own ambivalence toward the shrine. This ambivalence, which could hardly be detected in daily activities, had a very clear source. In the late 1970s, it was Ḥannah who relentlessly pushed Ya'ish to leave Beit She'an for Yavneh, where most of her siblings lived. But her wish was thwarted at the very last minute by the discovery of the Gate of Paradise. This lingering ambivalence may have contributed to the gloomy atmosphere that pervades the dream. But beyond that, the plot articulates the haunting issue of recognition. Having failed to obtain an answer that would confirm the shrine's identity, the visiting rabbi departs, leaving in his wake a strong sense of rejection: the shrine appears desolate and its owners ignored.

Yet, despite the absence of recognition from authority figures such as the chief rabbi of Beit She'an, Ya'ish's initiative did strike roots in the local community. The site's acceptance registered in the gush of dreams that followed the revelation. In the introduction, I suggested that these dreams functioned as self-generated sources of authority. But the glamour of the dreams should not blind us to the essential prerequisites for enduring sanctification. Visitational dreams played a decisive role in the charismatic phase of the foundation of the shrine, but their effects proved to be short-lived. To sustain the initial enthusiasm (which the dreams reflected and further enhanced), to lengthen the "shelf life" of the shrine by institutionalizing the charismatic phase of revelation, a critical set of preconditions had to be fulfilled. A new shrine cannot make a name for itself without a basic infrastructure to accommodate its visitors properly. This usually entails incessant struggles with municipal and state authorities—primarily to obtain permits for building public facilities on a private property—and this is a challenge that many saint agents fail to meet. No less important is launching an effective promotional campaign to attract people to the new shrine. The financial means to pursue these objectives must come from the community. All this calls for an agile and energetic agent, with considerable interpersonal, organizational, and leadership skills. Ya'ish, despite his impressive self-transformation, was far from possessing these skills. Lacking assertiveness and ill at ease in social situations, he could hardly impose his authority on the inner circle of activists who joined him in the project. Soon the debates among the community of believers over personal status and modes of preferred action grew into open feuds and divided them. The withdrawal of Me'ir, Raḥel, and other members involved in the shrine portended the beginning of its demise.

Epilogue: Afterlife

The life span of the Gate of Paradise was short. Erected in 1979, it ceased to exist around the end of the century. Yet Ya'ish's initiative had a peculiar afterlife in Beit She'an. Just two streets away from the defunct shrine, vibrant healing activity is now taking place in a new domestic site, the builder of which is none other than Raḥel, the prolific dreamer. The strong bond between Yaʿish and Raḥel was broken in the early 1990s, when Yaʿish started to suspect that she was trying to stake a claim in the shrine that he had erected. Banished from the place that had become her second home, Raḥel looked for a new outlet for her growing sense of calling. Capitalizing on the dream dialogues with Elijah and other zaddikim that she had cultivated under Yaʿish's sponsorship, she eventually emerged as a folk healer specializing in treating barren women. Elijah reappeared in Raḥel's dreams at a decisive moment in her life, after she had made up her mind to leave her apartment for a more spacious place. His nightly message was unequivocal: "My daughter, I came to warn you, don't leave this house; the value of the house depends only on the soul of the person [dwelling there]." Raḥel obeyed the message and stayed in her house, which later became a healing shrine, and Elijah the Prophet, with whom Raḥel had established an intimate liaison during the days of the Gate of Paradise, plays a cardinal role in her shrine. The same pattern—a near-executed plan to leave the old house annulled by the appearing saint—that had triggered the establishment of the Gate of Paradise triggered Raḥel's, as well as other, new shrines in Israel. In the same vein, Raḥel's willingness to reverse her decision and stay in the old place stands in sharp contrast to Yaʿish's uncontested move from Beit She'an. Raḥel maintains that Elijah is now dwelling in her house, two blocks away from his old abode. Following the tradition established by Yaʿish, she conducts the *hillulah* for Elijah every year at the beginning of the month of Elul. Even though the days of the Gate of Paradise are gone, its patron saint has not disappeared from the local scene, but rather moved to another house in the same neighborhood.

Sacred geographies in various religious systems are dynamic and shifting. This was particularly true of the premodern Christian orbit with its wandering saints, moving relics, and shifting sites.[35] Appropriations of saints and struggles over holy sites characterized Islamic Morocco, too.[36] Jewish saint worship in the Holy Land was also marked by displacements and the transformation of traditions in bounded geographical areas.[37] But the micro-dynamics of these processes have often escaped the historian's gaze. The ethnography of the vicissitudes of hierophany in Beit She'an lucidly illustrates the dynamic processes of continuity and change that typify the history of many holy places. Shrines may lose their popularity and disappear, but their underlying traditions can resurface unexpectedly in modified forms in other places. This fluidity, moreover, appears to be an inherent feature of popular sites that emerge outside institutionalized structures of authority and are empowered instead by "grassroots charisma" of the type embodied in visitational dreams. The trajectory and life span of these sites are informed by the creativity and vitality of self-generated, charismatic sources of authority, but also by their instability and fragility.

Chapter 4

Words, Images, and Magic:
The Protection of the Bride and
Bridegroom in Jewish Marriage Contracts

SHALOM SABAR

The Jewish marriage contract (*ketubbah*) exists between two worlds: the written text and material culture. Its primary feature and raison d'être is the text: the literal meaning of the word *ketubbah* is "that which is written," though it refers to the basic minimal sum of money, stipulated in the contract, that the talmudic rabbis deemed the husband should pay his wife upon the dissolution of their marriage.[1] But the *ketubbah* also developed into an object with a conspicuous physical presence in the wedding ceremony. In many communities, *ketubbot* were artistically ornamented, making them central objects of attention in the ceremony. This combination of text and image makes the *ketubbah* an invaluable source for the study of the Jewish past, including wedding practices and customs, visual traditions and aesthetic concepts, as well as fears of the unknown and the wish to protect the bridal couple.

The importance of the *ketubbah* for research into the daily life of Jewish communities also lies in its widespread use. According to Jewish law, a husband may not live with his wife even for one hour without a *ketubbah*, and if it is lost or destroyed, they must see to it that a replacement *ketubbah* (*ketubbah d'irkhesa*) is issued as soon as possible.[2] Surviving *ketubbot* attest to the weddings of individuals of all classes living in a broad geographic range of communities, about whom sometimes nothing is known besides what is contained in the *ketubbah* itself; in the case of certain villages or communities, the *ketubbah* is the only material evidence attesting to the existence of a Jewish community.

Between Written Text and Artistic Object

The presence of both textual and visual components in the *ketubbah* raises the question of their relative importance. Is the function of the *ketubbah* as a living physical object, enhanced with decorations made specifically for it, as important as that of the traditional text inscribed on it? In the field of Jewish studies, written texts are generally considered the most important sources for the study of the past. But the objects themselves and the images decorating them should not be overlooked; they attest to a greater range of social groups, including those who did not produce or use texts. Objects communicate differently from texts, and the proper investigation of their manufacture and place in society yields a type of information about the culture, time, and place in which they were produced that cannot be acquired from texts alone. The shape and design of the object as well as its decorations reflect ideas and beliefs, feelings and expressions, artistic tastes and aesthetic values. Each object from the past evokes a bygone world, embodying silent but faithful testimony to the life and, indeed, intimate experiences of the people who produced and used it.

Jewish artistic objects and illuminated manuscripts were not created as works of art to be admired solely for their aesthetic qualities. Rather, the objects were functional, and the images and other visual components were designed to enhance items that were part of the liturgy or had other ceremonial uses, in accordance with the talmudic concept *hiddur mitzvah* (beautification or adornment of a commandment).[3] Though the decoration of an object and its functional use are not mutually exclusive, three-dimensional Jewish objects such as boxes for the etrog (citron used ceremonially on the holiday of Sukkot), synagogue lamps, and Torah cases usually bear decorative inscriptions "justifying" or "explaining" their existence.[4] The inscriptions provide the biblical or other textual authority for the creation of the object and thus legitimate its use in the eyes of the text-centered tradition.

Ketubbot, by contrast, do not justify their existence as artistic objects. Rather, their texts perform a ritual function and are, in part, prescribed by Jewish law. From the talmudic period onward, rabbinic authorities attributed great importance to the text inscribed on this document for the proper consummation of Jewish marriage. As is evident in several tractates of the Babylonian Talmud, the rabbis of late antiquity spent a good deal of time formulating the precise wording and exact meaning of each clause in this important document. They apparently believed that the properly worded clauses would serve the rights of a married woman during her marriage as well as in the event that her marriage should be dissolved—whether by divorce or the husband's death in her lifetime. Moreover, in their endeavor to bolster the authority of this textual formula, some talmudic sages repeatedly attempted to demonstrate the biblical origin of the *ketubbah*, although the Hebrew Bible makes no mention of a written document in connection with the wedding ritual. Accordingly, halakhic authorities throughout the ages decreed the bridegroom forbidden to cohabit with his bride without having a *ketubbah* written and delivered to her before marriage. Even in modern times, though this document has lost much of its authoritative power, contemporary rabbinic treatises dedicate lengthy discussions to the correct spelling, meaning, and importance of every word in this document.[5]

Notwithstanding the halakhic importance of the *ketubbah*, its physical appearance had little or no influence on its authoritative rabbinic function. From a halakhic point of view, the *ketubbah* was effective even it was crudely and simply drawn—and indeed, it was the custom among some communities (for example, in Yemen) to inscribe their contracts on small and cheap pieces of paper, using plain ink and uneven lines. But in much of the Jewish world, the official rabbinic requirement served as a minimal starting point, thereby leaving a great deal of latitude for the document to develop along culturally and regionally specific trajectories. In some communities, sincere efforts and considerable resources were invested in producing *ketubbot* that were as attractive as possible. Costly materials were commissioned in advance, and professional scribes wrote the text in a large and calligraphic square Hebrew script. Skilled craftsmen were commissioned to design and create colorful decorations for the wide borders of the large pages, in which the required text sometimes occupied a small fraction of the overall layout. The marriage contract thus emerged in these communities as a striking artistic object that could attract much attention at the wedding ceremony. This development makes it possible to study the texts of *ketubbot* alongside their design programs in order to evaluate their respective contributions to the functions and meanings of the overall object.

The Text of the *Ketubbah*: Between Fixity and Variation

Despite the richness of source material in talmudic literature concerning the Jewish marriage contract as well as the meticulous care the rabbis took to formulate its various clauses, no fixed formula for the *ketubbah* text appears in the Babylonian or Palestinian Talmuds. It was only in subsequent centuries, during the Middle Ages, that rabbinic authorities in various places fixed an authoritative formulation. At the same time, the vast body of extant *ketubbot* from different locations and times demonstrates that, even in those communities that had adopted a relatively fixed formula, personal and local variation remained the norm. How was this perennial tension between fixity and variation sustained? And how did it manifest itself historically in various Jewish communities?

In the post-talmudic era, two basic methods of writing the rabbinic *ketubbah* developed, one Palestinian and one Babylonian. Surviving *ketubbot* from Erets Israel and Egypt discovered in the Cairo Genizah reveal that in the Palestinian tradition, no fixed formula existed throughout the Middle Ages; rather, *ketubbot* varied according to local traditions in which scribes composed and formulated *ketubbot* for individual weddings. Even the choice of language in the Genizah *ketubbot* remained flexible; scribes employed a variety of languages, primarily Aramaic and Hebrew, but also others, such as Arabic and Greek. Thus, these documents contain rich materials for illuminating the ongoing social, cultural, and legal diversity of Mediterranean Jewish life during the Middle Ages. The Palestinian tradition, however, all but disappeared from Jewish life following the destruction of Palestinian Jewry during the Crusades. By the early modern era, only incidental vestiges of this tradition could be found in the *ketubbot* of the Romaniote communities of the Balkans.[6]

Most other Jewish communities, including the Ashkenazim and Sefaradim of Christian Europe and the Jews of the Islamic world, followed the more dominant Babylonian tradition, which preferred a relatively fixed formula. Standard formulas according to the Babylonian-style *ketubbot* appear in the writings of several medieval authorities, representing various communities and traditions, such as Maimonides (1138–1204) for Sefaradi (Iberian) Jews and Eliezer ben Joel ha-Levi of Bonn (ca. 1140–1225) in Ashkenaz. The scribes of various communities followed the accepted authorities and, over the centuries, came to use the preferred Babylonian-style formula in nearly every *ketubbah*.

At the same time, even within the dominant tradition, local variation prevailed, retaining certain elements specific to particular countries and even towns. Thus, the *ketubbot* of Iran have much in common; but in Tehran, the scribes used a slightly different formula from that current in Isfahan. These microtraditions could be enormously stable: the highly localized formula of a given town was generally repeated from one document to another, generation after generation. The same is true for Damascus and Aleppo in Syria or Rome and Ancona in Italy. In Italy, the variation is even greater, reflecting the significant divergences within Italian Jewry; one can distinguish among Ashkenazi, Sefaradi, and Italian formulas in *ketubbot* from the city of Venice alone. This local dimension of the *ketubbah* is apparent in elements such as the *tena'im* (prenuptial conditions), which remained uniform over long periods of time for many communities, and the *tosefet ketubbah* (the additional money pledged by the groom in case of the marriage's termination), which, in many places, was fixed at a certain percentage of the dowry (for example, in Rome it was always one quarter of the dowry).

In some cases, the standardization of the text was even more extreme, such as among the Ashkenazim, who from the early Middle Ages onward used a fixed formula with few variations among documents. This formula includes almost no identifying personal details. The location of the wedding is not accompanied by the customary name of the nearest body of water; the bridegroom and bride are presented with their given names only, even after surnames had come into common use; and honorifics are generally avoided. Moreover, in the early Middle Ages the clause of the contract that usually reveals the most socially salient information, the bride's dowry and the bridegroom's *tosefet*, were completely standardized. One advantage of the standardized text was that a lost *ketubbah* could be replaced almost instantly. It is not surprising, therefore, that the Ashkenazi *ketubbah* lost its importance as a physical object in the wedding.[7] Typical of this situation is the incident mentioned by the German Jewish memoirist Glückel of Hameln at the turn of the eighteenth century about the wedding ceremony of her son: "When we stood all together under the huppah with the bride and bridegroom, we found out that in the great excitement the *ketubbah* had not been drawn up."[8] A scene like this would have been unthinkable among the Sefaradim or the Jews of the Islamic world.

The existence of instructional manuals produced for Jewish scribes demonstrates the nature of the fixed *ketubbah* text, whether among Ashkenazi Jewry in general or within the local traditions of other communities: the fixity of the document is not "sacred" but rather reflects specific disciplinary practices within the scribal profession. The importance of using a uniform set of textual formulas was reiterated periodically in such scribal manuals as *Naḥalat shiv'ah*, by the seventeenth-century Polish authority Samuel ben David ha-Levi, which instructs scribes in great detail concerning the correct wording and spelling in various kinds of contracts.[9]

The *ketubbah* outside Ashkenaz lent itself to a wide range of additions and variations, and came to reflect the diverse sociocultural tendencies of various Jewish communities. Unlike most other Jewish objects, the *ketubbah* is constructed to contain basic personal information on its "heroes," their families, time, and place. A fully preserved *ketubbah* sets the scene like a traditional play: it opens by presenting the exact date and location of the story, followed by the names of the main characters and the words recited by some of the participants such as the bridegroom and witnesses. In addition to the names of the witnesses and the fathers of the couple, *ketubbot* sometimes include names of other people involved in the wedding ceremony: the guardian of an orphan bride (occasionally also her mother's name), the public notary, the scribe, and the translator. Among the Spanish and Portuguese exiles in Morocco (*megorashim*), it became customary to write not only the names of the bridegroom's and bride's fathers in the *ketubbah*, but also their male ancestors going back several generations, with each name accompanied by a standard set of flowery honorifics. In the case of noted rabbinical figures, the scribe would add the positions that they held within the Jewish community and even the titles of the books that they had written.[10]

In some communities, these personal clauses were customarily emphasized and much expanded. Many Sefaradi and Italian communities found it appropriate to include not only the town's name but also all the water sources in its vicinity (for example, "the town of Ancona, which is situated on the border of the sea and on the rivers Aspio and Fiumicino"). In Sena (or Sanandaj, in northwestern Iran), the name of the town is accompanied in Aramaic by the name of a nearby mountain, Tur Oyder (Awyer in Kurdish, Abidar in Persian), possibly to identify the town's location even more precisely.[11]

The social standing of the families involved is usually evident in the value of the dowry the bride and her family bring and the bridegroom's *tosefet ketubbah*. In many of the *ketubbot* from the Cairo Genizah, the lists of the dowry items are exceptionally long and detailed; such lists provide abundant information regarding the material culture of the medieval Mediterranean.[12] Among some Sefaradi communities in Europe and in the lands of Islam, the tradition of enumerating dowry items continued into the modern era. Ordinarily, the items are listed in the vernacular (in Ladino or Judeo-Arabic), and their value is recorded in local coinage. Among the Jews of Yemen, such lists appear at times on the back of the contracts, while *ketubbot* from the Balkans list them in a framed, clearly visible section.[13] Customarily, the dowry items were listed on the contract only after being displayed in a public ceremony and appraised by community officials. The dowry texts attest to a ritual that would have involved the entire community, but their graphic representation on the contract itself reflects local scribal traditions.

Similarly, some Sefaradi communities include an additional section of text for the *tena'im* in a separate, graphically designed framework. The clauses in the *tena'im* section deal mainly with inheritance laws, especially the division of the dowry and other sums in case one of the partners in the marriage should die before producing offspring. Other conditions protect the bride's rights: the groom obligates himself to provide her with a legal bill of divorce (*get*) should he contract a serious illness and promises not to pressure her to renounce her rights to the dowry.[14] In Venice, Rhodes, Salonika, and Ragusa (modern Dubrovnik), the *tena'im* appear on the left in an arch of the same size and design as that of the main text, while in Livorno and Amsterdam, it is placed underneath the main text.[15] In many cases, the *tena'im* are written in smaller, cursive script, while the *ketubbah* text is in larger square letters. The practice of setting off the *tena'im* in a special section written in a more common, everyday script emphasizes its fluidity in contrast with the square "official" *ketubbah* formula above or at right.

Closely aligned with the tension between fixity and variation in the text of the *ketubbah* is the physical appearance of the contract. In communities where the formulation of the text mattered more and its variations encoded more highly personalized information, the *ketubbah* was generally more ornate than in communities that employed a more fixed text. In fact, the beginning of the phenomenon of *ketubbah* decoration, known to us from the Genizah *ketubbot* of medieval Egypt and Erets Israel, is undoubtedly associated with the aforementioned practice of displaying the items of the dowry, listing them in the *ketubbah*, and reading it aloud in front of the guests. Such displays called for the usage of a rather ornate document befitting the joyful public event. In Ashkenaz, by contrast, where the fixed text became the norm and the amounts of money were not made public within the document, *ketubbot* came to be written on small pieces of paper (more expensive parchment was far less common) and generally contained no decorations. In most cases, even the decorative blessings and verses that surrounded the text were limited to two words: the stock phrase *mazal tov*.

Ornate and attractive marriage contracts are characteristic of wedding practices among the European Sefaradim, the Jews of Italy, and the Jews of Islam, for whom the *ketubbah* continued its existence as a lively and meaningful textual object. Accordingly, the *ketubbot* of these communities were often written on costly pieces of parchment or large sheets of paper, the borders of which were attractively decorated in bright colors with illustrations and carefully selected biblical verses, blessings, and wedding poems. Like the variations in the text, the illustrations reflect the social status of the families, their aspirations and ideals, their aesthetic principles, their ideas about marriage, their Jewish beliefs, and, finally, their readiness to adopt decorative elements from the aesthetic traditions of the surrounding culture. Similarly, the selected motifs and designs and especially the general graphic layout of the page reflect local traditions, frequently repeated from one document to another. These colorful design elements convey the immediate time and place of their creation more directly than does the halakhically prescribed text. Moreover, they convey nuances of emotion that are not communicated through relatively fixed verbal formulas written in a language not understood by many of those present at the ceremony.

The variations in text of the *ketubbah*, amplified by a robust tradition of decorative design, transformed the Jewish marriage contract into one of the most fully personalized objects in the Jewish cultural repertoire. Communities in Italy, the Sefaradi diaspora, and the Islamic world, in particular, used the document as a living object, enhancing the text with personal modifications and additions. Their *ketubbot* thus contain a wealth of textual and visual information for several fields of Jewish studies.

Texts and Images as Amulets: The *Ketubbah* as a Protective Artifact

The juxtaposition of text and image imbues the *ketubbah* with a powerfully personalized quality. These two sources of information—text and image—enhance and complement each other, linking official and legal concerns with the festivity of the joyous event. While both elements contribute to this combination, the centuries-old standard formula—though amplified by personal texts—places more emphasis on the legal dimension of the document, while the decorative design highlights its celebratory elements. Accordingly (depending on region), the design may feature pictorial themes such as biblical heroes shown in their finest hours, the glorious Temple implements painted in shiny gold, the ideal heavenly Jerusalem, lavishly dressed imaginary portraits of the bridal couple, attractive allegorical representations pertaining to the wedding ideals, and magnificent architectural facades and gateways.

The most prominent and widespread elements in the repertoire of *ketubbah* decoration were drawn from the world of flora, especially in cultural contexts in which figurative images were frowned upon. The floral designs central to the decorative program of many *ketubbot* burst in bright and vivid colors, amplifying the cheerful sentiments conveyed by the richly illustrated contracts.

But these joyous images and laudatory blessings and verses hide one major, hitherto unnoticed, theme that would seem to contradict the ideal picture presented by the illustrated marriage contract: the worries and anxiety of the new couple and their families. The wedding, as a crucial moment of transition in the life cycle, is accompanied in many traditional societies by the fear that everything that could go wrong would go wrong unless the bridegroom and bride followed their society's protective customs and practices. Many Jewish communities deemed the *ketubbah* an appropriate vehicle for sublimating these fears. If the *ketubbah* had served as a mere legal formality intended to provide the marriage with public recognition, this palpable quality of personal fear and anxiety would not have formed such a prominent dimension of the contract. Especially in the countries where the elaborately decorated *ketubbah* was common, the generally joyous illustrations and decorative verses allude, either overtly or subtly, to such fears.

Some of the best-known customs associated with the wedding in various Jewish communities—breaking the glass in medieval Germany; dyeing parts of the body with henna in Islamic lands—were instituted to ward off evil spirits and protect the bridal couple. The scribes and artisans who produced the *ketubbot*, as well as their patrons, carefully selected verses and images for the purposes of sympathetic magic, to protect the bridal couple. In doing so, *ketubbah* makers closely followed the construction of Jewish amulets. Like *ketubbot*, Jewish amulets are generally composed of words and designs, both of which come from a corpus of elements associated with sympathetic magic in the Jewish tradition.[16] The *ketubbah* was itself used to provide protection for the bridegroom and bride, as were marital amulets.

The earliest decorated marriage contracts found in the Cairo Genizah already express hope for the success of the match. The appearance of such hopes on the Genizah *ketubbot* is certainly not accidental: it is closely related to the emerging practices of decorating the contract and of displaying the contract and reading its contents aloud at the wedding.[17] The public reading of the contract and its display set the social impetus for its decoration and forced the makers of the contracts to invest efforts in appropriate designs.

Today the custom is for the couple to display the *ketubbah* publicly after the wedding in their living room or elsewhere; but in premodern Jewish communities, it was shown briefly to the guests at the wedding while the officiant read or chanted its text. The document was subsequently rolled or folded up and put away—or, in some cases, even hidden as a safeguard for the bride. This was not only a legal safeguard, in keeping with the original function of the contract to protect the bride's rights and the financial obligations made in her favor, but a magical prophylactic.[18] The practice of hiding the contract and keeping it away from unwanted eyes reflected the fear that the contract might be used improperly should it fall into the hands of people wishing to harm the bridal couple or bring them bad luck.[19]

Other fears and hopes for the couple were reflected in the verses chosen to adorn the *ketubbah*. Although the illustrations on the Cairo Genizah *ketubbot* were limited to decorative motifs typical of Hebrew manuscript illumination in Islamic lands at the time, carefully selected blessings and verses give expression to the hopes held out for the bridal couple. The superscriptions were written spaciously in square letters. This section stands in sharp contrast with the text of the contract proper, which was usually inscribed in minuscule letters in crowded lines (Fig. 1).[20] Most common among superscriptions was the blessing *yivnu ve-yatsliḥu* ("May they build and prosper"; cf. 2 Chr 14:6). The spaces between sections of the blessings are often portrayed as alternating "bricks," representing the strong and steadfast home that the young couple will build. This feature was still a regular fixture of practically all the *ketubbot* produced in Yemen into the modern period.

The blessing *be-siman tov* ("under a good sign"), one of the most prominent written and illustrated wishes, carries with it a clear prophylactic connotation. It appeared as early as the medieval Genizah *ketubbot*, while in the *ketubbot* of Sefaradi and Italian Jews, it is written in Aramaic, *be-simana tava*, and is often followed by the phrase *u-ve-mazala me'alya* ("and under a favorable star"). The wish that the wedding be celebrated under a good constellation is further expressed in illustrations of the twelve signs of the zodiac. This is one of the most common motifs of Italian *ketubbot*, appearing on dozens of extant examples (Fig. 2).[21] Italian Jews expressed a deep belief in astral powers, especially in relation to marriage. Important decisions such as the proper match for one's child or the most favorable day for the wedding were often

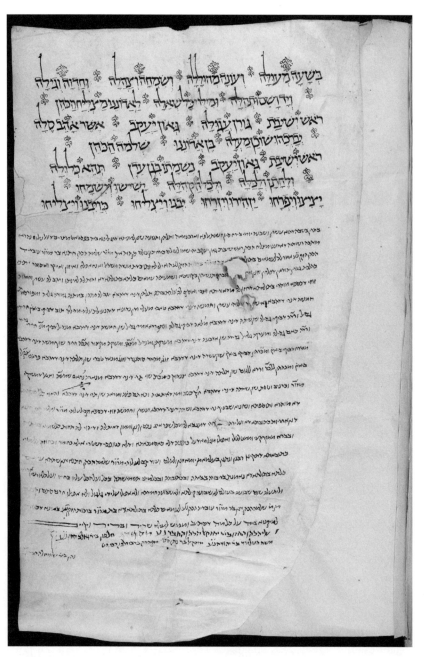

1. *Ketubbah,* Fustat, 1128. Oxford, Bodleian Library, University of Oxford, MS Heb. a 3, fol. 40r.

2. *Ketubbah,* Livorno, 1788. Jerusalem, the Schocken Institute for Jewish Research of the Jewish Theological Seminary of America, no. 14208/2.

made according to the position of the planets.[22] The importance of the signs of
the zodiac in Italian Jewish wedding customs can be seen in a letter in which
a sixteenth-century Jew from Ferrara describes the elaborate decorations at the
ceremony: "I wish you had been here at this wedding. . . . You would have
seen wonders, especially the figures of the twelve signs of the zodiac [*mazalot*]
on the tables, with lighted torches in their hands, with which they illuminate
the guests; and in four directions, four rolling hills, out of which come *putti*
pouring water on [the guests'] hands. And all these [models] were powered by
weights and internal clockwork devices."[23]

Hundreds of Italian *ketubbot* demonstrate that before 1800, nearly all
Jewish weddings in Italy were celebrated during the first fifteen days of the
Hebrew month, reflecting the belief that the waxing moon was a good sign for
fertility and blessing. Thus Leone Modena wrote in his *Historia de riti hebraici*
(Venice, 1637) that "the day for the wedding is set . . . usually in the increase
of the moon."[24] The bride was likened to the moon in more than one way: the
waxing moon was a symbol of her fertility and of the hope that she would "increase" on the wedding night. In this case, popular belief coincided with the
official halakhah: the exhortation to marry during the first fifteen days of the
month appears for exactly this reason in the *Shulḥan 'arukh* (first published in
Venice in 1566).[25]

The many shapes, designs, and forms that the zodiac signs assumed in
Italian *ketubbot* stand in marked contrast to the paucity of examples from
Sefaradi communities. Although Sefaradi Jews observed customs similar to
the Italian ones, such as including the blessing *be-simana tava* in the *ketubbah*
and holding the wedding within the first fifteen days of the month, Sefaradi
Jews very rarely used zodiac illustrations, and only a handful of Sefaradi *ketubbot* feature such motifs (Fig. 3).[26] A rabbi of Salonika, Abraham di Boton
(1545?–88), is the first Sefaradi authority to mention zodiac illustrations, and
he found them in a *ketubbah* that had been brought to his attention via a
halakhic query. Di Boton pointed to the halakhic problem of depicting this
idolatrous design, though he did not rule that the *ketubbah* in question should
be rendered invalid.[27] Similarly, the Sefaradi Jews of the Ottoman Empire generally avoided figurative representations, human ones in particular, including
those in the signs of the zodiac.

Nonetheless, other customs and practices related to the protection of the
bride and groom on their wedding night were common among the Sefaradi
Jews and demonstrate the centrality of prophylactic magic. Their *ketubbot*
favor other symbols and designs as the preferred means of protection. One,

3. *Ketubbah,* Jerusalem, 1844. Jerusalem, Wolfson Museum of Jewish Art, Hekhal Shelomoh.

borrowed from the realm of Hebrew amulets, was the hexagram, or shield of David. Several scholars have studied the history of this symbol before its adoption by the Zionist movement, but less well known is the role that it played in Jewish magic.[28] In Hebrew manuals for amulets, it occupies a central place, and its use is recommended for various circumstances. Jewish amulets made of paper, parchment, or metal featuring the shield of David were produced in diverse parts of the Jewish world, from the Ashkenazi communities of Germany and Poland to the Sefaradi communities of Italy, Greece, and Holland; they were most widely visible in the lands of Islam, including Iran, Iraq, Syria, Kurdistan, Morocco, and Ottoman Palestine (Fig. 4).

Magical protective powers were attributed to the design of two superimposed triangles as early as the Middle Ages.[29] Gershom Scholem hypothesized that the shield of David perhaps emerged as a protective symbol in the Islamic world, since the Qur'ān attributes magical power to David.[30] Hebrew amulets emphasize the protective quality of the shield of David by inserting a letter into each of the six triangles or wings of the hexagram, most commonly, making the Hebrew inscription "shield of David."[31] Other formulations are also common, such as *Taftayah* (the name of a protective angel), *Yerushalem* (Jerusalem), and *Qera' Satan* (rend Satan). In addition, the powerful three-letter divine name *Shaddai* is frequently inscribed in the center of the hexagram, or written twice in the six triangles; sometimes, the entire design is made of Hebrew "protective" texts, such as Psalm 121.[32]

In Sefaradi *ketubbot*, the shield of David usually appears without letters. Its central location at the top of the contract and its large size (for example, in the *ketubbot* of Salonika) demonstrate its importance. It is not only or always decorative, nor is it used merely as a standard Jewish symbol; rather, it serves to protect the bridal couple as evidenced by *ketubbot* in which the scribe-artist places inscriptions in the design. In the *ketubbot* of some towns in Bulgaria, for example, the center of the shield contains a four-line inscription abbreviating the priestly blessing (Nm 6:24–26; Fig. 5), one of the most frequent protective inscriptions cited on Hebrew amulets.[33] The earliest known set of Hebrew amulets, discovered at a burial cave in Ketef Hinnom (west of ancient Jerusalem) and dated to the seventh century B.C.E., are two tiny silver scrolls inscribed with this formula.[34] Abbreviating the formula makes the inscription more powerful as a way of hiding the name of God—a common method of forming protective divine names (*shemot*) in Jewish magic. Just as in these amulets, the six triangles in the Bulgarian *ketubbot* are inscribed with additional protective letters. Starting with the uppermost triangle, the seven letters

4. *Magen David* amulet, North Africa (Morocco?), late nineteenth century. Paint on tin and paper (43.2 x 38cm). Toronto, Beth Tzedec, Reuben & Helene Dennis Museum (Cat. #700, Roth Collection). Gift of Samuel and Israel Shopsowitz.

(the bottom triangle contains the last two) contain an abbreviation of Jacob's blessing to Joseph (Gn 49:22).[35] According to the Talmud, Joseph's modesty and steadfastness in the face of temptation rendered him "above the evil eye" (bBer 20a); he emerged among the Sefaradim and the Jews of the Islamic

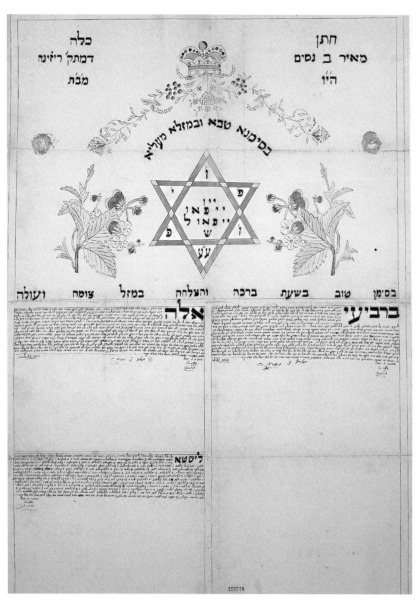

5. *Ketubbah,* Kyustendil, 1897. New York, Library of the Jewish Theological Seminary of America, Ket. 250. Courtesy of the Library of the Jewish Theological Seminary.

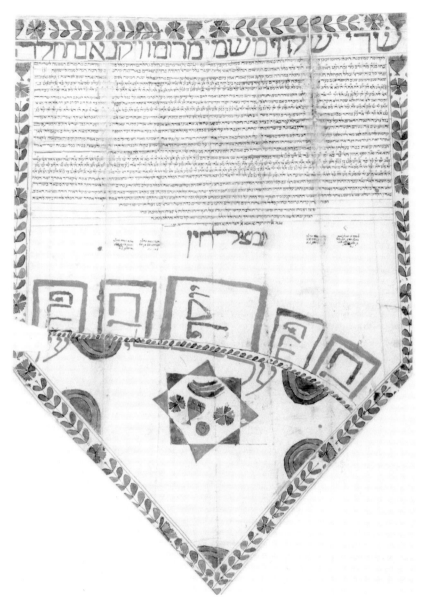

6. Qaraite *ketubbah,* Cairo, 1841. New York, Zucker Family Collection (Zucker Trust 2007).

world as an exemplary figure and symbol of blessing, protection, and fertility. Authorities such as the Ḥida (Ḥayyim Joseph David Azulai, 1724–1806), the Ottoman Jewish traveler and bibliophile, or Joseph Ḥayyim (Ben Ish Ḥai, ca. 1834–1909), the Baghdadi spiritual leader of the Jews of Iraq, wrote extensively about the special qualities of Joseph and found allusions in Scripture to demonstrate his wondrous abilities in providing abundance and fruitfulness.[36] Blessing the couple with these words provides them with protection and extends the wish that they increase and multiply.

Though Joseph's blessing has amuletic power in its abbreviated form, on some *ketubbot* the words of the verse are spelled out to make their meaning clear. In a Qaraite *ketubbah* produced in Cairo in 1841, only the first five words of the blessing were inscribed in monumental letters, so that everyone present at the wedding could see them (Fig. 6); in a Rabbanite *ketubbah* from Alexandria in 1835, all seven words are inserted into a magnificent shield of David shape (Fig. 7). In contrast to the Bulgarian *ketubbot*, each triangle contains one word, and the significant seventh, *'ayin* (which also means eye), is written in the center of the hexagram. Joseph's "protective eye" is set in a colorful background in the form of an open eye surrounded by rays of light. Depicting a yellow crescent underneath, the artist added an additional meaning: the design in the center of the "Jewish star" recalls the Ottoman official national emblem, an additional source of authority and protection for the Jewish community at the time.

The protective power of Joseph is enhanced on some contracts by additional, closely related motifs. In a *ketubbah* from Tiberias in 1889, the contract is topped by an image of two pairs of fish accompanied by the inscription: "Be fruitful and multiply like fish. Do not read *by the fountain* [*'alei 'ayin*] but *rising above the* [*power of the evil*] *eye* [*'olei 'ayyin*]" (bBer 20a; Fig. 8). The passage from which these words are taken associates Joseph with the fish, which live underwater and thus over whom "the evil eye has no power." Independently of the association with Joseph, pairs of fish as protective and fertility symbols are prominent in the *ketubbot* of Calcutta, Bombay, and Singapore, as well those of the Sefaradim in Vienna and elsewhere (Fig. 9).[37] In Salonika, the section of the *tena'im* is often topped by a monumental abbreviation, *Vilbah*, standing for Jacob's blessing of fertility to the sons of Joseph ("And let them grow [literally: multiply like fish] into a multitude in the midst of the earth," Gn. 48:16; Fig. 10). In Ottoman Jerusalem, the Sefaradim preferred to spell out the entire blessing.[38]

Closely related to the fish symbol is another protective design, the *khamsa*

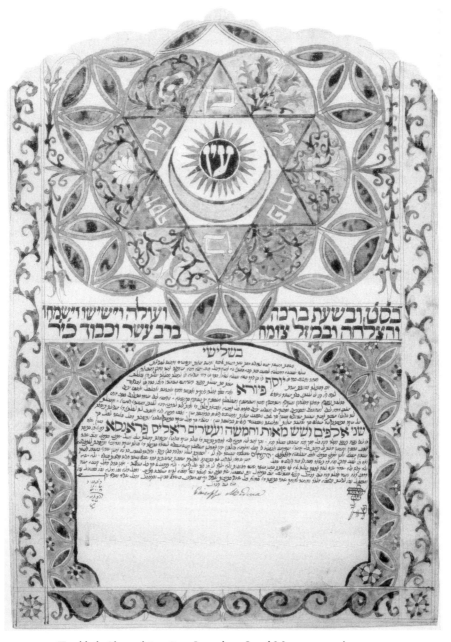

7. *Ketubbah,* Alexandria, 1835. Jerusalem, Israel Museum, 179/270.

8. *Ketubbah,* Tiberias, 1889. New York, Zucker Family Collection (Zucker Trust 2007).

(hand symbol), or number five. On Hebrew amulets from such places as Morocco, Algeria, Tunisia, as well as home amulets from Jerusalem, the *khamsa* and the fish designs are placed next to each other. In *ketubbot*, the motifs are generally separated—perhaps because each has a more distinct meaning in the context of marriage: while the fish emphasize fertility, especially meaningful for a young couple, the *khamsa* is more emphatically protective.

The *khamsa* is prominent in *ketubbot* from the western Ottoman Empire, particularly Istanbul and Rhodes. In one example from Istanbul in 1857, it is

9. *Ketubbah,* Calcutta, 1854. Bet Shemesh, Family Collection.

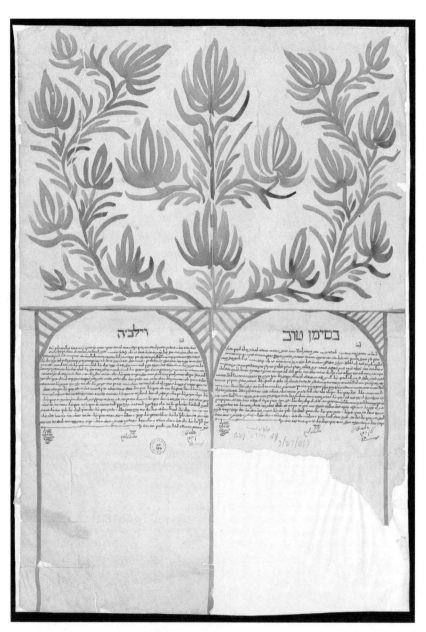

10. *Ketubbah*, Salonika, 1867. Jerusalem, Ben Zvi Institute, MS YBZ 44.

11. *Ketubbah,* Istanbul, 1857. Tel Aviv, Gross Family Collection.

12. *Ketubbah,* Herat, 1889. New York, Zucker Family Collection (Zucker Trust 2007).

depicted in the knob shape protruding above the rectangular page, as if it provides protection to everything beneath (Fig. 11).[39] This feature is also evident in one of the oldest illustrated *ketubbot* preserved from the Sefaradi community of Jerusalem in 1807.[40] In Morocco, where the *khamsa* is widespread and popular among both Muslims and Jews, selected *ketubbot* are decorated with a pair of palms in the position of the priestly blessing, imbuing this popular design with further sanctity.[41]

In their attempt to justify the widespread usage of the *khamsa* among

13. Decorative *ḥayy. Ketubbah,* Gibraltar, 1872 (detail). Toronto, Beth Tzedec, Reuben & Helene Dennis Museum (Cat. #598, Roth Collection). Gift of Samuel and Israel Shopsowitz.

the Jews of their communities, the Ḥida and other authorities pointed to the importance of the number five and the fifth letter of the Hebrew alphabet, *heh.* They argued that this letter represents the name of God; that the fish were created on Thursday, the fifth day of the week; that only after this letter had been added to Abram's name, making it Abraham, did he become "perfect";[42] that the Ten Commandments were divided into five on each tablet so that they would be immune to the evil eye; and that for the same reason Jacob divided the animals he presented to Esau in groups of five according to their sex (Gn 32:15–17).

In *ketubbot,* the protective number is expressed in curious ways. In some Afghan *ketubbot* from Herat, the upper section of the page is decorated with five small archways, paralleled at the bottom by five cartouches that the scribe-artist has marked for the witnesses' signatures (Fig. 12).[43] Ensuring that the number of witnesses added up to more than the required two was a good-luck measure. In some Sefaradi *ketubbot* from Erets Israel, the dowry and *tosefet* amounts are calculated so that they will contain the number five as many times as possible. In a *ketubbah* produced in Safed in 1911, the amount is "five thousand five hundred fifty-five *qurush*"; moreover, these words are inscribed

14. *Ketubbah,* Isfahan, 1921. Tel Aviv, Gross Family Collection.

in large capitals amid the small cursive script to enhance their visibility (cf. the dowry section in the *ketubbah* of Calcutta, 1854; Fig. 9).[44] The Moroccan Sefaradim calculated these amounts to eighteen hundred or eighteen thousand and wrote the enlarged word *ḥayy* (life, whose numerical equivalent is eighteen) in an ornamental manner (Fig. 13).[45] Based on this tradition, in modern Israel the word *ḥayy* has become an object that serves an amuletic function.

In rare cases, the creators of the *ketubbot* did not borrow elements from amulets but employed an entire form, design, or set of inscriptions usually

15. Pendant amulet with Psalm 67 as menorah. Iran, late nineteenth century. Tel Aviv, Gross Family Collection.

associated with Jewish magical objects. In Isfahan, the local decorative program is customarily dominated by a pair of lions with humanized suns on their backs; a contract of 1921 enhances this design with a familiar amuletic design, the *shiviti*-menorah plaque (Fig. 14).[46] Most often this qabbalistic representation of the presence of God appears as a separate plaque hung in the synagogue and is often used as a protective charm as well (Fig. 15). Here, it is embedded in the center of the familiar Isfahan upper border. This popular design, attested as early as the fourteenth century, is based on the qabbalistic association of Psalm 67 with the menorah used in the Jerusalem Temple. It links the forty-nine words of the psalm (seven times seven) and its seven verses

16. *Ketubbah,* Hawdiyān (Kurdish Iraq), 1936. Moshav Zechariah (Israel), Family Collection.

(not counting the first) with the seven branches of the menorah; the opening verse is written in the form of the menorah's flames.[47] The appearance of the symbol on the *ketubbah* brings the sanctity of the object and its multilayered mystical meanings into the wedding ceremony.

The magic depicted on *ketubbot* served to protect women during childbirth as well as the newborn. In a simple, undecorated *ketubbah* of 1936 from the village of Hawdiyān, in the region of Ruwanduz in Kurdish Iraq, the scribe flanked the customary wedding verses with the names of four biblical couples: Adam and Eve, Abraham and Sarah, Isaac and Rebecca, and Jacob and Leah (Fig. 16).[48] While it would seem appropriate to include the names of exemplary couples on a marriage contract, these names appear frequently on Jewish childbirth amulets.[49] That the names are intended as prophylaxis for childbirth is evident from the fact that the scribe did not couple Jacob with his beloved Rachel, but with Leah; since Rachel died in childbirth (Gn 35:18), she was omitted. The scribe joined the sphere of marriage with that of fertility and childbirth, citing ideal biblical couples to inspire and protect the young couple whose marriage this contract commemorates.[50]

The examples cited in these pages demonstrate a variety of magical practices related to the Jewish marriage ceremony. Ranging from the Middle Ages to the modern era and from Italy and other European countries to Yemen, Afghanistan, and Kurdistan, *ketubbot* include pictorial motifs and amuletic formulas that convey the tension and fears felt by the participants in the ceremony as well as various attempts to overcome them. By publicly displaying the protective texts and images, the wedded families felt more secure during these crucial moments of transition. The *ketubbah* emerged as a required official-legal document that was also enriched visually so that it might serve other critical—and more personalized—purposes in the Jewish wedding ceremony.

Text, Illustration, Amulet

The ketubbah developed over the ages as an object that functioned in two worlds: the official rabbinic world of halakhah and text; and the wedding ceremony, where it developed as a physical object with a pronounced presence and apotropaic functions. Especially among the Sefaradim, Italian Jews, and the Jewish communities in the lands of Islam, the appearance of the ketubbah was enhanced by decorative texts and colorful illustrations, and its brief exhibition during the wedding ceremony was sufficient reason to make special efforts and invest extra money into transforming it into a cheerful visual object. Its amuletic qualities transformed it into an apotropaic tool for coping with the fears and anxieties accompanying the wedding ceremony. Carefully selected verses and designs borrowed from the realm of "practical qabbalah" and the world of Jewish amulets filled the ketubbah with conjurations and protective designs and turned it into a protective artifact for the bride throughout her married life.

Each *ketubbah* is a unique object that uses standard formulas, designs, and motifs but also expresses the sociocultural ideas of the people for whom it was made. When properly investigated, *ketubbot* of the past provide insights into both the accepted and hidden norms of the society that produced and used them: the sentiments of the patrons, their wishes and ambitions, their religious and daily concepts, and their relationship with the norms of their culture.

PART II. DIASPORA

Chapter 5

The Dislocation of the Temple Vessels: Mobile Sanctity and Rabbinic Rhetorics of Space

RA'ANAN S. BOUSTAN

> Long residence enables us to know a place intimately, yet its image
> may lack sharpness unless we can also see it from the outside and
> reflect upon our experience.
>
> —Yi-Fu Tuan, *Space and Place: The Perspective of Experience*

Over the past two decades, a growing chorus of scholars and intellectuals, both within and beyond the field of Jewish studies, has advanced the claim that the notions of exile and diaspora, despite their apparent affinities, stand in profound tension with each other.[1] While "exile" is configured, in historical sources as well as contemporary scholarship, as an abnormal and unsustainable state of crisis governed by a narrative of sin, punishment, and longing for restoration, "diaspora" has come to signify a dynamic and even generative politico-spatial condition that is characterized by porous social boundaries and cultural vitality.[2] This revisionist interpretation of the Jewish discourse and experience of diaspora has been most powerfully articulated by Daniel Boyarin and Jonathan Boyarin in a series of provocative and incisive essays.[3] Blending historical analysis and political intervention, they advocate "a privileging of Diaspora, a dissociation of ethnicities and political hegemonies as the only social structure that begins to make possible a maintenance of cultural identity in a world grown thoroughly and inextricably interdependent."[4] This valorization of the essentially open-ended spatial horizons of diasporic existence glosses over the historical particularities of diasporic experience in specific times and places. As such, their formulation too readily assimilates "diaspora" in its heterogeneous historical forms to the highly particular phenomenon of "globalization" characteristic of capitalist postmodernity and its distinctive technologies of communication and movement (human, capital, and commodity).[5] Moreover, their critique of the Zionist project of re-territorializing the world's Jewish population within the borders of a nation-state in the area of Palestine runs the risk of establishing an equally teleological counter-narrative in which the postwar Jewish experience in Western Europe and especially North America displaces the State of Israel as a truer realization of Jewish historical processes. Still, the Boyarins have played an instrumental role in bringing about a salutary re(e)valuation of those forms of Jewish collectivity, both in the past and the present, that differ from, or even compete with, the model—and the ideal—of the modern liberal nation-state.[6]

This theoretical paradigm has called renewed attention to the rich spectrum of discursive and embodied practices through which Jewish diasporic communities have historically succeeded and continue to succeed in maintaining their collective identities. Most notably, Erich Gruen has recently argued that the Jews of the Hellenistic diaspora did not perceive their dispersion throughout the Mediterranean world as a condition in need of remedy, nor apparently did scriptural representations of the Babylonian exile as punishment for Israel's sin and the concomitant "doctrine of restoration" color their experience of their contemporary situation.[7] In fact, according to Gruen, the powerful image found in Greek-Jewish sources of the holy city of Jerusalem as the "mother city" (*metropolis*) of the scattered Jewish colonies (*apoikiai*) is an index of the profound sense of belonging that diaspora Jews felt in the local communities in which they and their more immediate ancestors made their lives.[8] Affective attachment to and financial support of the institutions of the geographic "center" in Jerusalem proved to be particularly effective strategies for sustaining numerous highly localized forms of diasporic Jewish identity throughout the Mediterranean world.

The Boyarins' diasporic model of Jewish social and cultural vitality has also productively informed the recent work of Charlotte Fonrobert on the historical emergence and significance of the rabbinic legal institution known as the 'eruv ḥatseirot, the ritual joining of courtyards, although her analysis also significantly modifies their assumptions about the nature of the relationship between the notions of territoriality and sovereignty.[9] Fonrobert argues that the *'eruv ḥatseirot* is a distinctive spatial practice that forges otherwise undifferentiated urban space into a residential community, thereby offering "a powerful model of a territory without sovereignty" that, "as such, would have much to offer the current discussions about diaspora cultures."[10] It would seem that, from the perspective of this paradigm, diasporic practices are not only highly admirable and adaptable, but also accord well with traditional Jewish piety; in sharp contrast, exile belongs to the naïve and ultimately dangerous sphere of "mythic" thinking that requires careful historical deconstruction lest it lead to the fetishization of territoriality.[11]

I think it important to stress that I myself am in full sympathy with these important "post-Zionist" correctives to the regnant approach to Jewish identity in nineteenth- and twentieth-century scholarship that was predicated on a cultural logic peculiar to the discourse of modern nationalism as well as to the institutional forms of the Western European nation-state.[12] This shift in perspective is particularly helpful when analyzing the sociocultural processes that obtained in the very different contexts of the multiethnic, multireligious, and multilingual empires of antiquity, with which this chapter is concerned. And the premodern cases, with their vast, contiguous territories and heterogeneous subject populations, in turn bear provocative similarities to the Russian, Ottoman, and Hapsburg Empires of the prewar period—and perhaps to contemporary, though still nascent, post-nationalist political arrangements as well.[13]

At the same time, I find something curious and even troubling in the way that the new scholarly discourse on diaspora maps so neatly onto traditional supersessionist narratives—both Christian and Jewish—concerning the replacement over the course of late antiquity of "cultic community" with "scriptural community" as the primary organizing principle for religious life. Indeed, the celebration in this scholarship of the mobility and dynamism of narrative, textuality, and hermeneutic creativity selectively recapitulates the perceived predilection within rabbinic Judaism—in its ancient and especially its modern forms—for Torah study as redemptive practice and its concomitant distaste for the sacred spaces of temple precincts, the genealogical exclusivity of priesthoods, and the bloody meat of animal sacrifices.[14] Insofar as the sacrificial cult of the Jerusalem Temple represents an atavistic embarrassment for many moderns, scholars included, there are enduring predispositions to prefer the text-centered scholastic piety of the rabbis to what might all too readily be seen as the spatial "obsessions" of the Temple cult.

It is, of course, undoubtedly the case that the period of late antiquity saw a profound historical shift in religious discourse and practice as societies throughout the ancient Mediterranean world ceased, albeit only gradually, to engage in animal sacrifice.[15] Yet, it would be deeply misleading to characterize this complex process as the inevitable "spiritualization" of what had suddenly come to seem empty ritual forms.[16] Blood cult remained the dominant paradigm for religious ritual and piety throughout late antiquity, providing the ritual logic and symbolic idiom for the novel modes of ritual-liturgical action that came to characterize Judaism and Christianity.[17] As Jonathan Klawans, Ishay Rosen-Zvi, Steven Fraade, and others have compellingly shown, many of the traditions found in rabbinic literature that describe the sacrificial and purity practices in force when the Jerusalem Temple was still in operation seem to be neither a simple record of pre-destruction practice nor the fruit of scriptural exegesis. Instead, these scholars have argued that these traditions reflect the rabbis' ongoing and creative engagement with—and even expansion of—cultic practice as they sought to address the contemporary religious and social concerns of post-destruction Judaism.[18]

Building on these insights into the enduring vitality of cultic discourse in late antique religions, I wish to explore in this essay how the spatial dislocation of the Temple vessels at the time of the destruction informs rabbinic attitudes concerning the physical reality and spatial fixity of the sacrificial cult. I will argue that the early rabbis of the second to fourth centuries articulated a far more nuanced attitude toward the dialectical tension between the "locative" dimensions of the physical cult and the more mobile forms of authority and piety that they sought to cultivate in the wake of the Temple's destruction.[19] I will focus on a series of early rabbinic sources of the third and fourth centuries that offer "eyewitness" testimonies concerning the cultic vessels that were taken from Jerusalem to Rome after the destruction of the Temple in 70 C.E. and, in some cases, detailed descriptions of their precise location and physical form.[20] I will suggest that these sources are not pursuing what is often taken as the relatively straightforward rabbinic agenda of supplanting the physical cult with an edifice of learned discourse and pious prayer.[21] Rather, these texts are marked by a palpable tension between appropriating the Temple cult to augment hermeneutically oriented rabbinic authority and prestige, on the one hand, and preserving sensual experience as a privileged site of religious meaning and authority, on the other. These rabbinic traditions betray an abiding fascination with the unique and inimitable power embodied in the concrete, but mobile, remains of a ritual system over which the rabbis are not quite able—or willing—to assert complete control. In emphasizing the visual accessibility of the Temple vessels outside the precincts of the Jerusalem Temple, these sources give expression to the productive tension that (some) Jews in late antiquity felt between the centering discourse of the traditional cult and the new spatial mobility of the sacred that characterized the post-Temple era in which willy-nilly they found themselves.

I wish to suggest that these traditions do not merely accord a central role to visual testimony in rabbinic halakhic debates concerning the form and function of the various Temple vessels, but in fact thematize the irrevocable visual power of these sacred objects. Visuality thus simultaneously indexes the experience of mobility, insofar as the act of seeing occurs in the imperial capital of Rome, and the enduring significance of the cultic center in Jerusalem, insofar as the very idiom of seeing hearkens to the materiality of the historical sacred center in Jerusalem.

In no sense, then, did rhetorics of space come to matter less to the production of Jewish identity in this period; nor were they replaced in rabbinic discourse, in any direct way, by rhetorics of textual authority. Rather, the spatial and material dimensions of the sacrificial cult—linked through the act of seeing—continued to function as primary parameters within which Jewish cultural forms evolved. It is thus my aim to show that a great deal is lost in our picture of early rabbinic Judaism if we emphasize its textual-exegetical nature to the exclusion of its deep and continuing engagement with the physical realities—both spatial and ritual—of the Jerusalem Temple.

I will thus suggest that at least some rabbinic sources betray an awareness that the new mobility of the post-destruction period did not merely present the potential for generating novel forms of religious authority and piety, but also generated a cultural and religious problematic that demanded far more than could be achieved through a straightforward supersessionist discourse. Instead, these sources transformed the long-standing link between visuality and cultic practice into a bridge between materiality and textuality, between the centripetal pull of the Jerusalem Temple and the centrifugal dynamism of the new "diasporic" piety of the rabbis.[22]

The Temple Vessels on Display in Rome: Rabbinic "Eyewitness" Testimonies

Following the protracted, but ultimately successful, siege of Jerusalem in 70 C.E., the Roman army under the command of Titus transported a variety of cultic implements from the now-destroyed Jerusalem Temple to Rome. Whether or not the Romans had initially intended to destroy the Temple complex and take its sacred vessels as war spoils,[23] these symbolically potent items were readily incorporated into the joint triumph celebrated by Vespasian and Titus at Rome circa June 71 C.E. for their victory in the (first) Jewish war.[24] This dramatic scene of the conquering Roman army parading the Temple vessels through the streets of Rome would subsequently be etched in stone for all time on the triumphal arch erected soon after the death of Titus, in 81 C.E.[25] Moreover, ancient sources report that Vespasian vowed—perhaps already during the triumphal ceremonies—to construct a temple to Peace in which the vessels would be placed on permanent public display.[26] This grand architectural project quite literally enshrined the Roman conquest of Judea within the public space of the imperial capital. Indeed, the Roman historian Fergus Millar has recently emphasized how significant this series of commemorative gestures was in legitimating the political aspirations of the new Flavian dynasty.[27]

The *Apocalypse of Baruch* (2 Baruch), an apocalypse set during the destruction of the First Temple by the Babylonians in 587/86 B.C.E. but written in response to the destruction of the Second Temple by the Romans, addresses quite candidly the anxieties of those who had experienced these events and were concerned about the fate of the Temple vessels.[28] The text reassures its audience in no uncertain terms that, at the bidding of the angelic emissary of God, the vessels will remain in or near Jerusalem, hidden beneath the earth: "'Earth, earth, earth, hear the word of the mighty God, and receive the things which I commit to you, and guard them until the last times, so that you may restore them when you are ordered, so that strangers may not get possession of them.' And the earth opened its mouth and swallowed them up."[29] This evocative image of the sacred vessels from the Jerusalem Temple, secreted away in or near the Land of Israel in preparation for the future renewal of the cult, echoes a long-standing literary tradition from the Second Temple period.[30] In resistance to the centrifugal forces of exile that had scattered the Judean population, the vessels are saved from the sacrilege of falling into the impure hands of the enemy. Yet, in the context of the events of 70 C.E., it is quite striking that the author of 2 Baruch refuses to acknowledge the fact that Titus and his victorious armies had, in very recent memory, paraded the sacred implements of the Jerusalem cult through the streets of Rome in triumphal procession, enshrined this celebration in monumental public art on the Arch of Titus, and even placed some of these items on display in the newly built Temple of Peace.[31]

The rabbis of Roman Palestine in the third and fourth centuries were also fascinated by the fate of the Temple vessels but apparently accommodated themselves to the reality of their dislocation to Rome. Reports concerning the viewing of the Temple vessels in Rome already make their appearance in the earliest strata of rabbinic literature. These sources present rabbinic visual testimonials concerning the physical form of a variety of Temple vessels, including the seven-branched candelabrum (menorah), the Temple veil (*parokhet*), and various vestments of the high priest. These testimonies concerning the Temple vessels in Rome form a tiny subgenre of their own. In the examples considered here, a rabbinic authority—either Rabbi Eleazar ben Yose or Rabbi Shim'on ben Yoḥai, both of whom lived in the second century C.E.—reports having seen one or another of the Temple implements during a visit to Rome. The formulation of the tradition is almost identical for both rabbis: the only difference is that while R. Eleazar merely reports what he "saw" in Rome, R. Shim'on adds a verb of motion ("When I *went to* Rome…") at the front of his report. As we will see below, this cluster of texts explicitly and repeatedly thematizes the act of visualization itself, linking these brief narrative snippets to a broader and highly contested discourse concerning the importance as well as the limits of visual access to the Temple vessels.

Because of the obvious similarities between these formulas, I would caution against the assumption that these third-, fourth-, and early fifth-century rabbinic sources represent transparent records of the actual experiences and words of second-century rabbis in the capital.[32] Moreover, I do not believe we are well served by trying to interpret these strikingly similar episodes in the biographies of R. Eleazar and R. Shim'on as historical events. Rather, I think it more productive to analyze these traditions within their immediate literary contexts in order to consider the place of cultic imagery within late antique Judaism in general and rabbinic culture in particular.

Almost from the beginning, these "eyewitness" reports appear within elaborate narrative, exegetical, or dialectical contexts, often to resolve a dispute concerning cultic law. These reports generally address either the precise design of one of the Temple implements or some sacrificial practice that has left a physical mark upon one of these vessels. Their emphasis on visualization builds upon widespread traditions concerning the public viewing of the Temple vessels by the laity during pilgrimage festivals, although it is worth stressing that these rabbinic "memories" of the Jerusalem cult likely do not reflect the actual historical practices performed before the destruction of the Temple when the sacrificial cult was still in force.[33]

Thus, for example, we read in the Tosefta (ca. mid-third century) that R. Eleazar ben R. Yose saw the Temple veil during a visit to Rome:

> And thus did he [the high priest] count [when sprinkling the sacrificial blood during the expiatory ritual on the Day of Atonement]: "One, one and one, one and two, one and three, one and four, one and five, one and six, one and seven." R. Judah said in the name of R. Eliezer: "One, one and one, two and one, three and one, four and one, five and one, six and one, seven and one." He went out to his left, along the veil [*parokhet*]. And he did not touch the veil. But if he touched it, he touched it. R. Eleazar b. R. Yose said: "I myself saw it [the veil] in Rome, and there were drops of blood on it. And they told me:[34] These [drops] are from the blood of the Day of Atonement."[35]

R. Eleazar's testimony is here appended to a series of relatively disconnected rabbinic dicta concerning the precise dynamics of the Yom Kippur ritual: mention of the *parokhet* seems to have prompted the redactor to include the R. Eleazar tradition, which does not otherwise substantiate or refute an argument.[36]

Details concerning R. Eleazar's sighting of the Temple vessels exhibit significant variation in the basic content of this tradition across the rabbinic corpora of the third and fourth centuries. For example, R. Eleazar elsewhere testifies that, while in Rome, he saw the head-plate (*tsits*) of the high priest— and not the Temple veil. More significantly, this tradition, which is found twice in the Jerusalem Talmud, likewise situates R. Eleazar's testimony within the context of halakhic debate regarding the precise appearance of the sacred object: "On the head-plate [*tsits*] there was written 'Holy unto the Lord.' 'Holy unto' [was written] below, while the divine name was above. Just as a king sits on his throne, so one [part of the phrase] is below and the divine name is above.' But R. Eleazar b. R. Yose said: 'I myself saw it in Rome, and actually, engraved upon it on one line was "Holy unto the Lord."'"[37]

The anonymous authority cited in this passage is apparently in possession of a received tradition that asserts that the words "Holy unto the Lord" were engraved upon the head-plate on two separate rows, with the divine name on top. This anonymous tradition does not rest on either an exegetical or an experiential rationale, but instead appeals to the obvious iconic function of the phrase: the vertical configuration not only embodies the elevated position of

God but also signifies the logical relationship between the priestly head-plate and God's divine kingship. By contrast, R. Eleazar grounds his conflicting position that the entire phrase was written on a single line in eyewitness testimony, which, while perhaps less graphically apt, carries with it the authority of visual experience.

Other tannaitic figures could similarly attract various cultic objects to their names. We find in the fragmentarily preserved halakhic midrash *Sifrei zuta* a statement attributed to R. Shim'on ben Yoḥai concerning the form of the menorah from the Jerusalem Temple, which he claims to have spent a long time inspecting while in Rome. But, unlike what is probably the earliest form of the R. Eleazar statement found in the Tosefta, R. Shim'on's report is here already embedded in a halakhic context and juxtaposed to an exegetical argument:

> From where [in Scripture do we know] that all the lamps [of the menorah] must be turned inward toward the middle lamp? Scripture teaches thus: "(When you set up the lamps, let the seven lamps give light) toward the front of (*el mul*) the lampstand" (Nm 8:2). And [elsewhere] it says: "(There is a people that came out of Egypt; it hides the earth from view) and it is settled next to me (*mimuli*)" (Nm 22:5). R. Shim'on said: "When I went to Rome and saw the menorah there, all of its lamps were turned inward toward the middle lamp."[38]

Perhaps unsurprisingly, this discussion in *Sifrei zuta* does not appeal to the authority of contemporary synagogue iconography. Instead, through midrashic exegesis, it substantiates its claim that the outer six lamps of the menorah were oriented toward the central lamp. The passage notes the echo of the verbal element *mul* ("in front of") in two unrelated verses from the Pentateuch—one stipulating how Aaron should arrange the lamps of the menorah and the other relating how the Moabite king Balak feared that he was being encircled by the people of Israel. The physical arrangement conjured up in the former verse is not, however, self-evident. The midrashist reasons that just as this element of the prepositional phrase implies encirclement in the Balak story, so should it be understood to do in the description of the menorah. The passage thus determines that the three candles on each side of the menorah were oriented inward toward the central flame. Unlike R. Eleazar's report concerning the head-plate, R. Shim'on's testimony confirms rather than contravenes the received tradition cited anonymously by the text.

Visualization of the Temple Cult among Jews and Christians

Beyond their varied halakhic aims, all these eyewitness testimonies participate in what seems to be an underlying cultural tradition—common in both early Judaism and early Christianity—that acknowledges the power and contentiousness of visual access to the Temple vessels. To report that one had laid eyes on the sacred objects of the Temple cult was no insignificant claim. Thus, for example, a noncanonical gospel (P. Oxyrhynchus 840), likely composed before the end of the second century c.e., not long before the motif would emerge in the Tosefta, relates that the high priest rebuked Jesus and his disciples for having entered the Temple sanctuary and gazed upon the Temple vessels in an impure state:

> And having taken them, he [Jesus] brought them [the disciples] into
> the place of purification [*eis auto to hagneutērion*] and was walking in
> the Temple. And having approached, a certain Pharisee, a chief priest
> whose name was Levi, joined them and said to the Savior: "Who
> gave you permission to enter this place of purification and to see
> these holy vessels [*tauta ta hagia skeuē*] when you have not washed
> yourself, nor have your disciples surely washed their feet? But you,
> in a defiled state, you have entered this temple, which is a pure place
> that no one enters nor dares to view these holy vessels without first
> having washed themselves and changed their clothes."[39]

Much about this passage remains obscure, not least whether the author of this gospel was familiar with the actual functioning of the defunct Jerusalem cult. Daniel Schwartz has noted that, in its equal emphasis on prohibitions against visual and physical violation of the cult, the passage is perfectly consistent with other Second Temple sources that likewise proscribe the improper viewing of the Temple utensils.[40] Here, of course, the author understands the actions of Jesus and his disciples as an outright rejection of the exclusivist posture of the Jerusalem priesthood. Schwartz suggests that the anti-priestly impulse in this text was also shared by the Pharisaic and rabbinic movements.

François Bovon, however, has recently pointed out that Schwartz's reading depends on the contradictory assertions that, on the one hand, the designation of the high priest as a "Pharisee" likely reflects later Christian criticism of Pharisaism rather than an accurate historical memory of the priest's identity, and, on the other, the document provides reliable insight into actual Pharisaic practice. Bovon instead argues, convincingly to my mind, that the gospel fragment should be read in the context of second-century Christian controversies concerning the need for purification during water baptism rather than as evidence for first-century Judaism or the historical Jesus.[41] He points out that the expression "the holy vessels" (*ta hagia skeuē*) is precisely the same language used by early Christians to describe the liturgical utensils employed in the ritual of the Eucharist. On this reading, the lost gospel tells us neither about the history of the actual Temple vessels nor about their fate, but about how their memory was appropriated in early Christian culture.

Unlike Second Temple Jewish sources—but very much in the spirit of P. Oxyrhynchus 840—rabbinic literature nowhere places restrictions on the viewing of the Temple vessels.[42] In a fascinating article, Israel Knohl has analyzed a variety of rabbinic sources that represent the laity's viewing of the Temple vessels during the Second Temple period as a sacred rite, one almost akin to a theophany.[43] Knohl's argument largely hinges on later rabbinic reports concerning sectarian controversy surrounding the display of the showbread table and the menorah outside the inner sanctuary of the Temple on pilgrimage festivals.[44] As I have suggested above, I doubt that these rabbinic sources can be used to reconstruct the history of actual cultic practice in the Jerusalem Temple.[45] Nevertheless, I do think he is fundamentally correct in identifying a strong "democratizing" or "popularizing" impulse within rabbinic literature itself. Quite clearly, the rabbinic authors of these texts wished to present the Temple vessels as the patrimony of all Israel—and not just the priesthood.

Yet, these diverse rabbinic traditions, including the eyewitness testimonies that I have analyzed above, are also marked by a provocative emphasis on the visual power of the Temple vessels. They carry within them a palpable and abiding interest in the very materiality of the cult. Of course, unlike early Christianity, late antique Judaism was relatively slow to develop liturgical practices and personnel that could be understood, however provisionally, to replace the Jerusalem cult; indeed, it was most likely not until the fifth century that the synagogue was gradually transformed, under considerable Christian influence, into a kind of surrogate temple.[46] But, while third- and fourth-century rabbinic sources do not provide the lost cultic implements with a tangible new referent comparable with the Christian Eucharist, rabbinic claims of special knowledge about the appearance and function of the Temple vessels paradoxically reaffirm their continuing cultural, religious, and political significance.

These rabbinic eyewitness reports serve as an antidote to the destruction of the Jerusalem Temple and the resulting dislocation of its cultic vessels. These conditions might have prompted the rabbinic authors to reflect on the fragility of a place-bound Temple cult or to interpret the capture of the Temple vessels as confirmation that proper knowledge of the Jerusalem cult should henceforth derive solely from Scripture. It is significant, therefore, that these particular rabbinic sources explicitly value visual confirmation over scriptural exegesis. Indeed, they stress that the physical acts of travel and visualization serve as the basis for rabbinic knowledge of and authority over cultic practice. This affirmation of the sheer physicality of the ritual implements of the Jerusalem cult complicates the traditional picture of the rabbis as the paragons of a post-Temple Judaism in which text trumps object. Moreover, this narrative image of the act of visualizing the Temple vessels in Rome encompasses both the experience of mobility and attachment to the cultic center in Jerusalem. The rabbis may have celebrated the power of their own mobility to bridge, however tenuously, the spatial rupture between their community in Palestine and the displaced sancta in Rome. But at least for some rabbis of the third and fourth century, the recognition that the sacred was an increasingly mobile phenomenon was compatible with their enduring attachment to the concrete realia of the Jerusalem Temple. In this regard, the rabbis of late antiquity could, at times, not only reinterpret but also reaffirm the religious power that was bound up in the sacrificial cult. Their cultivation of diasporic modes of continuity—in particular, hermeneutic authority and activity—stood in productive tension with the cultic idioms and images with which they remained very much in dialogue.

(Post)modern scholars, both Jewish and non-Jewish, may recognize their own values in the rabbinic embrace of the utopian potential of increasingly mobile and dynamic forms of religious community. Nevertheless, they should guard against adopting a supersessionist stance that relegates spatial and physical attachments to a more primitive phase of religious and cultural life, whether that stage is associated with the bloody sacrificial cult of the Jerusalem Temple or with the nationalist discourses of nineteenth- and twentieth-century European—and Jewish—modernity.

Chapter 6

Sacred Space, Local History, and Diasporic Identity: The Graves of the Righteous in Medieval and Early Modern Ashkenaz

Lucia Raspe

In 1470, the cantor of the Jewish community of Regensburg was questioned by Christian interrogators interested in hearing the Jewish view on Saint Emmeram, the city's patron saint. The cantor confirmed that his coreligionists believed that the saint had been a Jew named Amram and that he lay buried not in the abbey bearing Saint Emmeram's name, but in the Jewish cemetery. This was, he said, what he had been told by his parents. Although the grave was unmarked, the cantor was prepared to point out the hole in the ground that was believed to be the saint's burial place. It was said among the Jews, he added, that Amram "helped them."[1]

In the Rhenish city of Worms, a story was told of how the twelve *parnasim*, or Jewish community leaders, had met their deaths during the persecution of the First Crusade in 1096. Their supposed mass grave played a major role in local custom from at least early modern times. The rich tradition of *minhagim* preserved from that period gives a detailed picture of how, on various occasions throughout the year, the Jewish community would walk over to the cemetery outside the city walls, encircle its circumference, say prayers, and give charity. On the public fasts commemorating the persecution itself, people would prostrate themselves on the martyrs' grave and invoke their intercession with God to have mercy on the community.[2]

In Mainz, during the persecution of the First Crusade, the Jewish cemetery had apparently been desecrated. After a Jewish community had reestablished itself, great care was taken to place new markers upon the graves of some of the local sages. Although the cemetery was again vandalized in the fifteenth century, the purported resting place of the eleventh-century liturgical poet R. Shim'on ben Yitshaq continued to play a prominent role in the minds of local and not-so-local Jews; it is mentioned in several of the hagiographic legends connected with him. One narrator, apparently not from Mainz, insists that he had visited R. Shim'on's grave.[3] Another gives a description of the grave, noting that there was a miraculous spring nearby.[4] Later sources refer to the place as the "cave" (*me'arah*) of R. Shim'on. This would seem to indicate a certain degree of conflation with the rabbinic legends about the talmudic sage R. Shim'on bar Yoḥai, the presumed author of the Zohar, who was supposed to have spent several years in a cave while a miraculous spring kept him alive.[5] In a sense, then, a grave located in the Holy Land—and a particularly prominent one at that—had been transferred to Ashkenazi soil.[6]

Holy Graves and Normative Judaism

The role that the graves of the righteous—*qivrei tsaddiqim*—should play in the life of the community has been controversial in Judaism from ancient times. Although the biblical concepts of impurity connected with death may have been intended to rule out the development of any sort of a cult of the dead, pilgrimage to the graves of various biblical figures did take place in late antiquity, and pilgrimage to those of Hasidic rebbes or Moroccan Jewish saints is a familiar phenomenon in our own day.[7] Medieval Ashkenaz, on the other hand, is not known among scholars for its posthumous veneration of saints or their graves. However, research into the hagiographical legends of medieval Ashkenaz has drawn my attention to the way these tales appear to have taken on a life of their own as narrators "grounded" them in the physical reality of their own communities—most obviously at their heroes' real or putative graves.[8] These glimpses of a real-life *Sitz im Leben* of Ashkenazi hagiography are what have led me to suspect there may have been more going on at these sites than meets the eye. The present chapter will build upon these observations and place them in larger context, using a wider range of sources than the narrative texts that originally sparked my interest. At the same time, the connection thus forged between sanctity and topography may open a window onto the way in which premodern Ashkenazi Jews perceived their own existence in the German lands, as a minority group within Christian society and with regard to the larger question of their relationship to that more familiar repository of sanctity-in-space, the Holy Land.

The ubiquitous presence of the Christian veneration of saints in medieval Europe forms the backdrop to all the evidence we have of an analogous grass-roots phenomenon among Jews. While many Jews certainly reacted to saint veneration with ridicule or repulsion, the local adoption of Saint Emmeram of Regensburg as a Jewish patron saint shows something of the attraction that the Christian model may have held all the same. That Ashkenazi Jews should have felt a need for the kind of supernatural protection offered by a saint of their own seems natural enough in an age that earned Ashkenaz the title *erets gezeirah*, "the land of persecution."[9] Paradoxically, the very precariousness of their existence also strengthened their ties to their places of residence. As the case of Worms would seem to suggest, it was precisely a local history of Jewish piety and sacrifice that became manifest in the physical space of the cemetery and rendered that part of local topography hallowed ground.[10] This, in turn, raises the question of how the sacred space thus established on a local level was perceived vis-à-vis the more traditional orientation toward the Holy Land. The case of R. Shim'on ben Yitshaq of Mainz appears particularly suggestive in this respect. Perhaps only by associating his memory with that of a leading scholar of talmudic Palestine were Ashkenazi Jews able to sacralize the space that they were themselves inhabiting. Or had Ashkenaz indeed replaced the Holy Land in the minds of local Jews?

Pilgrimage to the Holy Land, as Elchanan Reiner has shown, never became a religious obligation; it is therefore rarely mentioned in medieval halakhic literature.[11] The same is all the more true for pilgrimage to holy graves within the diaspora. When the matter does come up in medieval responsa, it is viewed with suspicion. Such texts may be read as indirect testimony to an existing practice with which medieval rabbis were not entirely comfortable.[12] The *locus classicus* of this ambivalence is an oft-quoted responsum written by R. Hayyim Palti'el of Magdeburg at the end of the thirteenth century, in which he expresses astonishment at the way people made vows to visit cemeteries— a practice he found dangerously close to *doresh el ha-metim*, the "inquiring of the dead" expressly forbidden in the Bible.[13] Although R. Hayyim Palti'el was ready to admit that offering prayer at a place sanctified by the graves of the righteous might make one's supplications more likely to be accepted, he nevertheless felt that women and the unlearned should be discouraged from the practice. Apparently presumed either unable or unwilling to make such fine distinctions, they would invariably address the dead themselves. Hence, whenever people came to him in such a matter, he would absolve them of their vow and rule that they should give the sum that they would have spent on the trip to charity instead.

If R. Ḥayyim Palti'el thought that the problem was "inquiring of the dead," Yom Tov Lipman Mühlhausen (d. 1421), writing about a century later, was no less critical of what he perceived as the danger of idolatry inherent in addressing intermediaries in prayer.[14] His attack was directed primarily at Christian hagiolatry, since his *Sefer nitsaḥon* was intended as a handbook of interreligious polemic. But he, too, seems to have feared that some Jews might actually be drawn to such practices. Thus he closed his remarks with the admonition, "God forbid one should act in this way."[15]

Lest we be tempted to view such misgivings as an indication of a rift between learned and more popular culture, it should be noted that there were eminent medieval sages who not only condoned visiting cemeteries but did so themselves.[16] We need not even turn to *Sefer Ḥasidim*, the thirteenth-century compendium of Ashkenazi pietism ascribed to R. Yehudah he-Ḥasid (d. 1217), which perceives the relationship between the living and the dead as reciprocal in nature and expects those who refuse to acknowledge that reciprocity to be swiftly punished.[17] More noteworthy, perhaps, is the position taken by some of the leading halakhists of the fourteenth and fifteenth centuries. A passage in the ethical testament of R. Yehudah b. Asher of Toledo (d. 1349), for instance, records the prayer he used to say on "all those days" that he visited the graves of the righteous. It is true that the text of the prayer is phrased carefully so as not to address the dead themselves but to request their intercession in the third person. The practice itself, however, is something he completely takes for granted, a fact that has been interpreted as reflecting the Ashkenazi background of R. Yehudah's family.[18] Similarly, the Maharil, R. Ya'aqov Molin of Mainz (ca. 1360–1427), while warning explicitly that rather than addressing petitions to the deceased, a visitor to the cemetery should plead with God to have mercy on account of their merit, found the practice itself commendable.[19] One generation later, R. Israel Isserlein of Wiener Neustadt (1390–1460) was less scrupulous. The prayer he composed for his own use when visiting the graves of the righteous opens with an address to the dead interred in the plot before him; the invocation, preserved for posterity in his student's *Leqet yosher*, may be considered a forerunner of the genre of graveside prayer texts that began to flourish in the early modern period.[20]

Individual visits to cemeteries for the purpose of graveside prayer, then, represented one manifestation of the role that the graves of the righteous came to play in the religious life of medieval and early modern Ashkenaz. Two others were communal processions to the cemetery on fixed occasions and the desire to be buried in close proximity to specific graves. Let us consider each of these in turn.

Individual Pilgrimage to Holy Graves: Rabbinic Responsa and Material Evidence

Much of the evidence we have for individual pilgrimage to cemeteries is focused on the burial ground of Regensburg, which was renowned as the final resting place of R. Yehudah he-Ḥasid, although local Jews may also have been drawn to the unmarked grave of the rather more spurious R. Amram, mentioned at the beginning of this essay.[21] Pious travel to Regensburg from elsewhere is especially well documented for the fifteenth century. In 1519, when the Jews were expelled from the city, a Christian chronicler noted that the cemetery, which was destroyed, had been held in such veneration that Jews used to come there from as far away as Hungary.[22] In Jewish sources, we hear of such journeys almost exclusively in the context of rabbinic responsa dealing with vows, where the leniency instituted by R. Ḥayyim Palti'el came to be the dominant trend.

About 1415, R. Israel Isserlein vowed, as a youth in time of illness, to travel to Regensburg to the graves of his ancestors. However, when he fell ill a second time, he was absolved from his vow, since the journey would have posed a threat to his frail health.[23] Like Isserlein, individual pilgrims may often have aimed to visit the graves of their ancestors, as mobility was high and the Regensburg cemetery had long served the communities in all of Bavaria.[24] On the other hand, the phrase used in his case—to travel to Regensburg *'al qivrei avot*, literally, "to the graves of fathers"—seems unspecific. The rabbinic concept of *zekhut avot*, the merit of the fathers, after all, had originally referred to the biblical patriarchs, fathers of the nation in more than the biological sense; in rabbinic literature, it was extended to apply to any individual's own pious forebears. In our context, it seems to have come to include the founding fathers of the Ashkenazi community more generally. The case of a woman who had vowed to visit the cemetery in Regensburg at roughly the same time is a case in point. The Maharil gave another lenient ruling; more remarkable, perhaps, is the way in which the phrase used in the description of her case, "to go to the graves in Regensburg," turns into "to the graves of the righteous" in the sage's decision almost as a matter of course.[25] Indeed, in the second half of the fifteenth century, in a similar context, R. Moshe Mintz enumerated *qivrei avot, qivrei tsaddiqim,* and *qivrei qedoshim*—the graves of a person's own ancestors, of righteous persons, and of martyrs—as if there weren't really much difference between them, thus blurring the borders between individual heritage and communal patrimony in a way that is characteristic of the material throughout.[26]

Sources that allow us to hear the voices of pilgrims themselves are extremely rare. One such voice has been preserved in a final remark to one of the narratives about R. Shim'on b. Yitsḥaq, mentioned earlier in this essay. The text recounts a polemical debate, set in Bamberg, between this sage and a bishop, which results in R. Shim'on's banishment from the city and relocation to Mainz, thus providing an etiology of the rabbi's move to the city with which he is generally identified. As if to enhance the story's veracity, the narrator states that Mainz is where R. Shim'on was subsequently buried—and, he adds, "I have visited his grave."[27] The statement suggests that a topographical point of reference such as the sage's grave may have helped originally oral narratives to survive. Unfortunately, it tells us very little about the visit itself. Another text, likewise written by an Ashkenazi émigré to Italy, is less reticent. Copying out a list of medieval Tosafists and the date of each one's demise, Menaḥem Oldendorf—a well-known figure in old Yiddish letters—added a note of his own. R. Yehudah he-Ḥasid, he wrote, died in 1217 and was buried in Regensburg, "and on 29 Av 1472, I, Menaḥem b. Naftali, was at his grave, and I signed my name on his headstone."[28]

What appears as an early instance of the kind of tourist misbehavior often denounced as barbaric may tell us something about medieval Jewish piety that has left hardly a trace elsewhere. That Oldendorf remembered the exact date of his visit decades after the event is noteworthy enough; that he cared to set it down in writing would seem to testify to the importance he attached to the act of inscribing his name—an impression confirmed by his use of the verb *ḥatam*, to sign, which carries the connotation of affixing one's seal to a legally binding document.[29] Inscribing one's name at a pilgrimage site would appear to be more than an expression of what has been called the "I was here" syndrome, although religious and profane motivations for documenting one's own visit at a given place often appear intertwined.[30] Such inscriptions may function as a way of extending the pilgrims' presence at the site to remind the saint to continue bringing their concerns before God even after they have left.[31] The case of *qever Raḥel*, the tomb of the matriarch by the road from Jerusalem to Bethlehem, provides an instructive parallel. Binyamin of Tudela's travelogue of the twelfth century tells us that Jewish passersby regularly signed their names on her epitaph.[32] By the nineteenth and early twentieth centuries, with writing materials more readily available, visitors were in the habit of inscribing their names on scraps of paper and leaving them at the tomb; in the 1930s and 1940s, apparently in an effort to domesticate the practice, ledgers were provided at the site, encouraging pilgrims to sign their names and articulate their requests in a more orderly manner.[33] Similarly, while the custom of leaving paper notes is very much in evidence at the cemetery in Worms today, David Kaufmann, writing at the end of the nineteenth century, noted numerous inscriptions of names on the Maharil's tombstone. Some, he claimed, were still legible at the time; some are visible even today.[34]

The work that has been done on graffiti at Christian shrines suggests that, somewhat paradoxically, people feel compelled to assert their individual presence by inscribing their own names on walls, reliquaries, or pieces of art whenever they see that others have already done so.[35] It is unlikely, therefore, that Oldendorf's act was unique. What is more, the date recorded in his note would seem to indicate that he did not visit the rabbi's grave alone that day. The 29th of Av was the eve of the new moon. We have evidence from the late fourteenth century onward that 'erev rosh ḥodesh was a day of fasting for some in the community. At a later date, under the influence of Lurianic kabbalah, the day was observed as a "minor Yom Kippur" whose ritual often included visits to the cemetery.[36] What we have here, then, may be an early reference to a custom that was on the verge of becoming part of the communal life of Regensburg.

Collective Procession and Communal Fate

It has often been pointed out that, unlike Christianity, medieval Judaism— within Europe, at least—did not develop a system of organized public pilgrimage to particular graves.[37] Nevertheless, collective processions to the cemetery formed part of the ritual observed on fast days in many Ashkenazi communities, whether on the eves of Rosh Hashanah and Yom Kippur or, as we have seen, on 'erev rosh ḥodesh.[38] Precedent for this practice could be found in a passage in the Babylonian Talmud discussing fast days declared during a drought. Two reasons are given in the Talmud: one, that going to the cemetery is intended to make the community humble themselves before God, likening their own fate to that of the dead; the other, "so that the dead may beseech mercy on our behalf." The difference between the two reasons, the text goes on to explain, is that for purposes of the former, even a non-Jewish cemetery will do.[39] Communal visits to the cemetery after morning prayers on Tish'ah be-Av or the eves of the High Holidays are attested in the Ashkenazi realm by the end of the fourteenth century.[40] They may be implied in a note in the *Sefer ha-agudah* by Alexander Süßkind ha-Kohen of Erfurt (d. 1349), which mentions circumambulation of the burial ground in a way suggesting that the cemetery was believed to have absorbed a custom that had once been part of Temple liturgy.[41]

In addition to these traditional fast days punctuating the Jewish year, procession to the cemetery and circumambulation of its grounds also played a major role in the ritual designated for the public fasts that had been instituted by specific communities to commemorate persecutions in their more recent past. For this purpose, the community would direct their steps toward the graves of martyrs, ideally those who had died in the persecution in question, rather than toward those of "fathers" in either of the two senses discussed above. Although victims of mob or judicial violence were hardly ever given proper burial, the way the legend of the twelve *parnasim* was attached to a particular area in the cemetery at Worms suggests that the need to create a commemorative space could be strong enough to overcome this difficulty.[42] These collective trips to the cemetery must have contributed greatly to each community's sense of its own local history.

The graves of the righteous also figured prominently in liturgies devised ad hoc whenever a situation arose that required enlisting the assistance of the departed in an effort to avert impending communal disaster. The idea that heavenly decrees concerning future events (*gezeirot*, an expression also denoting persecutions) are made known beforehand to zaddikim, whether living or dead, is attested in the Talmud; so is the notion that they may step in to prevent their implementation.[43] Small wonder, then, if Ashkenazi Jews, fearing for their safety in a specific locality or as part of the Ashkenazi community at large, turned to graveside prayer to remind God of the merits of their righteous dead and to move these zaddikim to intervene on their behalf. Thus, the liturgy devised by the Maharil for a three-day fast intended to avert anti-Jewish rioting during the Hussite war of 1421 stipulated that the Jews of the German communities were to visit the graves after morning prayers, wherever that was permitted.[44] Similarly, in Wiener Neustadt in 1450, when R. Israel Isserlein ordered a fast during the weeks preceding the ultimate expulsion of the Jews from neighboring Bavaria, local Jews were enjoined to trundle to the cemetery in small groups in order not to attract the non-Jews' attention.[45] When the Jews of Frankfurt fled to their cemetery during the Fettmilch attack on the Judengasse in 1614, which occurred on the very day that had been declared a fast, they were acting in the same tradition.[46] And when the Jews were restored to Frankfurt after eighteen months of exile, a Yiddish song composed to commemorate the occasion framed the whole experience in terms of one long Yom Kippur. God had weighed the community's sins against the merits of their fathers; the merits had prevailed.[47] Such dramatic scenes went a long way toward making the holy graves a central locus of collective memory in that they provided a physical space linking the community's own past to its future in any given place. Somewhere along the way, the righteous "fathers" buried there were turned into local patron saints.

Sacred Proximity and Jewish Burial *ad Sanctos*

Let us see now what can be made of Ashkenazi Jews' desire to be buried in close proximity to certain graves. Time and again, we hear of individuals ready to go to great lengths to secure a burial site near their forebears' graves, which could be costly, particularly if they were no longer living in the same community and the right of burial had to be purchased.[48] Burial in family groups had been the norm in Jewish funeral practice since biblical times. More significant in our context is the way in which interment near the graves of *avot* in a wider sense appears to have been no less attractive to premodern Ashkenazi Jews.

It has been said that, contrary to Christian practice, there was no burial *ad sanctos*, "near the saints," in medieval and early modern Judaism.[49] If taken to mean that medieval churches served as burial grounds while synagogues did not, this is true. However, the idea behind the Christian practice—that burial near those among the previously departed whose portion in the world to come seemed assured might secure their patronage in one's own quest for salvation—may well be worth looking at in a Jewish context.[50]

Medieval Jewish cemeteries in present-day Germany are rare, and where they remain, researchers have been preoccupied with documenting inscriptions before they disappear and have thus had little time to study the patterns of the "geography of burial" that such inscriptions may reveal.[51] Let us first look at the Jewish cemetery of Mainz. When the Jews were expelled from that city in 1438, many, if not all, of its headstones were removed and used for various municipal building projects.[52] About two hundred of these, some complete, some mere fragments, have come to light since.[53] Among these was a grave marker for Shim'on b. Yitshaq, the eleventh-century liturgical poet mentioned earlier, which was unearthed during construction works in 1922 (Fig. 17). The epitaph was unusual in that it was undated; it simply read, "This is the grave of our master R. Shim'on b. Yitshaq. May his soul have eternal life."[54] The stone itself did not resemble those preserved from the eleventh century; both its shape and the execution of its inscription seemed closer to those of the twelfth or even the thirteenth century. Apparently, then, this was not the original tombstone but a later replacement, intended to mark the grave after the original had been lost, perhaps during the persecutions of the First Crusade. Similar undated markers were found for Rabbenu Gershom ("the Light of the Exile") of Mainz and the liturgical poet R. Meshullam b. Kalonymos, Shim'on's contemporaries and, like him, founding fathers of the local community and heroes of a narrative tradition that can be traced to the thirteenth century.[55] The Jews of Mainz, it seems, felt a need to mark the exact spot in which each of these sages had been buried, though possibly only several generations after the original headstones had disappeared. Although we lack textual sources to that effect, it stands to reason that their graves were visited even then.

Knowledge of the location of R. Shim'on's grave survived even the second, more permanent, expulsion of the Jews from Mainz that occurred in 1471, for, unlike that of Regensburg, the Mainz cemetery—bereft of its tombstones—appears to have remained accessible to Jews. Although no Jewish community had existed in the city for several decades by the time one narrator alluded to his own visit to R. Shim'on's grave in 1504, permission had been given in 1492 for a single Jew to reside in the city in order to provide accommodation to short-term visitors and, perhaps, to direct anyone thus inclined to the unmarked graves of the luminaries of the local past.[56] Moreover, those Jews remaining in the principality outside the city continued to bury their dead at Mainz, and the gravedigger appointed in 1515 came from a family that had served the community in that capacity for several generations.[57] Enough of a tradition, it seems, was kept alive. It was apparently revived when a Jewish community was reestablished in Mainz toward the end of the sixteenth century, and it must have gathered momentum when a description of R. Shim'on's grave appeared in print in the *Mayse bukh* of 1602.[58] It is from the mid-seventeenth century onward that we can follow the role that his grave played as the focal point in the hierarchy of sacred space emerging in the cemetery.

17. Mainz, "Denkmalfriedhof," undated epitaph of R. Shimʿon ben
Yitsḥaq. Photograph by the author, 2001.

We first hear of someone buried expressly near R. Shimʿon's grave in
1644, when R. Yehudah Löw, one of the first rabbis of the reestablished community, was laid to rest nearby—a fact of sufficient significance to be noted
by the rabbi's son Eliʿezer Liebermann Sofer, himself known primarily for his
augmented version of the *Maʿaneh lashon*, a collection of graveside prayers
that was to enjoy great popularity for several centuries.[59] By the eighteenth
century, it had become customary for the community's rabbis to find their
final resting place near Shimʿon's grave, unless they had been born in Mainz
and could be buried alongside their own ancestors. In 1762, the local *ḥevra
qaddisha* marked the site identified as his grave by dedicating a new epitaph
to his memory. Unfortunately, because of the dilapidated state of many of the
sandstone monuments, this memorial for Shimʿon b. Yitsḥaq can no longer
be located. However, it was seen by Jonas Bondi, then rabbi of the orthodox
community, who published its inscription in 1927.[60] Bondi also noted the
names of three rabbis buried nearby during the eighteenth century and several
more for the nineteenth, his own ancestors among them.[61] Although only
some of the cemetery's inscriptions have been deciphered to date and many
have become wholly illegible, several of the gravestones mentioned by Bondi
can still be identified. Their distribution indicates that Shimʿon's grave was

18. Mainz, Jewish cemetery, northwestern corner. Photograph by the author, 2006.

apparently located in the northwestern corner of the cemetery (Fig. 18). In addition to community rabbis, their wives, and their children, lay leaders and their families are strongly represented in this area.[62]

It is here, then, that the narrative of the cave and the spring associated with R. Shim'on ben Yitsḥaq, according to the *Mayse bukh*, must have manifested itself in some sort of tangible reality. Nothing of that can be seen today. Nevertheless, the appeal that burial near his grave appears to have carried for those sufficiently privileged to gain entry to this area is quite evident, although its precise meaning is never spelled out. Viewed against the backdrop of the narrative that presents the Ashkenazi sage as a saint of the rank of R. Shim'on bar Yoḥai, the evidence on the ground certainly is suggestive.

For what may be our best example of a Jewish practice analogous to Christian burial *ad sanctos*, we must go to Worms. How else are we to interpret the oft-repeated story of R. Me'ir (also known as the Maharam) of Rothenburg and Alexander Wimpfen? In 1307, Wimpfen, a wealthy and apparently childless Jew from Frankfurt, took it upon himself to ransom the Maharam's body, which had not been released for burial since the great rabbi had died in captivity fourteen years earlier.[63] In return for his effort, Wimpfen was granted the right to be buried by Rabbi Me'ir's side, a wish fulfilled only

19. Worms, Jewish cemetery, tombstones of R. Meʾir of Rothenburg and
Alexander Wimpfen. Photograph by the author, 2002.

months later. The inscriptions on the twin headstones erected for the two (Fig.
19) tell the full story.[64] Wimpfen's headstone provides an explicit record of
what was understood to have been the benefactor's prime motivation, expressing the hope that he merit the same place in paradise that he had received in
the cemetery—at the rabbi's right-hand side. The site has drawn pious visitors
since and continues to do so today. Like the grave of R. Shimʿon ben Yitsḥaq
in Mainz, it also attracted a number of communal functionaries who were laid
to rest in the vicinity.[65]

Again, the practice of Jewish burial *ad sanctos* did not go uncontested.
When the Maharil was buried in the cemetery at Worms in 1427, a spot was
chosen for his interment that was as far away from R. Meʾir's place of burial
as possible (Fig. 20, No. 1). Indeed, if it is true that the Maharil asked to have
no one buried within four cubits of his own grave (Fig. 20, No. 2), that request might have been intended to preclude burial *ad sanctos*.[66] It seems highly
ironic, therefore, that his grave, in turn, should have become the focal point
of the so-called "Rabbis' Valley" of the Worms cemetery (Fig. 20, No. 3), as
is commonly assumed.[67] But was the Maharil's grave really the focal point?
The first rabbi after the Maharil to be interred in this area was R. Eliyyahu
Loanz (Fig. 20, No. 4), a noted *baʿal shem* in his lifetime and after his death

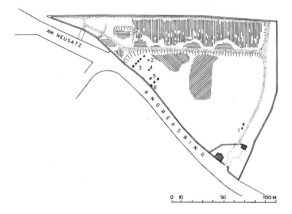

20. Worms, Jewish cemetery. Based on Otto Böcher, *Der Alte Judenfried-
hof zu Worms,* 5th ed. (Neuss, 1984). Used by permission of Rheinischer
Verein für Denkmalpflege und Landschaftsschutz.

in 1636.[68] In 1670, R. Shimshon Bacharach followed suit; in 1702, his son R.
Ya'ir Ḥayyim; and a year later, R. Ya'ir Ḥayyim's wife.[69] Now the tombstones
of the Bacharach family (Fig. 20, No. 5) are actually situated farther from the
Maharil than from a site already mentioned—the supposed mass grave of the
twelve *parnasim* of 1096, marked by a plaque in the cemetery wall (Fig. 20,
No. 6), which played a prominent role in the communal processions on the
fast days so well documented for seventeenth-century Worms. The emergence
of the "Rabbis' Valley" (Fig. 21) in precisely this area at precisely this time
can hardly be accidental.[70] As in Mainz, a son's taste for cemetery prayer and
the high status of his deceased father seem to have worked in concert here.
At the end of his *Ḥavot ya'ir,* the younger Bacharach mentions a promise that
he had made to his father to visit his grave with a quorum of ten men on the
day before each new moon and pray for his soul.[71] Perhaps the two did believe
that burial near the sainted martyrs would aid the deceased in gaining entry
to the heavenly abode reserved for zaddikim—if not directly and under their
protection, then possibly, as we have learned from R. Ḥayyim Palti'el, because
the son's prayer for his father's soul would have been more easily accepted if offered on ground hallowed by the presence of the martyrs' remains. Alexander
Wimpfen did not have a son; perhaps that was what led him to try to buy his
ticket to heaven by sticking close to his saint.

21. Worms, Jewish cemetery, "Rabbis' Valley," with the tombstones of the Bacharach family at center and a memorial plaque for the twelve *parnasim* on the cemetery wall at left. Photograph by the author, 2001.

Ashkenaz and the Holy Land

Like individual pilgrimage to specific graves and collective procession on particular days, Jewish burial *ad sanctos* would seem to illustrate how some of the functions related to sainted individuals' earthly remains, functions taken over by church buildings in medieval Christendom, remained within the confines of the cemetery among Jews, where those functions retained more of a presence than has previously been acknowledged. While possibly also catering to an unspoken need to have patron saints of their own, the emergence of holy graves in medieval and early modern Ashkenaz bespeaks an effort on the part of local Jews to invest the physical space they were inhabiting with meaning. This effort sheds light on various aspects of how they conceived of their own existence, both externally—vis-à-vis the local Christian population—and with respect to the larger, inner-Jewish question of their relationship to Erets Israel.

Outwardly, the way in which the cemeteries served to ground Ashkenazi Jews' sense of their own history in the very land may have been one way of stating that they, too—like the Christian majority—belonged.[72] Although defined locally, that claim of belonging did not necessarily require the continuous residence of a particular family in a particular place. On the contrary, with Jewish mobility within Germany as high as it was, the practice of undertaking occasional travel to visit the graves of one's forebears may have allowed individuals to maintain a sense of rootedness even where continuity of residence was lacking.[73] Moreover, the extension of the term *avot* to apply to the founding fathers of the community at large may testify to the emergence of a pan-Ashkenazi self-perception based on a shared history that went beyond individual lineage and narrow local attachments.

The cemeteries, especially those of the more ancient communities, played a crucial role here, providing tangible evidence of a long-standing Jewish presence while offering an opportunity for every Jew, no matter what his or her personal background, to forge links with that history by taking part in grave visitation. Hence the struggle when one of the cemeteries was threatened; hence the effort, wherever there had been a hiatus in settlement, to have the same piece of land restored to a reestablished community if at all possible, even though the new settlers were hardly ever themselves descended from the earlier ones.[74]

On an inner-Jewish level, the infusion of the local topography with the sanctity of holy graves may have functioned as a very down-to-earth way of legitimizing Jewish existence in the Ashkenazi diaspora. It is true that the way in which the grave of R. Shim'on ben Yitshaq was conflated with that of his talmudic namesake would seem to indicate that Palestine and the more distant past remained the point of reference against which the relative holiness of Jewish life in the diaspora was measured. At the same time, the very act of assimilating an Ashkenazi local hero to a talmudic model raised local history to a level of sanctity that allowed it to measure up to that standard. What is more, it enabled local Jews to have their own bit of the Holy Land within easy reach.

Recent studies have emphasized that, despite their deep spiritual ties to the Land, Ashkenazi rabbis of the high Middle Ages put relatively little stock in either short-term pilgrimage to Erets Israel or actual settlement there because the dismal conditions in Palestine could not support the kind of religious infrastructure that the Ashkenazi communities enjoyed at the time.[75] To some extent, then, the graves of the righteous may have played a role of increasing importance within the religious lives of individual and community in response to that situation. Practices traditionally related to sacred space came to be filled with local content, revaluing Ashkenaz as an alternative Holy Land.[76]

This process can be observed in several ways. At its most obvious, the proliferation of vows to visit specific cemeteries within Germany may be seen as a less demanding variation on the received practice of making a vow to go up to the Land of Israel.[77] From the late thirteenth century onward, as we have seen, some of the leading halakhic authorities in the German lands considered graveside prayer legitimate and, indeed, desirable, as long as petitioners took care to address themselves to God rather than to the deceased. The point of such prayer was that it was thought particularly efficacious when offered on ground sanctified by the presence of particularly righteous dead. Ḥayyim Palti'el, the first authority on record to argue along those lines, had illustrated his point by referring to the case of Kalev b. Yefunneh, who had supposedly prostrated himself at the graves of the patriarchs in Hebron.[78] A century later, the Maharil made the same argument for the local cemetery as the resting place of the righteous; in doing so, he used expressions such as "a sacred and pure place" and "holy ground" (*admat qodesh*), which had previously been reserved for the Holy Land.[79]

The phenomenon of Jewish burial *ad sanctos*, finally, would seem to lend itself to a similar interpretation. Traditionally, death "in an impure land" had been considered among the drawbacks of living in the diaspora.[80] Rabbinic literature of late antiquity mentions a practice of bringing the deceased of various diaspora countries to the Land of Israel for burial to expiate their sin of having lived elsewhere.[81] It has recently been argued that this practice shows that the respective diaspora countries did not serve as a focal point of identification and a symbol of continuity at the time.[82] By the same token, the hierarchy of funerary space that premodern German Jews developed within their own cemeteries may indicate that, at least to some minds, Ashkenaz did.

Chapter 7

Detours in a "Hidden Land": Samuel Romanelli's *Masa' ba'rav*

Andrea Schatz

In the eighteenth century, Ashkenazi Jews encountered the "orient" as an un-stable, shifting, and elusive place where they were said to be at home.[1] Chris-tian discourse described the orient as an archaic sphere of origins and insisted on situating the Hebrew language as well as Jewish religious and cultural practices within its remote scenery.[2] This had favorable as well as unfavorable implications. The orient was conceived as the cradle of mankind and depicted as the location of an infant stage of history. Ancient Jewish history thereby assumed universal significance, and noble origins were attributed to the Jew-ish nation.[3] But the orient was also described as having been in a state of permanent decline ever since its early days of splendor. Thus, in orientalizing approaches to rabbinic scholarship and culture, the Jews of Amsterdam and Berlin, Posen and Vilna, Prague and Livorno were denied creative power and written out of European history.[4]

Jewish authors of the eighteenth century were often critical of such ap-proaches and interpretations, but they did not dismiss the identification of Jews and Judaism with the orient out of hand. Rather, they challenged, sub-verted, and transformed Christian conceptions of oriental Judaism by estab-lishing their own Jewish orient.[5] The orient was perceived as a sometimes ideal, sometimes alien, place within the Jewish past, but it also attracted attention as part of the Jewish present. The authors of the Jewish Enlightenment were par-ticularly interested in the communities of the Ottoman Empire. According to

Naphtali Herz Wessely's famous treatise on educational reform, *Divrei shalom ve-emet* (Words of peace and truth), the "Ishmaelites" had established a liberal rule, allowing the Jews to practice their religion without hindrance and to pursue their chosen professions.[6] Wessely's vision of flourishing Jewish communities in the diaspora reflects his admiration for the cultures of what he terms "the East and the West" (*ha-mizraḥ ve-ha-ma'arav*), a translation of the Arabic terms for the Middle East and North Africa, *al-mashriq* and *al-maghrib*. Wessely's text unsettles the European distinction between orient and occident and questions the centrality and certainty of European perspectives by deferring to the languages of the "East," Arabic and Hebrew, with their own modes of orientation. His Hebrew translation of the Arabic terms removes "East" and "West" from their European contexts and addresses Europe as a "province," which—according to some languages and certain perspectives—is situated neither in the East nor in the West. In this shifting linguistic landscape, the dualism of Europe's terminology becomes untenable.

But it was not only the Ottoman Empire that provided a comparative and potentially subversive perspective. When Moses Mendelssohn pointed to the situation of Jews in the Islamic world in order to demonstrate that the legal restrictions imposed on Ashkenazi Jews were not an inevitable result of the diasporic condition, he turned to Morocco:

> In the present times, it may be true that, in Christian states, the condition of the Jews is better than in Mahometan; but in the latter, they have never been so cruelly persecuted, murdered, tormented, burnt, despoiled of their all, and driven out in a state of nakedness, as they were by the Christian governments, and ministers of religion in the middle ages. Even now, the Jews pay but a moderate poll-tax, in the Turkish territories, and endure not much more than the other inhabitants, or than is concomitant with the despotic government. The number of Jews in the Mahometan states, probably, is greater than in the Christian. It is there, that they more frequently attain wealth and distinction by excelling as physicians, or even statesmen. The present prime-minister of the Emperor of Morocco is a Jew, named Sumbul.[7]

Mendelssohn confirms Wessely's approach, in which the diaspora constitutes a frame of reference that transcends and cuts across European notions of East and West. Indeed, the two maskilim were not the first to compare the situation of Jews in Christian Europe with those in the Ottoman Empire and Morocco. Already in the seventeenth century, Simone Luzzatto and Menasseh ben Israel had been interested in the similarities between their own situation and that of Jews in Salonika, Constantinople, and Marrakech, because in each of these settings, Jewish communities were involved in negotiations over internal coherence and external acceptance.[8] At the same time, these authors recognized the widely varying contexts of such negotiations, comparing the challenges, constraints, and perils that Jews had to confront in non-Jewish societies. The maskilim took up this tradition of comparison and scrutinized Prussia's political and legal regulations as just one imperfect model among several historical possibilities, idealizing Ottoman and Moroccan arrangements rather than demonizing them.[9] The diaspora offered the possibility of recognizing sameness across boundaries of alleged "otherness," while it also provided material for comparative reflections on political and cultural differences. In this productive tension between similarity and difference, neither Europe nor the orient remained privileged points of reference. It was, rather, the situation of Jewish communities in their respective lands that determined their shifting relevance within the discourses of the Jewish Enlightenment.

In the eighteenth century, then, the "orient" emerged as both a Christian fantasy and a Jewish counter-fantasy. Jewish authors conceived it as an imagined and a real place, as a source of alienation and inspiration, as a sphere of sameness and difference. It is to this oscillating and resolutely overdetermined place that *Masa' ba'rav* (Travail in an Arab land), Samuel Romanelli's Hebrew book on his travels in Morocco, takes us. Romanelli was born in 1757 in Mantua, then a city of the Hapsburg Empire and a vibrant center of Jewish cultural life in northern Italy. After having received an excellent education in Hebrew and Italian subjects, Romanelli left Italy, traveled in various European countries, and spent some time in London. In 1786, he decided to return to Italy, but found himself unable to continue his journey beyond Gibraltar. Eventually, he joined a Christian merchant and his servant on their way to Morocco, where he attempted to make a living as an interpreter, accountant, and secretary. After the death of Sultan Sidi Muḥammad b. ʿAbdallāh, and amid the acts of violence committed against Jewish communities in 1790, Romanelli returned to Amsterdam. In the following years, we find him in Berlin, Vienna, and Trieste. After 1799, he lived in various northern Italian communities and became known as an admirer of Napoleon. He died in Casale Monferrato, Italy in 1814.

The Jewish Enlightenment of the eighteenth century did not inspire many writings (and certainly not many Hebrew writings) that attracted anything other than strictly scholarly attention. Among the few that did is Romanelli's travelogue, *Masa' ba'rav*, published in 1792 by the printing house of the maskilim in Berlin and reprinted at least four times during the nineteenth century.[10] Profound ambiguity informs Romanelli's descriptions, interpretations, and evaluations of Morocco. As Daniel Schroeter has already pointed out, Romanelli's account displays "an arrogant sense of superiority,"[11] while articulating a precarious sense of affiliation: "Quite unlike Christian European travelers, Romanelli became a participant in Moroccan Jewish society. In other words, despite the cultural differences between Romanelli and Moroccan Jewry, the two were still part of the same trans-national identity in which being Jewish transcended any type of national affiliation—for the Jews of both Europe and the Maghreb, civil society was still unknown."[12]

Schroeter states that the tensions in Romanelli's text indicate a turning point in the history of the Jewish diaspora, when national perspectives began to supersede transnational practices and sensibilities. Taking this observation a step further, I would like to suggest that *Masa' ba'rav* does not only exemplify the typical contradictions of a brief moment of transition. Neither the traveler nor the travel writer operates between "still" functioning diasporic modes of communication and already emerging national or colonial modes of dissociation and domination. Rather, the text makes visible the coexistence of transnational and national/colonial constellations and shows an amalgam of diverse and conflicting narrative strategies and interpretive practices that may be traced in Jewish travel (and other) writing throughout the colonial period.[13]

I would like to return to these contradictory and ambiguous strategies in Romanelli's text not in order to reconsider the contrast between them and earlier modes of transnational orientation, but rather to explore the contrast between them and later developments. A critical reading of Romanelli's text can hardly avoid asking whether this travelogue is not already part of the complex genealogy that underlies the twentieth-century rejection of the "orient" in Zionist representations of Jews from Muslim lands. Gabriel Piterberg characterizes this representational strategy as follows:

> The crux is that Orientalism is applied twice. Once it is used to depict the story of "decline" into which Oriental Jewry has fallen since the early sixteenth century, and to justify the fact that they must be "modernized" in order to join the new imagined community, which is part of Western civilization. Orientalism is then used again, this time to extricate the Oriental Jews from their cultural

context, so that the blame for the fact that they are "intellectually frozen, primitive and degenerated . . ." would not be pinned on their Jewish essence, but on their host societies, that is, the essentialized Orientalist notion of "Islam." . . . The implication that in a different—essentially national—environment the Oriental Jews can be introduced to Western modernity is rather obvious.[14]

At first glance, Romanelli's travelogue seems to provide an early example of this type of orientalism, adding "historical depth" to Piterberg's analysis of the emergence of later narratives and practices.

I argue that *Masa' ba'rav* significantly differs from later approaches in two respects. First, it makes Europe and its modes of orientation a target of both explicit and implicit critique. In Romanelli's travelogue, "modernity" is not yet "Western" territory. The Enlightenment, which figures prominently in the travelogue, is clearly, almost aggressively, deterritorialized. Second, the text never disentangles itself from the multiple and contradictory affiliations and commitments that both constitute and derive from the networks of Jewish communication and interaction in the diaspora. Although Morocco is perceived as part of the "orient," Tangier, Mogador, and other points on Romanelli's North African itinerary are also part of the Jewish diaspora. These are places where Jews live, from which they need to depart, and to which European Jews are invited to turn by reading about a traveler who wished to inhabit them and dwell there. Rather than negating the diaspora, the travelogue encourages readers to expand and complicate their understanding of it by incorporating Morocco's Jews within their purview. This type of recognition could facilitate colonial modes of integration and domination but also had the potential to disrupt European strategies of orientation, centralization, and control. Romanelli's account did not have much to offer to contemporary Moroccan Jews who were never addressed as readers. But it could, in Susan Miller's term, "disorient" Europe and, in doing so, encourage European Jews to explore possibilities of reorientation that were not entirely governed by Christian concepts of Jewish or other orients.[15]

"The Vast Difference in Everything on Passing Those Straits . . ."

Throughout the early modern period, there was substantial European interest in Morocco, the land of the Sharifian sultans that resisted the forces of the

Ottoman Empire and had, at the end of the seventeenth century, secured its sovereignty over the Atlantic coast against Portuguese, Spanish, British, and French troops. When Romanelli published his book in 1792, numerous accounts on the "present state" of Morocco circulated among English, French, and German readers.[16] The "Preface by the Translator" that accompanies the English edition of Chénier's *Recherches historiques sur les Maures et histoire de l'empire de Maroc* (1788) captures one of the major reasons for this heightened interest: "Of all the people with whom Europeans have any continued intercourse, those who inhabit the coast of Barbary seem to be the least known. This is the more extraordinary because that [*sic*] their manners, customs, government, and the ignorance in which they remain, when we recollect their proximity to Europe, are very remarkable."[17]

The Moroccan empire, which began just beyond the Strait of Gibraltar, was, from English and French perspectives, Europe's closest neighbor. A long history of "continued intercourse" involved European merchants, missionaries, and diplomats who stayed, often for years, in the country. Nonetheless, Morocco was perceived as remote and inhospitable—after all, it was not very susceptible to European influence and the rules of colonial "protection." The paradoxical image of a place that seemed at once visible and invisible, accessible and inaccessible, sustained considerable curiosity.[18]

A letter written by the English diplomat Alexander Jardine after he had crossed the Strait of Gibraltar points to an additional and closely related motive for such curiosity: "The vast difference in everything on passing those straits is perhaps greater than in any equal distance on our globe."[19] Morocco could be perceived as Europe's profoundly enigmatic next-door neighbor, because it represented—in the eyes of European writers and readers—an entirely unknown, and also an entirely different, world. The emphasis on "vast difference" was deeply rooted in early modern and Enlightenment political discourse, in which the relationship between "oriental despotism" and European monarchy was a major theme. Among the most important sources for the articulation of this relationship was Montesquieu's *Esprit des lois*. While Montesquieu emphasized that "most nations" are ruled by despotic governments, he singled out Persia, Turkey, and other "Mahometan countries," Morocco among them, as places where religion "is a fear added to fear" and where the princes rule over peoples that remain in a state of passivity, ignorance, and superstition.[20] At the same time, despotism was not perceived to be an entirely foreign variant within a range of political systems, but a degenerate form of monarchical rule.[21] Enlightenment writers insisted on a critical distance from which the flaws of both systems might be observed and from which neither monarchy with its seeds of despotism nor, of course, despotism itself could be viewed as desirable models. The empires of the Middle East and North Africa were thus construed as negative mirror images that reflected the broken promises and inherent dangers of European political systems. The emergence of republican political practices—whether in England, the Netherlands, or, after 1789, France—increased confidence in this interpretive approach. Finally, political analysis was translated into historical interpretation. Despotism was taken to be the same as European monarchical rule, except that "the same," in its decline, could no longer be recognized as such and became Europe's superseded "other." The political, religious, and cultural contexts of the Middle East and North Africa could not be captured on their own terms; they represented negation, degeneration, and, in the absence of any promise, stagnation.[22]

The convergence of such political reflections and historical interpretations can be observed in the manner in which Morocco was pictured as a profoundly different and, therefore, very distant place with respect to knowledge and its associated institutions. Morocco's scholars, manuscripts, and libraries were rarely mentioned in European travelogues and, if recalled at all, were cited in the context of historical decline.[23] Thus, Lemprière's depiction of "the Moors" after their expulsion from Spain emphasizes their rapid descent from a period of enlightenment into a state of ignorance: "Previous to that period, it is well known they were an enlightened people, at a time when the greater part of Europe was involved in ignorance and barbarism; but, owing to the weakness and tyranny of their princes, they gradually sunk into the very opposite extreme, and may now be considered as but a few degrees removed from a savage state."[24]

The idea that Islamic culture can be flexible—and that the historical affinities it had once shown to Europe were later erased in the Middle East and North Africa—is eloquently expressed in Jardine's letters. About Cordoba and Granada in Spain's Golden Age, he writes that if they had "fortunately continued to subsist in Europe . . . Christianity and Mahometism . . . might, from vicinity, arts, and intercourse, have been led into mutual forbearance and concessions, which, by degrees, might have produced a more comprehensive system of toleration than the world is now likely soon to enjoy."[25] According to Jardine, Islam in medieval Europe held promise for Christians and Muslims alike. This promise can still be remembered by the intellectuals of the Enlightenment, but after a history of degeneration that implicated both Europe and the orient, the prospect of its fulfillment is irrevocably lost.

The situation of the Jewish communities is a recurring, crucial, and often contradictory point of reference in European accounts of Islamic degradation. In the Moroccan case, the treatment of Jews is mentioned frequently as an example of the despotic and oppressive character of the sultan's reign and of the violent features of Moroccan society. European travelers to Morocco often characterize their Jewish hosts, interpreters, and mediators as "miserable," "unfortunate," and "unhappy" people. Lancelot Addison's description of Jewish life in Morocco, published in 1675, already emphasizes that "their present Condition under the *Moresco* Government" is "no other then [*sic*] a better sort of slavery,"[26] but attributes their misery to divine decree no less than to the rule of the "haughty and imperious Moor." A century later, "the Moors" alone have to take responsibility: Lemprière does not hesitate to claim that they "display more humanity to their beasts than to the Jews."[27] At the same time, he and his contemporaries also depict the influential position, affluence, education, and pleasant manners of the Jewish mercantile elite in whose houses they reside during their various missions. In this context, Mendelssohn's reference to the "present prime-minister of the Emperor of Morocco," the prominent court Jew Samuel Sumbal, does not come as a surprise. There are numerous sources from which he may have gleaned his knowledge.[28]

Romanelli's *Masa' ba'rav* forms part of the large body of "histories," "descriptions," and "letters" addressing Morocco in the eighteenth century. His narrative articulates European notions of the orient as a sphere of sameness and otherness constituted by relations across time but also takes up Jewish notions of the diaspora as a site of similarities and differences constituted by interrelations across space. The diaspora offers perspectives that Christian authors such as Jardine deemed lost after the expulsions from Spain, while Romanelli insists on reinscribing them within the present.

Detours

The first chapter of Romanelli's *Masa' ba'rav* is somewhat unusual for its time. Unlike many travel accounts from the period, this one does not begin with a departure: "Due to the turns of my fortune and the contrivances of the times in which I lived, I happened to be in Gibraltar's citadel heading toward Italy, my native land" (18). At the beginning of Romanelli's story, the traveler is already on his way home. But unfavorable circumstances have interfered with the course of his journey, which has been interrupted and come to a halt. We do not find the author in a state of cheerful or anxious expectation, in the moment of transition from familiar to unfamiliar terrain. Romanelli's travels are already oriented in a different way—he has turned away from the exploration of foreign places and wishes to arrive safely in his "native land" (*erets moladeti*). In the book, however, this return will never be accomplished. Rather, the reader encounters him in a state of frustration and resignation: "Surely many designs are in a man's mind, but it is what the Lord devises that will be accomplished."

In this brief first paragraph of the first chapter, Romanelli fashions himself according to an ancient poetical model—the figure of Ulysses. Romanelli was probably well acquainted with the *Odyssey*, given his admiration for Alexander Pope, the poet who translated the epic into English. Pope's translation begins as follows:

> The Man, for Wisdom's various arts renown'd,
> Long exercis'd in woes, oh Muse! resound.
> Who, when his arms had wrought the destin'd fall
> Of sacred Troy, and raz'd her heav'n-built wall,
> Wand'ring from clime to clime, observant stray'd,
> Their Manners noted, and their States survey'd.
> On stormy seas unnumber'd toils he bore,
> Safe with his friends to gain his natal shore.[29]

Like Ulysses, Romanelli has boarded a ship that should bring him home, but finds himself in adverse circumstances and subject to powers he cannot control. The character of the active and adventurous individual that governs early modern and modern travel literature is dismissed in favor of the antique persona of the patient hero who endures his fate with pious resignation—and with a sharp and cunning mind. Romanelli's introductory sentences are echoed throughout the book in numerous reflections on the unpredictable turns of fortune, and they are rhetorically reconfirmed in two further chapter openings, one dedicated to "treacherous . . . fickle and intriguing" fortune (35) and the other to its unsteady course: "So many changes of fortune! Time is true only in its vicissitudes" (78).

In the next paragraphs of his first chapter, the scene that was first presented in Greek terms now reveals its distinctly Jewish aspect. Finding himself without a ship, Romanelli cannot continue his journey overland because Gibraltar borders on Spanish territory where the Inquisition does not tolerate

Jews and is forever suspicious of conversos. For the Jewish traveler, the fortress, surrounded by the sea and the lands of the Inquisition, is a "closed-in place" (*misgar*). Having arrived "at the extremity of Europe" (*be-qitsvei ha-Eropa*), he finds it to be the end of his world of movement, of departures and returns.

It is at this impasse that Romanelli is offered the opportunity to cross the Strait of Gibraltar: "One of the respected merchants of the place, hearing me bemoaning my ill luck, called me aside and asked if I would be willing to go to Barbary with him. I replied that I would go" (19). We meet Romanelli as a reluctant explorer who neither chose the route he is going to follow nor intended to see the places he is going to describe. He is embarking on a journey without mission or purpose—not even with the aim to write. The travels he is going to narrate are not a sign of expanding technological, economic, or political power, but of limitation and uncertainty. In the absence of any supplementary documents, it is impossible to determine whether Romanelli's elaborate narrative actually captures something of his mood at the time or whether it aims to disguise the author's own initiative in order to present him as an unprejudiced traveler, without expectations or prior knowledge, whose approach is entirely fresh and original. What is obvious is that this opening marks a twofold departure—Greek and Jewish—from dominant contemporary modes of European travel writing.

We are still on the first page of the first chapter,[30] but Romanelli has already transferred the reader to new terrain, to a place whose significance cannot be rendered on a map because its geographical features are inextricably intertwined with political and cultural meanings that depend on the perspective of the observer and the practices of the traveler. For Christian travelers, Gibraltar's rock may signify a secure outpost, a place of connections and transitions, while in the eyes of Jewish travelers, for whom Spain is prohibited territory, it may be a precariously disconnected spot, an isolated island. Europe itself, the continent Romanelli is about to leave, dissolves as a unified signifier and assumes various meanings: while Italy is presented as the traveler's "native land," Spain remains inaccessible, the site of a history of violence, expulsion, and forced conversions. Europe, with its open and closed territories and with its multiple histories, is not introduced as a single and reliable point of departure, authorizing a travel account based on its central perspective and allowing the text to evolve around distinctions between Europeans ("us"/"here") and non-Europeans ("them"/"there"). Europe remains a fragmented, indefinable, and strangely distant presence throughout the book.

When Romanelli eventually embarks on his journey to Morocco, it is a departure after a departure, and when he returns to Europe, it is not an arrival home. Unlike Ulysses, Romanelli will not see his "native land" as long as the reader is with him. At the end of the book, Romanelli finds himself in Amsterdam and composes an elegy in which the place where he walks "peacefully" and "safely" is described again as a "shore," reminiscent of Gibraltar, located at the rim of the treacherous seas, from where the gaze of the author turns back to those of his people he has left behind. When we first encounter Romanelli, he already lives in foreign lands; his travels in Morocco are detours in yet another foreign land; and when we leave him, he has yet to return to his Italian "home." This narrative of departures dissociates "diaspora" from any promise of its transcendence, whether offered in religious or secular conceptualizations of exile and return.

Distance

When Romanelli eventually decides to cross the Strait of Gibraltar, the passage is surprisingly swift and easy—within four hours, he is in Africa. The few lines he dedicates to the voyage offer a perfect dramatization of the ambivalences that pervade European perceptions of Morocco: "We passed the fortresses of San Roque and San Felipe and the town of Algeciras, which stand one next to the other facing Gibraltar. We cut through the waters of the strait, whose current is swift at the sides, and within four hours we were between the mountains on our way to Africa" (19). Morocco may be remote, dangerous, and difficult to access, but at the same time it is a very close neighbor.

Like Ulysses, who "[w]and'ring from clime to clime, observant stray'd, [t]heir Manners noted, and their States survey'd,"[31] Romanelli becomes a keen observer as soon as he arrives in North Africa. His accounts, which include dialogues, letters, and other documents, are rich in detail. At the same time, it becomes clear that the author reverts, after having presented an unusual beginning, to rather conventional strategies of travel writing. Romanelli takes up a series of familiar dichotomies that inscribe his narrative into a body of citations and interpretations, which, in their recursive power, lend credibility to his observations.[32]

The first and perhaps most powerful of these dichotomies is built around the opposition between nature and culture. This pair makes its first appearance in a typical fantasy of easy conquest,[33] which is motivated, paradoxically, by Morocco's resistance to it: "Were it not for the fact that Barbary's geography defends it with steep cliffs along the seashore enclosing the points of entry and providing natural guard posts, I have no doubt that 100,000 brave soldiers skilled in European warfare would in a short while capture all the provinces of Morocco from one end to the other, if they could find some way to penetrate it and space wide enough to maneuver" (20). The observer has no European soldiers, but he identifies with their activities—he will find his own ways of "maneuvering," he will make use of his "penetrating" gaze, and he will capture nature's terrain with his active analytical mind and cultural skills.

On the road to Tangier, Romanelli finds many opportunities to emphasize difference by elaborating on the distinction between nature and culture. When he eventually encounters what is ostensibly a manifestation of culture—music at a wedding—he finds it quite ridiculous: "any resemblance between this and music was purely coincidental. Could any person control himself and not break out laughing at such a sight?" (23). At this point, the narrator quickly interrupts himself and questions whether the opposition on which he is about to build his narrative will indeed provide a framework for reliable knowledge: "But then man is vanity. The children of man are a fallacy on the face of the earth. Just as the practices of the North Africans seem strange to our eyes, so our practices seem strange to theirs. The truth is that all is vanity. We scoff at a child when we know his crying is for some immaterial reason, and the heavenly hosts above laugh at us because we are like infants until the time we become old and gray" (23).

A similar thought had already occurred to the traveler somewhat earlier. Admiring the stars on his first night in Morocco, Romanelli cites Fontenelle's *Plurality of Worlds*: "As I looked at them, I said in jest that perhaps even as I peek at the faces of these entities, their inhabitants are likewise gazing at my planet" (21). The observer may also be the observed; his perspective allows only for a partial view and does not support absolute claims. But rather than suggesting parity between himself and his Moroccan interlocutors, because no one escapes the particularity of his specific cultural perspective, Romanelli casts himself as a differentiated representative of the Enlightenment. He alone is the traveler who knows his limitations and so is able to transcend them. Since Fontenelle, Montesquieu, and Voltaire, the insight into the limits of human knowledge constituted a source of both humility and pride, circumscribing and reinforcing claims of authority at the same time.[34] Romanelli's recourse to an ideally universal perspective that needs to be integrated, tentatively, into the creation of self-reflective knowledge provides the narrative with its situated and recognizable forms of legitimation.

Romanelli's narrative dichotomies derive significantly from his identification with the intellectual and cultural practices of the Enlightenment. In
subsequent chapters, the opposition between nature and culture is abandoned
and gives way to other pairs of opposites: ignorance and knowledge and, intertwined with them, oppression and toleration. The third chapter offers the
following reflection on "the Arabs" and Islam: "The Arabs are an ignorant
people. They have no printers and no authors. The text of the Koran is all they
study. Even with regard to far-fetched ideas, it is the Divine Spirit that spoke
them all. It is all true, and anyone who questions them risks his life. . . . Thus
Muḥammad barred the door of science and investigation to them in order
to maintain them in their faith. . . . The wisdom of their sages in astronomy,
medicine, and mathematics is lost, and they have only inherited the occult
offshoots of these sciences" (40).

Here, Romanelli's narrative once more echoes the descriptions of other
travel writers and their confident generalizations and misconceptions. However, Romanelli seems interested in construing "the Arabs" as a stable and
negative point of reference not, primarily, because he wishes to establish a
contrast between them and "the Europeans" but because he wants to explore
the differences between Arabs and the Jews who live among them. Taking
up the ambivalences of the first paragraphs of his narrative, Romanelli depicts Europe once again as a nonentity, a double-edged signifier. He does not
hesitate to compare Islam with Catholicism: "As with the Catholics, deceitful
demagogues stir up the mob's emotion in the marketplace" (42). Romanelli
translates European anxieties about the possible identity between monarchism
and despotism—and the role of religion in them—into anxieties about the
similarities between Catholicism and Islam.

From Romanelli's Jewish perspective, Europe does not come into view as
a spatial, cultural, or historical unity. Romanelli identifies with the Enlightenment and its concepts of knowledge, "science," and "wisdom" but has no
stable geographical or symbolical place for it. Rather, it appears as the result of
individual commitments and local developments. Thus the Enlightenment is
dissociated from Christianity and Islam alike. If enlightened concepts can find
support in any religious context at all, it is within Judaism: "Judging anything
is always a matter of perception: thus, the Arab believes in his saints according
to the degree of his imbecility; the Christian venerates his saints in accordance
with their supposed miracles; while the holy man who is honored in Judaism
is he who walks in the path of wisdom and fear of God" (41).

The Enlightenment does not have a home. Romanelli frames it as a commitment to intellectual mobility that is absent among European Catholics or "catholic" Muslims but can become manifest among Moroccan Jews: "They are awed by dreams and terrified by vision. . . . Despite all this, their minds are not entirely blocked from reason, because they comprehend other matters perfectly well. In fact, sometimes their intelligence emits flashes of insight that reveal that it is not thick by nature, but only held down and mired in thick muck, like the sun when it is covered by a very dense cloud" (29).

The intellectual world of Moroccan Jews is, according to Romanelli, rather imperfect. Their ideas and attitudes are similar to those of their Muslim neighbors because political oppression and cultural assimilation have had their effects. This contextualization of local Jewish thought and practices does not, however, prevent Romanelli from observing a resemblance between Moroccan Jews and Jews in distant Eastern Europe as well: "Their style of sermon is like that of the Polish Jews and all who are hasty in their studies, becoming entangled in profundities whose meaning they do not know and whose context they distort" (36). In a similar vein, Romanelli writes about Moroccan liturgical hymns: "The subject matter of these poems is without value—like most of the books of interpretation and commentary by Polish authors" (86). The effect of these comparisons is ambiguous: Are Polish Jews orientalized? Are Moroccan Jews Europeanized? In Romanelli's narrative, with its multiplying points of reference and comparison, both operations become intertwined with each other. Eventually, however, Moroccan Jews are clearly dissociated from their Arab surroundings. In contrast to their neighbors, they demonstrate perfectibility; they are described as flexible and susceptible to education and reform. They, too, may enter the mobile world of the Enlightenment.

Romanelli describes several episodes that reveal the "covered" light of knowledge among Moroccan Jews. Thus he recounts his visit at the house of a beautiful Jewish woman in Tangier, who wrote Spanish and Arabic in Hebrew characters and recited by heart passages from Lope de Vega's works, while her husband chose the Hebrew language to greet his guest (39). In another episode, linked to the knowledge of languages, Romanelli enters a synagogue in Tangier, where he notices that the members of the community "follow the rite of the Sefaradim" and "pronounce the letters of the Holy Language correctly" (31–32). Romanelli explains that they make the appropriate phonological distinctions,[35] although in a different way from Sefaradi Jews, and he is amused by the results. Years later, he writes his *Grammatica ragionata italiana ed ebraica*, and he includes his observations regarding the script, pronunciation, and cantillation of Moroccan Jewry. The linguistic features of Moroccan Jewry are taken into consideration and become part of the process of determining normative linguistic practices for the Jewish communities of the diaspora.[36]

While the Christian world of Europe is depicted as a politically and culturally fragmented—and therefore indefinable—place, the Islamic world of Morocco is defined as a historically and culturally inflexible unity that vaguely mirrors European Catholicism. In contrast, Moroccan Jews are part of the interconnected and principally mobile sphere of the diaspora. Thus, Romanelli's descriptions of Muslims and Jews in Morocco—and his differentiation between them—establish his authority as a travel writer in two crucial, if contradictory, ways. They demonstrate his reliability because they simultaneously signal his critical distance from the world he describes and show him to be thoroughly involved and intimately acquainted with it. Romanelli situates his critical stance in the mobile world of the diaspora, which he embraces, and in opposition to the inflexibility of Christian and Islamic traditions, which he rejects. While his critique of Christian Europe offers insights into intriguing moments of resistance to orientalism and its dualistic "style of thought," his treatment of Islamic Morocco reveals his complicity with orientalist strategies of constructing a cultural and political "other." This contradiction is evident throughout the travelogue, as it oscillates between involvement and detachment, and it particularly informs the passages in which the author explicitly reflects on his methods as a travel writer.

"Here I Will Dwell . . ."

Romanelli will learn the language of Moroccan Jews, live in their houses, give sermons in their synagogues, pray and celebrate with them, get involved in their intrigues, and share their fate in dangerous times. He has not yet been long in the country when he realizes that he has lost his passport (36). He is upset and attempts to obtain new travel documents, but when—after several months—he is able to receive papers, he prefers not to make use of this opportunity to leave the country (55). At a certain point, he considers marriage, but then decides against it: "I would say as in the words of Pope on vice: We first endure, then pity, then embrace. But before I reached the brink, there was a turn of events that carried me off" (76). Later, he expresses his hope to establish his own business: "I thought to myself, 'Here I will dwell, for I desire it'" (132). Romanelli does not want to become part of the place but is unable to detach himself from it; he does not want to stay but does not leave. The detours become his life and leave their traces in his writing.

In his essay "Spatial Stories," Michel de Certeau points to two types of approaches to spatial relations: description and narration, the map and the tour: "Either it [the story] presents a *tableau* ('there are...'), or it organizes *movements* ('you enter, you go across, you turn')."[37] The first approach is exemplified by Lemprière's *A Tour from Gibraltar*, published at the same time as Romanelli's *Travail*.[38] Lemprière's book is about seeing and mapping what has been observed. In fact, it presents on its first pages a map reproduced, to this day, in practically every work on eighteenth-century Morocco. Lemprière is not interested in depicting and reflecting on interactions and complications that cannot be transformed into useful information or that may trouble his clear perspective and solid arrangements. The history of the production of his knowledge recedes into the invisible realms of "prehistory," a narrative strategy that de Certeau describes as follows: "The map, a totalizing stage on which elements of diverse origin are brought together to form the tableau of a 'state' of geographical knowledge, pushes away into its prehistory or into its posterity, as if into the wings, the operations of which it is the result or the necessary condition. It remains alone on the stage. The tour describers have disappeared."[39]

In Romanelli's book, the tour describer reappears. In contrast to Lemprière's work, it emphasizes movements, encounters, and entanglements, as Romanelli himself notes in his introduction: "I lived there and had the opportunity to mingle with all kinds of people great and small, learning their doings, knowing their comings and goings and almost all their ways. Nevertheless, I have been careful to report only that which I witnessed, and in relating my own personal history at length, I shall tell their history."

Romanelli's decision to base his writing on his "mingling" with "all kinds of people" results in a text with affinities to the emergent genre of the sentimental travel narrative. Mary Louise Pratt has argued that the sentimental travel narrative evolved as the result of a critical moment in the colonial endeavor, a moment when the failure of expeditions in Africa, anticolonial resistance, and Enlightenment concepts of democracy and reciprocity led to a certain sense of unease within the colonizing nations and to new modes of narrative negotiation. Pratt writes on Mungo Park's *Travels in the Interior Districts of Africa* (1799): "[He] did not write up a narrative of geographical discovery. . . . He wrote, and wrote himself, not as a man of science, but as a sentimental hero. He made himself the protagonist and central figure of his own account, which takes the form of an epic series of trials, challenges, and encounters with the unpredictable. . . . The textual space/time . . . is filled with (made out of) human activity, interactions among the travelers themselves or with people they encounter."[40]

Romanelli's departure from widely accepted conventions of travel writing in his first chapter, with its allusions to Ulysses, can now be read as the adoption of a contemporary alternative. Romanelli uses strategies of sentimental travel writing, because as a European Jew among European Christians, as a European among Arabs, and as a Jew among Jews, he, too, is constantly involved in negotiations over positions of strength and weakness, detachment and involvement. His movements within a tangled network of connections to both Europe and Morocco, and across varying constellations of difference and sameness, cannot be mapped—they demand narration or, in Romanelli's words, histories.

Departure

The complex and multifaceted world that supported Romanelli's travels and travel writing came abruptly to an end with the persecutions of Jews during the interregnum after Sultan Sidi Muḥammad's death in 1790. Romanelli's narrative turns into a somber vision of violence and destruction in some communities and of fear and severe repression in others.[41] It is under these circumstances that Romanelli eventually charts his departure from Morocco. Although the departure is not easy—he has to leave most of his belongings behind—it is achieved with surprising quickness and efficiency, mirroring his swift entry at the beginning. Romanelli describes his departure from Morocco as an "exodus": "I left and ran to the shore and never looked back. The moment the soles of my feet were off the dry land, I raised my voice to sing to the Lord for He has been good to me." A few lines later, he adds that he never turned back: "From that time on, I knew nothing about events in Morocco, nor did I inquire about them" (149–50).

Romanelli claims that he finally left behind the ambivalences of his detours. He is no longer both detached and involved; from now on, he resists involvement. His exit, described as an abrupt and complete dissociation from Morocco, reflects the violence that provoked it. Romanelli emphasizes a new sense of distance and difference. He does not return to Gibraltar, from where on a clear day Morocco would be visible, but boards a ship that will bring him to Amsterdam, from where he will be able to look back toward a coast receding into obscurity, toward a "land of darkness" (150). And it is this final assertion of mobility that will mark him as ultimately different from the Jews of Morocco, who are unable to leave. The only reminder of previous ambiguities is a memory of loss: Romanelli's book concludes with an elegy, expressing previous intimacy and present remoteness by mourning "the devastating ruin of the Daughter of my People" (151).

If, after having finished the book, we turn to its beginning, we realize that the traveler's claims regarding his disinterest in Morocco did not prevent his work as a travel writer. The writer looks back and creates a narrative that, with all its ambivalences, is not determined by the experiences that will be disclosed at the end of the book. The tension between Romanelli's desire to detach himself from the Jews of Morocco and his desire to engage with them remains unresolved. This is perhaps most obvious in the introduction, where Romanelli attempts to locate his writing within the framework of disciplined discourse. As we have already seen, Romanelli begins by fashioning himself as a sentimental travel writer, who, in relating his own "history," presents the "history" of the people among whom he dwelled. At the same time, the introduction is the place where Romanelli seeks to establish his "exteriority" vis-à-vis the "interior" he is going to describe. He "makes the Orient speak" like the scholars who, according to Edward Said, rendered "its mysteries plain for and to the West."[42] This is the first sentence of Romanelli's introduction: "The Israelite community presently living in the Arab territories of Africa's Barbary Coast under the rule of the Emperor of Mauretania, which is called nowadays *Marrakesh* in Arabic and *Maroc* in our languages, is almost entirely hidden from the eyes of the peoples living here in the countries of Europe" (15).

Romanelli alludes to, and takes up, a rhetoric familiar from other European travelogues. This rhetoric operates with the topos of the hidden land, the interior, and the scene behind the veil, which the European traveler—the diplomat or the ethnographer—will uncover and reveal to his readers.[43] At the same time, the image of the "hidden" scene is also reminiscent of Christian ethnographies, many of them written by converts, addressing the "secrets" of Jewish religious practice in the domestic sphere.[44]

But while the rhetoric in Romanelli's travelogue is clearly recognizable, he gives it a specific twist: the hidden Jewish community that exists beyond Christian lands is an integral part of the larger Jewish diaspora, thus constituting an other that is part of the self. The Jewish orient of Romanelli's present is evoked not as part of a single dualistic structure, in which a North African "interior" provides a defining counterpoint for the construction of identity and homogeneity within a European "exterior." Romanelli's exteriority is a highly individual accomplishment, attributed to his ability to distance himself from the collective ignorance of Christians, Muslims, and Jews alike. Thus, Romanelli describes the isolation of Moroccan Jewry as the result of various circumstances linked to Christian, Muslim, and Jewish contexts: Christian travelers do not know Jewish languages and mention Moroccan Jews only "as a part of the whole"; Muslims are depicted as ignorant and hostile toward Jews; and European Jews do not arouse "from their slumber of indifference" (15). Romanelli emphasizes the need to overcome the ignorance that generated the Moroccan-Jewish interior in the first place and to reinvigorate diaspora networks based on shared religious commitments and a shared language.[45]

At the same time, the orientalist overtones of his "exteriority" are apparent when he adopts a simpler interpretive framework, nourished by his negative notions of a stagnant Islamic Morocco, and points to the absence of two very important facilitators of communication. He finds almost no commercial exchange between Moroccan and European Jews. Moreover, in the eyes of this Italian Jew and agent of the Enlightenment, "the obstacle to disseminating information about Moroccan Jewry that surpasses all others is the absence of printing. For to this day, it has not been brought there, nor will it ever be" (16).[46] Romanelli's authority as a travel writer depends on the contrast between his mobile knowledge acquired in a land of printers and publishers and the absence of a printing press among Moroccan Jews, the emblem of their inability to communicate across boundaries and to represent themselves.[47]

Yet what remains absent throughout Romanelli's reflections, even when orientalist and colonial perspectives are clearly present, is the figure of an identifiable, stable, and powerful addressee; his text is not written "for and to the West," in Said's formulation. With his curiosity and willingness to "mingle" with "all kinds of people" and his decision to write his book in Hebrew, Romanelli fashions himself as an envoy not of this or that place but of an Enlightenment that is tied to mobility and of a diaspora that needs to be perpetually sustained by contact and communication.

In a "Hidden Land"

As an author, Romanelli never establishes a single and dominant perspective; he writes as a European and a Jew, as a migrant willing to stay in Morocco and as a traveler longing to leave, as the author of an autobiography interested in the exploration of his own self, and as an ethnographer interested in describing the world around him.[48] The resulting instabilities and indeterminacies produce a complex, vivid, and engaging text, but they also raise questions of authority, as posed by James Clifford: "[H]ow is unruly experience transformed into an authoritative written account? How, precisely, is a garrulous, overdetermined cross-cultural encounter shot through with power relations and personal cross-purposes circumscribed as an adequate version of a more or less discrete 'other world' composed by an individual author?"[49]

These questions respond to Edward Said's inquiries into the ways in which specific discursive practices and institutions govern the writing of individual scholars. Clifford asks how the texts of individual authors inscribe themselves in, and interfere with, such "governing bodies." Romanelli's narrative gives rise to similar questions: How did Romanelli try to gain control over his "unruly" material? How did his writing respond to a situation in which the "more or less discrete 'other world'" is also part of the "same world" of the Jewish diaspora and in which, therefore, the meanings of "cross-cultural encounter" become tangled and uncertain? How did Romanelli negotiate instability and indeterminacy to establish an authoritative text?

At first glance, instability and indeterminacy might seem to undermine the authority of the text, but Romanelli transforms these attributes into virtues by reinterpreting them as signs of physical, cultural, and intellectual mobility, of the ability to move between various places, people, and perspectives, and of the willingness to negotiate constantly between involvement and detachment. These authorial tactics emerge from, and contribute to, Romanelli's twofold commitment to Judaism and the Enlightenment. In Romanelli's text, these two frames of reference mirror each other in that they themselves are construed as ultimately defined by moments of mobility, by the capacity to create a critical distance from violently imposed conditions of immutability and immobility, and by the willingness to translate for present purposes the legacy of both the biblical "exodus" and Kant's "exit" from "immaturity."[50] Thus, Romanelli's authority vis-à-vis his Jewish or Christian readers in Amsterdam, Berlin, or Vienna rests on his ability to create an interpretive framework for his stories, autobiographical fragments, and philosophical reflections in which they speak of commitments that resonate with the insistence of his audience on the possibility of bringing together Judaism and Enlightenment.

At the same time, his book makes highly visible an aspect often present in works of the Jewish Enlightenment, but rarely explored in such a sustained

and complex manner: the strong commitment to intellectual and historical mobility goes along with uncertainty regarding its direction and desired
transcendence. After all, Christian modes of historical, political, and cultural
boundary formation in a world of emerging nation-states and colonial rule
were at odds with Jewish historical, political, and cultural orientations in the
diaspora.[51] Romanelli's text explores how it may be possible to insist on mobility while resisting Christian trajectories of progress and secular attempts to
map them on Jewish networks in time and space. Yet Romanelli's imaginative
critique of Christian Europe remains linked to his acceptance of orientalist notions regarding Moroccan Muslims and Jews. His authority as a travel writer
ultimately rests as much on his ability to deconstruct Christian perspectives
on Europe as on his willingness to reconstruct orientalist perspectives on Morocco. Thus, his book is as instructive in its failures as it is in its achievement as
a critical affirmation of the diaspora, with its disorienting as well as reorienting
potential, its disconcerting as well as reasserting effects. This affirmation can
be productively read as part of a European-Jewish interpretive tradition, entangled with Western strategies of domination, in which interrogation of the
diaspora resulted neither in its negation nor in assimilation.

Romanelli longs to "get out" (148) of the "hidden land," but he lingers,
and then, as a writer, he returns to it again and again. His detours seem not
only the result of circumstances beyond his control, but also the consequence
of a series of intended delays and deferrals, of periods of pausing and waiting
and staying. Like Romanelli, other Jewish authors in Europe around 1800
insisted on turning their gaze to other—hidden—places. While they clearly
wished to distance themselves from the orientalized Judaism of the Christian
world, they also insisted on engaging with a Jewish orient of their own. This
"Jewish orient" offered space for detours from linear narratives of arrival in
Christian Europe or return to Middle Eastern origins. It was imagined as a
site of difference that could support resistance to assimilation and to cultural
conversion. Romanelli's negotiation of this thoroughly overdetermined place
may represent, among other things, the articulation of an inclination to wait,
to pause, to explore other possibilities, and to inscribe what one has found—
like the vowels of Moroccan Hebrew—into an ongoing history of diasporic
communication.

Chapter 8

The Rhetoric of Rescue: "Salvage Immigration" Narratives in Israeli Culture

TAMAR KATRIEL

As "imagined communities,"[1] the nation-states of late modernity construct themselves in and through an array of globalized and localized discourses that often link notions of "homeland" and "diaspora." In a world characterized by large-scale population migrations, public discourses surrounding the issue of immigration make up a distinctive subclass of national and transnational discourses. Indeed, discourses on immigration and its regulation have been long-standing features of public debates concerning the construction and de-construction of national boundaries in many countries around the globe. Such discourses have found their articulation in such cultural-discursive arenas as the language of law and international agreements, popular press coverage, museum displays, school-related pedagogical materials, and commemorative occasions. Addressing large-scale immigrations as transformative junctures in the life of many modern nation-states, these public discourses serve to narrativize and make sense of mass immigration as a significant border-crossing phenomenon.

The centrality of immigration discourses in the construction of national identities is recognized by Nicolaus Mills in his introduction to a volume of essays concerned with the argument over immigration policies in the American context, where he points out: "We cannot discuss immigration these days without also talking about the kind of country we are."[2] Like other discourses of migration that form parts of the foundation mythologies of modern nation-states, such as the stories of the *Mayflower* and Ellis Island in the American context, the narratives of "salvage immigration" (*'aliyot hatsalah*) discussed in this essay thematize peoplehood through a particular construction of the immigration experience. In the Israeli and American cases alike, immigration is constructed as a moment of salvation, which simultaneously indexes a desire to become part of the new land and a decision to leave one's own homeland behind.[3]

Israeli discourses of aliyah—immigration conceptualized as "ascent"—have been crucially centered on the notion of rescue, marking the Zionist movement's goal of reestablishing the Jews' national homeland in Israel as a matter of personal and collective survival. While socialist versions of the Zionist movement have promoted a utopian vision of the Land of Israel as a site of national renewal, "catastrophic" versions of Zionism have foregrounded the hardships experienced by Jews in their lands of origins, as reflected in the labels *'aliyat metsuqah* (immigration of distress) and *'aliyat hatsalah* (salvage immigration).[4] In the parlance of immigration scholars, the Zionist construction of the Land of Israel as a haven for persecuted Jews highlights the "push factors" that encourage migration to places where life and dignity can be more easily sustained, whereas the construction of the Land of Israel as a privileged site for the cultivation of a utopian and authentic Jewish peoplehood constitutes a distinctive "pull factor."[5]

The hegemonic versions of Zionist immigration narratives have variously combined reference to push and pull factors, with one or the other foregrounded. Pull factors, in the form of the promise of enhanced social, national, and spiritual possibilities, dominated tales of utopian return to a Jewish homeland. In contrast, salvage immigration narratives foreground the push factors associated with leaving behind the hardships of diaspora life. These narratives refer to well-orchestrated "rescue operations" (*mivtsa'ei hatsalah*) that took place in pre-state years, continued into the early years of statehood, and were later launched from time to time as the occasion arose. These operations have resulted in the transfer to Palestine/Israel of practically entire Jewish communities (or what was left of them) from countries in which Jews experienced collective distress. Operations from postwar Europe, Iraq, Yemen, North Africa, Ethiopia, and the former Soviet Union have received worldwide media coverage and have been inscribed in Israeli-Jewish collective memory as crucial components of Israel's nation-building ethos. This subgenre of immigration narratives, in which aliyah is constructed as a form of rescue, will be at the center of my analysis.

In Israeli salvage immigration narratives, the nexus between immigration and rescue foregrounds the complementary sociopolitical roles of "rescuers" on the one hand and "rescued" on the other. The acknowledgment of these roles and their political implications takes us beyond transcendental tales of shared peoplehood and homecoming to the sociopolitical reality in which they are grounded. By addressing the cultural politics of Israeli immigration discourse, my goal is to attend to some of the ways in which notions of a Jewish homeland, Jewish diasporas, and the relationship between the two have been shaped and reshaped by the shifting historical circumstances of the past century.

The following discussion will problematize the rhetoric of rescue in Zionist discourse as it is articulated in stories of salvage immigration, exploring the role that they have played in the cultural politics of Israel's nation-building saga. In so doing, I hope to show how hegemonic versions of Israeli-Zionist immigration discourse, cast in transcendental terms, often mask the fact that they are grounded in concrete and politically situated communicative events and ritual practices. As my analysis will bring out, counter-discourses that contest the widely circulated, dominant versions of salvage immigration narratives have emerged from the very start, subtly destabilizing the meanings and power relations associated with the hegemonic narratives of rescue.

Salvage Immigration and Dialogic Narration

Edward Bruner and Phyllis Gorfain's notion of "dialogic narration," which they developed in exploring the role of the story of Masada in Israeli cultural politics, provides a conceptual framework for my analysis. Following their application of Bakhtin's dialogic linguistics to the study of narrative action, I propose to read Israeli salvage immigration narratives intertextually and in terms of the power relations that they encode.[6] In particular, Bruner and Gorfain's analysis helps to highlight the tension between the hegemonic, authoritative tellings of the national narrative and the counter-discourses that challenge its basic script. National narratives, of which the story of Masada is one example, serve "to integrate the society, encapsulate ideology, and create social order."[7] At the same time, the ambiguity and paradox that characterize such national narratives invite conflicting readings and dissident voices. Every act of narration is thus a polemic that either reproduces or contests the hegemonic version of the tale.

As an arena of "ideologies at war," the salvage immigration script is likewise subject to dialogic contestation. On the one hand, the script enjoys a privileged position that dominates official public performances and frames authoritative narratives that represent the official line. The power of the script both derives from the power of the state and reproduces it through each performative telling. On the other hand, resistant tellings often come in the form of "questions, interruptions, back-channel commentary, or argumentation in underground publications . . .. [T]hey are 'other' and always uttered in reaction to dominant tellings." Whatever shape the alternative narrations take, they are read as posing a challenge to the dominant telling, which they do not reproduce. Bruner and Gorfain summarize this multivocal dynamic as follows: "Authoritative voices attempt to fix meanings and stabilize order, whereas challenging voices question established meanings and tend to be deconstructive. Taken together, the various narrations and interpretations lead to what we call a process of dialogic narration." They characterize this process as involving interaction between voices in at least three domains, two of which will hold our attention here. The first relates to what they call the story's "intrinsic dialogue," which refers to the essential open-endedness, ambiguity, and paradox that attend great national stories, such that they tend to resist a single definitive interpretation. The second relates to what Bruner and Gorfain call the "historical dialogue," which refers to the fact that every telling "takes account of previous and anticipated tellings and responds to alternative and to challenging stories."[8]

This study adds to my previous attempts to understand Israeli national tales within an analytic framework first developed with respect to narratives of the Jewish settlement effort of 1936–39, known as Tower and Stockade (*Ḥomah u-Migdal*), and the discourse of kibbutz museums.[9] Juxtaposing settlement and immigration versions of the Zionist master narrative brings out implicit dimensions of the dialogic narration process. These two versions can be said to anchor two polar constructions of the place-making and people-making project of modern Zionism, both complementing and standing in tension with each other. The pioneering ideology celebrated through settlement narratives cultivates an image of the Land of Israel as a utopian site of personal and social renewal expressed in an ethos of productivity, sovereignty, and attachment to place. These narratives begin the tale of Israeliness where the catastrophic version of Zionism associated with the salvage immigration tale concludes—at the moment of arrival in the land.

Another intersecting discourse that indirectly amplifies the salvage immigration tale involves high-profile rescue narratives of state-sponsored struggles to release Israeli prisoners of war or hostages from captivity in enemy territory. The ongoing saga of Ron Arad and the rescue operation at Entebbe are prime examples of such narratives of rescue from captivity.[10] While these tales of rescue mark a different narrative trajectory from the one dealt with here, they are thematically related: both the captivity and the immigration versions of the rescue script foreground the values of communal commitment and joint action in salvage efforts. Not surprisingly, on some occasions the Jews waiting to be rescued from their plight in the diaspora are explicitly referred to as "captives," and their airlift to Israel labeled *pidyon shevu'im* (release of captives), an extremely important value in traditional Judaism.[11]

Keeping these framing narratives in mind, my analysis will trace the dialogic process at work in salvage immigration narratives. Most critically, rescue narratives involve an intrinsic relational ambiguity and paradox as they imply shared group affiliation and mutual commitment, on the one hand, and a power differential associated with the roles of rescuer and rescued, on the other. The historical dialogue relates to the struggle over the meanings of the salvage immigration script for Jews in various parts of the world at different points in time and with reference to the changing contours of Israeli and Jewish life.[12]

Immigration as Redemption, Homecoming, and Collaboration

The centrality of the trope of rescue in Israeli discourse on immigration emerged forcefully in the context of an ethnographic study I previously conducted in museums in the Haifa area, devoted to clandestine immigration to Palestine by Jews fleeing Nazi persecution between 1934 and 1948.[13] The struggle for Jewish immigration from Europe was waged by the organized Jewish community (the *yishuv*) in Palestine against the British blockade of Palestine's shores during the years of the Mandate. British restrictions on Jewish immigration were a response to the pressures of the majority Arab-Palestinian population, for whom the influx of Jews from Europe represented a demographic threat. The dramatic story of Jewish immigration during those years has come to epitomize the notion of rescue via immigration in Israeli collective memory.

This saga of clandestine immigration is narrated as a story of arduous journeys on rickety ships orchestrated by pre-state Jewish organizations inside and outside Palestine. Thousands of Jews undertook these risky journeys in their search for refuge in what they considered to be their old/new homeland. Clandestine immigration has provided a narrative paradigm for later immigration operations that have similarly combined elements of flight and rescue with elements of quest narratives. These versions of pre- and post-Holocaust journeys to the Land of Israel clearly hark back, in secularized form, to the ancient Jewish tale of the biblical Exodus. *Exodus* was also the name of the most famous of the ships involved in clandestine immigration, which the British seized in 1947, deporting the Holocaust survivors aboard back to Europe. These modern reincarnations of the Exodus story speak of Jewish redemption in national rather than religious terms, grafting a universalistic idiom of humanitarian intervention and rescue onto the Jewish national tale. However, the theme of rescue, as Ella Shohat has forcefully argued, carries additional, markedly orientalist, overtones when applied to the migration of Jews from Muslim lands to the Eurocentric state of Israel. The Zionist project has also cultivated a colonialist idiom of rescue whereby Jewish immigrants, seen as bearers of the Western culture of "progress," would save the "primitive," Levantine East from its backwardness.[14]

Israeli salvage immigration narratives express a particular relationship between Jewish diasporas and the Jewish homeland, simultaneously celebrating affinity and marking distance and hierarchy within one and the same narrative script. The trope of rescue, as applied to the plight of Jews in different countries of distress, is anchored in an ethos of mutual care and commitment that links disparate Jewish groups, an ethos articulated in the widely cited saying *kol yisra'el 'arevim zeh la-zeh*, "all the people of Israel are responsible for one another." Framing the arrival of Jews in the Land of Israel as a moment of redemption anchors their migration in experiences of loss and trauma, on the one hand, while creating a shared orientation to the Land of Israel as a Jewish homeland, on the other.

The discourse surrounding salvage immigration operations is resonant with stories of Jewish plight and migration. These accounts speak eloquently to the role that salvage immigration operations have played for Israelis as well as diaspora Jews as meaning-making mechanisms through which Zionist ideology, and especially its territorial tenet of "homecoming," have been repeatedly dramatized and reaffirmed.

Notably, and somewhat paradoxically, salvage immigration operations chart a Jewish geography grounded in the polarity between Israel/Zion and its various diasporas, while also joining the Jewish state and diaspora Jews in a collaborative project that reaffirms the shared affiliation of far-flung Jewish communities. The limits of collaboration in the salvage immigration enterprise mark the outer boundaries of the Jewish community. Salvage immigration narratives have thus emerged as central to the production of a worldwide sense of Jewish peoplehood in the postwar years, enacting basic tenets of Jewish commitment as well as the Jewish-Israeli national project of the "ingathering of the exiles" (*qibbuts galuyot*). I therefore refer to these narratives as "stories of peoplehood," a term recently proposed by Roger Smith that takes us beyond the language of nationalism and encompasses both "'pre'- and 'post'-national conceptions of community."[15] This usage emphasizes the fact that salvage immigration narratives are not only central to the Israeli national imaginary but are also part of a broader Jewish landscape of shared meanings and visions of communal action that links the Jewish state and the diaspora.

While some immigration efforts to transport Jews from a "country of distress" to Israel were defined as a collective project to begin with, others were only retrospectively included within the salvage immigration ethos. The question of inclusion became particularly significant for those isolated Jewish communities whose very Jewishness was put into question, such as the Jews of India in the 1950s, the Ethiopian Jews before the mid-1970s, Russian newcomers in the early 1990s, and the Christianized Falashmura of Ethiopia today. The analysis proposed in this chapter relates to those cases to which the salvage immigration script applies most readily. Such cases have often been labeled "operations" (sing., *mivtsa*'), a term with clear military connotations, and have become an essential part of Israeli collective memory. Prominent among them are: Operation Magic Carpet (less commonly known as Operation Eagles' Wings), which brought Jews from Yemen in 1949–50; Operation Ezra and Nehemiah (sometimes nicknamed Operation Ali Baba), which brought Jews from Iraq in 1950–51; and Operation Moses and Operation Solomon, which brought Jews from Ethiopia in 1985 and 1991. Other immigration efforts, such as the worldwide Jewish campaign to allow Jews to migrate from the Soviet Union to Israel in the 1980s, share at least some features of the salvage immigration script epitomized by the Magic Carpet, Ezra and Nehemiah, Moses, and Solomon operations. While my discussion draws most directly on these paradigmatic cases, I leave open the question of its applicability to more diffusely defined salvage immigration efforts.

The Salvage Immigration Script

As culturally resonant tales, salvage immigration narratives have generated a field of textual production that circulates and elaborates the theme of Jewish rescue and inscribes it in collective memory. This discursive field includes ephemeral fragments of the story as it unfolds in news reports or commemorative discourses designed to stabilize a particular version of the story over time. I draw on a variety of textual resources in building up my corpus: news stories derived from the mainstream Hebrew daily press; promotional materials used in fund-raising and public-relations campaigns in Israel and in the United States; personal testimonies published in such venues as the popular press, book-length memoirs, and photo albums by aliyah activists, journalists, immigrants, and scholars; commemorative texts produced on anniversary occasions for inclusion in communal publications, pedagogical materials, children's magazines, stamps and posters, and museum displays; popular histories exposing behind-the-scenes activities and often challenging the idealized hegemonic version of the politics of rescue; and academic studies concerning the mass immigrations to Israel and the public controversies that some of them generated.

As scholars of journalism have stressed in recent years, news reports are part of the ongoing cultural negotiation of meanings in modern societies and play an important role in shaping and propagating contemporary social myths.[16] While the press treated salvage immigration operations as "reportable events" between several weeks to several months after the events themselves, daily news accounts provided numerous facts and figures as well as a variety of human-interest stories featuring the newcomers and their journey. Commentaries in the press included discussions of Jewish vulnerability and survival, Jewish commitment, Jewish "return," and so on. As is most often the case with the circulation of cultural myths in news-telling, the state's immigration script remains dominant, even as counter-discourses that challenge some aspects of the official narrative are allowed to seep through, subtly destabilizing it in ultimately marginal but instructive ways.

News reports and commentaries that treat salvage immigration operations are often colored by a dramatic flair and partake of a self-reflexive mood. The inherent drama of the events is accompanied by a range of musings about the very meaning of Jewish national revival in Israel. In the wake of Operation Moses, which transported some 7,000 Jews from Ethiopia to Israel in 1984–85, the following editorial appeared in the high-circulation daily newspaper *Yedi'ot Aḥronot* under the title "A Collective Experience": "The aliyah of Ethiopian Jews is not only their experience; it is to no small degree the experience of all Israeli Jews. A well-known journalist, a Sabra, told us: 'The word Zionism was for me an abstract concept, it went in one ear and out the other. But here, seeing those Jews whom Zionism rescued from the worst plight, I felt like a Zionist for the first time in my life.'"[17]

The drama of the events is captured and highlighted in the many reports of specific salvage immigration operations in the mass media. Those reports have provided the narrative building blocks for the elaboration of a widely recognized script of Jewish rescue via immigration. While clearly not all components of the script appear in any particular retelling of the story, the script is part of Israelis' cultural repertoire.

Several components combine to make up the salvage immigration script. These include accounts of Jewish plight in the diaspora; the intercommunal politics of rescue; the polar images of rescuers and rescued; tales of the journey; the drama of arrival; and morning-after accounts of "surviving salvation."[18] Some newspaper headlines highlight the drama of a given salvage immigration operation as a whole. Metaphors such as "The Days of the Messiah" and the expression "On Eagles' Wings," for example, were commonly used in reference to the "rescue" of Yemenite Jews. Other headlines address specific components of the salvage immigration script.

Narratives that challenge some aspect of the salvage immigration saga have also been circulating all along. These challenges address every motif in the salvage migration script, deconstructing the cultural and ideological assumptions on which it rests. Indeed, against the background of these various challenges to the authoritative versions of the salvage immigration script, hegemonic retellings have become increasingly apologetic rather than celebratory. In what follows, I will use relevant newspaper headlines to explore the role played by this script and its various components in both constructing and challenging the hegemonic discourse surrounding immigration to Israel.

Jewish Plight in the Diaspora

Accounts of salvage immigration operations often include descriptions of the suffering of Jews in their countries of origin. The life of the Jews in particular diasporic settings is described as endangered by such threats as growing antisemitism, political instability, religious persecution, and acute economic hardship exacerbated by their ethnic affiliation.

The Holocaust epitomizes the Jewish plight in the diaspora, and its memory provides a readily available interpretive frame through which to construe the meaning of salvage immigration operations as a Zionist project. A lucid example of this is found in an article published in the daily newspaper *Ma'ariv* by the columnist (and later, politician) Yosef Lapid in response to Operation Moses. This oft-cited passage makes a direct link between the plight and rescue of Ethiopians and the Holocaust: "I became a Zionist on the day I fled with my mother from the Budapest ghetto and we had nowhere to hide. They wanted to kill us, and we had no place in the whole world to go. We had to return to the ghetto, but since then I have known that there has to be a place somewhere on the face of the earth that can offer haven to a Jewish child whose life is threatened by Nazis or by famine. In brief, that is what Zionism is. Welcome, my black brothers. You are helping us to understand what we are doing here."[19]

In the early 1950s, when the desire to gather Jews in the newly sovereign State of Israel was particularly great, the need to prioritize and pace the influx of newcomers created pressures and controversies. Accounts of the Jews' plight in a given diaspora affected public opinion and created pressure on the authorities to launch salvage immigration operations, and newspaper accounts of such plights became a tool in this internal political struggle over immigration priorities. This was the case in reporting the harassment that Jews suffered under the Iraqi regime in 1951. Forty years later, Israeli newspapers featured headlines such as "Economic Collapse and Hunger against the Background of Rebels' Victories and Hatred for the Regime"[20] (in Ethiopia) and "Concern in Israel for Ethiopian Jews Given the Uncertainties Following Mangisto's Flight."[21]

Over the years, a counter-discourse to these narratives of Jewish plight has emerged in the form of nostalgic tales associated with life in various communities previously identified as countries of distress. These nostalgic accounts give voice to the newcomers' sense of having been uprooted from their country of origin, the place they used to call "home." This nostalgia has had the effect of undermining the sense of "homecoming" associated with the new-comers' metaphorical return to the Land of Israel. A destabilizing component has thus been introduced into the basic salvage immigration script—the sense of rupture often associated with the immigration experience and the trauma of leaving one's home and life behind. Furthermore, the retrospective reaffirmation of Jewish diaspora experience by newcomers and their children has served to downplay the motif of communal plight associated with the salvage immigration script. At the same time, nostalgia foregrounds the possibility of cultural affinity between Jews and others within a non-Jewish environment and thus questions the sense of urgency that has accompanied the rescue operation project.

The Transnational Politics of Rescue

Launching a rescue operation represents a variety of interests and pressures at the communal, national, and international levels. These interests have affected the planning, timing, and execution of salvage immigration operations, which have often involved a range of diplomatic maneuvers, political pressures, economic enticements, and logistical efforts.

The religious establishment in Israel represents one such interest. A major underlying premise associated with the politics of salvage immigration operations is that only Jews recognized as such by the Israeli state can be transported to Israel. In some cases, this is an unproblematic issue, but in other cases, recognizing the Jewishness of those who wish to be rescued becomes a point of contention. The plight of Ethiopian Jews, to take the best-known example, was ignored until the Sefaradi chief rabbi Ovadiah Yosef recognized their Jewishness in 1973. As a result, they could be considered candidates for aliyah under the Law of Return.

The rescue of Ethiopian Jews has been implicated not only in the politics of religious-secular relations in Israel and the ongoing debate about criteria for Jewishness, but also in the politics of intercommunal relations between American Jews and the African American community in the United States.[22] American Jews prided themselves on their support of their dark-skinned brethren, using it to signal their liberalism vis-à-vis the American local ethnic landscape. They have generously and enthusiastically supported the Ethiopian (and other) rescue efforts, rallying behind the Jewish state's desire to increase its Jewish population.

Indeed, it is not always clear whose interests are foregrounded when a salvage immigration operation is launched: those of the Jews in search of rescue, those of the Jewish state eager to increase the number of its Jewish citizens, or those of Jewish communities in search of self-renewal through the enactment of Jewish solidarity.[23] When successful, the politics of rescue works to attain an acceptable balance among all three goals. Often, however, the power relations implicit in the rescue scenario cannot be avoided, resulting in the polarization of agents and beneficiaries of the rescue efforts.

Some counter-discourses have emerged that challenge the salvage immigration saga by casting doubt on the motivations of either the rescuers or those rescued, claiming that one or the other group was not so interested in the rescue operation in the first place. In one version of this challenge, ultra-orthodox Jews and post-Zionist historians have independently claimed that the Israeli leadership employed coercive measures in transporting reluctant Jews to the Land of Israel for the purpose of buttressing the Jewish population of the country. Specific accusations included putting pressure on Holocaust survivors in Displaced Persons camps and endangering various Middle Eastern communities by spreading Zionist agitation.

Narratives of reluctant or hesitant Jewish rescue efforts that were not forthcoming when called for—or that came too late, if at all—serve a similar purpose. The poignancy attending the highly tormented cultural conversation concerning the failure to rescue European Jews during the Holocaust has colored the elaborate mythology of Jewish rescue by immigration in the post-Holocaust years. Thus, for example, an American activist from the American Association of Ethiopian Jews (AAEJ) presented former vice president Bush with a copy of David Wyman's book *The Abandonment of the Jews: America and the Holocaust, 1941–1945* on the eve of the vice president's diplomatic mission to the Sudan in 1984.[24] Accusations by American-based aliyah activists against the Israeli government for its alleged unwillingness to act on behalf of the Ethiopian Jews before the mid-1980s have also invoked the Holocaust, to considerable effect.

Scripted Roles: Rescuers and Rescued

The hegemonic versions of the salvage immigration narrative reinscribe a polarization between the roles of rescuers and rescued even while reaffirming their shared communal affiliation. Both the sense of "otherness" and the possibility of bonding are expressed by Gideon Samet, a leading journalist, in "The Ethiopians as a Mirror," written in response to the arrival of Ethiopian Jews via Operation Moses. Underscoring the Ethiopian newcomers' "otherness," Samet nevertheless incorporates the new Ethiopian immigration into the Israeli scene by constructing a narrative that fits within the larger frame of the salvage immigration script. He accomplishes this rhetorically through references to the mass immigrations of the early years of statehood: "The effect of the rescue operation of Ethiopian Jews was tantalizing. . . . For many, the appearance of the beautiful black Ethiopians symbolized our own lost innocence. . . . In the midst of our banking scandals, these duplicates of Sallaḥ Shabati [humorist Ephraim Kishon's fictional figure of a newcomer from Morocco] and the Yemenites of the Magic Carpet suddenly appeared among us, as if emerging out of a time tunnel, looking like the models of a world we thought had already disappeared."[25]

A similarly two-pronged representational gesture is described in Kerri Steinberg's study of United Jewish Appeal promotional photographic fundraising campaigns.[26] Steinberg observes that these campaigns are rhetorically oriented toward constructing the inclusive trope of the "extended Jewish family" while at the same time preserving Western supremacy. The rescuers in these narratives are both individual and institutional agents. The individuals are appreciatively referred to as *sheliḥim* (emissaries) or *pe'ilei 'aliyah* (immigration activists). On a personal level, aliyah activists are presented as the quintessentially resourceful, ideologically committed, untiring and daring "doers" of the Zionist ethos. News reports, and especially retrospective accounts of salvage immigration operations, often describe individual agents as the unsung heroes of the nation-building saga who risked involvement in underground activities for what is repeatedly termed the "sacred mission" of bringing Jews to Israel, or, in the words of Israel's president after Operation Solomon, "the realization of a sacred goal."[27]

While highly responsive to the newcomers' plight, as an ideological construct and a lived reality, those who orchestrate the salvage immigration operations have nevertheless manifested a paternalistic—and, at times, orientalizing—attitude that constructs the dark-skinned Jews of the East as ahistorical and "authentic," romanticizing them as quasi-biblical figures whose religiosity is exemplary and pure.[28] The Jews rescued in salvage immigration operations are generally presented as helpless victims of harsh living conditions and oppression in their places of origin. Their role in deciding to leave their homes and undertake the arduous journey is blurred in official rescue accounts and remains barely recognized. The immigrants are not presented as mythical "doers," not even as agents, but mainly as the beneficiaries of others' actions, even when many of them walked thousands of miles in rugged terrain from remote villages to designated transit camps, where they sometimes were made to spend weeks, months, or even years before the transport to Israel was arranged.

In more recent years, possibly in response to latter-day critiques, the autobiographical narrations of the rescued Jews have increasingly found their way into the public arena, and the language of victimhood has given way to a discourse of voluntary personal sacrifice that comes closer to the heroic discourse of mainstream Zionist "doers." In particular, these accounts foreground the newcomers' agency. The suffering and losses associated with the Jews' departure and journey are reinscribed as sacrifices that they willingly made in order to reach the Holy Land. Their motives are associated with the reawakening of their dormant Zionism, which, in the case of Middle Eastern, North African, and Ethiopian Jews, is conceptualized in religious rather than in secular-revolutionary terms.[29] This narrative move is subversive precisely because it undermines the polarization of roles between rescuers, rescued, and enemy that is the hallmark of rescue narratives.

The Hardships of the Journey

At first, the numerous media reports of the Jewish newcomers' transport to Israel originated mostly in official sources and represented an institutional point of view. The coverage of the newcomers' journey thus involved a meticulous monitoring of numbers, places of departure and final destinations in Israel, the logistics of the operation, aircraft capacities, and so on. Depending on the circumstances, some of the operations have been shorter than others, and the media coverage of them has accordingly been more intense (with the 1991 Operation Solomon taking pride of place). The temporal compression heightens the sense of drama involved. The more protracted salvage immigration operations are accompanied by ongoing, repetitive, lower-profile reports regarding the pace and mechanics of various Jews' journeys to the Land of Israel.

Notably, the newcomers' own tales of the journey have a different temporality, as glimpsed in media reports and subsequent ethnographic interviews.[30] These stories go further back to painful scenes of departure, hardship, and loss, and they cover a much longer stretch of the journey, including the decision to leave. They detail that difficult stretch of the journey that brought Jews from Yemen or Ethiopia, for example, to transit camps on the way and later in Israel, going beyond the drama of departure and arrival compressed into the story of the airlift itself.

The Drama of Arrival

Jews' arrival in Israel is generally described as a moment of epiphany, an end to their long suffering in their country of origin and en route. The arrival of Ethiopian Jews via Operation Solomon in 1991 was heralded in one newspaper headline in celebratory tones: "A Whole Community Came to Find a Homeland." The article heading added this vivid and moving description of their first moments in the new land: "First the children came down. Then the others followed them down the stairs of the plane with some trepidation. They looked exhausted and afraid, and only few of them were able to express happiness or relief. A young man carried his elderly father on his shoulders, and both of them stooped to kiss the ground."[31]

News accounts covering the moment of arrival report on scenes of weeping and on emotionally charged encounters between long-separated relatives, but also on the newcomers' emotional restraint and dignified demeanor. In fact, for many of these newcomers, the arrival in Israel is a second arrival in a long journey that starts in a remote village and takes them through Israeli-run transit camps. These camps mark their first encounter with a Westernized environment, where they are clothed in modern garb and introduced to Western ways of hygiene and health care. Only upon arrival in Israel are they introduced to modern domestic technologies, a fact that was highlighted in some of the press coverage, sometimes giving rise to newspaper accounts that registered amusement at the newcomers' lack of familiarity with modern amenities such as electricity, refrigerators, or indoor toilets.

The public moments of heightened emotion that mark the newcomers' arrival in Israel are presented in press coverage and in retrospective memoirs. These episodes represent a climactic closure to the operation whose beneficiaries are not only the newcomers but all Israeli Jews. For the latter, the arrival of Jews from countries of distress is an authenticating moment of national purpose that transcends the doubts and disorientation of mundane reality. This is beautifully captured in the lead of the article "The Ethiopian Exodus 1991": "It was one of those rare moments, void of cynicism, in which everything is clear: what the state exists for, why, for whom. During one day and night in May, almost the entire Ethiopian Jewish community was brought to Israel. If there is nobody to whom one can say 'Let my people go,' at least there will be those who go to fetch them. The Jews of Ethiopia sat in Addis Ababa waiting for assistance from heaven. And that's where it came from."[32] What follows the moment of arrival is relegated to the category of *qelitah* (absorption), the anticlimactic "morning after" of the great drama of homecoming called aliyah.

Surviving Salvation

Immigration, however spiritualized, does not, of course, end with the transcendental moment of arrival. As numerous articles in the press remind readers, the phase of the immigration process in which newcomers become integrated into the new land begins only when the moment of aliyah is over. *Qelitah*, or absorption, is run by a range of government and Jewish Agency officials generally thought of as bureaucrats, not ideologically driven emissaries (*shelihim*). The epiphany of aliyah as a redemptive moment obscures the mundane reality of the process of adaptation that follows it.

The absorption of immigrants has been an enormous challenge and an ongoing source of strife and discontent in Israeli society since the mass immigrations of the late 1940s and early 1950s. Already in the late 1940s, the euphoria engendered by the tremendous influx of immigrants was accompanied by counter-discourses that fundamentally challenged the widely accepted categorical distinction between aliyah and *qelitah*, the moment of arrival and the morning after. Indeed, Ben-Gurion insisted on limitless support for aliyah in the post-independence years, despite the many complaints concerning the problems associated with the post-arrival phase. The new state's leadership felt overwhelmed by the enormous difficulties involved in procuring housing, health care, employment, and education for the masses of new immigrants. As Dvora Hacohen shows in her book on the mass immigrations of the 1950s, internal debates within the cabinet repeatedly included proposals to curb aliyah.[33] Even though attempts were made to keep these debates from public view, such policy proposals reached the press from time to time, undermining the hegemonic vision of Israel as unconditionally committed to offering a haven to all Jews. Later immigration operations have been accompanied by oft-repeated, public, and ritualistic resolutions "not to repeat the mistakes of the 1950s." These resolutions refer both to the regulation of immigration and to the administration of absorption efforts.

From the very beginning, the press has been full of stories relating to the immigrants' hardships, the insufficiency of the public programs prepared for them, and "alarmist" stories about the newcomers—their "primitiveness," the health threats they pose to the general population, the enormous resources they require, and so on.[34] As time has passed, stories have appeared about acute immigrant disaffection leading to vocal public demonstrations, which were sometimes contained by force. Against the background of such reports, the presumption that aliyah is in itself a moment of redemption has appeared less and less tenable. One newspaper headline succinctly captures the disappointment of some of the newcomers in Operation Moses: "When Will You Finally Allow Us to Feel That We Have Really Come Home?"[35]

Changing Trajectories of the Rhetoric of Rescue

Reading the salvage immigration script in conjunction with the counter-narratives and intersecting narratives that challenge it brings out the complex dynamics in which this highly charged "story of peoplehood" participates. The mythic status of the salvage immigration script is reinforced through frequent intertextual references that echo its central themes and connect different tellings of the story. Over the years, the cultural discourse about these rescue operations has developed its own lexicon and iconographic idioms. Photojournalistic images—of dark Jews embarking on a plane, huddling inside it, disembarking from it, and falling into one another's arms, carried by smiling (usually white) soldiers or other state representatives—are so repetitive that it is often unclear which immigration a given image depicts.

Many of the key words and images associated with salvage immigration stories have been incorporated into commemorative projects and become central fixtures of the Israeli nation-building ethos. Israeli public discourse is infused with discussions of antisemitism in the diaspora that emphasize the vulnerability of Jewish life outside Israel (echoing the "Jewish plight" theme) and of the so-called demographic problem in Israel, echoing anxieties about the loss of a Jewish majority and the erosion of the state's Jewish ethnic character.

Despite the tenacity of the salvage immigration saga and the imagery associated with it, the script seems to have lost some of its pertinence to the Israeli aliyah project. In 2004, a front-page notice in *Ha'aretz* under the headline "Sharon Wants Another Million *'Olim* [Newcomers], but Who Will Come?" declared a new era in Israeli immigration policy.[36] Contrary to the skeptical headline, the text itself recounted that the prime minister had taken time out of his busy schedule to initiate an in-depth consultation about ways to promote aliyah. One of his consultants reportedly explained that the new idea was to promote "aliyah out of choice" in place of the salvage immigration efforts of the past. No explanation was given for this unexpected narrative shift. Is it a response to the feeling that there are no more imperiled Jewish communities to be rescued? Or does it reflect the feeling that Israel is not much of a haven these days, given its relentlessly embattled situation?

Indeed, it seems to have become increasingly difficult to sustain the polarity between rescuers and rescued in charting contemporary relations between Jewish communities worldwide, especially between homeland and diaspora. Curiously, the particularistic narrative of Jewish rescue modeled on the story of Exodus appears to be losing its hold just when a globalized script of humanitarian rescue is becoming more prevalent. Rescue narratives represent the more rarified moments of "good news" in a media environment largely populated by tales of violence and suffering at the personal, social, national, or international levels. The particularistic as well as the globalized humanitarian rescue narratives provide paradigms for action, constituting discursive arenas in which human responsiveness, resourcefulness, and commitment are dramatized as practical possibilities. As such, they have a particularly important role to play in our increasingly globalized world, which confronts us with the ongoing moral dilemmas of spectatorship in the face of "distant suffering,"[37] whether the suffering of our own people or of "cultural others."

By modeling forms of effective action, rescue narratives of all kinds address a tension that is endemic to our spectator culture: the tension between the knowledge of others' suffering, as whispered by word of mouth or as viewed on our television screens; and the constraints (real or imagined) on our ability to act on this knowledge. As popular discourses, narratives of rescue celebrate the possibility of humanitarian intervention, while inviting reflection on its conditions and limits. Salvage immigration narratives thus negotiate their position in relation to particularistic discourses of Jewish identity within a globalized landscape of human suffering. As stories of peoplehood, they generate a Jewish idiom of suffering, efficacy, and morality, offering an uneasy, tension-filled response to the modern "crisis of pity"[38] of which the Jews have been prime victims and whose politics link Jewish diasporic communities and the Israeli state in multiple threads of commitment and struggle to this day.

PART III. TRADITION

Chapter 9

Judaism and Tradition: Continuity, Change, and Innovation

ALBERT I. BAUMGARTEN AND MARINA RUSTOW

> There is probably no time and place with which historians are concerned that has not seen the invention of tradition. However, we should expect it to occur more frequently when a rapid transformation of society weakens or destroys the social patterns for which "old" traditions had been designed.
>
> —Eric J. Hobsbawm

How and why did appeals to continuity become the principal means by which Judaism absorbed innovations? How, in short, did Judaism become a religion centered on tradition?

In his introduction to the classic volume *The Invention of Tradition*, Eric Hobsbawm distinguishes between "custom," the common set of behaviors that people observe in traditional societies, and "tradition," which, he argues, serves ideological functions, including that of legitimating and justifying power. Custom, Hobsbawm writes, "cannot afford to be invariant, because even in 'traditional' societies life is not so." He defines tradition, by contrast, as unvarying, repetitive, and frequently marked by rituals, costumes, and other appurtenances that no longer serve practical functions. "'Custom' is what judges do; 'tradition' (in this instance invented tradition) is the wig, robe, and other formal paraphernalia and ritualized practices surrounding their substantial action." For Hobsbawm, tradition is unvarying because it has pulled asunder from the course of everyday life. Indeed, "the wigs of lawyers could hardly acquire their modern significance until other people stopped wearing wigs."[1] In the ultraorthodox Jewish context, one might substitute the knickers, long coats, and fur hats of certain groups who continue to dress this way not in imitation of the Polish nobility, as is sometimes stated, but in deference to unalterable tradition—retroactively justified on the basis of talmudic prohibitions against changing even "the strap of a sandal" in times of persecution.[2]

That the era of modern nationalism saw the multiplication of invented traditions is by now nearly universally accepted. But the premises of Hobsbawm's argument are worth reconsidering. He pits custom or "genuine" tradition against the invented variety: "genuine" tradition characterizes premodern societies, while "invented" traditions are a hallmark of the modern. Custom is adaptive while invented tradition is static. Custom is unconscious and irrational, while invented traditions are consciously founded on acts of rupture and thus reflect artifice or manipulate the past. For Hobsbawm, then, invented traditions are an instrument or at least a symptom of false consciousness.[3] In this respect, he expands upon Marx's famous observation that "the tradition of all dead generations weighs like a nightmare on the brains of the living." Marx observed this in accusing the revolutionaries of 1848 of rummaging in the arsenal of the past in search of weapons to use in the service of legitimating their own authority: for Marx, precisely when people

> seem engaged in revolutionizing themselves and things, in creating something that has never yet existed, precisely in such periods of revolutionary crisis they anxiously conjure up the spirits of the past to their service and borrow from them names, battle-cries, and costumes in order to present the new scene of world history in this time-honored disguise and this borrowed language. Thus Luther donned the mask of the Apostle Paul, the Revolution of 1789 to 1814 draped itself alternately as the Roman Republic and the Roman Empire, and the Revolution of 1848 knew nothing better to do than to parody now 1789, now the revolutionary tradition of 1793 to 1795.[4]

For Marx and Hobsbawm, unmasking traditions as invented serves not just historiographic but political ends, challenging the legitimacy that rests on these invocations of tradition. Such unmasking also rests on the assumption that it is always possible to distinguish between "genuine" and "invented" traditions. But even if that distinction can be sustained in the context of political authority, which relies perforce on tactics of legitimation, we find it more difficult to sustain when it comes to religion, in which change is usually more problematic, and in which, accordingly, so much depends on invention or continual reinvention. For that reason, the concept of tradition still offers up ample fertile ground for analysis.

We take issue with two aspects of the "invented tradition" thesis. First, we find the distinction between "genuine" and "invented" traditions untenable in certain contexts and uninformative in others. There are instances in which a tradition is "genuine" and "invented" at the same time; and even when one can clearly distinguish between the two types, that distinction does not always yield analytical dividends. If we may borrow a term from mystery fiction, it is a red herring. We propose instead differentiating not between types of tradition but between types of appeal to tradition. The material from ancient, medieval, and modern Judaism that we will discuss in this essay has convinced us that a useful distinction can be made between appeals to tradition in a weak sense, that is, to a corpus of knowledge or practices handed down over the ages, and appeals to tradition in a strong sense, in which the past is construed so as to serve the needs of the present. Neither is more or less genuine. While we agree with Hobsbawm that constructions of the past always serve the needs of the present to some extent, our terminology—"weak" versus "strong"—obviates the need to make judgments of genuineness, which are often problematic or have an ideological motivation of their own. Our terminology also recognizes that some appeals to tradition that fit into our strong category have an excellent historical basis—a conclusion that Hobsbawm's terminology seems to preclude.

The second aspect of Hobsbawm's thesis with which we take issue is the presumption that "genuine" appeals to tradition cannot be made sincerely in modern, industrialized contexts—or perhaps more importantly, we take issue with its converse: that premodern appeals to tradition are necessarily organic, genuine, and uninvented. Premodern cultures occasionally contested the genuineness of claims to tradition, calling them spurious or literally invented, in precisely the same spirit as Hobsbawm in his arguments for the high artificiality of nationalist constructs. Accordingly, we question the distinction between the premodern and the modern that Hobsbawm's thesis presumes and argue that modern and premodern Jewish appeals to tradition and continuity share more than divides them. The more important issues are how appeals to tradition function in specific historical contexts and how traditions move beyond their origins and become accepted as legitimate. At certain key moments, we will argue, one witnesses a culture-wide complicity in accepting innovations as traditional despite the widespread understanding that circumstances have changed beyond recognition—or even precisely because of that understanding. It is not, then, that traditions are invented and the history of their invention is suppressed and discovered later by historians. Rather, people accept traditions as legitimate because historical conditions have changed in some decisive manner; and tradition, understood in our strong sense, papers over the change.

Gershom Scholem once made a similar point, arguing that in understanding the problem of tradition in Judaism, one "must distinguish between two questions. The first is historical: How did a tradition endowed with religious dignity come to be formed? The other question is: How was this tradition understood once it had been accepted as a religious phenomenon? For the faithful promptly discard the historical question once they have accepted a tradition; this is the usual process in the establishment of religious systems."[5] The analysis of tradition that we propose shares Scholem's emphasis on how traditions are received. It also accepts Hobsbawm's focus on the kind of "rapid transformation of society" that "weakens or destroys the social patterns for which 'old' traditions had been designed": change is the sine qua non, the condition of possibility, of tradition in our strong sense, even though tradition is about making claims to continuity, to things not having changed at all. But we try to extend these questions into premodern times and to ask whether the invention of tradition is necessarily a response to modernity—and if not, how its dynamics worked in premodernity.[6]

Understanding the seeming paradoxes of tradition in Judaism—acknowledging the intimate connection between tradition and change—helps explain the historical development of a specifically Jewish religious discourse from ancient Judaism to the modern era. In what follows, then, we will look at how tradition has functioned in Judaism at certain key moments of rupture: in the Second Temple period, in the centuries following the Islamic conquests, and in the nineteenth and twentieth centuries. Our concern throughout will be to understand how appeals to continuity became the means by which Judaism either absorbed and legitimated innovations or sacralized ancient practices.

Tradition: The Term, Its History, and Its Sacralization in Ancient Judaism

The era before the destruction of the Second Temple saw the birth of a new way of talking about the Jewish past, one encapsulated in a new term: in Hebrew, *masoret*; in Greek, *paradosis*. The term *paradosis* is attested in a specifically Jewish context as early as Paul. In discussing his past as a Jew, Paul explained that he persecuted the church in his extreme zeal for ancestral traditions.[7] *Paradosis* is also the regular designation in the Gospels and in Josephus for the special tradition of the Pharisees.[8] In one key passage, Josephus describes the difference between the Pharisees and the Sadducees: the former observed regulations, not found in the written law of Moses, that previous generations had supposedly handed down (*paredosan*) to them. While those laws admittedly fell outside the written canon, the Pharisees nonetheless claimed for them a pedigree in transmitted tradition. This view provoked extensive debate with the Sadducees, who denied the validity of the Pharisaic traditions. Josephus expressed this Pharisaic notion of tradition elsewhere, too: in explaining the policy of Salome Alexandra (76–67 B.C.E.), he wrote that she handed the real power to the Pharisees, who used it to restore the regulations from the traditions of their fathers (*kata tēn patrōian paradosin*) that had been abrogated by her father-in-law, John Hyrcanus (134–104 B.C.E.), a generation earlier when he deserted the Pharisees for the Sadducees. As early as the first century C.E., at the time of Josephus, our source for this story—but perhaps even several centuries earlier, at the time of John Hyrcanus—Pharisaic Jews recognized the power of tradition as a tactic of legitimation.[9]

As for the Hebrew term *masoret*, although it appears even earlier in the Hebrew Bible, there it bears a meaning different from tradition.[10] Nor does it appear in that sense in books of the later Second Temple period, including Ecclesiasticus (Ben Sira). Though attestations of the term *paradosis* suggest that *masoret* may have been prominent in Jewish discourse in Hebrew even before the destruction of the Temple, the earliest use of *masoret* to mean tradition appears in the tannaitic stratum of Hebrew sources (second–third centuries C.E.). In the Tosefta, fowl is said to be eaten permissibly "according to *masoret*," on the authority of tradition.[11] Here the term bears its simple, weak sense, a corpus of knowledge handed down over the generations, in this case, probably nothing more than a list of permissible birds. It means neither more nor less than that—even if its use here seems to invoke some vague body of transmitted knowledge in order to bolster the authority of laws whose origins were unknown.

Unlike this soft or weak meaning of tradition, one finds it used in the Mishnah in the stronger sense to describe the practice of the families of Rabban Gamaliel and R. Ḥananyah, who performed one more prostration than others in the Temple "since they had a tradition [*masoret*] from their ancestors that the ark was buried" in a particular place.[12] Here, the term *masoret* bears a more complex meaning. Precisely because the location of the lost vessels of Solomon's Temple was unknown, they carried important associations with claims to authority. This is apparent from 2 Maccabees, which begins with two epistles, followed by the epitome of Jason of Cyrene's account of the Hasmonean revolt. The second epistle relates the supposed discovery of the fire from the altar of the First Temple, hidden but allegedly preserved in liquid form. When the liquid was poured on the altar of the Second Temple in the days of Nehemiah, the fire flamed up once more, providing the Second Temple with legitimacy via a link of continuity.[13] The eventual discovery of the hidden vessels of the destroyed Temple also played a significant role in some millennial scenarios. This was already the case in a section of 2 Maccabees describing the time of the destruction of the First Temple, when Jeremiah supposedly reprimanded the Jews who wanted to mark the way to the place where he had hidden the vessels because "the place shall remain unknown, he said, until God finally gathers his people together and shows mercy to them" (2 Mc 2:7–8). Josephus similarly told the story of a Samaritan who promised to find the hidden vessels "where Moses had deposited them." Pontius Pilate ordered Roman troops to attack this Samaritan and many of his followers, and, according to Josephus, they were killed.[14] Pilate understood that this was not an innocent archaeological excavation, but an action fraught with eschatological meaning and a challenge to Roman rule. It was a claim about the past with important political implications for the present.

In the Mishnah, then, the knowledge of where the ark was hidden was not a simple matter of information passed down from generation to generation, but a special sort of claim to a connection with the past. Since no one knew where the vessels of Solomon's Temple were actually located, this was likely an invented tradition, in Hobsbawm's terms—in this case, one easily identified—but that is not the key point. What is crucial is that the families of Rabban Gamaliel and R. Ḥananyah reinforced this supposed knowledge with a demonstrative special practice—bowing one more time than everyone else—with the concomitant implication that they held the keys to the millennium. It was, in short, intended as a claim to these families' authority in the here and now (and perhaps to the status of the Mishnah's editor, Judah I, who claimed descent from Gamaliel and, in turn, from Hillel and King David). If so, this source is a first indication that, over and above its weak sense as the simple transmission of information, tradition bore a stronger meaning closely associated with matters of authority and status, in which the past was construed in such a way as to serve the needs of the present.

Appeals to the Past

Indeed, from the second century B.C.E. onward, Jews had begun to view the past very differently from before. The present had undergone radical changes, the new Hasmonean high priesthood and the achievement of independence from Seleucid rule being the most important ones. These transformations awakened hopes of imminent redemption that were quickly frustrated when, a few generations later, the Jews of Palestine once again found themselves subjugated to a world empire—this time, the Romans. Indicative of the transformative nature of these events are the differing attitudes toward the past expressed in three texts: the book of Ezra; *Miqtsat ma'aseh ha-torah* (Some precepts of the law), found at Qumran and known as 4QMMT; and the Mishnah. Admittedly, centuries separate these texts, and they come from different groups of ancient Jews. Nevertheless, their similarities are as worthy of note as their differences.

In the fifth century B.C.E., Ezra had painted the past as a stark lesson in how not to behave. The past was filled with unspecified errors for which he could feel only shame, and those errors had led to disaster. Even worse, the present was perpetuating the errors of the past, a dangerous practice that would inevitably culminate in the same destructive consequences.[15] True, God had seen fit to grant the exiles some measure of restoration at the hands of the Persian kings, but this would not last long if the current generation disregarded the divine commandments, as their ancestors had done. The same attitude characterized the appeals to the past of the Judahite exiles whom Jeremiah encountered in Egypt: as they saw it, they had been prohibited from worshiping the (non-Yahwistic) gods of their choice, and, as a result, the present was awful.[16] These exiles shared the same attitude toward the past as Ezra, even if they differed radically on the specific errors committed. For both camps, the past taught by negative example.

The author of 4QMMT, conventionally dated to the late second century B.C.E., saw the past as containing both good and bad examples, from which one might learn proper behavior by more than mere negation.[17] The "good" kings, David in particular, received God's aid and forgiveness and demonstrated that if one lived correctly, the consequences would be favorable. Similarly, Solomon's reign was an era of blessing, while the bad kings, such as Jeroboam, brought endless curses upon the people. The author of 4QMMT advised his addressee to learn from the past as follows: "Think of the kings of Israel and contemplate their deeds: whoever among them feared [the To]rah was delivered from troubles."[18]

For the authors of the first chapter of tractate *Avot* in the Mishnah, edited in the form we have it by the mid- to late third century C.E., the past had already become entirely authoritative. The past was the source of a binding tradition, handed down over the generations, and it was this past on whose stature the text meant to draw in citing the entire chain of transmission as an unbroken one, from the revelation at Sinai to the rabbis quoted in the Mishnah itself.[19] But this tradition remained controversial and far from accepted by all. The most important dissent in rabbinic sources appears in *Avot de-Rabbi Natan*, whose origins go back to the third century C.E. (even if its final redaction was later). There, the challenge to tradition was placed in the mouths of the Sadducees, who claimed that the Pharisees' adherence to tradition deprived them of legitimate pleasures in this world for no reason, since in the world to come they gained nothing.[20] The Sadducees were probably made to voice this belief because the authors of *Avot de-Rabbi Natan* held them to believe that the world to come was an illusion. Yet despite the critique that *Avot de-Rabbi Natan* attributed to them, it is likely, if not certain, that the Sadducees had their own way of connecting their special teachings to the past, one different from the Pharisaic way, but no less anchored in precedent. As suggested decades ago by Jacob Z. Lauterbach, the Sadducees based their claim to authority on the accumulated precedents of a priestly court meeting in the Temple in Jerusalem.[21] In one way or another, then, all the groups of the Second Temple era—whether they saw the golden age as recent or more distant, as adjacent to the present or separated from it by a huge chasm, as a source of favorable or unfavorable examples or of both at the same time—claimed the prestige of the past as one basis for their self-understanding.

This was even true of those groups who based themselves on new revelation, such as the Qumran group and the early Christians—despite the usefulness of revelation as a way of circumventing the need for claims to continuity with the past.[22] They could also accuse rivals of lacking continuity with the past, as Jesus criticized the Pharisees for violating the law of God by observing a tradition that was no more than a human creation, a tradition of men.[23] For that reason, Mishnah *Avot* can be said to reflect more than only the Pharisaic heritage of rabbinic Judaism. *Masoret* or *paradosis* was an important aspect of Pharisaic ideology; the Pharisees may even have employed the terms exclusively and others may have thus avoided them; but the Pharisees shared the turn to the past with the other groups of their era, all of whom used it to justify their version of how to live in the present. Conversely, the easiest way to discredit rival groups was to accuse them of having invented their way of observing the Torah, of following new inventions. Each group reserved for itself alone the claim to a legitimate connection with the past. As with Hobsbawm's critique of nationalist pageantry and Marx's of the pretensions of 1848, the ancient accusation of invented tradition served the interests of debunking claims to authority, continuity, and legitimacy. There is nothing modern about this strategy.

Enlisting the Weak in Defense of the Strong

The development of this strong sense of tradition led those who defended it to enlist tradition in its weak sense to help prop up particular strong traditions. One outstanding ancient example is a story told in various rabbinic texts about Hillel the Elder and his virtues in debating those who did not follow the rabbinic or Pharisaic tradition. As narrated in *Avot de-Rabbi Natan*:

> A certain man once stood before Shammai and said to him: "Master, how many Torahs do you have?" "Two," Shammai replied, "one written and one oral." Said the man: "The written one I am prepared to accept, the oral one I am not prepared to accept." Shammai rebuked him and dismissed him in a huff.
>
> He came before Hillel and said to him: "Master, how many Torahs were given?" "Two," Hillel replied, "one written and one oral." Said the man: "The written one I am prepared to accept, the oral one I am not prepared to accept."
>
> "My son," Hillel said to him, "sit down."
>
> He wrote out the alphabet for him [and, pointing to one of the letters,] asked him: "What is this?" "It is *aleph*," the man replied.

Said Hillel: "This is not *aleph* but *bet*. What is that?" he continued.
The man answered: "It is *bet*."
"This is not *bet*," said Hillel, "but *gimmel*."
[In the end,] Hillel said to him: "How do you know that this
is *aleph* and this *bet* and this *gimmel*? Only because our ancestors
of old handed it down to us that this is *aleph* and this *bet* and this
gimmel. Even as you have taken this in good faith, so take the other
in good faith."[24]

This text is not as simple as it might seem. It does indeed retroject later
rabbinic concepts such as the dual Torah, oral and written, onto the time of
Hillel the Elder, but this is not our prime concern here.[25] What is of particular
interest to us is that this text employs the alphabet—which is widely perceived
to be part of the common store of knowledge passed from generation to generation, a part of nature in the eyes of antiquity—in defense of the special
ways of life of Hillel and his fellow rabbinizing Pharisees, their "oral" law.[26] In
short, it employs tradition in our weak sense in defense of the claim to tradition in the strong sense.

This is not as surprising as it might seem. Mary Douglas argued persua-
sively that institutions classify and organize the world by means of analogy.
That is why there are so many classificatory schemes that use the human body
as their template or that are modeled on basic social or biological facts such
as the king–the people or male-female. As Douglas concluded, "the shared
analogy is a device for legitimizing a set of fragile institutions."[27] Douglas's
insight helps explain why, when one argues for the legitimacy of tradition in
the strong sense, the most appropriate analogy on which to base that claim is
tradition in the weak sense: it gives an aura of natural simplicity and continuity to a construct that is anything but simple and continuous. Paraphrasing E.
M. Forster's comment on "genius," Aleida Assmann notes that the very sound
of the word "tradition" "exempts us from discovering its meaning."[28] In its
weak sense, tradition's claim to authority is automatic and self-understood. It
is that sense of obvious legitimacy on which tradition in the strong sense seeks
to capitalize. The goal of bolstering tradition in the strong sense on the basis of
its weak sense is the same as the objective of every established order, as stated
by Pierre Bourdieu: to effect "the naturalization of its own arbitrariness."[29]

What, precisely, was at stake during the Hasmonean rebellion and the age
of Second Temple sectarianism? Why the prevalence of this particular type of
appeal to the past? This was an era of rapid change, with a new high priest-

hood, the attainment of political independence under the Maccabees, and then its loss with the Roman conquest. Appeals to the past at times like this are virtually guaranteed, but they reflect a paradoxical situation. Groups claim to base their novel responses to new circumstances on the past in order to ground as firmly as possible their way of coping with change. This suggests that innovation in response to new circumstances and claims to continuity with the past are bound up with each other. Tradition, in the strong sense of the term for which we are arguing here, was one strategy for coping with change, often the strategy of choice: it was intended to foreclose certain changes by claiming a monopoly on the past; that claim, in turn, was calculated to justify the assertion of a monopoly on a present and a future from which change was supposedly excluded. This claim ultimately served to legitimate specific changes in response to the new situation.[30] Like all such claims, it could be disputed, refuted, denied, or contested by competing claims; and whether those claims rested on an invented past is almost impossible to determine in many cases and ultimately of no consequence. What is important from our perspective is that the need to assert a monopoly on the past came in direct response to a radically different present; and that the claim to possess tradition gave this response an aura of antiquity. Tradition and change were therefore inextricably linked, like two sides of a single coin.

Tradition and Sacralization in the Middle Ages

Jews in the Middle Ages elevated claims on behalf of tradition from local, ad hoc arguments for the continuity between past and present—the role they play in the Second Temple and rabbinic texts discussed above—to general guarantors of the authenticity of the rabbinic variety of Judaism itself. This change arose partly because of a new tendency toward philosophical synthesis; but it reflected a change not just in style but in substance. The main causes were the adoption of new types of scholarship and new techniques for transmitting it; contact with Islamic scholasticism; and confrontation with the Qaraite challenge to the exclusive legitimacy of rabbinic Judaism.

The changes in this era were not merely intellectual but geopolitical. Though the Islamic conquests united Jewish communities politically, the resulting migrations also separated them from one another by distances exponentially greater than any in their entire previous history. This, among other things, must have created the sense that an irredeemable rupture had severed the biblical past from the present.[31] At the same time, Islamic religious discourse offered Jews new methods of pouring tradition into the fissures between past and present. The tension between continuity and change in the wake of the conquests can be seen most clearly in two innovations from which many others followed: Jews' adoption of the codex form for books and, along with it, the written rather than oral transmission of texts; and a proliferation of new types of historical claims on behalf of the antiquity of rabbinic interpretations. Both these trends reached their culmination in the tenth century.

Written and Oral Transmission

Though the codex had been in use among Christians since the second century C.E., particularly for biblical texts, Jews had generally avoided it in favor of the scroll, probably because of its association with Christian learning.[32] But after the Muslim embrace of the codex, Jews followed suit: the earliest reference to a Jewish codex appears in *Halakhot gedolot*, a legal compendium of ca. 800–850, and significantly, the word used for it is Arabic (*mushaf*).[33]

The codex did not eliminate the scroll as the traditional form of the Jewish book; it elevated it to greater importance. The scroll was now reserved as the vehicle for books that made special claims on tradition, such as the text of the Torah used in liturgical settings, which had been written on a scroll in accordance with late antique rabbinic law. Jews embraced the codex by sacralizing the older format, which now took on the significance of lawyers' and judges' wigs in Hobsbawm's essay: the halakhic insistence on scrolls of the law assumed new meaning once the scroll had become outmoded.

There is an irony in this: the type of Torah scroll that was sacralized was also something of a novelty by ancient standards. While the Temple was standing and in the years immediately following, there were very few copies of the entire Pentateuch in existence.[34] The Torah at the Temple, from which the high priest read on Yom Kippur, contained the entire Pentateuch, or so one understands from a section of the Mishnah in which the high priest explains that, although he has just read the relevant section from Leviticus from a scroll, he was reciting the section from Numbers by heart, even though the scroll contained it, too. He thereby called attention to the unusual nature of his scroll.[35] The finds from the Judean desert combined with rabbinic evidence suggest that the high priest's scroll on Yom Kippur as described in the Mishnah was one of very few full Torah scrolls at the time. Only one of the Judean desert Pentateuch fragments contains at least three books of the Pentateuch, and it was written in the first part of the second century C.E. Most other biblical scrolls from the Judean desert contain one of the five books of Moses (only roughly five scrolls include two books).[36] All this would change when the full Torah scroll, with two handles to cope with its huge dimensions, became not only widespread but obligatory in liturgical settings.[37] By the early Middle Ages, the tractate *Soferim* (3:4), which postdates the eighth century, prohibited writing a scroll with only two books of the Pentateuch.[38] This suggests that doing so had been a common practice. All Torah scrolls were now prepared according to a standard that had once applied only to the scroll(s) in the Temple. Arguably, only a vastly expanded trade and production of parchment after the Islamic conquests allowed these comparatively enormous scrolls to be produced in significant numbers. One of the earliest known full versions of the Pentateuch written in scroll form supports our conclusion. It is preserved in fragments in the Cairo Genizah, and it dates to between the eighth and tenth centuries.[39]

Meanwhile, the earliest Jewish codices, from the ninth century, are manuscripts of the Bible. Jews adopted the codex format for nonliturgical biblical texts and other books, not only unproblematically but rapidly and with great enthusiasm.[40] The chronological overlap between the legislation about Torah scrolls in *Soferim*, the earliest examples of full Torah scrolls, and the spread of the codex among Jews is significant. It suggests that sacralizing the old scroll form allowed for the acceptance of the codex, or that the new and more convenient codex allowed the scroll to be sacralized. Each development facilitated the other.

The Work of the Masoretes

As for the contents of those biblical codices, though the biblical canon had been a settled matter since the third century C.E., the texts of each book continued to reflect variations for more than a millennium. When in the late eighth, ninth, and early tenth centuries attempts were finally made to collate and systematize the text, the project assumed the name "Masorah," related to the word *masoret*, meaning transmitted tradition. The term reflects the claim that this version of the biblical text merely codified an accumulated oral tradition dating back to antiquity.

But what, in fact, was the masoretic text? First, there were various masoretic traditions, and their very multiplicity renders problematic the notion of the faithful transmission of some antique Urtext. Second, since even the consonantal text of the Bible was still not quite fully unified, the various masoretic texts retained important textual variations. (We would explain these as representing different recensions, while medieval scholars might have seen them as the effects of faulty transmission.) Third, the Masoretes added to the consonantal text a new system of vowel signs and neumes, or symbols for cantillation—in other words, they invented new written symbols to represent the sound of the text as it was supposed to have been transmitted orally. In that sense, the Masorah was a symptom of the growing dominance of written transmission: even the sound of the text was now represented in written form. Finally, though the surviving lists of masoretic scholars date the earliest masoretic work to the late eighth century, the earliest direct evidence of actual masoretic manuscripts dates to the end of masoretic activity in the late ninth; almost by definition, there is no evidence that the Masorah preserved some earlier oral mode of reading the text.[41] The Masorah presents the problem of tradition in a nutshell: it claimed to preserve but arguably created what was retroactively claimed to be "tradition." Just as paradoxically, the transmission of the Masorah helped to erode the oral tradition that it claimed to preserve by committing it to the authority of writing.

As with the shift from scroll to codex, the spread of the Masorah sacralized the old way of writing Torah scrolls, without vowels and neumes, so that texts read in synagogues had to be unvocalized. At the same time, the masoretic text quickly underwent its own process of sacralization, with the result that, by the twelfth century, it had been accepted universally as the canonical one, to the point that not just rabbinic Jews but Qaraites—who otherwise felt no particular attachment to the theory of tradition that the Masorah represented—expressed the view that the Torah had been revealed to Moses on Sinai with its masoretic marks already in place. This is a particularly remarkable belief when one considers that as recently as the eleventh century, the ge'onim of Baghdad had stated plainly that the original scroll given to Moses on Sinai contained consonants only. The opinion that the Masorah had been revealed on Sinai was so persuasive that it continued unchallenged until the sixteenth century, when the rise of humanism and the study of the Greek and Latin classics offered new methods of analysis for problems of textual transmission. Yet even then, the belief in the antiquity of the Masorah—or put another way, in the Masoretes' work as one of recovery and representation rather than innovation—was remarkably durable. In 1538, the Italian Jewish humanist Elia Levita (1469–1549) published *Masoret ha-masoret* (The tradition of the

Masorah), in which he argued that vowel points had been added to the consonantal text of the Bible only late in its diffusion; his view met with resistance from the Jewish humanist Azarya de' Rossi (ca. 1511–77) and the Christian Hebraist Johannes Buxtorf (1564–1629).[42]

The remarkable tenacity with which scholars and ordinary believers alike held the masoretic text to be ancient cannot be ascribed to the text itself or its singlehanded power to convince believers of its authenticity. One must seek the explanation instead in the history of the text's transmission and the dominance of the belief that the Jewish canon and Jewish practice were rooted in something ancient and revealed.

Naturalizing the Sacred

An index of the success of the masoretic project—particularly in its Tiberian form—is the degree to which it was not merely sacralized but naturalized. Almost as soon as masoretic codices began to circulate, Jewish scholars from Syria to Iberia expressed the belief not merely in the authenticity of the text it contained but in the purity and superiority of Hebrew as spoken—not read or written but *spoken*—by the Jews of Tiberias, as if they were heirs to a continuous practice of Hebrew pronunciation.[43] Thus did the "established order," to quote Bourdieu again, accomplish "the naturalization of its own arbitrariness."[44]

Among those who expressed this belief was 'Eli ben Yehudah ha-Nazir, a native of Tiberias, who wrote in a linguistic treatise of ca. 915 that when he had doubts about the accuracy of his work on the language of the Bible, in order to test his results, he would simply step outside. "I used to spend much time sitting in the squares and streets of Tiberias, listening to the speech of the marketplace and the simple people," he wrote. "I would observe their language and its grammar to see whether something in my grammar was lacking or there was something incorrect in my understanding and in the pronunciation of Hebrew and the various dialects of Aramaic, by which I mean the language of the Targum and so on, which is very close to Hebrew. . . . My findings turned out to be true and correct."[45]

The suggestion that Hebrew was spoken in Tiberias in the tenth century is far-fetched, especially given ha-Nazir's contention that "simple people" spoke it. Aramaic is more plausible: there must have been at least one, if not several, generations of bilingualism before Arabic fully replaced Aramaic as the spoken language of Jews in Palestine. But the historical verifiability of ha-Nazir's claim is not the point. Rather, it is that he believed Tiberian Hebrew to be superior to all other varieties. He also cast that belief in terms similar to contemporaneous arguments about the purity of bedouin Arabic in debates about the inimitability (*i'jāz*) of the language of the Qur'ān. Both those ideologies—the Jewish one elevating Tiberian Hebrew and the Muslim one elevating bedouin Arabic to the level of sacred paradigm—served as a means of claiming that the sacred was also natural. The identity of the sacred with the natural served as the ultimate safeguard of the authenticity of revealed Scripture. In the Jewish case, that belief emerged precisely at the point when the study of Hebrew was changing irrevocably under the impact of Arabic. This reflects a perennial pattern among Jews, particularly during moments of rapid change and intensified contact with new modes of cultural production: making claims for their distinctiveness from others (Hebrew as a uniquely Jewish inheritance) in terms shared with those others (the inimitability of qur'ānic Arabic).[46]

Nor did ha-Nazir's opinion reflect mere Tiberian partisanship. From the tenth through the twelfth centuries, Jews from the Atlantic to the Euphrates expressed similar views. In his *Kitāb hidāyat al-qārī* (Guide for the reader), the eleventh-century Palestinian Qaraite linguist Abū l-Faraj Hārūn ibn al-Faraj remarked:

> It is a commonplace that the way of the Land of Israel is the
> original, and this is what is called the Tiberian reading [*al-qur'ān
> al-tabarānī*]. What we have said is confirmed by the fact that any
> scholar [from Palestine] who travels to distant lands is eagerly
> begged by the exiles there to teach their children the reading of the
> Land of Israel: they absorb it from him and make him sit [among
> them] in order to learn it from him rigorously. Anyone who has
> come from the diaspora to the Land of Israel behaves like a for-
> eigner in his anxiety to learn the reading of the Land of Israel and in
> his abandonment of his own.[47]

Thus did Jews come to accept the idea that something new was, in fact, so hoary, ancient, and authentic that it could be explained only as autochthonous.

The parallel with bedouin Arabic may not be merely a case of "influence" or "cultural competition," even if the transformation of Hebrew literature in contact with Arabic was profound. It may have been a parallel development, a possibility suggested by parallels with other languages. Sanskrit, for instance, became the sacred language of a sacerdotal class under very specific historical circumstances, though the nature of the evidence prevents those circumstances from being clearly understood; it seems to have arrived from outside the area where it ultimately settled and assumed increasing prestige with the rise of its priestly champions. By the end of the first millennium B.C.E., Sanskrit was touted as a "natural," autochthonous product of the region to which it had migrated, which the early grammarians called the Āryāvarta (identified as the Indo-Gangetic plain). The Sanskrit scholar and grammarian Patanjali (second century B.C.E.), in his *Mahābhāṣya*, describes the Āryāvarta as the native country of the *śiṣṭa*s, Brahmans who used classical Sanskrit as true native speakers without having studied its grammar. According to the classical grammatical tradition, grammars existed not in order to explain how to use Sanskrit, but to enable students to recognize the *śiṣṭa*s, who possessed grammatical knowledge despite the fact that they had not studied it. In short, Sanskrit's prestige rose under specific historical conditions but was quickly naturalized and granted metaphysical status. The traces of the transformation were covered over in a halo of sacralization: the language's prestige now became eternal, and its link to the Āryāvarta was presumed to be natural.[48]

Similarly, most of the statements on behalf of the purity and authenticity of Tiberian Hebrew actually postdate the acceptance of the Tiberian Masorah as the authoritative version of the biblical text. This suggests that, as with Sanskrit, beliefs about Tiberian Hebrew's prestige were a function of the spread of the masoretic text. The causality was, of course, understood the other way around. After all, the circumstances of Jewish life and of Hebrew textual transmission had by now changed beyond recognition and no one could remember what they had been in late antiquity and the early Islamic period. Jews not only accepted the authenticity of the Masorah but made statements claiming for it an even greater authenticity than it claimed for itself—precisely because they could no longer imagine the process that brought it into being.

Oral and Written Transmission

In the ninth and tenth centuries, the transmission of the biblical text served as a motor of the spread of the codex among Jews, just as it had among Christians in the third and fourth. For Jews, it also served as a motor of the spread of the techniques of written textual transmission. In time, rabbinic conceptions of writing and orality changed radically, and they came to provoke their own protests on behalf of the sacredness of written texts—and of oral transmission. In this case, both the old and the new methods were sacralized, but for different purposes: written texts of the Bible became sacred objects for use in liturgical contexts, while the oral transmission of rabbinic texts began to carry new weight as a claim to authenticity, even when those texts were, in fact, transmitted in writing.

The changing roles of oral and written transmission were partly a function of the codex and the spread of paper manufacture in the Near East after the eighth century, which made books much more widely available than before. But the technological explanation can never stand alone. New ideologies of orality and writing played a large role in these changes. In principle, both Jewish and Muslim religious specialists believed in the importance and even the necessity of oral transmission as a safeguard on the authenticity of tradition, even if in practice, written transmission became widespread in both traditions. But the specialists of each religion reacted differently to the contradiction between theory and practice. The Muslim scholarly class (*'ulamā'*) claimed so profoundly to mistrust written transmission that they required books to be copied not from other manuscripts but by having their contents recited aloud and copied from the aural model. They championed this method of transmission not just for sacred works but for any form of knowledge, and authors continued to declaim their works before audiences who transcribed them and then became licensed to transmit them orally themselves.[49] In theory, the oral intermediary was necessary to the work's proper transmission; in practice, licenses (*ijāzāt*) were granted even to children who had sat through a work's recitation before learning how to write. The system of granting licenses, then, in reality constituted a mechanism for maintaining some scholarly control over the transmission of knowledge. Such control must have seemed the best way to safeguard the authenticity of tradition during a period when conversion to Islam multiplied the number of Muslims exponentially, and those Muslims were dispersed over a geographically broad area.

Gregor Schoeler has argued convincingly that this system of transmission via an oral intermediary had its origin in Hellenistic models of education, which distinguished rigorously between private notes to aid memory (*hypomnēmata*) and the official redaction and declamation of a work (*syngramma*). Only the latter was appropriate for transmission. Schoeler follows Saul Lieberman's discovery of this distinction in wide use among late antique Jews, who based themselves on Hellenistic models in expressing prohibitions on transmitting written matters orally and oral matters in writing—even if in practice they, too, may have kept written texts.[50] Strangely, however, by the time Muslims adopted this system for transmitting knowledge, Jews had abandoned it and had begun transmitting even rabbinic literature in writing. Not only that, but Jews never developed a system of licensing transmission. They simply copied books from other books. This is odd, given that rabbinic teachers stood at the end of a long history of using the very same methods of oral recitation that their Muslim contemporaries now strived to use.

By the tenth century, in fact, the oral monopoly on textual transmission had eroded so completely among Jews that it applied to only one Jewish text: the Babylonian Talmud. The ge'onim at the two rabbinic academies in Baghdad continued to insist that the Babylonian Talmud be learned orally. Yet even that insistence was, in some cases, merely theoretical, since the Babylonian Talmud had already been copied and mailed to followers of the ge'onim throughout the Mediterranean basin. And by the eleventh century, even the theoretical precedence of the oral transmission of the Babylonian Talmud had eroded. Hayya bar Sherira, ga'on of Pumbedita in Baghdad (1004–38), plainly admitted that written copies of the Babylonian Talmud were circulating within the yeshiva and that, in some instances, the version of the text they contained was more reliable than the one transmitted orally.[51] Even in the one place where claims to oral transmission still inspired veneration, it was giving way to writing.

The difference between Muslim suspicion of writing and the Jewish embrace of it may owe to the simple fact that there were fewer Jews than Muslims: small numbers helped scholars to preserve institutional monopolies on texts like the Talmud, even over great distances. There were fewer scholarly networks to be controlled. Nonetheless, the change to written transmission should not be understated. Talya Fishman has convincingly argued on behalf of a similar change attendant on increased book production in medieval Ashkenaz. She argues that there, "the textualization of rabbinic Judaism affected every aspect of Jewish life and culture; the authority of the text supplanted the master-disciple relationship through which tradition had been transmitted for centuries."[52] Yet effects are not causes. Even with their smaller numbers, the Jewish move "from ear to eye," as Colette Sirat has put it, must be explained.[53]

Rina Drory has offered a suggestive explanation. She emphasized the role of the Qaraites in this transformation, arguing that their enthusiastic adoption of certain literary innovations had, by the tenth century, helped break the traditional Jewish patterns of oral transmission in most fields of knowledge.[54] Before the tenth century, new works of rabbinic literature had striven to fit themselves into the old canonical genres, hidden behind collective authorship, anonymity, or pseudepigraphy, and had poured themselves into compendia organized mnemonically and/or associatively—for example, the midrash collections or the apocalypses compiled in Palestine during the early centuries of Islamic rule. Starting in the tenth century, rabbinic literature embraced innovations such as individual authorship, the use of an authorial voice, and new genres such as the monograph. The result was a remarkable outpouring of scholarly works in new forms and genres, and in a new literary language, Judeo-Arabic.

The figure who did the most to import the new models into the rabbinic canon was Se'adyah ben Yosef al-Fayyūmī, ga'on of Sura (928–42). This may seem paradoxical, given that he was a vehement anti-Qaraite and a champion of Babylonian rabbinic supremacy. In fact, one of Se'adyah's most effective tactics against those he opposed was to adopt the best of their arguments and systems to his own purposes. He accordingly produced works in disciplines and genres that had previously been the purview of Qaraites, Muslims, or Palestinian Rabbanites and ignored by the relatively closed circle of the academies in Baghdad: systematic theology, linguistics, liturgical poetry, polemics, biblical exegesis, and Judeo-Arabic Bible translations. Robert Brody has aptly called Se'adyah a "revolutionary champion of tradition."[55] Emblematic of Se'adyah's paradoxical radicalism was a traditionalist contention that may have seemed extreme even in its own time. In his *Book of Beliefs and Opinions*, Se'adyah argued that the Bible and its commandments remain opaque to human understanding without their accompanying rabbinic commentaries. To establish this conclusion, Se'adyah followed in the footsteps of Hillel the Elder in the story of the man who refused to accept the oral Torah: he enlisted the weak sense of tradition in support of the strong, claiming that without tradition, it would be impossible to know anything with certainty—even, as he put it with characteristic hyperbole, whether one is "the son of his mother, let alone the son of his father."[56] In Se'adyah's hands, scholarly continuity within chains of rabbinic discipleship turned into an epistemological necessity, the sole means of legitimating religious knowledge and of interpreting the various commandments set forth in the Bible.

The Qaraite challenge to tradition echoed Jesus' critique of the Pharisees' invented traditions as quoted in Mark 7:8–9 ("Their teachings are but rules taught by men"), in turn echoing Isaiah 29:13. Several Qaraites argued that rabbinic law was no more than "a commandment of men" rather than of God and "learned by rote" rather than through reason.[57] But one of the unintended consequences of this challenge was to drive Rabbanites such as Se'adyah to articulate ever more extreme arguments on behalf of the unbrokenness of rabbinic transmission and its centrality for understanding God's commandments.

Chains of Transmission

As paper manufacture and the volume of textual production in the Arabic-speaking world increased, Jews continued to defend oral transmission while furthering its erosion as a method of scholarship. For Babylonian Rabbanites, that erosion presented a particularly difficult dilemma: they were deeply committed to oral transmission, even if geographic circumstances did not allow them to make good on that commitment. Their dilemma is evident in the increasingly vehement claims they lodged on behalf of oral transmission as the best way to ensure the continuity of rabbinic tradition.

Though classical rabbinic literature contains implicit claims about the continuity of rabbinic discipleship and quotes teachers in the names of their students, the chains of transmission are never as long as among Muslim *ḥadīth* transmitters. Nor did rabbinic literature in late antiquity develop a thoroughgoing theory of transmission, as Islamic jurisprudence did. But a change is evident in a new use to which the single chain of rabbinic tradition in the first chapter of Mishnah *Avot* was put: the ge'onim 'Amram bar Sheshna (857–75) and Se'adyah elevated it to a new status by including its recitation in their liturgies for the Sabbath, probably as a traditionalist polemic. By the eleventh century, it was an established practice to read *Avot* aloud weekly, and it was likely evident to all that the targets of the recitation were the Qaraites.[58]

Contemporary parallels suggest that 'Amram and Se'adyah were not the only Jewish traditionalists in Baghdad. In the mid-tenth century, an Iraqi named Natan ha-Bavli arrived in Ifrīqiya and composed a profoundly tendentious account of the Jewish academies in Baghdad and the ostensibly special place that the Jews held at the caliph's court. Most telling was Natan's description of the ritual surrounding the installation of the exilarch in terms that evoked the ceremonial of an Abbasid court dominated by condottieri who had reduced the caliph to a mere puppet. Thus did Natan ha-Bavli try to convince the Jews of Ifrīqiya to offer the Iraqi yeshivot their allegiance, though at the time of his writing, Sura was probably already closed and would remain so for more than four decades (943–87). Natan's account is a quintessential instance of tradition in the strong sense, recorded for the consumption of out-siders with embellishments just at the moment when both the customs that it claimed to describe and the political power on which they rested were in steep decline. Similarly, in 986–87, Sherira bar Ḥananyah, ga'on of Pumbedita (968–1004), sent a responsum to the Jews of Qayrawān in Ifrīqiya in which he explained how the Mishnah and the Talmud were composed, detailing the entire chain of transmitters from biblical times to the ge'onim of Babylonia. His account must have assumed increased urgency in light of Sura's closure and the great distance from the yeshiva at which his followers now lay.

Over the tenth century, then—precisely the period when oral transmis-sion was eroding most rapidly—gaonic literature of Iraqi provenance elevated chains of tradition from local statements of discipleship to general guarantees of the authenticity of the entire body of rabbinic tradition. Claims to tradition were a means of suturing over a situation that had, in fact, changed.

The Qaraite Adoption of Tradition

By the tenth century, even Qaraites had begun accepting historical arguments as a means of expressing claims to religious authority—even though, prima facie, Qaraites had no reason to defend their own legitimacy on grounds other than reason: Of what use are historical claims to a group that has rejected the authority of tradition?[59] Yet by the tenth century, Qaraites began to trace their origins to 'Anan ben David, a scion of the Babylonian exilarchal house who was active in Baghdad during the reign of the Abbasid caliph al-Manṣūr (754–75)—before any Qaraites had existed.[60] The paradox that this represents is worthy of consideration. The Qaraite embrace of historical claims shows the effect of rabbinic thinking on Qaraism; it also shows the extent to which both schools of Judaism responded to some perceived crisis, one that was supposed to be remedied by new modes and methodologies of transmission but was only deepened by them. Most importantly, there is something to be learned about the ideological system of Judaism in general and its relationship to tra-dition in particular from the fact that the Qaraites, too, adopted claims to an-tiquity and continuity. A stance of pure innovation was unsustainable within the established vocabulary of Jewish religious self-legitimation.

Tradition as Change

The dynamic of tradition to which we are pointing differs from the mere use of precedent to justify innovations. Medieval Jewish sources are filled with appeals to tradition and appeals to the past. After the crusader massacres of 1096, when the Jews of the Rhineland opted to sacrifice their own children and commit suicide rather than submit to conversion to Christianity, their chroniclers justified their decision by calling it martyrdom and invoking biblical precedents such as Abraham's binding of Isaac. Thus did they use precedents to justify what was, in its own context, an innovation—perhaps even an innovation in response to the Christian ethos of crusading martyrdom, and thus an instance of Jews expressing their distinctiveness in the language of those from whom they strove to distinguish themselves. But it was still basically a simple invocation of the past to legitimate a present innovation.[61]

The examples above demonstrate something beyond this point: that there is an intrinsic, not merely an oppositional, relationship between rupture and tradition; that claims to continuity are most vocal precisely during times of rapid change; and that creating tradition involves strategies for underlining ruptures and discontinuities, not merely by making them appear as continuous with the past, but by calling attention to them as sacred.

Tradition and Sacralization in the Modern Period

From the late eighteenth century onward, tradition continued to serve as Judaism's main method of legitimating changes to religious practice and of confronting change.

Tellingly, this was as true for the modernizers as for the traditionalists. Moses Mendelssohn (1729–86) used the tools of enlightened reason to defend Judaism's time-honored practices and habits; but Moses Schreiber (known as the Ḥatam Sofer, 1762–1839) summoned arguments from the past—including the self-contradictory claim that Judaism was immutable and he was restoring the old ways—to justify practices that were unprecedentedly strict and thus entirely new. Whether one sees this as a case of custom trumping law or law trumping custom depends on how warmly one embraces his innovations. Either way, the Ḥatam Sofer was hardly alone in buttressing ever higher edifices of piety with building materials scavenged from history.[62]

A similar dynamic was at work in the movement that historians alternately call orthodoxy or neo-orthodoxy (we shall ask below what the prefix means), which arose in the 1840s in response to the reforms instituted in synagogues as far apart as Seesen and South Carolina. The challenge and the riposte shared the presumption that Judaism was subject to change over time, but the conclusions they drew were diametrically opposed: the reformers declared themselves no longer bound by the legal and ritual demands of Judaism, but only by its moral code as represented in the prophetic books of the Bible; the orthodox mounted a defense in the form of rigorous observance of the law. But orthodoxy, too, especially the early strain of it propounded by Samson Raphael Hirsch (1808–88), was entirely nontraditional in its methods, models of education, practices, and beliefs—particularly in its emphasis on the study of the Bible rather than Talmud. Despite their differences, the reformers and the orthodox both introduced changes into the synagogue service, including sermons in the vernacular, the use of a choir, and a clerical uniform. In that sense, Michael Meyer is correct to insist that each wing of the nineteenth-century struggle over Jewish religious practice should, in its own way, be understood as a mode of reform: by calling nineteenth-century orthodoxy a type of reform, he is bracketing its claim on tradition and understanding it instead as a response to modernity.[63] That the same religious phenomenon can be labeled traditionalist by its adherents and reformist by scholars underlines the dual nature of tradition to which we wish to call attention in this essay.

Sacralization, too, played an important role in Jewish movements in the modern period. A particularly demonstrative instance of this in the twentieth century was the championing of rabbinic infallibility, by which increasingly comprehensive claims for rabbis' stature attempted to prop up a position obviously felt to be weakened. Another session of rummaging around in the storehouse of sacred texts produced the notion of *da'at Torah*. This phrase first appears in the Babylonian Talmud, where it describes a well-founded conclusion, something certain and supported by reason, in contrast to a *da'at notah*, a probable interpretation without absolute certainty.[64] In the Hebrew translations of medieval Arabic philosophical works, *da'at Torah* was contrasted with *da'at ha-pilosofim* (the view of the philosophers) or *da'at ha-hamon* (the opinion of the common people), in order to emphasize the sophistication of the "Torah view" in theological points of contention. But in the twentieth century, *da'at Torah* was understood to be what made the rabbi master of all areas of knowledge and gave him the authority to decide on issues beyond the bounds of halakhah. In order to play this part, so the theory went, rabbinic authority had to be pure—the rabbi's world had to be based on the Torah and the Torah only; he could not be polluted by external knowledge. The more ignorant the rabbi was in conventional terms, the more natural and absolute his authority. Those propounding the notion of *da'at Torah* recognized that there was little in standard rabbinic texts that gave the rabbi this kind of authority. Nevertheless, they believed that exclusive immersion in the world of the Torah granted him a prophet-like status, so that he could speak authoritatively in the name of God on all subjects—making him, effectively, infallible.[65] As Gershon Bacon has noted, the parallel with Pius IX's proclamation of papal infallibility in 1870—precisely when nationalist forces finally broke the Vatican's hold on Rome—is hardly accidental.[66] Where geopolitical events deprived religious figures of authority, religious theory would restore it to them. Thus was the modern rabbi granted a new status made to appear traditional through sacralization.

Religious change among nineteenth-century Jews has been analyzed abundantly and convincingly enough elsewhere to exempt us from presenting more examples. We wish only to emphasize one point: the problem of change—and the solutions of tradition and sacralization—were not new to the modern period. Modern traditions were, in that sense, neither more nor less invented than those of earlier periods.

What, then, are we to make of the terms orthodoxy and neo-orthodoxy? The question also consumed nineteenth-century German Jews in the trenches of religious movements, with each camp accusing the other of having invented an inappropriate label. The reformers called the traditionalists *der sogenannte Orthodoxen* ("the so-called orthodox," or variations with "ostensibly" and "fake"); Samson Raphael Hirsch, in turn, accused them of having invented the epithet to denigrate the traditionalists.[67] Those who describe nineteenth-century religious innovation as orthodoxy are similarly faced with the dilemma of what to call what came before. The only viable alternative, "traditional Judaism," begs the question of what one means by "traditional." But if we admit that orthodoxies are subject to change and that self-proclaimed orthodoxies preceded the nineteenth century, we have to embrace the prefix.[68] And if we embrace the prefix, we must explain: What was really new about orthodoxy in the nineteenth century? Our research into premodern Judaism has led us to dispense with the untenable distinction between spontaneous, genuine tradition and the invented variety; likewise, the modes and methods of nineteenth-century orthodoxy were not so very different from those of the Mishnah or Se'adyah. Nor is the claim of invented tradition—with which Jesus criticized the Pharisees, medieval Qaraites dismissed the Rabbanites, and historians explain the nineteenth-century orthodox movement—a different tactic across periods. What differs is only the particular configuration of power that it challenges.

We emphasize this point because by the late twentieth century, historians of Judaism had reached a near-universal consensus that Jewish modernity was characterized by the diminished hold of religion on the lives of Jews, the weakening of institutional sources of authority and communal structures, and the reorganization of the Jewish community on a voluntary basis. The locus classicus of this argument is Jacob Katz's *Tradition and Crisis*, which posited an emerging space that he described alternately as "neutral" or as "semi-neutral" (again, the qualifying prefix is important) and that finally broke the power of the old society. According to Katz, the old society was relatively stable and always "saw the present as no more than an attempt—always unsuccessful—to maintain the ideals of the past." Though Katz noted in passing that the old world had endured a certain degree of change over time, he nonetheless held that premodern Jewish society "had achieved its full character at the very latest by the start of the Diaspora period [in 70 C.E.] and subsequently underwent merely minor changes in the many lands where Jews settled" until the challenges of modernity. Thus Katz's search for Weberian ideal types led him, by his own admission, to "gloss over many distinctions between German, Moravian-Bohemian, and Lithuanian-Polish Jewries of the sixteenth through eighteenth centuries," societies in which, he argued, "even the most serious events"—including the revolutions of 1648 and the Sabbatean movement of 1666—"were likely to evoke reactions only within the framework of traditional modes of thought and action." Katz was forced to admit that, at some point, the old structure buckled and collapsed. Pressed to identify causes, he found them in the cataclysmic challenges presented by Hasidism in Eastern Europe and the Jewish Enlightenment (Haskalah) in the West.[69] The fact that both were internal challenges has often been noted in pointing out the nationalist and internalist underpinnings of Katz's historiosophy. Both Hasidism and Haskalah, in his view, led to the ruin of the old institutional structures of education, the family, and the communal and administrative function of the synagogue. Modernity, in sum, was characterized by a waning commitment to the institutions of Jewish self-governance and to Jewish collective life.

Anyone who has taken even a desultory look at the letters of eleventh- and twelfth-century rabbis and other communal officials preserved in the Cairo Genizah—we offer the example of this historical setting because its communal life is the most densely and richly documented of any in premodern Jewish history—will concede that none of those problems was new to modernity. To take only the most representative change, a loose historiographic consensus dates the beginning of the decline of the Jewish community as an administrative body with authority over its members either to the migration across Europe of Iberian conversos returning to a Judaism that they hardly knew or to the rise of the modern European nation-state. But Genizah documents show that even in the eleventh and twelfth centuries, many Jews were indifferent to the demands of Jewish law or, even more frequently, were ignorant of them. Others failed to pay their dues to the community or otherwise attempted to remain on its margins. Rabbis and other communal officials were well aware of this and complained vociferously and repeatedly of the lack of authority they wielded over their congregants. Some explicitly admitted that they rarely exerted the power to coerce or persuade their followers to do anything. They imposed excommunications, which were easily evaded when the banned party moved to another town or converted to Islam, or when the community simply ignored the ban; the weakness of the punishment deterred more than one rabbi or ga'on from administering it. In extreme cases, there was the unpalatable option of petitioning the government to do the Jewish community's dirty work by imprisoning offenders.[70] Waning commitment to purportedly traditional modes of Jewish living must not, then, be seen as an innovation of modernity.[71] That is not to say that nothing distinguishes modernity from premodernity. But to argue for the dynamic of tradition as a distinguishing factor is to risk misunderstanding that dynamic in both periods.

The debate over the nature and rate of legitimate change continues to animate debates within Judaism and among those who study it. Traditions in the strong sense regularly emerge as central to those debates. The shared presumption is that these problems sprouted and grew in the soil of modernity. Yet that presumption rests on a notion that we find difficult to accept in light of the evidence we have examined—as though prior to modernity, Jews were unflaggingly pious, heirs to a continuous, organic, and unselfconscious tradition, and entirely lacking in the tools, the wherewithal, or the necessity to call upon arguments from the past with self-conscious intent. The converse presumption is also worth reexamining: that the effort to revive the past, to return it, and to find continuity with it is less genuine (or more manipulative) when it is made by modern people.

A major contribution to this debate was made more than a decade ago by Haym Soloveitchik, who asked just what, if anything, orthodox Jews at the end of the twentieth century had in common with the ancestors whose way of life they insisted they were practicing. Soloveitchik argues for signal differences between modern Jews and their predecessors: mass literacy; the easy availability of inexpensive reprints of rabbinic works; and a penchant for following stringent rulings. This argument is difficult to grasp if one insists on seeing tradition in Hobsbawmian terms. On the one hand, the past to which the Jews Soloveitchik describes sought to return was really there in the old books—in that sense, it was "genuine." On the other hand, it was illusory, because these books had not in the past served as a guide to religious life. The rulings that self-styled orthodox Jews now followed had had little use in the past, when life was governed instead by a living mimetic tradition (in the weak sense), and few people paid attention to the norms that the books prescribed. Here we meet the ultimate paradox: modern Jews became even more pious than their supposedly "traditional" predecessors by virtue of modern innovations. The change in this case was not merely offset printing, which allowed the average yeshiva student to own a library more vast than those of all but the most outstanding—and wealthy—scholars of previous generations. Now these Jews paid attention to what was written in books and asserted that, by doing so, they were taking their religious obligations seriously, basing their conduct on the most authoritative written sources, in contrast to other contemporary Jews whose lifestyles they meant to repudiate. One need only note the irony that a modern technological change helped feed a reaction against other aspects of modernity, and not for the first time. Like those before them, the communities Soloveitchik describes followed a model of the past itself already deeply altered because, of necessity, it was first filtered through the present.[72]

Toward a New Understanding of Tradition

If what we call "tradition in the strong sense"—claims of continuity with the past that serve the needs of the present—is not the same as Hobsbawm's "invented tradition," it is also not so far apart. We take issue, rather, with the implied judgments of value attendant on the distinction between genuine and invented traditions; and the implied homology between genuine tradition and the premodern, on the one hand, and invented tradition and the modern, on the other. Tradition in the weak sense is not permanently tied to short life expectancy, low levels of education, subsistence agriculture, sparse settlement, and unending starvation. Nor will modernity finally eradicate the unconscious devotion to tradition, leaving only the most headstrong and self-aware of revivalists among its proponents.

We are not the first to make this point. Edward Shils, in his 1981 book on tradition, launched a stalwart defense of the permanence of tradition as a part of human experience.[73] His argument responded to social scientific denunciations of tradition by his generation of scholars and launched a critique of the notion of progress, or at least of the presumption that progress is always good. Shils argued cogently that tradition is a permanent feature even of social settings that do not consciously profess to follow it. But while he seemed to recognize, here and there, the connection between change and tradition in the strong sense for which we are arguing, the main thrust of his book remained an apology for tradition. In the end, Shils was correct about the connection between change and tradition, but for a reason we believe that we can articulate more explicitly than he did: tradition, in our strong sense, is no stranger to innovation. It is, perhaps, even the most intimate companion of change, especially of rapid change.

Tradition, as we wish to understand it, can support existing authority structures or challenge them. It can be deployed by "churches" as well as by "sects." It can serve oral societies as much as literate ones, societies in which there are textual communities and a canon of authorized works or those in which everything is still up for grabs. The deployment of "strong" traditions differs from one social context to another; what remains constant is the link between those traditions, innovation, and change. Accordingly, the primary goal of historical analyses of tradition should not be to distinguish between the genuine and the invented types, but to explain the links between the specific claims made on tradition's behalf and the changes taking place when those claims are made.

What is at stake in this argument is making what may seem paradoxical—the appeal to tradition at times of great change—appear logical and explicable. The distinction between "genuine" and "invented" tradition lessens the paradox and thus fails to resolve it: one still has to explain why traditions are invented when they are, and why and how they become accepted as tradition. As Elias Bickerman noted, paraphrasing Vico, "people accept only the ideas for which their previous development has prepared their minds, and which, let us add, appear to be useful to them."[74] This understanding helps situate the dynamic of tradition not in an autonomous category of its own, but in the larger range of explanations for change and how change is legitimated. How can something new possess authority? This problem is especially crucial if the central institutions of a culture happen to be invisible or seem wholly natural, and they often do if they work. Claims to tradition in the strong sense are one solution to the problem.

Hannah Arendt, in her lectures on Kant, claimed that, in the modern period, tradition had lost the potential to grant authority. The authority of a founding political event such as the French Revolution consisted instead in its future continuity and its universal significance for posterity.[75] This is similar to Marx's claim that when a revolution appeals to the past, it betrays the revolutionary principles for which it stands, or Hobsbawm's division between self-conscious modernity and the innocent past. The fundamental presumption on which our analysis rests, by contrast, is that premodern appeals to tradition are not, by definition, more successful bids for legitimacy than modern ones.

Our analysis convinces us that questions of tradition might be productively brought back into the purview of broader problems of cultural memory, a point made in other guises by Aleida Assmann and Mark Salber Phillips.[76] But what distinguishes tradition in the strong sense from the other forms of cultural memory—in its objectives, its structure, and the means that it employs—is its consciousness of change. To deploy arguments from tradition is, by definition, to acknowledge historical change on two separate counts: it is to admit that the present is no longer what the past once was, and to argue that the future should be different from the present. In this sense, traditionalists are not always the guardians of stasis but can be the greatest proponents of change.

We close as we began: by returning to the Jewish experience and asking how and why Judaism absorbed innovations principally via appeals to continuity and became a religion centered on tradition. The sheer number of geographic and chronological contexts in which Jews have lived and thrived—and the flexibility and range of solutions they have devised in order to survive as a minority among empires and nation-states—offers part of the answer. Why, then, choose appeals to continuity rather than, for example, proclaiming innovation? One reason is that the living—especially when deprived of political power—need the support of the dead. G. K. Chesterton said this with characteristic paradox: "Tradition means giving votes to the most obscure of all classes, our ancestors. It is the democracy of the dead. Tradition refuses to submit to the small and arrogant oligarchy of those who merely happen to be walking about. All democrats object to men being disqualified by the accident of birth; tradition objects to their being disqualified by the accident of death."[77]

Or, as Orwell put it more darkly in *1984*, "'Who controls the past,' ran the Party slogan, 'controls the future: who controls the present controls the past.'"[78] In less cynical terms, groups in the present that hope for a future need ways to claim a connection with the past, whatever intellectual somer-saults and sleights of hand are necessary to establish that tie. Denied, after the Hasmonean period, the appeal to mass conversion, denied the overwhelming success in numbers that Christianity and Islam achieved, and deprived of po-litical power as a means of either demonstrating or imposing the truth of their way, Jews appealed instead to the past and to the success of continuity—a no-tion that consequently provokes particularly acute anxiety in organized Jewish communities in the diaspora today and a somewhat different anxiety within Israel. The appeal to tradition, in the strong sense for which we have argued, is one of those sleights of hand.

Chapter 10

In the Path of Our Fathers:
On Tradition and Time from Jerusalem
to Babylonia and Beyond

Sylvie Anne Goldberg

The Hebrew terms *masoret* and *qabbalah*—both meaning "tradition"—offer us a concise, concrete overview of the dual dimensions of the concept of tradition in Judaism. While the verb *masar* means "to transmit," the verb *qibbel* means "to receive." Both terms convey the idea of some sort of movement.

To delve more deeply into their semantic meaning, one must consider the contexts in which they were originally used. The two sources of the term *masoret* are the prophecy of Ezekiel and Mishnah *Avot*.[1] Ezekiel describes the biblical covenantal tradition as *masoret ha-berit* (the *masoret* of the covenant), while in *Avot*, there appears the notion that rabbinic tradition is a protective fence around the laws of the Torah, *masoret siyag la-torah* ("the *masoret* is a fence around the Torah"). While the biblical *masoret* suggests the handing down of tradition as a complete source of revelation, the rabbinic *masoret* allows making additions to a tradition that is constructed over time. One should also take into account the expression *divrei qabbalah* ("words of tradition"), the traditions of the prophets, in which the emphasis is on revelation rather than reception. These are the threads that one has to unravel to glimpse what the term "tradition" refers to in the common conception of classical Judaism.

Moses, transmitting to the people of Israel the laws that he received on Mount Sinai, accomplished the move that led to the Covenant becoming a covenantal tradition (*masoret ha-berit*). The mishnaic sage Rabbi Joshua ben

Levi warned that all the teachings of the Bible, Mishnah, Talmud, and aggadah (that is, all the teachings of the tradition) had already been given to
Moses at Sinai, and so tradition was binding to the same degree as the written
Torah.[2] According to one set of statements in rabbinic literature, tradition is
as binding as law: "'What is the meaning of the verse "and I will give thee the
tables of stone, and the law and the commandments which I have written to
teach them" (Ex 24:12)?' asked Rabbi Levi ben Ḥama in the name of Rabbi
Shimʻon ben Laqish. *The tables of stone* are the Ten Commandments, the *Law*
is the Pentateuch, the *commandments* is the Mishnah, 'which I have written'
are the Prophets and the Hagiographa, 'to teach them' is the Gemara. This
exegesis teaches us that all these things were given at Sinai."[3]

Viewed from this perspective, the written and the oral law are two parts
of a whole, constituting what Judaism understands as "tradition." This conclusion is troublesome primarily in two situations: when a change or an adaptation of the law is required; and in the case of competing traditions or texts that
challenge a given tradition.

This chapter discusses a historical event in which both these situations
occurred: the controversy about the calendar that divided the Jewish world
during the tenth century, in which a would-be legislator had to grapple with
incompatible views concerning the authenticity of an established Jewish tradition, in a context in which the meaning and direction of Jewish time called
for rethinking. This controversy—which has become known to us only since
the discovery of the Cairo Genizah material—entangled the leading scholars
of the day in fierce polemics, lively debates, and argumentation over obscure
points.[4]

The Jewish World in the Tenth Century

What did the inner Jewish world in the early tenth century look like? It is still
worthwhile to ask this question, despite the numerous works already published about the geʼonim (640–1040) and the period of the Cairo Genizah
(900–1250): scholarship has carefully documented many facts but drawn few
conclusions about the development and maturation of the Jewish world in
that period.[5] Reunited by the Islamic conquests of the seventh century, the
whole Near East had become, for the first time since Alexander the Great in
the fourth century B.C.E., a single political entity. This meant that the Jews of
Palestine, Persia, and Iraq (or Babylonia, as they called it in the Jewish world)

were subjects of one and the same empire until the breakup of the caliphate in the tenth century. Although the Jews of Erets Israel and Babylonia had inherited diverse traditions reflecting the differences between the Greco-Roman and Persian civilizations in which they lived, they all had to cope with the new patterns of government that the rulers imposed upon them. The cultural differences then salient in the Jewish communities derived primarily from centuries of rivalry over political leadership between the rabbis of Palestine and those of the diaspora.

This period is one in which the main legal authority over the Jewish world was the ge'onim, be they in Babylonia (Iraq) or Palestine (the ga'on of Palestine supplanted the now obsolete function of the *nasi*).[6] Connections between the Jews of Palestine and Babylonia were improving and the two communities were becoming more interdependent. The first Qaraite settlement had been established in Jerusalem around 880.[7] Meanwhile in Babylonia, a quarrel between the ge'onim and the exilarch blurred the question of who was supposed to constitute the legitimate authority and gave increasing precedence to the spiritual power over the temporal one.[8] As far as it is possible to know, this was the context in which the calendar controversy broke out in 4681 A.M., around 921 C.E.

Calendrical and Geographic Differences

Since setting the calendrical order was the exclusive prerogative of the Sanhedrin, the proclamation of the months, the New Year, and the *'ibbur* (intercalary thirteenth month) was a duty reserved for the *nesi'im*, and later the ge'onim, of the Land of Israel.[9] Avoiding entering into the details of what still remains obscure, one should mention only that while Jerusalem, led by the ga'on Ben Me'ir (whose first name may have been Aaron), announced that the year 4682 would be proclaimed a regular short year, the leaders of Babylonian Jewry defended a different calculation and decided that the current year should be a leap year. If they were not able to reach an agreement, such a discrepancy would make Rosh Hashanah fall on a Tuesday in Jerusalem and a Thursday in Babylonia. Despite an exchange of vehement letters, neither of the two opposing sides renounced claims of its own legitimacy in declaring the calendar.[10] We are told by a well-known witness of the confrontation, the Christian historian Elijah of Nisibis, that "the year 309 [A.H.] began on the Sabbath of 22 Iyar, in the year 1232 of the Greek era [May 922 C.E.], and . . .

in this year, a schism broke out between the Eastern and Western Jews in relation to the dates of the feasts. The Western Hebrews began their year on a Tuesday, the Eastern on a Thursday."[11] Consequently, the two parts of the rabbinic Jewish world "had become an object of shame among the Gentiles and of derision amongst the heretics," adds a Qaraite contemporary, Sahl ben Matsliaḥ.[12] In more concrete terms, this means that in the year 4683 A.M., 922–23 C.E., while some Jews were fasting for the Day of the Atonement, others were eating; and that while some were celebrating Passover and were eating only unleavened bread, others were still eating without any restrictions.[13] It is easy to understand that each party saw the other as breaking the law, and consequently placed the other under a ban of excommunication.[14]

Given that the unification of the empire had blurred the previous distinct geographic and cultural divides, how could someone assert that he actually considered himself a "westerner" or an "easterner"? Taking for granted that all the Jews of Palestine were on the "western" side of the conflict and all those from Babylonia on the "eastern" would offer an erroneous picture. For it was not a conflict based on a geographic repartition of identities, but more significantly, one that arose because anyone living anywhere could adhere to one synagogue or another and by the same token embrace a whole lattice of different traditions. Babylonian and Palestinian synagogues coexisted in every large town and provided different understandings of rituals and traditions while competing to affiliate members.[15] Furthermore, it is possible to figure out from extant sources that some Jews of Palestine did not follow the injunctions of Ben Me'ir, and some of those from Babylonia did not agree with the calculations of the Babylonian gaonate.[16]

The Meanings of the Controversy

To make sense out of what might appear to be a strange incident, one might try to assess the available historical data about the declarations made by the two opponents. One might assess the halakhic validity of their competing techniques insofar as they were permitted by laws and by tradition as methods of declaring the beginnings of the year for all Jews settled in the Land of Israel or in the diaspora.[17] Another way—the one I have chosen to follow in this chapter—would be to examine closely the scanty material that has reached us in order to decipher the nature of the arguments on both sides. One might try to discover what caused such a great schism that both parties addressed their letters to "the divided House of Israel"[18] while still referring to their own tradition of determining the calendar. If the differences between them were really only a matter of hours or days, one might wonder why those differences became important at this moment in time and not earlier.

According to one hypothesis, observation of the appearance of the new moon, which allowed the proclamation of the entire cycle of the feasts of the year, was done in the month of Nisan in Erets Israel, according to the ancient tradition that set the creation of the world in that month. On the other hand, in Babylonia, the tradition held that the world was created during the month of Tishri, and made the new moon of Tishri the starting point for calculating the length of the year. This was also the starting point of their disagreement in calculating the *annus mundi*, the number of years since the creation of the world.[19] Another strand of interpretation tells us that since the talmudic period, the Palestinian method of proclaiming the annual calendar had rested on a combination of observing the sky and the ripeness of the crops in Palestine,[20] a technique based on the privilege and sanctity accorded to the Land of Israel; in Babylonia, astronomical calculation (rather than observation) gained the favor of scholars who had perhaps been trained in astronomy at the Abbasid schools. From the exchange of correspondence, it is clear that the manifest content of the disagreement rested on how the conjunction (the *molad ha-zaqen* or *ḥai*) and the parts of hours (*ḥalaqim*) were reckoned.[21] But as the then-unknown Babylonian delegate stated, "You set the calendar according to your custom, and we also follow the custom of our fathers and we set the calendar in our own way," a statement that suggests that there might have been more than merely astronomical considerations behind the disagreement.[22]

Now that rabbinic Jews live according to a standardized and normalized calendar, the substance of this discussion is difficult to grasp. Is the calendar a matter of custom (*minhag*) or a question of law (halakhah)? As Ben Me'ir wrote in a letter, the Talmud simply forbids the calculation of the *'ibbur* (intercalary month of the year) outside the Land of Israel.[23] And *Pirqei de Rabbi Eliezer* explicitly teaches: "Even when the prophets are outside the land and common people alone remain, the intercalation is conducted by them," thus placing the exclusive privilege of determining the calendar upon the Jews of Erets Israel.[24]

In order to understand what lies behind this question, it is impossible to avoid discussing the historical development of the struggle against the Palestinian prerogative. The Holy Land, considered the receptacle of the *Shekhinah* (divine presence), always claimed the privilege of precedence over the countries of the diaspora.[25] Even when adverse circumstances reduced its Jewry to indigence in numbers, wealth, and intellectual activities, the aura of the glorious past was entirely concentrated in its distinctive monopoly on ordering and fixing time for the entire Jewish world.[26] When the Romans forbade Jews from living in Jerusalem itself, the Sanhedrin and later academies continued to proclaim the calendar from Tiberias. When the Muslims once again opened Jerusalem to the Jews, they returned and restored the academy, and purchased property on the Mount of Olives for the Jewish community to hold public convocations on the three pilgrimage festivals.[27]

At the same time, Jerusalem became the center of attraction for the members of the Qaraite group.[28] As the academies of Babylonia considered themselves the authentic possessors of leadership and erudition, they developed arguments to fuel the age-old rivalry based partly on their sense of legitimacy and partly on the suspicion that the Jews of Palestine were somehow contaminated by Qaraite influence. This is attested by the many accusations that the Babylonians leveled regarding the supposedly corrupt traditions of Palestine. Trying to depreciate the Palestinian customs, the Babylonians claimed that they were mainly the product of the numerous persecutions that the Jews of Palestine had undergone under Roman and Byzantine rule, and were based at best on lack of knowledge and at worst on *minhag shemad*, "custom [that developed because of] persecution."[29]

Se'adyah's Role in the Controversy

A hitherto unknown scholar, having just arrived from Egypt and called Se'adyah al-Fayyūmī, entered into the battle, writing in the name of the Babylonians. Considered rightly by his biographer, Henry Malter, as a "founder of a new epoch in Jewish history,"[30] Se'adyah was born in 882, left Egypt sometime before 915, and lived in various parts of Palestine, Syria, and Babylonia until he was appointed as the head, or ga'on, of the academy of Sura (Babylonia) in 928. Considered an exceptionally broad-minded scholar, Se'adyah introduced a systematic revolution into the Jewish thought of the time and left a legacy of works ranging from poetry to halakhah, the first full book of prayers, a pioneering philosophical work, a commentary to the *Sefer yetsirah*, works of Hebrew grammar, and numerous treatises of law and exegesis based on the Talmud and the Bible.[31] His greatest achievement was endowing Judaism with an elaborate theology.[32] He also had an incomparable penchant for getting embroiled in disputes, from which he usually emerged the winner.[33]

When the material concerning the calendar controversy emerged from the Genizah, both protagonists were unknown and the Babylonian writer had not yet been identified as Se'adyah. It took some time for scholars to discover the name of this Babylonian hero. When it appeared that the Babylonian letters were to be attributed to him, the discovery shed new light on this period. More important, it turned what seemed to be a local disagreement into an event of major importance for all of Jewish history.[34]

Just as we do not know why Se'adyah left Egypt to become a wandering scholar in his early years, we can only conjecture about his personal hostility and pugnacity toward those ideas and practices that he believed deviated from true religion. Even before he left Egypt, he had written a booklet against Anan, the founder of a new group that later merged with the Qaraites.[35] It was the first landmark of his lifelong struggle against Qaraism.[36] It is our concern here not to discuss the contents of these polemics but to try to locate in the extant sources the meaning of Se'adyah's approach to tradition, an approach that has left an unparalleled imprint on the Jewish theological system.

To understand this issue, we must return to the dual dimensions of the Jewish "tradition" mentioned at the beginning of this chapter. The proclamation of the yearly calendar was supposed to rely on secrets that the sages transmitted during the period of the Sanhedrin, supposedly through oral tradition. Babylonian scholars now pretended to be able not only to surpass but to inherit the Palestinians' unique prerogative in that matter. This is the argument Se'adyah made in one of his letters:

> To be sure, in earlier generations the rabbis of Babylonia would
> send and ask for the Palestinian rabbis' yearly decisions regarding
> the months of the year, because they [the Babylonians] were not
> expert in the order of intercalation in the same way [as the Palestinians]. Therefore, they used to write to them. But many years ago,
> sages from Babylonia went up to the Land of Israel and studied
> with its sages in the court of intercalation, and searched and inquired into this matter, until they understood it very well. And now,
> for many years, they have set the month on their own in Babylonia, and the sages of the Land of Israel also calculate and set the
> months on their own. And all these years, their calculation has been
> the same and there has been no difference between them; for the

calculation is well established, the festivals are sanctified according
to the same rule and the same principle, and the calculations were
all given by the same rule and the same principle, and the calculations were all given by the same shepherd. We have never seen such
a disruption or breach. . . . Behold, there are elders in the yeshivot
(of Babylonia) who are advanced in years and who are very old, and
none of them remembers that the Babylonians ever needed to ask
the Palestinians about intercalating the years and setting the month.
Rather, you set the calendar according to your custom, and we also
follow the custom of our fathers and we set the calendar in our own
way, but the calendar is one and the same.[37]

In spite of this firm assertion, when one reads the letters exchanged during the polemic, one discovers that the main difference in calculation rested on
Se'adyah's introduction of an algorithmic rule for calculating the calendar without resort to empirical observation.[38] Only a few years later, in 926, Se'adyah
amplified his claims on behalf of the legitimacy of the Babylonian system by
claiming that it dated back to time immemorial: "The very year in which we
are now living is the year 1238 since the reign of Alexander; it is 4686 since
the world was created according to our computation. Others [Palestinian Jews]
reckon it as 4687 since the creation of the world, but this is not plausible, since
this calculation [of ours] is the right one; our predecessors transmitted the tradition to us through the Talmud, that there is a discrepancy of two years between
the *Seder 'olam* and the Kingdom of Alexander,[39] and they noticed it."[40]

This last claim allows a better understanding of Se'adyah's use of rhetoric.
In the first letter, he claims that in the early days, the Babylonian scholars
came to Palestine to study—in his argument, an admission on their part of the
anteriority of Palestinian tradition. He then adds, maliciously, that this event
took place so long ago that no one could even remember it. He specifies that
the Babylonians took back with them the science of reckoning and proclaiming the calendar—again, as a way of conceding the previously acknowledged
Palestinian superiority in computing the calendar. By contrast, in the second
extract of another of his letters, he decisively dismisses the way the Palestinians
reckoned time, implying that since their discrepancy was already noticed by
the redactors of the Talmud, it is mistaken, while the Babylonian way is the
only right one.

Se'adyah gives away his game in an additional piece of writing in which
he contends that the Babylonian rabbinic system of the calendar was of re-

motest antiquity: all the commandments related to its reckoning, postpone-
ments, and intercalations, he argues, were revealed simultaneously during the
biblical epoch.[41] To be sure, this was his authentic position, since elsewhere,
he does not hesitate to include in the original revelation all the material that
later came to constitute the corpus of the Mishnah and the Talmud.[42] Transmitted orally from ancient times, all this material was written down only
under the pressure of circumstances: "When our forefathers saw that the
multitude was dispersed throughout the land and feared lest the [divine]
speech be forgotten, they gathered every word that they had transmitted from
ancient times . . . and called them Mishnah . . . and they feared lest they be
forgotten and gathered them as well and called them Talmud, five hundred
years after the first time."[43]

Seʻadyah and Tradition

When one remembers the different meanings given to the term "tradition" in
Jewish sources, one notices that Seʻadyah is taking the position defended in
both Talmuds, by Rabbi Joshua ben Levi in the Yerushalmi and by Rabbi Levi
ben Ḥama in the Bavli (in the name of the Palestinian Resh Laqish).[44] Both
rabbis maintained that the entire content of all the rabbinic teachings were
revealed on Sinai. It is possible to infer from this that Seʻadyah was playing a
strange game. As a scholar well acquainted with the most complex aspects of
Jewish history, he could not ignore the contrary position that the calendar as
well as the Mishnah and Talmud were written by human hands—all the more
since he declared elsewhere that one cannot rely upon the aggadah, because it
reflects individual opinions not formally accepted by all scholars.[45]

Nevertheless, another problem remains unsolved: On what basis could
Seʻadyah distinguish between a revealed tradition (one that relies on divine
revelation) and human custom (which relies only on decisions)? One way to
understand his position may be found in the introductory part of the prayer
book that he composed. Explaining his purpose in committing the prayers
to writing, he claims that as he wandered and observed people making omissions, additions, and abridgments to the Jewish liturgy, he decided "to collect and arrange the established prayers, praises, and benedictions so that the
original form should be restored. But as to the omissions and additions, I shall
point out which are contrary to the fundamentals of prayer and which are not:
the former I prohibit; the latter I permit though they have no foundation in

tradition."[46] But on what grounds could he have decided "which are contrary to the fundamentals of prayer and which are not"?

Se'adyah answers the question when he cites a precise and scientific tool that he used in almost all his works: *sekhel* (reason), *ketuv* (Scripture), and *mequbbal* (received tradition). The first concept is related to rationalism; the second to revelation; and the third, the most troublesome in this context, remains ambiguous, like the notion of tradition in Se'adyah's oeuvre in general: Does he mean tradition as received through revelation, or tradition as established by human decision? Se'adyah claimed to have investigated every prayer and custom, its historical development, its textual basis, and its grounding in tradition. He concluded that the historical development of the prayers that he had collected fit into present time via the logic of rationality, the logic of textuality, and ultimately via its placement within tradition. Taking into account the many differences in practice and ritual among the various Jewish communities, he allows himself to express an opinion as to whether they should be perpetuated or abandoned. Elaborating his categories of validity and classification, he writes: "With regard to prayers and benedictions, we relied on the tradition people had received from the prophets of God. And they had two orders: one for the time of the kingdom and one for the time of the exile. This is why it is necessary to collect the prayers of our time, the epoch of the exile."[47]

Se'adyah's construction of the notion of tradition seems to be built upon the usual duality of transmission and reception (*masar/qabal*). But spurred on by new historical conditions, he makes a totally innovative contribution to a theory of tradition by introducing a new criterion: knowledge.[48] In that sense, two seminal things mediate human beings' relationships to God, the world, and the commandments: historical time and language. Since God stands outside history and time while human beings do not, the only way for human beings to understand God and the world and to perform the commandments appropriately is to apprehend them in the historical present with the mediating use of language, that is, knowledge.[49]

The Land, Time, and Tradition

Having probably spent some years studying in the Palestinian cultural center of Tiberias, Se'adyah was well acquainted with Palestinian traditions of both scholarship and everyday life.[50] Paradoxical though it may seem for a Babylonian ga'on, the fact that Se'adyah grew up in an area of Palestinian cultural influence in Egypt also has importance in this case: he is renowned for having introduced the Palestinian Talmud into the world of talmudic learning in Babylonia, which almost exclusively used the Babylonian Talmud;[51] he also championed the renewal of the Hebrew language, traditionally a Palestinian field of expertise.[52] In brief, Se'adyah cannot be accused of being hostile toward everything that originated from Palestine.

One must now consider that Se'adyah's position about fixing the calendar cannot be disconnected from the Qaraite appeal to Jews to settle in Jerusalem.[53] Viewing Qaraism in the perspective of a messianic movement, Se'adyah fought to end this outright dissidence, which endangered the Rabbanites' exclusive leadership. But it would be far too simple to explain Se'adyah's inauguration of the notion of "historical time" as a tool in the defense of Judaism.[54] Rather, Se'adyah's substitution of what was once the ritual sanctification of the month with a new astronomical and mathematical determination in effect created an abstract continuum of time, cutting it off from the age-old order of time that had been related to the sanctity of the Holy Land.[55] In so doing, intending a development in historical time, Se'adyah endowed the "time of the exile" with legal contents, albeit exilic ones.[56] Furthermore, stigmatizing variations in the calendrical order was a tactic to stigmatize and outlaw the dissidents and simultaneously provide unity for the dispersed Jewish communities.[57] Just as Se'adyah severed the Jewish calendar from its tie to the Land of Israel, so did he endow it with metaphysical value. Disconnected from geography, time escaped from the jurisdiction of the rabbis. And once standardized in a calendar identical throughout the Jewish world, time became an abstraction, nearly inconceivable, out of its mathematical sphere of dimension. This liberated calendar could then function perpetually in every Jewish community in every place on the globe. The liberation of the Jewish calendar from the Land of Israel meant the neutralization of the messianic idea anchored in the ground of Erets Israel. Once the messianic idea is reduced to an abstract order of time and detached from the land, it may become neutralized without losing its expression of hope. Messianic hope remains, while messianic politics is neutralized: messianism is removed from the present, not from the future.

Se'adyah thus blurred the boundaries between law and custom (halakhah and *minhag*) by claiming the ironclad status of law for custom, in this case, the custom of determining the calendar. But in so doing, he invented something radically new: the sense of a "true" tradition—not a static tradition wholly determined by its having been handed down in the past, but a living and dynamic tradition based on the world and the commandments, that is, on historical time and language.

Se'adyah was committed to the importance of the Land of Israel and its customs, but considering himself directly inspired and enlightened by God, his primary allegiance was to the future of the Torah and the future of the Jewish people.[58] Before he became the leader of the Babylonian academy of Sura, during the debate over the calendar, Se'adyah chose as his weapon the argument of "tradition," the most controversial subject of his time. Then, when he was appointed ga'on and took on the task of inaugurating a prayer book for the use of individuals, he expanded and elaborated this argument more fully in his introduction. Building his argument on philosophical grounds, he introduced three concepts in a theological frame: *sekhel*, *ketuv*, and *mequbbal*, which were all related in some way to his position toward the Land of Israel and its inheritance. Through *sekhel* (reason), he introduced his pioneering conceptualization of "historical time," and transformed "the time of the exile" into a host of laws applicable now in the "present day" and in this worldly world. Through *ketuv* (Scripture), he presented himself as continuing the work of the sages of the past. Through *mequbbal* (received tradition), he continued improvising, readjusting all the time. Generally, he alternated judiciously between continuity and change. He sometimes broke tradition, allowing himself, for example, the right to remove a sentence from the benedictions introducing the *Shema'* prayer, in spite of their established usage in Palestine as well as at Sura, and its entire third benediction. In both cases, the material removed bore a highly messianic tone of redemption.[59] Moreover, he was not afraid to reshuffle the ritual, introducing new prayers, songs, and penitential poems into the liturgy.[60] He left to his successors the task of revisiting anew the transformations that he introduced and to decide for the needs of their own time what would have to be removed as accretions or maintained as genuine traditions.

This is how Se'adyah demonstrated that acting to enforce tradition gives one the possibility of choosing at which end of the rope one stands: one has either to transmit (*limsor*) or to receive (*leqabbel*). That is why the ga'on summoned the approaches of both Ezekiel and Joshua ben Levi to find a midpoint between transmission and reception that he would call "true" tradition, which is a mixture of both. Se'adyah was undoubtedly attached to the Land of Israel and paid the highest respect to its traditions; nevertheless, he was convinced that the future of the Jewish people now required a move toward exilic time.

Chapter 11

Prayer, Literacy, and Literary Memory in the Jewish Communities of Medieval Europe

Ephraim Kanarfogel

Our knowledge and understanding of the popular history of the Jews in Christian Europe during the high Middle Ages has been significantly enriched in recent years, largely due to new archival research.[1] Nonetheless, large gaps remain. The partial results that are sometimes presented on the basis of rabbinic literature reveal the methodological problems inherent in sketching popular history on the basis of the literature of the rabbinic elite, whose educational levels were presumably much higher than those of the average person. Much can be learned from the rabbinic oeuvre about the lives and the intellectual capabilities of scholars. Far less can be learned about the common folk, whose achievements (and frustrations) are not typically included or reflected in this corpus.[2]

With regard to the literacy of the Jewish layman in the medieval period,[3] a number of scholars have assumed that many (or even most) males could read, since they participated in the recitation of the liturgy in synagogue services throughout Europe and the East.[4] It is impossible, however, to demonstrate this contention with any certainty on the basis of the sources or texts that have been adduced to this point. Needless to say, prayer stands at the heart of Jewish tradition and custom. Liturgical formulations are found within the Bible itself, and talmudic and rabbinic literature attribute aspects of the daily prayer order (as well as occasional liturgies) to various biblical figures. This study seeks to understand the dynamics of how medieval Jewry negotiated and sustained the performance of these traditional rites in light of the realia and educational levels of the period, which did not so easily support this endeavor.

Passages that discuss various public prayer practices from the twelfth through the early fourteenth centuries, in both Ashkenaz and Sefarad, have not been analyzed in terms of lay literacy. Although these texts are found in rabbinic works, they summarize and describe popular customs and practices, as well as the attempts of rabbinic scholars and halakhic decision makers to come to grips with congregational prayer practices that appeared to contradict talmudic and post-talmudic legal formulations and traditions. Judging by the efforts of the leading rabbinic authorities and scholars to justify and integrate these popular practices, we can learn about the level of lay literacy or, more precisely, literary memory (*memoria ad verba*). Mary Carruthers has argued that this concept, which connotes people's ability to remember great quantities of written material precisely and to recite it by heart, was closely linked with people's ability to read.[5]

In the mishnaic and talmudic periods, orality was valued as a means of preserving the accurate transmission of the body of the Mishnah and various talmudic texts.[6] The state of affairs in pre-Crusade Ashkenaz is difficult to trace, at best, although the written text of the Oral Law as an accurate repository of talmudic teachings surely made important strides through the eleventh century.[7] By the twelfth century, the rabbinic elite of medieval Ashkenaz did not eschew written texts as a means of preserving rabbinic teachings and traditions. To the contrary, even though texts were not always available, the Tosafists presumed that they were generally the most accurate records of the Oral Law, and their interpretations and analysis proceeded according to the best readings available to them.[8]

To be sure, medieval rabbinic scholars still had to commit a great deal of material to memory, owing to the paucity or shortage of texts. As the following citation from mid-thirteenth-century northern France demonstrates, scholars welcomed the opportunity to check particular readings in written texts as they became available: "When I arrived in northern France (Tsarefat), I saw in the *Bereshit Rabbah* [text] of my teacher R. Yeḥi'el [of Paris] and also in the *Bereshit Rabbah* [text] of my teacher R. Tuvyah [of Vienne] that [the phrase in question] was found in them as it was in my [copy]."[9]

Carruthers characterized *memoria* as an aid to or as an outgrowth of the reading of texts (rather than as a hindrance).[10] These models would seem to apply equally to rabbinic scholars as to monastic scholars and their successors in the cathedral schools, as characterized, for example, by Jean Leclerq.[11] Rabbinic scholars during the High Middle Ages studied from written texts, or memorized those texts on the basis of a written version.

There is no doubt that the Tosafists themselves (as well as their rabbinic counterparts in Islamic and Christian Spain during the twelfth and thirteenth centuries) were literate. The vast written corpus they produced makes it clear that they could make sense of unfamiliar Hebrew texts and compose new ones. These highly literate rabbinic figures provide the data and context for the main issue to be discussed in this study: What was the literary memory of laymen with respect to prayer? Although laymen have not left us records of their own abilities or of deliberations in this matter, the assessments of the rabbinic scholars emerged from and were meant to address the broad ranks of Ashkenazi and Sefaradi society. This is not an instance of elite rabbinic figures ruling or commenting only for themselves or for their closest followers and confidants.

Although the bulk of the discussion will center on laymen's capacity to recall liturgical texts (*memoria*) and will not often refer to full-fledged literacy, this study has implications for both the capacity of laymen to recollect Scripture more broadly and for their overall literacy level as well. When prayer books, or *maḥzorim*, were more widely available in Ashkenaz (for example, on the High Holidays and other festivals, when the complexity and uniqueness of the prayers required written versions), rabbinic authorities report that lay members of the congregation were able, on the whole, to read from them without difficulty.[12]

Reciting Liturgical Verses by Heart in Ashkenaz

Let us begin our analysis with a passage found in a fifteenth-century collection of Byzantine sermons that preserves earlier Ashkenazi material. The passage will help us to understand the nature of an ongoing halakhic problem related to public prayer, as well as the solutions that medieval Jewish scholars proposed: "[T]he German Pietists were accustomed to reciting the *Shemaʿ* from a written text, as was the communal prayer leader (*shaliaḥ tsibbur*) in particular. R. Meʾir of Rothenburg [d. 1293] wrote that it is prohibited to recite [the *Shemaʿ*] without a written text, and certainly [it is forbidden to recite] other Torah portions [that are part of the liturgy without a written text]. Therefore, Ashkenazi prayer leaders in all locales recite the *Shemaʿ* to themselves [*be-laḥash*]."[13]

The halakhic dilemma that stands at the center of this passage emerges from an uncontested talmudic ruling stating that sections from the Written Torah or Law ("written matters") may not be recited by heart.[14] The German Pietists suggested that this difficulty could be solved if the congregation, and especially the cantor or prayer leader, read all the biblical verses found in the liturgy from a written text. The (unnamed) Pietists apparently preferred that everyone present read from a written text, not merely the cantor, since if the cantor alone read from a written text, others would fulfill their obligation to recite the verses by listening to his reading—and thus not from a written text. Me'ir of Rothenburg remained concerned that, in most instances, even the cantor would be forced to recite biblical verses in the liturgy by heart because of the relative paucity of prayer books. Thus the passage states that, in cases where the cantor does not have a written prayer text in front of him, he should recite the verses by heart quietly to himself, in a low voice, so that other worshipers will not be able to hear him and will therefore not attempt to fulfill their obligation through his recitation. Me'ir of Rothenburg's formulation suggests that members of the congregation could recite the verses in the liturgy by heart for themselves, at least in a situation in which no prayer books were available.

That people throughout northern France and Germany in the twelfth and thirteenth centuries could, in fact, do so is made explicit by two parallel Tosafot texts.[15] Both discuss the talmudic stricture against reciting "written matters" by heart and interpret it as applying only when the person reciting the biblical verse(s) by heart intends to help others fulfill their obligation. But, they say, reflecting the view of Ri (R. Isaac of Dampierre, d. 1189), this prohibition does not apply to those who recite verses by heart only for themselves, suggesting rather strongly that this was a widespread practice.

Ri derived his view from a talmudic passage according to which the high priest was allowed to recite the final part of the Torah reading for Yom Kippur by heart and was not required to read it from a Torah scroll.[16] The reason was that the high priest read the Torah only for his own sake, not in order to fulfill others' obligation to hear the reading. Ri extends this allowance to cover verses of the liturgy.[17] The Tosafot texts conclude: "The custom is to recite the *Shema'* silently, and every member of the congregation should recite it for himself. The prayer leader may not recite verses [aloud] by heart in order to help the congregation to fulfill their obligation."

Other texts make it clear that the question of reciting written texts by heart was a widespread concern among rabbinic leaders of the twelfth and thirteenth centuries. For Eliezer b. Samuel of Metz (d. 1198), even the un-learned knew the verses of the *Qedushah* prayer by heart, although it appears that many of them knew other liturgical verses by heart as well.[18] A number of other contemporaneous scholars also commented on the relationship be-tween orality and writing in the synagogue liturgy. R. Eliezer b. Joel ha-Levi (Rabiah), a leading German halakhist in the late twelfth and early thirteenth centuries, writes that the prohibition against reciting verses from the Writ-ten Law by heart applies only to a prayer leader "who wishes thereby to ful-fill the obligation of his congregation." Rabiah also writes that the entire congregation was accustomed to reciting the biblical verses preceding the morning *'Amidah* as well as the *Shema'* prayer by heart, provided that the cantor did not specifically intend to fulfill the obligation of others through his recitation.[19]

Another Tosafot passage composed in northern France attests that the prohibition against reciting the Written Law by heart should be narrowed along similar lines.[20] The concluding observation in this text is that "one need be concerned [about violating the prohibition] only when others are fulfilling their obligation [on the basis of his recitation by heart]."[21] Although the pri-mary aim of this passage is to delineate the scope of the talmudic prohibition, this Tosafot formulation (like those of Ri, R. Eliezer of Metz, and Rabiah) notes (and justifies) the widespread practice in the synagogues of northern France and Germany: most, if not all, of the worshipers (including the can-tors) typically recited the prayers by heart, including the various biblical verses that were part of the liturgy.

As they did in other cases, Ri of Dampierre and his Tosafist successors in northern France and Germany preserved the long-standing practice of reciting liturgical verses from memory by limiting or neutralizing a potentially prob-lematic talmudic prohibition through a somewhat novel understanding of the talmudic texts in question.[22] All the Ashkenazi formulations and interpreta-tions that we have seen to this point understood the talmudic prohibition that "written matters" may not be recited by heart as a public or congregational prohibition only. Moreover, we have evidence of this practice as early as the first half of the twelfth century. The earliest German rabbinic scholar to jus-tify and allow it was R. Eliezer b. Nathan (Raban), a leading figure in Mainz. Raban was asked by his son-in-law, Samuel b. Natronai, "How is it that we recite the scriptural portions of the sacrifices, *Shema'*, and *pesuqei de-zimrah* each day [by heart]" in light of the talmudic prohibition against reciting "writ-ten matters" by heart?[23] Raban suggested two ways of resolving this dilemma.

First, where it is impossible to observe the talmudic prohibition on reciting verses of the written Torah by heart without jettisoning a religious obligation—for example, when one has no text and is forced to attempt to fulfill his religious obligations by reciting scriptural verses in the liturgy by heart—one may ignore the talmudic prohibition; this is based on the scriptural and rabbinic notion that "there is a time when, in order to act for the Almighty, one is bidden to abrogate Your Torah."

Similarly, in order for the masses to continue to pray effectively, as they were accustomed, the talmudic prohibition may be set aside. Raban links this resolution to a talmudic passage that relates to the converse prohibition that the Oral Law may not be written down.[24] The rabbis allowed the Oral Law to be written down when it became impossible for it to be properly remembered without committing it to a fixed literary form. As Raban notes, "when the later generations of the amoraim saw that the capacity for study had decreased, and in order that the [Oral] Torah not be forgotten, they asserted the principle that 'it is time to act for the Almighty.' For a similar reason and concern, reciting liturgical verses by heart may also be countenanced." Although the talmudic passage does not specifically extend the permissive rationale "it is time to do for the Almighty" to the prohibition on reciting "written matters" by heart, Raban proposes its extension to the parallel prohibition of writing down "oral matters" to justify the common prayer practice in Ashkenaz. To this end, he musters additional talmudic texts as well. As far as I can tell, however, only one other Ashkenazi authority (his own grandson, Rabiah) cited or endorsed this approach.[25]

Raban's second explanation is closer to the standard approach among Ashkenazi Talmudists, namely, that the talmudic prohibition applies only when one is attempting to fulfill the obligations of others. Raban bases this interpretation on two talmudic passages. The first permits the *anshei mishmar* (who oversaw the Temple service) to recite verses by heart.[26] The second concludes that even though a blind man may not write a Torah scroll because Scripture must be copied from a written text, Rabbi Me'ir (who was blind) could copy a Scroll of Esther because "Rabbi Me'ir was different." Since the words of the biblical text were entrenched (*shegurim*) and clearly established (*meyusharim*) in his mouth so that he could write them properly, it was as if he was writing them on the basis of a written text."[27] In a parallel ruling, the Talmud concludes that a scribe may write the Torah passages that are to be placed in tefillin or mezuzot by heart because these portions are relatively short and are entrenched in the memories of all. According to this approach, all biblical verses that are firmly established in the memories of the members of the congregation may also be recited by heart, for the people will not err in their recitation.[28]

A nearly identical explanation is preserved in *Sefer or zarua'* and *Sefer Mordekhai* in the name of Rabbenu Tam, a slightly younger contemporary of Raban in northern France. "How do we recite the Song of the Sea and the sacrificial portions in the synagogue by heart? As we know, the Written Law may not be recited by heart. Rabbenu Tam responded that the situation of prayer is different, since the prayers are easily and accurately recited."[29] Similarly, Ri of Dampierre also preserved in his legal rulings the loosened prohibition as formulated by his uncle Rabbenu Tam: "Although we hold that the Written Law may not be recited by heart, the *Shema'* and other verses in which people are proficient are permitted. The Talmud rules similarly in tractate *Megillah* that tefillin and mezuzot that are written not on the basis of a written copy are permitted, since the [biblical verses included in] prayers are easily and accurately recited."[30]

We have thus far identified two dominant interpretations or justifications among the Tosafists and leading halakhists in medieval Ashkenaz: that "the prayers are established in the mouths of all" and thus do not require resort to written texts; and that the prohibition of reciting verses by heart applies only when fulfilling the obligation of others. Both these approaches suggest a shared reality: most, if not all, of the people in the synagogue, including the cantors, did not have written prayer books in front of them. Moreover, both rabbinic approaches assumed that the vast majority of people could recite the many liturgical verses by heart without any difficulty. For this reason, the cantors in Ashkenaz could be instructed to lower their voices when reciting verses so that the congregation would not be able to hear their recitation. Similarly, the approach that "the prayers are established in the mouths of all" presumes that the verses included within the prayer service were fixed in the memories of most of the congregation.[31]

A Paucity of Prayer Books in Ashkenaz

What was the situation in twelfth- and thirteenth-century Ashkenaz with respect to the availability of prayer books?

Israel Ta-Shma has demonstrated the general dearth of prayer books through the end of the thirteenth century and beyond in Ashkenaz. Although the earliest known Ashkenazi prayer book was copied in England at the end of the twelfth century, it and others like it could be found only in the hands of wealthy people. Although prayer books (for the regular prayers and for festivals) were copied in increasing quantities during the thirteenth century, the average person "in the pews" had neither a prayer book nor a copy of the Torah or other biblical texts in his hands during synagogue services.[32] In addition, no comprehensive collections of biblical verses were written on the synagogue walls.[33]

The German Pietists, who were inclined toward stringency, required at least the cantor (if not the rest of the congregation) to pray from a written text so that the obligations of anyone listening would be fulfilled according to the strict interpretation of the halakhah. Similarly, *Sefer Ḥasidim* itself writes that "a person who cannot have the proper intentions during prayer if he does not have a prayer book, as well as a sated person who cannot recite the grace after meals with proper intention [without a written text before him], should read these [from a prayer book or] from a book that has the grace after meals text in it. If the individual did not have the proper intention during his silent recitation of the *'Amidah*, he should have the proper intention during the cantor's repetition and recite every word along with him."[34] In this passage, *Sefer Ḥasidim* is suggesting that a written text helps to focus a person's intentions during prayer, this being a lofty goal for the German Pietists. More importantly for our purposes, it suggests that if an individual has no prayer book, he may fulfill his obligation by reciting the words along with the cantor's repetition of the *'Amidah*. However, as far as any biblical verses are concerned, the cantor may undertake this role only so long as he has a written prayer text in front of him.

To be sure, it is clear from these and other sections that *Sefer Ḥasidim* preferred that a capable individual pray by heart and concentrate very deeply. This level of concentration would facilitate counting the letters of the prayers and other pietistic techniques designed to unlock their hidden meanings and intentions. *Sefer Ḥasidim* also suggests postures for initiated worshipers, for those relatively unfamiliar with the act and mechanics of reading and praying, and for the pietistic adept who wished to achieve pietistic goals.[35] Indeed, even the pietist mode of prayer depended on the availability of proper written texts for the counting of letters. Thus, several sections in *Sefer Ḥasidim* stress the importance and effectiveness of copying siddurim. As in other issues of religious practice, *Sefer Ḥasidim* expresses the concern that prayer texts be copied only by appropriate, worthy people.[36]

There were locales in Ashkenaz in which the community owned a siddur

or a *maḥzor* for the use of the prayer leader. In addition, leading rabbinic figures possessed or compiled *maḥzorim* to establish and direct the components
of the communal prayer services as well as to fix customs and procedures
related to prayer.[37] Nonetheless, during the days of Me'ir of Rothenburg (late
thirteenth century), a widow's bequest of a large prayer book to the community for the use of the cantor was still considered noteworthy.[38] In reality,
twelfth- and thirteenth-century Ashkenazi cantors were thought of as "living
prayer books" who could faithfully present the daily and Sabbath liturgies by
heart, in addition to providing appropriate liturgical poetry for a range of occasions.[39] The paucity of siddurim and *maḥzorim* suggested by these examples
corroborates the situation we have noted in the rulings of the Tosafists and
other Ashkenazi halakhists: the members of the congregation typically prayed
by heart.

There were, however, distinctions with respect to the prayers on festivals
and the High Holidays. Rabiah writes that on the three pilgrimage holidays
(Passover, Shavuot, and Sukkot), cantors could simply say, "as it is written in
Your Torah [*ka-katuv be-toratekha*]," which would obviate the need for them
to recite the biblical verses that described the sacrificial service as they applied specifically to each festival. On Rosh Hashanah and Yom Kippur, however, the cantors recited all appropriate biblical verses in the liturgy, since they
(and many of the congregants) had written copies of the *maḥzorim* in front of
them.[40] It is clear that in such a situation, the congregants could fulfill their
obligation to recite the verses by means of the cantor's recitation from his
maḥzor even if they did not have their own *maḥzorim*. Nonetheless, the implication of this passage is that there was an effort to copy *maḥzorim* for the High
Holidays in particular, in order to obviate this problem entirely. Moreover,
this passage serves to confirm that the congregants were sufficiently literate to
read from *maḥzorim* and siddurim when they were available.[41]

A passage in *Sefer Mordekhai* (late thirteenth century) makes a similar distinction between the daily prayers and those of the High Holidays: "Although
the *'Amidah* is recited silently throughout the days of the year (as per the
talmudic characterization of the prayer of Hannah), on Rosh Hashanah and
Yom Kippur it is recited aloud so that each congregant will thereby teach the
other to pray with proper intention. We are not afraid that they will cause one
another to err, since they have *maḥzorim* and prayer books in their hands."[42]
Here again, the passage confirms the situation that we have described: for
weekdays, Sabbaths, and perhaps on the festivals as well, most people in the
congregation did not have siddurim.[43]

The logistics of synagogue lighting in medieval Ashkenaz also had implications for the use of prayer books. Isaac b. Moses of Vienna, the author of
Sefer or zarua', cites a passage from the *Sefer ha-terumah* by Barukh b. Isaac (a
northern French Tosafist, d. 1211) on the prohibition against reading on the
Sabbath near a lamp, lest the reader tilt it.[44] The passage also discusses the use
of lamps in the synagogue on Yom Kippur and on the festivals:

> On Yom Kippur eve, the congregation recites *Selihot* and supplica-
> tions by candlelight, and each person reads from the [prayer] book by
> himself (*ve-qor'in ba-sefer yehidi*) without being concerned lest he tip
> the candle, since, in this case, the fear of Yom Kippur is upon him,
> as well as the fear of the congregation [who are standing by] and the
> need to recite many supplications. But on the eve of a festival that
> occurs on the Sabbath, the cantor *cannot* recite the *Ma'ariv* prayer
> and its liturgical poem from the *mahzor* alone by the light of the
> candle, since there is not such a pressing need to recite the poem. And
> similarly, when the first night of Passover falls on the Sabbath and
> one wants to recite the Haggadah alone, he must have another person
> reading along with him. If, however, the other person with him can-
> not read at all [or if it is a woman], his presence is not helpful in this
> regard. And if, by perusing each section from the text in advance, he
> can then finish reciting it without [the text], that is a good thing.[45]

The underlying presumption of Barukh's ruling is that most males could and
did read from written prayer texts when they were available to them (as on
Yom Kippur in the synagogue, or for those who had a Passover Haggadah for
their use at home).

Isaac *Or zarua'* ruled even more leniently in the public contexts just described. The cantor may recite by candlelight the liturgical poems for a festival
that falls on the Sabbath (and not only the *Selihot* for Yom Kippur). Isaac's
reasoning is that any individual in the congregation (and not only the cantor)
can be confident that he will not tip the lamp, since "it is impossible that no
one from the congregation will see this and not prevent him from doing so.
Therefore it is permissible on Yom Kippur eve for everyone to pray from his
prayer book. And the cantor may recite the poem by candlelight . . . when a
festival coincides with the Sabbath [as well], since the fear [and vigilance] of
the congregation are upon him."[46] The presence of *mahzorim* on Yom Kippur
was, then, not uncommon.

Up to this point, we have described the relationship between Jewish law and actual ritual performance as reflected in Ashkenazi prayer practices. Tosafists and other rabbinic authorities resolved the contradiction between the talmudic prohibition against reciting biblical passages by heart and common practice by asserting that the Talmud had, in fact, meant to apply the prohibition only when the recitation fulfilled the obligation of others. They also maintained that there had never been any prohibition on an individual writing down teachings and formulations of the Oral Law for his own use. Only when it became necessary to provide a textual version of the entire corpus of the Oral Law for everyone's use did it also become necessary to invoke a large-scale allowance based on the principle that "there is a time to act for the Almighty."[47] A second prevalent view held that the prohibition of reciting verses by heart did apply to an individual who was doing so for himself, but the prohibition could be set aside (or perhaps had never been established) for verses deeply etched into the memories and mouths of those praying (*shegurim be-fihem*).[48] Both these approaches presumed that many or most members of the communities in medieval Ashkenaz could recite the verses found in the liturgy by heart. Within the broader Ashkenazi community, *memoria* (as an indication of basic literacy) was considered to be strong and active.[49]

Literary Memory in Sefarad

The situation in medieval Iberia at first blush appears similar. Sefaradi rabbinic scholars suggest that the availability of prayer books was, generally speaking, rather limited. Thus, for example, David b. Joseph Abudarham of Seville notes in several places in his overarching commentary to the liturgy (ca. 1340) that neither the cantor nor the members of the congregation had prayer books in front of them.[50]

In fact, Sefaradi talmudists and legal authorities reacted differently from their Ashkenazi counterparts to the talmudic prohibition against reciting "written matters" by heart. Rabbenu Yonah of Gerona (mid-thirteenth century), a leading rabbinic figure and communal leader in Catalonia, wrote that the prohibition applies only in the absence of an absolute halakhic or customary requirement to recite the verses in question. If they are required, however, one may recite them by heart. This is the opposite approach from what we have seen among the Ashkenazi rabbis, who were troubled by the talmudic prohibition precisely when the verses in question were required. Rabbenu

Yonah based his position on a different understanding of the permission given to the high priest to read by heart the final part of the Torah reading on Yom Kippur. According to the talmudic passage, the high priest was required to read the verses and therefore permitted to recite them by heart. Only when the recitation of verses was completely optional was it necessary to read them from a text (and thus prohibited to recite them by heart). According to this approach, one person could recite liturgical verses by heart on behalf of another, provided that the verses were part of the standard, required liturgy.[51]

To be sure, the Sefaradi rabbis did not always agree with one another on the specifics of the prohibition, even if their positions reflect a shared material reality. R. Yom Tov b. Abraham Ishvilli (Ritba), one of the leading Sefaradi talmudic interpreters and legal authorities (d. ca. 1325), cites a passage in the Talmud Yerushalmi that stresses that the high priest could recite by heart only the final part of the Torah reading on Yom Kippur, the sacrifices recorded in Numbers 29:7–11, instituted to give added meaning and significance to the events of the day.[52] The first (and main) part of the Torah reading had to be read from a scroll. Similarly, Ritba argues, the verses that are part of the daily liturgy are not considered to be an obligatory public reading on par with the main part of the Yom Kippur Torah reading. Rather, they are additional praises and statements of thanksgiving that are added to the core prayers to give them greater substance, import, and beauty. Thus, all these verses may be recited by heart.[53] While Rabbenu Yonah permits obligatory readings or verses to be recited by heart, Ritba proscribes it.

Both their solutions presuppose that the average Sefaradi congregant could not recite liturgical verses by heart. According to both, the cantor was permitted to recite all verses on behalf of the congregation, even if he was doing so by heart. This was, in fact, the common practice in medieval Christian Iberia, as we shall see shortly.

In Ashkenaz, however, cantors were forbidden from reciting verses on behalf of the congregation, and all the various Ashkenazi authorities whose views we have surveyed denied the permissibility of this practice. One early German Tosafist, R. Isaac b. Asher (Riba) ha-Levi of Speyer (d. 1133), cites the passage from the Talmud Yerushalmi on the basis of which Ritba allowed the cantor to fulfill the liturgical obligation of the members of the congregation by reciting verses by heart. However, neither Riba of Speyer nor any other Ashkenazi scholar cited the passage for this purpose.[54]

The differences between the Sefaradi and Ashkenazi approaches to the question are even more striking when we consider that both Rabbenu Yonah and Ritba were familiar with Ashkenazi traditions. Rabbenu Yonah had studied at the Tosafist study hall in Evreux, Normandy, and was well aware of the teachings of various northern French Tosafists. Ritba also received a great deal of Tosafist material from both northern France and Germany and cites it throughout his talmudic commentaries. But both are conspicuously silent when it comes to the Ashkenazi approaches to the matter of reciting "written things" (biblical verses) by heart. This development reflects, to my mind, a fundamental difference between Ashkenaz, where worshipers possessed a high level of literary memory, and Sefarad, where the level was lower.[55]

In ignoring Ashkenazi precedent, were Rabbenu Yonah and Ritba influenced by earlier Sefaradi sources or precedents? To the best of my knowledge, no Sefaradi sources prior to Rabbenu Yonah address this issue directly. Perhaps Rabbenu Yonah was moved to raise this halakhic problem explicitly based on what he had seen and learned from his teachers in northern France, even if he did not propose their solutions to the problem. Even Maimonides, the most systematic and comprehensive Sefaradi authority in his treatment of halakhic problems, does not mention the talmudic prohibition against reciting "written matters" by heart. Interpreters of Maimonides have suggested that he omitted it because he linked it to the related prohibition against formulating "oral matters" (*devarim she-be-'al peh*) in writing.[56] That prohibition could not ultimately be upheld: because of the vicissitudes of the times (so the rabbinic argument runs), it became necessary to write down the Oral Law (or at least to formulate it in a unified literary form). Similarly, these commentators suggest, Maimonides held that the prohibition of reciting biblical verses by heart had also fallen into disuse owing to the troubles of the day and thus never mentioned it in his writings.[57]

Although Maimonides omits the prohibition on reciting "written matters" by heart, he does mention in a responsum the principle that "there is a time to act for the Almighty" in order to justify a synagogue practice in effect in exceptional cases: on festivals when a large number of congregants were present, or even on a weekday when the hour was late, the cantor would commence his recitation of the *'Amidah* out loud immediately, without first engaging in silent prayer. He would thereby fulfill the obligation for all those present, both those who did not know how to pray (*einam beqi'im*) and those who did (although the latter were expected to recite each word quietly to themselves together with the cantor). The questioners had informed Maimonides that there were certain congregations in Egypt in which the cantor recited the *'Amidah* in this manner even on behalf of those who were generally capable of praying for themselves (for example, in the *Musaf* service on Rosh Hasha-nah), so that they would not err.[58] His answer suggests that he did not expect everyone to know the prayers by memory.

In another responsum, Maimonides was asked about locales in which the cantors prayed aloud twice, first to fulfill the obligations of those incapable of praying and second to uphold the obligation of "repeating the *'Amidah*." Maimonides responded that it would be better to have only one recitation by the cantor.[59] In neither case does he mention the prohibition on reciting biblical verses by heart. His silence perhaps served as a halakhic precedent for Rabbenu Yonah and Ritba, who effectively detached the prohibition from the recitation of prayers, and retained it only with respect to the study and recita-tion of biblical texts for their own sake.

Gaonic Precedents

All these Sefaradi authorities presume that prayer books were rare, even if they presume that congregants had different levels of competence in recit-ing the liturgy from memory. This shared presumption may seem surprising, given that several of their predecessors, including the Iraqi ge'onim 'Amram bar Sheshna (d. 875) and Se'adyah al-Fayyūmī (d. 942), had authored prayer books, copies of which were sent to individuals and even entire communities within their orbits. Nevertheless, it seems that the average Jew in the Islamic world during the seventh to eleventh centuries did not have a prayer book in his hand when he prayed.[60]

This observation is at the core of an article by Louis Ginzberg, who reaches the somewhat radical conclusion that the general absence of prayer books during this period resulted from a purposeful halakhic ruling rather than the high cost of copying books or the absence of qualified copyists.[61] The Talmud prohibits an individual from holding anything in his hands while reciting the *'Amidah* lest he be distracted.[62] For this reason, according to Ginzberg, Yehudai Ga'on (mid-eighth century) ruled that the cantor himself should never hold a prayer book, except on the High Holidays and other similar occasions when the liturgy is more complicated than usual. Two ge'onim at Sura, Sar Shalom (d. ca. 859) and Natronai (d. 865), omitted the recitation of sacrificial verses during the *'Amidah* on Sabbaths and holidays for a similar reason: they thought that it would be impossible for cantors to recite all of them correctly by heart. The presumption is that cantors did not have prayer books in front of them.[63]

Ginzberg's theory is difficult to accept. He assumes that the ge'onim were prospectively legislating that the cantor should not hold a prayer book. But it seems to me more reasonable to suggest that they were simply reacting to a state of affairs in which prayer books were unavailable because of cost or difficulties in production. Indeed, Se'adyah writes in his authorized and annotated version of the prayer book that someone familiar with the biblical texts about sacrificial offerings should include them in his recitation of the 'Amidah during Musaf on festivals, while someone who is not should omit them.[64] Neither Se'adyah nor any other Iraqi ga'on explicitly mentions the talmudic prohibition on reciting biblical verses by heart. This suggests that they assumed the prohibition was not in force.

Ginzberg's argument on behalf of a continued rabbinic prohibition on reciting the liturgy from a written text extends even beyond the period of the ge'onim. He holds that, as late as the thirteenth century, Rabbenu Yonah maintained that it was prohibited to hold a prayer book while praying.[65] Indeed, according to Ginzberg, it was only a ruling by Israel Isserlein in fifteenth-century Ashkenaz that permitted a prayer book to be held if it helped one to have the proper intentions.[66] In fact, Rabbenu Yonah did permit a prayer book to be held if it would help one achieve the proper level of intention.[67] This was also the view of Sefer Ḥasidim, whose impact on Rabbenu Yonah has been documented.[68]

Other evidence against Ginzberg's theory comes from the work of Zedekiah b. Abraham ha-Rofe min ha-'anavim (Italy, d. 1260). Zedekiah permits the cantor to pray from a prayer book to avoid mistakes. In doing so, he considers the talmudic prohibition against praying from a written text, but rejects it. He cites the view of Rabbenu Ephraim, a student of Isaac Alfasi (d. 1103), that the cantor alone should not use a prayer book, based in turn on the talmudic law that the cantor is required to "organize his prayers" (lehasdir et tefillato) while the congregation is reciting the silent 'Amidah. If the cantor were allowed to use a siddur, Rabbenu Ephraim reasons, why would he be required to "organize his prayers"? Zedekiah disagrees with Rabbenu Ephraim, concluding that even the talmudic prohibition against writing down prayers was in effect only throughout the talmudic period.[69] Since, however, the rabbis had already permitted the prayers to be written down for quite some time (based on the principle that "there is a time to act for the Almighty"), the cantor may pray from a prayer book.[70] Thus, well before the thirteenth century, any halakhic problem related to praying from a written text had been effectively neutralized, and cantors were allowed to use prayer books.

What emerges from this part of our discussion is that no Sefaradi legist, neither Maimonides, Rabbenu Yonah, Ritba, nor their gaonic predecessors, assumed that the average member of the congregation could recite liturgical verses by heart. Ashkenazi halakhists, by contrast, presumed that most, if not all, of those who prayed could recall and recite correctly and unfailingly the various biblical verses that were part of the prayers, and when they made exceptions, it was only as a means of limiting the scope of the talmudic prohibition. Their Sefaradi counterparts allowed the cantor to fulfill the obligation of the members of the community in all prayers—including those that contained biblical verses, whether he was reciting them from a written text or by heart—because they did not imagine that all their congregants could recite the prayers on their own without help.

Literacy in Ashkenaz and Sefarad

In light of Carruthers's findings about the relationship between liturgical memory and literacy, the difference between the Ashkenazi and Sefaradi positions tells us something about levels of liturgical memory and literacy in the two regions. Other rabbinic sources confirm these findings.

Menaḥem b. Aaron ibn Zeraḥ's encyclopedic work *Tsedah la-derekh* (composed ca. 1370) reflects Jewish life in Navarre and Toledo.[71] Delineating the requirement for every Jewish male to study Torah, irrespective of his socioeconomic status or prior education, Ibn Zeraḥ explains that one should set aside time for study in the morning and in the evening: "And even if he is unable to learn but can read from the prayer book, he should read Psalms in the mornings and the evenings and will thereby fulfill his obligation to establish periods for Torah study. And if he cannot even read from the prayer book . . . he should provide monetary support for others who are studying Torah, and it will be considered as if he were studying as well."[72]

This passage does not, of course, provide us with the percentages or the breakdown of those who could read and those who could not, although it does perhaps reflect the fact that prayer books were becoming more available. It suggests, however, that those able to read the prayers could do so mainly because they had recited them often enough. They could not necessarily read and comprehend new texts on their own.

The limited degree of literacy in Sefarad is confirmed by the following passage from a responsum of Ritba. The responsum deals with the suitability of a blind person to serve as cantor, a particularly vexing problem, since the extent of a blind person's obligation in the precepts of the Torah (including the obligation to pray) was generally a matter of great debate. According to Ritba, the problem was exacerbated in his day, since many sighted worshipers could not pray for themselves and relied completely upon the cantor's prayer to fulfill their obligations. Ritba writes:

> There are in our day a number of ignorant people who do not know the Torah portion that discusses *tsitsit*, which must be recited each day, perhaps even as an obligation from the Torah itself (*mitsvah de-oraita*), as well as the first verse of *Shemaʿ*, which, according to all, is a [*mitsvah*] *de-oraita*. There are a number of ignorant people who cannot pray at all, and the cantor fulfills their obligation for them. For these reasons, it appears to me . . . that now that, due to our sinfulness, ignorant people are numerous (*nefishei ʿammei ha-arets*), it is inappropriate to appoint as a permanent cantor either a person who is blind from birth or one who lost his sight later.[73]

Throughout Sefarad, then, neither widespread literacy nor a strong degree of literary memory (*memoria*) could be presumed. R. Isaac bar Sheshet (Ribash, late fourteenth century), a leading rabbinic figure who had studied in Gerona, confirms this when he writes that the custom for the cantor to recite the *ʿAmidah* of *Musaf* on Rosh Hashanah immediately, without the congregation first praying silently, "was adopted in those Sefaradi locales because most of [the people there] are ignorant and can pray from a written text only with great difficulty, due to the number and length of the blessings. For this reason, they all pray together with the cantor, similarly to one person reading [prayers] for another."[74]

In contemporaneous Ashkenazi rabbinic literature, by contrast, the presumption is that most people know how to read and write. *Sefer Ḥasidim* devotes a number of sections to encouraging those who could not study Talmud (or even the Bible) nonetheless to study legal or aggadic texts, or simply to read or copy holy texts.[75] The average Jewish male's possibilities for Torah study were apparently much richer in Ashkenaz than in Sefarad, at least to judge by *Tsedah la-derekh*. In Ashkenaz, those who could not engage in more systematic or complex study nonetheless took part in Hebrew reading, writing, and copying scholarly texts.

We can detect the same patterns in a comparison of the views of medieval

Ashkenazi and Sefaradi authorities on whether someone called up to the Torah during synagogue services is required to read his portion in an undertone along with the official reader or should serve as the public reader if he can. The tendency in northern France and Germany was for someone called to the Torah to read along wherever possible. In Sefarad, on the other hand, Judah al-Bargeloni writes in his *Sefer ha-'ittim* (ca. 1100) that typically "the cantor reads [from the Torah] and the one who goes up [to the Torah] is silent."[76]

Although al-Bargeloni himself and subsequent Sefaradi authorities decried the practice of calling to the Torah someone who was unable to read from it or did not understand its contents, the practice of calling illiterate people to the Torah continued in Sefarad unabated—presumably because there were few other choices. In the mid-fourteenth century, David Abudarham railed against those "who were ascending to the Torah and cannot read even one letter. . . . They should be prohibited from being called up [to the Torah]."[77] In Ashkenaz, however, it was relatively rare for someone unable to read to be called to the Torah, as indicated by formulations of both Ephraim of Regensburg (d. 1175) and Isaac *Or zarua'*.[78] Indeed, it would appear that as late as the days of Me'ir of Rothenburg, there were places in Germany where the person called up to the Torah was still primarily responsible for executing the public reading of that section.[79]

Educational Practices

The different levels of literacy in Ashkenazi and Sefaradi communities are at least partly dependent on the educational approaches in these societies. In Ashkenaz, tutors taught young boys to read Hebrew in order to read verses of the Bible so that they could recite them by heart during the course of prayer. The cantor could fulfill the obligation to read parts of the prayer service that did not consist of biblical verses or that could not be readily memorized. Although not every child studied with a tutor, reading liturgical verses was one goal of tutors or *melammedim* employed by parents to teach their sons. *Melammedim* were available even to children of the poor through individual subsidy or benefaction, and their teaching assignments often included the rudiments of biblical interpretation and mishnaic and talmudic reading and interpretation as well. This suggests that reading biblical verses was taught at the initial phase not merely as an aid to liturgical memory but as a first step toward a more developed form of literacy.[80]

Eleazar of Worms offers a sense of how the educational trajectory proceeded after basic reading instruction: "At the beginning, the tutor should instruct [the child] to recognize the letters, and afterward, how they are put together to form words, and after that, the [Torah] verse, and then the weekly portion, and then the Mishnah, and then the Talmud." The reading of biblical verses was among the first stops on the road toward mastering the reading process, but it was not always the last.[81]

Other Ashkenazi sources suggest that even before the child was formally brought to a tutor, his father taught him to recognize the letters of the Hebrew alphabet and read verses from the Torah.[82] Nonetheless, it was deemed appropriate and beneficial to hire a tutor to teach the basics of reading.[83] Isaac *Or zarua'* describes tutors who taught the weekly Torah portion and the *haftarot* together with the Aramaic translations or Rashi's commentary. He also mentions a tutor who was hired to teach a "book" or "half a book" of the Bible.[84] Already in the days of Rabbenu Gershom of Mainz (d. 1028), there had been discussion concerning a tutor hired to teach a boy "all of Scripture," and the tutor maintained that he had successfully discharged his mission.[85] Here again, the goal was far more than providing familiarity with the content of the liturgy.

In Islamic lands, as Goitein suggests, teaching the reading process initially familiarized young boys with liturgical verses so that they could memorize them. Similarly, providing books to follow the reading of the Torah and Prophets was intended as an aid to memory. For many, however, these were the end goals of reading instruction.[86]

In Iberia, the educational process appears to have been even less successful in some respects. Yom Tov Assis has shown that elementary education was disorganized and uneven. There was little provision to educate the children of the poor.[87] And here is how Rabiah, the leading German halakhist at the beginning of the thirteenth century, characterized the level of literacy in the Sefaradi world of his day: "I have seen responsa that indicate that even today (*'od ba-yamim ha-elu*), the custom in Spain and Babylonia is that the cantor conducts the Passover seder in the synagogue on behalf of ignorant people who are not well versed enough in the Haggadah to recite it (*mipnei 'ammei ha-arets she-ein beqi'in ba-haggadah le-omrah*)."[88] That Rabiah was aware of the gap between Ashkenaz and Sefarad is indicated by his positions on reciting biblical verses in prayer.[89]

Admittedly, there were ignorant people in Ashkenaz who could not read Hebrew and people in Spain who could.[90] Nonetheless, judging by the rabbinic practices, policies, and descriptions that we have seen, the level of Hebrew literacy and literary memory among males in these two regions appears to have differed substantially. These differences depended on their respective structures of education, if not on more basic societal attitudes.[91]

Literacy and *Memoria ad Verba* in Ashkenaz and Sefarad

This study has sought to provide a new window onto the level of *memoria* and, to a lesser extent, actual Hebrew literacy in the Jewish communities of medieval Europe. In the relative absence of texts that describe or report these phenomena, the rabbinic rulings on liturgical practices shed light on the question. During the twelfth and thirteenth centuries, few Jewish males actually read their prayers owing to the general unavailability of written texts. At the same time, Ashkenazi Jews' capacity for *memoria* (and indeed, their ability to read from liturgical texts when available, and even to read and understand new material) was greater than that of their Iberian counterparts.

Each center's attitude toward Torah study may also have played a role. Ashkenazi Jewish communities sought to produce not only successful businesspeople but also as many talmudic scholars as possible. *Sefer Ḥasidim* even laments that most young men were schooled in order to attain the highest levels of talmudic study, even if their intellects, abilities, and proclivities were not prepared for this challenge. In the view of *Sefer Ḥasidim*, these students should instead have considered focusing on other texts (such as Scripture and midrash), or simply copying Torah and rabbinic texts.[92] Nonetheless, as far as basic levels of literacy are concerned, my findings agree with Robert Chazan's assertion that "the already high level of cultural achievement [in northern France during the Tosafist period] indicates a successful educational system."[93]

Iberian Jewry, on the other hand, did not aspire to the same levels of educational achievement for all.[94] Lower levels of expectation and opportunity help explain the fact that *memoria* and basic literacy developed differently in medieval Spain. Certainly for most, familiarity with biblical verses and Hebrew texts was desirable for facilitating recitation of prayers and reading the weekly Torah portion, but expectations did not rise much beyond this. The level of *memoria* in medieval Spain, at least as presumed by its leading rabbinic authorities, apparently fell short even of these expectations.

This study has used rabbinic literature and halakhic formulations to reflect Jewish life and experience on the ground and to identify and distinguish between shared religious traditions. It should be correlated with archival and similar materials. Aspects of the elusive social history of ordinary Jews in medieval Europe during the High Middle Ages still lie among these materials, awaiting further research. It is only through a fuller appreciation of this history that the dynamics of tradition and custom can be properly calibrated.

Chapter 12

A Temple in Your Kitchen: *Hafrashat Hallah*—The Rebirth of a Forgotten Ritual as a Public Ceremony

Tamar El-Or

> Speak to the Israelite people and say to them: "When you enter the land to which I am taking you and you eat of the bread of the land, you shall set some aside as a gift to the Lord: as the first yield of your baking, you shall set a side a loaf as a gift; you shall set it aside as a gift like the gift from the threshing floor."
>
> —Nm 15:18–20

> For three sins women die in childbirth: for neglecting the laws of menstruation, of first dough, and of lighting the [Sabbath] lamp.
>
> —mShab 2:6

Women's Range of Action and Participation in the Religious Jewish World

At the center of this chapter is the ritual of *hafrashat hallah*: a Jewish precept (or mitzvah, in Jewish parlance) that requires a woman, when she bakes bread, to separate out, sanctify, and discard a portion of dough as an offering to God. The commandment appears in the book of Numbers. The rabbis who translated the precepts of the Torah into practical rules made this ritual incumbent on women, one of the three principal observances with which they are charged. Nevertheless, until recently, it was a private rather than public ceremony. In the modern age, many women buy rather than bake bread, including *hallah*, the special Sabbath loaf. Furthermore, the ritual is required only when baking bread (or, in some cases, cake or other baked goods) from a large quantity of dough—a quantity containing at least 3 2/3 pounds of flour. Many observant women, even those who bake at home, never have occasion to perform *hafrashat hallah* or to see it performed by someone else. The other two principal observances are more familiar. Lighting Sabbath candles is a popular ritual widely performed even by women who are not observant. Adherence to the laws of *niddah*—the separation of a woman from her husband during and after her menstrual period and her subsequent purification in a ritual bath (*miqveh*)—is also familiar beyond the bounds of the orthodox community.[1] In contrast, *hafrashat hallah* has become marginal to the life of most religious Jewish women.

Women's range of action and participation in the Jewish religious world are constrained by their gender. Most rituals are reserved for the patriarchy that manages that world, and it devises secondary roles for other participants. Women play limited roles at the margins of the central sites of Jewish religious life (synagogues and study halls), principally as the wives, mothers, or daughters of men. More distant from these sites, where they are somewhat freer from religious formality, women have created their own traditions. In the form of ceremonies and spiritual work—the one integrated into the patriarchy and the other more distant from it—these traditions are undergoing significant changes in the wake of the gender revolution that began at the beginning of the twentieth century. Roughly put, women have penetrated the hegemonic circles and broadened them, and certain men and new participants in spiritual work have entered these non-hegemonic "feminine" religious spaces and intensified the importance of "popular religion." The movement toward increasing numbers of participants, men and women, in both circles has forced the religious patriarchy to think and respond.

In some communities (especially, but not only, in modern orthodox ones), these changes have invited increasing involvement from women in the central areas of Jewish practice. Religious women have chosen to blaze a trail into religion's fortified strongholds. The trail first entered areas of study, then moved into the spaces of prayer and ritual, and afterward returned to women's bodies and their supervised sexuality. Rituals that were kept within women's spaces (bat mitzvah, the birth of a daughter, immersion in the *miqveh*) have emerged from these distant areas and moved closer to the hegemonic spaces, in turn affecting the entire community. They have entered discussions between study partners, public organizations, media, and art. The gender distinction has not faded; it remains a supreme organizing category of the worship of God. But the negotiation over its nature has brought men's and women's areas of prayer, ritual, and study closer together and has brought both men and women closer to halakhic discourse.

Each community conducts its gender and religious relations in different ways, and there is no discernible linear or progressive movement toward a single goal. The significance of the movement lies within its precise context. In *ḥaredi* communities, for example, most of the gender change occurs as broadening opportunities for women (and men) to engage in nonreligious studies and their entry into professional areas of knowledge. It may be that this entry will lead *ḥaredi* women to a demand broader knowledge of halakhah as well.

The Sefaradi community in Israel, on which this work focuses, comprises women and men who live according to the halakhah, as well as others who are in negotiation with it. It is a heterogeneous community that seeks to include under a single roof individuals with broad and varied histories of education, lifestyle, and religious customs. Rabbi Ovadiah Yosef, the most prominent religious authority in this community, envisages all its members united under a single halakhic canopy. But the community's sociology and cultural conduct do not automatically conform to this goal.[2] With regard to the gender order, the Sefaradi community has had few difficulties providing extra-religious knowledge to women. The first general education college for *ḥaredi* women in Israel was established by Rabbi Yosef's daughter. But there is no place today where *ḥaredi* women can pursue religious and halakhic education in *midrashot* (institutes of religious study for women) similar to those found in the religious Zionist and modern religious communities (which have many Sefaradi members).

Rather, the religious gender change in Sefaradi communities can be sought at the margins of the synagogues, in home gatherings, in classes for women, and in the areas of para-religious ceremonies and rituals. There is no point in describing this activity as a "feminist revolution." The terminology is foreign to this context. Yet one can see how the needs of new adherents create transformations and innovations in the spaces of women's activity while also creating new spaces. The recent return to religion—*teshuvah* in Hebrew—includes private and organizational initiatives offering "spiritual experiences" to the public at large. These include organized pilgrimages to the graves of famous rabbis and miracle workers, participation in special festivals commemorating these figures, weekends of Torah study, and talks by men and women who have become religious. Among this plethora of experiences aimed specifically at women and girls are public celebrations of *hafrashat ḥallah*. Such events have become accepted as a kind of "spiritual leisure activity," even among *ḥaredi* and orthodox women who are not newly observant.[3]

This essay centers on a detailed description of such a ceremony in a neighborhood in central Israel.[4] My reading and analysis of the ethnographic material move between halakhic interpretations of the precept of *hafrashat ḥallah* and its significance on the one hand, and sociological and anthropological interpretations of the ceremony on the other. Together these yield the blueprint of a space of public spiritual activity for women and its cultural and political context. This neoteric ceremony offers a unique window on women's religious activity and on the creation of tradition. It links halakhah with the kitchen, a religious precept with creation, consumerism with qabbalah, and the Holy Temple with the corner grocery store. It is the story of a "comeback," of an "invented" tradition whose impact lies not merely in its use of the past for the present, but in its impact on the future.

The renaissance of *hafrashat ḥallah* is an "event." A halakhic practice, observed only in limited situations, has been refashioned to suit contemporary audiences. It has become a celebration of womanhood, an opportunity to shop, to pray, and to learn new recipes. It is an invitation to women to take part in *tiqqun 'olam*—the "repair" or "mending" of the world through the observance of the Torah's commandments. The new ceremony serves as a school in which women learn about their religious responsibilities and as a theater in which they act out new roles. It is a social gathering—a mélange of aromas, stories of tribulations and miracles, of spinsters and orphans. The mass *hafrashat ḥallah* ceremonies are policing entertainments, fun targeted toward education and discipline, and a good traded in a bustling and competitive spiritual market. These ceremonies mark a gendered old-new realm of action and a creative initiative within the *teshuvah* industry.

The ethnography of this event describes it "as it happened." The analysis that follows is limited in this context to two aspects: the agency of the participants; and the juxtaposition of the kitchen and the Temple.

Hafrashat Ḥallah—July 15, 2002

Four days before the fast of the Ninth of Av, 5763 (2002), at the height of the July heat, Mira and a group of other *ḥaredi* women organized a public *hafrashat ḥallah* ceremony in Pardes Katz. They contacted the *ḥaredi* charity Ḥasdei Naʿomi, which produces such evenings, and spread word of the event among their friends. Mira also pasted small flyers around the neighborhood to gain a larger audience. I heard about the event from the neighborhood's community worker, who put me in touch with Mira. I phoned her and introduced myself as a researcher who studies religious women, and Mira saw no problem with my attending and observing the ceremony.

I arrive at the synagogue wearing a black jumper over a long-sleeved shirt. Taking advantage of the lenient atmosphere with which I am familiar from other Sefaradi synagogues, I wear sandals without socks. But I nevertheless put on a hat out of respect, in keeping with the orthodox stricture for married women to keep their hair covered. It is the first time I have covered my head since I completed my work with the women of the Gur Hasidic community in Tel Aviv. Nearly ten years have gone by in the meantime, but the hat doesn't feel peculiar to me. This time, I leave a ponytail showing in back, walking the edge a little. At the entrance to the synagogue sits a woman who collects a ten-shekel entrance fee. The synagogue is a comfortable temperature thanks to its central air conditioning, and a small number of women sit on the benches. I search for a woman in advanced pregnancy and identify one who meets that description. She is tall, thin except for her belly, and she is pushing benches around, organizing the synagogue into a makeshift classroom. None of the other women is helping her.

"Mira?" I hazard.

"Yes."

"I'm the Tamar who spoke to you on the phone."

"Ah, hi." She shakes my hand. "As you see, they're coming in dribs and drabs. Turns out that at the Gold wedding hall, there's some sort of food fair or something. A lot of them went there, and they'll come here afterward. You know, last night, in the middle of the night, I couldn't sleep. I said to my husband, let's take a walk. We walked to downtown B'nei Brak, to Rabbi Akiba Street, three in the morning, maybe. What a scene, people pasting up posters one on top of the other, what competition. Lectures, events . . . the city is humming, everyone has something to advertise, covering up one another's posters, a real scene."

At a quarter to nine, two women and a man lug large cases and amplification equipment into the synagogue and set up a sound system. At nine, one of the women, Anat, takes the microphone, introduces herself, and begins to talk fluently. She speaks in a monotonic, almost mechanical voice. It does not rise, fall, or change with the story she tells, whether she speaks of quantities of flour, *tiqqun 'olam*, or a profusely bleeding woman in labor who observed the precept of *hafrashat hallah* on her hospital bed when her fetus was in danger.

I take a flyer offering a trip to the Ashkeluna water park and begin to write on its back. What follows is taken from my on-site notes, which could not keep pace with Anat's speech. I fleshed them out from memory. She stood on the dais in the front of the sanctuary, and, as she spoke, she held up large, plastic-covered posters in phosphorescent yellow, pink, and green. The posters contained keywords that served as overhead projections.

Anat is very nice looking. On her head is a Bukharan straight-sided cloth cap of the type that religious Zionist women often wear. The bun that peeks out from behind is covered in black fabric. Over her long, loose dress, she wears a long gray vest. She is delicately made up, and a silver Star of David hangs from a long black leather lace around her neck. Her socks and platform clogs are of the same color, black. She expresses herself well and seems intelligent and experienced. She has prepared the dough beforehand with the help of Orly, who came with her, and now makes the *hallah*, not describing what she is doing. When asked for details, she says that everything is written on the sheet (which she later sells). When she finishes the dough, she says:

> I knead with my hands, not with a mixer, so that my limbs will be
> partners in the mitzvah. It is written that limbs that are occupied
> in a mitzvah do not get hurt. For example, they told Queen Jezebel
> that her body would be mutilated, and indeed, after her death dogs
> ate her body, but they left her two hands and feet and her head,
> because she used to rejoice with brides at their weddings, singing to
> them and dancing and clapping her hands. So let your hands take
> part in the mitzvah. After the dough is ready, cover it with plastic
> and put a box of matches on it, because the sulfur in the matches
> accelerates the rising of the dough.

Anat takes the dough out of the air-conditioned synagogue and puts it in the hot courtyard. She apparently knows that the lecture will be long enough for the dough to rise. At the height of the evening, there are about fifty women in the hall.

> Women! [This is how she addresses them throughout the evening,
> avoiding the terms "righteous women" or "souls," which have

recently become fashionable.] Women are commanded to observe three precepts. [She raises a poster.] They have the initials Ḥ.N.H., like the name Ḥannah: *ḥallah*, *niddah*, and *hadlaqat nerot* [lighting the Sabbath candles]. *Niddah*: those who observe it, who observe it carefully, observe it. *Hadlaqat nerot*: women who are very far [from religious observance] also observe it, even those who don't keep the Sabbath or keep kosher light candles [before the Sabbath]. So why do we leave *hafrashat ḥallah* to a few righteous women? Why do most of us not perform this excellent mitzvah? Today, with God's help, we will learn the mitzvah of *hafrashat ḥallah*. This is a very spiritual mitzvah. It is a mitzvah in which every woman makes her home into a Holy Temple in miniature. From the day that the Temple was destroyed, there were no more sacrifices; the priests ceased to serve, and here, we are commanded to observe such a great mitzvah that contains a commemoration of the sacrifices. This mitzvah has great potency, huge powers. It is a mitzvah that you do by yourself; no one sees you, no one hears you, there's no performance. I cry about what is going badly with me, what I am bitter about. I ask and plead and, as always in prayer, I ask first for the entire public, for the collectivity, and then for me, and I don't cry over my husband because a woman's tears over her husband burn him up. First I'll read you a few letters from women who have heard my lecture and who wrote me letters. I have them here with personal details and telephone numbers, and you can call them and everything.

Anat does not actually have the letters in hand and does not read from them. Instead, she refers to an edited text she has compiled.

The first is Meital from Elʿad. She was about to give birth and felt a discharge coming out of her and thought that her water had broken. Suddenly, she looks and sees that it's blood, a really strong stream of blood, like a river. Her husband was paralyzed and couldn't manage to call an ambulance. Meital herself, with her very last bit of strength, slipped a coin into the charity box at home and began to pray. In the end, they somehow got to the hospital, where she asked her husband to call Rabbi Kneibsky, so that he would go to *kolelim* [seminaries for married men to engage in advanced

religious studies] and give her name for the students to pray for
her, because the doctors said that the situation was very bad. The
placenta had become detached from the uterus, and without that,
the baby can't receive oxygen. She had a hemoglobin count of eight,
which means that she had really lost a lot of blood. Suddenly, her
mother came to the hospital with a bowl and dough, and the doctor
asked if they were going to make doughnuts, because it was Hanuk-
kah. But her mother gave her the opportunity to do the mitzvah of
hafrashat ḥallah. From that moment, the bleeding stopped and she
gave birth in good fortune to a healthy, whole son.

I've got a letter here from a girl named Osnat, who was at my
lecture in Lod. She came in jeans and a tank top and short hair
and lots of earrings. She said to herself that if I made any comment
on the way she looked, she'd get up and leave. God forbid, I never
make any comments. I'm a newly religious woman myself. When
she went home, she saw on television that they were looking for a
home for a lonely old woman, and she decided to try to help. She
made maybe fifteen phone calls, and really prayed in her heart that
she would have the luck to do a mitzvah and meet someone who
would lift her up because she didn't have the strength alone to go
the distance. In the end, she reached someone and talked with him
from eleven at night until three in the morning. Half an hour about
the old woman, and the rest on Torah and precepts and *teshuvah.*
In the end, she met the boy, a *ḥaredi* boy with a pure soul. Osnat
is, God be blessed, married today to that boy. Do you know Rabbi
Ofer from Ḥolon? Do you listen to him on the holy radio stations
[pirate radio stations run by religious parties and organizations], the
precepts he observes and the mending [of souls] that he does? His
assistant, Rabbi Ḥayyim Gad, that's her husband. Their wedding
was the holiest and most moving thing I ever saw in my life.

The third and last story I'll read you is about a girl from Afulah,
a newly religious woman whose husband didn't become religious
with her. He's a son of Holocaust survivors. His parents taught
him not to throw out a single crumb. So he wouldn't let her do
hafrashat ḥallah, and there were literally shouts and arguments, and
he'd tell her about all the horrors of the Holocaust. The *ḥallot* she
made came out like concrete. Five years she was married, and she
didn't have children. He didn't let her throw out [the dough taken

as an offering] and forbade her to bake *ḥallot*. She was at one of my lectures, and I gave her instructions on the phone how to do it, and her *ḥallot* came out excellent. Her husband didn't believe that she baked them and asked to stand by her the next time she made them. You know what it's like when your husband stands next to you and you have to succeed? He saw her *ḥallot* and walked out of the house in anger. Afterward, he came back with tefillin in his hand. Your *ḥallot* are too holy to eat [he said]. I have to put on tefillin first. Today, God be blessed, he is studying [religious texts], and the good news that she adds in the letters is that she's in her fourth month of pregnancy.

Anat then presents her audience with letter and word games, which appear on the posters that she holds up one after the other. The woman sitting next to me draws a small notebook out of her purse and tries to copy what is written on the posters. She says that the letters of the word *ḥallah*, *ḥ-l-h*, stand for *ḥeleq le-ʿolam ha-baʾ*, a share in the world to come. *Hafrashat ḥallah*, in an anagram, becomes *tafraḥ shaḥalah*, "to stitch an ovary," meaning that the ovary will catch the seed, she explains: that it will be fertilized. The women are extremely impressed with this wordplay, and Anat continues with a wealth of further examples, some of them clever and some of them forced. In the end, she says:

Someone showed me something clever and new recently, after what happened on September 11. How many aircraft took part in the attack? Four; that's the four matriarchs. How many in the end succeeded? Three, because one went down on the way, that's the three patriarchs. What are the Twin Towers of the World Trade Center? The two tablets. And one is the Pentagon—God. Those who forget the four matriarchs and the three patriarchs and the Torah and God become the target of terrorist attacks. That is how God teaches us, via the Gentiles, and reminds us where we ought to go.

The dough needs more time to rise, so there is time for some other business. Anat looks into the distance, beyond the door, and asks Orly: "Has the rabbi come? He's here. Okay, now I'll invite Rabbi [I didn't catch the name] of the Ḥasdei Naʿomi organization to say a few words."

A man in "Lithuanian" dress—a dark suit, white shirt, and black homburg—enters, fairly young, speaking without an accent and addressing the women as a "public" (*tsibbur*). The category of "public" has implications in Jewish law. In general, only men can constitute a public with obligations beyond those of the individual. By addressing the women in the audience in this way, the rabbi implies that they have collective responsibilities, elevating them symbolically to a new status. He describes Ḥasdei Naʿomi as a charity that helps Israelis of all walks of life and all communities.

In the meantime, the man who arrived with Anat and Orly walks among the women and checks whether they are filling out the bank order forms that he has passed out. Only one of the fifty women—Mira's unmarried sister, who is not in *ḥaredi* dress—fills out the form. On the spot, she receives a framed copy of the "blessing for the home" with a talisman from Rabbi Kaduri, a Sefaradi qabbalist believed to have great powers, as well as some virgin olive oil blessed by another mystic. Some of the women tell the rabbi's assistant that they already have bank orders; he thanks them and does not badger them with further questions. Then there are those who say that they must consult with their husbands, an explanation that he accepts with understanding, asking that they fill out their personal information anyway so that he can call to follow up. Others evade his glance, and he smiles shyly and passes them by. Meanwhile, the rabbi on the dais continues to describe how the virgin olive oil succeeded in saving a woman who was on the operating table and how it cured children.

The rabbi leaves, the risen dough returns, and things begin to buzz. Anat has prepared a large table covered with a plastic tablecloth, where she will show how to braid beautiful *ḥallot*. But first, she turns to the ceremony that is the main part of the evening: the study and practice of *hafrashat ḥallah*.

Anat asks, "Who will do the *hafrashah*, Mira?" "Yokhi, Yokhi," Mira replies. Then Anat says, "Come on, Yokhi, come over here. Now, Mira, you bought the flour, right? So tell Yokhi that you are giving her the flour as a gift." "I give you, Yokhi, the flour as a gift," Mira recites.

"Great." Anat proceeds. "At home, at this point it's a good idea to light a candle for a righteous man that you are connected to, and when you light it you can say: 'I hereby light this candle in honor of the righteous man... , may it be his will that by the merit of lighting this candle, my prayer will be accepted and his merit will protect us and all the Jewish people.' Now, Yokhi, go wash hands, without a blessing, with the washing cup, alternating hands. After washing say, 'I hereby come to observe the precept of *hafrashat ḥallah* to correct its root in the high place, to give contentment to our maker, the will of our creator.'"

Yokhi reads from a sheet that Anat holds in front of her. "Now we will say the blessing twice together." She holds up a huge poster with the blessing so that we can all read it. "May the favor of the Lord, our God, be upon us; let the work of our hands prosper, O prosper the work of our hands!" (Ps 90:17).

"Now you, Yokhi, read the prayer from this." Yokhi reads the prayer. From the way she reads, I presume that she is not familiar with the prayer, even though she grew up in a *haredi* home.

> May it be before you the Lord our God and God of our fathers
> that by the merit of this mitzvah and by the merit of this taking of
> the priestly tithe, the transgression of Eve, the mother of all living,
> who brought death on Adam, who is the dough of the world, [be
> removed] and that by the merit of this mitzvah death be removed
> from the world and a tear wiped from every face and a blessing sent
> upon our homes [Anat adds: "and the sick and the wounded healed
> and the soldiers protected"], amen may it be his will, and may it be
> before you that you bless our dough as you sent a blessing on the
> dough of our mothers Sarah, Rebecca, Rachel, and Leah, and may
> the verse be realized with us: "You shall further give the first of the
> yield of your baking to the priest, that a blessing may rest upon
> your home" (Ez 44:30), amen, may it be his will.

Anat then resumes her presentation. "Now we take the four corners of the dough and create a small lump the size of an olive (and less than the size of an olive for the Sefaradim), and we will tear off this quantity and wrap it in one piece of aluminum foil, and then in another piece, because holy things are wrapped twice, and now lift it up in your right hand and say: 'Behold, this is *hallah*.'"

Yokhi lifts up the wrapped dough and declares: "Behold, this is *hallah*." Anat continues: "Now, women, we will turn to the tabernacle, and open our hands to heaven, and pray from deep in the heart, first for the entire Jewish people and then each one of you her own prayer."

The women pray. I close my eyes and say to myself a few supplications for the public and then for myself. When I open my eyes, some of the women are still swaying from side to side, their eyes closed and their lips moving, and others have already completed their prayer. Anat turns back to us and goes on to the part that elicits the most interest: the braiding of the dough. First, she tells the women what to do with the portion that was taken out:

The best thing is to put it on the gas on an open flame, not one that has a pot on it, until it is good and burned. You can also put it in the oven when you bake the *ḥallot*, but the aluminum gives off poisons into the food, and it's not good. After it has burned, you put it into a plastic bag and then that bag in another plastic bag, and you throw it into the garbage can.

I have a few kitchen items you can buy afterward. A wonderful bowl with a lid, don't even ask how useful it is. It's also great for couscous. I've got a Tupperware rolling pin, I've got only six more like it, and it costs fifty shekels [about US$13] but it's worth every shekel. This is Paka dry yeast, which stays good for an entire year in the refrigerator and doesn't smell at all. Okay, I take small balls from the dough—they shouldn't be too heavy—and roll them out, first so that they will be airy. Afterward, I make them into strands. Orly, come help me.

Orly skillfully takes the balls from Anat, kneads and rolls out strands. Anat, in a magic act, shows the women different ways of braiding the *ḥallot*. She is quick, and every so often, the women ask her to repeat some shape ("It's all on the sheets that you can buy," she says). The *ḥallot* indeed come out beautifully, rounded and long, in the shape of a flower or a braid. She teaches them how to make a pretzel shape and a small *ḥallah* like those served at weddings, and the women are excited and happy. Anat arranges the *ḥallot* on an aluminum pan and says, "Here I am using aluminum, but don't bring it into your homes. It's literally poison, aluminum emits poison in heat. I put waxed paper between the *ḥallot* so that they won't stick to one another, because then when I separate them, they won't be whole, and you won't be able to say the Sabbath blessing over them."

One of the women who seems very *ḥaredi* and who has already made several comments tells her: "I actually heard from Rabbanit Kneibsky that it's best to take two *ḥallot* that were stuck to each other and break them on the head of child who has speech problems, who stutters." Anat replies: "I haven't heard about that, but I'm always learning. That's what's good about these lectures—I hear new things all the time."

At the end, the women throng around Anat, who asks them to be patient so that she won't get confused giving them their change. Most of the women buy the two laminated sheets with the *hafrashat ḥallah* blessings, the recipes, and the braiding patterns, at twelve shekels each. A few also buy the bowl with the lid. No one buys the Tupperware rolling pin, even though Anat has only six of them left, and even though they are worth every one of the fifty shekels that they cost.

The Holy Temple versus the Gold Hall: The Ceremony's Interpretive Space

If we could center Jewish cosmology on a single symbol, as the anthropologist Sherry Ortner did with Hindu-Tibetan cosmology, this interpretive project would be relatively simple.[5] Yet the power given to Western scholars studying "other" societies dissipates in studies done at home. Those conducted elsewhere seem more recently to have eschewed reduction in favor of a cautious complexity. Nevertheless, reduction—that is, the organization of the phenomenal world around a primal, fundamental component—is still seductive. As a method, it can be powerful and offer valuable insights.

It is hardly risky to designate the Holy Temple that once stood in Jerusalem as a central symbolic site for Judaism. This is especially true if the designation is based on social and cultural rather than religious discourse. In trying to explain the cultural and social significance of this space, the sociologist Georg Simmel designated it as a "pivotal point" for Jews. He was, of course, interested in the special situation in which the culture's pivotal point is absent and the members of the culture are dispersed geographically. The fact that the sacrificial service ended with the destruction of the Temple meant that Jerusalem had no replacement: "Sacrifices could only be made in Jerusalem; Yahweh had no other sacrificial altar in any other place. . . . A rigid choice: here or nowhere."[6]

Living with the choice between "here" and "nowhere" produced spaces of longing. Loss and absence became constitutive experiences in Jewish culture, giving rise to various ways of mourning and comforting, and to lesser substitutes for the Temple. "From the day that the Temple was destroyed," Anat tells the women in her audience, "there were no more sacrifices, the priests ceased to serve, and here, we are commanded to observe such a great mitzvah that contains a commemoration of the sacrifices." The placement of the *hafrashat hallah* ceremony in the Temple context is the interpretive linchpin in my reading of the ethnography. Added to this are common interpretations of the deed that view the ceremony as a type of *tiqqun 'olam*, or repair of the world. The fact that the destroyed Temple reconstitutes itself for a few moments in the kitchen of each woman who performs the ceremony of *hafrashat ḥallah* makes the home, the kitchen, and the food produced there critical components in the observance of rituals in general and, in particular, those relevant to women.[7]

Foodstuff, the sustenance processed by culture into food (organic and/or spiritual), is a subject beloved by anthropologists. Ortner is not the only one to address its theoretical aspects. She follows a solid tradition, the most prominent of whose founders were the structuralists Claude Lévi-Strauss and Mary Douglas.[8] The transition to research on Western capitalist societies placed food within the broader context of consumerism. Food is, on the one hand, a principal component in the living expenses of poor individuals and families and, on the other, a part of the culture of plenty, of fashion, and of overconsumption. In this ceremony, a commandment that first appeared in the Torah and that was then assigned to women fell into neglect; the directors and impresarios here have revived it, but in a world of consumption and plenty. Leaving aside for the moment the cultural economy of the *hafrashat ḥallah* ceremony, I will focus in what follows on the organizers and attendees as a learning group and the metamorphosis of the kitchen into a Holy Temple in miniature.

"All Rights Reserved to Anat": The Ceremony's Organizers and Audience as a Learning Group

The three letters that Anat chose to read to her audience present three heroines, each situated in a different position in the field of religious observance and return to religion. Meital is *ḥaredi*, Osnat is a nonreligious woman who is searching, and the woman from Afulah has found her way to religious Judaism, but her husband has not yet joined her. Fragments of details point to their Sefaradi or Ashkenazi ethnicity, but all three have entirely modern Israeli names and live at varying degrees of remove from the densely populated Tel Aviv metropolitan area. Meital lives in El'ad, a new *ḥaredi* town in central Israel; Osnat in Lod, a Jewish Arab city between Tel Aviv and Jerusalem that suffers from poverty and neglect; and the unnamed woman in Afulah, a city in the Jezreel Valley in the country's north. Anat apparently assumes that this range of individuals and locations will invite most of her listeners to find a character with whom they can identify.

Each letter centers on a dramatic narrative. Even though Anat reads only a few lines to the women, it is easy to imagine the event, the protagonist, the secondary characters, and, especially, the role that the *hafrashat ḥallah* ceremony plays in the chain of events. Meital, who is taken to the hospital bleeding, is presented as a pious and competent woman. She calls an ambulance when her husband is paralyzed, gives charity, and prays, and asks her husband to see to it that Torah scholars recite psalms for her. Yet this battery of religious acts and the efforts of the doctors have no effect. Meital's mother, rather than the famous Rabbi Kneibsky, the dough rather than prayer and charity, produce the miracle. The choice of a drama leading to the "happy ending" of the safe birth of a son hardly needs explication within orthodox Jewish discourse.

Osnat, the next heroine, blends two critical and connected processes: returning to religion and finding a good match. In her case, the *hafrashat hallah* ceremony is not the successful end of the drama but its beginning. After attending one of Anat's ceremonies, something is kindled in Osnat's heart. The same "something" that sent a girl with "short hair and lots of earrings" who would not let anyone comment on her appearance to the ceremony is the "something" that would not let her sleep afterward.[9] The letter describes a turbulent night that ended with the holiest and most moving wedding that Anat had ever witnessed. The union of the punk girl and "*haredi* boy with a pure soul" is a variation on a classic template in the genre of back-to-religion tales. Chance and romance are interwoven and lead to the acknowledgment of a guiding hand that mends torn souls.

Osnat's story is the one for the girls in the audience who are unsure which way to choose in life and who have not yet found love. For those who are already on the path of religious observance but are having difficulty bringing their husbands along, and who are also having trouble getting pregnant, Anat presents the girl from Afulah. Her letter depicts harsh scenes of fighting and suspicion. He is a son of Holocaust survivors, and she is an unsuccessful baker. After attending a *hafrashat hallah* ceremony and receiving telephone guidance from Anat, all her problems are solved. Her husband believes in God, her *hallot* come out perfectly, and of course she becomes pregnant.

Anat knows that she is not alone in the back-to-religion and spirituality marketplace. She knows that some of the women have heard such stories before, have attended spiritual events, have listened to rabbis of various sorts preach on religious radio stations or at live events. Despite their fundamental willingness to be open to her messages, she knows that they are also always somewhat skeptical. So she tells them that she has the full names, addresses, and telephone numbers of the heroines of her stories, and a binder full of additional stories of women "you can call and everything." Anat's rhetorical and ritual work seeks to create an open space that many women can enter. It promises them a chance to cope with what popular religious culture considers "the most basic problems of the female sex": finding a husband, giving birth to healthy children, and running a successful household.

Anat offers this package deal explicitly, almost crudely. But alongside it are secondary benefits made possible by the fact that the person conducting the ceremony is a woman and that the letters were written by women and are read before women. The process of empowerment runs from Meital's mother to Meital herself, skipping over the doctors who disparage them, and even over the Torah scholars who read psalms for them. It extends from Osnat, who demands that no one comment on her appearance, to Anat, who would "God forbid never make any comments." The process extends from Lod to Afulah. It portrays an inept housewife as a person who has an opportunity to point her family along the right road. Anat's mention of her return to religion invites other women into the changing community. It indicates to them that they can succeed there and that those who succeed do not forget where they come from. The destination remains clear, but many women in the synagogue and at other ceremonies that Anat runs know that they are still far from reaching that point. Yet their very presence in the hall makes them potential heroines in future letters. The *hafrashat hallah* ceremony that they attend is not only a way of fulfilling a commandment but also an opening for the repair of the world.

Kneading Flour and Water to Mend the World: The Temple and the Kitchen

> The sin of the Tree of Knowledge caused a general imperfection and accomplished a separation of corporeality from divinity, and there-fore its repair is in the commandment of *hallah*. . . . It is written in the midrash that the commandment of *hallah* repairs the sin of the Tree of Knowledge, and therefore the commandment was given to women. Because she spoiled the *hallah* of the world [i.e., Adam], she must repair this through the commandment of *hallah*.
> —Rabbi Menachem Mendel Schneerson

In his book *Divinity and Experience: The Religion of the Dinka*, the anthropologist Godfrey Liendhardt recounts the creation story of the Dinka, an East African tribe.[10] Instead of Adam and Eve, the Dinka tell him about Abuk and Garang. Instead of the Garden of Eden, Abuk and Garang have a field and a single seed of millet that their god gives them each day. One day, the woman, "because she was greedy," tries to cultivate more than one seed. She raises her hoe and deals a blow to the god. He retreats to his place in the sky, leaving behind parched land, hunger, death, and disease. He cuts the rope that linked sky and earth.

There are many parallels between the two stories, but the most important one for this study is the subject of ruin and repair. With her greed, the Dinka woman causes the god to retreat and unlink heaven and earth. Eve "ruins" Adam, whom the midrash describes as "the *hallah* of the world." In the view of the last Lubavitcher rebbe, Rabbi Menachem Mendel Schneerson, the spiritual leader of Ḥabad Hasidism—and in the view of other traditional commentators—this "ruin" is the separation between the material and the spiritual, between the mundane and the divine. He views Eve's choice as having set off a chain of binary separations that deepen the breach between the sacred and the profane, between the creator and his created beings, and among the created beings themselves. Before the "ruin," the world was hybrid. God and his created beings functioned in the same ecology, which was good and benevolent. Man's divine image needed no additional reinforcement (such as "knowledge"), and there were no differences between different kinds of human beings.

After the sin, the biblical story is one of differentiations. Humans are differentiated from animals, man from woman, brother from brother, one language from another, righteous men from evil men, and so on. The *hafrashat hallah* ceremony is one of mixing, of kneading, of unifying two distinct materials into a single dough. Flour is mixed with water, and the *hallah* is eaten by men and women, "so that food is unified with man and becomes blood and flesh of his flesh, and by this man lives," writes the rebbe. The goal of observing the commandment of *hafrashat hallah* is, according to Rabbi Schneerson, "to act on it in the words of the authority so that they are unified with the divine." In the dough, "flour and water are mixed, where the flour is individual crumbs, separate points, and by the water the separate points are united and made a single entity, and its spiritual meaning is that corporeal things, which are separate things, like the separate points of the flour, are united by the Torah, which is symbolized by water." In Ḥabad's theology, it is another way in which the Torah hints that distant things must be brought together.[11] Therefore, Anat does not just seek to perform the ceremony among the members of her family, but to go out and seek "separated points" and then "knead" them into the "water"—the Torah. The uniqueness of the ceremony lies in the fact that the sanctification or rising is performed on the raw material before it becomes food.

The fact that all human beings treat raw material in one form or another before turning it into food has made this work a common subject of anthropological research. This processing separates us from animals and marks the "treatment" of food as a cultural process laden with meaning. It is hardly surprising, then, that structuralist anthropologists, especially Lévi-Strauss and Douglas, spent some time at this intersection between the distinctions among foods (pure and impure) and their preparation. They, and Ortner after them, presumed that deconstructing these actions would reveal the cultural foundations that construct their subjects' worlds. Ingesting food into the human body makes humans like animals, who must also consume food in order to survive. The fact that humans often eat animals makes this similarity especially problematic. Human beings view their bodies as having been created in the image of God, yet they turn out to be material bodies with physical needs. The preparation of food is thus an act of paradoxically distancing oneself from the material, an attempt to approach the spiritual.

In Rabbi Schneerson's explanation of the reasons for the *hafrashat hallah* ritual, he explicates the Hebrew word *terumah*, which appears in the Torah verses on this precept. The usual translation of the word is "gift," but the rebbe instead focuses on the meaning of the root on which the verb is built, which connotes "rising" or "raising up." Man is commanded to raise up the dough from which he will bake bread by giving a part of it as a gift. The bread will be elevated, and all food will be elevated with it: "When the dough is baked and becomes bread, man can choose to raise up the bread, and in this manner the bread can raise up the man," writes Rabbi Schneerson.[12] The mending act is thus a double one, and, like all acts of mending, it is meant to act on and be acted on by the material and the spiritual, to exert its influence both below and above. Human actions in this world are meant to shape the cultural reality in which humans live. This reality is meant to affect heaven and to repair what has been broken by the acts of other human beings. The first human act of breakage or damage is attributed to the first woman, and the precept of *hafrashat hallah*, which the Bible did not assign to women (and which apparently became associated with women because of their kitchen work), is interpreted as offering them the possibility of repairing that damage, of engaging in *tiqqun 'olam*.

Anat seeks to resuscitate an opportunity that has, for whatever reason, been allowed to gather dust. She seeks to walk the sure path that directs women into the kitchen, and to create there a Temple in miniature. For one night, the path leaves the house and leads to the synagogue, where Anat and the participants occupy the building's sanctuary. Anat stands on the bimah (the raised platform at the front of the room from which the prayers are led and the Torah scrolls read). The folding table, placed before the bimah and covered with an oilcloth on which there are flour, water, rolling pins, bowls, and yeast, brings something of the kitchen into the synagogue. From the very first step, when Anat prepares the dough, she addresses the links between body and spirit. "I knead with my hands, not with a mixer, so that my limbs will be partners in the mitzvah." She presents unmediated, sensuous touch as a link between the road and the destination, between the material and the spiritual. When the dough is taken outside to rise, Anat takes up the reasons behind the precept. She reiterates its centrality in the life of women, alongside the commandments of lighting the Sabbath candles and observing the laws of ritual purity. She regrets that this mitzvah is not as widely observed as the other two, and presents it as "very spiritual." It "contains a commemoration of the sacrifices," Anat says, and locates the women who observe it as continuing, in their way, the devotions of the high priest, who in the past oversaw the rituals of the Temple. The audience has already heard about the practical efficacy of the observance from the letters that Anat read them. So, after the reading of the letters, which tell of this world's tribulations and its wonders, Anat tells of other worlds.

Anat makes the existence of these worlds real by playing with letters and numbers. She uses anagrams, letter replacements, and number symbols to play with the significance of coincidence, subjecting it to a transcendental order. The women in the audience are amazed by the way in which the letters *ḥ-l-ḥ* become the first letters of "share in the world to come," and how rearranging the letters of *hafrashat ḥallah* produces a phrase promising pregnancy. They are impressed by the interpretation of the events of September 11, in the form of an updated version of the Passover song "Who Knows One." This numerology can inhabit their own kitchens. It is another form of empowerment that links their bodies, their private fears, and the fears of their nation into something that they can grasp. The Temple as a "key symbol" in Jewish culture, and the kitchen as an existential locus of women, come together and create a point on the map of symbols where women can stand erect.

Ortner's theory about "key symbols" divides them into binary clusters. One side of this division collects individual components and connects them into a coherent picture. This side ratifies and sanctifies the culture and the social order that derives from it and is meant to strengthen commitment to them. The other side of the division opens and broadens the exegetical horizon. It offers broad metaphors that can develop new thoughts and fresh strategies of action. In modern American society, for example, Ortner places the national flag on the summarizing, uniting side and the "machine" or the "computer" on the elaborating metaphorical side. Ortner realizes that the two sides are connected by a spectrum of intermediate states, but she prefers to work with their ideal types. The *hafrashat ḥallah* ceremony now renewing itself in *ḥaredi* society indicates an even more complex situation. The symbols, and the scenarios of action derived from their meanings, can move from one side to the other. This movement can be a challenge to the social structure, or create an alternative. The actual kitchen and the absent Temple are an example of this situation.

The kitchen as a real or symbolic area of women's living is, without a doubt, a summarizing symbol. The call "Women to the kitchen!," which came with Western feminism of the second half of the twentieth century, sought to send women back to their "natural place." The kitchen is that internal region of the home that both sends out food for the sustenance of the home's inhabitants and gathers in the leavings and the dirt. In this small, warm enclosure, women's work is conducted routinely and cyclically.

The symbolic distance between the Temple and the home kitchen is obvious. This distance derives from the divergence between the sacred and the mundane, the public and the private, the ceremonial and the routine, the male and the female. The destroyed Temple can be seen as an elaborating symbol from which are derived a multitude of metaphors that sustain Jewish culture in a variety of ways. But the similarity between the two sites is no less interesting. The sacrifices in the Temple turned it into a type of large slaughterhouse, the altar into the largest work surface in the region, and the priests into butchers of a sort. The Temple and its personnel occupied themselves with food—firstfruit offerings, priestly gifts, and tithes. They mixed, kneaded, sprinkled, and fed. The placement of the Temple and the kitchen side by side in the public *hafrashat ḥallah* ceremony challenges the division between the public and the private, between the male and the female, between summarizing and elaborating symbols. The biblical commandment, which is meant to be carried out in the public space of the Temple, moves into the home. The hands of male priests are replaced by the arms of women. The culturing of the dough into food, the elevation of bread into a means of *tiqqun 'olam*, is made a duty of the daughters of Eve. Instead of a private act accomplished by each woman inside her house, the ceremony offers a public spiritual event. The synagogue becomes, for a time, a Temple and a kitchen, a place of leisure, enjoyment, and shopping, a site of induction of new participants into the life of halakhah and religion, offering a real and symbolic elaboration for women within their lives.

On Tradition

> The derivation of the legitimacy of an order from a belief in the sanctity of tradition is the most universal and most primitive case. The fear of magical penalties confirms the general psychological inhibitions against any sort of change in customary modes of action.
>
> —Max Weber

Within sociological discourse, the definition of tradition in modern societies goes back to Max Weber. His understanding of the power of tradition as "the most universal and most primitive case" of deriving legitimacy for social action served as a point of departure for most scholars.[13] A common interpretation of his understanding situates tradition vis-à-vis autonomy, or logical thinking. On this interpretation, tradition entails the repetition of customs rather than a rational decision to pursue a certain goal or choose an original way of acting. Raymond Aron, for example, reads traditional action à la Weber as "action that is dictated by customs, by beliefs, [has] become habitual and second nature, as it were, so that to act according to tradition the actor need not imagine a goal, or be conscious of a value, or be stirred to immediate emotion; he simply obeys reflexes that have become entrenched by conditioning."[14]

Aron's interpretation pictures the actor who follows tradition as a conditioned one, a "he" who "simply obeys reflexes." Much has been written on tradition since Weber and Aron. Modern, autonomous, and logical social action has been problematized, and tradition has been portrayed (among other things) as a forceful mechanism made anew or invented to suit changing social and political situations.[15] Yet it seems as if the space between the natural appearance of tradition and the actual creation of that tradition is the most suggestive one. This space does not necessary exclude Weber's actor from the scene, since he might claim (and feel) that he is repeating a habit as he performs something new or different. But the social ability to create new practices and perform them in a way that allows them to be taken for granted and habitual turns tradition into something dynamic.

In his research on Purim celebrations in the early days of Tel Aviv (1908–36), Hezki Shoham talks about tradition in a fresh way. Via the case study of the Purim festivals, he challenges the dichotomy between tradition and modernity, the temporal affiliation of traditions to the past, and the distinctions between big and small traditions. He claims that the discourse of tradition was (and is) the creation of a modern culture to legitimize new social actions, social orders, and the emergence of new cultural agents. Hobsbawm likewise differentiated between authentic and invented traditions, marking the later as manipulative. But Shoham wishes to take the industry of tradition invention seriously, to show that beyond the use of the past to serve the present, it has an important impact on the future. While Weber saw tradition as a means to bend the present to the past, Shoham argues that invented tradition can tie the present to a future while relating to the past. Thus it offers paths for historical continuities, essential in the creation of modern societies. Following the anthropologists Redfield and Singer, he claims that only "frozen societies" lacking any notion of time and history can afford to live without tradition. The rest need traditions in order to change. The new Zionist culture in the Land of Israel offered an ideal case study to check these assumptions, though Shoham believes that they hold true in any modern culture.[16]

The urgency of tradition in a religious culture such as the one discussed in this chapter is acute. Yet the need for constant dialogue with "the past" creates endless new possibilities for conversations with the present and for the future. In this study, the actor is a she, whether it is Anat, who runs the ceremony (and holds the "copyright"), or Mira, who put a group of *haredi* women together in order to shake up their everyday reality. The women who gathered in the synagogue came at the initiative of a local action group that organizes activities of various types—field trips, vacations, exercise classes, lectures, and group discussions. The group was established by women and for women, without the precedent of former such groups and without official male oversight. A fuller description and analysis of the group's activities (of which this event is only a part) reveals the practice of teaching tradition, in a new market of initiators and clientele.

The designation of the women as a public obligated to observe commandments, the public instruction of women aimed at teaching them to observe commandments carefully, the resuscitation and innovation of praxes meant for and permitted to women as areas of activity abounding in spiritual power all join together to make a new force. It is a force that makes a place for women, a force that reorganizes the living compounds of religion and its ceremonies, a force that negotiates patriarchal definitions of high versus popular religion, not from the margins of the synagogue but at its very heart. A vital force, the industry of *teshuvah*.

You can pray, sing, move, and perform the work of God in an embodied manner, engraved on your skin, burned in your flesh, saved in your memory after years of watching your mother, aunt, and grandmother do it. You may perform these actions in a newly learned manner, as your teacher does it, as you saw it done in the synagogue, as your friend does it, or as you have grown accustomed to doing it yourself. Paradoxically, then, tradition is a social work that is never complete, acted out over and over again like an ancient deed, over and over again like a new act.

Chapter 13

Judaism and the Idea of Ancient Ritual Theory

Michael D. Swartz

Ritual, despite its universality as a form of human activity, is remarkable for its resistance to definitive interpretation. Indeed, some have argued that its very opacity is indispensable to its effectiveness. As Catherine Bell has pointed out, in many cases ritual is invalidated if it is understood: if we understood the (supposedly) "real" reasons why we shake hands, knock on wood, or throw rice at a wedding, there would be no reason to do so. This idea can be traced to Pierre Bourdieu's notion of misrecognition. Describing the process of gift-giving, Bourdieu argues that the appearance of a disinterested voluntary exchange masks the real economy of reciprocal and hierarchical relations that occurs in a gift-exchanging society.[1] Likewise, Bell maintains that a successful operation of a ritual involves what she calls a "strategic 'misrecognition' of the relationship of one's ends and means."[2] This opacity led Frits Staal to characterize ritual as a set of "rules without meaning."[3]

Yet ritual practitioners do, in fact, give account of their own rituals and offer interpretations of them. At times, a ritual explicitly interprets itself, as when a priest, presenting the Eucharist, announces that it is the body and blood of Christ; or when, in a synagogue service, a Torah scroll is held up and pronounced to be "the Torah that Moses placed before the children of Israel from the mouth of God, by the hand of Moses." However, these utterances do more than explain—indeed, one could argue that explanation is not their major purpose. Some, applying J. L. Austin's speech-act theory, call such utterances performative, transforming the status of those objects by the very fact of being uttered.[4]

One way or another, these arguments show us the dual nature of language in relationship to ritual: that it can be a way of embedding meaning in a ritual situation; and that, at the same time, it has a function that goes beyond the informative or explanatory. In other words, language functions *in* ritual and communities create language *about* ritual. On the one hand, discourse is embedded in ritual, including speech acts and signs encoded for communicating with deities or intermediary beings.[5] On the other hand, when we step back from this closely integrated level of ritual discourse, we come to the act of interpreting and systematizing ritual practices. These practices can range from practical discussions about how a ritual should be carried out to wide-ranging theoretical discussions about the nature and purpose of ritual and its various forms.

This chapter concerns one type of discourse about sacrifice as it was imagined in a period of crisis in ancient Judaism—what will be called ancient ritual theory in this essay. It describes how, during the centuries following the destruction of the Temple in 70 C.E., two distinct groups, the rabbis quoted in the Mishnah and the liturgical poets of the Palestinian synagogues, recounted one of ancient Judaism's central sacrifices—the ritual of purification for Yom Kippur (the 'Avodah)—in different ways for their own purposes. The main sources for this study are the tractate *Yoma* of the Mishnah, Tosefta, and Palestinian Talmud, and the 'Avodah *piyyutim*, the liturgical compositions recited on Yom Kippur that recount that sacrifice in verse. It will be argued that for the rabbis and synagogue poets who wrote systematic accounts of the lost sacrifices, this act served both as an activity embedded in ritual itself and as a theoretical examination of its meaning and purpose. These writers were not only interested in establishing the meaning of ritual in theological and conceptual terms. Rather, in the process of commenting on ritual actions and actors, they also engaged in social analysis and critique. Ancient ritual theory, then, must be understood as a historically situated discourse that responded to specific transformations in sacrificial practice and reflected competing social hierarchies that contested religious authority.

Ancient Ritual Theory

Ritual theory, the endeavor to make ritual understandable as a form of human activity, is a characteristic feature of the modern study of religion. However, systematic discourse about the meaning and function of ritual has also been carried out in societies that do not engage in the study of religion. The term "ancient ritual theory" alerts us to occasions in which a premodern culture turns to systematic discourse about ritual.

These occasions deserve notice as a historical phenomenon. They are partly a result of the very opacity of ritual described above. This opacity creates a tension between the performance of ritual, which, in many cases, relies on a type of misrecognition for its success, and its interpretation, which is occasioned by those very mechanisms of misrecognition. The process of interpretation can take various forms, from the embedding of explanatory discourse within a ritual itself to construction of a fully formed philosophical system around a set of ritual prescriptions.

A culture's interest in speaking about ritual systematically is not fully realized in all places and times. Some people are particularly adept at thinking about rituals reflectively, phenomenologically, or historically. Victor Turner, for example, found such a person in Muchona the Hornet, a wandering Ndembu healer whom he saw as a kindred spirit.[6] But it is one thing to say that the talents and urges that motivate contemporary anthropologists and students of religion also motivate participants in ritual traditions; it is another thing to find that a society has turned from the conscientious practice of ritual to a concerted effort to explain it and has built systems of discourse around it. Because rituals can go on for generations without occasioning more than casual attempts at theorization or explanation, we should ask ourselves why ritual theory takes place at particular moments in history, and what the conditions are in which discourse about ritual flourishes. Thomas Kasulis uses the term "metapraxis" for such discourse and observes that it requires certain conditions: "First, a religious praxis always involves effort, and the effort must be justifiable. Second, where there is awareness of other traditions with different praxes, one's own praxes necessarily undergo scrutiny."[7] Kasulis's insights alert us to how we must pay attention to historical context when examining discourse about ritual.

Historically, ancient ritual theory has taken several forms. In some cases, communities or intellectual circles have constructed a set of symbols, constituting a kind of allegorical pattern, around the materials and acts of a ritual system. In this way, every object or action stands for something else, so that the participants in the ritual are seen to be enacting a kind of symbolic drama. The Passover Haggadah provides a good example of this conception, as it makes the interpretation of symbols an indispensable part of the ritual itself.[8]

At other times, ancient ritual theory has served as a philosophical justification for a given set of rituals. In classical Christianity, it has taken the form of ritual theology. In the Purva Mīmāṃsā, the complex philosophical tradition of Vedic interpretation that arose in Hinduism in the fifth century B.C.E., it constituted an encompassing conceptual system based on the premise that the ritual system is deeply foundational to the makeup of the world.[9] Other related forms of discourse on ritual have taken the form of redescribing an older ritual in such a way that it became intelligible to a community that needed to make sense of it. In this case, the "theorizing" did not inhere in the explicit formulation of abstract principles. Rather, the authors' use of symbolism, emphasis and connotation, and narrative flow tell us how the ritual has been conceived and reinterpreted.

Finally, ancient ritual discourse has also been known to constitute a form of ritual itself. That is, the act of speaking about ritual, in the form of philosophical or legal study, recitation of ritual prescriptions, or the creation of artistic works portraying existing rituals, can itself become a ritualized activity and thus enter a liturgical system. It is in this last function, as a form of embedded ritual activity, that the rubric of ancient ritual theory is most relevant to this discussion. Jewish texts from late antiquity on the sacrificial system provide excellent examples of these dynamics. The rabbis and poets who applied themselves to the Yom Kippur sacrifice were striving both to arrive at a conception of the function of sacrifice and its participants and to mirror some of those functions in the very act of describing them.

Sacrificial Theory in Mishnah *Yoma*

Sacrifice was the central ritual in the ancient world.[10] By end of the second century C.E., only two communities of any significance in the Mediterranean basin did not hold sacrifices: Jews and Christians. For the rest of the Greco-Roman world, sacrifice was at the very heart of religion. This point is important because subsequent history and the triumphs of Christianity and rabbinic Judaism seem to make sacrifice's obsolescence inevitable. As Peter Brown, Jonathan Z. Smith, and others have argued, late antiquity marked a major shift in paradigms of holiness, especially the transfer of the locus of holiness from place to person.[11] Therefore, any consideration of how successive generations of Jews in late antiquity understood rituals involving sacred places such as the Jerusalem Temple must pay attention to how the social dimensions of ritual are understood as well.

To set the stage for understanding Jewish conceptions of sacrifice in late antiquity, we must ask ourselves what, exactly, the destruction of the Temple entailed. To be sure, it entailed human tragedy and physical destruction, but its theological meaning went beyond that. The Temple was considered to be the locus of what Baruch A. Levine calls the potent presence of God, which was said to descend on the Holy of Holies when the high priest invoked it on Yom Kippur.[12] The function of purification and attraction of this presence, not only atonement, lay at the heart of Yom Kippur. The loss of the Temple therefore meant the departure of that presence from the world, an idea that persisted well beyond the first century.[13]

Often, accounts of the rabbinic response to the destruction focus on statements attributed to such figures as Yoḥanan ben Zakkai, who is said to have declared, "We have another means of atonement, effective as Temple sacrifice. It is deeds of lovingkindness."[14] But a better indication of the early rabbis' response is the first systematic expression of the rabbinic world view, the Mishnah, which devotes more than a third of its bulk to the sacrificial system and its ramifications. Indeed, the rabbis declared that the study of the laws of sacrifice was tantamount to the actual performance of sacrifice in the Temple.[15]

One of the first scholars to express awareness of this problem was Jacob Neusner, who dealt with the question of mishnaic theories of sacrifice in his article "Map without Territory."[16] Neusner surveys the order *Qodashim* of the Mishnah to consider whether it offers a theory of sacrifice. For Neusner, the material of the order itself adds little to Scripture's prescriptions for the cult—this in contrast to the order of *Toharot*, which made many remarkable innovations. The novelty of *Qodashim* is to be found in its matter-of-fact description itself, in a context in which the Temple had been destroyed and practical hopes for its restoration had been dashed. Tractate *Yoma* (in the order *Mo'ed*), by contrast, presents a different portrait of the cult, reflecting the ideology of the early rabbis in representing the Yom Kippur ritual.

Yoma belongs to a category of Mishnah tractates distinguished by their unusual style. Rather than presenting legal principles and rulings in a prescriptive fashion, *Yoma* is structured as a narrative, describing the Yom Kippur ritual from the week of preparation preceding the day to the evening at the close of the holiday when the high priest rejoins his family. *Yoma* shares this narrative style with a few other tractates that describe pivotal institutions of the lost Temple system.[17] The narrative character of *Yoma* has further ramifications for its function as a text to be recited. Starting with the early rabbinic period, it played a role in the synagogue liturgy for Yom Kippur.

This dual nature of the tractate corresponds to two ways in which it expresses early rabbinic theories of sacrifice. The first is in how the tractate narrates the ritual so as to imagine the sacrifice in a new way. This redescription places a new emphasis on the social dimension of the ritual and, in so doing, mounts a critique of the priesthood. At the same time, the tractate follows the biblical source in understanding the ultimate purpose of the sacrifice to be purification through blood. The second way the tractate tells us about the nature of sacrifice is through its function as a scholastic text to be memorized and performed.

Persons and Politics

One of the most striking characteristics of *Yoma* is its social and political concerns. In Leviticus 16, Aaron is the sole human character in the sacrificial drama. He alone is portrayed as the one who offers the sin offering, slaughters the bulls, sends the goat to Azazel, and, above all, enters the Holy of Holies to encounter the divine presence. The active verbs in the chapter belong to him.

Yoma presents a different picture entirely. The tractate cannot contradict the Torah's instructions, but it contextualizes the priest's performance of his duties in a radically different way. The Mishnah depicts the sacrifice as it took place in the Second Temple of the first centuries B.C.E. and C.E. Aaron, the ancestor of all priests, is represented in this depiction by a Zadokite high priest, a member of the Sadducean party of the Second Temple period. However, the high priest is depicted as acting under the strict supervision of the sages, who are identified with the Sadducees' opponents, the Pharisees. In the eyes of the early rabbis in the wake of the destruction of the Temple, these Pharisaic sages were the spiritual ancestors of the rabbis themselves and symbolized the rabbinic way of life: the emphasis on the study of Torah and the individual's performance of the mitzvot in contrast to the collective, sacrificial, and priest-centered cult.

The high priest is portrayed in the Mishnah as utterly passive. In the first chapters of the tractate, most of the active verbs concern actions not of the high priest himself but of the sages, a category missing entirely from Leviticus 16.[18] They sequester him, prepare a new wife for him in case he is suddenly bereft of a household for which to atone, keep him awake while they lecture him, walk him from one chamber to another in the Temple complex, and instruct him in the order of sacrifice to such an extent that they must even pass bulls and sheep before him so that he will be familiar with them.[19] It is assumed that the high priest is likely to be an ignoramus or a heretic. When the time comes for the priest to read and expound on the Scripture's instructions for performing the ceremony, the sages enjoin him, "My lord high priest! Recite with your own mouth—or perhaps you have forgotten or did not learn!"[20] When it comes time to charge the high priest with the solemnity of what he is about to do, the sages do so with this speech: "My lord high priest! We are the representatives of the court, and you are our representative and the messenger of the court. We adjure you by the One who caused his name to dwell in this house not to change a thing of what we have told you." Then the Mishnah adds, "He turned aside and wept, and they turned aside and wept."

This poignant moment encapsulates a major theme in the tractate: the tension between the high priest and the sages is cast against the background of the sectarian strife of the Second Commonwealth. According to the Mishnah, the elders needed to ensure that the high priest would perform the sacrifice according to Pharisaic law and therefore made him swear to that effect on penalty of death. Indeed, the Tosefta tells a story in which a Sadducean priest offers the incense his way and not in the order prescribed by the Pharisees. As the story goes, "Three days did not go by before they put him in his grave."[21] This story emphasizes two things: the gravity of proper performance of the procedure and the degree to which it was the focus of intense political struggle. In the opening mishnayot, then, the tractate introduces two elements to Leviticus's narrative of the procedure: the social dimension of the ritual; and a deep ambivalence about the main actor in the sacrifice, the high priest.

Efficacious Elements of the Ritual

Yet the structure of the Yom Kippur sacrifice demands that the high priest be the focus of the procedure. Therefore, the tractate is organized around him. It follows him step by step, detailing which actions he performs, where he stands, and those with whom he relates. This, however, does not prevent the Mishnah from criticizing the high priest and from departing from that structure to linger on several details. These details can give us an idea of what the Mishnah considers to be the most efficacious elements of the ritual.

Often, those departures take the form of excurses on specific artifacts used for the ceremony. An important theme of *Yoma* is the nature and history of the objects necessary for the cult. The tractate is especially concerned with how the objects are made and their social history. In the course of describing the containers that held the lots for the scapegoat, the Mishnah remarks that although "they had been made of boxwood, Ben Gamla made them of gold" (mYom 3:9). The Mishnah goes on to list other praiseworthy donations of sacred implements (mYom 3:10), but then turns to those who were remembered unfavorably (mYom 3:11). The examples are those of clans or individuals identified with the priestly establishment who refused to teach their craft to others, such as the House of Garmu, who were unwilling to teach making the Bread of Presentation, and Hygros ben Levi, who knew a singing technique but was unwilling to teach it.

These mishnayot interrupt the narrative and were apparently inserted at one point, as the next mishnah describes the high priest shaking the urn.[22] But, like the Mishnah's description of the ignorant priest in chapter 1, this interpolation expresses the Mishnah's ambivalence toward the priestly establishment. The clans and persons mentioned in Mishnah *Yoma* 3:11 are unambiguously condemned. Through these examples, the Mishnah teaches that the respect due the priestly clan is conditional on its piety.

Another important element of the Mishnah's narrative is how it follows the high priest through the geography of the Temple as he carries out his ritual. The tractate describes with precision which direction the high priest faces as he holds the goat, where he steps at each stage, and how he enters the Holy of Holies. A striking example of the methodical, repetitive style that characterizes this description appears in *Yoma* 5:5: "He began purifying downward. From where did he begin? From the northeast corner, to the northwest, to the southwest, and to the southeast. From the place that he began purifying the outer altar, from there he would finish doing so on the inner altar."

The passage, with its recitation of the four corners, takes us through the process of expiation of the altars. It draws a kind of diagram of the priest's movements as he purifies both altars and, in specifying each direction, allows us to imagine each step.

Also notable is the Mishnah's description of the high priest's entrance into the Holy of Holies, according to the opinion that there were two curtains: "He reached the northern end, he faced the south, and walked to his left with the curtain, until he reached the ark" (mYom 5:1). Saul Lieberman showed that this movement corresponded to common Greco-Roman practices for entering sanctuaries with proper respect.[23] This methodical description of the geography of the Temple serves not only to fill in legal details of the cult, but to provide the reader or listener with a vivid verbal map of the lost sanctuary.

The high priest is thus at the center of the ceremony in the Mishnah's description. However, his role is not simply as a representative of Israel before God. His main role, in the view of the Mishnah, is as a dispenser of blood, which is the principal agent of activity in the ritual system of *Yoma*. Immediately after the animal is slaughtered, the blood is collected in bowls and used to purify the most sensitive places in the sanctuary. The narrative follows the blood at every step, from the moment of slaughter to when it runs down the drains to be sold as fertilizer. At *Yoma* 5:4, the Mishnah includes a litany that counts the number of times the priest whips the blood onto the altar: "And this is how he would count: 'one, one and two, one and three, one and four, one and five, one and six, one and seven.'" The effect of this recitation is to carry the listener through the process of the distribution and disposal of the blood moment by moment.

The second most important substance in the ceremony is the incense. The Mishnah follows the incense in the fire pan into the sanctuary with the priest, commenting on the high priest's requirement to follow the sages' procedure against the Zadokite practice. The Mishnah states that the public perceived the moment inside the Holy of Holies as fraught with danger; the high priest was not to prolong his prayer there lest the people panic (mYom 5:1). However, it is not stated explicitly that he encounters the divine presence.

Perhaps the most famous component of the Yom Kippur ceremony is the scapegoat ritual, in which two goats are presented at the altar, one to be slaughtered "for the Lord" and one "for the people," to be cast out into the wilderness bearing Israel's sins. In the Mishnah's description, this procedure becomes a drama about Israel's fate. The narrative makes it clear that the masses of people observing the ceremony are primarily concerned with the portents connected with that ceremony and what they mean for the nation's destiny for the coming year: whether the lot designating the goat "for the Lord" comes up in the priest's right hand; and, at the end, whether the crimson thread tied to the door of the sanctuary turns white to indicate that the goat has reached the wilderness and God has forgiven the people.[24]

The Purpose of Sacrifice

According to the Mishnah, therefore, the purpose of the Yom Kippur sacrifice is the purification of the altar through blood. This statement might seem uncontroversial; after all, is this not the purpose of the biblical sacrifice? But there are cases where the Mishnah transforms biblical rituals into enterprises not self-evident from the biblical texts. Baruch Bokser's classic study *The Origins of the Seder* provides such a case, in which the sacrificial nature of the biblical Passover is transformed in the hands of the Mishnah's description of the rite in *Pesaḥim*.[25]

But does the Mishnah's account of the Yom Kippur ritual add up to an early rabbinic theory of sacrifice? On the face of it, there is little explicit theorizing. The Mishnah and Tosefta do not explain, for example, why animals are to be killed or sent out into the wilderness, what exactly the blood does to the altar, and whether the presence of God actually resides in the Holy of Holies. Nevertheless, *Yoma*'s narrative constitutes a subtle but meaningful discourse on the expiation ritual and its meaning.

The first message that *Yoma* conveys is, to paraphrase a famous work of Jewish anthropology, that ritual is with people.[26] Whereas Leviticus 16 presents the story of a man, his bull, and his goats, *Yoma* presents a full tableau depicting a complex institution peopled with sages, priests, guilds, and throngs of anxious worshipers. Yom Kippur is a collective occasion for expiation of the community and its central institution, as we can see from the text's account of how many classes and professions contribute to the success of the ritual (mYom 3).

At the center of the activity is the priest himself. The Mishnah necessarily adheres to the structure of Leviticus as it follows the high priest in his steps through the process of sacrificing, offering incense, and sending the scapegoat to Azazel. At the same time, the Mishnah displays a deep ambivalence toward the high priest as a person morally and intellectually qualified to carry out his solemn task. The idea advanced so aggressively in *Yoma* that an ignorant high priest is still somehow suited to perform the ceremony deserves serious consideration. To understand this concept, we must assume that the requirements for performance of the sacrifice are largely material. His pedigree, his physical stature, and his appointment to the office represent his qualifications to perform the sacrifice. The effect of this emphasis is to make the priest into an impersonal agent of the process of expiation.

We can also draw at least one negative conclusion about the Yom Kippur sacrifice as seen through early rabbinic eyes. Those theories that see sacrifice principally in terms of the victim and the violence done to it, such as those of René Girard and Walter Burkert, would find little reception among the authors of our Mishnah and Tosefta.[27] Whereas the scapegoat ceremony is discussed in chapter 6, and the death of the scapegoat is described graphically, the scapegoat is not equated with animals slaughtered on the altar in an explicit way. But if the Mishnah does not say much about the sacrificial victim as victim, it does say a good deal about blood. The tractate is quite concerned with where it is dashed and in what direction, how it is collected in bowls, and even what happens to it when it is drained out of the altar. Sacrifice on Yom Kippur, it turns out, is primarily a way of getting purifying blood.

Recently, Kathryn McClymond has come to similar conclusions in her study of sacrifice in Vedic Hinduism compared with the Yom Kippur sacrifice as described by Leviticus and the Mishnah.[28] Whereas most theorists of sacrifice focus on the killing of the victim as the central, dramatic, and indispensable moment in the sacrificial procedure, McClymond argues that both Vedic and Jewish conceptions of sacrifice see it as a way of manipulating substances that represent the essence of the animal (*medha*, or breath, in the case of Hinduism; and blood in the case of Judaism). The effect of this comparison is thus to dislodge the idea of sacrifice from its association with violence and death and to place it into a broader framework as a ritual way of working with essential and quotidian substances.

We have seen that Mishnah *Yoma* functions as a systematic statement about the nature of the Yom Kippur sacrifice. This statement introduces a social component to the ritual lacking in the biblical source. In addition, its implication that the high priest acts as an agent of purifying blood draws attention to the function of the sacrifice for purification. At the same time, the language of the tractate bears a performative dimension, in that the memorization and recitation of the tractate's narrative is meant to carry the student through the procedure. These functions suit the rabbinic context of the tractate well, for they emphasize that the actions of the high priest are dependent on a community of learned sages; the student is thus meant to identify with the sages in the process of learning the tractate.

The theoretical and performative functions of *Yoma* also found their way to the ancient synagogue, but with different results.

The 'Avodah *Piyyutim*

Yoma is not the only cohesive statement about the meaning of the Yom Kippur sacrifice stemming from late antiquity. An equally extensive and systematic rendering of the ceremony can be found in a complex and fascinating genre of liturgical poetry known as the 'Avodah *piyyutim*. These compositions constitute both a form of ancient ritual theory and a ritual in itself.

In late antiquity, when the Talmuds and midrash were being formed, a rich and complex literature of Hebrew liturgical poetry was also flourishing. This literature, called *piyyut*, was composed and performed by prayer leaders (*payyetanim* or *ḥazzanim*) whose artistry earned them fame in Palestinian synagogues. They created intricate compositions informed by deep acquaintance with the mythic, political, exegetical, and legal traditions of ancient Palestine, and displaying interesting affinities to the Byzantine liturgical poetry of the same era.[29] The poetry of the synagogue presents valuable evidence not only of the history of ideas about sacrifice, but of the social history of the rabbinic period. While historians of Hebrew literature have advanced our knowledge of the literary characteristics of *piyyut* considerably, it has only recently received consideration as evidence for Judaism in late antiquity.[30] In *piyyut*, we have systematic statements on many subjects, from the binding of Isaac to the zodiac. We can also encounter ideas and aspirations expressed less frequently or forcefully in the rabbinic canon. The Mishnah tractate *Yoma* itself entered the synagogue liturgy soon after its composition. The tractate's narrative style made it conducive to liturgical recitation.[31] Apparently by early post-mishnaic times, a liturgical recitation of the tractate had evolved known as the 'Avodah service.[32] The earliest version of this service, called *Shiv'at yamim*,[33] follows the Mishnah closely, with a few changes. By the fourth or fifth century, the custom had grown into a full-fledged poetic genre with a distinct formal structure. This structure is best exemplified in two early masterpieces, "Az be-ein kol," a massive anonymous *piyyut* published recently for the first time by Yosef Yahalom; and Yose ben Yose's "Azkir gevurot Elohah," published by Aaron Mirsky.

The 'Avodah *piyyut* is an epic form. The constituent poems customarily begin with an account of creation, and then describe each major generation, culminating in the selection of Aaron as priest. After this mythical-historical preamble, the service in the Temple is described according to the order in the Mishnah. In these *piyyutim*, practically every major detail of the Mishnah is treated poetically. Although these poems are based on Mishnah *Yoma*, they represent a distinct ideological view of the Yom Kippur sacrifice that places the sacrificial system and its priesthood in a central place in Israel's mythic universe. This interest in the details and cosmic ramifications of sacrifice is not simply a product of rabbinic literature's influence on the poets, or their tendency to elaborate every subject presented to them. The earliest named poet, Yose ben Yose, wrote more 'Avodah poems than poems in any other genre, not to mention other compositions lamenting the destruction of the Temple. In addition, there is evidence that the 'Avodah served as a model for later genres of *piyyut*.[34] The 'Avodah was thus central to early *piyyut*, and sacrifice was a major concern for these liturgical poets.

The 'Avodah's conception of sacrifice has three main components: the idea that the sacrificial cult is essential to the creation of the world; the valorization of the high priest as a heroic embodiment of Israel and an evocation of the divine world; and the redescription of the sacrificial procedure and its purpose. After describing these three components, this chapter will evaluate their implications for the idea of ancient ritual theory.

Creation and Cult

One of the most striking characteristics of the 'Avodah is its literary organization. These compositions are characterized by a peculiar two-part epic structure, in which the description of the Temple sacrifice is preceded by a lengthy historical preamble. The *piyyutim* begin, after an initial passage praising God, with an account of God's creation of the universe by the agency of Torah, and wend their way through Israel's sacred history until the erection of the tabernacle. Only after this do they proceed to narrate the service on Yom Kippur.

This very structure serves as a meditation on the meaning of sacrifice and its institutions, in which the 'Avodah asserts that the Temple cult was knitted into the fabric of creation—indeed, that it was bound up with God's purpose in creating the universe. This section of the *piyyutim* emphasizes a teleological view of creation, in which every created thing has a purpose in later history. This motif offers an interesting parallel to the idea that the Torah was the blueprint for the world, expressed most prominently in Genesis Rabbah 1:1 and based on interpretations of Proverbs 8. This will set the stage for the passages immediately preceding the description of the sacrifice, in which creation and history culminate in the building of the tabernacle and the selection of Aaron as priest. This section begins by describing how God used the Torah to create heaven and earth:

Looking into [the Torah], You carved out
the pillars of the heavens
before there was primordial chaos[35]
on which the rafters could rest.

The next stanza elaborates this idea further:

By [its] weaving
loops and twisted chains
until you were to [   ]
to build Your tent.[36]

As Yahalom points out, according to *Shabbat* 99a, the clasps in the loops that
held the curtains of the tabernacle to each other according to Exodus 26:6
looked like stars in the sky.[37] The poet then seems to be expressing the idea
that the earthly tabernacle that was to be built had a primordial supernal
counterpart.

This stanza introduces a section that emphasizes the role of the Torah in
God's planning of future events. They follow a specific pattern, as can be seen
in these examples:

With [the Torah's] pools You increased
fins and fowl
until You were to give commands
concerning a fish and a raven.[38]
. . . .
By its delight
You created the world in six days,
until repose came to You
and You rested from labor.

The first line refers to an attribute of Torah, identified with wisdom, to which
specific powers are attributed. The second line describes an act of creation,
such as the separation of the waters and appearance of the land. The third and
fourth lines are in the imperfect, implying either that God did that action
subsequently in history or will do the action in the future. The stanzas follow
the six days of creation. Other examples of this motif refer to eschatology. For
example, the Behemoth and Leviathan were created for the express purpose of

serving as a meal for the righteous in the world to come, as stated in this passage from Yose ben Yose's "Atah qonanta 'olam be-rov ḥesed":[39]

> You made, as a sign, for those who know You,[40]
> those who are clad with scales,
> and a fleeing serpent[41]
> for the meal in eternity.
>
> Did You not make out of the earth
> in great abundance
> cattle and crawling creatures
> and the beasts of the earth?[42]
>
> You set signs to be known
> of edibility for purity,
> and for the company of the righteous
> You made the Behemoth fit to eat.[43]

The point of this passage is that God explicitly made animals to be eaten by the righteous, thoughtfully placing signifiers of kashrut on pure animals and preparing the great beasts for the world to come. Here, then, the eschatological details are placed into the context of the whole of sacred history. At the same time, the purity system and sanctuary are part of God's original plan for the makeup of the universe. For these poets, the cult is therefore a fundamental element of creation. The *piyyutim* employ the myth found in several midrashim that the world was created outward from the foundation stone (*even shetiyyah*) in the Temple. "Az be-ein kol" describes the high priest in this way:

> He began to perform the sacrifice
> of the lamb for the daily offering,[44]
> offering it entirely
> over that which is entirely beautiful.[45]

Here the poetic substitution (*kinnui*) used by the poet is based on a rabbinic exegesis of Psalms 50:2 ("From Zion, perfect in beauty, God appeared"), in which the verse is interpreted to mean that the world was created from the foundation stone on the Temple Mount.[46] By linking it with this midrash, the poet implies that the Temple is the place from which creation began. The first component of the 'Avodah's conception of sacrifice is therefore the notion that the sacrificial system is an essential part of creation, and the Temple where it took place is not simply the site of a ritual but the place where the world originated.

Valorization of the Priest

The second major feature of the 'Avodah *piyyutim* is the valorization of the high priest. In contrast to their mishnaic source, in which the high priest is depicted very much as a man of flesh and blood, of dubious education and orthodoxy, the *piyyutim* depict him as a virtuous man, of heroic moral and physical dimensions. The priest, his appearance, his actions, and his encounter with the divine form the organizational principle of the section of the *piyyutim* that deals with the actual sacrifice in the Temple.

The poets accomplish this in two ways. First, the *piyyutim* tend to downplay or elide events from the Mishnah's narrative that cast the high priest in a negative light. For example, in Mishnah *Yoma* 1:3, the sages admonish the high priest to perform the ritual according to their procedure. At this point, says the Mishnah, "He turned aside and wept, and they turned aside and wept." In contrast, the early anonymous 'Avodah *piyyut* "Atah qonanta 'olam me-rosh" describes him as an active and engaged participant:

> For seven days
> he studied, in our Temple,
> the laws of the procedure
> and the service of the day,

> For the elders of his people
> and the sages of his brothers
> perpetually surrounded him
> until the day arrived.

> "See before whom
> you are entering,
> to a place of fire,
> a burning flame.

"Our community's congregation
relies on you
and by your hands
will be our forgiveness."

They commanded him and taught
him until the tenth day
so that he would be accustomed
to the order of the 'Avodah.[47]

According to the *piyyut*, the priest did not listen passively; rather, he "studied in our Temple." To be sure, he was surrounded by the sages and warned of the solemn nature of what he was about to do; but he seemed to take the lesson in good faith. He is depicted as performing the ritual joyously and reverently.[48] More remarkable is how the *piyyutim* focus on the body and appearance of the high priest as a glorious man of heroic proportions, whose very limbs and garments are laden with significance. According to Leviticus 21:10, the high priest is supposed to be "greater than his brothers" (*gadol me-eḥav*). Building on rabbinic interpretations of this verse, the *piyyutim* portray him as literally "larger than his brothers," a man whose strength and stamina equip him to carry out the arduous labor of the sacrifice. Thus "Az be-ein kol" marvels how

his stature
rose to the height of a cedar
when he was fit with embroidered garments
to ornament his body.[49]

So, too, in Yose ben Yose's "Azkir gevurot Elohah":

He displayed his great strength
and pushed aside the curtain. [50]

Elsewhere in that poem, the priest is described in almost mythic terms:

Wrapped in a blue robe,
as bright as the firmament,
His rounded arms
filled the sleeves.[51]

Notable in this stanza is the use of celestial imagery. It is clear that the 'Avodah *piyyutim* wish to glorify the high priest by describing his physical splendor. But their goal goes further than this. By concentrating on his accouterments, they indicate exactly what his role is in the performance of the Yom Kippur sacrifice. The classical 'Avodah *piyyutim*, especially "Azkir gevurot Elohah" and "Az be-ein kol," contain long excursuses on the vestments of the priest, describing them in lavish detail.[52] As described in Exodus 28 and 39, the high priest wore a breastplate containing twelve precious stones, engraved with the names of the twelve tribes. In addition, two shoulder straps on the ephod contained stones, designated as "stones of remembrance of the children of Israel."[53] The high priest thus brings Israel with him into the Temple, engraved on his chest and shoulders. This apparatus inspired a remarkable amount of interpretive activity in antiquity, from Second Temple times to the Middle Ages. In rabbinic literature, the notion of the priest as representative of Israel is most clearly articulated in an exegetical essay on the significance of the basic elements of the costume that appears in the Palestinian and Babylonian Talmuds and in several Palestinian midrashim.[54] The vestments become the focus of a semiotic system in which each garment stands for one class of Israel's sins and effects atonement. For example, the linen tunic atones for the sins of Joseph's brothers, who sold him over his sleeved tunic. This idea becomes a major feature of the 'Avodah *piyyutim*. Thus in "Azkir gevurot Elohah," Yose ben Yose makes more explicit what the Talmud implies: that Israel atones for its sins against Joseph when the priest's tunic, the antithesis of Joseph's blood-stained tunic, enters the Temple.[55] Likewise, Yose ben Yose equates the voice of the bells of the robe with the voice of malicious gossips:[56]

> When, [the bells] struck each other,
> the voice of one with the other,
> they atoned for the voice
> of one who strikes his neighbor in secret.[57]

"Az be-ein kol" takes the role of the vestments further. According to this poem, it is the duty of the garments not just to represent Israel but to arouse God's compassion for his people on the Day of Judgment and to dispel the malevolent forces. Thus he says of the bells:

> He set golden bells
> and wove them into his hem

to recall [God's] love
of [the one of whom it is said,] "How beautiful are your steps."[58]

In "Az be-ein kol," the active properties of the vestments extend to their role
in dispelling the hostile forces preventing purification. Returning to the bells
on the robe, the poem makes it clear that their function is not only atonement but to announce, noisily, the presence of the priest. He steps into the
sanctuary:

> When his soles moved
> they gave voice
> like him who called in the wilderness
> to make a path straight.[59]

> The servants of the *Shekhinah*
> were fearful of him,
> for the robe was named
> after the One who wears justice.[60]

That is, the hostile angels in the sanctuary, who are essentially bodyguards
fending off intruders in the sacred precinct, are frightened by the sound of
the bells, which carries with it divine authorization. This notion is close to
Heikhalot literature's depiction of the rabbis' ascent into the heavenly realm,
in which the traveler must ward off angelic guards using the authorization of
esoteric divine names.

This function of the robe hints at another aspect of the vestments according to the 'Avodah *piyyutim* and a few midrashim: the idea that the priest is
not only a representative of Israel but of the divine world as well. This motif
can be traced back to Malachi 2:7, in which the priest is called *mal'akh*, which
can be interpreted as messenger or angel. Yose ben Yose's 'Avodah poem "Atah
qonanta 'olam be-rov ḥesed" describes the priest in heavenly terms:

> His likeness was like Tarshish,
> like the look of the firmament
> when he put on the blue robe,
> woven like a honeycomb.[61]

"Az be-ein kol" describes the headdress in this way:

Sparks of the seraphim
recoiled from it,
for its image
was like that of a helmet of redemption.
. . . .
And he placed on his forehead
the frontlet, the holy diadem,
and his eyes
shone like the heavens.

And on it was written
the letters of the Great Name,
"Adonai" above
and "Holy" below.

And the supernal demigods
made room for him
lest their eyes be filled with [the sight of him]
and grow dim.[62]

Here we see the last two themes combined: not only does the priest evoke the heavenly world, but he does it so successfully that the creatures in the sanctuary make way for him as he enters. Thus he becomes a representative not only of Israel, but of the divine realm. The second component, then, of the 'Avodah's conception of sacrifice is the centrality of the priest. The poets' effort to valorize him stands in contrast to the Mishnah and Tosefta, which seek to downgrade the virtue and sanctity of the priests as a class.

We can learn something from this theme about the rise of ritual theory in late antiquity and about the sociopolitical context of this literature. Priestly themes occur in early *piyyut* to a surprising degree, and some forms of priestly piety are preserved mainly in *piyyut*. Most notable is the tradition, apparently widespread in the Galilee at one time, of composing poems for the *mishmarot*, the priestly "watches" that visited the Temple when it was standing.[63] Recently, scholars have pointed out that many of the early *payyetanim*—such as Yose ben Yose, Pinḥas ha-Kohen, and Ḥaduta—are supposed to have been priests; in fact, the last two poets wrote cycles for the *mishmarot*.[64] Although the poets were learned in rabbinic Torah, the *beit midrash*, the house of study, was not identical with the *beit kenesset,* the synagogue.[65] In late antiquity and the early

Middle Ages, synagogue leaders often encouraged the free expansion of the liturgy through *piyyut*; at times, this tendency provoked controversy with rabbinic authorities.[66] The poets therefore constituted an alternative source of cultural power. Temple imagery was also a prevalent theme in the iconography of the ancient synagogue.[67] An excellent illustration of this connection between temple and synagogue appears in the synagogue mosaic from Sepphoris, which depicts the sacrificial animals, the priest in his robes, and the offerings of the first fruits.[68] By glorifying the priest, then, the synagogue poets reinforce what is important to them in contradistinction to the rabbis. The 'Avodah depicts a Temple-centered cosmos, in which God, with the assistance of the Torah, made a world maintained by Temple sacrifice and an Israel that lives or dies dependent on its performance. By evoking that world centuries after it has disappeared, the poet, taking the place of the priest, reminds his congregation of its continuing relevance.

The Ritual Procedure

The third component in the 'Avodah's conception of sacrifice concerns how the poems portray the ritual itself. While the poets' description of the priest and his accoutrements is elaborate, their account of the sacrificial procedure itself is remarkably concise. The language describing the sacrificial procedure is rather businesslike, although not without nuance. But a few details of the procedure stand out. The 'Avodah *piyyutim* follow the Mishnah in stressing the disposition of the blood of the goat and bull. The poet notes how the priest hands it to his assistant, who stirs it to prevent it from coagulating and, following the Mishnah, repeats the method by which he counts the seven times the blood is sprinkled. Thus, like the Mishnah, the *piyyutim* recognize the blood's role as a purifying agent and follow its progress from the slaughter of the animals to its sprinkling on the altar.

Another focal point of the ceremony is the high priest's entrance into the Holy of Holies to present the incense. Just as the Mishnah says that the priest would not spend too long in prayer lest the people be afraid that something had happened to him, the 'Avodah poems are also brief at this point. They culminate in the moment when the entire process is completed and the scarlet thread that had been tied to the door of the sanctuary miraculously turns white. Echoing Isaiah 1:18, the miracle is an assurance that Israel's sins have been forgiven. For the authors of the *piyyut*, the Yom Kippur sacrifice is both about purification and atonement; more than this, it is about Israel's fate for the coming year. The crucial distinction between the 'Avodah's conception of the ritual and the Mishnah's is the high priest's role in securing these blessings.

The Purpose of the 'Avodah

We can now consider what the 'Avodah tells us about ancient ritual theory. Like the Mishnah, this literature does not focus on the status and suffering of the victim. The goat and bull do not stand for a suffering Israel, the Messiah, or God. Likewise, sacrificial blood is understood as an agent of purification and of atonement. In this way, the 'Avodah *piyyutim* are in accordance with their mishnaic sources. But the 'Avodah's dual depiction of the priest as an exemplary man and exemplar of the divine presence constitutes a significant difference. The priest stands in a liminal position between the presence of God and the community. In fact, a frequent poetic substitution (*kinnui*) for the priest is *tsir*, "emissary." At the same time, his encounter with the divine presence puts him in a zone of sanctity touched by the divine radiance. This aspect is emphasized in an appendix to the 'Avodah common in many rites that goes back to chapter 50 of Ben Sira (Ecclesiasticus), describing the radiance on the face of the priest as he emerges from the Holy of Holies.[69] This recalls some interpretations of sacrifice, such as those of Edmund Leach and Hubert and Mauss, in which its purpose is to place the community in a realm of sanctity through the union of sacrificer and victim, and to bring both into consonance with the deity.[70] The poets of the 'Avodah did indeed think about the meaning of sacrifice; for them, it was a medium for encounter with the divine presence.

At the same time, the 'Avodah, even more than the Mishnah, functions performatively. Its status as a prayer text places it in the ritual context of the synagogue, an echo of the sacred place. But more than this, the poet seeks to create in the listener a kind of dramatic empathy with the high priest. The prayer leader takes the congregation vicariously through the numinous experience of the priest. In the 'Avodah service, the congregation reenacts the high priest's pronouncement of the powerful divine name, the prostrations that accompanied it, and the priest's confession for the people. It also hears of the radiance on the face of the priest that results from his encounter with the divine presence. At some point in the development of the 'Avodah, this mimetic experience was reinforced when it became customary for the congregation to prostrate themselves upon hearing of the pronouncement of the divine name in the confession.[71] This action allows them to reenact a key moment in the Temple sacrifice.

Ancient Ritual Theory and Its Function

It has been argued here that systematic discourse about ritual, identified here as ancient ritual theory, arises in response to specific historical circumstances, especially when the ritual system is challenged or undergoes a deep transformation. This condition certainly applies to the period following the destruction of the Temple. Moreover, the process by which holiness is said to have shifted from sacred place to sacred person in late antiquity is reflected in the way both communities, the compilers of the Mishnah and the *payyetanim*, portray the Yom Kippur sacrifice. These factors suggest ways in which each community met these challenges and to what use each put its concerted thought about sacrifice.

First, each corpus suggests the prominence of the notion of sacred person over sacred place in late antiquity. The Mishnah concentrates on the interaction between the sages and the high priest and so conveys the messages that sanctity is to be found in the rabbi, the embodiment of Torah, and that this embodiment allows the sacred place to function properly. The 'Avodah focuses on the holy man in the person of the priest, but to different effect. By valorizing the high priest, the poet places him in a crucial position between heaven and earth. At the same time, the poet identifies himself with the priest by taking him through his paces in the narration and reciting his confessions.

But these values still stood in tension with an older notion of sacred space, at least in the way the Temple and its rituals were remembered. The Mishnah's narrative depends on bringing the student through the topography of the Temple no less than negotiating the sociopolitical landscape of the Second Temple period. In the 'Avodah, too, the *payyetan*, who was often both the author and performer, would bring the community into the Temple with him, behind the curtain where he offered incense, prayed for Israel's welfare, and basked in the divine presence. Thus a remarkable transformation occurred: an act of discourse about sacrifice became a virtual form of sacrifice itself.

The rabbis alluded to this transformation themselves when they referred to the study of the sacrificial system as an effective equivalent to sacrifice in the Temple.[72] The *payyetanim* likewise presented verbal offerings in the *miqdash me'at*, the smaller sanctuary.[73] In this way, legal and liturgical texts on ritual served as both theory and practice.

Epilogue

Toward an Integrative Approach in Jewish Studies: A View from Anthropology

HARVEY E. GOLDBERG

I approach the task of writing this epilogue with gratification and humility: gratification because this book makes it clear that cross-fertilization between anthropology and Jewish studies is taking place; and humility in the face of the quality of work that historians and scholars of religion who look beyond texts, and anthropologists who incorporate textual analyses and diachronic perspectives into their ethnographic work, have begun to produce. In this epilogue, I reflect more generally on the challenges of linking anthropology to the study of Jewish history and texts. That link has, until recently, proved particularly elusive, since the discipline of history and the field of Jewish studies take as their primary methods the study of written texts, an approach that does not always share much with the ethnographic methods at the heart of anthropology.

With some trepidation, I turn to what once was a catchphrase of anthropology in the United States: the holistic approach. The notion of viewing cultures as integrated "wholes" now often raises eyebrows. But much about this volume conjures up what is best about a holistic approach, which can still raise questions and challenges that are worthwhile for Jewish studies. The chapters in the book at hand span the expanse of Jewish space and the range of Jewish history. Placing them in a single volume overrides epochs, embraces expressions of Judaism over four continents, and defies regional definition.

Implicitly, the volume assumes some sort of Jewish "wholeness" that allows such studies to be brought together and compared.

Before turning to the utility of holism as a starting point for advocating an integrative approach to Jewish studies, let me discuss what it has implied within the discipline of anthropology. There have been at least three levels of anthropological holism, none completely distinct from the others. The first stresses that social facts—institutions, practices, symbols—cannot be understood in isolation; rather, they are interlinked and have to be placed in their local contexts. This approach was associated with functionalist theory, which posited that societies should be viewed as "functioning wholes" within which individual practices help to maintain the entire system. The second level focuses on culture and highlights "meaning," whether cognitive, affective, symbolic, or embodied in practice. This kind of anthropology insisted that cultural traits are organized into "patterns" and "configurations," beyond meanings attached to isolated acts. A third, somewhat different, type of holism is characterized by a comparative approach that entailed an encompassing view of human experience in its striking historical and regional variety. Anthropology in the United States and Great Britain was divided into four subdisciplines: physical (biological) anthropology, archaeology (mostly prehistoric), linguistics (stressing spoken language), and cultural or social anthropology.[1] This third type of holism sought to bring all four kinds of anthropological analysis together into a single discipline focused on the comparative study of mankind across its entire temporal and geographic existence.

These intersecting types of holism have significant implications for the Jewish case. I first came to understand some of these implications early in my career as an anthropology student interested in Jews from the Middle East. In 1961, during my first year of graduate work, I audited a course required of all students in Middle East Studies at Harvard University. The course was taught by several historians, none of whom pretended to be able to handle all the different historical periods the course covered (Hellenistic, Arab-Muslim, Turkish-Ottoman). I wondered how the holistic approach, used by anthropologists who studied small-scale societies ethnographically, might work in the historically documented Middle East. The one existing attempt to provide a comprehensive anthropological view of the Middle East, a region that remained under-explored in the discipline, demonstrated the limitations of a holistic approach that ignored history. Carleton Coon's *Caravan: The Story of the Middle East* skipped rapidly from prehistoric archaeology to recent times, omitting much of the intervening historical evolution and variation documented by textual scholars with the requisite linguistic and archival skills. If anyone could supply a holistic view of the region, I felt, it was more likely to be a historian than an ethnographer. The experience made me simultaneously aware of the limits of ethnography when applied to textual societies and the necessity of a holistic approach that ranged across historical periods.[2]

In the same course, I was struck by a question raised by Hamilton A. R. Gibb, one of the leading authorities on the Arab world, during his lecture on the emergence of Islam and its historical setting. Why, he asked rhetorically, did the course assignments not include excerpts from the Qur'ān? Gibb answered that there were two ways of reading the Qur'ān: that of a devoted believer or that of a scholar equipped with philological and historical methods. Since most participants in the course fit neither category, he reasoned, it was better not to study the text at all. This stance puzzled me. My prior Jewish education had convinced me that knowing classical or canonical texts was the principal means by which one came to understand a tradition. Admittedly, such knowledge could not be gained in a single course. But to keep students from gaining some familiarity with classic Islamic texts did not make sense to me. Given that an imperative in anthropology enjoined the ethnographer to begin with the "native's point of view," it seemed odd to bypass texts in cases in which the people under study regarded them as central to their tradition.

As these initial observations settled into what became my research agenda, I came to appreciate that if anthropology's vaunted holistic approach was to be applied to the study of Jews, that approach must be historical and textual no less than ethnographic.[3] In what follows, I spell out how the chapters in this book illustrate two reorientations in research on Jewish studies that I see as feeding into an integrative view of Judaism. The first is the movement away from the exclusively textual focus that has long characterized Jewish studies. This shift requires scholars to possess a wider methodological repertoire in order to examine the very phenomena of textuality, literacy, and the entire range of everyday practices and institutions that textual prescriptions have never entirely determined. One important implication of this methodological expansion is that it facilitates investigation into the experiences of the non-rabbinic elite, including women. The second reorientation is the move toward greater attention to the range of Judaic historical experiences beyond the European context. This comparative approach remains open to placing records of Jewish life from the remote past side by side with those from subsequent eras in order to see how they illuminate one another, or to allow one to venture workable generalizations.

To be sure, an integrative perspective harbors potential limitations and dilemmas, related not least to the kind of naïve essentialism for which the older holistic approaches have been criticized. But an integrative perspective need not begin or end with a totalizing view of Jewish life as a systemic whole that can be placed on permanent exhibit.[4] To the contrary, a tempered holistic approach provides an analytic scaffolding that can enlarge our perceptions of what is included in Jewish culture and history. This scaffolding can be taken apart and reassembled as modifications to our understanding of the ever-shifting structures of Jewish life become necessary. An integrative approach to Jewish studies, then, delves into texts while attending equally to the full range of activities in which Jews of all social rungs, genders, and provenances have been involved. Such an approach fits well at the crossroads of disciplines and subfields as they are articulated across the academy. Anthropologists have paid increasing attention to texts and historical concerns. At the same time, the core humanistic disciplines of Jewish studies—history, literature, and religious studies—have adopted approaches that, to quote Lawrence Hoffman, go "beyond the text."[5] The present book succeeds in moving in both these directions.

Beyond the Text

Favoring a hermeneutic approach to texts, Jewish historians have often skipped over elementary questions about the forms and extent of literacy in a given period. One of the first attempts to open up this line of inquiry was made by Aaron Demsky, whose investigation of literacy in the biblical period drew upon the work of the anthropologist Jack Goody.[6] Two chapters in the present book underline the importance of understanding the dynamics of Judaic literacy in medieval settings. Ephraim Kanarfogel (Chapter 11) shows that the relative unavailability of written prayers had a significant impact on the liturgy as it was performed in medieval Ashkenaz. In a way that is rare in the writing of Jewish history, he provides a historical-ethnographic glimpse of the extent of literacy, of the links between written and oral transmission, and of the various modes of participation in liturgy. Similarly, Albert I. Baumgarten and Marina Rustow's investigation of critical transitions in ancient and medieval rabbinic culture (Chapter 9) demonstrates how the mechanics of transmission—for example, the spread of paper manufacture and the distinct valorizations of oral and written traditions—energized and sacralized the notion of the "Oral Torah" while also contributing to the ascendancy of textual authority.

Several other contributions point to how textual production is embedded in spatial, material, and graphic practices. Lucia Raspe's study of the graves of sainted rabbis in Ashkenaz (Chapter 6) runs counter to the research habitus of previous scholarship, which has focused on burial inscriptions while paying little attention to the spatial organization of Jewish graveyards. Raspe demonstrates that there was, in fact, a contentious tradition of seeking to be buried in physical proximity to the graves of sainted rabbis. At the same time, she offers insights into the dynamic interface between pilgrimage practice—visiting the graves of zaddikim—and its textual treatment. Although pilgrimage was not typically subject to written halakhic injunctions in post-Temple Jewish life, the textualization of pilgrimage in Ashkenaz began no later than the thirteenth century, with the appearance of written pilgrimage guides describing sanctified sites in the Land of Israel that were identified as the graves of biblical figures or rabbis known from the Talmud.[7] In medieval Ashkenaz, rabbis further concerned themselves with the practice, since pilgrims often took vows and thereby engaged in a practice of abiding halakhic concern. Halakhic literacy has also been actively engaged at contemporary pilgrimage sites, as Yoram Bilu's ethnography of a modern Israeli shrine (Chapter 3) demonstrates. In that case, one rabbi registered and authorized his resistance to the legitimacy of a popular local pilgrimage site in sanctioned written expression. These chapters offer a nuanced appreciation of the fluctuating spatial and ritual borderlines between textual expression and extra-textual matters.

The interplay between textual and nontextual modes of engagement with Jewish practice runs thematically throughout several other chapters in this volume. Shalom Sabar's study of *ketubbot* (Chapter 4) points to the expanded insights arising from the synergy between textual analysis and sensitivity to visual forms. He demonstrates the intricate connections between texts and decorative-aesthetic communication, phenomena that may be overlooked when they are relegated to a separate specialty of "Jewish art." Sabar shows that images on *ketubbot* hold evidence about the social status of the implicated families and about the function of the document as a prophylactic amulet against supernatural forces. J. H. Chajes (Chapter 2) demonstrates the prevalence of Jewish "magic" not as a counterpoint to textual forms of "religion" but as an ambivalent constituent within them. Like Raspe, Chajes demonstrates the caution that one must use in separating out the culture of the "learned elite" from the practices of the untutored. In this vein, Tamar El-Or (Chapter 12) shows how women assert symbolic links between activities in the kitchen and those that took place in the Temple in Jerusalem. This appropriation of central religious symbols, often taken to be confined within an exclusively male domain, represents an audacious step that the women involved authorize by reference to rabbinic hermeneutics.[8] These chapters reveal that speaking or writing about "Judaism" while ignoring activity at the borders of textuality offers, at best, a truncated view of a lived and evolving tradition.

Comparative Jewish Studies

The chapters in this volume also raise the question of how comparing diverse Jewish groups contributes to grasping the scope of Jewish life, particularly when comparative cases cross the line distinguishing Ashkenaz (Franco-Germany and, later, Eastern Europe) from Sefarad (the Iberian Peninsula and its later Mediterranean diaspora). For starters, such comparisons help us to reconsider the rigidity of the dividing line itself. Raspe's discussion of Jewish hagiography in Ashkenaz provides a case in point. She indicates that some sources refer to the purported resting place of the eleventh-century liturgical poet Shim'on ben Yitshaq in Mainz as his "cave" (*me'arah*), and takes this to be an allusion to rabbinic legends about Shim'on bar Yohai, the second-century talmudic sage who was supposed to have found extended refuge in a cave. This allusion appears with comparable force in southern Morocco, where cemeteries are often referred to by the term *me'arah*. In that case, the connection with Bar Yohai revolves around his putative authorship of the Zohar, the central qabbalistic text that is closely linked to burial institutions in North Africa.[9] Whether the common use of the term *me'arah* across the Ashkenaz/Sefarad divide was the result of independent developments or the outcome of paths of transmission of which we are unaware, the similarity underlines the value of comparison even while attending to localized Jewish experience.

Another advantage of comparison is that parallel historical scenarios in widely separated contexts highlight dimensions of Jewish existence often taken for granted and thus left unexamined. Sylvie Anne Goldberg (Chapter 10) explains how debates surrounding the regulation of the ritual calendar in tenth-century Iraq and Palestine posed basic challenges to authority within the world's major centers of rabbinic activity. Over time, the vast majority of both Eastern and Western Jews accepted a standardized calendar. Yet calendar coordination remained, until recently, a concern among Jews scattered in distant regions of northern Ethiopia.[10] There, rather than generating crises of authority, as it did when the yeshivot in Baghdad were the hub of a vast communication network linking far-flung regions of Jewish habitation, the will to keep a unified calendar encouraged Jews in Ethiopia to maintain community and continuity across dispersed settlements. Thus, a basic but dynamic feature of Jewish life, the necessity of reconciling the lunar and solar elements of the ritual calendar, appeared in very different configurations of authority and the changing possibilities of its enforcement. This comparison suggests the wisdom of analytically separating the cultural-symbolic aspects of religious life from their sociopolitical implications, so that the interaction of these planes may be examined in each context with greater precision.

Comparisons like these, across the widest possible geographic and temporal scales, cut against the grain of particularist sensibilities in both anthropology and history. Suggesting that historical comparison belongs in an integrative approach to Jewish studies therefore requires some brief comments on the ambivalent place of diachronic approaches within early to mid-twentieth-century anthropology. The anthropological focus on the "ethnographic present" emerged in British and American anthropology partly as a reaction to an earlier pseudo-historical approach based on rigid models of social evolution. In England, Bronislaw Malinowski and Alfred R. Radcliffe-Brown each developed somewhat different versions of what came to be called functionalist theory. Both stressed that documentary or archaeological evidence was lacking for most of the societies that anthropologists studied; rather than speculate about an unobservable past, it made sense to see how those societies cohered in the present. Malinowski, often viewed as the father of ethnographic "participant observation," showed how an ethnographer's extensive daily contact with a "native" group could reveal links among aspects of a society that were not apparent when those cultures were disassembled into "traits." Radcliffe-Brown coined the term "conjectural history" to emphasize a similar rejection of attempts to reconstruct the past of "primitive" societies. Inspired by the functionalist theories of Emile Durkheim, Radcliffe-Brown instead focused on how specific practices and institutions in a society contribute to maintaining the social whole in the present.[11]

Anthropologists in the United States did not abandon history to the extent of their British counterparts, but the ethnography of societies in the present began to hold center stage in the American transformation of the discipline as well. The call to view cultures as "wholes" emerged strongly in Ruth Benedict's influential book *Patterns of Culture*.[12] In line with the diffusionist model then prevalent in American anthropology, Benedict admitted that regional contacts between cultures are an important part of their development, but focused on how each group "selected" individual traits and brought them together into patterns.[13] Similarly, Benedict's colleague Edward Sapir was interested in the spatial distribution of languages, since the absence of writing in Amerindian languages made comparative linguistics the only way to draw inferences about the pre-Columbian past. (In the 1930s, Sapir hosted and inspired the Yiddish linguist Max Weinreich, a fact that demonstrates that Sapir's research interests extended to historically documented languages.)[14] But despite the interest of American anthropologists in the past, their work was still perceived as substantively and methodologically separate from what was ordinarily understood as "history."

The weaknesses of downplaying history are now well understood within anthropology. Even though documentation may be scarce, there are no societies that are "without history."[15] Viewing some groups as "isolated" seems less tenable when one considers that events originating in Europe affected and changed "remote" societies even before direct conquest and colonization. As the chapters in this volume demonstrate, comparison within an integrative approach to Jewish studies therefore entails full appreciation of the global contacts and confrontations though which Jewish societies and cultures have generally taken shape. One promising approach to this comparativist challenge lies in viewing Judaism as an integrated tradition that has emerged dynamically, across time and geography, in public practices such as liturgy, magic, pilgrimage, and the wide array of other activities traced in this volume. Despite the striking differences in social and historical circumstances in the cases examined here, these activities all rely on traditionalizing modes by which the same set of building blocks or, as Victor Turner suggested in another context, "alphabet blocks" of Jewish culture may be put together in diverse circumstances in the search to gain and to convey coherence.[16] The notion that Judaism has accommodated to changing conditions over the centuries by returning to and reconfiguring the same storehouses of texts is not new.[17] What the chapters in this volume show is that not only texts but also practices, visual images, and other articulations of culture are central to the emergence of tradition as a dynamic historical process.

Tradition, in this expanded sense, provides an integrative rubric under which to develop a comparative approach within Jewish studies. For example, Ra'anan S. Boustan (Chapter 5), Michael D. Swartz (Chapter 13), and Tamar El-Or (Chapter 12) all emphasize the enduring power of the image of Temple rites as they have been variously refigured over time and across space. Boustan identifies sources showing how the rabbis "transformed the long-standing link between visuality and cultic practice into a bridge between materiality and textuality." Swartz, who appreciates this bridging, also points out that the rede-scription of a biblical account of sacrifice in Mishnah *Yoma* "mounts a critique of the priesthood." At a later period, medieval *piyyutim* tended to valorize the priesthood in the liturgy of the Day of Atonement, reinstating an enhanced priestly image that survives to our day. El-Or similarly traces this legacy into the expanding religious world of Sefaradi women in Israel, who interpret their reinvigorated domestic rituals in the kitchen "as continuing . . . the devotions of the high priest, who, in the past, oversaw the rituals of the Temple." The modular unit constituted by Temple–priesthood–sacrificial ritual thus consti-tutes a node of stability even when limited, criticized, or used as leverage for change. Its symbolic presence within Jewish tradition is maintained, even as its direct practice was annulled close to two millennia ago.

Local historical actors themselves often make comparisons that traverse time in full self-awareness that they are asserting an authorizing claim to the continuity of a tradition, as several chapters in this volume demonstrate. Riv-Ellen Prell (Chapter 1) documents that sense of continuity in the controversy over calling Black Jews to the Torah at Camp Ramah in the 1960s. Recalling the difference of opinion that the camp's rabbinic leaders voiced, one camper stated that she felt she was witnessing a real rabbinic *maḥloqet*, a dispute based on different text-based halakhic positions. At the same time, some par-ties to the controversy self-consciously articulated traditional notions of con-tinuity while also acknowledging present social conditions. As Prell shows, camp educators aimed to turn "an American issue . . . into a Jewish issue," and worked with the assumption that "Judaism was completely compatible with a liberal democracy." Traditions do not necessarily emerge organically from the past; they are points of contestation as much as of continuity, and often consciously so.

Along these lines, Baumgarten and Rustow take up Hobsbawm and Ranger's notion of "invented tradition"[18] in order to show that sensitivity to the fabrication of traditions is not restricted to dispassionate modern schol-arship. Rather, self-invested Jews have observed and debated the novelty of tradition at critical historical junctures. One may speculate as to whether the medieval liturgical poets who re-valorized the status of the priesthood were self-conscious about how they invoked images and texts from the past in order to authorize change. We must be careful, indeed, to avoid simplistic comparisons, whether in illuminating the past through modern parallels or evaluating recent events in terms of valued ancient scenarios. Baumgarten and

Rustow put the challenge of examining such diverse examples comparatively as follows: "[T]he claim of invented tradition—with which Jesus criticized the Pharisees, medieval Qaraites dismissed the Rabbanites, and historians explain the nineteenth-century orthodox movement—[is not] a different tactic across periods. What differs is only the particular configuration of power that it challenges." This formulation highlights the importance of keeping cultural processes analytically separate from the social fields in which they operate. With this distinction in mind, one even may examine Jewish life as a "tradition of invention."[19]

Integration without Essentialism

Calling attention to the integration of diverse realms of Jewish experience within local contexts and across them does not necessarily entail presenting a picture of an essentialized or transhistorical Judaism. Anthropology and Jewish studies have both appreciated this lesson, though each has struggled to overcome somewhat different hurdles. Drawing on Marxist social theories that focused on the fissures and conflicts within society, anthropologists came to reevaluate the holistic emphasis on the internal coherence of cultural configurations. In the postcolonial moment, depictions of culture as internally coherent and harmonious, or possessed of timeless "essences," grew increasingly suspect. The relationship between colonial domination and the epistemological entailments that might reduce a society to a set of defining and enduring characteristics made any attempt to broadly characterize another (an "other") society susceptible to the charge of essentialism. At the same time, the postcolonial theorist Gayatri Chakravorty Spivak drew attention to the process of "strategic essentialism" mobilized by subaltern groups to present themselves, when beneficial, in reductive terms. Anthropologists, too, began to struggle with the ethnographic reality that various subaltern groups essentialized themselves to some degree, in ethnic or national terms, in attempts to attain a political voice.[20]

Within Jewish studies, this paradox of essentialism immediately conjures up twentieth-century criticisms of the Wissenschaft des Judentums school of Jewish history in nineteenth-century Germany.[21] While not subject to domination from overseas or a concomitant colonial "gaze," these scholars made holistic and essentialist statements about "Judaism" in order to demonstrate their worthiness of legal emancipation and equal rights.[22] Ismar Schorsch has noted that early Wissenschaft scholars "were ready to identify the ruling ideas of Jewish history," but that this kind of essentialism "was never intended as an end in itself. On the contrary, it was forged and employed by the intellectuals of an embattled minority as the most effective instrument for handling the formidable challenge of emancipation."[23]

At the same time, certain aspects of this evolving historical school, including its insistence on linguistic and philological exactitude, militated against reifying Judaism and led to an emphasis on the particularities of historical cases. Likewise, there developed some skepticism toward those who moved too easily from the "scientific" study of texts to theological or "philosophical" generalizations.[24] While the nineteenth century saw the emergence of a wide range of religious and cultural ideologies concerning Judaism and its future, almost all those engaged in research took for granted that Judaism evolved historically. Simplistic reductions of Judaism did not sit well with the internal differences and tensions that this historical approach recognized.

These competing nineteenth-century visions of Judaism, one essentializing and the other particularizing, continue to define much of Jewish studies today. There remains the challenge of finding a conceptual and methodological middle road for the study of Judaism as it bridges specific places and periods. Such a middle path would exhibit an interpretive openness to patterns and cultural associations that seem to reappear with more than coincidental repetition. It would appreciate contestation and countervailing strains within Jewish life while also remaining cautious about generalizations that overstep the bounds of legitimate inferences from texts and other sources.

Chajes's chapter operates explicitly in this middle ground. On the one hand, Chajes appreciates the consistencies in magical practices over the *longue durée*. On the other hand, alone among the authors in this volume, he writes of "Judaisms," a plural form that emphasizes how Jewish practice and precept have varied and been contested.[25] He notes that medieval rabbis debated the latitude that talmudic texts allowed for magic, hedging their own acceptance of some magical concepts and practices while leaving room for early modern Jews both to engage in magic and to leave records of their ambivalent experiences. Similarly, Tamar Katriel's discussion of the rhetoric of rescue in Israeli narratives of immigration (Chapter 8) focuses squarely on contestation within Jewish discourse. Highlighting competing and dialogic discourses within Israeli society, Katriel traces both the hegemonic Zionist narratives that celebrate the heroic role of the state in "rescuing" immigrants and the development of counter-narratives focusing on the historical agency of the immigrants themselves. As she shows, Jews from Ethiopia portray their journey to Israel as a voluntary personal sacrifice rather than as their passive "rescue" by the state. In recent years, these counter-hegemonic narratives have also appeared in the public event known as Jerusalem Day (28 Iyyar). This national Israeli ritual has become the annual occasion to recognize publicly the special saga and suffering of the Jews of Ethiopia in their trek and eventual airlift to the Land of Israel. It has also become the public stage on which the contribution to Zionism of Jews from the former Soviet Union has moved from the recesses of memory to fuller recognition: immigrants who are veterans of that former country's victory over Nazi Germany parade in their decorated uniforms.

Swartz's chapter further exemplifies how an integrative approach to Jewish studies works against essentialism rather than reinforcing it. Swartz emphasizes the dialogic tensions within the 'Avodah prayer, the section of the Yom Kippur liturgy that focuses on priestly activity in the ancient Temple. He points to at least three discursive planes within the 'Avodah. One is the biblical account of the temple rites prescribed for Yom Kippur (Lv 16). A second is the portrait of the rites in Mishnah *Yoma* that challenge the centrality of certain aspects of that biblical account. A third is the representation of those rites in medieval liturgical poems. All these levels are woven into the standard liturgy of the Day of Atonement as it has existed for centuries. Swartz's exposition illuminates both the continuities and the tensions between these literary levels, the coexistence of which creates the potential for divergent interpretations and reactions to the liturgy. Does this example then allow us to infer that Jewish literary and liturgical compositions exhibit a penchant toward the dialogic addition of new layers that run against the grain of earlier texts without discarding them? Is one of the impulses of liturgy to promote a sense of harmony between distinct sources? If so, may we see the Yom Kippur liturgy as a mechanism through which Jewish tradition "essentializes itself" while simultaneously preserving and acknowledging the diversity of religious expressions that have entered it over time?

This is precisely the process that Goldberg explores in her discussion of Se'adyah Ga'on's calendrical innovations and their far-reaching consequences for time-based Jewish ritual. Jewish tradition subsequently naturalized Se'adyah's innovations and took them for granted, dulling later appreciation of the "revolution" that they effected. Goldberg's depiction of this process places Se'adyah within a middle ground of "tradition," between the "reception" (*qab-balah*) of norms from the past and the changes entailed by "transmission" (*masorah*) to future generations. A dual sense of the stem *m-s-r* is preserved in modern Hebrew, in which one can be committed (*masur*) to something already extant, such as an idea or a person, but also transmit a "message" (*messer*, or, if it is an SMS, *misron*). By guiding us through the fraught processes by which a uniform Jewish calendar emerged under particular political circumstances, Goldberg demonstrates how even the most "essential" features of Jewish tradition are the products of historical contingency.

That an integrative approach to Jewish studies need not rely on naïve forms of essentialism is further illuminated by the ways in which several authors in this volume attend to the problem of defining the boundaries of Jewish life. In her examination of Samuel Romanelli's account of his sojourn in Morocco in the late eighteenth century (Chapter 7), Andrea Schatz shows the pitfalls of classifying people, practices, and writing as belonging either to the "internal" Jewish or "external" world. She shows how Romanelli's Jewish orient "is a site of multiplying forms of difference and sameness" and his perceptions of Jews in Morocco are informed by "the possibility of bringing together Judaism and Enlightenment." Chajes similarly asserts that internal traditions were "in constant dialogue with the myriad environments in which Jews lived," and Raspe shows that while the practice of visiting the graves of famous rabbis echoed the saint veneration of Christian Europe and was the subject of much ambivalence, "there were eminent medieval sages who not only condoned visiting cemeteries but did so themselves."

Internal variations and oscillations like these may discourage the comparative search for any static or transcendent core of Judaic tradition or Jewish experience, but there is still room for an integrative approach based upon middle-range generalizations and comparisons that look beyond highly specific historical situations or cultural patterns. This approach might also serve as a useful middle path for seeking broader, tentative, and testable statements, open to ongoing revision, about Jewish history and cultural patterns.

A Conversational Approach in Jewish Studies

Scholars select and categorize materials of interest in ways that can never completely be disentangled from current ideologies. Those ideologies, of course, shift with time, sometimes dramatically and sometimes imperceptibly. Study of the Hebrew Bible can provide a point of reflection on the intermingling of ideologies and research orientations. At the turn of the twentieth century and for decades thereafter, many Jews viewed the "higher" biblical criticism of nineteenth-century

German Protestant scholars as potentially undermining Jewish self-worth and religious commitment. Writing in opposition to the documentary hypothesis and railing against it on pulpits, Jewish apologists saw the slicing up of the Hebrew Bible into diverse literary and historical documents as an existential threat.[26] But how might these defenders of the Bible have responded to "charges" of multiple authorship had the documentary hypothesis appeared in the age of "deconstruction," "fragmentation," and the "decline of master narratives"? It may be significant that precisely when the Hebrew Bible was first being subjected to literary-historical analysis, the text emerged as the locus classicus of the intersection between the emergent fields of Jewish studies and anthropology. In this context as well, Jewish scholars were suspicious of an approach that compared Judaism with the "primitive" and "less developed" cultures against which the superiority of Christianity was defined.[27] In the mid-twentieth century, the leading British anthropologists Edmund Leach and Mary Douglas boldly resuscitated an anthropological interest in the Hebrew Bible. Although some biblical scholars were at first skeptical of colleagues who could not read the original text, many took up anthropological concepts, as in Jacob Milgrom's edition of Leviticus in the Anchor Bible series.[28] Although none of the preceding chapters applies anthropological methods to the Hebrew Bible, El-Or can now compare a creation story among the Dinka of East Africa with that in Genesis without worrying about ideological sensibilities.[29]

Post-Zionist discourse is another ideological terrain that scholars of Judaism must navigate, as Katriel's chapter illustrates. Boustan tests this terrain when he introduces his discussion of images of the Temple vessels by alluding to the work of Daniel Boyarin and Jonathan Boyarin. As Boustan notes, these authors "[b]lend . . . historical analysis and political intervention" when they prioritize Jewish existence in diaspora settings. In an effort to keep these spheres apart, Boustan interrogates the view that the mobile text superseded attachment to physical objects and space; his analysis traces a "nuanced attitude" among early rabbis as they articulated a "dialectical tension between the 'locative' dimensions of the physical cult and the more mobile forms of authority and piety that they sought to cultivate." Boustan may have his own ideological commitments, including an "anti-supersessionist" position that resists a historical trajectory in which ideas that originated in Judaism give way to Christian ones, but he uses it to raise questions about Boyarin and Boyarin's stance even while sharing the same general orientation with them. There is a general lesson here: as much as a given scholarly critique may reveal bias, the critique itself carries its own ideological components.

We thus are led to acknowledge that the presence of ideological factors is something with which scholarship will always have to contend. It is therefore useful to retain a sense of proportion about one's work and to recall that a researcher is ultimately in the same boat as the people being studied. Both, navigating broad societal waves and currents, select from the repertoire of interpretive schema available to them. Schatz's discussion of Romanelli, for example, echoes inner tensions in Romanelli's own writing, which includes several different and opposing representations of Jews in Morocco. Indeed, several authors in this book note that some analytical insights formulated in modern scholarship may also be found in earlier and even ancient texts, as when Chajes reveals definitions of magic common to modern anthropology and the Babylonian Talmud. Even more powerfully, a fieldworker or a historian may allow voices found in research data to modify the rigidities of ideological or disciplinary preconceptions. Katriel points out how Ethiopian immigration stories, which portray "painful scenes of departure, hardship, and loss," subvert the ideology of the Zionist narrative by undermining "the polarization of roles between rescuers, rescued, and enemy that is the hallmark of [hegemonic] rescue narratives." Raspe's success in fleshing out a systematic pattern of attachment to rabbinic graves in Ashkenaz implicitly critiques an assumption that such popular practices are found primarily among Middle Eastern communities.[30] And Kanarfogel, attentive to medieval texts that reflect the practices of ordinary male Jews, gently leaves behind Isadore Twersky's insistence that Jewish studies "focus on the leaders, the intellectuals, the elite of the Jewish religious community."[31]

It may thus be useful to envision the way forward as an expanding series of conversations that cross conventional boundaries. Such conversations might venture to unsettle, to puncture, or at times to bridge the dividing lines that this volume challenges: between texts and extra-textual expression, between learned elites and "ordinary Jews," between highly specified studies and the audacity of encompassing statements about Jewish life, between synchrony and diachrony, and between what is perceived as "within" and "outside" Jewish life. Anthropologists in these pages take history seriously, as exemplified by Bilu's demonstration that ethnographic data gathered over consecutive years can be productively organized into a diachronic framework. Anthropologists are now more attuned to textual readings than in the past: El-Or's ethnography of religious women in Israel pays attention to both practice and literacy; Prell begins with a short story by Bernard Malamud to frame a discussion about race and identity in a Jewish summer camp. Conversely, in his study of ancient ritual, Swartz cites Pierre Bourdieu's concept of "misrecognition," demonstrating how historians in Jewish studies draw on theoretical insights growing out of ethnographic work.

Likewise, the chapters in this volume help us to consider the methodological implications of the recognition that Jewish societies and culture have always been shaped by their surroundings, even when Jews have experienced periods of relative political and territorial autonomy. The chapters in this book invoke the relevance to Jewish experience of ancient Rome, medieval Baghdad and the Rhineland, early modern Italy, recent rural Morocco, "the sixties" in the United States, and contemporary Israel. Each contribution demonstrates the author's command of relevant non-Jewish contexts. That knowledge may have been acquired through differing disciplinary trajectories. Some scholars may have gained expertise in Jewish texts before turning to broader disciplinary concerns; others may have acquired a deep familiarity with the wider historical context before focusing on the Jewish case. Suppose, however, that the model for approaching Jewish topics were more "conversational" or collaborative, requiring researchers interested in Jews to carry out a project together with a partner more oriented toward the society "as a whole." Might not such an institutional modification be a step toward encouraging new ways of thinking?

If such collaborative research remains in the realm of suggestion, this volume is the product of a more modest trend that has brought together scholars across an unprecedented range of fields, disciplines, methodological commitments, regional proficiencies, and historical foci. This effort has been a long time in coming. In addition to overcoming institutional barriers and set attitudes, this effort perhaps requires the basic apperception that interest in the sublime concerns encoded in hoary texts can, and even must, go hand in hand with placing the creators and users of those texts in their social and material contexts. This stance was stated succinctly by S. D. Goitein in the first volume of his magisterial *A Mediterranean Society*: "[W]e cannot afford to neglect any kind of writing which has come down to us, for life is one single undivided unit. [W]e cannot form a proper idea of the spiritual aspirations of a society if we do not pay some attention to its daily life and economic foundations."[32]

Goitein negotiated a middle ground in a number of spheres. *A Mediterranean Society* deals with the economic and social structures of communal and religious life revealed in texts from the Cairo Genizah, but it came after that trove had been combed for classics of Jewish literature. His use of the phrase "the Geniza people" reveals his strong impulse toward providing the portrait of a whole society. As attested in many footnotes in *A Mediterranean Society*,

Goitein's earlier ethnographic research on the social life, language, and litera-ture (oral and written) of Jews from Yemen was constantly on his mind as he worked with medieval documents. His appreciation of the Jews in Yemen as reflecting their Arab Muslim milieu—he called them "the most Jewish and the most Arab of all Jews"—went hand in hand with his sensitivity to centuries-long continuities in aspects of Jewish life.[33]

What allowed Goitein, master of textual details, to make such presump-tuous supra-epochal inferences? How was he able to appreciate cultural inte-gration and stability while also being keenly aware of change? Perhaps a hint is to be found in his brief autobiographical sketch from 1975: "I started out as an essentially medieval being," for whom "there exists only one real issue in life, overriding all others: religion. I have remained, I believe, a *homo religio-sus*, but have become a thoroughly modern man."[34] This evolution must have entailed much internal personal dialogue, to which were added the conversa-tions he carried out with a range of disciplines and scholars, as outlined in the epilogue to the last volume of his work. Among them were two anthropolo-gists: Erich Brauer, a friend and fellow immigrant to Mandate Palestine from Germany who also researched Jews from Yemen; and Clifford Geertz, whose programmatic statements about cultural analysis Goitein acknowledged as resonant with his own.[35] One way of envisioning the contribution of the pres-ent volume is that it transposes and extends the conversation-based middle ground that Goitein achieved from the realm of a single scholarly virtuoso into the collective habitus of future researchers into Jewish history, society, and culture.

Notes

1. On problems associated with categories of analysis in the study of religion, see Talal Asad, *Genealogies of Religion: Discipline and Reasons of Power in Christianity and Islam* (Baltimore, 1993). With respect to Judaism in particular, see Gershom G. Scholem, "Revelation and Tradition as Religious Categories in Judaism," in *The Messianic Idea in Judaism and Other Essays on Jewish Spirituality* (New York, 1971), 282–303; William Cutter, "Jewish Studies as Self-Definition: A Review Essay," *Jewish Social Studies* 3 (1996): 158–76; Jonathan Boyarin, "Jewish Ethnography and the Question of the Book," *Anthropological Quarterly* 64 (1991): 14–29; Jonathan Boyarin and Daniel Boyarin, eds., *Jews and Other Differences: The New Jewish Cultural Studies* (Minneapolis, 1997); David Nirenberg, "The Birth of the Pariah: Jews, Christian Dualism, and Social Science," *Social Research* 70 (2003): 201–36; and Daniel Boyarin, *Border Lines: The Partition of Judaeo-Christianity* (Philadelphia, 2004).

2. See, e.g., Todd M. Endelman, ed., *Comparing Jewish Societies* (Ann Arbor, Mich., 1997); David Biale, ed., *Cultures of the Jews: A New History* (New York, 2002); Howard Wettstein, ed., *Diasporas and Exiles: Varieties of Jewish Identity* (Berkeley, Calif., 2002); and André Levy and Alex Weingrod, eds., *Homelands and Diasporas: Holy Lands and Other Places* (Stanford, Calif., 2005).

3. Pathbreaking early examples of this approach, both by now canonical, include Gershom G. Scholem, *Major Trends in Jewish Mysticism*, rev. ed. (New York, 1946); and S. D. Goitein, *A Mediterranean Society: The Jewish Communities of the Arab World as Portrayed in the Documents of the Cairo Geniza*, 6 vols. (Berkeley, Calif., 1967–93). For recent reflections on these trends, see Barbara Kirshenblatt-Gimblett, "The Corporeal Turn," *Jewish Quarterly Review* 95 (2005): 447–61; and Scott Jaschik, "The New Jewish Studies," in *Inside Higher Ed*, December 21, 2005, http://www.insidehighered.com/news/2005/12/21/jewish (accessed January 17, 2010).

4. Scholem famously took a nominalist approach in his "Shelumei emunei Yisra'el be-fi doram," in *'Od davar: Pirqei morashah u-teḥiyah* (Tel Aviv, 1989), 98–104, reprinted from his 1958 response to R. J. Zwi Werblowsky, "Hirhurim 'al Shabbetai Tsevi shel G.

Shalom," *Molad* 15 (1957): 113–37. Against Werblowsky's defense of "normative" Judaism, Scholem proposed with the title phrase of his essay ("those who are peaceable and faithful in Israel," 2 Sam 20:19) a definition of Judaism as what Jews do in the name of the tradition, those "who saw themselves as obligated by the heritage (*yerushah*) of the generations and as obligated to the tradition (*masoret*) of historical Judaism" (103). For the classic methodological statement advocating a "polythetic" rather than "monothetic" or "normative" approach, see J. Z. Smith, "Fences and Neighbors: Some Contours of Early Judaism," in *Imagining Religion: From Babylon to Jonestown* (Chicago, 1982), 1–18.

5. The embrace of anthropology in Jewish studies also draws on developments within the discipline of anthropology itself. See Harvey E. Goldberg, "Introduction: Reflections on the Mutual Relevance of Anthropology and Judaic Studies," in *Judaism Viewed from Within and from Without: Anthropological Studies*, ed. idem (Albany, N.Y., 1987), 1–43; Barbara Kirshenblatt-Gimblett, introduction to *Life Is with People: The Culture of the Shtetl*, ed. M. Zborowski and E. Herzog, 2nd ed. (New York, 1995 [1952]), ix–xlviii; Gelya Frank, "Jews, Multiculturalism, and Boasian Anthropology," *American Anthropologist* 99 (1997): 731–45; and Marcy Brink-Danan, "Anthropological Perspectives on Judaism," *Religion Compass* 2 (2008): 674–88.

6. The non-Western orientation of Jewish anthropology has been significantly counterbalanced by the prominence of the United States and Europe as loci of ethnographic research. See Riv-Ellen Prell, *Prayer and Community: The Havurah in American Judaism* (Detroit, 1989); Jack Kugelmass, *The Miracle of Intervale Avenue: The Story of a Jewish Congregation in the South Bronx* (New York, 1996); and Matti Bunzl, *Symptoms of Modernity: Jews and Queers in Late-Twentieth-Century Vienna* (Berkeley, Calif., 2004). Israeli anthropology was, until recently, concerned almost exclusively with immigrants from non-Western contexts. For discussion, see Harvey Goldberg and Orit Abuhave, eds., *Perspectives on Israeli Anthropology* (Detroit, 2009).

7. Formative observations on the confluence of anthropology and history include E. E. Evans-Pritchard, *Anthropology and History: Essays in Social Anthropology* (London, 1962); Claude Lévi-Strauss, "History and Anthropology," in *Structural Anthropology* (New York, 1963), 1–27; and Marc Bloch, *The Historian's Craft*, trans. P. Putnam (New York, 1953). For groundbreaking exemplars of the interpretive turn in anthropology and the social sciences, see Clifford Geertz, *The Interpretation of Cultures* (New York, 1973); and Paul Rabinow and William M. Sullivan, eds., *Interpretive Social Science: A Reader* (Berkeley, Calif., 1979). In history, see Carlo Ginsburg, *The Cheese and the Worms: The Cosmos of a Sixteenth-Century Miller* (Baltimore, 1980); and Natalie Zemon Davis, *Fiction in the Archives: Pardon Tales and Their Tellers in Sixteenth-Century France* (Stanford, Calif., 1987). On the study of textual practices, see the introduction to Jonathan Boyarin, ed., *The Ethnography of Reading* (Berkeley, Calif., 1993); and Mary J. Carruthers, *The Book of Memory: A Study of Memory in Medieval Culture* (New York, 1990).

8. Examples in which anthropological theory has been brought to bear on textual Jewish studies include Jacob Neusner, *The Talmud as Anthropology* (New York, 1979); Lawrence A. Hoffman, *Beyond the Text: A Holistic Approach to Liturgy* (Bloomington, Ind., 1987);

Howard Eilberg-Schwartz, *The Savage in Judaism: An Anthropology of Israelite Religion and Ancient Judaism* (Bloomington, Ind., 1990); Ivan G. Marcus, *Rituals of Childhood: Jewish Culture and Acculturation in the Middle Ages* (New Haven, Conn., 1996); Mary Douglas, *Leviticus as Literature* (Oxford, 1999); and Lawrence Fine, ed., *Judaism in Practice: From the Middle Ages through the Early Modern Period* (Princeton, N.J., 2001). Ethnographic studies of Jewish textual culture include Harvey E. Goldberg, "The Zohar in Southern Morocco: A Study in the Ethnography of Texts," *History of Religions* 29 (1990): 233–58; Shlomo Deshen, *The Mellah Society: Jewish Community Life in Sherifian Morocco* (Chicago, 1989); and Jonathan Boyarin, "Voices around the Text: The Ethnography of Reading at Mesivta Tifereth Jerusalem," *Cultural Anthropology* 4 (1989): 399–421. Folklore has provided another field in which Jewish texts have been mined "ethnographically" for cultural material: Joshua Trachtenberg, *Jewish Magic and Superstition* (New York, 1939), is an early example; Galit Hasan-Rokem, *Web of Life: Folklore and Midrash in Rabbinic Literature* (Stanford, Calif., 2000), is a recent one.

9. Benedict Anderson's *Imagined Communities: Reflections on the Origin and Spread of Nationalism*, rev. ed. (London, 2006) has been especially influential in focusing attention on the relationship between print capitalism and modern nationalism. The now-extensive anthropological literature on textual power deals largely with Islamic societies. See Dale F. Eickelman, *Knowledge and Power in Morocco: The Education of a Twentieth-Century Notable* (Princeton, N.J., 1985); idem, "Mass Higher Education and the Religious Imagination in Contemporary Arab Societies," *American Ethnologist* 19 (1992): 643–55; Andrew Shryock, *Nationalism and the Genealogical Imagination: Oral History and Textual Authority in Tribal Jordan* (Berkeley, 1997); and Gregory Starrett, *Putting Islam to Work: Education, Politics, and Religious Transformation in Egypt* (Berkeley, Calif., 1998). Our use of textual hegemonies draws on Brinkley Messick's *The Calligraphic State: Textual Domination and History in a Muslim Context* (Berkeley, Calif., 1996).

10. On the notion of textual hegemony, see Teresa E. P. Delfin, "Postcards from the Andes: Politics of Representation in a Reimagined Peru," in *Ecosee: Image, Rhetoric, Nature*, ed. S. I. Dobrin and S. Morey (Albany, N.Y., 2009), 203–22; Lata Mani, *Contentious Traditions: The Debate on Sati in Colonial India* (Berkeley, Calif., 1998); and Charles L. Briggs, "The Politics of Discursive Authority in Research on the 'Invention of Tradition,'" *Cultural Anthropology* 11 (1996): 435–69. On the hegemony of texts in postwar modern Orthodoxy, see Haym Soloveitchik, "Rupture and Reconstruction: The Transformation of Contemporary Orthodoxy," *Tradition* 28 (1994): 64–131; and Jeremy Stolow, "Communicating Authority, Consuming Tradition: Jewish Orthodox Outreach Literature and Its Reading Public," in *Religion, Media, and the Public Sphere*, ed. B. Meyer and A. Moors (Bloomington, Ind., 2006). On contemporary Jewish liturgical performance, see Samuel C. Heilman, *Synagogue Life: A Study in Symbolic Interaction* (Chicago, 1976); and Arnold M. Eisen, *Rethinking Modern Judaism: Ritual, Commandment, and Community* (Stanford, Calif., 1998).

11. On the authority of visual experience in Judaism, see, esp., Chapters 3–6 of this volume.

12. On the relationship between scribal and priestly authority in ancient Near Eastern contexts, see David M. Carr, *Writing on the Tablet of the Heart: Origins of Scripture and Literature* (Oxford, 2005), 111–73; and Karel van der Toorn, *Scribal Culture and the Making of the Hebrew Bible* (Cambridge, Mass., 2007), 75–108. On rhetorical authority in the ancient Judaism, see, esp., Martin S. Jaffee, "The Oral-Cultural Context of the Talmud Yerushalmi: Greco-Roman Rhetorical Paideia, Discipleship, and the Concept of Oral Torah," in *Transmitting Jewish Traditions: Orality, Textuality, and Cultural Diffusion*, ed. Y. Elman and I. Gershoni (New Haven, Conn., 2000), 27–73; and Jaffee, *Torah in the Mouth: Writing and Oral Tradition in Palestinian Judaism, 200 B.C.E.–400 C.E.* (New York, 2001).

13. On the importance of priestly-scribal power focused on Jerusalem and its temple throughout the Second Temple period, see Martha Himmelfarb, *A Kingdom of Priests: Ancestry and Merit in Ancient Judaism* (Philadelphia, 2006), esp. 11–52. On Jewish *paideia*, see Catherine Hezser, *The Social Structure of the Rabbinic Movement in Roman Palestine* (Tübingen, 1997). On medieval textual canonization, see Lawrence A. Hoffman, *The Canonization of the Synagogue Service* (Notre Dame, Ind., 1979). On the impact of new writing technologies on Judaism, see Marina Rustow, *Heresy and the Politics of Community: The Jews of the Fatimid Caliphate* (Ithaca, N.Y., 2008), 37–52.

14. See David Sorkin, *The Berlin Haskalah and German Religious Thought: Orphans of Knowledge* (London, 2000); idem, *The Religious Enlightenment: Protestants, Jews, and Catholics from London to Vienna* (Princeton, N.J., 2008); David Ruderman, *Jewish Enlightenment in an English Key: Anglo-Jewry's Construction of Modern Jewish Thought* (Princeton, N.J., 2000); Shmuel Feiner, *The Jewish Enlightenment* (Philadelphia, 2002); and Sarah Abrevaya Stein, *Making Jews Modern: The Yiddish and Ladino Press in the Russian and Ottoman Empires* (Bloomington, Ind., 2004).

15. For critical reevaluations of secularism, see José Casanova, *Public Religions in the Modern World* (Chicago, 1994); Talal Asad, *Formations of the Secular: Christianity, Islam, Modernity* (Baltimore, 1993). For alternative views of modern Jewish secularism, see Daniel J. Schroeter, "A Different Road to Modernity: Jewish Identity in the Arab World," in *Diasporas and Exiles: Varieties of Jewish Identity*, ed. H. Wettstein (Berkeley, Calif., 2002), 150–63; and Yehouda Shenhav, "Modernity and the Hybridization of Nationalism and Religion: Zionism and the Jews of the Middle East as Heuristic Case," *Theory and Society* 36 (2007): 1–30.

16. On the Alliance Israélite Universelle in a global context, see Aaron Rodrigue, *French Jews, Turkish Jews: The Alliance Israélite Universelle and the Politics of Jewish Schooling in Turkey, 1860–1925* (Bloomington, Ind., 1990). For reflections on Ḥabad Judaism as a transnational phenomenon, see Jonathan Boyarin, "Jews in Space; or, the Jewish People in the Twenty-First Century," in idem, *Thinking in Jewish* (Chicago, 1996), 160–82.

17. See Jana Evans Braziel and Anita Mannur, *Theorizing Diaspora: A Reader* (Malden, Mass., 2003). On the anthropological turn toward diaspora, see Akhil Gupta and James Ferguson, eds., *Culture, Power, Place: Explorations in Critical Anthropology* (Durham, N.C., 1997); and Engseng Ho, *The Graves of Tarim: Genealogy and Mobility across the Indian Ocean* (Berkeley, Calif., 2006). For reflections on the Jewish genealogy of diaspora as an

anthropological concept, see Gelya Frank, "Melville J. Herskovits on the African and Jewish Diasporas: Race, Culture and Modern Anthropology," *Identities* 8 (2001): 173–209. For evocative portraits of premodern Jewish diasporic mobility, see Amitav Ghosh, *In an Antique Land: History in the Guise of a Traveler's Tale* (New York, 1992); Ammiel Alcalay, *After Jews and Arabs: Remaking Levantine Culture* (Minneapolis, 1993); and Erich S. Gruen, *Diaspora: Jews amidst Greeks and Romans* (Cambridge, Mass., 2002). For a particularly rich re-theorization of diaspora and the extent to which imagined communities rest on (mis)translation, see Brent Hayes Edwards, *The Practice of Diaspora: Literature, Translation, and the Rise of Black Internationalism* (Cambridge, Mass., 2003).

18. For an early, provocative statement in praise of diaspora, see Gerson D. Cohen, "The Blessings of Assimilation in Jewish History," commencement address, Hebrew College, Boston, June 1966, reprinted in *Jewish History and Jewish Destiny* (New York, 1997), 145–56. For an influential statement on the new Jewish diaspora studies, see Jonathan Boyarin and Daniel Boyarin, "Generation: Diaspora and the Ground of Jewish Identity," *Critical Inquiry* 19 (1993): 693–25. We are convinced by the Boyarins' careful unmooring of Jewish identity from fixed territorial grounds, but startled by the way they obscure territoriality as a historically entrenched facet of generational transmission itself. Other recent celebrations of diaspora include David Biale, *Power and Powerlessness in Jewish History: The Jewish Tradition and the Myth of Passivity* (New York, 1986); Caryn Aviv and David Scheer, *New Jews: The End of the Jewish Diaspora* (New York, 2005); and Melanie Kaye/Kantrowitz, *The Colors of Jews: Racial Politics and Radical Diasporism* (Bloomington, Ind., 2007). For a review of these trends, see Arnold Band, "The New Diasporism and the Old Diaspora," *Israel Studies* 1 (1996): 323–31. For a critique of the new diaspora theorists, see Allan Arkush, "From Diaspora Nationalism to Radical Diasporism," *Modern Judaism* 29 (2009): 326–50.

19. In this volume, see, esp., the chaps. in Part 2.

20. On the tension between diaspora and territory, see Eyal Ben-Ari and Yoram Bilu, eds., *Grasping Land: Sacred Space and Place in Contemporary Israeli Discourse and Experience* (Albany, N.Y., 1997); Sander Gilman and Milton Shain, eds., *Jewries at the Frontier: Accommodation, Identity, Conflict* (Urbana, Ill., 1999); Jasmin Habib, *Israel, Diaspora, and the Routes of National Belonging* (Toronto, 2004); and Charlotte Elisheva Fonrobert and Vered Shemtov, "Introduction: Jewish Conceptions and Practices of Space," *Jewish Social Studies* 11 (2005): 1–8, and the articles that follow.

21. Ivan Davidson Kalmar and Derek Penslar, eds., *Orientalism and the Jews* (Waltham, Mass., 2005). On the dualistic reflex in studies of Jewish diaspora, see William Safran, "The Jewish Diaspora in a Comparative and Theoretical Perspective," *Israel Studies* 10 (2005): 36–60.

22. On orientalizing representations of Jews in Europe, see R. Po-chia Hsia, "Christian Ethnographies of the Jews in Early Modern Europe," in *The Expulsion of the Jews: 1492 and After*, ed. R. B. Waddington and A. H. Williamson (New York, 1994), 223–35; and Yaacov Deutsch, "Polemical Ethnographies: Descriptions of Yom Kippur in the Writings of Christian Hebraists and Jewish Converts to Christianity in Early Modern Europe," in

Hebraica Veritas: Jews and the Study of Judaism in Early Modern Europe, ed. A. P. Coudert and J. S. Shoulson (Philadelphia, 2004), 202–33. On the intersecting treatment of Jews and colonial subjects, see Jonathan Boyarin, *The Unconverted Self: Jews, Indians, and the Identity of Christian Europe* (Chicago, 2009); idem, *Storm from Paradise: The Politics of Jewish Memory* (Minneapolis, 1992); and Aamir Mufti, *Enlightenment in the Colony: The Jewish Question and the Crisis of Postcolonial Culture* (Princeton, N.J., 2007).

23. On the application of orientalism to Jews to the east and south of the European center, see Daniel Schroeter, "Orientalism and the Jews of the Mediterranean," *Journal of Mediterranean Studies* 4 (1994): 183–96.

24. On Jewish ethnic categories, see Ella Shohat, "The Invention of the Mizrahim," *Journal of Palestine Studies* 29 (1999): 5–20; and Harvey E. Goldberg, "From Sephardi to Mizrahi and Back Again: Changing Meanings of 'Sephardi' in Its Social Environments," *Jewish Social Studies* 15 (2008): 165–88. The politics of Ashkenazi identity followed a similar trajectory when German-speaking Jews from Central Europe discriminated against the "oriental" Jews of Eastern Europe (*Ostjuden*). See Jack Wertheimer, *Unwelcome Strangers: East European Jews in Imperial Germany* (New York, 1991); Noah Efron, "Trembling with Fear: How Secular Israelis See the Ultra-Orthodox, and Why," *Tikkun* 6 (1991): 15–22, 88–90; Aziza Khazzoom, "The Great Chain of Orientalism: Jewish Identity, Stigma Management, and Ethnic Exclusion in Israel," *American Sociological Review* 68 (2003): 481–510; and Arieh Bruce Saposnik, "Europe and Its Orients in Zionist Culture before the First World War," *Historical Journal* 49 (2006): 1105–23.

25. Within Israel, the same division of labor has conventionally prevailed; see Harvey E. Goldberg and Chen Bram, "Sephardic/Mizrahi/Arab-Jews: Reflections on Critical Sociology and the Study of Middle Eastern Jewries within the Context of Israeli Society," in *Sephardic Jewry and Mizrahi Jews*, ed. P. Y. Medding (Oxford, 2007), 227–58.

26. For recent trends in the anthropology of European Jews, see above, n. 6, and Sascha L. Golubuff, *Jewish Russians: Upheavals in a Moscow Synagogue* (Philadelphia, 2003). On North African and Middle Eastern Jewries, see Daniel Schroeter, *Merchants of Essaouira: Urban Society and Imperialism in Southwestern Morocco* (Cambridge, 1988); Joel Beinin, *The Dispersion of Egyptian Jewry: Culture, Politics, and the Formation of a Modern Jewish Diaspora* (Berkeley, Calif., 1998); Yaron Tsur, *Qehilah qeru'ah: Yehudei Maroqo ve-ha-le'umiyyut, 1943–1954* (Tel Aviv, 2001); and Emily Benichou Gottreich, *The Mellah of Marrakesh: Jewish and Muslim Space in Morocco's Red City* (Bloomington, Ind., 2006).

27. On the fluid boundaries and contested borderlines between Christianity and Judaism, see, esp., Daniel Boyarin, *Dying for God: Martyrdom and the Making of Christianity and Judaism* (Stanford, Calif., 1999); and the essays in Adam H. Becker and Annette Yoshiko Reed, eds., *The Ways That Never Parted: Jews and Christians in Late Antiquity and the Early Middle Ages* (Tübingen, 2003; repr. Minneapolis, 2007). For criticism of an overly simplistic bifurcation of rabbinic and priestly Judaisms in late antiquity, see Ra'anan S. Boustan, *From Martyr to Mystic: Rabbinic Martyrology and the Making of Merkavah Mysticism* (Tübingen, 2005), 139–47, 264–81. On the gradual emergence of Qaraism and rab-

binic Judaism's response, see, most recently, Rustow, *Heresy and the Politics of Community*, 33–34, 45–47, 52–65.

28. On global Jewish connections across modern national, regional, and imperial boundaries, Daniel J. Schroeter, *The Sultan's Jew: Morocco and the Sephardi World* (Stanford, Calif., 2002); Sarah Abrevaya Stein, *Plumes: Ostrich Feathers, Jews, and a Lost World of Global Commerce* (New Haven, Conn., 2008); Lisa Moses Leff, *Sacred Bonds of Solidarity: The Rise of Internationalism in Nineteenth Century France* (Stanford, Calif., 2006); Oren Kosansky, "Tourism, Charity and Profit: The Movement of Money in Moroccan Jewish Pilgrimage," *Cultural Anthropology* 17 (2002): 359–400; Elliot Horowitz and Moises Orfali, eds., *The Mediterranean and the Jews: Society, Culture, and Economy* (Ramat Gan, 2002); and Resianne Fontaine, Andrea Schatz, and Irene E. Zwiep, eds., *Sepharad in Ashkenaz: Medieval Knowledge and Eighteenth-Century Enlightened Jewish Discourse* (Chicago, 2008).

29. On Zionist historiography, e.g., see David N. Myers, *Re-inventing the Jewish Past: European Jewish Intellectuals and Zionist Return to History* (New York, 1995). On the limits of national models in the study of Jewish identity, see Schroeter, "Different Road to Modernity."

30. For a recent example, see Emily Benichou Gottreich and Daniel J. Schroeter, eds., *Jewish Culture and Society in North Africa* (Bloomington, Ind., 2010).

31. See Chapter 1 of this volume. On the laboratory model in comparative Jewish studies, see Endelman, *Comparing Jewish Societies*, 13–18. Several of the chapters in that volume, in fact, work explicitly against the comparativist approach—most notably, Zachary Lockman, "Railway Workers and Relational History: Arabs and Jews in British-Rule Palestine," 235–66.

32. David Nirenberg offers a notable exception in his studies of the genesis of a racialized converso class in fifteenth-century Iberia. Nirenberg, "Conversion, Sex, and Segregation: Jews and Christians in Medieval Spain," *American Historical Review* 107 (2002): 1065–93; idem, "Mass Conversion and Genealogical Mentalities: Jews and Christians in Fifteenth-Century Spain," *Past and Present* 174 (2002): 3–41; idem, "Enmity and Assimilation: Jews, Christians, and Converts in Medieval Spain," *Common Knowledge* 9 (2003): 137–55; idem, "Une société face à l'altérité: Juifs et Chrétiens dans la péninsule Ibérique 1391–1449," *Annales. Histoire, Sciences Sociales* 62 (2007): 755–92.

33. Marcus, *Rituals of Childhood*, 11.

34. Biale, preface to *Cultures of the Jews*, xvii and xxi.

35. The organ/organism metaphor is from Biale, preface to *Cultures of the Jews*, xvii. At the same time, Biale's preface levels a thoughtful critique of the notion of assimilation along lines similar to those we are suggesting here.

36. The idea of invented tradition was developed most influentially in Eric J. Hobsbawm and Terence Ranger, eds., *The Invention of Tradition* (Cambridge, 1989). The ensuing literature is vast. For critiques and applications in religious studies, see James R. Lewis and Olav Hammer, eds., *The Invention of Sacred Tradition* (Cambridge, 2007). With respect to Judaism, see Jack Wertheimer, ed., *The Uses of Tradition: Jewish Continuity in the Modern Era* (New York, 1993), esp. Michael K. Silber, "The Emergence of Ultra-Orthodoxy: The

Invention of a Tradition," in ibid., 23-84. For an anthropological reflection with relevance to the present arguments, see Briggs, "Politics of Discursive Authority." In this volume, see Part 3, esp. Chapters 9 and 12.

37. Jacob Katz, *Tradition and Crisis: Jewish Society at the End of the Middle Ages*, trans. B. D. Cooperman, rev. ed. (New York, 1993), presents an overly schematic model of modernity and tradition. Katz's influence has proved durable and has been extended beyond the European context in which he worked; his reification of this dichotomy has been applied, e.g., in Reeva S. Simon, Michael M. Laskier, and Sara Reguer, *The Jews of the Middle East and North Africa in Modern Times* (New York, 2003). Cf. Kosansky, "The Jews of the Middle East and North Africa in Modern Times (Review)," *Shofar* 24 (2006): 196–98. For a summary of critical revisions within Jewish studies, see Bernard Dov Cooperman's afterword in Katz, *Tradition and Crisis*, 236–53. On the emergence of ritual strictness and textual constraint in modern orthodoxy, see Soloveitchik, "Rupture and Reconstruction"; Stolow, "Communicating Authority"; and Adam S. Ferziger, *Exclusion and Hierarchy: Orthodoxy, Nonobservance, and the Emergence of Modern Jewish Identity* (Philadelphia, 2005). On the flexibility of Jewish traditions in premodern and modern Arab contexts, see Zvi Zohar, *Tradition and Change: Halakhic Responses of Middle Eastern Rabbis to Legal and Technological Change* (Hebrew) (Jerusalem, 1993).

38. For an early statement, see Asad's programmatic *The Idea of an Anthropology of Islam*, Occasional Papers of the Center for Contemporary Arab Studies (Washington, D.C., 1986); see also idem, *Genealogies of Religion*; and idem, *Formations of the Secular*. For reflections on Asad's influence, see David Scott and Charles Hirschkind, eds., *Powers of the Secular Modern: Talal Asad and His Interlocutors* (Stanford, Calif., 2006). Michael L. Satlow has suggested the utility of Asad's discursive approach for the study Judaism in "Defining Judaism: Accounting for 'Religions' in the Study of Religion," *Journal of the American Academy of Religion* 74 (2006): 837–60; and idem, *Creating Judaism: History, Tradition, Practice* (New York, 2006).

39. In *Idea of an Anthropology of Islam*, Asad moves rather quickly over the textual entailments of discursive traditions. With respect to Islam, he refers to "the founding texts of the Quran and the ḥadith" as the textual place where Muslims "begin" (14). This brevity has led to misreadings: Satlow ("Defining Judaism," 850) takes Asad to suggest that discursive traditions are first and foremost textual, a reading at odds with Asad's emphatic focus on instituted practice and apt performance (*Idea of an Anthropology of Islam*, esp. 14–17). Asad attends more fully to the role of texts in the regulation of religious bodies in his discussions of medieval Christianity (e.g., *Genealogies of Religion*, 83–167).

40. Scholem's phenomenological approach is especially evident in *Sabbatai Sevi: The Mystical Messiah, 1626–1676*, trans. R. J. Z. Werblowsky (Princeton, N.J., 1976 [1957]); see also above, nn. 3–4. Jacob Neusner's corpus is vast. A characteristic statement on the open-endedness of "Torah" can be found in *Major Trends in Formative Judaism*, 2nd ser. (Chico, Calif., 1983), 38–47. Satlow's claim ("Defining Judaism," 844–45) that Neusner reduces Judaism to the rabbinic movement mistakes Neusner's hermeneutic totalism, which is rightly criticized, for a transhistorical claim that he clearly rejects. The movement

in Jewish studies toward the textual peripheries can be seen in works such as Michael Swartz, *Scholastic Magic: Ritual and Revelation in Early Jewish Mysticism* (Princeton, N.J., 1996); Chava Weissler, *Voices of the Matriarchs: Listening to the Prayer of Early Modern Jewish Women* (Boston, 1998); Ephraim Kanarfogel, *Peering Through the Lattices: Mystical, Magical, and Pietistic Dimensions in the Tosafist Period* (Detroit, 2000); and J. H. Chajes, *Between Worlds: Dybbuks, Exorcists, and Early Modern Judaism* (Philadelphia, 2003). In this volume, see Chapters 3 and 6 on hagiographic texts and practices; and Chapters 2 and 4 on magic.

41. The Moroccan example is taken from Kosansky, "All Dear unto God: Saints, Pilgrimage, and Textual Practice in Jewish Morocco" (Ph.D. diss., University of Michigan, 2003), 123–30. For critiques of the distinction between the great and little traditions and related two-tiered models of religion, see Asad, *Idea of an Anthropology of Islam*, 15–16; and Peter Brown, *The Cult of the Saints: Its Rise and Function in Latin Christianity* (Chicago, 1981), 16–22. For critical engagement of the model within the anthropology of Judaism, see Harvey E. Goldberg "Torah and Children: Some Symbolic Aspects of the Reproduction of Jews and Judaism," in idem, *Judaism Viewed from Within and from Without*, 107–70.

42. See, e.g., Swartz, *Scholastic Magic*, 173–208; and Ra'anan S. Boustan, "The Emergence of Pseudonymous Attribution in Heikhalot Literature: Empirical Evidence from the Jewish 'Magical' Corpora," *Jewish Studies Quarterly* 14 (2007): 18–38. For a theoretical statement on the authorizing function of generic forms, see Charles L. Briggs and Richard Bauman, "Genre, Intertextuality, and Social Power," *Journal of Linguistic Anthropology* 2 (1992): 131–72.

43. On the relative intermediacy of social actors and texts within a discursive tradition, see Messick, *Calligraphic State*, 1–15. The ethnography of Judaism, as represented by many of the chapters in this volume, often works with such intermediate social actors.

44. For an exemplary study of the contested process of canonization and marginalization, by Jews and Christians of various stripes, of one particularly important and fraught text from the Second Temple period, see Annette Yoshiko Reed, *Fallen Angels and the History of Judaism and Christianity: The Reception of Enochic Literature* (Cambridge, 2005).

45. Messick, *Calligraphic State*, 1.

46. The notion of textual tradition as a centripetal force is from Satlow, *Creating Judaism*, 12. Biale, preface to *Cultures of the Jews*, xxii, similarly suggests that Jewish cultural unity "rested on" the Hebrew Bible. On the effects of modern Jewish iconoclasm on Jewish studies, see Kalman Bland, *The Artless Jew: Medieval and Modern Affirmations and Denials of the Visual* (Princeton, N.J., 2000); and Naomi Seidman, "Review: Carnal Knowledge: Sex and the Body in Jewish Studies," *Jewish Social Studies* 1 (1994): 115–46.

47. This excellent collection offers compelling accounts of Jewish oral, visual, and embodied practices across a range of experiences. Somewhat paradoxically, however, the analyses it contains are based almost exclusively on textual evidence, something of which the volume's title gives no indication.

48. On the question of Jewish orthodoxy versus orthopraxy, see Marina Rustow, "Karaites Real and Imagined: Three Cases of Jewish Heresy," *Past and Present* 197 (2007): 35–37; for Islam, see Devin J. Stewart, *Islamic Legal Orthodoxy: Twelve Shiite Responses to the Sunni Legal System* (Salt Lake City, 1998), 45–48. On the ethnographic representation of European Jews, see n. 22 above. On Christian representations of excessive Jewish materiality and carnality, see, e.g., Sander Gilman, *The Jew's Body* (New York, 1991); and Derek Penslar, *Shylock's Children: Economics and Jewish Identity in Modern Europe* (Berkeley, Calif., 2001). For a prominent recent example of the folklorization of North African and Middle Eastern Jewries, see Issachar Ben-Ami, *Saint Veneration among the Jews in Morocco* (Detroit, 1998).

49. For renewed attention to subaltern Jewish textual traditions, see Alcalay, *After Jews and Arabs*; Stein, *Making Jews Modern*. The contribution of scholars working in postcolonial academic diasporas has been crucial to this development, e.g., Haïm Zafrani, *Littératures dialectales et populaires juives en Occident musulman: L'écrit et l'oral* (Paris, 1990); and Joseph Chetrit, *Written Judeo-Arabic Poetry in North Africa: Poetic, Linguistic, and Cultural Studies* (Hebrew) (Jerusalem, 2004). Examples of the growing literature on the gendered hierarchies of Jewish textuality include Susan Starr Sered, *Women as Ritual Experts: The Religious Lives of Elderly Jewish Women in Jerusalem* (Oxford, 1996); Weissler, *Voices of the Matriarchs*; and Tamar El-Or, *Next Year I Will Know More: Literacy and Identity among Young Orthodox Women* (Detroit, 2002). On Moroccan pilgrimage as a textual practice, see Kosansky, "All Dear unto God."

50. See Chapter 11 of this volume.

51. On the textual production of Jews, see Goldberg, "Torah and Children"; idem, *Jewish Passages: Cycles of Jewish Life* (Berkeley, Calif., 2003); Samuel Heilman, *The People of the Book: Drama, Fellowship, and Religion* (New Brunswick, N.J., 2002); and Marcus, *Rituals of Childhood*.

52. In *Idea of an Anthropology of Islam*, 15, Asad is clear about the analytical starting point for the study of discursive traditions: "the proper theoretical beginning [for a discursive approach] is . . . an instituted practice (set in a particular context, having a particular history) into which Muslims are inducted as Muslims." Our emphasis on the disciplinary mechanisms of transmission follows from what we take to be the most important arguments forwarded in Boyarin and Boyarin, "Generation." Recent studies have attended to the formation of Jewish subjects and subjectivities in non-pedagogical institutional contexts, including medical ones. See Susan Martha Kahn, *Reproducing Jews: A Cultural Account of Assisted Conception in Israel* (Durham, N.C., 2000); and Mitchell Bryan Hart, *The Healthy Jew: The Symbiosis of Judaism and Modern Medicine* (Cambridge, 2007).

53. Satlow's claim that "Messianic Jews and Black Hebrews have, from a non-normative perspective, every right to call themselves 'Israel,' but through their rejection of postbiblical Jewish literature they have largely ceased to engage in the same conversation as other Jewish communities" (*Creating Judaism*, 15) is analytically imprecise. It would be more accurate to say that many Jews reject the claims of messianists, just as the latter reject some canonical Jewish texts.

54. Biale, *Power and Powerlessness*, focuses predominantly on assertions of Jewish

agency and power in the diaspora. Satlow is even clearer on this point: "Communities become Jewish first and foremost because they say they are" ("Defining Judaism," 849). His claim that Christian ideas of Judaism had "some impact" on Jews themselves seems naïve in the face of the Spanish Inquisition and the Nazi extermination.

55. On the dialects of Jewish identity in the French Empire, see Rodrigue, *French Jews, Turkish Jews*; and Schroeter and Chetrit, "Emancipation and Its Discontents." On Jewish identity as a product of European colonial representational practices more generally, see Barbara Kirshenblatt-Gimblett, *Destination Culture: Tourism, Museums, Heritage* (Berkeley, Calif., 1998).

56. Albert Memmi, one of the twentieth century's major theorists of fractured colonial subjectivity, provides a pronounced counterpoint to David Biale's claim that Jews and "non-Western colonized peoples under Western Colonialism" share a similarity insofar as their identities have been formed in "a rich dialectic" with "majority" cultures (preface to *Cultures of the Jews*, xx). In fact, Jews numbered among the colonized, and the conditions of their identity formation were often violent. See, esp., Memmi, *The Colonizer and the Colonized*, trans. Howard Greenfield (Boston, 1965 [1957]).

57. On the comparable tendency to exaggerate the religious subjectivity of Muslims, see Asad, *Idea of an Anthropology of Islam*, 13; and Michael Gilsenan, *Recognizing Islam: Religion and Society in the Middle East* (London, 2000), 9–26.

58. In this volume, see, esp., Chapters 1, 8, and 10.

59. Asad (*Idea of an Anthropology of Islam*, 9–11) similarly critiques exaggerated views of Islamic sectarianism; cf. Satlow, *Creating Judaism*, 11, and idem, "Defining Judaism," 843–47, for the idea that normative Judaism is a "second-order" crutch for Jewish identity formation.

60. On the difficulty of finding common Jewish identity within even a single national context, see Jack Wertheimer, *A People Divided: Judaism in Contemporary America* (Waltham, Mass., 1997).

61. For one recent approach to Jewish syncretism and hybridity, see David Frankfurter, "Syncretism and the Holy Man in Late Antique Egypt," *Journal of Early Christian Studies* 11 (2003): 339–85.

CHAPTER 1. "HOW DO YOU KNOW THAT I AM A JEW?"

I wish to thank the funders who supported this research: the College of Liberal Arts, University of Minnesota; the Center for Advanced Judaic Studies, University of Pennsylvania; the Lucius Littauer Foundation; and the Hadassah Brandeis Institute. I appreciate the comments of Deborah Dash Moore, Steven S. Foldes, Eric Goldstein, Elaine Tyler May, Sara M. Evans, Rabbi Morris J. Allen, and especially Ra'anan S. Boustan on earlier drafts of this chapter. A different version of this chapter appeared as "Jewish Summer Camping and Civil Rights: How Summer Camps Launched a Transformation in American Jewish Culture, the Bellin Lecture," published by the Frankel Center for Judaic Studies, University of Michigan, 2007. I first presented this material in 2000 as a paper called "Experiencing 'Others' in Jewish Summer Camps: Constructing a Postwar Identity," at Institute for the Advanced Study of Religion, Yale University. I appreciate the thoughtful comments that I received from members of the seminar.

1. Bernard Malamud, "Angel Levine," in idem, *The Magic Barrel* (New York, 1972 [1958]).

2. Manischewitz is the name of a line of very popular and widely advertised kosher products. Virtually any Jewish reader and many non-Jewish ones would make this obvious association.

3. Malamud, "Angel Levine," 49–58.

4. Ibid., 57.

5. In general social theory, authority is most often linked to institutions, or to the translation of ideas or authorizing texts through offices. Types of authority may be differentiated—e.g., sacred versus political—as a way to understand how they operate. The dynamic of authority, however, requires a more process-oriented approach. See Bruce Lincoln, *Authority: Construction and Corrosion* (Chicago, 1994), 1–10.

6. Technically, the proper transliteration of the name is ha-Tsaʿad ha-Rishon. However, libraries and scholars writing about the group archive their materials with the spelling Hatzaad Harishon.

7. Ivan G. Marcus, *Rituals of Childhood: Jewish Acculturation in Medieval Europe* (New Haven, Conn., 1996), 4.

8. Talal Asad, "The Construction of Religion as an Anthropological Category," in idem, *Genealogies of Religion: Discipline and Reasons of Power in Christianity and Islam* (Baltimore, 1993), 37.

9. There are two archival collections related to Hatzaad Harishon: the American Jewish Committee in New York in the folder on black Jews; and the Schomburg Manuscripts, Archives, and Rare Books branch of the New York Public Library in the Hatzaad Harishon collection. See also Janice W. Fernheimer, "The Rhetoric of Black Jewish Identity Construction in America and Israel: 1964–1972" (Ph.D. diss., University of Texas, 2006).

10. See Deborah Dash Moore, *To the Golden Cities: Pursuing the American Jewish Dream in Miami and L.A.* (New York, 1994); Edward S. Shapiro, *A Time for Healing: American Jewry since World War II* (Baltimore, 1992); and Riv-Ellen Prell, "Community and the Discourse of Elegy: The Postwar Suburban Debate," in *Imagining the American Jewish Community*, ed. J. A. Wertheimer (Hanover, N.H., 2008).

11. See Prell, "Community and the Discourse of Elegy."

12. Idem, "Summer Camp, Post-War American Jewish Youth, and the Redemption of Judaism," in *The Jewish Role in American Life: An Annual Review*, ed. B. Zukerman and J. Schoenberg (West Lafayette, Ind., 2007), 5:77–106.

13. See, esp., the essays included in Michael M. Lorge and Gary Zola, eds., *A Place of Our Own: The Rise of Reform Jewish Camping* (Tuscaloosa, Ala., 2006); and Shuly Rubin Schwartz, "Camp Ramah, the Early Years 1947–1952," *Conservative Judaism* 11 (1987):

12–42. Daniel Isaacman has produced the most complete survey of Jewish summer camping in the 1960s, including a useful historical discussion of the various types of camps sponsored by Jewish organizations, in "Jewish Education in Camping," *American Jewish Yearbook* (1966): 245–52. See also Jenna Weissman Joselit and Karen S. Mittleman, eds., *A Worthy Use of Summer: Jewish Summer Camping in America* (Philadelphia, 1993), which provides a catalog and collection of essays related to an exhibition on Jewish summer camping. Jonathan Sarna provides a partial chronology of Jewish educational camps in "The Crucial Decade in Jewish Camping," in *A Place of Our Own*, ed. Lorge and Zola, 27–51.

14. According to a number of historians I have consulted who are experts on orthodox Judaism in America, there is no extant written source on the history of this camp. The general consensus is that the camp began after World War II during the 1940s.

15. See Marc Lee Raphael, "Diary of a Los Angeles Jew, 1942–1972 (An Excerpt)," *American Jewish History* 92 (2006): 299–311.

16. The concept of liminality was developed by the anthropologist Victor W. Turner in *The Ritual Process: Structure and Antistructure* (Ithaca, N.Y., 1977).

17. Interview with Moshe Davis by Pamela Jay in 1990, cited in Jenna Weissman Joselit, "The Jewish Way of Play," in *A Worthy Use of Summer*, ed. Joselit and Mittleman, 18–19.

18. Mordecai Kaplan, "Editorial," *Reconstructionist* 7 (1956): 6–7.

19. The details of the experiment were included in the program book of the Union Institute, Oconomowoc, Wisc., July 14, 1961, Intermediate Session I, July 11–23, 1961. These documents were unprocessed at the American Jewish Archive at the time of my research in 1968. Campers learned that "Blik" was a neologism for "black kike" and that "WASP" stood for White Anglo-Saxon Protestant.

20. Interview with Walter Ackerman, May 2001, Jerusalem. All interviews are with the author unless noted. In 1968, following the assassination of Dr. Martin Luther King, Jr., Jane Elliott, an Iowa schoolteacher, created an "experiment" in her classroom in which she separated out children with blue eyes, declaring them superior, while denying other children privileges. She wanted students to "experience the emotional impact of race bias." This experiment was the subject of a documentary in 1970, and Elliott subsequently offered workshops that re-created the experiment for adults (Public Broadcasting System, "An Unfinished Crusade: An Interview with Jane Elliott," http://www.pbs.org/wgbh/pages/frontline/shows/divided/etc/crusade.html, accessed June 17, 2009).

21. Ackerman explained that he grew up working-class in Boston and was a member of the Labor Zionist youth group ha-Shomer ha-Tsa'ir. He described the group as putting a "wall" between themselves and the rest of America, adding that they met across the street from a park where other "outsiders" congregated, women to run track and Jamaicans to spend time together. His identification with African Americans, he reported, came from the world of his youth. He also described the depth of his commitment to civil rights, which led him to join the famous March 9, 1965, civil rights march in Selma, Ala. He was one of several rabbis from Southern California who joined the march. Interview with

Ackerman, May 2001, Jerusalem; and interview with Regina Morantz (a counselor at the camp), by phone to Ann Arbor, Mich., August 2006.

22. Interview with Rabbi Shelly Podwol, November 7, 2000, by phone to Chicago.

23. The opera *The Circus of Life* was written and scored by Rabbi Efry Spectre. It was translated into Hebrew and adapted by Stuart Kelman and Rabbi Jack Bloom. The Hebrew and English manuscript is in Spectre's files. Rabbi Spectre was music director of Camp Ramah Poconos between 1960 and 1963. The actual year of the performance does not appear on the script. Interview with Rabbi Efry Spectre, New York, 2000.

24. Interview with Chaim Potok, November 9, 2000, by telephone to Philadelphia.

25. Nathan Glazer, "The Jewish Revival in America," *Commentary* 21 (1956): 24.

26. There is an extensive literature on the relationship between Jews and African Americans. A foundational history of the immigrant period is Hasia Diner, *In the Almost Promised Land: Jews and Blacks 1915–1935* (Baltimore, 1995).

27. Eric L. Goldstein, *The Price of Whiteness: Jews, Race, and American Identity* (Princeton, N.J., 2006), 186–70.

28. Ibid., 196–98.

29. Arthur Goren, "A Golden Decade for American Jews," in *The American Jewish Experience*, ed. J. Sarna (New York, 1997), 299–300.

30. Goldstein, *Price of Whiteness*, 201.

31. Cheryl Lynn Greenberg, *Troubling the Waters: Black-Jewish Relations in the American Century* (Princeton, N.J., 2006), 97–99.

32. Victor W. Turner, *Schism and Continuity in an African Village: A Study of Ndembu Village Life* (Manchester, 1957).

33. Interview with Joseph Lukinsky, October 2000, New York. The American Seminar is also described in Lukinsky, "Teaching Responsibility: A Case Study in Curriculum Development" (Ph.D. diss., Harvard University, 1968).

34. Robert Cover went on to a distinguished, if too brief, career as a legal scholar on the faculty of Yale University, and died at a tragically young age from heart disease.

35. Interview with Ann Mintz, February 2000, New York.

36. I was told by Joseph Lukinsky and others two different versions of the initial contact. One person (I was not given permission to cite him/her directly) said that the National Camp Ramah director was contacted; Lukinsky said that he himself had been contacted directly by a teacher in the youth group from Harrison, N.Y.

37. Several different groups call themselves Black Jews. Howard Brotz, *The Black Jews of Harlem: Negro Nationalism and the Dilemma of Negro Leadership* (Glencoe, Ill., 1964), offers a history of the community and a study of its leader. He describes the Black Jews of Harlem as a distinct religious sect that makes no claim to practice Judaism the way descendants of European Jews do.

38. My information about the organization comes from the American Jewish Committee Blaustein Library in its folder "Black Jews."

39. Ultimately, after five years of unsuccessful requests for Jewish communal funding, in 1969 the group received support for programming from the New York Jewish Federa-

tion. Its board of both Black Jews and what they called "white" Jews included virtually every prominent rabbi, scholar, and communal leader of European descent in the United States during the period. The group dissolved in the late 1970s because of conflict over the treatment of a group of Black Jews in Israel.

40. Interview with Ann Mintz, February 2000, New York.

41. On discussions of Black Jews, see Brotz, *Black Jews of Harlem*, 50–51; and Fernheimer, "Rhetoric of Black Jewish Identity," esp. chap. 1.

42. Fernheimer, "Rhetoric of Black Jewish Identity," 140. Reaffirmation suggests that they were not "converts," which would undercut their claim to authenticity. However, it is possible that the *beit din* viewed the issue differently.

43. Rabbi Zucker was affectionately called the "Gaonic poseq" to indicate that he felt more comfortable in the period of the ge'onim (roughly seventh to eleventh century C.E.). Interview with Sylvia Ettenberg, November 2000, New York.

44. Interview with Stephen Donshik, May 2001, Jerusalem.

45. Interview with Mintz, February 2000, New York.

46. Interview with Lukinsky, October 2000, New York.

47. Interview with Mintz, February 2000, New York.

48. Interview with Danny Margolis, November 2000, by telephone to Boston.

49. Interview with Mintz, February 2000, New York.

50. Interview with Israel Francus, June 16, 2004, New York.

51. Lukinsky, "Teaching Responsibility," 105.

52. Interview with Margolis, November 2000, by telephone to Boston. Others have corroborated these events in informal conversations.

53. Interview with Rabbi Joshua Elkin, November 28, 2000, Boston.

54. Interview with Donshik, May 2001, Jerusalem.

55. Jewish social scientists advanced these formulations in the 1960s. On "folk" versus "elite," see Charles Liebman, *The Ambivalent American Jew* (Philadelphia, 1973). On ethnicity and Judaism, see Marshall Sklare, *Conservative Judaism: An American Religious Movement* (New York, 1972).

56. Greenberg, *Troubling the Waters*, 9.

CHAPTER 2. RABBIS AND THEIR (IN)FAMOUS MAGIC

1. Surveys of the historiography of magic are not difficult to find. For a fine recent summary, see R. Schmitt, *Magie im Alten Testament* (Münster, 2004), chap. 1. The important recent books by G. Bohak and Y. Harrari appeared too late to be considered here.

2. P. Schäfer, "Magic and Religion in Ancient Judaism," in *Envisioning Magic: A Princeton Seminar and Symposium*, ed. P. Schäfer and H. G. Kippenberg (Leiden, 1997), 33. Schmitt's work (n. 1 above) proposes a more complex developmental scheme in biblical literature, while I emphasize here only the dominant polemical use.

3. Idolatry, often conflated with magic, was defined talmudically in terms of its struc-

tural resemblance to the licit cult. A telling statement to this effect is that "the Torah prohibits only what resembles what is within the Temple" (bAZ 50a). Cf. R. Kieckhefer, "The Holy and the Unholy: Sainthood, Witchcraft, and Magic in Late Medieval Europe," *Journal of Medieval and Renaissance Studies* 24, no. 3 (1994): 355–85; and S. Clark, *Thinking with Demons: The Idea of Witchcraft in Early Modern Europe* (Oxford, 1997).

4. We should not fail to mention the very significant "othering" of magic to be found in rabbinic literature that is intrinsic to the denoting of certain forms of forbidden magic as *darkhei ha-Emori* (Amorite practices). This terminology seems to represent a conflation of all the Canaanite nations whose forms of worship were stigmatized in Dt 18 into one of them, the Amorites (Gn 10:16; Ex 8:17). Although specific actions are categorized as such, no theorizing of the term in rabbinic literature explains the logic behind the categorization. There is, however, a negative principle invoked: no practice that is intended to provide medical relief falls under the category. See G. Veltri, "The 'Other' Physicians: The Amorites of the Rabbis and the Magi of Pliny," *Korot* 13 (1998): 37–54; and idem, *Magie und Halakha: Ansätze zu einem empirischen Wissenschaftsbegriff im spätantiken und frühmittelalterlichen Judentum* (Tübingen, 1997), 93–220.

5. As the very definition of magic is at the heart of what has been at stake in this long history, I take the liberty of refraining from offering yet another. My strong preference is, in any case, to analyze the internal understandings of the magical in discrete cultural contexts. References to scholarship in which a definition of magic is proffered would include nearly every study cited here; some scholars have even offered different definitions in different articles. For a recent attempt to deal with the problem by applying Wittgenstein's theory of family resemblances, see Y. Harari, "What Is a Magical Text? Methodological Reflections Aimed at Redefining Early Jewish Magic," in *Officina Magica: Essays on the Practice of Magic in Antiquity*, ed. S. Shaked (Leiden, 2005), 91–124.

6. See R. Kieckhefer, *Magic in the Middle Ages* (Cambridge, 1990), 14–16; and S. Tambiah, "Magic, Science, and Religion in Western Thought: Anthropology's Intellectual Legacy," in idem, *Magic, Science, Religion, and the Scope of Rationality* (Cambridge, 1990), 1–31.

7. Jewish tradition, in fact, developed a rich euphemistic vocabulary to designate beliefs, practices, and objects that, from an academic standpoint, would generally be taken to be magical—though without using the *kishshuf* word: *qamea', segulah, hashba'ah, yiḥḥud*, etc.

8. bSan 67b. On this material, see M. Idel, *Golem: Jewish Magical and Mystical Traditions on the Artificial Anthropoid* (Albany, N.Y., 1990), 27–30.

9. But cf. Abraham Yagel (1553–ca. 1623), who attempted to demonstrate the equivalence of the Hebrew *mekhashef* and the Latin *magus* in his *Beit ya'ar ha-Levanon*. Yagel insisted that the Hebrew term was generic and that it could refer to one who performs permissible as well as forbidden magic. See D. B. Ruderman, *Kabbalah, Magic, and Science: The Cultural Universe of a Sixteenth-Century Jewish Physician* (Cambridge, Mass., 1988), 110.

10. Cf. M. Idel, "On Judaism, Jewish Mysticism, and Magic," in *Envisioning Magic*, ed. Schäfer and Kippenberg, 204.

11. There were, of course, early scholarly works on magic that were exceptional in

their relative lack of apologetics or ridicule for their subject matter, such as those of Moses Gaster, whose works include *The Sword of Moses: An Ancient Book of Magic from a Unique Manuscript* (London, 1896).

12. For a brief and provocative survey to this effect, see Idel, "On Judaism, Jewish Mysticism, and Magic."

13. Nevertheless, leading scholars can still be found who take a negative, judgmental view of magic and its relation to Judaism. Thus, for example, in his introduction to a recent collection of Gershom Scholem's essays on magical topics, Yehudah Liebes, "Introduction: Magic and Kabbalah" (Hebrew), in *Shedim, ruhot, u-neshamot: Mehkarim be-dimonologia me-et Gershom Scholem*, ed. E. Liebes (Jerusalem, 2004), 5–6, attempts to exonerate Ḥoni the Circle Drawer from the sin of magical performance while seemingly praising Shim'on ben Shetaḥ for his witch hunts:

> The manipulation [Ḥoni] enacted upon high by means of that circle was not technical, but personal-emotional [*ishit rigshit*]. This was also recognized by no less than the stern establishment man Shim'on ben Shetaḥ in his statement "if you were not Ḥoni, I would decree a ban upon you, but what can I do, for you plead before the Place and thus make your will like [that of] the son who pleads before his father and does his will" (bTa'an 19a, 23a). And, indeed, Shim'on ben Shetaḥ understood witchcraft [*keshafim*] full well, and fought to annihilate it (apparently hanging eighty witches in Ashkelon, mSan 6:4).

14. Gideon Bohak devoted his remarks to this effect at a plenary session on Jewish magic at the Fourteenth World Congress of Jewish Studies in Jerusalem (summer 2005).

15. On these egodocuments more generally, see J. H. Chajes, "Accounting for the Self: Preliminary Generic-Historical Reflections on Early Modern Jewish Egodocuments," *Jewish Quarterly Review* 95 (2005): 1–15.

16. On the appropriateness of the *longue durée* approach to the subject of magic, see, e.g., A. Murray, "Missionaries and Magic in Dark-Age Europe," in *Debating the Middle Ages: Issues and Readings*, ed. B. H. Rosenwein and L. K. Little (Malden, Mass., 1998), 94; and O. Davies and W. d. Blécourt, eds., *Beyond the Witch Trials: Witchcraft and Magic in Enlightenment Europe* (Manchester, 2004), 3.

17. Also on the level of the *longue durée*, Moshe Idel's argument that the centrality of performance operates in so many forms of Judaism points to the "integral magic" of these Judaisms, as well as their readiness to incorporate magical lore from their environments. See Idel, "On Judaism, Jewish Mysticism, and Magic," 206.

18. Cf. Charles Mopsik's statement: "Nous reservons le mot magic aux actes ayant une visée surnaturelle qui sont accomplish dans un but étranger aux preoccupations et aux valeurs de la religion instituée" (C. Mopsik, *Les grands textes de la cabale: Les rites qui font Dieu, pratiques religieuses et efficacité théurgique dans la cabale, des origines au milieu du XVIIIe siècle* [Lagrasse, 1993], 39). This usage is adduced and endorsed in B. Huss, *Sockets of Fine Gold: The Kabbalah of Rabbi Shim'on ibn Lavi* (Hebrew) (Jerusalem, 2000), 219.

19. J. Trachtenberg, *Jewish Magic and Superstition: A Study in Folk Religion* (New York, 1939), 16.

20. The magical work that best exemplifies the coupling of proximity and danger is *Sefer ha-razim* (The book of secrets), wedding as it does Heikhalot-style material written in fine rabbinic Hebrew and practical instruction in techniques explicitly forbidden in classical Jewish sources. On the enigmas of this work, see P. S. Alexander, "*Sefer ha-Razim* and the Problem of Black Magic in Early Judaism," in *Magic in the Biblical World: From the Rod of Aaron to the Ring of Solomon*, ed. T. Klutz (London, 2003), 170–90. For English translation, see M. A. Morgan, trans., *The Book of the Mysteries* (Chico, Calif., 1983).

21. For the classic statement to this effect, see M. Idel, "The Curriculum of R. Yohanan Alemanno" (Hebrew), *Tarbiz* 48 (1980): 303–31. On the Jewish Renaissance context of this conception more generally, see M. Idel, "The Magical and Neoplatonic Interpretations of the Kabbalah in the Renaissance," in *Jewish Thought in the Sixteenth Century*, ed. B. D. Cooperman (Cambridge, Mass., 1983), 186–242; and Ruderman, *Kabbalah, Magic, and Science*, 102–20.

22. I. Gruenwald, "The Writing, the Writing Implements, and the Tetragrammaton: Magic, Spirituality, and Mysticism" (Hebrew), in *Masu'ot: Mehqarim be-sifrut ha-qabbalah u-be-mahshevet yisra'el muqdashim le-zikhro shel Prof. Ephraim Gottlieb*, ed. M. Oron and A. Goldreich (Jerusalem, 1994), 75–98. See also the discussion of medieval views emphasizing Maimonides' exceptional belief in the natural origins of the Hebrew language, in M. M. Kellner, *Maimonides' Confrontation with Mysticism* (Oxford, 2006), 155–78.

23. See the recent critical edition: Y. Harari, *Harba de-Moshe* (Jerusalem, 1997).

24. The responsum dates from the period of Rav Hayya's tenure as ga'on, which began with his father's death in 1004. It was most recently printed in S. Imanuel, *Teshuvot ha-ge'onim ha-hadashot: Ve-'iman teshuvot, pesaqim u-ferushim me-et hakhmei Provans ha-rishonim* (Jerusalem, 1995), §115. A historical review of the use of the term *ba'al shem* may be found in G. Nigal, *Magic, Mysticism, and Hasidism: The Supernatural in Jewish Thought* (Northvale, N.J., 1994), 3–22. "Path jumping" is discussed there, 33–49, as well as in M. Verman and S. H. Adler, "Path Jumping in the Jewish Magical Tradition," *Jewish Studies Quarterly* 1 (1993): 131–48. Recent historical treatments of the eighteenth-century Eastern European *ba'al shem*—with an emphasis on Israel Ba'al Shem Tov, or the Besht—include I. Etkes, *The Besht: Magician, Mystic, and Leader*, trans. S. Sternberg (Waltham, Mass., 2005); and M. Rosman, *Founder of Hasidism: A Quest for the Historical Ba'al Shem Tov* (Berkeley, Calif., 1996).

25. Idel, "On Judaism, Jewish Mysticism, and Magic," 207–12. Cf. J. Garb, "Mysticism and Magic: Opposition, Indecision, Integration" (Hebrew), *Mahanayim* 14 (2002): 97–109.

26. On class, magic, and the barber-surgeon, see Kieckhefer, *Magic in the Middle Ages*, 61–64. Cf. the association between magic and trade secrets noted briefly in M. Halbertal, *Seter ve-gilui: ha-Sod u-gevulotav ba-masoret ha-yehudit bi-mei ha-beinayim* (Jerusalem, 2001), 27 n. 38.

27. P. Katzenellenbogen, *Yesh manhilin* (Jerusalem, 1986).

28. Ibid., 97; and Etkes, *Besht*, 18.

29. Thus, while most Jewish sources would concur with Stanley Tambiah (applying Austin's notion of speech acts) that in ritual settings, "saying something is doing something as a conventional act," they would nevertheless maintain a distinction between acts in the realm of speech (*dibbur*) and action (*ma'aseh*). See S. Tambiah, "The Magical Power of Words," in *Culture, Thought, and Social Action: An Anthropological Perspective* (Cambridge, Mass., 1985), 17–59; and J. L. Austin, *How to Do Things with Words*, ed. J. O. Urmson and Marina Sbisa, 2nd ed. (Cambridge, Mass., 1975). For an application of speech-act theory in the study of ancient Jewish magic, see R. M. Lesses, "The Adjuration of the Prince of the Presence: Performative Utterance in a Jewish Ritual," in *Ancient Magic and Ritual Power*, ed. M. Meyer and P. Mirecki (Leiden, 1995), 185–206. It should be noted that, notwithstanding Katzenellenbogen's repeated references to warnings against magical activity in the medieval *Sefer Ḥasidim* (on which we will have more to say below), the very situation he describes—and its cure—is in *Sefer Ḥasidim* as well, and it would not have been necessary for him to learn it from an itinerant *ba'al shem* (R. Margalioth, ed., *Sefer Ḥasidim* [Jerusalem, 1957], §411; cf. §680).

30. Vital never seems to have truly abandoned an active interest in alchemy. See G. Bos, "Hayyim Vital's 'Practical Kabbalah and Alchemy': A 17th Century Book of Secrets," *Journal of Jewish Thought and Philosophy* 4 (1994): 55–112. Vital's work may be found in English translation in M. M. Faierstein, *Jewish Mystical Autobiographies: Book of Visions and Book of Secrets* (New York, 1999). On Jewish alchemists, see R. Patai, *The Jewish Alchemists: A History and Source Book* (Princeton, N.J., 1994).

31. On this manuscript, see Bos, "Hayyim Vital's 'Practical Kabbalah and Alchemy.'" According to Scholem, "what came to be considered practical Kabbalah constituted an agglomeration of all the magical practices that developed in Judaism from the talmudic period down through the Middle Ages." See G. Scholem, *Kabbalah* (New York, 1974), 183.

32. J. H. Chajes, *Between Worlds: Dybbuks, Exorcists, and Early Modern Judaism* (Philadelphia, 2003), 71–85. On the return of classical magical exorcism elements into the purged Lurianic technique, see idem, "Rabbi Moses Zacuto as Exorcist: Kabbalah, Magic, and Medicine in the Early Modern Period" (Hebrew), *Pe'amim* 96 (2003): 121–42.

33. R. J. Z. Werblowsky, *Joseph Karo: Lawyer and Mystic* (Philadelphia, 1977), 72.

34. The distinction, however, was "more apparent than real," the difference being merely that the former forbidden variety is used for mystical ascents, and the latter permitted variety for "bringing about the reverse flow of the divine light and its infusion into the soul" (ibid., 72–73).

35. On Maimon, see, most recently, A. P. Socher, *The Radical Enlightenment of Solomon Maimon: Judaism, Heresy, and Philosophy* (Stanford, Calif., 2006).

36. S. Maimon, *Solomon Maimon: An Autobiography*, trans. J. C. Murray (Boston, 1888), 158–59.

. 37. See J. Emden, *Megillat sefer* (Jerusalem, 1979). On R. Moshe David, see C. Wirszubski, *Between the Lines* (Hebrew) (Jerusalem, 1990), 189–209.

38. See Rosman, *Founder of Hasidism*, 23–24. On Emden and Falk, see M. Oron, *Mi-*

ba'al shed le-ba'al shem: Shmuel Falk, ha-Ba'al Shem mi-London (Jerusalem, 2002), 47–50, 93–96.

39. For a restatement and critique of this possibility, see Rosman, *Founder of Hasidism*, 17–26.

40. E. Reiner, "The Figure of the Besht—History Versus Legend," *Studia Judaica* 3 (1994): 52–66. See D. Ben-Amos and J. R. Mintz, eds., *In Praise of the Baal Shem Tov (Shivhei ha-Besht)* (New York, 1984), 173–74; and M. Piekarz, *The Beginning of Hasidism* (Hebrew) (Jerusalem, 1978), 136–37. See also Nigal, *Magic, Mysticism, and Hasidism*, 1–31.

41. Cf. P. Burke, "Rituals of Healing in Early Modern Italy," in idem, *The Historical Anthropology of Early Modern Italy: Essays on Perception and Communication* (Cambridge, 1987), 207–20.

42. Lore gathered by Zacuto over the course of his travels in Eastern Europe was preserved in his *Shorshei ha-shemot*, as well as in *Sefer ha-sodot she-qibbalti mi-rabbotai* (The book of secrets I received from my teachers), MS Günzburg 1448 (Jerusalem, Institute for Hebrew Microfilmed Manuscripts, no. 48570). The former work was published from an expanded eighteenth-century manuscript: M. Zacuto, *Shorshei ha-shemot*, 2 vols. (Jerusalem, 1995). An early witness to this phenomenon of travel to study magic was discovered by I. Yuval, on which see his "An Ashkenazic Autobiography from the Fourteenth Century" (Hebrew), *Tarbiz* 55 (1986): 552 n. 34.

43. See I. Etkes, "Der Rabbi Israel Ba'al Schem Tov: Seine beiden Funktionen als professioneller Magier und Beschützer der Juden," in *Der Magus: Seine Ursprünge und seine Geschichte in verschiedenen Kulturen*, ed. A. Grafton and M. Idel (Berlin, 2001), 196–97.

44. See S. Fishbane, "'Most Women Engage in Sorcery': An Analysis of Sorceresses in the Babylonian Talmud," *Jewish History* 7 (1993): 27–42; and M. Bar-Ilan, "Sorceresses," in *Some Jewish Women in Antiquity* (Atlanta, 1998), 114–31. The medieval *Sefer Ḥasidim* and *Megillat Ahima'ats* also told tales of witches; those in *Sefer Ḥasidim* were Jews, while those in *Megillat Ahima'ats* were of uncertain origin. See the discussion in E. Yassif, *The Hebrew Folktale: History, Genre, Meaning*, trans. J. S. Teitelbaum (Bloomington, Ind., 1999), 352–54.

45. I discussed the nature of the authority of these women in J. H. Chajes, "Women Leading Women (and Attentive Men): Early Modern Jewish Models of Pietistic Female Authority," in *Jewish Religious Leadership: Image and Reality*, ed. J. Wertheimer (New York, 2004), 237–62.

46. On this motif, see C. Weissler, *Voices of the Matriarchs: Listening to the Prayers of Early Modern Jewish Women* (Boston, 1998), 38–44.

47. Chajes, *Between Worlds*, 92–95.

48. Trachtenberg, *Jewish Magic and Superstition*, 16–17.

49. Chajes, *Between Worlds*, 84–85.

50. On Albom, see M. Benayahu, *Toldot ha-Ari* (Jerusalem, 1967), 299–306.

51. Bos, "Hayyim Vital's 'Practical Kabbalah and Alchemy.'"

52. Chajes, *Between Worlds*, 165, 176.

53. S. Shtober, ed. *Sefer divrei Yosef le-R. Yosef Sambari* (Jerusalem, 1994), 414.

54. This episode is discussed in Chajes, *Between Worlds*, 104–13.

55. Ibid., 168.

56. Oron, *Mi-baʿal shed le-baʿal shem*.

57. See, e.g., ibid., 131.

58. See G. Nigal, *Dybbuk Stories in Jewish Literature* (Hebrew) (Jerusalem, 1994), 51.

59. On spirit possession as a form of theater, see the classic study of B. Kapferer, *A Celebration of Demons: Exorcism and the Aesthetics of Healing in Sri Lanka* (Bloomington, Ind., 1983). The propagandistic potential of public exorcisms to demonstrate the power of the sacraments and the authority of the Church was explored in D. P. Walker, *Unclean Spirits: Possession and Exorcism in France and England in the Late Sixteenth and Early Seventeenth Centuries* (Philadelphia, 1981).

60. See, e.g., the editorial "The Dybbuk Is Political," *Haʾaretz*, December 23, 1999.

61. Mark R. Cohen, ed. and trans., *The Autobiography of a Seventeenth-Century Venetian Rabbi: Leon Modenaʾs Life of Judah* (Princeton, N.J., 1988), 108.

62. Oron, *Mi-baʿal shed le-baʿal shem*, 137–38.

63. On this phenomenon, see J. Garb, *Manifestations of Power in Jewish Mysticism: From Rabbinic Literature to Safedian Kabbalah* (Hebrew) (Jerusalem, 2005), 190. Cf. Huss, *Sockets of Fine Gold*, 219–24. It is worth noting that one of the most interesting questions about Falk's activity, largely unanswered by either his own or his assistant's notebooks, is the extent and nature of his involvement with the Freemasons as well as his position vis-à-vis Christianity. For diverging opinions, see Oron, *Mi-baʿal shed le-baʿal shem*, 51–63; and M. K. Schuchard, "Dr. Samuel Jacob Falk: A Sabbatian Adventurer in the Masonic Underground," in *Jewish Messianism in the Early Modern World*, ed. M. D. Goldish and R. H. Popkin (Dordrecht, 2001), 203–26.

64. See, e.g., I. b. S. Perfet, *Shut ha-Ribash* (Brooklyn, 1994), §92; and D. b. S. ibn Zimra, *Shut ha-Radbaz* (New York, 1966), vol. 3, §405.

65. This very question opens the responsum in *Shut ha-Radbaz*, §405.

66. For a discussion and survey of the dream question technique (*sheʾelat halom*) for divination, see M. Idel, "Investigations in the Methodology of the Author of *Sefer ha-Meshiv*" (Hebrew), *Sefunot* n.s. 17 (1983): 201–20.

67. So reads A. Berliner in his *Hayyei ha-yehudim be-Ashkenaz bi-mei ha-beinayim* (Tel Aviv, 1968), 78 n. 211. He identifies *wegerich* with the perennial "weed" plantain, Plantago major.

68. Margalioth, *Sefer Hasidim*, 194, §205.

69. Katzenellenbogen, *Yesh manhilin*, 89.

70. Ibid., 93. For a fuller discussion of this material, see Etkes, *Besht*, 14–24.

71. The term "bother" (*matrihim*) is used in this context in Margalioth, *Sefer Hasidim*, 195, §206.

72. G. Scholem, "*Havdalah de-Rabbi Akiva*: A Source for the Tradition of Jewish Magic during the Gaonic Period" (Hebrew), in *Shedim, ruhot, u-neshamot*, ed. Liebes, 178–79.

73. Alnakar was an eighteenth-century North African rabbi who lived most of his life in Fez and Tunis; the last decade or so of his long life he spent in Livorno. His manuscript of *Shorshei ha-shemot*, which includes numerous additions of his own as well as those of R. Eliyahu Shapira, was the basis of the published edition that first appeared in 1995, M. Zacuto, *Shorshei ha-shemot*.

74. Zacuto, *Shorshei ha-shemot*, 2:170.

75. See Chajes, *Between Worlds*, 82, and bibliography cited therein.

76. See Vital's explanation to that effect. For a rabbi whose magical prowess depended upon his engagement with the demonic in particular, see Y. Bilu, *Without Bounds: The Life and Death of Rabbi Ya'aqov Wazana* (Detroit, 2000).

77. Cf. J. Katz, "Halakhah and Kabbalah as Competing Disciplines of Study," in *Jewish Spirituality*, ed. A. Green, 2 vols. (New York, 1987), 2:34–63.

78. See n. 18 above.

79. In the talmudic narrative, knowledge leads to action. Although arguably more "experimental" and heuristic than necessary or practical (a meaningful distinction in some theories of magic), it is hard to overlook the utility and thriftiness of such a Sabbath meal.

80. Cohen, *Autobiography of a Seventeenth-Century Venetian Rabbi*, e.g., 90, 110–11.

81. M. Pachter, *Milei de-shemaya le-R. El'azar Azikri* (Tel Aviv, 1991), 176. As Pachter shows, many of Azikri's dreams express his fervent wish for a son (57–69).

82. M. Ginsberger, *Die Memoirien des Ascher Levy aus Reichshofen im Elsass (1598–1635)* (Berlin, 1913), 40. On R. Asher, see, recently, Debra Kaplan, "The Self in Social Context: Asher ha-Levi of Reichshofen's *Sefer Zikhronot*," *Jewish Quarterly Review* 97 (2007): 210–36.

83. Faierstein, *Jewish Mystical Autobiographies*, 61.

84. See e.g., Oron, *Mi-ba'al shed le-ba'al shem*: 133, line 365; 138, line 503; 146, line 693.

85. A book of prayers and qabbalistic *tiqqunim* (rectifications) by Natan (Nata) Hannover (d. 1683), based on Lurianic principles, published dozens of times from 1662 onward.

86. See Oron, *Mi-ba'al shed le-ba'al shem*, 138.

87. A synoptic presentation of the Epistle in English may be found in Etkes, *Besht*, 272–81. For a discussion of the Epistle, see Jonathan Dauber, "The Baal Shem Tov and the Messiah: A Reappraisal of the Baal Shem Tov's Letter to R. Gershon of Kutov," *Jewish Studies Quarterly* 16 (2008): 210–41.

88. Ben-Amos and Mintz, *In Praise of the Baal Shem Tov*, 54–58; and A. Rubenstein, ed., *Shivhei ha-Besht* (Jerusalem, 1991), 91–94. This parallel text is discussed in Etkes, *Besht*, 91–97.

89. G. Scholem, "Sidrei de-shimmusha rabba," in *Shedim, ruhot, u-neshamot*, ed. Liebes, 121–22, 135–36. Scholem discusses whether such techniques were ever actually practiced, 129–36.

90. See I. G. Marcus, *Rituals of Childhood: Jewish Culture and Acculturation in the Middle Ages* (New Haven, Conn., 1996), 47–73. Cf. G. Bos, "Jewish Traditions on

Strengthening Memory and Leone Modena's Evaluation," *Jewish Studies Quarterly* 2 (1995): 39–58; and M. D. Swartz, *Scholastic Magic: Ritual and Revelation in Early Jewish Mysticism* (Princeton, N.J., 1997), 33–50.

91. The expression is from mAvot 2:8; Karo's dream question may be found in J. Karo, *Maggid meisharim* (Petah Tiqvah, 1990), 344–45.

92. This account, along with a number of additional parallels, is adduced in Margalioth, *Sefer Ḥasidim*, 194 n. 205 to §205. It appears in the thirteenth-century *Sefer mitsvot qatan*, sec. 3; see the discussion and notes in E. Kanarfogel, *Peering Through the Lattices: Mystical, Magical, and Pietistic Dimensions in the Tosafist Period* (Detroit, 1999), 85–86, 208–13. Kanarfogel also adduces contrary material in which R. Judah figures as the author of charms; see, e.g., 203 n. 32 and esp. 212 n. 49 for references to manuscripts that include amulets and charms attributed to R. Judah. Eli Yassif has also suggested that the anonymous sage in *Sefer Ḥasidim* stories should be taken as referring to R. Judah and that these stories reflect a transitional stage in his emergence as a hagiographical hero. See E. Yassif, "The Exemplary Story in *Sefer Ḥasidim*" (Hebrew), *Tarbiz* 57 (1988): 217–55.

93. M. A. da Fano, *Kanfei yonah* (Jerusalem, 1998), 116–17 (I §110). Adduced in Margalioth, *Sefer Ḥasidim*, 194 n. 205 to §205.

94. See n. 72 above. Cf., with slight changes, MS Parma in J. H. Wistinetzki, ed., *Sefer Ḥasidim* (Berlin, 1891), 76–77, §212.

95. Eleazar ben Judah of Worms, *Sefer ha-shem* (Jerusalem, 2004), 1. The translation is from E. R. Wolfson, *Through a Speculum That Shines: Vision and Imagination in Medieval Jewish Mysticism* (Princeton, N.J., 1994), 239. See the entire discussion there, 238–42. The ritual and its magical parallels are discussed in G. Scholem, "Tradition and New Creation in the Ritual of the Kabbalists," in *On the Kabbalah and Its Symbolism* (New York, 1996), 135–37; and J. Dan, *The Esoteric Philosophy of the German Pietists* (Hebrew) (Jerusalem, 1968), 74–75. Dan's reading of this text as "speculative" rather than magical in nature is contested in M. Idel, *Kabbalah: New Perspectives* (New Haven, Conn., 1988), 323 n. 171; and Wolfson, *Through a Speculum*, 190.

96. Scholem, "Tradition and New Creation," 136–37.

97. Yassif, *Hebrew Folktale*, 530 n. 99.

98. T. Alexander, "Rabbi Judah the Pious as a Legendary Figure," in *Mysticism, Magic, and Kabbalah in Ashkenazi Judaism: International Symposium Held in Frankfurt a. M. 1991*, ed. K. E. Grözinger and J. Dan (Berlin, 1995), 129. In the tales included in the *Ma'ase buch*, R. Samuel's use of magic does bring him to repent; after a self-imposed exile of seven years, he returns home to father Judah (M. Gaster, ed., *Ma'aseh Book* [Philadelphia, 1934], 320ff.).

99. Gaster, *Ma'aseh Book*, 357–58, §171.

100. Ibid., 172–73, §172.

101. Ibid., 366–67, §173. R. Eleazar does not seem to have shared his master's grave concern with the consequences of using names. If the hagiographical literature has R. Eleazar receiving a magical initiation from R. Judah, we have seen that R. Eleazar's own writings preserve an actual initiation ceremony in which the master passes on the powerful divine names to his qualified disciple. Eleazar ben Judah of Worms, *Sefer ha-shem*, 1.

102. Gaster, *Ma'aseh Book*, 370, §174; also in A. Jellinek, ed., *Beit ha-midrash*, 6 vols. (Jerusalem, 1967), 6:140. A similar tale about a R. Joseph, "who was one of the *ba'alei shemot*," was included in a collection of stories assembled by R. Judah himself. See J. Dan, "Demonological Stories from the Writings of R. Judah the Pious" (Hebrew), *Tarbiz* 30 (1961): 288–89, §29. See also the discussion in Yassif, *Hebrew Folktale*, 355–58.

103. Cited in Kanarfogel, *Peering Through the Lattices*, 210–11, esp. n. 44.

104. Alexander, "Rabbi Judah the Pious," 138. Cf. idem, "A Sage and a Saint: Rabbi Luria and Maimonides in Folk Literature" (Hebrew), in *Jerusalem Studies in Hebrew Literature* 13 (1992): 29–64.

105. On Maimonides' historical attitude toward magic, see the discussion and bibliography in D. Schwartz, *Astral Magic in Medieval Jewish Thought* (Hebrew) (Ramat Gan, 1999), 92–121; and, most recently, Kellner, *Maimonides' Confrontation with Mysticism*.

106. Moses of Kiev, *Sefer shoshan sodot* (Petah Tikvah, 1995), 81. On this letter, see G. Scholem, "From Philosopher to Kabbalist: The Kabbalistic Legend on Maimonides" (Hebrew), *Tarbiz* 6 (1934): 90–98. Proof of its forgery was established in J. L. Meises, "Responsum on Maimonides and Kabbalah," *Bikkurei ha-'ittim* 11 (1830): 131–42. On the qabbalistic reception of Maimonides, see M. Idel, *Maïmonide et la mystique juive*, trans. C. Mopsik (Paris, 1991).

107. Such examples could be multiplied. See, e.g., the image of Rashi discussed in L. Zunz, *Toldoth Rashi*, trans. S. Bloch (Warsaw, 1862); and E. Yassif, "Rashi Legends and Medieval Popular Culture," in *Rashi, 1040–1990: Hommage à Ephraim E. Urbach*, ed. G. Sed-Rajna (Paris, 1993), 483–92.

CHAPTER 3. DREAMERS IN PARADISE

1. Yoram Bilu, "The Sanctification of Space in Israel: Civil Religion and Folk-Judaism," in *Jews in Israel: Contemporary Social and Cultural Patterns*, ed. U. Rebhun and C. I. Waxman (Lebanon, N.H., 2004), 371–93; and Rivka Gonen, ed., *To the Tombs of the Righteous: Pilgrimage in Contemporary Israel* (Jerusalem, 1998).

2. Issachar Ben-Ami, *Saint Veneration among the Jews in Morocco* (Hebrew) (Jerusalem, 1984).

3. bEruv 19a. "With regard to Gan Eden, Reish Lakish said: if it is in Eretz Israel, Beis Shean is its entrance." Translation from *Talmud Bavli*, ed. Hersh Goldwurm and Nosson Sheman (New York, 1990).

4. Vittorio Lanternari, "Dreams as Charismatic Significants: Their Bearing on the Rise of New Religious Movements," in *Psychological Anthropology*, ed. T. R. Williams (The Hague, 1975), 221–35. For Lanternari, "charismatic significants" are dreams "in which the dreamer is convinced he has gained control of the source of some extraordinary charismatic power" (233).

5. On visitational dreams in Maghrebi culture, see Yoram Bilu and Henry Abramovitch, "In Search of the Saddiq: Visitational Dreams Among Moroccan Jews in Israel,"

Psychiatry 48 (1985): 83–92; Vincent Crapanzano, "Saints, Jnun, and Dreams: An Essay in Moroccan Ethnopsychology," *Psychiatry* 38 (1975): 145–59; and Benjamin Kilborne, "Moroccan Dream Interpretation and Culturally Constituted Defense Mechanisms," *Ethos* 9 (1981): 294–312.

6. On "swing concepts," see Waud H. Kracke, "Reflections on the Savage Self: Interpretation, Empathy, Anthropology," in *The Making of Psychological Anthropology*, ed. M. M. Suarez-Orosco, G. Spindler, and L. Spindler (Fort Worth, Tex., 1994), 195–222.

7. Ben-Ami, *Saint Veneration*, 79–84.

8. On the articulation of psychological experiences through cultural idioms, see Gananath Obeyesckcre, *Medusa's Hair: An Essay on Personal Symbols and Religious Experience* (Chicago, 1981); idem, *The Work of Culture* (Chicago, 1990); Melford E. Spiro, "Collective Representations and Mental Representations in Religious Symbol Systems," in *Culture and Human Nature*, ed. B. Kilborne and L. L. Langness (Chicago, 1987), 161–84; and Peter Stromberg, "The Impression Point: Synthesis of Symbol and Self," *Ethos* 13 (1985): 56–64.

9. I deliberately refrain from discussing the immediate experience of the dream as dreamed, given its epistemologically precarious nature.

10. John Eade and Michael Sallnow, *Contesting the Sacred: The Anthropology of Christian Pilgrimage* (London, 1991).

11. Clifford Geertz, *Islam Observed: Religious Development in Morocco and Indonesia* (Chicago, 1968); Ernest Gellner, *Saints of the Atlas* (Chicago, 1969); Dale Eickelman, *Moroccan Islam: Tradition and Society in a Pilgrimage Center* (Austin, Tex., 1976); Paul Rabinow, *Symbolic Domination: Cultural Forms and Historical Change in Morocco* (Chicago, 1975); and Edvard Westermarck, *Ritual and Belief in Morocco*, 2 vols. (London, 1926).

12. Ben-Ami, *Saint Veneration*; and Norman A. Stillman, "Saddiq and Marabout in Morocco," in *The Sephardi and Oriental Jewish Heritage: Studies*, ed. I. Ben-Ami (Jerusalem, 1982), 485–500.

13. Rabinow, *Symbolic Domination*, 19–30; and Westermarck, *Ritual and Belief*, 1:35–126.

14. Ben-Ami, *Saint Veneration*, 33–38.

15. Harvey E. Goldberg, "The Mellahs of Southern Morocco: Report of a Survey," *Maghreb Review* 8 (1983): 61–69.

16. Yaron Tsur, *A Torn Community: The Jews of Morocco and Nationalism, 1943–1954* (Hebrew) (Tel Aviv, 2001).

17. Ben-Ami, *Saint Veneration*, 164–65.

18. Ibid., 208; Norman A. Stillman, *Sephardi Religious Responses to Modernity* (Luxembourg, 1995), 73–74; and Alex Weingrod, *The Saint of Beersheba* (Albany, N.Y., 1990), 75.

19. The following mapping of Jewish Moroccan saint worship in Israel is based on Ben-Ami, *Saint Veneration*, 207–13; Yoram Bilu, "Jewish Moroccan 'Saint Impresarios' in Israel: A Stage-Developmental Perspective," *Psychoanalytic Study of Society* 15 (1990): 247–69; idem, "Sanctification of Space"; Avraham Sasson, "Ha-Tahalikh ha-'amami shel

hitqadshut qevarim be-Yisra'el," *Kivvunim ḥadashim* 4 (2001): 153–70; and Weingrod, *Saint of Beersheba*, 93–111.

20. Yoram Bilu and Eyal Ben-Ari, "The Making of Modern Saints: Manufactured Charisma and the Abu-Hatseiras of Israel," *American Ethnologist* 19 (1992): 29–44; and Uri M. Kupferschmidt, "A Moroccan Tzaddiq in Israel: The Emergence of the Baba Sali," *Bijdragen en Mededelingen* 11 (2002): 233–55.

21. Issachar Ben-Ami, "The Folk-Veneration of Saints Among Moroccan Jews, Traditions, Continuity and Change: The Case of the Holy Man, Rabbi David u-Moshe," in *Studies in Judaism and Islam*, ed. S. Morag, I. Ben-Ami, and N. Stillman (Jerusalem, 1981), 283–345; Yoram Bilu, "Dreams and the Wishes of the Saint," in *Judaism Viewed from Within and from Without: Anthropological Explorations in the Comparative Study of Jewish Culture*, ed. H. Goldberg (New York, 1987), 285–314.

22. Peter Brown, *The Cult of the Saints* (Chicago, 1981); and Bilu, "Saint Impresarios."

23. On the association between Elijah and the Garden of Eden, see bBM 114b; and *Yalqut Shim'oni, Bereshit* 5 §42.

24. Spiro, "Collective and Mental Representations"; and Claudia Strauss and Naomi Quinn, *A Cognitive Theory of Cultural Meaning* (Cambridge, 1997).

25. The agricultural nature of Jewish Oulad Mansour was so exceptional compared with the other Jewish communities of Morocco that Pierre Flamand depicted it as "un accident de l'economie juive" (*Diaspora en terre d'Islam: Les communautés israélites du Sud-Marocain, essai de description et d'analyse de la vie juive en milieu berbère* [Casablanca, 1959], 84).

26. Ben-Ami, *Saint Veneration*, 440; Yoram Bilu and André Levy, "Nostalgia and Ambivalence: The Reconstruction of Jewish-Muslim Relations in Oulad Mansour," in *Sephardi and Middle Eastern Jewries: History and Culture in the Modern Era*, ed. H. Goldberg (Bloomington, Ind., 1996), 288–311.

27. Cf. Yoram Bilu, *Without Bounds: The Life and Death of Rabbi Ya'aqov Wazana* (Detroit, 2000), 68–69.

28. Bilu and Abramovitch, "In Search of the Saddiq."

29. For traditional images of paradise, see Yehudah D. Eisenstein, *Otsar midrashim* (B'nei Brak, 1990), 84.

30. The same precipitating factor—a firm decision to leave one's hometown for a more central place, forestalled by a saintly apparition—appeared in the reports of most saint agents I studied in the 1980s. For the significance of this recurring theme for the development towns in which the new sites were built, see Yoram Bilu, *The Saints' Impresarios* (Brighton, Mass., 2010).

31. Ben-Ami, *Saint Veneration*, 23.

32. Cf. Greg Urban, *Metaphysical Community: The Interplay of the Senses and the Intellect* (Austin, Tex., 1996), 241–58.

33. Johannes Fabian, "Dreams and Charisma: 'Theories of Dreams' in the Jamaa Movement (Congo)," *Anthropos* 61 (1966): 544–60; and Jackson S. Lincoln, *The Dream in Primitive Societies* (Baltimore, 1935).

34. Yoram Bilu, "Oneirobiography and Oneirocommunity in Saint Worship in Israel: A Two-Tier Model for Dream-Inspired Religious Revivals," *Dreaming* 10 (2000): 85–101.

35. Brown, *Cult of the Saints*; Patrick J. Geary, *Furta Sacra: Thefts of Relics in the Central Middle Ages* (Princeton, N.J., 1978); and David Sox, *Relics and Shrines* (London, 1985).

36. Vincent Crapanzano, *The Ḥamadsha: A Study in Moroccan Ethnopsychiatry* (Berkeley, Calif., 1973); and M. A. Marcus, "The Saint Has Been Stolen: Sanctity and Social Change in a Tribe of Eastern Morocco," *American Ethnologist* 12 (1985): 454–67.

37. Elchanan Reiner, "Pilgrims and Pilgrimage to Erets Israel, 1099–1517" (Hebrew) (Ph.D. diss., Hebrew University of Jerusalem, 1988), 295–305; and idem, "Bein Yehoshua' le-Yeshu': Mi-sippur miqra'i le-mitos meqomi," *Zion* 61 (1996): 281–317.

CHAPTER 4. WORDS, IMAGES, AND MAGIC

1. Cf. Mordechai A. Friedman, *Jewish Marriage in Palestine: A Cairo Geniza Study*, 2 vols. (Tel Aviv, 1980–81), 1:239–41.

2. bBK 89a; *Shulḥan 'arukh, Tur even ha-'ezer*, 66:3; and cf. Maimonides, *Mishneh Torah*, Hilkhot Ishut, 10:10.

3. For this concept in the talmudic literature, see the entry *"Hiddur mitzvah*," in *Talmudic Encyclopedia*, ed. S. Zevin (Jerusalem, 1957), 8:271–84; for a discussion of examples of artistic objects for the Sabbath and holidays created for the "beautification of commandments," see Isaiah Shachar, *The Jewish Year* (Leiden, 1975), 1–21.

4. Cf. Shalom Sabar, "The Uniqueness of Hebrew Script in the Development of Jewish Art," in *Continuity and Change: 92 Years of Judaica at Bezalel*, ed. M. Ben-Sasson (Jerusalem, 1999).

5. For example, Binyamin Adler, *Sefer ha-nissu'in ke-hilkhatam* (Jerusalem, 1985), 1:278–355; and Yitzhak Ratzabi, *Sefer tofes ketubbot* (B'nei Brak, 1995).

6. Friedman, *Jewish Marriage in Palestine*, 1:43, 190; and cf. Shalom Sabar, "Two Millennia of *Ketubbot* in Eretz Israel," in *A Local Wedding: Ketubbot from Eretz Israel, 1800–1960*, ed. N. Behrouzi (Tel Aviv, 2005), 10 (English section).

7. Cf. Shalom Sabar, "The Beginnings of *Ketubbah* Decoration in Italy: Venice in the Late Sixteenth to the Early Seventeenth Centuries," *Jewish Art* 12–13 (1986–87): 101–2.

8. B. Z. Abrahams, ed. and trans., *The Life of Glückel of Hameln, 1646–1724, Written by Herself* (New York, 1963), 79.

9. Samuel ben David ha-Levi, *Nahalat shiv'ah* (Amsterdam, 1667).

10. For the importance of such lists for genealogical studies, see Abraham I. Laredo, *Les noms des Juifs du Maroc: Essai d'onomastique judéo-marocaine* (Madrid, 1978), 35–38. For an example of one such flowery list, see Shalom Sabar, "Sephardi Elements in North African Hebrew Manuscript Decoration," *Jewish Art* 18 (1992): 191 n. 82.

11. Cf. Abraham Ben-Yaacob, *Kurdistan Jewish Communities* (Hebrew) (Jerusalem, 1980), 148.

12. See Yedida K. Stillman, "The Geniza *Ketubbot* as a Source for Medieval Female Attire" (Hebrew), *Te'uda* 1 (1980): 149–60; Friedman, *Jewish Marriage in Palestine*, 1:288–309; and see the specific examples in ibid., vol. 2.

13. For Yemen, see Aharon Gaimani, "Shetar ha-ketubbah shel aḥot Maharits," in *Bat teiman: 'Olamah shel ha-ishah ha-yehudiyyah*, ed. S. Seri (Tel Aviv, 1994), 70–72. For Balkan examples, see Shalom Sabar, *Ketubbah: Jewish Marriage Contracts of the Hebrew Union College Skirball Museum and Klau Library* (Philadelphia, 1990), 275 (Bucharest, 1854), 285 (Semlin, 1845). In a rare *ketubbah* from Patras, Greece, written in 1566, the detailed dowry list is inserted into the standard text, but more lines are dedicated to this section than to the rest of the document. The Library of the Jewish Theological Seminary of America, Ket. no. 154 (described and analyzed in a forthcoming book by this author).

14. These two clauses are taken from the *ketubbot* of Livorno; cf. Sabar, *Ketubbah*, 108.

15. For examples from these towns, see Sabar, *Ketubbah* (index, s.vv.).

16. E.g., texts containing *shemot* ("names of God"), names of angels, "effective" biblical verses, abbreviations of selected verses and prayers, and images such as triangles, squares, hexagrams, etc. For a general introduction to the topic, see T. Schrire, *Hebrew Amulets: Their Decipherment and Interpretation* (London, 1966). See n. 29 below for additional literature.

17. Attempts to prove that *ketubbot* were decorated in earlier periods have yielded no evidence. Franz Landsberger, e.g., hypothesized: "The adorning of [Jewish] marriage contracts may have begun when the Jews still partook of the Hellenistic predilection for the beautiful; that is to say, in the last pre-Christian or in the first Christian centuries" ("Illuminated Marriage Contracts with Special Reference to the Cincinnati Ketubahs," *Hebrew Union College Annual* 26 [1955]: 505). See, however, Shalom Sabar, "The Beginnings and Flourishing of *Ketubbah* Illustration in Italy: A Study in Popular Imagery and Jewish Patronage during the Seventeenth and Eighteenth Centuries" (Ph.D. diss., University of California at Los Angeles, 1987), 21–31; and idem, *Ketubbah*, 6–8. On the public reading of the *ketubbah* in medieval Egypt, see Friedman, *Jewish Marriage in Palestine*, 1:96, 296, 467; 2:186.

18. For the practice in medieval Egypt, see S. D. Goitein, *A Mediterranean Society*, 6 vols. (Berkeley, Calif., 1967–93), 3:113–14. Goitein cites a case where the *ketubbah* was kept "for reasons of safety" in another town. The most extreme contemporary example of such practices is among the Jews of Georgia, who have customarily hidden *ketubbot* even after the woman passed away, placing it with her in her tomb. Cf. Rachel Arbel, "Georgian *Ketubbot*" (Hebrew), *Rimonim* 6–7 (1999): 37.

19. When the curators at the Museum of the Jewish Diaspora in Tel Aviv conducted a survey for a major exhibition on the Jews of Georgia, they had difficulty locating *ketubbot* from that region because of this practice and the families' fear of exposing their personal contracts in public. See the catalog for the exhibition: Rachel Arbel and Lily Magal, eds., *In the Land of the Golden Fleece: The Jews of Georgia—History and Culture* (Tel Aviv, 1992); and Arbel, "Georgian *Ketubbot*," 37.

20. In one of the examples cited by Friedman, *Jewish Marriage in Palestine*, 2:217–26

(no. 21), dated 1084, the epithalamium occupies more than half of the entire document (cf. ibid., 1:95).

21. For a detailed discussion of the zodiac in Italian (and some related) *ketubbot*, see Sabar, "Beginnings and Flourishing of *Ketubbah* Illustration," 178–213. For examples, see idem, *Mazal Tov: Illuminated Jewish Marriage Contracts from the Israel Museum Collection* (Jerusalem, 1993), pls. 7, 10–12, and 22. The twelve signs of the zodiac are likewise popular on childbirth amulets, especially from Germany and Holland (one rare example is known from Iran). For a survey of the zodiac motif in Jewish art, see Iris Fishof, ed., *Written in the Stars: Art and Symbolism of the Zodiac* (Jerusalem, 2001).

22. For the position and views of magic and astrological beliefs in the Italian Renaissance, see Eugenio Garin, *Astrology in the Renaissance: The Zodiac of Life* (London, 1983); and Paola Zambelli, *L'ambigua natura della magia: Filosofi, streghe, riti nel Rinascimento* (Milan, 1991).

23. The letter was first published by Isaiah Sonne, "Eight Sixteenth-Century Letters from Ferrara" (Hebrew), *Zion* 17 (1952): 154. Cf. Sabar, "Beginnings and Flourishing of *Ketubbah* Illustration," 208–9.

24. The quotation is from the English translation of Modena's work by Simon Ockley, *The History of the Present Jews throughout the World* (London, 1707), 169.

25. *Tur yoreh de'ah*, 179:2.

26. One from the island of Minorca, 1751: *Encyclopaedia Judaica*, s.v. "Ketubbah," pl. 2. A second is from Salonika, 1790: Shalom Sabar, "Decorated *Ketubbot*," in *Sephardi Jews in the Ottoman Empire: Aspects of Material Culture*, ed. E. Juhasz (Jerusalem, 1990), pl. 54. A third comes from the old Sefaradi community of Jerusalem, 1844: Sabar, "Two Millennia of *Ketubbot*," 41 pl. 3. Apart from these isolated examples, the zodiac was a popular motif in the *ketubbot* of Corfu, but these were created under the influence of Venice, which ruled the island.

27. In pointing to the halakhic problem, Di Boton was following many previous authorities, both Sefaradi and Ashkenazi, who based their prohibition on talmudic rulings that associate the images of the sun, moon, and stars with idolatry (see, e.g., bAZ 43b). Cf. David Kotlar, *Art and Religion* (Hebrew) (Tel Aviv, 1971), 118–21, 158–59; and Vivian B. Mann, ed., *Jewish Texts on the Visual Arts* (Cambridge, 2000), 20–24.

28. For example, Gershom Scholem, "The Star of David: History of a Symbol," in idem, *The Messianic Idea in Judaism and Other Essays on Jewish Spirituality* (New York, 1971), 257–81; and Gerbern S. Oegema, *The History of the Shield of David: The Birth of a Symbol* (Frankfurt am Main, 1996).

29. In the Hebrew "magical" manual *Sefer Raziel ha-mal'akh* (Amsterdam, 1701), the star of David appears several times, but in one case, the triangles are arranged base to base within inscribed concentric circles, with the names of the four rivers of paradise in the corners. The same composition appears on another page, where the two triangles are superimposed in the familiar hexagram design. See E. A. Wallis Budge, *Amulets and Superstitions* (New York, 1978), 226–27; Schrire, *Hebrew Amulets*, 62–63. The power of the triangle to ward off evil spirits by reducing their strength is illustrated in the Talmud (bPes 112a) with

the name of an evil spirit (*Shabriri, briri, riri, iri, ri*) inscribed in a triangular shape (cf. Schrire, *Hebrew Amulets*, 60).

30. Scholem, "Magen David," *Encyclopaedia Judaica*, 11:688. Note, however, that in Islamic culture the hexagram is commonly referred to as Solomon's Seal, based on legendary accounts of the wondrous signet that the biblical king received from heaven. For examples of Solomon's Seal in Islamic art and culture, see Rachel Milstein, ed., *King Solomon's Seal* (Jerusalem, n.d. [1995]).

31. In contrast to what Schrire writes (*Hebrew Amulets*, 68), the expression *melekh David* (King David) is far less common.

32. Examples of Hebrew amulets are reproduced and discussed in Schrire, *Hebrew Amulets*; Isaiah Shachar, *Jewish Tradition in Art: The Feuchtwanger Collection of Judaica* (Jerusalem, 1981), 237–317; Eli Davis and David A. Frenkel, *The Hebrew Amulet: Biblical-Medical-General* (Hebrew) (Jerusalem, 1995); Nitza Behrouzi, ed., *The Hand of Fortune: Khamsas from the Gross Family Collection and the Eretz Israel Museum Collection* (Hebrew and English) (Tel Aviv, 2002); and Elka Deitsch, ed., *Kabbalah: Mysticism in Jewish Life* (New York, 2003).

33. Another example from Kyustendil was made a year earlier than the 1897 *ketubbah* preserved in the Library of the Jewish Theological Seminary of America (private collection in New York, unpublished).

34. Gabriel Barkay, "The Priestly Blessing in Silver Plaques: The Significance of the Discovery at Ketef Hinnom" (Hebrew), *Cathedra* 52 (1989): 37–76. Barkay suggests the amulets were "probably worn on the body, maybe forerunners of tefillin."

35. The word בן is abbreviated as 'ן, which, among the Sefaradim, commonly indicates "son of" (as in the Arabic *ibn*).

36. See Ḥayyim Joseph David Azulai, *Petaḥ ʿeinayim* (Jerusalem, 1959; 1st ed., Livorno, 1790), vol. 1, 18a–18b; Joseph Ḥayyim, *Adderet Eliyyahu* (Jerusalem, 1968; repr. of Livorno, 1864), 21b. Cf. Shalom Sabar, "From Sacred Symbol to Key Ring: The 'Hamsa' in Jewish and Israeli Society," in *Jews at Home: The Domestication of Identity*, ed. S. J. Bronner (Oxford, 2010), 140–62.

37. For the Indian examples, see Shalom Sabar, "The Illuminated *Ketubbah*," in *The Jews of India: A Story of Three Communities*, ed. O. Slapak (Jerusalem, 1995), 166–202, nos. 1, 14, 15, 17. An example from Vienna, 1831, is reproduced in Sabar, *Ketubbah*, 239. For this motif, see also an example from Jerusalem, 1893, in Sabar, "Two Millennia of *Ketubbot*," 58.

38. For examples from Jerusalem, see Sabar, "Two Millennia of *Ketubbot*," 58, 68–70.

39. Gross Family Collection, Tel Aviv. Cf. Behrouzi, *Hand of Fortune*, 18.

40. Sabar, *Mazal Tov*, pl. 18.

41. See the example issued for Moroccan families in Pará, Brazil, 1911, reproduced in Sabar, *Ketubbah*, 366–68.

42. This notion is already implied in the midrash in *Numbers Rabbah* 18:21. This interpretation depends upon *gematria* (numerology): the numerical value of the letters in

"Avram" is 243, but when the *heh* is added to his name, the total reaches 248, according to rabbinic tradition the number of limbs in the human body. In a recent work on the evil eye in Jewish tradition, however, the Sefaradi rabbi Yitshak Peha explains that the *heh* was added to protect Abraham (Peha, *Sefer 'olei 'ayin* [Jerusalem: 1990], 210).

43. For example, Herat, 1880, No'am Bar'am-Ben Yossef, ed., *Brides and Betrothals: Jewish Wedding Rituals in Afghanistan* (Jerusalem, 1998), 84, and Herat, 1895 (Sabar, *Ketubbah*, 304).

44. Even when the sums did not reach the said amounts, at least the tens and units added up to fifty-five. See also the examples illustrated in Sabar, "Two Millennia of *Ketubbot*" (e.g., 41, 43, 46, and 47).

45. This practice was also followed by the Moroccan families who immigrated to Gibraltar, as our example shows.

46. An earlier example, dated 1898, is preserved in the collection of the Israel Museum, Jerusalem (Ket. 179/157); see Sabar, *Mazal Tov*, pl. 36. The term *shiviti* derives from the first word of the verse quoted on this plaque: "I have set [*shiviti*] the Lord always before me" (Ps 16:8). Among the Jews of Islam, this plaque is generally called menorah, after its central design component (see below).

47. For the history, meaning, and analysis of the Shiviti Menorah in Jewish art and thought, see Esther Juhasz, "The 'Shiviti-Menorah': A Representation of the Sacred—Between Spirit and Matter" (Ph.D. diss., Hebrew University of Jerusalem, 2004).

48. In 1933, only two Jewish families were recorded in the village. Cf. Ben-Yaacob, *Kurdistan Jewish Communities*, 99. The *ketubbah* is preserved by the descendants of the original couple, who reside in Zechariah (a moshav near Jerusalem).

49. Cf. Shalom Sabar, "Childbirth and Magic: Jewish Folklore and Material Culture," in *Cultures of the Jews: A New History*, ed. D. Biale (New York, 2002), esp. 683, and figs. 9–11, 15, 19.

50. The decoration of the *ketubbah* with biblical figures who bear the same names as those of the bridal couple was especially common in Italy. In some communities, it was more common to inscribe names of ideal biblical couples—in particular, Ruth and Boaz—but the names of the patriarchs and matraiarchs are rare.

CHAPTER 5. THE DISLOCATION OF THE TEMPLE VESSELS

1. See, esp., the general framework presented in the introduction to Howard Wettstein, ed., *Diasporas and Exiles: Varieties of Jewish Identity* (Berkeley, Calif., 2002).

2. The theoretical and historical literature on the notion of diaspora as well as on specific diasporic communities is vast. Recent Jewish studies scholarship in this field has been profoundly shaped by its dialogue with a series of seminal studies, published in the 1980s and 1990s, on the historical emergence of the modern nation-state as the dominant politico-social form characteristic of "European modernity" and its contemporary ("postmodern") crises and transformations, most prominently: Benedict Anderson, *Imagined*

Communities: Reflections on the Origin and Spread of Nationalism, rev. ed. (London, 1991); Roger Rouse, "Mexican Migration and the Social Space of Postmodernism," *Diaspora* 1 (1991): 8–23; idem, "Questions of Identity: Personhood and Collectivity in Transnational Migration to the United States," *Critique of Anthropology* 15 (1995): 351–80; Paul Gilroy, *The Black Atlantic: Modernity and Double Consciousness* (Cambridge, Mass., 1993), esp. 187–224; Homi Bhabha, *The Location of Culture* (New York, 1994), esp. 199–244, 303–37; James Clifford, "Diasporas," *Cultural Anthropology* 9 (1994): 302–38; Smadar Lavie and Ted Swedenburg, introduction to *Displacement, Diaspora, and Geographies of Identity*, ed. S. Lavie and T. Swedenburg (Durham, N.C., 1996), 1–25; Vijay Mishra, "The Diasporic Imaginary: Theorizing the Indian Diaspora," *Textual Practice* 10 (1996): 421–47; and Arjun Appadurai, "Sovereignty without Territoriality: Notes for a Postnational Geography," in *The Geography of Identity*, ed. P. Yaeger (Ann Arbor, Mich., 1996), 40–59.

3. Daniel Boyarin and Jonathan Boyarin, "Diaspora: Generation and the Ground of Identity," *Critical Inquiry* 19 (1993): 693–725; and idem, *Powers of Diaspora: Two Essays on the Relevance of Jewish Culture* (Minneapolis, 2002).

4. Boyarin and Boyarin, "Diaspora," 723.

5. See, esp., Boyarin and Boyarin, *Powers of Diaspora*, esp. 6–11; and Jonathan Boyarin, "Space, Time, and the Politics of Memory," in idem, *Remapping Memory: The Politics of Timespace* (Minneapolis, 1994), 1–38. By contrast, Engseng Ho, *The Graves of Tarim: Genealogy and Mobility across the Indian Ocean* (Berkeley, Calif., 2006), 3–5, cautions strongly against using "globalization" as the dominant framework for understanding the historical experiences of long-standing diasporic communities. As Ho observes, the practices that produced and sustained these diasporas in fact "expand the time and space of social life, rather than compress them" (4).

6. See now, however, David Goodblatt, *Elements of Ancient Jewish Nationalism* (Cambridge, 2006), which offers a thoroughgoing but, I think, ultimately unsuccessful defense of applying the category of nationalism to forms of Jewish collectivity in antiquity. For a critical assessment of Goodblatt's inattention to the fundamental structural differences in the distribution of power between the imperial states of antiquity and the modern system of nation-states, see Steven Weitzman, "On the Relevance of Ancient Jewish Nationalism: A Brief Response to David Goodblatt's *Elements of Ancient Jewish Nationalism*," *Jewish Social Studies* 14 (2008): 165–72.

7. Erich S. Gruen, *Diaspora: Jews amidst Greeks and Romans* (Cambridge, Mass., 2002); and idem, "Diaspora and Homeland," in *Diasporas and Exiles*, ed. Wettstein, 18–46.

8. See, esp., Gruen, *Diaspora*, 232–52, here 243.

9. Charlotte Elisheva Fonrobert, "The Political Symbolism of the Eruv," *Jewish Social Studies* 11 (2005): 9–35.

10. Ibid., 29.

11. See Israel J. Yuval, "The Myth of the Jewish Exile from the Land of Israel: A Demonstration of Irenic Scholarship," *Common Knowledge* 12 (2006): 16–33, which argues that the connection between the destruction of the Second Temple and the notion of exile developed only gradually over the course of late antiquity and, in fact, represents a Jewish

appropriation of an originally Christian, anti-Jewish claim. The author seems to be suggesting that the Jewish notion of "exile" not only masks its own hybrid origins, but is both politically and ethically problematic. The article was first published in Hebrew in *Alpayim* 20 (2005): 9–25.

12. See the discussion in Ra'anan S. Boustan, "Imperialisms in Jewish History, from Pre- to Post-Modern," *AJS Perspectives* (fall 2005): 8–10; and Jonathan Boyarin, "Jews, Christians, and the Identity of Christian Europe," *AJS Perspectives* (fall 2005): 12–13.

13. Sarah Abrevaya Stein, "Modern Jews and the Imperial Imagination," *AJS Perspectives* (fall 2005): 14–16.

14. See Jonathan Klawans, *Purity, Sacrifice, and the Temple: Symbolism and Supersessionism in the Study of Ancient Judaism* (New York, 2006), esp. 175–211, which shows that much scholarship on rabbinic Judaism presumes the narrative of spiritual progress already found in some rabbinic texts in which the sacrificial cult of the Jerusalem Temple was replaced by increasingly meaningful forms of religious piety, such as prayer, Torah study, and good deeds.

15. See the classic statement of Peter Brown concerning the far-reaching process that occurred in late antiquity whereby a mobile class of exceptional individuals eclipsed the traditional Temple cults as the locus of the holy in "The Rise and Function of the Holy Man in Late Antiquity," in *Society and the Holy in Late Antiquity* (London, 1982), 103–52; and J. Z. Smith, *Map Is Not Territory: Studies in the History of Religion* (Leiden, 1978), 172–89.

16. For a thoroughgoing critique of the use of the concept of "spiritualization" in modern scholarship, see Klawans, *Purity, Sacrifice, and the Temple*, esp. 147–74, 213–54; and idem, "Interpreting the Last Supper: Sacrifice, Spiritualization, and Anti-Sacrifice," *New Testament Studies* 48 (2002): 1–17. For a nuanced and dialectical account of the "end" of sacrifice in ancient Mediterranean religions generally, see Guy G. Stroumsa, *La fin du sacrifice: Les mutations religieuses de l'antiquité tardive* (Paris, 2005).

17. On sacrificial cult as the paradigm for ritual action in late antique religions, see Stroumsa, *Fin du sacrifice*, 105–44, as well as the contribution in this volume by Michael Swartz.

18. Klawans, *Purity, Sacrifice, and the Temple*, 175–211; Ishay Rosen-Zvi, "Bodies and Temple: The List of Priestly Bodily Defects in Mishnah *Bekhorot*, Chapter 7" (Hebrew), *Jewish Studies* 43 (2005–6): 49–87; and Steven D. Fraade, "The Temple as a Marker of Jewish Identity Before and After 70 C.E.: The Role of the Holy Vessels in Rabbinic Memory and Imagination," in *Jewish Identities in Antiquity: Studies in Memory of Menahem Stern*, ed. L. I. Levine and D. R. Schwartz (Tübingen, 2009), 235–63. I would like to thank Steven Fraade not only for generously sharing his paper with me in advance of its publication, but also for engaging with me in productive and enjoyable dialogue about the meaning of the rabbinic representations of the Temple vessels—about which we have come to strikingly complementary conclusions.

19. On the "locative" worldview of religious systems that are built around traditional sacrificial cults, see Smith, *Map Is Not Territory*, esp. 101–3, 132–43, 160–70, 185–89, 291–94, 308–9. For an important attempt to modify and nuance Smith's dichotomy be-

tween "locative" and "utopian" religions, see Sarah Iles Johnston, "Working Overtime in Afterlife; or, No Rest for the Virtuous," in *Heavenly Realms and Earthly Realities in Late Antique Religions*, ed. R. S. Boustan and A. Y. Reed (New York, 2004), 85–100.

20. I analyze here only those traditions that are found in rabbinic compilations from Palestine from the third and fourth centuries (i.e., the Mishnah, the Tosefta, the halakhic midrashim, and the Palestinian Talmud). For discussion of the subsequent development of this material in later rabbinic and "para-rabbinic" literature, see my companion study, "The Spoils of the Jerusalem Temple at Rome and Constantinople: Jewish Counter-Geography in a Christianizing Empire," in *Antiquity in Antiquity: Jewish and Christian Pasts in the Greco-Roman World*, ed. G. Gardner and K. Osterloh (Tübingen, 2008), 327–72. A number of recent studies have also addressed various aspects of these traditions: Fraade, "Temple as a Marker of Jewish Identity"; Steven Fine, "When I Went to Rome . . . There I Saw the Menorah . . .": The Jerusalem Temple Implements During the Second Century C.E.," in *The Archaeology of Difference: Gender, Ethnicity, Class and the "Other" in Antiquity, Studies in Honor of Eric M. Meyers*, ed. D. R. Edwards and C. T. McCullough (Winona Lake, Ind., 2007), 171–82; and David Noy, "Rabbi Aqiba Comes to Rome: A Jewish Pilgrimage in Reverse?," in *Pilgrimage in Graeco-Roman and Early Christian Antiquity: Seeing the Gods*, ed. J. Elsner and I. Rutherford (Oxford, 2005), 373–85.

21. See n. 14 above.

22. For a characterization of rabbinic Judaism as a fundamentally "diasporic" religious and cultural formation, see Boyarin and Boyarin, "Diaspora," esp. 718–23.

23. See now James Rives, "Flavian Religious Policy and the Destruction of the Jerusalem Temple," in *Flavius Josephus and Flavian Rome*, ed. J. Edmondson, S. Mason, and J. Rives (Oxford, 2005), 145–66, which argues that the destruction of the Jerusalem cult by the Romans was an intentional strategy for dispiriting and thus subduing the rebellious population of Judea.

24. The fullest source on the triumph is Josephus, *Jewish War*, 7.118–62. On Vespasian and Titus's triumph, see, esp., Michael McCormick, *Eternal Victory: Triumphal Rulership in Late Antiquity, Byzantium, and the Early Medieval West* (Cambridge, 1986), 14–17; and Mary Beard, *The Roman Triumph* (Cambridge, Mass., 2007), 152–53.

25. I follow the date for the erection of the arch given in Michael Pfanner, *Der Titusbogen* (Mainz, 1983), 91–92. For the most comprehensive discussion of the spoils panel of the arch, see Leon Yarden, *The Spoils of Jerusalem on the Arch of Titus: A Re-investigation* (Stockholm, 1991).

26. Suetonius, *Ves.* 9.1; Josephus, *Jewish War*, 7.158. On the Templum Pacis, see, esp., James C. Anderson, Jr., *The Historical Topography of the Imperial Fora* (Brussels, 1984), 101–18; Eva Margareta Steinby, ed., *Lexicon Topographicum Urbis Romae*, 6 vols. (Rome, 1993–2000), 4:67–70; and Lawrence Richardson, Jr., *A New Topographical Dictionary of Ancient Rome* (Baltimore, 1992), 286–87.

27. Fergus Millar, "Last Year in Jerusalem: Monuments of the Jewish War in Rome," in *Flavius Josephus and Flavian Rome*, ed. Edmondson et al., 101–28.

28. On the dating of the text to the period between the fall of Jerusalem (70 C.E.) and

the Bar Kokhba revolt (132–135/36 C.E.) and, more specifically, between 100 and 130 C.E., see A. F. J. Klijn, "2 (Syriac Apocalypse of) Baruch," in *The Old Testament Pseudepigrapha*, vol. 1: *Apocalyptic Literature and Testaments*, ed. J. H. Charlesworth (New York, 1983–85), 615–52, esp. 616–17.

29. 2 Bar 6:8 (Klijn, "2 Baruch," 623).

30. 2 Mc 2:1–8. Close parallels also appear in 4 Bar (*Paraleipomena Jeremiou*) 3:7–20; *Vit. Proph.* 2:11–14. On this theme, see Steven Weitzman, *Surviving Sacrilege: Cultural Persistence in Jewish Antiquity* (Cambridge, Mass., 2005), 96–117; and Isaac Kalimi and James D. Purvis, "The Hiding of the Temple Vessels in Jewish and Samaritan Literature," *Catholic Biblical Quarterly* 56 (1994): 679–85.

31. On the image of the hidden vessels as a strategy of cultural resistance, see Weitzman, *Surviving Sacrilege*, 96–117; and idem, "Myth, History, and Mystery in the Copper Scroll," in *The Idea of Biblical Interpretation: Essays in Honor of James L. Kugel*, ed. H. Najman and J. H. Newman (Leiden, 2004), 239–55.

32. In my view, neither Fine, "When I Went to Rome," nor Noy, "Rabbi Aqiba Comes to Rome," provides sufficient justification for reading these sources as straightforward historical reports. For a critique of their positions, see Boustan, "Spoils of the Jerusalem Temple," 339–41.

33. See Fraade, "Temple as a Marker of Jewish Identity," which demonstrates convincingly that sources from the Second Temple period provide no evidence for the public display of the Temple vessels and explains the appearance of this tradition in post-destruction Jewish and Christian sources as a reflex of the growing importance that the visualization of the sacred held in late antique religions. See below for further discussion of this issue.

34. yYom 5:5 (42d) offers a slightly different version of this phrase, in which it is R. Eleazar who is the speaker: "I said: These [drops] are from the blood that they would sprinkle upon it on the Day of Atonement."

35. tKipp 2:16 (Lieberman); my translation. Cf. bYom 57a.

36. R. Eleazar's testimony is absent in the Mishnah's parallel description of the sacrificial ritual carried out by the high priest on the Day of Atonement.

37. yYom 4:1 (41c); my translation. Cf. yMeg 1:9 (71d); bShab 63b.

38. *Sifrei zuta, be-ha'alotekha*, 8:2 (Horovitz, 255); my translation.

39. P. Ox. 840, 2:1–3. I have followed the text and translation in François Bovon, "Fragment Oxyrhynchus 840, Fragment of a Lost Gospel, Witness of an Early Christian Controversy over Purity," *Journal of Biblical Literature* 119 (2000): 705–28, esp. 714–15. The text is also translated in Wilhelm Schneemelcher, ed., *New Testament Apocrypha*, trans. R. McL. Wilson, 2 vols., rev. ed. (Louisville, Ky., 1991), 1:94–95. It was originally published in Bernard P. Greenfell and Arthur S. Hunt, *The Oxyrhynchus Papyri* (London/Oxford, 1908), vol. 5, no. 840.

40. Daniel R. Schwartz, "Viewing the Holy Utensils (P Ox V, 840)," *New Testament Studies* 32 (1986): 153–59. For example, Schwartz cites Josephus's report that when Pompey and his men entered the Temple and saw various cultic vessels, they "saw what it was unlawful for any but the high priest to see" (Josephus, *Antiquities of the Jews*, 14:71–72).

41. For his assessment of Schwartz's argument, see Bovon, "Fragment Oxyrhynchus 840," 711–12.

42. This fact was already stressed by Abraham Sulzbach, "Zum Oxyrhynchus-Fragment," *Zeitschrift für die neutestamentliche Wissenschaft und die Kunde der älteren Kirche* 9 (1908): 175–76.

43. Israel Knohl, "Post-Biblical Sectarianism and Priestly Schools of the Pentateuch: The Issue of Popular Participation in the Temple Cult on Festivals," in *The Madrid Qumran Congress*, ed. J. T. Barrera and L. Vegas Montaner, 2 vols. (Leiden, 1992), 2:601–9; also published as "Participation of the People in the Temple Worship—Second Temple Sectarian Conflict and the Biblical Tradition" (Hebrew), *Tarbiz* 60 (1991): 139–46.

44. This material is found in increasingly expansive forms at mHag 3:8; tHag 3:35; yHag 3:8 (79d); bHag 26b. Knohl finds echoes of the debate between the Pharisees and Sadducees described in these sources in an ordinance found in the Qumran Temple Scroll, col. 3, lines 10–12. Knohl's view is in keeping with the interpretation of the rabbinic sources in Ya'akov Sussman, "The History of the Halakhah and the Dead Sea Scrolls: Preliminary Talmudic Observations on *Miqsat Ma'ase ha-Torah*," appendix 1 in Elisha Qimron and John Strugnell, *Qumran Cave 4*, vol. 5: *Miqsat Ma'ase ha-Torah* (Oxford, 1994), 199; Saul Lieberman, *Tosefta kifshutah*, 10 vols. (New York, 1973), 5:1336. But for a contradictory interpretation, see Joseph M. Baumgarten, "Immunity to Impurity and the Menorah," *Jewish Studies Internet Journal* 5 (2006): 141–45, which attributes Sadducean ridicule of the Pharisaic practice of purifying the menorah not to their rejection of Pharisaic liberalism (i.e., allowing the public to come into contact with the vessel) but to their conviction that the menorah was itself immune to impurity because of "the purifying power of its radiance" (145).

45. See also Fraade, "Temple as a Marker of Jewish Identity."

46. Lee I. Levine, *The Ancient Synagogue: The First Thousand Years*, 2nd ed. (New Haven, Conn., 2005), esp. 236–49, 630–32. But a higher degree of continuity with earlier periods is emphasized in Steven Fine, *This Holy Place: On the Sanctity of the Synagogue during the Greco-Roman Period* (Notre Dame, Ind., 1997).

CHAPTER 6. SACRED SPACE, LOCAL HISTORY, AND DIASPORIC IDENTITY

1. Raphael Straus, ed., *Urkunden und Aktenstücke zur Geschichte der Juden in Regensburg 1453–1738* (Munich, 1960), 29–31. For the full narrative, see the Yiddish *Mayse bukh* (Basel, 1602), now available in facsimile: Astrid Starck, ed. and trans., *Un beau livre d'histoires: Eyn shön Mayse bukh*, 2 vols. (Basel, 2004), no. 241.

2. Israel Mordechai Peles, ed., *R. Juda Löw Kirchheim: The Customs of Worms Jewry* (Hebrew) (Jerusalem, 1987), 251–54; Binyamin Shlomo Hamburger and Eric Zimmer, eds., *Wormser Minhagbuch des R. Jousep (Juspa) Schammes* (Hebrew), 2nd ed. (Jerusalem, 1992), 1:102–7.

3. London, British Library, MS Add. 18695 (G. Margoliouth, *Catalogue of the Hebrew*

and Samaritan manuscripts in the British Museum, vol. 2 [London, 1905], no. 683; Institute of Microfilmed Hebrew Manuscripts, Jerusalem [IMHM], no. 4981), fol. 56r.

4. *Mayse bukh*, no. 187, introduction.

5. bShab 33b–34a. On the way the posthumous image of R. Shimʿon ben Yitshaq was modeled on that of his talmudic namesake, see Lucia Raspe, "Payyeṭanim as Heroes of Medieval Folk Narrative: The Case of R. Shimʿon ben Yishaq," in *Jewish Studies Between the Disciplines/Judaistik zwischen den Disziplinen: Papers in Honor of Peter Schäfer on the Occasion of His Sixtieth Birthday*, ed. K. Herrmann, M. Schlüter, and G. Veltri (Leiden, 2003), 354–69.

6. For an account of the pilgrimage to Meron in the Galilee, where Shimʿon bar Yohai's grave was located from the fifteenth century onward, see Elchanan Reiner, "Pilgrims and Pilgrimage to Erets Yisrael, 1099–1517" (Hebrew) (Ph.D. diss., Hebrew University of Jerusalem, 1988), 237–39, 295–305.

7. Robert L. Cohn, "Sainthood on the Periphery: The Case of Judaism," in *Saints and Virtues*, ed. J. S. Hawley (Berkeley, Calif., 1987), 87–108; repr. in *Sainthood: Its Manifestations in World Religions*, ed. R. Kieckhefer and G. D. Bond (Berkeley, Calif., 1988), 43–68, esp. 46–47. On late antiquity, see, e.g., Allen Kerkeslager, "Jewish Pilgrimage and Jewish Identity in Hellenistic and Early Roman Egypt," in *Pilgrimage and Holy Space in Late Antique Egypt*, ed. D. Frankfurter (Leiden, 1998), 99–225; for contemporary practices, see Shifra Epstein, "Les pèlerinages hassidiques en Pologne," *Cahiers du Judaïsme* 8 (2000): 100–111; and Oren Kosansky, "Tourism, Charity, and Profit: The Movement of Money in Moroccan Jewish Pilgrimage," *Cultural Anthropology* 17 (2002): 359–400.

8. Lucia Raspe, *Jüdische Hagiographie im mittelalterlichen Aschkenas* (Tübingen, 2006); for a summary in English, see idem, "Jewish Saints in Medieval Ashkenaz: A Contradiction in Terms?" *Frankfurter Judaistische Beiträge* 31 (2004): 75–90.

9. Thus R. Yaʿaqov b. Asher (d. 1340), author of the *Arbaʿah turim*, in a letter dated 1329 advising a German rabbi to follow his example and emigrate to Spain. Published by Alfred Freimann, "Erets gezeirah," *ha-Soqer* 2 (1934): 37–38; on the subsequent fate of the addressee, see Moses A. Shulvass, "Würzburg," in *Germania Judaica*, vol. 2, part 2, ed. Z. Avneri (Tübingen, 1968), 933 no. 11. The same phrase recurs in the ethical testament of Yaʿaqov's brother Yehudah: Israel Abrahams, ed., *Hebrew Ethical Wills* (Philadelphia, 1926), 166; for an impression of the controversy that it has raised in recent historiography, see Michael Toch, *Die Juden im mittelalterlichen Reich* (Munich, 1998), 121.

10. Cf. Michael Toch, "Jüdisches Alltagsleben im Mittelalter," *Historische Zeitschrift* 278 (2004): 329–45, esp. 341–42.

11. Reiner, "Pilgrims and Pilgrimage," 14–15.

12. Elliott Horowitz, "Speaking to the Dead: Cemetery Prayer in Medieval and Early Modern Jewry," *Journal of Jewish Thought and Philosophy* 8 (1999): 303–17; Mordechai Breuer and Yacov Guggenheim, "Die jüdische Gemeinde, Gesellschaft und Kultur," in *Germania Judaica*, vol. 3, pt. 3, ed. A. Maimon, M. Breuer, and Y. Guggenheim (Tübingen, 2003), 2088 n. 57. See also Hirsch Jakob Zimmels, "Erez Israel in der Responsenliteratur des späteren Mittelalters," *Monatsschrift für Geschichte und Wissenschaft des Judentums* 74 (1930): 49 n. 1.

13. Raphael Nathan Neta Rabbinovicz, ed., *Sefer she'elot u-teshuvot Maharam bar Barukh* (Lemberg, 1860), fol. 13a, no. 164. On the responsum's author, see Ernst Daniel Goldschmidt, "Magdeburg," *Germania Judaica*, vol. 2, part 2, 507–8; Yitshaq S. Lange, "Identifying R. Haim Paltiel" (Hebrew), *Alei Sefer* 8 (1980): 140–46; on *doresh el ha-metim* (Dt 18:11), see Horowitz, "Speaking to the Dead," 305, 310–11.

14. *Sefer ha-nitsahon* (Altdorf, 1644); repr. ed. Frank Talmage (Jerusalem, 1983), 86, no. 132. See Talmage, "Angels, Anthems, and Anathemas: Aspects of Popular Religion in Fourteenth-Century Bohemian Judaism," *Jewish History* 6 (1992) (= *The Frank Talmage Memorial Volume*, ed. B. Walfish, vol. 2): 13–20, esp. 14–15; on the author more generally, Ora Limor and Israel Jacob Yuval, "Skepticism and Conversion: Jews, Christians, and Doubters in *Sefer ha-Nizzahon*," in *Hebraica Veritas? Christian Hebraists and the Study of Judaism in Early Modern Europe*, ed. A. P. Coudert and J. S. Shoulson (Philadelphia, 2004), 159–80.

15. *Sefer ha-nitsahon*, ed. Talmage, 16, no. 12; and 82, no. 127.

16. This point has been made by Chava Weissler, *Voices of the Matriarchs* (Boston, 1998), 245–46 n. 61. For modern efforts to defend the practice from a halakhic point of view, see Yehiel M. Tykochinsky, *Sefer gesher ha-hayyim*, 2nd ed. (Jerusalem, 1960), vol. 2, chap. 26; Avraham Mordekhai ha-levi Horovitz, "Hishtathut 'al qivrei tsaddiqim u-meqomot ha-qedoshim," *No'am* 12 (1969): 169–238. For a more critical view, see Yechezkel Shraga Lichtenstein, *Consecrating the Profane: Rituals Performed and Prayers Recited at Cemeteries and Burial Sites of the Righteous* (Hebrew) (Tel Aviv, 2007).

17. *Sefer Hasidim,* in Jehuda Wistinetzki, ed., *Das Buch der Frommen nach der Rezension in Cod. de Rossi No. 1133* (Hebrew), 2nd ed., with introduction and indices by Jacob Freimann (Frankfurt am Main, 1924), nos. 270 (= 1537) and 273; cf. Horowitz, "Speaking to the Dead," 310. On the intercession of the dead for the living, see *Sefer Hasidim*, nos. 227, 274, 355, and cf. Joseph Dan, "Demonological Stories in the Writings of R. Yehuda Hehasid" (Hebrew), *Tarbiz* 30 (1960–61): 288, no. 27; for an account of a community punished for abandoning its dead, *Sefer Hasidim*, no. 269.

18. Abrahams, *Hebrew Ethical Wills*, 183–84; cf. Horowitz, "Speaking to the Dead," 309–10. Incidentally, what R. Yehudah recalled praying for was to be blessed with offspring, a concern often thought specific to women. See, e.g., Susan Starr Sered, "Rachel's Tomb: Societal Liminality and the Revitalization of a Shrine," *Religion* 19 (1989): 27–40.

19. Shlomoh J. Spitzer, ed., *The Book of Maharil: Customs by Rabbi Yaacov Mulin* (Hebrew) (Jerusalem, 1989), 270, Hilkhot ta'anit no. 18, a passage that is cited by several of the later authorities.

20. Jacob Freimann, ed., *Leket Joscher des Joseph b. Mose: Collectaneen seines Lehrers Israel Isserlein* (Hebrew) (Berlin, 1903–4), 1:116; cf. 140. For the early modern reception of this text, see ibid., 116 n. 313a; Weissler, *Voices of the Matriarchs*, 246 n. 64. Earlier formulations avoiding direct address of the dead can be found in Shlomoh J. Spitzer, ed., *Decisions and Customs of Rabbi Shalom of Neustadt* (Hebrew) (Jerusalem, 1977), 161, no. 490.

21. For evidence of pilgrimage to the cemeteries of the time-honored Rhenish communities of Mainz, Worms, and Speyer, see *Leket Joscher*, ed. Freimann, 2:25, a case dated

to ca. 1428 in Reinhard H. Seitz, "Augsburg," in *Germania Judaica*, vol. 3, part 1, ed. A. Maimon (Tübingen, 1987), 63 n. 293. The vow of a woman to visit the cemetery in Landshut in about 1450 is mentioned in the responsa of R. Israel Bruna: Moshe Hershler, ed., *She'elot u-teshuvot ha-ma'or ha-gadol ha-mefursam Yisra'el mi-Bruna* (Jerusalem, 1960), 264–65, no. 245.

22. Straus, *Urkunden*, 386, citing Christophorus Ostrofrancus.

23. *Leket Joscher*, ed. Freimann, 2:24. For the dating of Isserlein's vow, see Peter Herde, "Regensburg," in *Germania Judaica*, vol. 3, pt. 2, ed. A. Maimon, M. Breuer, and Y. Guggenheim (Tübingen, 1995), 1217 n. 344.

24. Zvi Avneri, "Regensburg," in *Germania Judaica*, vol. 2, pt. 2, 686.

25. Yitzchok Satz, ed., *Responsa of Rabbi Yaacov Molin Maharil* (Hebrew) (Jerusalem, 1979), 214, no. 118.

26. Yonatan Shraga Domb, ed., *She'elot u-teshuvot rabbeinu Mosheh Mintz* (Jerusalem, 1991), 2:377, no. 79. Tykochinsky, *Gesher ha-ḥayyim*, vol. 1, chap. 29, no. 9, makes a distinction between prayer at the graves of parents and relatives designed to assist their souls and that at *qivrei tsaddiqim* intended to aid the living. The adult Isserlein, on the other hand, is reported to have said the same prayer at the graveside of every single *gadol* as well as the graves of his relatives: *Leket Joscher*, ed. Freimann, 1:140.

27. British Library, MS Add. 18695 (written ca. 1504), fol. 56r. For the text and a full discussion, see Raspe, *Jüdische Hagiographie*, 306–10.

28. Moscow, Russian State Library, MS Günzburg 109 (IMHM, no. 6789), fol. 528v. See Ephraim Kupfer, "Menakhem Oldendorfs oytobiografishe fartseykhenungen un notitsn in a hebreishn ksav-yad," *Di Goldene Keyt* 58 (1967): 214 and 220 n. 15. Israel M. Ta-Shma, "A New Chronography on the Thirteenth-Century Tosafists" (Hebrew), *Shalem* 3 (1981): 324, interprets this passage as referring to the Ninth of Av. I prefer Kupfer's reading over Ta-Shma's for reasons of *lectio difficilior*; see below. My thanks to Abraham David and Elchanan Reiner for their help in this matter.

29. I owe this observation to Martha Keil.

30. Detlev Kraack, "Die Magie des (Wallfahrts-)Ortes und der Zwang zur Verewigung: Religiöse und profane Mobilität im Spiegel vormoderner (Pilger-)Graffiti," http://edoc.hu-berlin.de/conferences/conf2/Kraack-Detlev-2002-09-08/HTML (accessed June 23, 2010). For a survey of scholarly work on similar inscriptions that have been preserved at a variety of pilgrimage sites, beginning in late antiquity, see Detlev Kraack and Peter Lingens, *Bibliographie zu historischen Graffiti zwischen Antike und Moderne* (Krems, 2001), esp. 30–36; for an exemplary exercise in both documentation and interpretation, see Gerhard Schober, "Die Votiv- und Graffitifunde in der Laurentiuskapelle Unterbrunn," *Bayerisches Jahrbuch für Volkskunde* (1976–77): 227–45.

31. Charles Pietri, "Graffito I (Lateinisch)," *Reallexikon für Antike und Christentum* 12 (1983): 638.

32. Marcus Nathan Adler, ed. and trans., *The Itinerary of Benjamin of Tudela* (London, 1907; repr. New York, n.d.), 26. For a similar custom observed at the Western Wall in Jerusalem, see ibid., 224; cf. the photograph of 1865 in Eli Schiller, ed., *The First Photographs*

of Jerusalem: The Old City (Hebrew) (Jerusalem, 1978), 79, and Schiller's comments, ibid., 242.

33. Eli Schiller, *Qever Raḥel* (Jerusalem, 1977), 17, 31–37; Sered, "Rachel's Tomb," passim. For similar developments at Christian shrines, see Lenz Kriss-Rettenbeck, *Ex Voto: Zeichen, Bild und Abbild im christlichen Votivbrauchtum* (Zürich, 1972), 47–53; Walter Heim, *Briefe zum Himmel: Die Grabbriefe an Mutter M. Theresia Scherer in Ingenbohl. Ein Beitrag zur religiösen Volkskunde der Gegenwart* (Basel, 1961), 10–29.

34. David Kaufmann, "Der Grabstein des R. Jakob b. Mose ha-Levi in Worms," *Monatsschrift für Geschichte und Wissenschaft des Judentums* 42 (1898): 228. The Hebrew names inscribed on the chair long identified as Rashi's in the seventeenth-century *beit midrash* adjacent to the synagogue in Worms, read as the scribbling of schoolchildren by Otto Böcher, *Die alte Synagoge zu Worms* (Worms, 1960), 112–14 nos. 16–21, may reflect a similar mix of tourism and piety. To what extent the custom of leaving notes at holy graves is a carryover from modern-day Hasidism has not been studied to date. On the *kvitlekh* originally addressed to the rebbe while he was alive, see Aaron Wertheim, "Traditions and Customs in Hasidim," in *Essential Papers on Hasidism: Origins to Present*, ed. G. D. Hundert (New York, 1991), 378–82.

35. Kriss-Rettenbeck, *Ex Voto*, 47. For an example involving the delicate woodwork of the Torah shrine at the synagogue of Old Cairo, see Benjamin Richler, "New Inscriptions from the Synagogue of the Palestinians in Fustat" (Hebrew), *Alei Sefer* 5 (1978): 182–85; Menahem Ben-Sasson, "The Medieval Period: The Tenth to Fourteenth Centuries," in *Fortifications and the Synagogue: The Fortress of Babylon and the Ben Ezra Synagogue, Cairo*, ed. P. Lambert (London, 1994), 201–23, esp. 219–23.

36. The custom is mentioned in the glosses to *Sefer mitsvot qatan* edited from a late fourteenth-century manuscript by Yitshaq Ya'aqov Har-Shoshanim-Rosenberg, ed., *Sefer ha-sm"q mi-tsurikh ve-hu sefer 'amudei golah* (Jerusalem, 1973–82), 1:54; and in *Leket Joscher*, ed. Freimann, 1:47, 116. See Gershom Scholem, *Zur Kabbala und ihrer Symbolik* (Zürich, 1960), 199–202 and 278 n. 62; Hamburger and Zimmer, *Wormser Minhagbuch*, 1:65–66 n. 1; and see below at n. 71.

37. See e.g. Breuer and Guggenheim, "Gemeinde," 2088.

38. Herman Pollack, *Jewish Folkways in Germanic Lands (1648–1806): Studies in Aspects of Daily Life* (Cambridge, Mass., 1971), 47–49.

39. bTa'an 16a. The debate over the status of non-Jewish cemeteries—and, implicitly, over intercessory prayer as the primary motivation of such visits—continues into the *Shulḥan 'arukh*, Oraḥ ḥayyim, no. 579:3, and the commentaries ad loc. Indeed, Zalman Tsvi of Offenhausen's *Yudisher teryaq* (Hanau, 1615), fol. 15b, chap. 2, no. 32, insists that German Jews of his time did visit non-Jewish cemeteries on fast days when there was no Jewish burial place at hand. See also Yuzpa Kosman, *Noheg ka-tson Yosef* (Hanau, 1718; repr. Tel Aviv, 1969), 250, 'Erev tish'ah be-Av, no. 10.

40. Yonah Y. Dissen, ed., *Minhagim (Customs) of Rabbi Abraham Klausner* (Hebrew) (Jerusalem, 1978), 131, no. 138:8, which is itself cited in *Sefer Maharil*, ed. Spitzer, 247, no. 14. See also *Sefer Maharil*, 273, Hilkhot rosh ha-shanah, no. 3, and the Tosafot on

bTaʻan 16a, s.v. *yotsʼin le-veit ha-qevarot*. More detailed description can be found in the local *minhagim* literature of the seventeenth and eighteenth centuries. For Worms, see Liva Kirchheim's *Customs*, ed. Peles, 95, 134, 271, as well as Yuzpa Shammes's *Minhagbuch*, ed. Hamburger and Zimmer, 1:127, 143, 172–73; for Frankfurt, Yuzpa Hahn, *Sefer Yosif omets* (Frankfurt am Main, 1723; repr. 1928), 212, nos. 956–57; 219, no. 986, and Yuzpa Kosman's *Noheg ka-tson Yosef*, 262, ʻErev rosh ha-shanah, no. 4, and 250, ʻErev tishʻah be-Av, no. 10; for Fürth, Israel and Koppel Gumpel, *Sefer ha-minhagim de-qehilateinu* (Fürth, 1767), fol. 4b, no. 20; fol. 6a, no. 30. Regarding Prague, a Hebrew chronicle of 1648 bemoans the fact that due to the Swedish siege of the city, the Jews "were not able to go to the cemetery on Tisha bʼAv or on Erev Rosh Hashanah and Yom Kippur" of that year. Cited in Rachel L. Greenblatt, "The Shapes of Memory: Evidence in Stone from the Old Jewish Cemetery in Prague," *Leo Baeck Institute Year Book* 47 (2002): 43.

41. *Sefer ha-agudah* (Krakow, 1571; repr. Jerusalem, 1966), fol. 172a, commenting on *Masekhet semahot* 6:11. See Michael Higger's edition of the latter (New York, 1931), 134, as well as his introduction, 75–77, and Ernst Roth, "Das Licht im jüdischen Brauchtum," *Udim* 3 (1972): 106–7. Horovitz, "Hishtathut ʻal qivrei tsaddiqim," 175, has linked this source to a passage in *Sefer Ḥasidim*, ed. Wistinetzki and Freimann, no. 630, which describes Hayya Gaʼon conducting the *haqqafot* that were formerly part of the Temple ritual at the Mount of Olives, itself a cemetery. See also Reiner, "Pilgrims and Pilgrimage," 184–85. Although the passage in *Sefer ha-agudah* is far from clear, several early modern authors make reference to this source when discussing communal visits to the cemetery. Thus Mosheh Mat, *Sefer mateh Mosheh* (Frankfurt am Main, 1720), fol. 83b, no. 789; and Yeshayahu Horowitz, *Sefer shenei luhot ha-berit* (Amsterdam, 1649), fol. 213b.

42. See Lucia Raspe, "The Black Death in Jewish Sources: A Second Look at *Mayse Nissim*," *Jewish Quarterly Review* 94 (2004): 471–89. On the paucity of medieval tombstones dedicated to martyrs, as opposed to those mentioning a martyred parent, see Michael Brocke, "Märtyrer in Worms und Mainz: Eine epigraphische Studie zu *qadosh*," in *Aus den Quellen: Beiträge zur deutsch-jüdischen Geschichte. Festschrift für Ina Lorenz zum 65. Geburtstag*, ed. A. Brämer, S. Schüler-Springorum, and M. Studemund-Halévy (Hamburg, 2005), 14.

43. The rabbinic sources are discussed in Arthur Marmorstein, "Beiträge zur Religionsgeschichte und Volkskunde," *Jahrbuch für jüdische Volkskunde* 25 (1923): 280–319; 26–27 (1924–25): 51–62; Rudolf Mach, *Der Zaddik in Talmud und Midrasch* (Leiden, 1957), 112 n. 2. According to *Sefer Maharil*, ed. Spitzer, 602, Hilkhot semahot, no. 10, this is why a wicked person should not be buried near a zaddik (cf. bSan 47a), a concern also in evidence in *Sefer Ḥasidim*, ed. Wistinetzki and Freimann, nos. 265–67, since a *rashaʻ* listening in will cause future events to be hidden from the righteous person in the grave nearby.

44. Israel Jacob Yuval, "Jews, Hussites, and Germans according to the Chronicle *Gilgul Bʼnei Hushim*" (Hebrew), *Zion* 54 (1989): 317.

45. *Leket Joscher*, ed. Freimann, 1:115; cf. ibid., 112.

46. See Rivka Ulmer, ed., *Turmoil, Trauma, and Triumph: The Fettmilch Uprising in Frankfurt am Main (1612–1616) according to Megillas Vintz* (Frankfurt am Main, 2001),

114–19, 138–39, and the editor's comments, ibid., 71–73; cf. Isidor Kracauer, "Die Juden Frankfurts im Fettmilch'schen Aufstand 1612–1618," *Zeitschrift für die Geschichte der Juden in Deutschland* 4 (1890): 351–57. For a parallel from late eighteenth-century Morocco, see Samuel Romanelli, *Ketavim nivḥarim: Masa' ba'rav, leqet shirim, qeta'im mittokh maḥazot*, ed. Ḥayyim Schirmann (Jerusalem, 1968), 132.

47. *Megillas Vints*, ed. Ulmer, 144–45 no. 49, and Ulmer's comments, ibid., 74.

48. For one example, ca. 1500, see Hans Jürgen Wunschel, "Rothenburg ob der Tauber," in *Germania Judaica*, vol. 3, part 2, 1255 and 1267 n. 88. Note also the provisions made in the testament of one Eleazar of Mainz (d. 1357) in Abrahams, *Hebrew Ethical Wills*, 217–18; cf. *Sefer Ḥasidim*, ed. Wistinetzki and Freimann, nos. 306 and 312.

49. Robert Bonfil, *Jewish Life in Renaissance Italy*, trans. A. Oldcorn (Berkeley, Calif., 1994), 280–81.

50. A classic study of Christian practices is Bernhard Kötting, *Der frühchristliche Reliquienkult und die Bestattung im Kirchengebäude* (Cologne, 1964). See also Philippe Ariès, *L'homme devant la mort* (Paris, 1977), 37–93; and Yvette Duval, *Auprès des saints, corps et âme: L'inhumation "ad sanctos" dans la chrétienté d'Orient et d'Occident du IIIe au VIIe siècle* (Paris, 1988).

51. The phrase is Christopher Daniell's. See his *Death and Burial in Medieval England, 1066–1550* (London, 1997), chap. 4. For an overview of medieval Jewish cemeteries preserved in Germany, see Michael Brocke and Christiane E. Müller, *Haus des Lebens: Jüdische Friedhöfe in Deutschland* (Leipzig, 2001), esp. 137–39 (Würzburg), 145–46 (Mainz), 149–52 (Worms), 156–58 (Frankfurt am Main).

52. Friedrich Schütz, "Mainz," in *Germania Judaica*, vol. 3, pt. 2, 805.

53. Those found before 1926 were placed in a "Denkmalfriedhof" section of the cemetery set up that year, where a majority remains today. See Sali Levi, *Beiträge zur Geschichte der ältesten jüdischen Grabsteine in Mainz* (Mainz, 1926). The fullest published list of medieval Jewish epitaphs from Mainz, including those found in the aftermath of World War II, is Eugen Ludwig Rapp, *Chronik der Mainzer Juden: Die Mainzer Grabdenkmalstätte* (Mainz, 1977).

54. Siegmund Salfeld, "Mainzer jüdische Grabsteine, gefunden im Jahre 1922," *Mainzer Zeitschrift* 17/19 (1921–24): 63, no. 2.

55. For R. Gershom's epitaph, see Levi, *Beiträge*, 12–13, no. 1; for R. Meshullam's, Avraham Grossman, *Ḥakhemei Ashkenaz ha-rishonim* (Jerusalem, 1981), 49–50 n. 78; and Bernd A. Vest, *Der alte jüdische Friedhof in Mainz*, 2nd ed. (Mainz, 2000), 17, pl. 3. Narratives concerning either of the two are discussed in Sara Zfatman, *The Jewish Tale in the Middle Ages: Between Ashkenaz and Sefarad* (Hebrew) (Jerusalem, 1993), 81–158; and Raspe, *Jüdische Hagiographie*, 285–86 and 300.

56. Schütz, "Mainz," 806; and idem, "Die Geschichte des Mainzer Judenviertels," in *Juden in Deutschland*, ed. M. Matheus (Stuttgart, 1995), 39.

57. Friedrich Schütz, "Weisenau," in *Germania Judaica*, vol. 3, part 2, 1566.

58. See n. 4, above. On the reestablishment of the community and the year 1583 as the *terminus ante quem*, see Schütz, "Judenviertel," 39–40.

59. See Eliezer's note on his father's grave in the epigraph to his *Zemer na'eh le-shabbat shaḥarit* (Prague, ca. 1657), no pagination [fol. 12v], cited in Moritz Steinschneider, *Catalogus librorum Hebraeorum in Bibliotheca Bodleiana* (Berlin, 1852–60), 475–76, no. 3161; cf. idem, "Jüdisch-Deutsche Literatur," *Serapeum* 9–10 (1848–49) (repr. Jerusalem, 1961), no. 174. On R. Yehudah himself, see Leopold Löwenstein, "Zur Geschichte der Rabbiner in Mainz (1615–1848)," *Jahrbuch der Jüdisch-Literarischen Gesellschaft* 3 (1905): 221, no. 5; on the various editions of the *Ma'aneh lashon*, first printed in Prague, ca. 1615, see Steinschneider, *Catalogus*, 965–67, no. 5010; 1178, no. 5492.

60. Jonas Bondi, "Der alte Friedhof," *Menorah* 5 (1927): 720–21.

61. Ibid., 726–27.

62. For a detailed map of the cemetery, see Vest, "Friedhof," 96. I am grateful to Martina Strehlen for providing me with a corresponding list of inscriptions deciphered during her tenure in office at the Landesamt für Denkmalpflege Rheinland-Pfalz.

63. For background, see Irving A. Agus, *Rabbi Meir of Rothenburg*, 2nd ed. (New York, 1970), 125–55; Ephraim E. Urbach, *The Tosafists: Their History, Writings, and Methods* (Hebrew), 5th ed. (Jerusalem, 1986), 541–45.

64. For the text, see Ludwig Lewysohn, *Nafshot tsaddiqim: Sechzig Epitaphien von Grabsteinen des israelitischen Friedhofes zu Worms* (Frankfurt am Main, 1855), 35–39, no. 21 and 39–41, no. 22; cf. the readings of David Kaufmann, "Die Grabsteine R. Meïr's von Rothenburg und Alexander Wimpfen's in Worms," *Monatsschrift für Geschichte und Wissenschaft des Judentums* 40 (1896): 126–30.

65. See Lewysohn, *Nafshot tsaddiqim*, 42 no. 23 (Shemu'el b. Shenei'or, 1310); ibid., 57–58, no. 31 (Naftali Yehudah Liva b. Mosheh Yitsḥaq Hoheneck, 1622). Note also the way the latter's headstone (Fig. 19, to the left behind the Maharam's epitaph) is designed to appear as a virtual replica of the two erected three centuries earlier.

66. The Maharil's request is reported in Lewysohn, *Nafshot tsaddiqim*, 48–50, no. 28. Cf. the strictures against burying ordinary people near great sages ascribed to both Maharil and Shalom of Neustadt in a manuscript cited by Israel Peles and Shlomo Spitzer, "Qeta'im ḥadashim mi-torat ha-Maharil," *Moriah* 19, nos. 1–2 (1993): 10. Implicit criticism of burial *ad sanctos* may perhaps also be found in the thirteenth-century commentary of the *Ḥizquni* on Dt 34:6. See Ḥayyim Dov Chavel, ed., *Ḥizquni: Perushei ha-torah le-rabbenu Ḥizqiyyah bar Manoaḥ* (Jerusalem, 1981), 606–7.

67. Vest, "Friedhof," 59–61; and Brocke and Müller, *Haus des Lebens*, 151.

68. Lewysohn, *Nafshot tsaddiqim*, 59–60, no. 32.

69. Ibid., 62–68, no. 35; 71–74, no. 38; 74–75, no. 39.

70. In seventeenth-century Frankfurt, too, rabbis were buried near an area reserved for *qedoshim* (called *har shel qedoshim* or *Kedauschim-Platz*); by that time, that term had come to include the victims of any sort of violent death. See Dietrich Andernacht, Michael Lenarz, and Inge Schlotzhauer, "Frankfurt am Main," in *Germania Judaica*, vol. 3, part 1, 351, and references in ibid., 376 n. 222; for the semantic shift in the use of *qadosh*, see Brocke, "Märtyrer," 13.

71. Shim'on Ben-Tsion ha-kohen Kutas, ed., *Sefer she'elot u-teshuvot Ḥavot Ya'ir*

(Ramat Gan, 1997), 2:683–85, no. 238. On Bacharach's interest in the tale of the Maharam and Alexander Wimpfen, see David Kaufmann, *Jaïr Chajjim Bacharach (1638–1702) und seine Ahnen* (Trier, 1894), 104, 131; for his awareness of the medieval pogroms, see n. 74, below.

72. For an account of a similar process of sanctification of space as an expression of a slow-forming attachment to a given locality taking place, somewhat ironically, in contemporary Israel, see Yoram Bilu, "Moroccan Jews and the Shaping of Israel's Sacred Geography," in *Divergent Jewish Cultures: Israel and America*, ed. D. Dash Moore and S. I. Troen (New Haven, Conn., 2001), 72–86.

73. Marginal notes recording the location of the writer's own ancestors' or relatives' graves can be found in many medieval manuscripts. See, e.g., David Kaufmann, "Anglo-Judaica: Three Centuries of the Genealogy of the Most Eminent Anglo-Jewish Family before 1290," *Jewish Quarterly Review* o.s. 3 (1890/91): 561 (again relating to the grave of Shim'on ben Yitshaq).

74. Breuer and Guggenheim, "Gemeinde," 2087–88. See the comment of Ya'ir Hayyim Bacharach remarking on the fact that the fasts commemorating the medieval pogroms in Worms were still observed in his time, even though there was no biological link between the victims and the community of his day; cited in Eric Zimmer, "The Persecutions of 1096 as Reflected in Medieval and Modern *Minhag* Books" (Hebrew), in *Facing the Cross: The Persecutions of 1096 in History and Historiography*, ed. Y. T. Assis et al. (Jerusalem, 2000), 157 n. 1. For examples of the efforts made to save the cemeteries at times of imminent expulsion, see Michael H. Wehrmann, "Die Rechtsstellung der Rothenburger Judenschaft im Mittelalter (1180–1520): Eine rechtsgeschichtliche Untersuchung" (Ph.D. diss., Universität Würzburg, 1976), 155–55a [*sic*] n. 2; Straus, *Urkunden*, 392–93, no. 1052; for the attempt, often made at these times, to prove a community's great antiquity by pointing to extravagantly ancient headstones found in its cemetery, see Böcher, *Alte Synagoge*, 24; and Grossman, *Hakhemei Ashkenaz ha-rishonim*, 2.

75. See Israel M. Ta-Shma, "The Attitude to Aliya to Eretz Israel (Palestine) in Medieval German Jewry" (Hebrew), *Shalem* 6 (1992): 315–18, as well as his earlier "Eretz Israel Studies" (Hebrew), *Shalem* 1 (1974): 81–95; Reiner, "Pilgrims and Pilgrimage," 50–118, 139–56; Ephraim Kanarfogel, "The '*Aliyah* of 'Three Hundred Rabbis' in 1211: Tosafist Attitudes Toward Settling in the Land of Israel," *Jewish Quarterly Review* 76 (1986): 191–215.

76. Israel Yuval has discussed how the Hebrew Crusade narratives paint Mainz as a latter-day Jerusalem and the burning of the city's synagogue in 1096 as a replica of the destruction of the Second Temple. See his "Heilige Städte, heilige Gemeinden: Mainz als das Jerusalem Deutschlands," in *Jüdische Gemeinden und Organisationsformen von der Antike bis zur Gegenwart*, ed. R. Jütte and A. P. Kustermann (Vienna, 1996), 91–101. A similar point has been made for Cologne: Matthias Schmandt, *Judei, cives et incole: Studien zur jüdischen Geschichte Kölns im Mittelalter* (Hannover, 2002), 10 n. 10. For a discussion of how the Jews of medieval Rome styled their place of residence into "a fantasy Palestine" by means of narrative, see Yosef Levanon, "The Holy Place in Jewish Piety: Evidence of Two Twelfth-Century Jewish Itineraries," *Annual of Rabbinic Judaism* 1 (1998): 104.

77. In fact, while Zimmels, "Erez Israel," 49 n. 1, has addressed grave visitation within Ashkenaz in the context of a discussion of vows to visit or settle in the Land of Israel, the relationship between the two remains unexplained.

78. According to the talmudic elaboration of Nm 13:22 in bSot 34b.

79. This has been pointed out by Breuer and Guggenheim, "Gemeinde," 2088. See *Sefer Maharil*, ed. Spitzer, 270, Hilkhot ta'anit, no. 18.

80. Am 7:17; cf. bKet 111a.

81. See the discussion in Isaiah M. Gafni, *Land, Center and Diaspora: Jewish Constructs in Late Antiquity* (Sheffield, 1997), 79–95. For a more skeptical view interpreting the relevant passages as a matter of ideology rather than actual—let alone widespread— practice, see Tessa Rajak, "The Rabbinic Dead and the Diaspora Dead at Beth She'arim," in *The Talmud Yerushalmi and Graeco-Roman Culture*, ed. P. Schäfer (Tübingen, 1998), 1:349–66.

82. Nissan Rubin, *The End of Life: Rites on Burial and Mourning in Talmud and Midrash* (Hebrew) (Tel Aviv, 1997), 134.

Chapter 7. Detours in a "Hidden Land"

This chapter is the result of an ongoing research project on Jewish translations of the "orient" in the eighteenth and early nineteenth centuries. My fellow Fellows at the Center for Advanced Judaic Studies and in the Society of Fellows at Princeton University; William J. Bulman, Mary Harper, Martin Jacobs, and Richard Payne; and the editors of this volume offered many stimulating suggestions and comments. I remain very grateful to all of them.

1. In the first decades of the eighteenth century, the "orient" emerged as a rather flexible concept. Although it could denote—in a dualistic "style of thought" (Edward Said)— the "other" just beyond the borders of Christian Europe, it could also become a highly complex signifier, disorienting and reorienting static notions of the "East" as well as of the "West." See, esp., Lisa Lowe, *Critical Terrains: French and British Orientalisms* (Ithaca, N.Y., 1991); and Ali Behdad, *Belated Travelers: Orientalism in the Age of Colonial Dissolution* (Durham, N.C., 1994).

2. The orientalist and theologian Johann David Michaelis was among the most remarkable proponents of this approach. On Michaelis's attitude toward Jews and Judaism, see Jonathan M. Hess, *Germans, Jews, and the Claims of Modernity* (New Haven, Conn., 2002), 51–89; and Jonathan Sheehan, *The Enlightenment Bible: Translation, Scholarship, Culture* (Princeton, N.J., 2005), 214–17.

3. A characteristic remark on this subject can be found in Lancelot Addison, *The Present State of the Jews (More Particularly Relating to Those in Barbary.) Wherein Is Contained an Exact Account of Their Customs, Secular and Religious. . . .* (London, 1675): "For this people, if any under heaven, may boldly glory of the Antiquity and Nobless of their Descent. There being no Nation can prove its Pedigree by such clear and Authentique Heraldry as the

Jews. . . . So that all other Nations must have recourse to the Jewish Records, to clear their Genealogies, and attest their Linage" (2).

4. See, e.g., Christian Wilhelm Dohm, *Über die bürgerliche Verbesserung der Juden* (Berlin/Stettin, 1781–83), 1:8. On Dohm's interest in external as well as internal colonies, see Hess, *Germans, Jews, and the Claims of Modernity*, 1–4, 25–41.

5. A significant number of studies have examined Jewish approaches to the "orient" in the nineteenth and twentieth centuries. See, esp., the contributions to Ivan D. Kalmar and Derek J. Penslar, eds., *Orientalism and the Jews* (Lebanon, N.H., 2005).

6. Naphtali Herz Wessely, *Divrei shalom ve-emet*, pt. 2: *Rav tuv le-veit Yisra'el* (Berlin, 1782), fol. 28a–b.

7. Moses Mendelssohn, *Jerusalem: A Treatise on Ecclesiastical Authority and Judaism*, trans. M. Samuels (London, 1838), 1:14 (preface to the German translation of Menasseh ben Israel's *Vindiciae Judaeorum*); and idem, *Gesammelte Schriften: Jubiläumsausgabe*, ed. A. Altmann et al. (Stuttgart, 1971–2005), 8:35.

8. Simone Luzzatto already speculated on the advantages of living in "the Turkish State" in his *Discorso* (1638), written in defense of Venetian Jewry. His argument was taken up by Menasseh ben Israel in reflections that precede the remarks on which Mendelssohn comments; see Simone Luzzatto, *Discorso circa il stato de gl'hebrei* (Venice, 1638; repr. Bologna, 1976), 89v–90r, trans. F. Giovanelli, *Commentary* 3 (1947): 477; and Menasseh ben Israel, *To His Highnesse the Lord Protector of the Common-wealth . . . the Humble Addresses* (London, 1641), 5–7.

9. Their assessment, however, was not entirely unfounded. Daniel Schroeter observes that "[p]rior to the French Revolution and emancipation" Jews "would have enjoyed much more freedom of movement in Morocco than in much of Europe. In Morocco and elsewhere in the Muslim world, Jews, together with other religious groups, were in theory free to move anywhere subject to the same rights and disabilities everywhere. Moreover, Jews experienced far fewer impediments in the Muslim world to practicing different trades than in pre-emancipation Europe, even if they tended to concentrate in specific professions" (*The Sultan's Jew: Morocco and the Sephardi World* [Stanford, Calif., 2002], 56).

10. See Moshe Pelli, "Masa' ba'rav le-Shemu'el Romanelli: ha-Masa' ha-gadol shel maskil el yahadut bi-mtsuqah," in *Kinds of Genre in Haskalah Literature: Types and Topics* (Tel Aviv, 1999), 208. Today it is the only book of the maskilic printing press in Berlin available in modern Hebrew and English editions: Samuel Romanelli, *Ketavim nivharim: Masa' ba'rav, leqet shirim, qeta'im mittokh mahazot*, ed. H. Schirmann (Jerusalem, 1968); and Samuel Romanelli, *Travail in an Arab Land*, trans. Y. K. Stillman and N. A. Stillman (Tuscaloosa, Ala., 1989).

11. Daniel Schroeter, "Orientalism and the Jews of the Mediterranean," *Journal of Mediterranean Studies* (1994): 184.

12. Ibid., 185.

13. For an illuminating discussion of the highly ambiguous relations between "East" and "West" in Jewish ethnographic writing at the beginning of the twentieth century, see Harvey E. Goldberg, "The Oriental and the Orientalist: The Meeting of Mordecai ha-

Cohen and Nahum Slouschz," *Jewish Culture and History* 7 (2004): 1–30. See also Oren Kosansky's meticulous and stimulating analysis of strategies of "distance and intimacy" (95) in the ethnographic writings of French and Moroccan Jews during the decades of the French Protectorate, in particular in the works of Nahum Slouschz, Elie Malka, and Y. D. Sémach: "All Dear unto God: Saints, Pilgrimage, and Textual Practice in Jewish Morocco" (Ph.D. diss., University of Michigan, 2003), 71–131.

14. Gabriel Piterberg, "Domestic Orientalism: The Representation of 'Oriental' Jews in Zionist/Israeli Historiography," *British Journal of Middle Eastern Studies* 23 (1996): 135–36.

15. Susan G. Miller, *Disorienting Encounters: Travels of a Moroccan Scholar in France in 1845–1846: The Voyage of Muḥammad aṣ-Ṣaffār* (Berkeley, Calif., 1992).

16. Pidou de Saint-Olon, Laugnier de Tassy, and Labat were some of the earlier authors whose descriptions of North Africa were translated into English and cited throughout the eighteenth century. Among the later works that were considered authoritative was, above all, Louis de Chénier's *Recherches historiques sur les Maures et histoire de l'empire de Maroc* (Paris, 1787). The third volume, dedicated to the "present state" of Morocco, was translated into English (London, 1788) and German (Leipzig, 1788). In England, William Lemprière's *A Tour from Gibraltar to Tangier, Sallee, Mogodore, Santa Cruz, Tarudant ... to Morocco* (London, 1791) was reprinted at least four times, until 1813.

17. Louis de Chénier, *The Present State of the Empire of Morocco* (London, 1788), 1:i.

18. In 1764, Sultan Sidi Muḥammad ibn ʿAbdallāh established the port of Essaouira (Mogador), concentrating and supporting European trade on the Moroccan coast in this newly built city. This new opportunity for commercial exchange may have contributed to the growing number of European travelogues on Morocco in the second half of the eighteenth century. On the relations between the court and Jewish merchants in the eighteenth century, see Schroeter, *Sultan's Jew*.

19. Alexander Jardine, *Letters from Barbary, France, Spain, Portugal, etc.* (London, 1788), 12.

20. Montesquieu, *The Spirit of Laws*, 5:14, trans. T. Nugent, 2nd rev. ed. (London, 1752), 86, 88.

21. In Montesquieu's *Persian Letters*, Usbek, one of the Persian travelers, remarks on "the king of France": "He has often been heard to say that that of all the world's governments, that of the Turks, or that of our august sultan, pleased him most. So highly does he esteem Oriental statecraft!" (Montesquieu, *Persian Letters*, trans. G. R. Healy [Indianapolis, 1999], 63 [letter 37]).

22. For a concise analysis of the larger theoretical and political contexts in which these developments became possible, see Talal Asad, "Two European Images of Non-European Rule," in *Anthropology and the Colonial Encounter*, ed. T. Asad (London, 1973), 103–18. Cf. Ann Thomsen, *Barbary and Enlightenment: European Attitudes towards the Maghreb in the Eighteenth Century* (Leiden, 1987), 54–57.

23. Chénier, however, refers frequently to Leo Africanus. For Chénier and his French predecessors, see Oumelbanine Zhiri, *Les sillages de Jean Léon l'Africain, du XVIe au XXe siècle* (Casablanca, 1995).

24. Lemprière, *Tour from Gibraltar*, 98–99.

25. Jardine, *Letters from Barbary*, 18–19. The author had chosen as his motto a sentence from Montesquieu ("Il s'agit de faire penser, et non de faire lire"), thereby visibly placing his work within an Enlightenment tradition of political thought.

26. Addison, *Present State of the Jews*, 7.

27. Lemprière, *Tour from Gibraltar*, 190. Lemprière's description of the oppression of the Jews is mentioned explicitly in the review of the German translation in the renowned scholarly journal *Neue Allgemeine Deutsche Bibliothek* 39, no. 1 (1798): 160.

28. See, e.g., Høst's report on the role and activities of "Sumbel" in his *Nachrichten von Marókos und Fes*, 145, and Jardine's description of his encounters with "Sombel" in his *Letters from Barbary*, 44–46.

29. Alexander Pope, trans., *The Odyssey of Homer* (London, 1725), 3–4.

30. In the first edition published by Ḥevrat ḥinnukh ne'arim: Samuel Romanelli, *Masa' ba'rav* (Berlin, 1792), 1.

31. Pope, *Odyssey*, 4.

32. As Edward Said notes, "Orientalism is after all a system for citing works and authors" (*Orientalism: Western Conceptions of the Orient* [New York, 1978], 23; see also 176–77).

33. Cf. Lemprière, *Tour from Gibraltar*, 6.

34. See, e.g., Mendelssohn's early version of this ambivalence in *Qohelet musar*, his first Hebrew work, in part translated by Edward Breuer and David Sorkin, "Moses Mendelssohn's First Hebrew Publication: An Annotated Translation of the *Kohelet Mussar*," *Leo Baeck Institute Yearbook* 48 (2003): 3–23.

35. Only their *tzade* is not as correct as the one in Amsterdam (30).

36. Samuel Romanelli, *Grammatica ragionata italiana ed ebraica con trattato, ed esempi di poesia* (Trieste, 1799), 4–5, 22.

37. Michel de Certeau, *The Practice of Everyday Life*, trans. S. Rendall (Berkeley, Calif., 1984), 119.

38. See n. 16, above.

39. De Certeau, *Practice of Everyday Life*, 121.

40. Mary Louise Pratt, *Imperial Eyes: Travel Writing and Transculturation* (London, 1990), 75.

41. Schroeter offers a brief account of the political situation in Morocco at the end of the eighteenth century that puts Romanelli's and other reports in perspective, especially regarding the pogrom in Tetouan: "From Dhimmis to Colonized Subjects: Moroccan Jews and the Sharifian and French Colonial State," *Studies in Contemporary Jewry* 19 (2003): 104–23, esp. 105–9.

42. Said, *Orientalism*, 20–21.

43. Behdad, *Belated Travelers*, 19.

44. Elisheva Carlebach, *Divided Souls: Converts from Judaism in Germany, 1500–1750* (New Haven, Conn., 2001), 181.

45. The famous letters of Lady Montagu (first published in 1762) may be described as

a similar project: Montagu emphasizes the unique intimacy between Turkish women and herself, making this the starting point of a trenchant critique directed against European modes of governing women and writing about the Ottoman Empire (see, e.g., her letter to Lady Mar, dated April 1, 1717, in Robert Halsband, ed., *The Complete Letters of Lady Mary Wortley Montagu*, 3 vols. [Oxford, 1965–67], 1:325–30).

46. Portuguese Jews established a Hebrew printing press at Fez quite early. The press operated between 1516 and 1524; but 250 years later, this moment seems to have fallen into oblivion.

47. It is significant that the presence of "Berberiscos" as merchants and diplomats in the Sefaradi communities of Europe, in particular in London and Amsterdam, remains unacknowledged in Romanelli's account, although he had lived in London for some time; see Schroeter, *Sultan's Jew*, 55–76.

48. Moshe Pelli offers interesting observations on these tensions, while discussing them from a strictly literary-historical point of view: "The Literary Genre of the Travelogue in Hebrew Haskalah Literature: Shmuel Romanelli's *Masa Ba-'Arav*," *Modern Judaism* 11 (1991): 241–60, esp. 246–53; and idem, "Masa' ba-'arav," 220–25, 232–36.

49. James Clifford, "On Ethnographic Authority," in *The Predicament of Culture: Twentieth-Century Ethnography, Literature, and Art* (Cambridge, Mass., 1988), 25.

50. Immanuel Kant, "An Answer to the Question: What Is Enlightenment? (1784)," in *What Is Enlightenment? Eighteenth-Century Answers and Twentieth-Century Questions*, ed. and trans. J. Schmidt (Berkeley, Calif., 1996), 58.

51. Cf. Ella Shohat's observations on the transformation of Ashkenazi-Sefaradi relationships in the eighteenth century: *Taboo Memories, Diasporic Voices* (Durham, 2006), 206.

Chapter 8. The Rhetoric of Rescue

A research grant from the Memorial Foundation for Jewish Culture is gratefully acknowledged.

1. Benedict Anderson, *Imagined Communities: Reflections on the Origin and Spread of Nationalism*, rev. ed. (London, 1991).

2. Nicolaus Mills, "The Era of the Golden Venture," in *Arguing Immigration*, ed. N. Mills (New York, 1994), 15.

3. See Aviva Halamish, "Aliyah Policy in the 1930s: Between *Ge'ulah* and *Hatsalah*" (Hebrew), *Zemanim* 58 (1997): 86–98.

4. On the ideological role of the meta-narratives of "utopian Zionism" versus "catastrophic Zionism," see Pnina Lahav, *Judgment in Jerusalem: Chief Justice Simon Agranat and the Zionist Century* (Hebrew) (Tel Aviv, 1999). For the centrality of rescue and the catastrophic view of Jewish life, see Ilan Troen and Benjamin Pinkus, *Organizing Rescue: National Jewish Solidarity in the Modern Period* (London, 1992).

5. See Tamar Horowitz, "Integration or Separatism," in *Children of Perestroika in Israel*, ed. T. Horowitz (New York, 1999), 1–21.

6. Edward Bruner and Phyllis Gorfain, "Dialogic Narration and the Paradoxes of Masada," in *Text, Play and Story: The Construction and Reconstruction of Self and Society*, ed. E. Bruner (Washington, D.C., 1994), 56–75.

7. Ibid., 56.

8. Ibid., 56–60.

9. See Tamar Katriel and Aliza Shenhar, "Tower and Stockade: Dialogic Narration in Israeli Settlement Ethos," *Quarterly Journal of Speech* 76 (1990): 359–80; and Tamar Katriel, *Performing the Past: A Study of Israeli Settlement Museums* (Mahwah, N.J., 1997).

10. On the still-unresolved Ron Arad case, see Keren Tenenboim-Weinblatt, "Fighting for the Story's Life: Non-Closure in Journalistic Narrative," *Journalism* 9 (2008): 31–51. For a discussion of the rescue operation of Entebbe, see Yishayahu Ben-Porat, Eitan Haber, and Ze'ev Schiff, *Entebbe Flight 139* (Hebrew) (Tel Aviv, 1991).

11. See Ilan S. Troen, "Organizing the Rescue of Jews in the Modern Period," in *Organizing Rescue*, ed. Troen and Pinkus, 3–19; and Y. Bildstein, "The Redemption of Captives in Halakhic Tradition: Problems and Policy," in ibid., 20–30.

12. The Palestinian narrative of dislocation and dispersal emplots Jewish immigration to Palestine/Israel as part of a colonial-settler project. This is the clearest counter-narrative challenging Zionist discourses of aliyah and settlement but is not addressed in this essay.

13. Tamar Katriel, "'From Shore to Shore': The Holocaust, Clandestine Immigration and Israeli Heritage Museums," in *The Holocaust and Visual Culture*, ed. B. Zelizer (New Brunswick, N.J., 2001), 198–211.

14. See, for example, Ella Shohat, *Israeli Cinema: East/West and the Politics of Representation* (Austin, Tex., 1989); and idem, "Sephardim in Israel: Zionism from the Standpoint of Its Victims," *Social Text* 19/20 (1988): 1–35. For a discussion of the rhetoric of rescue in the broader context of postcolonialist discourse, see Kinneret Lahad, "The Representations of the Call for Help and Rescue Scripts in Postcolonial Cinema" (Hebrew) (M.A. thesis, Hebrew University of Jerusalem, 2004).

15. Roger M. Smith, *Stories of Peoplehood: The Politics and Morals of Political Membership* (New York, 2003), 70.

16. For recent examples, see Jack Lule, *Daily News, Eternal Stories: The Mythological Role of Journalism* (New York, 2001); and Ya'acov Yadgar, *Our Story: The National Narrative in the Israeli Press* (Hebrew) (Haifa, 2004).

17. Editorial, "A Collective Experience" (Hebrew), *Yedi'ot Aḥronot*, January 6, 1985.

18. The phrase "surviving salvation" has been taken from Ruth Westheimer and Steven Kaplan, *Surviving Salvation: The Ethiopian Jewish Family in Transition* (New York, 1992).

19. Cited in Louis Rapoport, *Redemption Song: The Story of Operation Moses* (San Diego, 1986), 182.

20. Nitzan Horowitz, "Economic Collapse and Hunger against the Background of Rebels' Victories and Hatred for the Regime" (Hebrew), *Ha'aretz*, May 26, 1991.

21. Eitan Rabin et al., "Concern in Israel for Ethiopian Jews Given the Uncertainties

Following Mangisto's Flight" (Hebrew), *Ha'aretz*, May 22, 1991. For examples of the popular literature published in the wake of salvage immigration operations, see Tudor Parfitt, *Operation Moses: The Untold Story of the Secret Exodus of the Falasha Jews from Ethiopia* (New York, 1985); Mitchell G. Bard, *From Tragedy to Triumph: The Politics behind the Rescue of Ethiopian Jewry* (London, 2002); Edward Trueblood Martin, *I Flew Them Home: A Pilot's Story of the Yemenite Airlift* (New York, 1958); Tudor Parfitt, *The Road to Redemption: The Jews of the Yemen 1900–1950* (Leiden, 1996); and Dena Merriam and Zion Ozeri, *Operation Exodus: The Making of a Miracle* (New York, 1995).

22. See Riv-Ellen Prell's chapter in this volume.

23. Two notable (and controversial) books that have challenged mainstream historiography on the study of illegal immigration operations are Idith Zertal, *From Catastrophe to Power: Jewish Illegal Immigration to Palestine, 1945–1948* (Berkeley, Calif., 1998); and Yosef Grodzinsky, *Good Human Material* (Hebrew) (Or Yehuda, 1998).

24. David Wyman, *The Abandonment of the Jews: America and the Holocaust, 1941–1945* (New York, 1998).

25. Gideon Samet, "The Ethiopians as a Mirror" (Hebrew), *Ha'aretz*, January 8, 1985.

26. Kerri Steinberg, "The Ties That Bind: Americans, Ethiopians, and the Extended Jewish Family," *Race, Gender & Class* 6 (1999): 135–51.

27. *Yedi'ot Ahronot*, May 26, 1991.

28. Steinberg, "Ties That Bind."

29. See Yehouda Shenhav, *The Arab Jews: Nationalism, Religion, and Ethnicity* (Hebrew) (Tel Aviv, 2003).

30. Gadi Ben-Ezer, *The Ethiopian Jewish Exodus: Narratives of the Migration Journey to Israel, 1977–1985* (London, 2002).

31. Anat Tal-Shir, "A Whole Community Came to Find a Homeland" (Hebrew), *Yedi'ot Ahronot*, May 26, 1991.

32. David Lavie, "The Ethiopian Exodus 1991" (Hebrew), *Ma'ariv*, "Ma'ariv Today" special issue, May 26, 1991.

33. Dvora Hacohen, *Immigrants in Turmoil: Mass Immigration to Israel and Its Repercussions in the 1950s and After* (Syracuse, N.Y., 2003).

34. Conflicting attitudes toward immigration are not, of course, unique to the Israeli case. See Leo R. Chavez, *Covering Immigration: Popular Images and the Politics of the Nation* (Los Angeles, 2001).

35. Nadav Shraga'i, "In a Meeting of Chief Rabbis with Ethiopian Religious Leaders: 'When Will You Finally Allow Us to Feel That We Have Really Come Home?'" (Hebrew), *Ha'aretz*, February 7, 1985.

36. Amiram Barkat, "Sharon Wants Another Million *'Olim*, But Who Will Come?" (Hebrew), *Ha'aretz*, March 12, 2004.

37. Luc Boltanski, *Distant Suffering* (New York, 1999).

38. Ibid., 149–92.

CHAPTER 9. JUDAISM AND TRADITION

1. Eric J. Hobsbawm and Terence O. Ranger, eds., *The Invention of Tradition* (Cambridge, 1992), 2–3.

2. bSan 74b.

3. Mark Salber Phillips, "What Is Tradition When It Is Not Invented? A Historiographical Introduction," in *Questions of Tradition*, ed. M. S. Phillips and G. Schochet (Toronto, 2004), 6–14.

4. Karl Marx, *The Eighteenth Brumaire of Louis Bonaparte*, in *Karl Marx: Selected Writings*, ed. D. McLellan (Oxford, 1977), 300.

5. Gershom Scholem, "Revelation and Tradition as Religious Categories in Judaism," in *The Messianic Idea in Judaism and Other Essays on Jewish Spirituality* (New York, 1971), 283.

6. Cf. John Rogister and Anne Vergati, "Introduction: Tradition Revisited," *History and Anthropology* 15 (2004): 201–5. This issue of the journal brings the question of religion into the framework built by Hobsbawm and Ranger but focuses on the twentieth century.

7. Gal 1:14.

8. E.g., Mk 7; on Josephus, see next note.

9. Josephus, *Antiquities of the Jews*, 13:297, 13:408.

10. See Ez 20:37–38. The meaning of the Hebrew is uncertain; the New Jewish Publication Society translates *be-mesoret ha-berit* as "the *bonds* of the covenant." The Greek translation rendered the word *en arithmōi*, understanding the clause as God "numbering" his people, i.e., making them pass muster.

11. tBekh 1:12.

12. mSheq 6:1. On the Temple vessels and their fate in rabbinic literature, see Ra'anan S. Boustan's essay in this volume.

13. 2 Mc 1:18–2:18. See, e.g., Steven Weitzman, *Surviving Sacrilege: Cultural Persistence in Jewish Antiquity* (Cambridge, Mass., 2005), 96–117.

14. Josephus, *Antiquities of the Jews*, 18:85–87. See also Isaac Kalimi and James D. Purvis, "The Hiding of the Temple Vessels in Jewish and Samaritan Literature," *Catholic Biblical Quarterly* 56 (1994): 679–85.

15. Ezr 9:6–7.

16. Jer 44:15–19.

17. Elisha Qimron and John Strugnell, *Qumran Cave 4*, vol. 5: *Miqsat Ma'ase ha-Torah* (Oxford, 1994). All references to 4QMMT below follow this edition.

18. 4QMMT C: 25–26; C: 18; C: 19–20; C: 23–24. The attitude toward hortatory and exemplary uses of the past, with the emphasis on both good and bad figures, is much the same in Ben Sira's "Praise of the Fathers," 47:23–25, 49:4–6.

19. See Elias J. Bickerman, "The Chain of the Pharisaic Tradition," in *Studies in Jewish and Christian History: A New Edition in English including the God of the Maccabees*, ed. A. Tropper, 2 vols. (Leiden, 2007), 1:528–42; and Amram Tropper, *Wisdom, Politics, and Historiography: Tractate Avot in the Context of the Graeco-Roman Near East* (New York, 2004).

20. Solomon Schechter, ed., *Aboth de Rabbi Nathan* (New York, 1967), 26.

21. Jacob Z. Lauterbach, *Rabbinic Essays* (Cincinnati, 1951), 51–159.

22. Moshe D. Herr, "Continuum in the Chain of Torah Transmission" (Hebrew), *Zion* 44 (1979): 43–56.

23. Mk 7:8–9. Cf. the Qaraite criticism of the rabbis, first voiced by Daniel al-Qūmisī on the basis of Is 29:13, below at n. 57.

24. *Avot de-Rabbi Natan* A, 15, in Schechter, *Aboth*, 31. Translation based on Judah Goldin, *The Fathers according to Rabbi Nathan* (New Haven, Conn., 1955), 80. See also bShab 31a.

25. See Gerald Blidstein, "The Sources of the Term *Torah SheBe'Al Peh*" (Hebrew), *Tarbiz* 43 (1974): 496–98.

26. See also Albert I. Baumgarten, "The Pharisaic *Paradosis*," *Harvard Theological Review* 80 (1987): 63–77.

27. Mary Douglas, *How Institutions Think* (London, 1987), esp. 45–54; quotation on 49.

28. Aleida Assmann, *Zeit und Tradition: Kulturelle Strategien der Dauer* (Cologne, 1999), 63.

29. Pierre Bourdieu, *Outline of a Theory of Practice* (Cambridge, 1977), 164.

30. Compare the claim to a monopoly on the future made through eschatological visions, which in turn also have consequences in the present.

31. On one set of strategies to bridge this rupture through claims of Davidic descent, see Arnold Franklin's forthcoming book from the University of Pennsylvania Press.

32. L. D. Reynolds and N. G. Wilson, *Scribes and Scholars: A Guide to the Transmission of Greek and Latin Literature* (Oxford, 1991 [1968]), 34–35; and Maria Luisa Agati, *Il libro manoscritto: Introduzione alla codicologia* (Rome, 2003), 134–47.

33. Malachi Beit-Arié, *Hebrew Manuscripts of East and West: Towards a Comparative Codicology* (London, 1993), 10–11. See also Cambridge University Library, Taylor-Schechter 6 H 9–21, a papyrus codex containing liturgical poems (*piyyutim*) by Yosef ben Nisan of Neve Qiryatayim (sixth century C.E.), copied eighth–ninth century C.E.

34. Emanuel Tov, *Scribal Practices and Approaches Reflected in the Texts Found in the Judean Desert* (Leiden, 2005), esp. 75–76. See next note for details.

35. mYom 7:1. This conclusion is supported by the rabbinic references to the three Torah scrolls in the Temple courtyard. See mMQ 4:3, MidTannDt 105 and ySan 2:6 (20c), and tKelim BM 5:8 (Zuckermandel, 584).

36. Mur1, from Wadi Murabba'at, contains selections from Genesis, Exodus, and Numbers. Although there are at least five finds with consecutive books from Cave 4 at Qumran (4QGen-Exod[a]; 4QpaleoGen-Exod[l]; 4QExod[b]; 4QExod-Lev[f]; and 4QLev-Num[a], summarized in Tov, *Scribal Practices*, 75, table 10), it is questionable whether any of them was part of a complete Torah scroll, as Tov rightly concludes with caution (ibid., 76). Cf. Yossi Baruchi, "Fragmentary Biblical Scrolls from Bar Kokhba Revolt Refuge Caves" (Hebrew), *Meghillot* 3 (5765 [2005]): 177–90.

37. The only two scrolls preserved in full at Qumran are 1QIsa[a] and 11QT[a]. 1QIsa[a] is

7.34 meters long and has 54 columns. 11QT^a, as reconstructed, has 67 columns and is 8.75 meters long. These two scrolls are among the longest found at Qumran, even when compared with scrolls whose estimated length has been reconstructed (Tov, *Scribal Practices*, 76, table 11). Our Torah scrolls by convention have 248 columns, by the standards of 1QIsa^a or 11QT^{b,}, an estimated 30 meters long. Our Torah scrolls would have been "monsters" by ancient standards.

38. On the dating of *Soferim*, see Hermann L. Strack and Günther Stemberger, *Introduction to the Talmud and Midrash* (Minneapolis, 1992), 248.

39. Colette Sirat, "Les rouleaux bibliques de Qumran au moyen âge: Du livre au sefer tora, de l'oreille à l'oeil," *Comptes rendus de l'Académie des Inscriptions et Belles Lettres* (1991): 427 (Cambridge University Library, Taylor-Schechter NS 2.16). See also Colette Sirat, Michèle Dukan, and Ada Yardeni, "Rouleaux de la Torah antérieurs à l'an mille," *Comptes rendus de l'Académie des Inscriptions et Belles Lettres* 138 (1994): 861–87, discussing Torah fragments found as palimpsests of Greek manuscripts in the Bibliotheca Laurentina in Florence.

40. E.g., British Library, MS Or. 4445, on which see Aron Dotan, "Reflections towards a Critical Edition of Pentateuch Codex Or. 4445," in *Estudios Masoréticos (X Congreso de la IOMS) en memoria de Harry M. Orlinsky*, ed. E. F. Tejero and M. T. Ortega Monasterio (Madrid, 1993), 39–51. See also the colophon of the Cairo Codex of the Prophets, published in Paul Kahle, *The Cairo Geniza*, 2nd ed. (Oxford, 1959 [1947]), 110–14; and Mordechai Glatzer, "The Aleppo Codex: Codicological and Paleographical Aspects" (Hebrew), *Sefunot* 19 (1989): 250–59.

41. Cf. Bruno Chiesa, *The Emergence of Hebrew Biblical Pointing* (Frankfurt am Main, 1979), 36–40, 84 n. 133; assuming twenty-five-year generations, we date the Tiberian Masoretes to ca. 775–925.

42. Ibid., 5–8. Chiesa also cites a lone twelfth-century statement that the original Torah scroll was not pointed, cited in the *Mahzor Vitry*; but both this and the gaonic statements should be understood not as historical evidence of the Masorah's early date but as justifications for using unpointed texts for liturgical purposes.

43. Ibid., 9–13.

44. Bourdieu, *Outline of a Theory of Practice*, 164.

45. Taylor-Schechter Ar. 32.17, verso, lines 9–17; published in Nehemya Allony, "'Eli ben Yehuda ha-Nazir and His Treatise *Kitāb uṣūl al-lugha al-'ibrāniyya*" (Hebrew), *Leshonenu* 34 (1969–70): 97–104.

46. On this dynamic, see, esp., David Biale, ed., *The Cultures of the Jews: A New History* (New York, 2002), xx–xxi.

47. Quoted in Chiesa, *Emergence of Hebrew Biblical Pointing*, 31, 33, from Saint Petersburg, Russian National Library, 2 Firk. 2390, 5b (we have slightly modified his translation). The author of the treatise is identified and the text published in Ilan Eldar, *The Art of Correct Reading of the Bible* (Hebrew) (Jerusalem, 1994).

48. Madhav M. Deshpande, *Sanskrit and Prakrit: Sociolinguistic Issues* (Delhi, 1993), esp. 61–64; Sheldon Pollock, *The Language of the Gods in the World of Men: Sanskrit, Cul-*

ture, and Power in Premodern India (Berkeley, Calif., 2006), 47–50; and Ashok Aklujkar, "The Early History of Sanskrit as Supreme Language," in *The Ideology and Status of Sanskrit: Contributions to the History of the Sanskrit Language*, ed. J. E. M. Houben (Leiden, 1996), 59–85. Our thanks to Federico Squarcini and Phyllis Granoff for helping us clarify this point.

49. Gregor Schoeler, *The Oral and the Written in Early Islam*, trans. U. Vagelpohl, ed. J. E. Montgomery (London, 2006), first published as a series of articles in *Der Islam* in the 1980s; cf. Michael Cook, "The Opponents of the Writing of Tradition in Early Islam," *Arabica* 44 (1997): 437–530.

50. Saul Lieberman, *Hellenism in Jewish Palestine* (New York and Jerusalem, 1994), 87–88; Gregor Schoeler, "Oral Torah and *Ḥadīth*: Transmission, Prohibition of Writing, Redaction," in *Ḥadīth: Origins and Development*, ed. H. Motzki (Aldershot, 2004), 69 n. 10, 68 n. 3. See also Martin S. Jaffee, *Torah in the Mouth: Writing and Oral Tradition in Palestinian Judaism, 200 B.C.E.–400 C.E.* (New York, 2001), 126–56; and idem, "The Oral-Cultural Context of the Talmud Yerushalmi: Greco-Roman Rhetorical Paideia, Discipleship, and the Concept of Oral Torah," in *Transmitting Jewish Traditions: Orality, Textuality, and Cultural Diffusion*, ed. Y. Elman and I. Gershoni (New Haven, Conn., 2000), 27–73.

51. Quoted in Robert Brody, *The Geonim of Babylonia and the Shaping of Medieval Jewish Culture* (New Haven, Conn., 1998), 157–58; cf. his interpretation there.

52. Talya Fishman, "The Rhineland Pietists' Sacralization of Oral Torah," *Jewish Quarterly Review* 96 (2006): 14.

53. Sirat, "Les rouleaux bibliques de Qumran au moyen age," 417–32.

54. Rina Drory, "Le rôle de la littérature karaïte dans l'histoire de la littérature juive au xᵉ siècle," *Revue des études juives* 159 (2000): 107–8; idem, *Models and Contacts: Arabic Literature and Its Impact on Medieval Jewish Culture* (Leiden, 2000); and idem, *The Emergence of Jewish-Arabic Literary Contacts at the Beginning of the Tenth Century* (Hebrew) (Tel Aviv, 1988).

55. Brody, *Geonim of Babylonia*, 239–48. In a parallel vein, Martha Himmelfarb uses the phrase "radical traditionalism" to characterize the Hasmoneans' attitude toward Hellenistic culture in Elias Bickerman's interpretation ("Elias Bickerman on Judaism and Hellenism," in *The Jewish Past Revisited: Reflections on Modern Jewish Historians*, ed. D. N. Myers and D. B. Ruderman [New Haven, Conn., 1998], 203–5). On Seʿadyah, see also Sylvie Anne Goldberg's chapter this volume.

56. Brody, *Geonim of Babylonia*, 244–45; see also 245–48.

57. Among Qaraites, the accusation was first voiced by Daniel al-Qūmisī (fl. ca. 870–900); Oxford, Bodl. MS Heb. d 36.15r, line 1, and 17 r, line 22, published in Jacob Mann, "A Tract by an Early Karaite Settler in Jerusalem," *Jewish Quarterly Review* 12 (1921–22): 273–98, republished and translated in Leon Nemoy, "The Pseudo-Qumisian Sermon to the Karaites," *Proceedings of the American Academy of Jewish Research* 43 (1976): 49–105. It was repeated by Sahl ben Matsliah (mid-tenth century), in his polemical treatise against the Rabbanite Yaʿaqov ben Shemuʾel, published in Simḥa Pinsker, *Lickute Kadmoniot: Zur*

Geschichte des Karaismus und der karäischen Literatur (Vienna, 1860), app. 2, 31, and translated in Nemoy, "The Epistle of Sahl ben Masliah," *Proceedings of the American Academy for Jewish Research* 38–39 (1970–71): 145–77; and by Yūsuf ibn Nūḥ (early eleventh century), published in Nemoy, "Nissi ben Noah's Quasi-Commentary on the Decalogue," *Jewish Quarterly Review* 73 (1983): 328.

58. Alexander Guttman, "Tractate Abot: Its Place in Rabbinic Literature," *Jewish Quarterly Review* 41 (1950): 190–93. Guttman also argues that the rabbinic chain of tradition in *Avot* was a late stratum added under the influence of *ḥadīth* scholarship.

59. This question was first raised in Fred Astren, *Karaite Judaism and Historical Understanding* (Columbia, S.C., 2004). On arguments from history in the service of tradition, see Scholem, "Revelation and Tradition"; Gerson D. Cohen, *A Critical Edition with a Translation and Notes of the Book of Tradition (Sefer ha-qabbalah)* (Philadelphia, 1967); and Yosef Hayim Yerushalmi, *Zakhor: Jewish History and Jewish Memory* (Seattle, 1982).

60. Haggai Ben-Shammai, "Between Ananites and Karaites: Observations on Early Medieval Jewish Sectarianism," in *Studies in Muslim-Jewish Relations*, ed. R. L. Nettler (Chur, 1993), 19–29.

61. On the medieval retelling of this story as an anti-conversion narrative, see Elisheva Baumgarten and Rella Kushelevsky, "From 'the Mother and Her Sons' to 'The Mother of the Sons' in Medieval Ashkenaz" (Hebrew), *Zion* 71 (2006): 301–42.

62. Michael Silber, "The Emergence of Ultra-Orthodoxy: The Invention of a Tradition," in *The Uses of Tradition: Jewish Continuity in the Modern Era*, ed. J. Wertheimer (New York, 1992), 23–84. See also Jacob Katz, "Towards a Biography of the Hatam Sofer," in *Divine Law in Human Hands: Case Studies in Halakhic Flexibility* (Jerusalem, 1998), 403–43.

63. Michael Meyer, *Response to Modernity: A History of the Reform Movement in Judaism* (Detroit, 1988), esp. 77–79.

64. bHul 90b.

65. Gershon Bacon, "*Da'at Torah* and the Birth Pangs of the Messiah" (Hebrew), *Tarbiz* 52 (1983): 497–508; and Lawrence Kaplan, "Daas Torah: A Modern Conception of Rabbinic Authority," in *Rabbinic Authority and Personal Autonomy*, ed. M. Sokol (Northvale, N.J., 1992), 1–60.

66. Bacon, "*Da'at Torah*," 502 n. 26.

67. See Jeffrey C. Blutinger, "'So-Called Orthodoxy': The History of an Unwanted Label," *Modern Judaism* 27 (2007): 310–28. They preferred to call themselves "Torah-true" Jews but eventually accepted the label "orthodox."

68. The question of orthodoxy versus orthopraxy—often raised in discussions of Judaism that mistakenly claim that it is a religion of praxis rather than belief—need not detain us here. We use the term "orthodoxy" to encompass practices sustained by beliefs, and vice versa.

69. Jacob Katz, *Tradition and Crisis: Jewish Society at the End of the Middle Ages*, trans. B. D. Cooperman (New York, 1993 [1958]), esp. pt. 3; 183–84, 195.

70. On the limits of Jewish communal autonomy in the Middle Ages, see Salo W.

Baron, *The Jewish Community: Its History and Structure to the American Revolution*, 3 vols. (Philadelphia, 1942), 1:21–25, 2:220–28; idem, *Social and Religious History of the Jews*, 17 vols., 2nd ed. (New York, 1957), 5:45–46, 56–58, 3312 n. 55, 316 n. 69; S. D. Goitein, *A Mediterranean Society: The Jewish Communities of the Arab World as Portrayed in the Documents of the Cairo Geniza*, 6 vols. (Berkeley, Calif., 1967–93), 2:330–34; Elka Klein, *Jews, Christian Society, and Royal Power in Medieval Barcelona* (Ann Arbor, Mich., 2006), esp. 26–51; Jonathan Ray, *The Sephardic Frontier: The Reconquista and the Jewish Community in Medieval Iberia* (Ithaca, N.Y., 2006), 104–11; and Marina Rustow, *Heresy and the Politics of Community: The Jews of the Fatimid Caliphate* (Ithaca, N.Y., 2008), 67–108.

71. Moshe Rosman, "The Postmodern Period in Jewish History," in *How Jewish Is Jewish History?* (Oxford, 2007), 56–81.

72. Haym Soloveitchik, "Rupture and Reconstruction: The Transformation of Contemporary Orthodoxy," *Tradition* 28 (1994): 64–130; Soloveitchik explicitly notes his debt to Menahem Friedman, "Life Tradition and Book Tradition in the Development of Ultra Orthodox Judaism," in *Judaism from Within and from Without: Anthropological Studies*, ed. H. E. Goldberg (Albany, N.Y., 1987), 235–55. What Soloveitchik describes is similar to the talmudization of medieval Judaism as described in Fishman, "Rhineland Pietists' Sacralization." See also Moshe Samet, "The Beginnings of Orthodoxy," *Modern Judaism* 8 (1988): 249–69.

73. Edward Albert Shils, *Tradition* (Chicago, 1981).

74. Elias Bickerman, *The Jews in the Greek Age* (Cambridge, Mass., 1988), 304–5.

75. Hannah Arendt, *Lectures on Kant's Political Philosophy*, ed. R. Beiner (Chicago, 1982), 54–57.

76. Phillips, "What Is Tradition?"; and Assmann, *Zeit und Tradition*, esp. 88–90.

77. G. K. Chesterton, *Orthodoxy* (Garden City, N.J., 1959), 48.

78. George Orwell, *1984* (New York, 1950), 29. Thus did Orwell's Oceania ally itself with Eastasia in war against Eurasia, concealing the fact that only four years earlier the alignment had been precisely the converse: "Officially, the change of partners had never happened. Oceania was at war with Eurasia: therefore Oceania had always been at war with Eurasia" (ibid.).

CHAPTER 10. IN THE PATH OF OUR FATHERS

1. Ez 20:37; and mAvot 3:13.

2. yPe'ah 2:4 (17c).

3. bBer 5a.

4. On the discoveries of the Cairo Genizah, see Paul E. Kahle, *The Cairo Geniza* (Oxford, 1959); Stefan C. Reif, *Hebrew Manuscripts at Cambridge University Library* (Cambridge, 1997), introduction and esp. 30; idem, "The Impact on Jewish Studies of a Century of Geniza Research," in *Jewish Studies at the Turn of the Twentieth Century*, ed. J. Targarona Borrás and A. Sáenz-Badillos, 2 vols. (Leiden, 1999), 1:577–608; and S. D. Goitein, *A

Mediterranean Society: The Jewish Communities of the Arab World as Portrayed in the Documents of the Cairo Geniza, 6 vols. (Berkeley, Calif., 1967–93), vol. 1, introduction.

5. Goitein summed up the transformations before and during what he called the "Geniza period" in his "Political Conflict and the Use of Power in the World of the Geniza," in *Kinship and Consent: The Jewish Political Tradition and Its Contemporary Uses*, ed. D. J. Elazar (Ramat Gan, 1981), 169–82.

6. See Robert Brody, *The Geonim of Babylonia and the Shaping of Medieval Jewish Culture* (New Haven, Conn., 1998). For extensive insights, see Goitein, *Mediterranean Society*.

7. There is a profuse bibliography on Qaraism. See, e.g., Zvi Ankori, *Karaites in Byzantium: The Formative Years, 970–1100* (New York, 1959); Moshe Gil, *Palestine during the First Muslim Period (634–1099)* (Hebrew), 3 vols. (Tel Aviv, 1983); idem, *A History of Palestine, 634–1099*, trans. Ethel Broido (Cambridge, 1992); Philip Birnbaum, ed., *Karaite Studies* (New York, 1971); Steven Wasserstrom, *Between Muslim and Jew: The Problem of Symbiosis under Early Islam* (Princeton, N.J., 1995); and Nathan Shur, *History of the Karaites* (Frankfurt am Main, 1992). On the settlement in Jerusalem, see Daniel al-Qumisi's appeal to return to Zion, in Jacob Mann, "A Tract by an Early Karaite Settler in Jerusalem," *Jewish Quarterly Review* 12 (1921–22): 257–98; and Leon Nemoy, *Karaite Anthology: Excerpts from the Early Literature* (New Haven, Conn., 1980 [1952]), 38. On al-Qumisi himself, see Haggai Ben-Shammai, "Daniel al-Qumisi ve-toledot Erets Yisrael," *Shalem* 3 (1980–81): 295–305; and idem, "The Karaites," in *The History of Jerusalem: The Early Muslim Period 638–1099*, ed. J. Prawer and H. Ben-Shammai (Jerusalem, 1996), 201–24.

8. Attested via the *Iggeret Rav Sherira Ga'on*, ed. B. M. Lewin (Haifa, 1922). On the *Iggeret*, see Jacob Neusner, *A History of the Jews in Babylonia*, 9 vols. (Leiden, 1965–67), 1:154–55; and Brody, *Geonim of Babylonia*, 20–25.

9. Abraham ha-Nasi Savasorda bar Hiyya, *Sefer ha-'ibbur*, ed. H. Filipowski (London, 1851), 6:97.

10. The letters have been collected in the pioneering work of Hayim Yehiel Bornstein, *Mahloqet Rav Se'adyah Ga'on u-ven Me'ir be-qevi'at shanot: Sefer ha-yovel le-Nahum Sokolov* (Warsaw, 1904).

11. Friedrich B. Baethgen, ed., *Fragmente syrischer und arabischer Historiker* (Leipzig, 1884), 84 (Syriac), 141 (German); Bornstein, *Mahloqet Rav Se'adyah Ga'on*, 21–22; English translation, Salo Wittmayer Baron, *A Social and Religious History of the Jews*, 18 vols. (New York, 1952–93), 8:374 n. 62; idem, "Saadiah's Communal Activities," in *Saadia Anniversary Volume: Texts and Studies*, ed. B. Cohen (New York, 1943), 2:9–74, 38 n. 81; and Samuel Poznanski, "Ben Meir and the Origin of the Jewish Calendar," *Jewish Quarterly Review* 10 (1898): 152–61. See the letter written by the end of summer 922 c.e. (1233 of the Seleucid era) in Bornstein, *Mahloqet Rav Se'adyah Ga'on*, 104–5; and Michael Friedländer, "Life and Works of Saadia Gaon," *Jewish Quarterly Review* 5 (1893): 177–99, esp. 197–99.

12. See Sahl ben Matsliah, in Simha Pinsker, *Lickute Kadmoniot: Zur Geschichte des Karaismus und der karaischen Literatur* (Jerusalem, 1968 [1860]), 36.

13. "None of the people dare to profane the festivals of God willfully, to eat leav-

ened bread on Passover, and eat, drink, and work on the Day of Atonement. May it be the will [of the Lord] that there be no stumbling block or pitfall in your place or in any other place in Israel. Pray, answer this letter." Henry Malter, *Saadia Gaon: His Life and Works* (Philadelphia, 1921), 83; Bornstein, *Maḥloqet Rav Se'adyah Ga'on*, 67–71, 69; and Solomon Schechter, *Saadyana: Geniza Fragments of Writings of R. Saadya Gaon and Others* (Cambridge, 1903), 25.

14. Poznanski, "Ben Meir and the Origin of the Jewish Calendar," 154, mainly based on the testimony of Sahl ben Matsliaḥ. See above, n. 12.

15. Goitein, *Mediterranean Society*, 2:52.

16. Louis Ginzberg, e.g., argued that the Academy of Sura had been under the influence of Erets Israel since its founding: *Ginzei Schechter: Genizah Studies in Memory of Doctor Solomon Schechter*, 2 vols. (New York, 1969 [1928–29]), 2:508.

17. For the technical, mathematical, and astronomical aspects of the dispute, see, among others, Malter, *Saadia Gaon*, 73–78; and Sacha Stern, *Calendar and Community: A History of the Jewish Calendar, 2nd Century B.C.E.–10th Century C.E.* (Oxford, 2001), 264–75.

18. Malter, *Saadia Gaon*, 85; see Bornstein, *Maḥloqet Rav Se'adyah Ga'on*, 26–27, 61.

19. mRosh 1:1; bRosh 2b, 11b. On discrepancies in beginning the year of the Seleucid era in autumn or in spring in eastern and western areas of the Jewish worlds, see Eduard Mahler, *Handbuch der jüdischen Chronologie* (Hildesheim, 1967 [1916]), 133–36. See also the testimony of al-Bīrūnī (late tenth or early eleventh century) about the discrepancies he observed between the Jews in counting the cycles (*maḥzorim*) and introducing the intercalations of months: Abū l-Rayḥān al-Bīrūnī, *The Chronology of Ancient Nations or Vestiges of the Past*, trans. Edward Sachau (Frankfurt am Main, 1969 [1879]), 64–65.

20. Compare with the episode of Rabban Gamaliel and the two witnesses he sent whom he did not believe on their return, reported in bRosh 24b–25a (cf. mRosh 2:8).

21. For the technical aspects of the conflict, see above, n. 17.

22. Bornstein, *Maḥloqet Rav Se'adyah Ga'on*, 88–89.

23. ySan 1:2 (18d–19a); and yNed 6:13 (39d–40a).

24. bSan 5a, 11b. See Ḥayyim Meir Horowitz, ed., *Pirqei de-Rabbi Eliezer* (Jerusalem, 1972 [1888]); and Gerald Friedlander, ed., *Pirke de rabbi Eliezer, according to the Text of the Manuscript Belonging to Abraham Epstein of Vienna* (London, 1981 [1916]), 8.

25. Midrash *Tanḥuma Yelamdenu*, Ex 10; Sg *Rabbah* 2:9.

26. Bornstein, *Maḥloqet Rav Se'adyah Ga'on*, 22–23.

27. See Salmon ben Yeruḥim, Commentary on Ps 30; English translation in Gil, "The Jewish Community," 166; al-Bīrūnī, *Chronology of Ancient Nations*, 277; and Gil, *History of Palestine*, 626–29.

28. See above, n. 7.

29. As shown in the Babylonian pamphlet written against Palestinian customs and liturgy by Pirqoi ben Baboi: Ginzberg, *Ginzei Schechter*, 2: 504–73; on "customs of persecution," see, esp., 506–7, 559. See also Mann, "Pirqoi ben Baboi," *Revue des Études Juives* 70 (1920): 113–48; and Brody, *Geonim of Babylonia*, 113–17.

30. Malter, *Saadia Gaon*, 16.

31. See Malter's bibliography of his works, *Saadia Gaon*, 306–419. Cf. Aron Freimann, "Saadia Bibliography," in *Saadia Anniversary Volume*, ed. Cohen, 327–39; Israel Davidson, Simḥa Assaf, and B. Issachar Joel, eds., *Siddur R. Saadja Gaon (Kitab gami as-salawat wat-tasabih)* (Rubin, Mass., 2000 [1941]); and Y. Qafiḥ, ed., *Sefer Yetsira: Perush ha-ga'on rabbenu Se'adyah bar Yosef Fayyumi* (Jerusalem, 1972). On *Sefer yetsira*, see, among others, Georges Vajda, "Le commentaire de Saadia sur le Séfer Yeçira," *Revue des Études Juives* 106 (1941–45): 65–85; Steven Wasserstrom, "Sefer Yetsira and Early Islam: A Reappraisal," *Journal of Jewish Thought and Philosophy* 3 (1993): 1–30; and idem, "Further Thoughts on the Origins of *Sefer Yesirah*," *Aleph* 2 (2002): 201–21. See also the other articles dedicated to the *Sefer yetsirah* in this same issue, 167–221; and Yehuda Liebes, *Ars poetica in Sefer yetsirah* (Hebrew) (Jerusalem, 2000); Joseph Dan, "Three Phases of the History of the *Sefer Yezira*," *Frankfurter Judaistische Beitrage* 21 (1994): 7–29; idem, *Jewish Mysticism*, vol. 1: *Late Antiquity* (Northvale, N.J., 1998): 155–87; Nicolas Sed, "Le Sefer Yesira, l'édition critique, le texte primitif, la grammaire et la métaphysique," *Revue des Études Juives* 132 (1973): 513–28; Moïse Ventura, *La philosophie de Saadia Gaon* (Paris, 1934), 17–30; and Joseph Derenbourg, ed., *Œuvres complètes de R. Saadia ben Iosef al-Fayyoûmi*, 9 vols. (Paris, 1893–99); 2 vols. (Hildesheim, 1979).

32. The work that is considered Se'adyah's masterpiece is *The Book of Beliefs and Opinions*, translated into Hebrew as *Sefer ha-nivḥar be-emunot ve-de'ot: ha-Emunot ve-ha-de'ot le-rabbenu Se'adyah ben Yosef Fayyumi*, ed. Y. Qafiḥ (Jerusalem, 1970); for the English, see Samuel Rosenblatt, trans., *Saadia Gaon, The Book of Beliefs and Opinions* (New Haven, Conn., 1976 [1948]).

33. The titles of at least six polemical works by Se'adyah have survived, all of them combating what he considered heretical arguments.

34. The first emergence of this controversy was the discovery of Ben Meir's name in fragments of Se'adyah's *Egron* and *Sefer ha-galui* found in the library of Saint Petersburg, published in the Russian Hebrew periodical *ha-Melits* (26, 27) by Abraham Firkovich in 1868. It took another twenty-five years to unearth the extant material related to it and for scholars to identify with certainty the "Babylonian" spokesman as the ga'on Se'adyah. See Malter, *Saadia Gaon*, 69, 409–19, for the whole history of the fragmented publications of manuscripts up to Bornstein's work (*Maḥloqet Rav Se'adyah Ga'on*), updated in Stern, *Calendar and Community*.

35. Abraham Harkavy, *Studien und Mitteilungen aus der Kaiserlichen Öffentlichen Bibliothek zu St. Petersburg* (Saint Petersburg, 1903), vol. 8.

36. Samuel Poznanski, "The Anti-Karaïte Writings of Saadiah Gaon," *Jewish Quarterly Review* o.s. 10 (1898): 238–76; repr. in *Karaite Studies*, ed. Birnbaum, 89–127.

37. Bornstein, *Maḥloqet Rav Se'adyah Ga'on*, 88–89; see also the English translation in Stern, *Calendar and Community*, 267.

38. Bornstein, *Maḥloqet Rav Se'adyah Ga'on*, 37–40, 66–70, 75–78, 113–16; Solomon Gandz, "Saadia Gaon as a Mathematician," in *Saadia Anniversary Volume*, ed. Cohen, 141–95; and Stern, *Calendar and Community*, 193.

39. This discrepancy was well known during the Middle Ages, and rabbis everywhere were aware of it when they spelled out the different dates according to the various traditions for drawing up contracts. The discrepancy apparently originated in counting the Seleucid era beginning the year in autumn or spring. Thus, according to the Palestinian reckoning recorded in *Seder 'olam*, the destruction of the Second Temple occurred in 68 rather than in 70.

40. Reported by Abraham bar Ḥiyya, *Sefer ha-'ibbur*, 3:7, 97; B. M. Lewin, *Otsar ha-ge'onim: Thesaurus of the Gaonic Responsa and Commentaries* (Hebrew), 13 vols. (Jerusalem, 1944 [1928]): 5:1, 3, 15. See also Edgar Frank, *Talmudic and Rabbinical Chronology: The System of Counting Years in Jewish Literature* (New York, 1956), 36; Ḥayim Yeḥiel Bornstein, "Ta'arikhei Yisrael," *ha-Tequfah* 8 (1920): 281–338, and 9 (1920): 202–64, esp. 223; and see Sylvie Anne Goldberg, *La Clepsydre: Essai sur la pluralité des temps dans le judaïsme* (Paris, 2000), 209.

41. "Sa'adia asserted that the [length of the] months have always been determined by calculations. It is only after Tsadoq and Bœthos, the disciples of Antigonos, rebelled and contended that the Torah prescribes fixing the New Moon by observing the moon that we began to assign witnesses to proclaim the New Moon after having demonstrated that calculation and observation exactly coincide." Poznanski, "Anan et ses écrits" *Revue des Études Juives* 44 (1901–2): 161–87 (esp. 176–77) and 45 (1902): 50–69, 176–203; idem, "The Anti-Karaïte Writings," 273, repr. in *Karaite Studies*, ed. Birnbaum, 124; and Goldberg, *La Clepsydre II, Temps de Jérusalem, temps de Babylone* (Paris, 2004), 220–21.

42. See the arguments by the Qaraite scholar Ya'qūb al-Qirqisānī, in Georges Vajda, "Études sur Qirqisâni," *Revue des Études Juives* 107 (1946–47): 52–98, esp. 73–74.

43. Schechter, *Saadyana*, 5. See the English text in Brody, *Geonim of Babylonia*, 246.

44. yPeah 2:4 (17c); and bBer 5a.

45. See Se'adyah's commentary on bBer 7a., *Perush rav Se'adyah 'al masekhet Berakhot*, ed. S. A. Wertheimer, 2nd ed. (Jerusalem, 1927 [1908]); see also the end of the introduction to Se'adyah's commentary on *Sefer yetsirah*, where he said that the Mishnah had been transmitted orally before it was written down: Qafiḥ, ed., *Sefer Yetsira*, 33; and Mayer Lambert, ed., *Commentaire sur le Sefer Yesira ou Livre de la création par le gaon Saadya de Fayyoum* (Paris, 1891), 19–20.

46. Davidson et al., eds., *Siddur R. Saadja Gaon*, 10–13; and Ginzberg, "Saadia's Siddur," in *Saadia Studies*, ed. A. A. Neuman and S. Zeitlin (Philadelphia, 1943), 315–63, esp. 327.

47. Davidson et al., eds., *Siddur R. Saadja Gaon*, 10; and Goldberg, *La Clepsydre II*, 191–92.

48. Cf. Georges Vajda, "Autour de la théorie de la connaissance chez Saadia," *Revue des Études Juives* 126 (1967): 135–89, and esp. 127 (1967): 375–97. See also Goldberg, *La Clepsydre II*, 289.

49. On a more specifically philosophical approach to Se'adyah's relation to *kalām* and free will, see Tamar M. Rudawski, *Time Matters: Time, Creation, and Cosmology in Medieval Jewish Philosophy* (New York, 2000), 112–15. For a different perspective, see Z. Diesend-

ruck, "Saadya's Formulation of the Time-Argument for Creation," *Jewish Studies in Memory of George A. Kohut*, ed. S. W. Baron and A. Marx (New York, 1935), 145–58.

50. Brody, *Geonim of Babylonia*, 136; the biographical sketch in Malter, *Saadia Gaon*, 53–68; and Abraham A. Neuman, "Saadia's Relation to Palestine," in *Saadia Studies*, ed. Neuman and Zeitlin, 109–32.

51. Thus it is possible to understand the later declaration of Hayya Ga'on: "We do not rely upon the Palestinian Talmud in connection with any matter that is definitively decided in our Talmud." Simḥa Assaf, ed., *Teshuvot ha-Geonim: Responsa geonica, ex fragmentis Cantabrigiensibus* (Jerusalem, 1970 [1929]), 125–26; and Neuman, "Saadia's Relation to Palestine," 125. On the decline of the authority of the Palestinian Talmud, see Louis Ginzberg, *Introduction to the Palestinian Talmud* (Philadelphia, 1941), repr. in idem, *On Jewish Law and Lore* (Philadelphia, 1955), 3–57, esp. 33.

52. Nehemya Allony, ed., *ha-Egron le-Rasag* (Jerusalem, 1969).

53. See above, n. 7.

54. For Sacha Stern, Se'adyah was "the first to use the term *zeman*, or at least its Judeo-Arabic equivalent and cognate *al-zamān*, in the sense of 'time' as a general category" (*Time and Process in Ancient Judaism* [Oxford, 2003], 89).

55. Goldberg, *La Clepsydre*, 302–4.

56. See Se'adyah's introduction, in Davidson et al., eds., *Siddur R. Saadja Gaon*, 10.

57. As may be seen from the fact that there has always been a question of the calendar in the many sectarian dissidences attested since antiquity. See, e.g., the numerous works written about Qumran regarding the calendar, synthesized in James C. Vanderkam, *Calendars in the Dead Sea Scrolls: Measuring Time* (London, 1998); and Goldberg, *La Clepsydre*, 282–300.

58. As shown explicitly in *Sefer ha-galui*: "God does not leave his nation in any period without a scholar whom he inspires and enlightens, so that he in turn may so instruct and teach her, that her condition shall be thereby bettered." *Sefer ha-galui*, ed. A. E. Harkavy, *Zikkaron le-rishonim: Leben und Werke des Saadjah Gaon* (Saint Petersburg, 1891), 5:155.

59. The sentence removed from the *Yotser* is: *Or hadash al-tsiyyon ta'ir* ("May a new light shine on Zion"); from the *Shema' Yisra'el*, it is: *Tsur yisra'el ve-go'alo* ("the Holy One and his Redeemer"). See Naphtali Wieder, "Fourteen New Genizah Fragments of Saadya's *Siddur* Together with a Reproduction of a Missing Part," in *Saadya Studies: In Commemoration of the One Thousandth Anniversary of the Death of R. Saadya Gaon*, ed. E. J. Rosenthal (Manchester, 1943), 245–83.

60. Malter, *Saadia Gaon*, 149–53; Brody, *Geonim of Babylonia*, 324–27; and Yosef Tobi, *Piyyutei Rav Se'adyah Ga'on: Mahadurah madda'it (shel ha-yotsrot) u-mavo' kelali le-yetsirato* (Jerusalem, 1982).

CHAPTER 11. PRAYER, LITERACY, AND LITERARY MEMORY
IN THE JEWISH COMMUNITIES OF MEDIEVAL EUROPE

1. See, e.g., Avraham Grossman, *Pious and Rebellious Women* (Hebrew) (Jerusalem, 2001), 10–11.

2. See, e.g., Jay Harris, "Among the Giants," *Bulletin of the Center for Jewish Studies at Harvard University* 17 (1999): 1–5. Cf. Moshe Idel, "Kabbalah and Elites in Thirteenth-Century Spain," *Mediterranean Historical Review* 9 (1994): 5–19.

3. We shall deal here only with Hebrew literacy. On literacy in French and Latin of the Jews in northern France, see William Chester Jordan, *The French Monarchy and the Jews* (Philadelphia, 1989), 15–21; and Ephraim Kanarfogel, *Jewish Education and Society in the High Middle Ages* (Detroit, 1992), 15–16, 119. Cf. F. H. Bauml, "Varieties and Consequences of Medieval Literacy and Illiteracy," *Speculum* 55 (1980): 237–49; and Kirsten Fudeman, "'They Have Ears but Do Not Hear': Gendered Access to Hebrew and the Medieval French Wedding Song," *Jewish Quarterly Review* 96 (2006): 542–49.

4. See, e.g., Simon Schwartzfuchs, *The Jews of France in the Middle Ages* (Hebrew) (Tel Aviv, 2001), 127–28 (who distinguishes correctly between the ability to read and the ability to write); Stefan Reif, "Aspects of Medieval Jewish Literacy," in *The Uses of Literacy in Early Medieval Europe*, ed. R. McKitterick (Cambridge, 1989), 145–52; S. D. Goitein, *A Mediterranean Society: The Jewish Communities of the Arab World as Portrayed in the Documents of the Cairo Geniza*, 6 vols. (Berkeley, Calif., 1967–93), 2:174–75, 181–82; and idem, *Jewish Education in Muslim Countries, Based on Records from the Cairo Geniza* (Hebrew) (Jerusalem, 1962), 36–40. Cf. Shaul Stampfer, "Yedi'at qero u-khetov etsel yehudei mizraḥ Eropah ba-tequfah ha-ḥadashah: Heqsher, qorot ve-hashlakhot," in *Temurot ba-historiyyah ha-yehudit ba-'et ha-ḥadashah*, ed. S. Almog et al. (Jerusalem, 1988), 459–62; M. T. Clanchy, *From Memory to Written Record* (Cambridge, 1977), 182–95; James Foley, "Orality, Textuality and Interpretation," in *Vox Intexta: Orality and Textuality in the Middle Ages*, ed. A. N. Doane and C. B. Pasternak (Madison, Wisc., 1991), 34–35; Brigitte Bedos-Rezak, "The Confrontation of Orality and Textuality: Jewish and Christian Literacy in Eleventh and Twelfth-Century Northern France," in *Rashi, 1040–1990*, ed. G. Sed-Rajna (Paris, 1993), 541–58; Goitein, *Jewish Education*, 41–45; and the next note.

5. Mary Carruthers, *The Book of Memory: A Study of Memory in Medieval Culture* (Cambridge, 1990), 9–11, 46–48, 106–112, 122–23, 161–72, 258–59; M. Carruthers and J. M. Ziolkowski, eds., *The Medieval Craft of Memory* (Philadelphia, 2002), 1–23; Ivan Illich, *In the Vineyard of the Text* (Chicago, 1993), 34–45; Charles Jones, "The Book of the Liturgy in Anglo-Saxon England," *Speculum* 73 (1998): 659–66; Matei Calinescu, "Orality in Literacy: Some Historical Paradoxes of Reading," *Yale Journal of Criticism* 6 (1993): 175–90; and Stefan Reif, *Judaism and Hebrew Prayer* (Cambridge, 1993), 147–52.

6. See, e.g., Y. N. Epstein, *Mavo le-nosaḥ ha-Mishnah* (Jerusalem, 1964), 692–706; idem, *Mevo'ot le-sifrut ha-amora'im* (Jerusalem, 1962); Yaakov Elman, *Authority and Tradition* (Hoboken, N.J., 1994); Martin Jaffee, *Torah in the Mouth: Writing and Oral Tradition in Palestinian Judaism, 200 B.C.E.–400 C.E.* (Oxford, 2001); and Shelomoh Na'eh, "Omanut

ha-zikkaron, mivnim shel zikkaron ve-tavniyyot shel teqst be-sifrut Hazal," in *Mehqerei Talmud*, ed. Y. Sussmann and D. Rosenthal, 3 vols. (Jerusalem, 2005), 2:543–89.

7. See, e.g., Avraham Grossman, *Hakhemei Ashkenaz ha-rishonim* (Jerusalem, 1981), 110–11, 158–60, 250–52, 316–18, 383–84; and idem, *Hakhemei tsarefat ha-rishonim* (Jerusalem, 1995), 226–38, 438–39, 583–84.

8. See, e.g., E. E. Urbach, *Ba'alei ha-Tosafot* (Jerusalem, 1980), 1:50–51, 71–73, 97, 154–55, 299–301, 371; 2:680–86, 700; and Y. S. Spiegel, *'Amudim be-toledot ha-sefer ha-'ivri: Haggahot u-maggihim* (Ramat Gan, 2005), 104–7, 111–56. Cf. Talya Fishman, "Rhineland Pietist Approaches to Prayer and the Textualization of Rabbinic Culture in Medieval Northern Europe," *Jewish Studies Quarterly* 11 (2004): 313–31; idem, "The Rhineland Pietists' Sacralization of Oral Torah," *Jewish Quarterly Review* 96 (2006): 9–16; and Shraga Abramson, "Ketivat ha-Mishnah 'al da'at ge'onim ve-rishonim," in *Culture and Society in Medieval Jewry: Studies Dedicated to the Memory of Haim Hillel Ben-Sasson* (Hebrew), ed. R. Bonfil et al. (Jerusalem, 1989), 27–52.

9. Paris, Bibliothèque Nationale, MS Heb. 260, fol. 92v.

10. See also Jack Goody, *The Interface between the Written and the Oral* (New York, 1987), 189–90; and David Olson, *The World on Paper* (Cambridge, 1994), 100–101.

11. Jean Leclerq, *The Love of Learning and the Desire for God* (New York, 1961), 18–22, 90. See also Douwe Draaisma, *Metaphors of Memory* (Cambridge, 2000), 31–34; and Alberto Manguel, *A History of Reading* (New York, 1996), 57–60. Cf. Carruthers, *The Book of Memory*, 88–111.

12. See below, nn. 41–46.

13. Cambridge, University Library, MS Add. 1022.1, fol. 100v; and cf. below, n. 54. On the Cambridge manuscript, see Marc Saperstein and Ephraim Kanarfogel, "A Byzantine Manuscript of Sermons: A Description and Selections about Prayer and the Synagogue" (Hebrew), *Pe'amim* 78 (1999): 164–84.

14. *Devarim she-bikhtav i attah rashai le-omran 'al peh*; bGit 60b, bTem 14b.

15. The first is a passage in *Tosafot ha-Rosh* (to bYom 68b), which was compiled by Me'ir of Rothenburg's student R. Asher b. Yehi'el (Rosh) but typically reflects earlier material from the classic Tosafot of Ri and his student R. Samson of Sens (d. 1214). The second passage is found in the so-called *Tosafot yeshanim* to bYom (70a), which are (for the most part) the Tosafot of R. Judah Sirleon of Paris (d. 1224), who was also a student of Ri (and refers to him here as his teacher, *m[ori] r[abbi]*).

16. bYom 70a.

17. These include the verse of the daily sacrificial service, the psalms of *pesuqei de-zimrah*, the verses associated with the Song of the Sea and the verses of *Shema'*.

18. See *Sefer yere'im ha-shalem* (Jerusalem, 1973), sec. 268.

19. *Sefer Rabiah*, ed. A. Aptowitzer (New York, 1982), 3:640.

20. See the Tosafot to bTem 14b, s.v. *devarim she-bikhtav*.

21. According to Urbach (*Ba'alei ha-Tosafot*, 2:671), the standard Tosafot to bTem were compiled in the study hall of the brothers of Evreux (Normandy) in the mid-thirteenth

century; cf. Kanarfogel, *Jewish Education and Society*, 74–79. See also Simcha Krauss, "Devarim she-bikhtav i attah rasha'i le-omran be'al peh," *Or ha-mizraḥ* 49 (2004): 101–4.

22. Kanarfogel, "Halakhah and Metsi'ut (Realia) in Medieval Ashkenaz: Surveying the Parameters and Defining the Limits," *Jewish Law Annual* 14 (2003): 193–201.

23. See *Sefer Raban*, sec. 42, fol. 16a (cited in brief in *Sefer semaq mi-Tsurikh*, 1:247, precept 104, *liqqutim*); and cf. *Sefer ha-orah*, ed. Solomon Buber, sec. 12 (p. 9). Cf. Israel Ta-Shma, *ha-Tefillah ha-ashkenazit ha-qedumah* (Jerusalem, 2003), 30.

24. See bGit 60a.

25. *Sefer Rabiah*, 3:642–43. This reason is based in part on the talmudic *sugya* of the Torah reading by the high priest on Yom Kippur. Cf. *Sefer kol bo*, sec. 2, and below, n. 48.

26. bTa'an 28b.

27. bMeg 18b.

28. This explanation is also cited in *Sefer Rabiah*, pt. 3, 643.

29. R. Isaac b. Moses, *Sefer or zarua'* (Zhitomir, 1862), pt. 1, Hilkhot tefillin, sec. 545; *Sefer Mordekhai le-massekhet Gittin*, sec. 407, ed. Mayer Rabinowitz (Jerusalem, 1990), 628–29; and *Sefer Mordekhai, Halakhot qetanot*, fol. 14, s.v. *zeh*. On the preservation of Rabbenu Tam's teachings by *Sefer or zarua'*, cf. Rami Reiner, "Rabbenu Tam u-venei doro: Qesharim, hashpa'ot, ve-darkhei limmud ba-Talmud" (Ph.D. diss., Hebrew University of Jerusalem, 2002), 61–62.

30. *Teshuvot u-pesaqim le-Ri ha-zaqen*, in *Shitat ha-qadmonim 'al massekhet 'Avodah Zarah*, ed. M. Blau (New York, 1991), 3:228, sec. 110/3; and *Teshuvot Maharam mi-Rothenburg* (Prague, 1895), no. 313. Cf. Simcha Emanuel, "Teshuvot shel Maharam she-einan shel Maharam," *Shenaton ha-mishpat ha-'ivri* 21 (1998–2000): 160, 202.

31. In his response to his son-in-law (above, at n. 23), Raban maintains that he assumed on the basis of this construct (*shegurin be-fi kol*) that verses in all sections of the prayer service were known to those who prayed regularly.

32. See Ta-Shma, *ha-Tefillah ha-ashkenazit ha-qedumah*, 26–32. Cf. Jones, "Book of the Liturgy," 696–702; Eric Palazzo, *A History of Liturgical Books*, trans. M. Beaumont (Collegeville, Minn., 1998), 238–40; and Draaisma, *Metaphors of Memory*, 31–36. On the paucity of collections of biblical verses that were available in medieval Ashkenaz, see, e.g., *Sefer Mordekhai* to bEruv 67b, sec. 513. Cf. *Shibbolei ha-leqet*, sec. 9, and Goitein, *Mediterranean Society*, 2:181.

33. See, e.g., T. C. Hubka, *Resplendent Synagogue* (Hanover, N.H., 2003), 91, 105–8, 192–93.

34. *Sefer Ḥasidim* (Bologna), ed. Reuven Margoliot (Jerusalem, 1957), sec. 18 (p. 81).

35. See Ta-Shma, *ha-Tefillah ha-ashkenazit ha-qedumah*, 51–52; and Ephraim Kanarfogel, *ha-Ḥinnukh ve-ha-ḥevrah ha-yehudit be-Eropah ha-tsefonit bimei ha-beinayim* (Jerusalem, 2003), 198–205. Cf. Fishman, "Rhineland Pietist Approaches to Prayer," 326–27.

36. *Sefer Ḥasidim* (Parma), in Jehuda Wistinetzki, ed., *Das Buch der Frommen nach der Rezension in Cod. de Rossi No. 1133* (Hebrew), 2nd ed., with introduction and indices by Jacob Freimann (Frankfurt am Main, 1924), secs. 404–5, 710, 1621; and *Sefer*

Ḥasidim (Bologna), ed. Margoliot, sec. 249. Cf. H. Soloveitchik, "Three Themes in the Sefer Ḥasidim," *Association for Jewish Studies Review* 1 (1976): 330–35; C. Heyman, "L'écrit dans les croyances, les superstitions et la psychologie du 'pietiste,'" in *La conception du livre chez les pietistes ashkenazes au Moyen Age*, ed. C. Sirat (Geneva, 1996), 119–21; Ta-Shma, *ha-Tefillah ha-ashkenazit ha-qedumah*, 51–52, and below, n. 68.

37. See Ta-Shma, *ha-Tefillah ha-ashkenazit ha-qedumah*, 30.

38. *Responsa of R. Meir of Rothenburg* (Berlin, 1891), 371 (no. 293). Cf. I. A. Agus, *R. Meir of Rothenburg* (Philadelphia, 1947), 1:251–52 (no. 189); *Responsa of R. Meir* (Prague, 1897), no. 120; and *Responsa of R. Ḥayyim Or Zarua'* (a student of R. Meir) (Jerusalem, 1960), no. 2.

39. See, e.g., Leo Landman, *The Cantor: An Historic Perspective* (New York, 1972), 29–32; Grossman, *Ḥakhemei Ashkenaz ha-rishonim*, 292–93, 390–91; idem, *Ḥakhemei Tsarefat ha-rishonim*, 126, 173–74, 255–59; *'Arugat ha-bosem le-R. Avraham ben Azri'el*, ed. E. E. Urbach (Jerusalem, 1963), 4:71, 102, 108; and Ta-Shma, *ha-Tefillah ha-ashkenazit ha-qedumah*, 33–35, 52–53.

40. *Sefer Rabiah*, vol. 2, 222–23 (sec. 536).

41. On the ability of the members of the congregation to read from and to utilize *mahzorim*, see also, e.g., *Sefer Rabiah*, 3:439; the liturgical interpretation by R. Samuel of Falaise, cited in *Sefer or zarua'*, Hilkhot pesaḥim, sec. 256, fol. 57, col. 4; *Sefer Mordekhai* to bBets 11b, sec. 659, ed. Makhon Yerushalayim (Jerusalem, 1983), 37–38; and Tosafot Yom 54a–b (reflecting a responsum of R. Me'ir of Rothenburg; see Urbach, *Ba'alei ha-Tosafot*, 2:610).

42. *Sefer Mordekhai* to *Yoma*, sec. 725, ed. Makhon Yerushalayim (Jerusalem, 1989), · 69–70. See also *Arba'ah turim*, Oraḥ ḥayyim, sec. 582 (end); *Beit Yosef*, ad loc. (and to sec. 101); and Ta-Shma, *ha-Tefillah ha-ashkenazit ha-qedumah*, 29 n. 58. On prayer in a low voice during the weekdays in northern France, cf. Paris, Biblothèque Nationale de France, MS Heb. 167, fol. 91a; Eric Zimmer, "Tenuhot u-tenu'ot ha-guf bi-she'at qeri'at shema'," *Assufot* 8 (1994): 363–67; *Sefer ha-makhkim le-R. Natan b. Yehudah*, ed. Judah Freimann (Jerusalem, 1968), 123–24, s.v. *la-menatseaḥ*; and I. Ta-Shma, "Matsavei yeshivah va-'amidah bi-qeri'at shema' u-virkhotehah," in *Kenishta*, ed. Y. Tabory (Ramat Gan, 2001), 1:53–61. See also *Sefer or zarua'*, pt. 1, sec. 115, and pt. 2, Hilkhot shabbat, sec. 42 (fol. 10a, col. 2, end), for the ability of laypeople to read from the Torah in the synagogue.

43. It should be noted that the convention of simply stating "as it is written in the Torah" on festivals, without having then to recite the verses themselves (which would certainly have made things easier for those who did not have *mahzorim* in front of them) was also referred to by Rabbenu Tam (who expressed his disapproval), by Rashi and his school, and by Raban. See *Sefer Rabiah*, 2:222–23 (and Aptowitzer's notes there). See also *Siddur Rashi* (Berlin, 1912), 80; and Ta-Shma, *ha-Tefillah ha-ashkenazit ha-qedumah*, 30.

44. *Sefer ha-terumah*, sec. 219. On R. Barukh's locale, see S. Emanuel, "Barukh b. Isaac" (Hebrew), *Tarbiz* 69 (2000): 423–40. On the date and circumstances of his death, see I. Ta-Shma, "Keroniqah ḥadashah li-tequfat ba'alei ha-tosafot me-ḥugo shel Ri ha-zaqen," *Shalem* 3 (1981): 320–23; and cf. Kanarfogel, "The Aliyah of 'Three Hundred

Rabbis' in 1211: Tosafist Attitudes Toward Settling in the Land of Israel," *Jewish Quarterly Review* 76 (1986): 202–4.

45. *Sefer or zarua'*, pt. 2, sec. 32 (laws of *'erev Shabbat*), fol. 8a, cols. 1–2. Cf. *Sefer kol bo*, sec. 68.

46. R. Isaac also discusses a prevalent (parallel) custom in his region of the Slavic lands (*be-khol yom be-malkhutenu be-erets kena'an*) to read from a siddur the psalms for the wedding feast that are recited on the eve of the Sabbath, without concern that the candles will be tilted. On the absence of illumination and light sources as a cause for prayers being recited by heart, cf. Ta-Shma, *ha-Tefillah ha-ashkenazit ha-qedumah*, 29.

47. It should be noted that for many medieval Ashkenazi rabbinic scholars, the Mishnah was not written down as a fixed text in the days of Rabbi Judah the Prince. Rather, an authoritative version was established that could be uniformly preserved by memory; see below, n. 49.

48. *Sefer kol bo*, a halakhic compendium composed anonymously in Provence ca. 1300, notes that Rabbenu Perets of Corbeil (one of the last of the northern French Tosafists, d. 1298) also supported the first interpretation or method of justification, as apparently did his northern French predecessor in the first half of the thirteenth century, R. Moses of Coucy. See *Sefer kol bo*, sec. 2 (cited also by *Beit Yosef, Orah hayyim*, sec. 49), and *Sefer mitsvot gadol, mitsvot 'aseh mi-de-rabbanan*, sec. 4, Hilkhot megillah. See also *Sefer or zarua'* (above, n. 229); *Arba'ah turim*, Orah hayyim, sec. 49; *Sefer ha-maskil*, ms. Bodl. 2287, fol. 6v; and Y. N. Epstein, *Mehqarim be-sifrut ha-Talmud u-vi-leshonot shemiyyot* (Jerusalem, 1984), 1:303–4.

49. In light of this, a passage attributed to R. Isaac (Ri) of Dampierre (in Barukh b. Isaac, *Sefer ha-terumah*, sec. 245; *Sefer mitsvot gadol, Lo ta'aseh* 65, fol. 16d; *Sefer Mordekhai* to *Shabbat* 116a, s.v. *alibba*) requires further discussion. Cf. above, at n. 23; see also B. M. Lewin's introduction to his edition of *Iggeret R. Sherira Ga'on* (Haifa, 1921), 26 n. 1; Epstein, *Mavo le-nusah ha-Mishnah*, 692–706; Abramson, "Ketivat ha-Mishnah"; and Yaacov Sussmann, "Torah she-be'al peh: peshutah ke-mashma'ah," in *Mehqerei Talmud*, ed. idem and Rosenthal, vol. 3, pt. 1, 209–38, 318–31, 369–70.

50. *Perush Abudarham ha-shalem* (Jerusalem, 1963), 48, 79–80, 238.

51. See *Perushei talmidei Rabbenu Yonah le-massekhet Berakhot* (5a, s.v. *lo hifsid*, in the name of R. Solomon of Montpellier), cited in *Beit Yosef* to Orah hayyim, sec. 49.

52. Ritba studied with the leading scholars of Catalonia and served as rabbinic leader in Saragossa, Aragon. See Israel Ta-Shma, *ha-Sifrut ha-parshanit la-Talmud be-Eropah u-vi-Tsefon Afriqah: qorot, ishim ve-shitot* (Jerusalem, 1999), pt. 2, 69–74; Moshe Goldstein, ed., *Hiddushei ha-Ritva le-massekhet 'eruvin* (Jerusalem, 1974), 7–28; and Ephraim Kanarfogel, "Between Ashkenaz and Sefarad: Tosafist Teachings in the Talmudic Commentaries of R. Yom Tov b. Abraham Ishvilli," in *Between Rashi and Maimonides: Themes in Medieval Jewish Thought, Literature, and Exegesis*, ed. E. Kanarfogel and M. Sokolow (Jersey City, N.J., 2010): 237–73.

53. See *Hiddushei ha-Ritva le-Yoma* 70a, s.v. *le-fi*, and cf. *Sefer kol bo* (and *Beit Yosef*, above, n. 48).

54. See *Tosafot yeshanim le-Yoma* and *Tosafot ha-Rosh le-Yoma*, above, n. 15. Cf. *Teshuvot Maharam mi-Rothenburg*, ed. Lemberg, no. 437, and *Sefer Tashbets*, sec. 185.

55. After presenting the Ashkenazi approach (in the name of Rosh and Semag), *Shiltei ha-gibborim* (to bMeg 14a, in the pagination of the Rif), whose author was among those exiled from Spain, suggests a completely different approach that is similar at its core to that of Rabbenu Yonah and Ritba. Only an individual is prohibited from reciting biblical verses by heart. But when the congregation is reading with him ("they are reading all together in one voice"), there is no prohibition on reciting the biblical verses by heart. Thus, whenever the congregation reads biblical verses aloud publicly, this prohibition is not in force.

56. See, e.g., Y. M. Epstein, *'Arukh ha-shulḥan* to *Oraḥ ḥayyim*, sec. 49:3.

57. This type of argument had been made in Germany in the mid-twelfth century by R. Eliezer b. Nathan (Raban) of Mainz, although, as noted above (n. 25), it did not have much impact on subsequent Ashkenazi authorities.

58. *Teshuvot ha-Rambam*, ed. A. H. Freimann (Jerusalem, 1934), no. 36; and ed. J. Blau (Jerusalem, 1986), 469–76 (no. 256).

59. *Teshuvot ha-Rambam*, ed. Blau, no. 258. Cf. Gerald Blidstein, *ha-Tefillah be-mishnato ha-hilkhatit shel ha-Rambam* (Jerusalem, 1994), chap. 7, esp. 176–81. Maimonides mentions "one of the rabbinic scholars in Christian lands" (*eḥad me-ḥakhemei Edom*) who suggested something similar to his proposal. It is difficult, however, to identify this scholar and his precise locale from the text of the responsum. Freimann, in his edition (4 n. 12), suggests, relying on Moshe Lutski, "Five Autographed Responsa of the Rambam" (Hebrew), *ha-Tequfah* 30–31 (1946): 689–93, that Maimonides was referring here to R. Pinḥas Dayyan of Alexandria, whose origins were in southern France.

60. See Robert Brody, *The Geonim of Babylonia and the Shaping of Medieval Jewish Culture* (New Haven, Conn., 1998), 192–93, 253–54, 260; Goitein, *Mediterranean Society*, 2:159–65; and idem, *Jewish Education*, 51–54. Cf. Moshe Gil, *Palestine during the First Muslim Period (634–1099)* (Hebrew) (Tel Aviv, 1983), 160–63, 190–94.

61. L. Ginzberg, "Saadia's Siddur," *Jewish Quarterly Review* 34 (1942–43): 315–24 (= idem, *'Al halakhah va-aggadah* [Tel Aviv, 1960], 171–77).

62. bBer 24b.

63. See also Ginzberg, *Geonica* (New York, 1968), 1:119–21; 2:26, 119.

64. Israel Davidson, Simḥa Assaf, and Yissachar Joel, eds., *Siddur rav Se'adyah Ga'on* (Jerusalem, 1941), 152–53. Cf. *Perush Abudarham*, 238.

65. See *Perush talmidei Rabbenu Yonah le-massekhet berakhot*, fol. 14b, in the pagination of Alfasi's *Halakhot*, s.v. *sakkin*. See also *Sefer ha-yir'ah le-rabbenu Yonah*, ed. Binyamin Zilber (Jerusalem, 1959), 24, sec. 89; and cf. R. Isaac of Corbeil, *Sefer mitsvot qatan*, end of sec. 11.

66. See Isserlein, *Terumat ha-deshen*, sec. 17.

67. See *Perush talmidei Rabbenu Yonah le-massekhet berakhot*, fol. 15b in the Alfasi pagination, s.v. *asur*; and *Beit Yosef, Oraḥ ḥayyim*, sec. 96 (end) and sec. 97 (end).

68. *Sefer ḥasidim* (Bologna), sec. 249 (above, nn. 34 and 36, and the additional sections noted there). On Rabbenu Yonah's awareness of *Sefer ḥasidim*, see Ephraim Kanar-

fogel, *Peering through the Lattices: Mystical, Magical, and Pietistic Dimensions in the Tosafist Period* (Detroit, 2000), 27, 54 n. 59, 62–65, 72.

69. bShab 116b.

70. See *Shibbolei ha-leqet*, sec. 12. On the identity of R. Ephraim in this passage, see Ginzberg, *Geonica*, 120 n. 1; and A. Aptowitzer, *Mavo la-Rabiah*, 325–26.

71. On the nature of *Tsedah la-derekh* (which has been compared with the encyclopedia by Bartholomew of England, who taught in Paris ca. 1225) and its communal underpinnings and origins, see Kanarfogel, *ha-Ḥinnukh ve-ha-ḥevrah*, 47–48, 555; Shelomo Eidelberg, "ha-Sefer *Tsedah la-Derekh* u-meḥabro R. Menaḥem b. ha-Qadosh R. Aharon b. Zeraḥ," *Proceedings of the Sixth World Congress of Jewish Studies* 3 (Jerusalem, 1977): 15–30; and Y. Galinsky, "Arba'ah turim ve-ha-sifrut ha-hilkhatit shel sefarad ba-me'ah ha-14" (Ph.D. diss., Bar Ilan University, 1999), 300–301.

72. *Tsedah la-derekh*, unit 1, pt. 3, chap. 20.

73. *Responsa of the Ritba*, ed. Y. Qafiḥ (Jerusalem, 1959), no. 97. Cf. B. S. Hamburger, *Shorashei minhag Ashkenaz* (B'nei Brak, 1994), 4:170–73.

74. *Responsa of Rivash*, ed. David Metzger (Jerusalem, 1993), no. 37.

75. *Sefer Ḥasidim* (Parma), sec. 748. See also secs. 745, 765, 796, 824–25; and cf. Ephraim Kanarfogel, "R. Judah he-Ḥasid and the Rabbinic Scholars of Regensburg," *Jewish Quarterly Review* 96 (2006): 36 n. 55, and the literature cited there.

76. *Sefer ha-'ittim* (Krakow, 1903), 264.

77. *Perush Abudarham*, 131 (cited in *Beit Yosef, Oraḥ ḥayyim*, sec. 139).

78. See R. Ephraim's formulation in *Sefer Rabiah*, pt. 2, sec. 551; and *Sefer or zarua'*, pt. 2, sec. 42.

79. *Teshuvot R. Me'ir mi-Rothenburg* (Lemberg, 1860), no. 149. For a thorough discussion of this issue, based on all the relevant medieval and early modern rabbinic sources, see Hamburger, *Shorashei minhag Ashkenaz*, 4:205–53.

80. On the widespread availability of *melammedim* in medieval Ashkenaz (despite the relatively informal educational structure) and expectations of them, see Kanarfogel, *Jewish Education and Society*, 19–32.

81. *Sefer Roqeaḥ* (Jerusalem, 1967), 11. Cf. Carruthers, *Book of Memory*, 29–30, 107–21.

82. See Kanarfogel, *ha-Ḥinnukh ve-ha-ḥevrah*, 55 n. 40 (and app. 2, 196–97).

83. *Sefer Ḥasidim* (Parma), sec. 829. On Hebrew as a spoken language, cf. *Sefer Ḥasidim* (Parma), secs. 99, 902, 1368; and N. Morris, *Toledot ha-ḥinnukh shel 'am Yisra'el*, pt. 2 (Tel Aviv, 1977), 1:85, 324–25.

84. *Sefer or zarua'*, pt. 1, Hilkhot qeri'at Shema', sec. 12; pt. 2, sec. 389; pt. 3, *Pisqei Bava Metsia'*, sec. 242.

85. *Teshuvot Ragma*, ed. S. Eidelberg (New York, 1955), sec. 71. Cf. *Sefer ḥuqqei ha-torah* (transcribed in Kanarfogel, *ha-Ḥinnukh ve-ha-ḥevrah*, 191–95), lines 60–72, 134–35, 170–80.

86. See Goitein, *Mediterranean Society*, 2:174–75, 182; and idem, *Jewish Education*, 36–43.

87. See Assis, "'Ezrah hadadit u-se'ad bi-qehillot Yisra'el bi-Sefarad," in *Moreshet Se-farad*, ed. H. Beinart (Jerusalem, 1992), 276–77; and idem, "Ḥinnukh yaldei Yisra'el bi-Se-farad ha-notserit ba-me'ot ha-13–14: Bein qehillah la-ḥavurah," in *Ḥinnukh ve-historiyyah*, ed. R. Paldahi and I. Etkes (Jerusalem, 1999), 145–65. Cf. Kanarfogel, *Jewish Education and Society*, 42–65.

88. *Sefer Rabiah*, pt. 1, 179, responsum 168. Cf. *Maḥzor Vitry*, ed. S. Hurvitz, 3.

89. See above, nn. 19, 40, and 45 on the reading of the Haggadah in Ashkenaz accord-ing to *Sefer or zarua'*, whose author had studied with Rabiah.

90. On those in Ashkenaz who were ignorant of Hebrew, see, e.g., *Sefer or zarua'*, pt. 1, *Hikhot qeri'at Shema'*, sec. 12, and above, nn. 18 and 45. On the enlarged circle of read-ers in Spain in the late thirteenth and fourteenth centuries, see Galinsky, "Arba'ah Turim," 102–11.

91. For a similar problem in the realm of religious behavior and observance, see Ephraim Kanarfogel, "Rabbinic Attitudes toward Nonobservance in the Middle Ages," in *Jewish Tra-dition and the Non-Traditional Jew*, ed. J. Schachter (Northvale, N.J., 1992), 3–35.

92. See, e.g., Kanarfogel, *Jewish Education and Society*, 86–91.

93. Robert Chazan, *Medieval Jewry in Northern France* (Baltimore, 1973), 20, 52.

94. See, e.g., Mordechai Breuer, "Le-ḥeqer ha-tippologiyyah shel yeshivot ha-ma'arav bimei ha-beinayim," in *Studies in the History of Jewish Society in the Middle Ages and the Early Modern Period Presented to Prof. Jacob Katz* (Hebrew), ed. I. Etkes and Y. Salmon (Jerusalem, 1980), 45–55.

CHAPTER 12. A TEMPLE IN YOUR KITCHEN

1. On *niddah* and ritual immersion as a custom observed outside the orthodox world, see Inbal Sicoral, "Madua' hen tovlot" (M.A. thesis, Ben-Gurion University, 1998); and Rahel R. Wasserfall, ed., *Women and Water: Menstruation in Jewish Life and Law* (Hanover, N.H., 1999).

2. Nissim Leon, "Sefaṙadim ve-ḥaredim" (M.A. thesis, Tel Aviv University, 1999).

3. As such, they are an example of the religious arena's large-scale dialogue between those born into the observant community and those who have joined it, between religious Israelis and religious Jews from the U.S. and Europe, and between men and women. This complex dialogue explains some of the dynamism of orthodox and *ḥaredi* communities.

4. From 1999 to 2003, I conducted fieldwork in the neighborhood of Pardes Katz in the largely orthodox city of B'nei Brak, near Tel Aviv. The neighborhood is inhabited mainly by Jews whose families came to Israel from the Islamic world. This research con-tinues my study of the connections between women, religion, and knowledge. Previous projects focused on women in the *ḥaredi* and religious Zionist communities in Israel: see El-Or, *Reserved Seats: Religion, Gender and Ethnicity in Contemporary Israel* (Hebrew) (Tel Aviv, 2006), in English at http://www.tamarelor.com/index.php/books/reserved-seats/; idem, *Educated and Ignorant: On Ultra-Orthodox Women and Their World* (Boulder, Colo.,

1993); and idem, *Next Year I Will Know More: Literacy and Identity among Young Orthodox Jewish Women* (Detroit, 2002).

5. Sherry B. Ortner, "Tibetan Circles" (M.A. thesis, University of Chicago, 1966); and idem, "Food for Thought: A Key Symbol in Sherpa Culture" (Ph.D. diss., University of Chicago, 1970).

6. David Frisby and Mike Featherstone, eds., *Simmel on Culture* (London, 1997), 151.

7. See the work of Susan Starr Sered, who studied the participation of elderly women in Jerusalem in religious and spiritual life, esp. *Women as Ritual Experts: The Religious Lives of Elderly Jewish Women in Jerusalem* (New York, 1992). Sered gives a prominent place to women's occupation with food.

8. Claude Lévi-Strauss, *The Savage Mind* (Chicago, 1966); and Mary Douglas, *Purity and Danger* (New York, 1966).

9. The hair and earrings are the "*teshuvah* hammer." At many *teshuvah* gatherings, the organizers shear ponytails off young men who decide to become religious and remove earrings and piercing jewelry from the bodies of young men and women. Some organizers hang the sheared hair and jewelry on the walls, where they remain like the crutches of the miraculously cured at holy sites in Lourdes or Czestochowa.

10. Godfrey Liendhardt, *Divinity and Experience: The Religion of the Dinka* (Oxford, 1961).

11. *Mi-siḥat ha-rabbi me-Lyubavitch: Torat-Menaḥem—hitvaʾaduyot* 23 (1958): 83–91, online at www.chabad.org.il.

12. Ibid.

13. Max Weber, *The Theory of Social and Economic Organization*, trans. A. M. Henderson and T. Parsons (Glencoe, Ill., 1947), 131.

14. Raymond Aron, *Main Currents in Sociological Thought* (New York, 1967), 186–87.

15. Eric J. Hobsbawm and Terence Ranger, eds., *The Invention of Tradition* (Cambridge, 1983).

16. Hezki Shoham, "So, We Created Some Tradition" (Hebrew), *Reshit* 1 (2009): 305–24; the reference to Redfield and Singer appears on 307.

CHAPTER 13. JUDAISM AND THE IDEA OF ANCIENT RITUAL THEORY

1. Pierre Bourdieu, *Outline of a Theory of Practice* (Cambridge, 1977), 171–83.

2. Catherine Bell, *Ritual Theory, Ritual Practice* (New York, 1992), 108–10, 114–17.

3. Frits Staal, *Rules without Meaning: Ritual, Mantras, and the Human Sciences* (New York, 1989).

4. J. L. Austin, *How to Do Things with Words*, ed. J. O. Urmson and M. Sbisa, 2nd ed. (Cambridge, Mass., 1975); on some implications of Austin for ritual language, see Stanley J. Tambiah, "A Performative Approach to Ritual," in *Culture, Thought, and Social Action*

(Cambridge, Mass., 1985), 123–66; Roy Rappaport, "Liturgies and Lies," *Internationales Jahrbuch für Wissens- und Religionssoziologie* 10 (1976): 75–104; Benjamin Ray, "Performative Utterances in African Ritual," *History of Religions* 13 (1973): 16–35; and Rebecca M. Lesses, *Ritual Practices to Gain Power: Angels, Incantations, and Revelation in Early Jewish Mysticism* (Harrisburg, Pa., 1998). Cf. Wade Wheelock, "The Problem of Ritual Language: From Information to Situation," *Journal of the American Academy of Religion* 50 (1982): 49–71.

5. On semiotic communication in Jewish magical and divinatory rituals from the Cairo Genizah, see Michael D. Swartz, "Understanding Ritual in Jewish Magic: Perspectives from the Cairo Genizah and Other Sources," in *Officina Magica: The Workings of Magic*, ed. M. J. Geller (Leiden, 2005), 235–55.

6. Victor W. Turner, "Muchona the Hornet, Interpreter of Religion," in *In the Company of Man: Twenty Portraits by Anthropologists*, ed. J. P. Casagrande (New York, 1960), 334–55; repr. in Turner, *The Forest of Symbols: Aspects of Ndembu Ritual* (Ithaca, N.Y., 1967), 131–50.

7. Thomas P. Kasulis, "Philosophy as Metapraxis," in *Discourse and Practice*, ed. F. Reynolds and D. Tracy (Albany, N.Y., 1992), 169–95.

8. On the Passover seder, see Baruch M. Bokser, *The Origins of the Seder: The Passover Rite and Early Rabbinic Judaism* (Berkeley, Calif., 1984). Another striking case is the modern holiday Kwanzaa, which was developed consciously around a set of seven symbolic objects. For a description of Kwanzaa by its founder, see Maulana Karenga, *Kwanzaa: A Celebration of Family, Community, and Culture* (Los Angeles, 1998).

9. On the Purva Mīmāṃsā as a form of ritual theory, see Francis X. Clooney, *Thinking Ritually: Rediscovering the Purva Mīmāṃsā of Jaimini* (Vienna, 1990).

10. The literature on theories of sacrifice is vast, indicating the centrality of the topic as well as the range of interpretations given to it by modern students of religion and culture. For a recent collection of essays on the meaning of sacrifice, see Jeffrey Carter, ed., *Understanding Religious Sacrifice: A Reader* (London, 2003).

11. Peter Brown, "The Rise and Function of the Holy Man in Late Antiquity," in *Society and the Holy in Late Antiquity* (London, 1982), 103–52; Jonathan Z. Smith, "Towards Interpreting Demonic Powers in Hellenistic and Roman Antiquity," *Aufstieg und Niedergang der Römischen Welt* 2.16.1 (Berlin, 1978), 425–39; and idem, "The Temple and the Magician," in *Map Is Not Territory* (Leiden, 1978), 172–89. On Judaism, see, e.g., William Scott Green, "Palestinian Holy Men: Charismatic Leadership and Rabbinic Tradition," *Aufstieg und Niedergang der Römischen Welt* 2.19.2 (Berlin, 1979), 619–47. For a more concise argument for how this shift is reflected in the sources analyzed in this chapter, see Michael D. Swartz, *Place and Person in Ancient Judaism: Describing the Yom Kippur Sacrifice*, The International Rennert Center Guest Lecture Series 9 (Ramat Gan, 2000); and idem, "The Topography of Blood in Mishnah Yoma," in *Jewish Blood: Metaphor and Reality in Jewish History, Culture, and Religion*, ed. M. Hart (London, 2009), 70–82.

12. See Baruch A. Levine, *In the Presence of the Lord* (Leiden, 1974); idem, "The Presence of God in Biblical Religion," in *Religions in Antiquity: Essays in Memory of E. R.*

Goodenough, ed. J. Neusner (Leiden, 1968), 71–87; and idem, *The JPS Torah Commentary: Leviticus* (Philadelphia, 1989).

13. See, e.g., the depiction of the departure of the *Shekhinah* in *Avot de-Rabbi Natan* A, chap. 34; Solomon Schechter, ed., *Aboth de Rabbi Nathan* (New York, 1967), fols. 51b–52a.

14. *Avot de-Rabbi Natan* A, chap. 4; B, chap. 4 (ed. Schechter, fol. 11a). For a survey of rabbinic statements on sacrifice and the cult, see Naftali Goldstein, "'Avodat ha-qorbanot be-hagut hazal she-le-ahar hurban bet ha-miqdash," *Daat* 8 (1982): 29–51; cf. Yakov Genack, "Mitsvat sukkah ba-halakhah shel hazal: Bein bayit le-miqdash," *Daat* 42 (1999): 283–98.

15. See, e.g., *Avot de-Rabbi Natan* A, chap. 4; bMeg 31b; and bMen 110a.

16. Jacob Neusner, "Map without Territory: Mishnah's System of Sacrifice and Sanctuary," in idem, *Method and Meaning in Ancient Judaism* (Chico, Calif., 1979), 133–53.

17. On this style, see Martin Jaffee, "Writing and Rabbinic Oral Tradition: On Mishnaic Narrative, Lists, and Mnemonics," *Journal of Jewish Thought and Philosophy* 4 (1994): 129–30, and the sources cited there; see, esp., J. N. Epstein, *Mevo'ot le-sifrut ha-tanna'im* (Jerusalem, 1957), 28–29.

18. I would like to acknowledge Kevin Osterloh for emphasizing this contrast in the use of verbs in a seminar paper presented at the Ohio State University.

19. mYom 1:1–5.

20. mYom 1:3.

21. tKip 1:8.

22. See Jacob Neusner, *A History of the Mishnaic Law of Appointed Times*, 5 vols. (Leiden, 1982), 3:81.

23. Saul Lieberman, *Hellenism in Jewish Palestine* (New York, 1962), 164–67.

24. See mYom 6:8.

25. Bokser, *Origins of the Seder*.

26. Mark Zborowski and Elizabeth Herzog, *Life Is with People: The Jewish Little-Town of Eastern Europe* (New York, 1952).

27. René Girard, *Violence and the Sacred* (Baltimore, 1977); and Walter Burkert, *Homo Necans: The Anthropology of Ancient Greek Sacrificial Ritual and Myth*, trans. P. Bing (Berkeley, Calif., 1983).

28. Kathryn McClymond, "Death Be Not Proud: Reevaluating the Role of Killing in Sacrifice," *International Journal of Hindu Studies* 6 (2002): 211–42; and idem, *Beyond Sacred Violence: A Comparative Study of Sacrifice* (Baltimore, 2008).

29. See Jefim Schirmann, "Hebrew Liturgical Poetry and Christian Hymnology," *Jewish Quarterly Review* 44 (1953–54): 123–61; and Joseph Yahalom, "*Piyyut* as Poetry," in *The Synagogue in Late Antiquity*, ed. Lee I. Levine (New York, 1987), 111–25.

30. See, e.g., Yosef Yahalom, *Piyyut u-metsi'ut ba-zeman ha-'atiq* (Tel Aviv, 1999); Jeffrey Rubenstein, "Cultic Themes in Sukkot Piyyutim," *Proceedings of the American Academy for Jewish Research* 59 (1993): 185–209; Michael Fishbane, "The Holy One Sits and Roars: Mythopoesis and the Rabbinic Imagination," *Journal of Jewish Thought and Philosophy* 1

(1992): 1–21; and Seth Schwartz, *Imperialism and Jewish Society: 200 B.C.E. to 640 C.E.* (Princeton, N.J., 2001), 262–74.

31. See bYom 36b and 56b, which describe a prayer leader who recites his version of the Mishnah before the amora Rava on Yom Kippur. It is unclear whether bYom 36b refers to full recitation of the Mishnah. See Zvi Zohar, "U-mi metaher etkhem—avikhem ba-shamayim: Tefillat seder ha-'avodah shel Yom ha-Kippurim: Tokhen, tifqud u-mashma'ut," *Association for Jewish Studies Review* 14 (1989): 4–5.

32. For an introduction to the 'Avodah as well as texts and translations of the major early 'Avodah compositions, see Michael D. Swartz and Joseph Yahalom, *Avodah: Ancient Poems for Yom Kippur* (University Park, Pa., 2005), and the bibliography there; all translations of 'Avodah *piyyutim* here are from this volume. For a comprehensive study of the 'Avodah service and *piyyutim* from the perspective of the history of Hebrew literature, see Zvi Malachi, "ha-'Avodah le-yom ha-kippurim: Ofiyah, toledoteiha ve-hitpathutah ba-shirah ha-'ivrit" (Ph.D. diss., Hebrew University, 1974). For further editions and discussions of 'Avodah *piyyutim*, see Yosef Yahalom, *Az be-ein kol: Seder ha-'avodah ha-erets-yisra'eli ha-qadum le-yom ha-kippurim* (Jerusalem, 1996); Daniel Goldschmidt, ed., *Mahzor le-yamim nora'im* (Jerusalem, 1970), 2:18–25; and Aaron Mirsky, *Piyyutei Yose ben Yose*, 2nd ed. (Jerusalem, 2001). For further elaboration of some of the arguments made here, see Michael D. Swartz, "Ritual about Myth about Ritual: Toward an Understanding of the *Avodah* in the Rabbinic Period," *Journal of Jewish Thought and Philosophy* 6 (1997): 135–55; and idem, "Sage, Priest, and Poet: Typologies of Leadership in the Ancient Synagogue," in *Jews, Christians, and Polytheists in the Ancient Synagogue: Cultural Interaction During the Greco-Roman Period*, ed. S. Fine (London, 1999), 101–17.

33. Published in J. Elbogen, *Studien zur Geschichte des jüdischen Gottesdienstes* (Berlin, 1907), 103–17; cf. the edition in Malachi, "ha-'Avodah," 2:127–31. For a translation, see Swartz and Yahalom, *Avodah*, 53–67.

34. Michael Rand, "The *Seder Beriyot* in Byzantine-Era *Piyyut*," *Jewish Quarterly Review* 95 (2005): 667–83.

35. Heb., *tohu va-vohu*.

36. "Az be-ein kol," lines 35–38: Yahalom, *Az be-ein kol*, 67; and Swartz and Yahalom, *Avodah*, 104–5.

37. Yahalom, *Az be-ein kol*, 67.

38. Referring to the fish that swallowed Jonah and the ravens that fed Elijah in 1 Kgs 17:2–6.

39. Lines 18–20; Swartz and Yahalom, *Avodah*, 296–97; and Mirsky, *Piyyute Yose ben Yose*, 180–81.

40. I.e., for Israel.

41. See Is 27:1. Here the poet is referring to the Leviathan.

42. The rhetorical question is placed here for the sake of the acrostic; the first line in the stanza (line 19) begins *ha-lo*.

43. Heb., *hikhsharta*; i.e., "You made the Behemoth kosher."

44. The *Tamid*.

45. Lines 738–39; Swartz and Yahalom, *Avodah*, 200–201; Yahalom, *Az be-ein kol*, 143.

46. tKip 2:14.

47. "Atah qonanta 'olam me-rosh," lines 2–6 of the second section; Goldschmidt, ed., *Maḥzor*, 2, 20; and Swartz and Yahalom, *Avodah*, 76–77.

48. Lines 8–9.

49. Lines 551–52; Yahalom, *Az be-ein kol*, 124; and Swartz and Yahalom, *Avodah*, 176–77.

50. Line 229; Mirsky, *Yose ben Yose*, 167; Swartz and Yahalom, *Avodah*, 278–79.

51. Line 165: Mirsky, *Yose ben Yose*, 157; Swartz and Yahalom, *Avodah*, 264–65.

52. On descriptions of the vestments of the high priest, see Michael D. Swartz, "The Semiotics of the Priestly Vestments in Jewish Tradition," in *Sacrifice in Religious Experience*, ed. A. I. Baumgarten (Leiden, 2002), 57–80.

53. Ex 28:20.

54. yYom 7:3 (44b); bZev 88b; b'Arak 16a; Lv Rabbah 10:6, Mordecai Margulies, ed., *Midrash Vayikra Rabbah* (New York, 1993), 210–12; and a fragment related to Tanḥuma published by Jacob Mann, *The Bible as Read and Preached in the Old Synagogue* (New York, 1971 [1940]), 1:258 (Hebrew); see also Sg *Rabbah* 4:5.

55. *Azkir gevurot*, lines 159–60; Mirsky, *Yose ben Yose*, 159–60; Swartz and Yahalom, *Avodah*, 264–65.

56. Ibid., line 166.

57. Verbally, through slander.

58. Lines 559–69, quoting Sg 7:2; Yahalom, *Az be-ein kol*, 125; and Swartz and Yahalom, *Avodah*, 176–77.

59. Cf. Is 40:3; see Yahalom, *Az be-ein kol*, 32.

60. *Az be-ein kol*, lines 565–70; Yahalom, *Az be-ein kol*, 126; Swartz and Yahalom, *Avodah*, 178–79; cf. Is 59:17.

61. Line 103; Mirsky, *Yose ben Yose*, 192; and Swartz and Yahalom, *Avodah*, 318–19.

62. Lines 645–46, 651–54; Yahalom, *Az be-ein kol*, 134–35; and Swartz and Yahalom, *Avodah*, 188–91.

63. On these *piyyutim*, see Paul Kahle, *Masoreten des Westens* (Stuttgart, 1927), 81–87, 1*– 59* and 1–23 (Hebrew sec.); Menahem Zulay, "Le-toledot ha-piyyut be-Erets-Yisra'el," *Yedi'ot ha-makhon le-ḥeqer ha-shirah ha-'ivrit* 5 (1939): 107–80; Ezra Fleischer, "Shivta'ot ḥadashot 'al mishmarot ha-kehunah la-payyetan Rabbi Pinhas," *Sinai* 61 (1967): 30–56; "Le-'inyan ha-mishmarot ba-piyyutim," *Sinai* 62 (1968): 13–40; "Piyyut le-Yannai ḥazzan 'al mishmarot ha-kohanim," *Sinai* 64 (1969): 176–84; and Joseph Yahalom, "The Temple and the City in Liturgical Hebrew Poetry," in Joshua Prawer and Haggai Ben-Shammai (eds.), *The History of Jerusalem: The Early Muslim period, 638–1099* (Jerusalem, 1996), 274–75. Samuel Klein, *Beiträge zur Geographie und Geschichte Galiläas* (Leipzig, 1909), 64–70, cited this genre as evidence that the priestly watches emigrated from Jerusalem to the Galilee after the Bar-Kokhba rebellion. This conclusion is disputed by Dalia Trifon, "Ha-im 'avru mishmarot ha-kohanim mi-Yehudah la-Galil aharei mered Bar-Kokhba?," *Tarbiz* 59 (1980): 77–93; cf. Zeev Safrai, "Matai 'avru ha-kohanim la-Galil? Teguvah le-ma'amarah shel Dalia Trifon," *Tarbiz* 62 (1993): 287–92.

64. See, esp., Yahalom, *Az be-ein kol*, 56–57; and Salo Wittmayer Baron, *A Social and Religious History of the Jews* (New York, 1958), 7:90–92.

65. See Dan Urman, "The House of Assembly and the House of Study: Are They One and the Same?," *Journal of Jewish Studies* 44 (1993): 236–57. On the term *hazzan*, see Hyman I. Sky, *Redevelopment of the Office of Hazzan through the Talmudic Period* (San Francisco, 1992).

66. See Lawrence Hoffman, *The Canonization of the Synagogue Service* (Notre Dame, Ind., 1979), 66–71; and Baron, *Social and Religious History*, 7:100–105.

67. On the relationship of the synagogue to the Temple, see Steven Fine, *This Holy Place: On the Sanctity of the Synagogue during the Greco-Roman Period* (Notre Dame, Ind., 1997); Joan R. Branham, *Sacred Space in Ancient and Early Medieval Architecture* (Cambridge, forthcoming); and idem, "Vicarious Sacrality: Temple Space in Ancient Synagogues," in *Ancient Synagogues: Historical Analysis and Archaeological Discovery*, ed. D. Urman and P. V. M. Flesher (Leiden, 1995), 2:319–45.

68. On the synagogue and its mosaic, see Ze'ev Weiss and Ehud Netzer, *Promise and Redemption: A Synagogue Mosaic from Sepphoris* (Jerusalem, 1996), where parallels in rabbinic literature are suggested; for another interpretation of the mosaic and its function in the context of the synagogue, see Steven Fine, "Art and the Liturgical Context of the Sepphoris Synagogue Mosaic," in *Galilee through the Centuries: Confluence of Cultures,* ed. E. M. Meyers (Winona Lake, Ind., 1999), 227–37.

69. See Swartz and Yahalom, *Avodah*, 343–47; and Goldschmidt, *Mahzor*, 2:483–84.

70. Edmund Leach, "The Logic of Sacrifice," in *Culture and Communication: The Logic by Which Symbols Are Connected* (Cambridge, 1976), 81–93; and H. Hubert and M. Mauss, *Sacrifice: Its Nature and Function* (Chicago, 1964).

71. It is unclear as to when this custom arose. For an early citation, see the responsum of Hayya Ga'on published in B. M. Lewin, *Otsar ha-ge'onim*, 13 vols. (Jerusalem, 1934), 6:18–19; cf. *Beit Yosef Orah hayyim*, 621. On the custom and its implications, see Zohar, "U-mi metaher etkhem," 22–23.

72. See, e.g., Sifre Dt *'Eqev* 41 (ed. Finkelstein, 87–88); and yYom 4:1 (7a). On substitutes for sacrifice in rabbinic thought, see Michael Fishbane, *The Exegetical Imagination: On Jewish Thought and Theology* (Cambridge, Mass., 1998), 123–219; and Goldstein, "'Avodat ha-qorbanot."

73. On the implications of this idea for the 'Avodah, see Swartz, "Kohah u-teqifah shel ha-shirah ha-'ivrit be-shalhei ha-'et ha-'atiqah," in *Continuity and Renewal: Jews and Judaism in Byzantine-Christian Palestine*, ed. L. I. Levine (Jerusalem, 2004), 542–62.

Epilogue

1. A classic example of this view is found in a volume put together by Franz Boas with the collaboration of many of his students. See his *General Anthropology* (Boston, 1938).

2. Carleton S. Coon, *Caravan: The Story of the Middle East* (New York, 1951). An eth-

nographic account of an "isolated" Jewish community in Algeria represents the approach to anthropology found in Coon's *Caravan*: Lloyd C. Briggs and Norina L. Guède, *No More for Ever: A Saharan Jewish Town* (Cambridge, Mass., 1964). Coon is among the "technical consultants" acknowledged in the preface (p. x), along with Shelomo Dov Goitein and Isadore Twersky. One might speculate regarding the extent to which Twersky's ambivalent perception of anthropology was shaped by this encounter.

3. See Harvey E. Goldberg, ed., *Judaism Viewed from Within and from Without: Anthropological Studies* (Albany, N.Y., 1987), 1–43, 3–29; and idem, *Jewish Passages: Cycles of Jewish Life* (Berkeley, Calif., 2003), 1–27.

4. On the dilemmas of exhibits, see Barbara Kirshenblatt-Gimblett, *Destination Culture: Tourism, Museums, and Heritage* (Berkeley, Calif., 1998).

5. Lawrence A. Hoffman, *Beyond the Text: A Holistic Approach to Liturgy* (Bloomington, Ind., 1987).

6. Aaron Demsky, "Writing in Ancient Israel and Early Judaism. Part One: The Biblical Period," in *Miqra: Text, Translation, Reading and Interpretation of the Hebrew Bible in Ancient Israel and Early Judaism*, ed. M. J. Mulder (Assen and Philadelphia, 1988), 1–20; idem, *Literacy in the Biblical Period* (Hebrew) (Jerusalem, forthcoming); and Jack Goody, ed., *Literacy in Traditional Societies* (Cambridge, 1968).

7. Elchanan Reiner, "Pilgrims and Pilgrimage to Erets Israel, 1099–1517" (Hebrew) (Ph.D. diss., Hebrew University of Jerusalem, 1988).

8. See Chava Weissler, *Voices of the Matriarchs: Listening to the Prayers of Early Modern Jewish Women* (Boston, 1998), chap. 6, who provides a parallel analysis of lighting Sabbath candles in an Ashkenazi context.

9. Harvey E. Goldberg, "The Zohar in Southern Morocco: A Study in the Ethnography of Texts," *History of Religions* 29 (1990): 233–58.

10. Hagar Salamon, "Journeys as a Means of Communication among the Beta-Israel in Ethiopia" (Hebrew), *Pe'amim* 58 (1993): 104–19.

11. See Alan Barnard, *History and Theory in Anthropology* (Cambridge, 2000), chaps. 3–5; and George Stocking, *After Tylor: British Social Anthropology, 1888–1951* (Madison, Wisc., 1996).

12. Ruth Benedict, *Patterns of Culture* (Boston, 1934). There eventually appeared one attempt to characterize rabbinic Judaism in terms of these intellectual trends: Max Kadushin, *The Rabbinic Mind* (New York, 1952).

13. Benedict, *Patterns of Culture*, 42–43.

14. Barbara Kirshenblatt-Gimblett, "Coming of Age in the Thirties: Max Weinreich, Edward Sapir, and Jewish Social Science," *YIVO Annual* 23 (1996): 1–103, esp. 23.

15. Eric Wolf, *Europe and the People Without History* (Berkeley, Calif., 1982).

16. Victor Turner utilized the notion of "alphabet blocks" combined to create larger ritual patterns in referring to the work of Arnold Van Gennep. See Goldberg, *Judaism Viewed*, 322.

17. Judah Goldin, "On Change and Adaptation in Judaism," *History of Religions* 4 (1965): 269–94, esp. 278.

18. Eric J. Hobsbawm and Terence O. Ranger, eds., *The Invention of Tradition* (Cambridge, 1992).

19. Harvey E. Goldberg, "A Tradition of Invention: Family and Educational Institutions among Contemporary Traditionalizing Jews," in *National Variations in Modern Jewish Identity*, ed. S. M. Cohen and G. Horenczyk (Albany, N.Y., 1999), 85–106.

20. See the editorial introduction by Daniel A. Siegel, "Resisting Identities: A Found Theme," *Cultural Anthropology* 11 (1996): 431–34.

21. Salo W. Baron, "Ghetto and Emancipation: Shall We Revise the Traditional View?," *The Menorah Journal* 14 (1928): 515–26; and Gershom Scholem, "Mi-tokh hirhurim 'al ḥokhmat Yisra'el," in *Devarim be-go*, 2 vols. (Tel Aviv, 1976), 2:385–403.

22. See Jonathan Boyarin, *Storm from Paradise: The Politics of Jewish Memory* (Minneapolis, 1992); and, more recently, Ivan D. Kalmar and Derek J. Penslar, eds., *Orientalism and the Jews* (Waltham, Mass., 2005), who show that "orientalism" regarding Jews preceded the era of colonial domination. Boyarin, *Storm*, 80, takes issue with Gayatri Spivak, who does not accept the comparison between colonial domination and disenfranchised groups in Europe. See also Shmuel Trigano, "L'invention sépharade de la modernité juive," in idem, ed., *Le monde sépharade*, vol. 1: *Histoire* (Paris, 2006), 243–78, esp. 259–62.

23. Ismar Schorsch, "Ideology and History in the Age of Emancipation," in *Heinrich Graetz: The Structure of Jewish History and Other Essays*, ed. and trans. I. Schorsch (New York, 1975), 9.

24. Harvey E. Goldberg, "Becoming History: Perspectives on the Seminary Faculty at Mid-Century," in *Tradition Renewed: A History of the Jewish Theological Seminary of America*, ed. J. Wertheimer, 2 vols. (New York, 1997), 1:353–437, esp. 378–79.

25. Jacob Neusner has advocated writing about "Judaisms" in contrast to "Judaism," e.g., in his *Judaism in Modern Times: An Introduction and Reader* (Cambridge, Mass., 1995).

26. A prime example of this reaction may be found in the edition of the Hebrew Bible, with English translation, commentary, and supplemental essays, prepared by Joseph H. Hertz, ed., *The Pentateuch and Haftorahs: Hebrew Text, English Translation and Commentary* (London, 1938). See also Harvey W. Meirovich, *A Vindication of Judaism: The Polemics of the Hertz Pentateuch* (New York, 1998).

27. In the view of Howard Eilberg-Schwartz, *The Savage in Judaism: An Anthropology of Israelite Religion and Ancient Judaism* (Bloomington, Ind., 1990), some Christian scholars were also sensitive about the disparaging perceptions of the Old Testament implied by applying anthropological methods to understanding its content.

28. Jacob Milgrom, *Leviticus: A New Translation with Introduction and Commentary*, 3 vols. (New York, 1991–2000); and Alan Cooper, "Biblical Studies and Jewish Studies," in *The Oxford Handbook of Jewish Studies*, ed. M. Goodman (Oxford, 2002), 14–35.

29. See Harvey E. Goldberg, "The Voice of Jacob: Jewish Perspectives on Anthropology and the Study of the Bible," *Jewish Social Studies* n.s. 2 (1995): 36–71; and idem, "Cambridge in the Land of Canaan: Descent, Alliance, Circumcision, and Instruction in the Bible," *Journal of the Ancient Near Eastern Society* 24 (1996): 9–34.

30. See also Yoram Bilu, "The Sanctification of Space in Israel: Civil Religion and Folk-Judaism," in *Jews in Israel*, ed. U. Rebhun and C. I. Waxman (Hanover, N.H., 2004), 371–93. Using a different analytic approach, Bilu stresses that visits to graves of sainted rabbis can be understood beyond the framework of Jewish customs in Morocco.

31. Jay Harris, "Among the Giants," *Bulletin of the Center for Jewish Studies at Harvard University* 17, no. 1 (1999): 1–5.

32. S. D. Goitein, *A Mediterranean Society: The Jewish Communities of the Arab World as Portrayed in the Documents of the Cairo Geniza*, 6 vols. (Berkeley, Calif., 1967–93), 1:26.

33. See Abraham Udovitch's foreword in Goitein, *Mediterranean Society*, 5:x. That this was a perspective Goitein reached over time is suggested by an earlier, less subtle, statement: "[I]t has been deeply and rightly felt by many that the Yemenites were the most Jewish of all Jews" ("The Yemenite Jews in the Israel Amalgam," in *Israel: Its Role in Civilization*, ed. M. Davis [New York, 1956], 178).

34. S. D. Goitein, "The Life Story of a Scholar," in *A Bibliography of the Writings of Prof. Shelomo Dov Goitein*, ed. R. Attal (Jerusalem, 1975), xiii–xxviii.

35. Goitein, *Mediterranean Society*, 5:498–501. On Brauer, see Orit Abuhav, "The Human Countenance: The Contribution of the Ethnologists Erich Brauer and Raphael Patai to the Anthropology of the Jews" (Hebrew), *Jerusalem Studies in Jewish Folklore* 22 (2002): 159–77; and Clifford Geertz, *The Interpretation of Cultures* (New York, 1973).

Contributors

ALBERT I. BAUMGARTEN is a professor of Jewish history at Bar-Ilan University. He specializes in the Second Temple period, with a particular interest in understanding that era with the help of the social sciences. One result of that focus is his *The Flourishing of Jewish Sects in the Maccabean Era: An Interpretation* (1997). His most recent book is *Elias Bickerman as a Historian of the Jews: A Twentieth Century Tale* (2010).

YORAM BILU is a professor of anthropology and psychology at the Hebrew University of Jerusalem. His most recent publication is *The Saints' Impresarios: Dreamers, Healers, and Holy Men in Israel's Urban Periphery* (2010).

RA'ANAN S. BOUSTAN is an associate professor in the Departments of History and Near Eastern Languages and Cultures at the University of California, Los Angeles. His publications include *From Martyr to Mystic: Rabbinic Martyrology and the Making of Merkavah Mysticism* (2005) and a number of coedited volumes, including *Violence, Scripture, and Textual Practice in Early Judaism and Christianity* (2010) and *Heavenly Realms and Earthly Realities in Late Antique Religions* (2004).

J. H. (YOSSI) CHAJES is an associate professor in the Department of Jewish History at the University of Haifa. He is author of *Between Worlds: Dybbuks, Exorcists, and Early Modern Judaism* (2003) and numerous articles on early modern Jewish culture.

TAMAR EL-OR is associate professor in the Sarah Allen Shaine Chair in Sociology and Anthropology at the Hebrew University of Jerusalem. Her *Meqomot shemorim* (2006), on orthodox women in the Mizraḥi-Sefaradi community, is the third in a trilogy on gender, religion, and knowledge in Israel.

HARVEY E. GOLDBERG is professor emeritus in the Sarah Allen Shaine Chair in Sociology and Anthropology at the Hebrew University of Jerusalem. He has authored *Cave Dwellers and Citrus Growers* (1972), *Jewish Life in Muslim Libya* (1990), and *Jewish Passages: Cycles of Jewish Life* (2003) and edited *Judaism*

Viewed from Within and from Without (1986), *Sephardi and Middle Eastern Jewries* (1996), and *The Life of Judaism* (2001).

SYLVIE ANNE GOLDBERG is a professor of Jewish history at the École des Hautes Etudes en Sciences Sociales, Paris. Her field of interest is cultural and conceptual history, from the building of Jewish communities in Western and Eastern Europe to their dissolution. Her books include *La Clepsydre* (2 vols., 2000–2004) and *Crossing the Jabbok: Illness and Death in Ashkenazi Judaism in Sixteenth- through Nineteenth-Century Prague* (1996).

EPHRAIM KANARFOGEL is the E. Billi Ivry Professor of Jewish History at the Bernard Revel Graduate School of Jewish Studies at Yeshiva University. His most recent book is *The Intellectual History of Medieval Ashkenazic Jewry: New Perspectives* (2010).

TAMAR KATRIEL is a professor of communication and education at the University of Haifa. She is author of *Talking Straight: "Dugri" Speech in Israeli Sabra Culture* (1986), *Communal Webs: Communication and Culture in Contemporary Israel* (1991), *Performing the Past: A Study of Israeli Settlement Museums* (1997), *Keywords: Patterns of Culture and Communication in Israel* (Hebrew) (1999), and *Dialogic Moments: From Soul Talks to Talk Radio in Israeli Culture* (2004).

OREN KOSANSKY, an assistant professor of anthropology at Lewis & Clark College, is the author of articles and book chapters on religious modernity, Jewish textual practice, and saint pilgrimage in colonial and postcolonial Morocco.

RIV-ELLEN PRELL, an anthropologist, is a professor of American studies at the University of Minnesota. Her recent publications include an edited volume, *Women Remaking American Judaism* (2007), and "Triumph, Accommodation, and Resistance: American Jewish Life from the End of World War II to the Six-Day War," in *The Columbia History of Jews and Judaism in America*, ed. Marc Lee Raphael (2008).

LUCIA RASPE teaches in the Jewish studies department of Johann Wolfgang Goethe-Universität, Frankfurt am Main. She is author of *Jüdische Hagiographie im mittelalterlichen Aschkenas* (2006). Her current work focuses on the Ashkenazi diaspora in Italy in the fifteenth and sixteenth centuries.

MARINA RUSTOW is the Charlotte Bloomberg Associate Professor in the Humanities in the Department of History at Johns Hopkins University. She is author of *Heresy and the Politics of Community: The Jews of the Fatimid Caliphate* (2008), which won the Salo Wittmayer Baron Book Prize for an outstanding first book in Jewish studies.

SHALOM SABAR is a professor of Jewish art and folklore at the Hebrew University of Jerusalem and the academic director of the Revivim Honors Program for the Training of Jewish Studies Teachers. His books include *Ketubbah: Jewish Marriage Contracts of the Hebrew Union College Skirball Museum and Klau Library* (1990), *Mazal Tov: Illuminated Jewish Marriage Contracts from the Israel Museum Collection* (1994), *Jerusalem—Stone and Spirit: 3000 Years of History and Art* (with Dan Bahat, 1997), and *The Life Cycle* (Hebrew) (2006).

ANDREA SCHATZ is a lecturer in Jewish studies at King's College London and author of *Sprache in der Zerstreuung: Zur Säkularisierung des Hebräischen im 18. Jahrhundert* (2009). In her books and articles, she explores Jewish and postcolonial perspectives on language, religion, secularism, and "the orient."

MICHAEL D. SWARTZ is a professor of Hebrew and religious studies at the Ohio State University. He is author of *Mystical Prayer in Ancient Judaism* (1992) and *Scholastic Magic: Ritual and Revelation in Early Jewish Mysticism* (1996); and coauthor, with Lawrence Schiffman, of *Hebrew and Aramaic Incantation Texts from the Cairo Genizah* (1992) and, with Joseph Yahalom, of *Avodah: Ancient Poems for Yom Kippur* (2005). He served as Judaica editor for the second edition of the *Encyclopedia of Religion*.

Index

masoret ha-berit (*masoret* of the covenant), 238
Masoret ha-masoret (The tradition of the Masorah) (Levita), 220–21
Masoretic texts: and problem of tradition, 220–21; and revelation to Moses on Sinai, 219–21; sacralization and historical claims for antiquity of, 219–23; Tiberian Masorah, 221–23; written symbols to represent oral sounds of the text, 220, 221, 388n42
Mauss, M., 315
Mayse bukh (1602), 156, 158
medieval Judaism: changing roles of oral and written transmission, 7, 26, 218–19, 223–28; ge'onim, 225, 227–28, 240, 263–65; literacy and literary memory (*memoria ad verba*), 250–70; liturgical-legal hegemony, 7; reuniting of Jewish world under Islamic rule, 217–18, 239–40, 241; standardization of the fixed *ketubbah* formula, 106–7; tenth century and Jewish tradition, 217–29, 232–33, 239–40. *See also* calendar controversy; magic in medieval and early modern rabbinic culture
A Mediterranean Society (Goitein), 333–34
Meir of Rothenburg (Maharam): and practice of burial *ad sanctos*, 158–59, *159*, 377n65; and practice of calling someone to the Torah, 267; and prayer books, 258; and proscription against public prayer, 252–53
Memmi, Albert, 345n56
Menaḥem Azariah of Fano, 75–76
Menaḥem b. Aaron ibn Zeraḥ, 265
Mendelssohn, Moses, 165–66, 171, 229
Meshullam b. Kalonymos, 156
messianic Jews, 19, 344n53
"metapraxis," 296
Mishnah: and past authority and status, 212–13; *Qodashim*, 298; sacrifice focus and rabbinic responses to the Temple's destruction, 297–98; and Torah scrolls before/after Jewish adoption of codices, 218–19; tractate *Avot*, 214–15, 227–28, 238; tractate *Avot de-Rabbi Natan*, 214–16, 227–28; tractate *Soferim*, 219; tractate *Yoma* and theories of sacrifice, 297–306, 316–17. *See also* Mishnah *Yoma*
Mishnah *Yoma* and Yom Kippur sacrifice, 297–306, 316–17, 326; blood and, 302, 304; community involvement, 303; criticism of priestly establishment, 299–301,

303, 309; and early rabbinic theories of sacrifice, 299; and geography of the Temple, 301–2; the high priest's actions, 300–302; the incense, 302; liturgical recitation, 299, 305–6, 315–16; narrative style, 298–99; performative functions, 304; purification and, 303, 304; the scapegoat ritual, 302, 304; social and political concerns, 299–300, 304, 316; tensions between the Sadducees and Pharasaic sages, 299–300. *See also* ancient ritual theory and Yom Kippur sacrifice; 'Avodah *piyyutim* and Yom Kippur sacrifice
Mizraḥi ("oriental") Jews, 46–47
"Mizraḥi studies," 11
Modena, Leon, 67–68, 72–73, 114
modernity and tradition: discursive tradition and, 14–15; modern technologies and innovations that return attention to written texts, 234; and movement of orthodoxy (neo-orthodoxy), 230–34; reappraisal of Jewish textual hegemony, 8–9; sacralization and tradition in modern period, and the secular, 8, 84; 229–34; Shoham's study of Purim festivals, 292; waning commitment to Jewish life, 233
monothetic vs. polythetic views of Judaism, 3
Montagu, Lady, 382n45
Montesquieu, 169–70, 381n21, 382n25
Moroccan Jewish shrines and visitational dreams in contemporary Israel, 23–24, 27, 80–101, 322; charismatic phase of shrine foundation, 99, 101; cult of saints, 80, 83–85, 97, 100–101; demise and afterlife of shrines, 82–83, 96–101; dream communities (oneirocommunities), 91–96; dreams as "charismatic significants," 81, 96, 358n4; dreams as "swing concepts," 81–82; Elijah the Prophet and, 80–81, 86, 90–91, 100; female dreamers, 91, 94–100; Gate of Paradise shrine in Beit She'an, 80–83, 85–101; *hillulah* for patron saints, 81, 85; innocence theme, 89; nostalgic, idealized affection for Morocco, 86–87; patron saints, 83–84, 90–91; precipitating factors, 84, 88, 90, 100, 360n30; rabbinic approval problem, 97–99, 322; *se'udah* dreams, 90–91; symbolic translocation of "migrant saints," 85; textual precedents/talmudic traditions, 80–81, 86; zaddikim and notion of *zekhut avot*, 83, 86

textual hegemony *(cont.)*
7; print capitalism, 7–8; and refined distinctions between modernity and tradition, 8–9; rhetorical hegemony, 6–7; scribal hegemony, 6–7
textual heterogeneity and discursive tradition, 15–19, 342n39; authority in texts/authority of texts, 17; marginal texts, 15–16; relationship of texts and practices, 19; textual canonicity and, 6–7, 15–17, 342n39
Tiberian Hebrew, 221–23
tiqqun 'olam (repair of the world), 274, 283–84, 286–88, 290–91
Titus, 139–40
Torah scroll: adoption of the codex and sacralization of, 218–19; Yom Kippur readings in medieval Ashkenaz and Sefarad, 253, 258, 259, 261
Tosafists and reciting "written matters" by heart, 251–56, 260–62, 398n15
Tosefta: and proper performance of Yom Kippur, 300; and rabbinic "eyewitness" testimonies of the Temple vessels in Rome, 142, 144; term *masoret* and authority of tradition, 211
tradition, "invented," 14; accusations of, 215, 231–32, 336; and appeal to tradition in times of change, 210, 216–17, 229, 235–37; custom and, 208; false distinction between "genuine" and, 207–10, 215, 234–36, 292, 326–27; and *hafrashat ḥallah* ceremonies in contemporary Israel, 274, 292; Se'adyah and, 248
tradition, Jewish, 14–22; as both written and oral law, 239; boundaries of Jewish tradition, 11–14, 19–21, 191, 323, 330, 344n53; competing discourses in tenth-century Jewish world, 238–49; custom and the calendar controversy in medieval Judaism, 242–43, 248–49; discursive tradition, 5, 14–22; and *paradosis*, 211, 215; *masoret*, 211–13, 238–39, 386n10; *qabbalah*, 238–39; "invented" tradition, 14, 207–10, 215–17, 229, 234–37, 274, 292, 326–27; Jewish normativity and, 21–22; modernity and, 8–9, 14–15, 229–34, 292; rethinking local and global extents of, 21–22; rethinking textual canonicity and textual heterogeneity, 15–17, 342n39; and revelation to Moses on Sinai, 219–21, 238–39, 246; Se'adyah and, 246–49. *See also* ancient

ritual theory and Yom Kippur sacrifice; calendar controversy; *hafrashat ḥallah* ceremonies; literacy and literary memory (*memoria ad verba*) in medieval Ashkenaz and Sefarad; tradition and appeals to the past during periods of change
tradition and appeals to the past during periods of change, 25–26, 207–37, 321, 326–27; beliefs in antiquity of the Masorah, 219–21; and book of Ezra, 213; chains of transmission, 227–28; claims for the antiquity of rabbinic interpretations, 219–23; development of strong sense of tradition, 213–15; differentiating between weak and strong appeals, 209–10, 234–36; enlisting tradition in its weak sense to defend the strong sense, 215–17, 226; and false distinction between "genuine" and "invented" tradition, 207–10, 215, 234–36, 292, 326–27; ge'onim and, 225, 227–28; and lost/hidden vessels of Solomon's Temple, 212–13; *masoret*, 211–13, 238–39, 386n10; Middle Ages (tenth century), 217–29, 232–33; Mishnah tractate *Avot*, 214–15, 227–28; modern period, 229–34; notion of *da'at Torah* and rabbinic infallibility, 230–31; oral and written transmission of texts, 218–19, 223–28, 321; and orthodoxy (neo-orthodoxy), 230, 231–34, 390n68; *paradosis*, 211, 215; Pharisees, 211, 215; Qaraites, 220, 225–27, 228; Qumran group and early Christians, 214–15; sacralization, 217–23, 229–34; Sadducees and Pharisees, 214–15; Second Temple period, 211–17; and spoken Tiberian Hebrew, 221–23; tradition's association with authority and status, 212–13, 214–15
travel writing, eighteenth-century, 173, 178–82, 184; colonialism and, 167, 168, 179, 184; spatial relations and narrative strategies, 179. *See also* Romanelli, Samuel
Tsedah la-derekh (Ibn Zeraḥ), 265, 266
Turner, Victor, 44, 296, 325, 411–16

United Jewish Appeal, 197

Vedic Hinduism, 297, 304
Vespasian, 140
Vital, Ḥayyim, and magical work in rabbinic culture, 64–69, 73

Acknowledgments

The editors would like to thank David Ruderman and the staff at the Herbert D. Katz Center for Advanced Judaic Studies at the University of Pennsylvania for their support throughout the process of completing this volume; Hannah Ferreri and Alice Mandell for their contributions in the preparation of the manuscript; Daniel Kelley and Kate Rubick for their bibliographic assistance; Holly Knowles for her excellent work on the index; and Leah Boustan, Piero Capelli, and Julie Hastings for their patience, help, and advice.